New Accountabilities, New Challenges

New Accountabilities, New Challenges

Edited by John Wanna, Evert A. Lindquist and Penelope Marshall

Australian National University

PRESS

ANU PRESS

School of Government
the Australia and New Zealand

Published by ANU Press
The Australian National University
Acton ACT 2601, Australia
Email: anupress@anu.edu.au
This title is also available online at http://press.anu.edu.au

---

National Library of Australia Cataloguing-in-Publication entry

Creator:	Wanna, John, author.
Title:	New accountabilities, new challenges / John Wanna, Evert A. Lindquist and Penelope Marshall.
ISBN:	9781925022070 (paperback) 9781925022087 (ebook)
Subjects:	Government accountability. Politics, Practical. Public administration.
Other Authors/Contributors:	
	Lindquist, Evert A., author. Marshall, Penelope, author.
Dewey Number:	321.8

Cover design and layout by ANU Press

Contents

Part I. Systemic Accountabilities

Part II. Policy Processes

List of Abbreviations and Acronyms

AAT	Administrative Appeals Tribunal
ABS	Australian Bureau of Statistics
ACCC	Australian Competition and Consumer Commission
ACER	Australian Council for Educational Research
ACT	Australian Capital Territory
ACTU	Australian Council of Trade Unions
ADJR Act	Administrative Decisions (Judicial Review) Act 1977 (Cth)
AEU	Australian Education Union
ALP	Australian Labor Party
ALRC	Australian Law Reform Commission
ANAO	Australian National Audit Office
ANZSOG	Australia and New Zealand School of Government
APS	Australian Public Service
APSC	Australian Public Service Commission
ARC	Administrative Review Council
CDEP	Community Development Employment Project
CGovC	Compact Governance Committee
CGrC	Commonwealth Grants Commission
CJPA	cross-jurisdictional performance audit
COAG	Council of Australian Governments
DEETYA	Department of Employent, Education, Training and Youth Affairs
DES	Department of Education and Science
DETYA	Department of Education, Training and Youth Affairs
DEWR	Department of Employment and Workplace Relations
DHHS	Department of Health and Human Services
FaCSIA	Department of Families, Community Services and Indigenous Affairs
ERC	Expenditure Review Committee
EU	European Union
FOI	freedom of information
FPP	first past the post
GAO	Government Accountability Office
GBE	Government Business Enterprise
GDP	gross domestic product
GST	Goods and Services Tax
ICC	Indigenous Coordinating Centre
ICCS	Institute for Citizen-Centred Service

IGA	intergovernmental agreement
IMF	International Monetary Fund
INTOSAI	International Organisation of Supreme Audit Institutions
IPS	Information Publication Scheme
ITARI	integrity, transparency, accountability, responsiveness, and inclusiveness
JCPAA	Joint Committee of Public Accounts and Audit
LNP	Liberal–National Party
MCEETYA	Ministerial Council for Education, Employment, Training and Youth Affairs
MFP	multifactor productivity
MMP	mixed member proportional
MoU	Matter of Urgency
MP	Member of Parliament
MPI	Matter of Public Importance
MTEF	medium-term economic framework
MYEFO	Mid-Year Economic and Fiscal Outlook
NAO	National Audit Office
NBN	National Broadband Network
NCC	National Competition Council
NCP	National Competition Policy
NFP	not-for-profit
NGO	non-governmental organisation
NPM	new public management
NPP	National Partnership Payment
NSW	New South Wales
NT	Northern Territory
NTER	Northern Territory Emergency Response
OAIC	Office of the Australian Information Commissioner
OECD	Organisation for Economic Cooperation and Development
PBS	Portfolio Budget Statement
SA	South Australia
SPP	Specific Purpose Payment
SAI	supreme audit institution
WA	Western Australia

Foreword

This present collection of essays and research reports by 14 academic commentators and senior practitioners brings together a diverse set of contributors unified in the belief that reform initiatives are imperative for better government and public policy. All these contributions have connections with ANZSOG — the Australia and New Zealand School of Government, established in 2002–03 as an innovative collaboration between the Australian and New Zealand governments and a range of prestigious universities across both countries. Some of the essays were commissioned research papers by experts in the field on topics of multi-jurisdictional concern, others were research papers in which ANZSOG played a role and that were subsequently presented to ANZSOG for publication, and others were first given as keynote speeches at public events hosted by ANZSOG or involving ANZSOG staff members. Of the 14 contributors, eight are academics by profession (at various stages, five have been members of ANZSOG faculty), and six are senior executives with wide-ranging government experience. They each approach their topic with critical engagement, providing constructive suggestions and recommendations for future reform.

This title, *New Accountabilities, New Challenges,* is the latest in the ANU Press/ ANZSOG series which now runs to over 40 titles covering diverse areas of public policy and administration. (ANZSOG also publishes web-based occasional papers, often with jurisdictional partners.) It is the fourth collection of essays ANU Press and ANZSOG have published since the series began in 2006. The first was *A Passion of Policy: Essays in public sector reform* (2007), the second *Improving Implementation: Organisational change and project management* (2007), and the third was *Critical Reflections on Australian Public Policy: Selected essays* (2009). Each of these previous collections has been well received and consistently attracted high downloads. I am sure that this collection will not disappoint readers, and feel confident that it will surpass the take-up and dissemination accorded to the earlier collections. I commend the volume of essays to our stakeholders and readers and look forward to the debates it will undoubtedly stimulate.

Professor John Wanna
Sir John Bunting Chair in Public Administration, RSSS, ANU, and National Director of Research, ANZSOG

Contributors

John Wanna holds the Sir John Bunting Chair of Public Administration at the Research School of Social Sciences, The Australian National University and is Director of Research for the Australian and New Zealand School of Government (ANZSOG).

Chris Eccles was appointed Secretary of the Victorian Department of Premier and Cabinet in December 2014. He previously held the positions of Director General, NSW Department of Premier and Cabinet (2011–2014) and Chief Executive, South Australian Department of Premier and Cabinet (2009–2011). Prior to this, he worked in a variety of government and private sector senior management positions.

Derek Drinkwater holds a BA with First Class Honours in government from the University of Queensland and a PhD in political science and international relations from The Australian National University. He worked for 20 years in the Department of the Senate and for a decade as a public administration adviser at the Australian Public Service Commission. His publications include *Sir Harold Nicolson and International Relations: The practitioner as theorist* (Oxford University Press, 2005) and *The Biographical Dictionary of the Australian Senate: 1901–1929* (Melbourne University Press, 2000) of which he was assistant editor. He has also contributed to *The Oxford Dictionary of National Biography*.

Daniel Stewart is a senior lecturer at the ANU College of Law, The Australian National University and a consultant to Sparke Helmore Lawyers. He was a National Undergraduate Scholar and received First Class Honours degrees in economics and law from The Australian National University. He has a Masters in law from the University of Virginia, where he was a John M. Olin Fellow in law and economics. He has practiced as a solicitor, been employed with the Corporate Law Economic Reform Program in the Commonwealth Attorney-General's Department, and was associate to Justice A. M. North of the Federal Court. His publications have considered the role of the distinction between public and private in administrative law, access to information and privacy.

Harshan Kumarasingham holds the Smuts Research Fellowship in Commonwealth Studies, University of Cambridge, and is a fellow of Wolfson College, Cambridge. He completed his doctorate at Victoria University of Wellington in comparative politics. His current research examines how the Westminster system was exported across the world. His publications include *Onward with Executive Power: Lessons from New Zealand 1947–57* (Victoria University of Wellington, 2010) and *A Political Legacy of the British Empire: Power and the parliamentary system in post-colonial India and Sri Lanka* (I. B. Tauris, 2013). He is also a senior research fellow at the Institute of Commonwealth Studies, University of London, and Alexander von Humboldt Research Fellow at Ludwig Maximilian University in Munich.

John Power is an emeritus professor in political science at the University of Melbourne. His current research interests are focused on reforming the roles of heads of state, so that they can take a leading role in the strengthening of what he calls 'fiducial governance'. In the development of these interests, he has looked to comparative governance, especially in semi-presidential regimes.

Evert Lindquist is professor and director, School of Public Administration, University of Victoria, British Columbia, and editor of *Canadian Public Administration*.

Jeffrey Harwood is a political scientist whose research interests include intergovernmental relations, fiscal federalism, and science communication. He is an adjunct lecturer at the John Curtin Institute of Public Policy, Curtin University, where he was a research fellow from 2007–2011. He is the co-author of *Government and Democracy in Australia*, 2nd ed. (Oxford University Press, 2009) (with Ian Cook and Mary Walsh). His recent publications include the commissioned reports 'The Effects of COAG's National Reform Agenda on Central Agencies' (ANZSOG, 2012) (with John Phillimore), and 'Common Cause: Strengthening Australia's cooperative federalism' (Council for the Australian Federation, 2009) (with John Wanna, John Phillimore and Alan Fenna).

John Phillimore has been Executive Director of the John Curtin Institute of Public Policy, Curtin University, since 2007, where he is also a professor in public policy. He lectured in policy at Murdoch University for 10 years and has had over 10 years' experience in senior government positions in the Western Australian State Government as chief of staff and adviser to several Ministers. He was also director of intergovernmental relations, where he advised the Western Australian Premier on COAG and other federalism-related matters. He currently works on a range of policy issues, including federalism, higher education, and innovation policy, and writes and comments on state and federal politics.

Ian Marsh is a visiting professor at the UTS Business School, University of Technology, Sydney. His most recent publication is *Democratic Decline and Democratic Renewal: Political Change in Britain, Australia and New Zealand* (Cambridge University Press, 2012) (with Raymond Miller).

John Butcher has worked as a policy and performance analyst in state and Commonwealth line and central agencies. He has a long-standing scholarly interest in the relationship between the formal institutions of government and civil society. He is especially interested in the political framing of the not-for-profit sector and its role as a vehicle for the delivery of public policy. For his PhD dissertation, he undertook a comparative case study of cross-sector policy frameworks in Australia, New Zealand, the United Kingdom and Canada.

Wendy Jarvie was a public servant for more than 20 years, including seven years as a deputy secretary in the Commonwealth Department of Education, Science and Training. She is currently a visiting professor at the School of Business, University of NSW at Canberra as well as undertaking early childhood education work for the World Bank.

Trish Mercer is an ANZSOG visiting fellow at The Australian National University. As a former senior executive, Trish has extensive experience in Commonwealth policy and program formulation, particularly in education, employment and training. Her research projects include early childhood education and schools reforms, and she is engaged in teaching through the executive education courses offered by ANU Australian National Institute of Public Policy.

Patricia Gerald received her Masters degree in public administration from the University of Victoria, Canada, in 2013. She has worked as a performance auditor at Australian National Audit Office and at the Office of the Auditor-General of British Columbia. In 2012, she received an Australia Award Endeavour Research Fellowship to further her research on performance audit, and was hosted by ANZSOG in Canberra. She currently works as a policy advisor for the Government of Alberta, in Edmonton, Canada.

1. Introduction — Embracing New Accountabilities, Confronting New Challenges: Canvassing options for next generation improvements

John Wanna

For several decades now Australian governments have been increasingly active in policy-making across traditional as well as new policy sectors, yet often remain ineffective in dealing with some of the more intransigent social and economic problems our nation faces. Governments seem unable to solve or mitigate the inherent problems in many specific areas of policy responsibility, such as child welfare and protection; dignified aged care (especially for the frail and aged); dealing with Indigenous well-being and closing the gap between Indigenous health indicators and those of the wider community; the management of mental health problems and care of those afflicted; dealing with chronic substance abuse across generations; the provision of effective education and health services; delivering sustainable energy and reducing carbon emissions; and improving environmental management and mitigating climate change and preparing for adaptation. This is just to name a few of these intractable policy problems of limited effectiveness.

However, despite recent rhetoric about the end of the age of entitlement, there is no evidence of a lack of appetite among either politicians or government officials in addressing areas they feel *need* attention — including behavioural change and forms of social engineering. Although politicians and media commentators like to think that the real motivation for this activity is entirely down to rising electoral expectations (see Tingle 2012), politicians and senior officials are also to blame for fanning such demands. Arguably there is more supply-side willingness to increase state responsibilities than demand-side expectations. Even in fiscally stringent times, governments have continued to demonstrate a real propensity to commit to long-term unfunded liabilities (their so-called 'signature projects'), locking in future governments and parliaments to generous funding plans conceived in today's opportunistic politics. There is still a mentality of 'let's try to fix everything' among the political elite, arguably guided today less by ideology and more by a desire to be seen to be doing something and to spawn legacy initiatives. There is also an attitude within government that substantial funding cannot be withdrawn from existing programs, even from those that may be of dubious worth, and that we will continue pouring good money after bad, even into programs that are not working well.

In making this critique of public policy, we need not go so far as to agree with the former US President Ronald Reagan when he asserted in his presidential campaign of 1980 that governments *are the problem*, not the solution. But we should recognise that governments often contribute towards the dimensions of the problem, and can make problems worse by their actions or inaction. Governments have their own serious limitations which often prevent them from optimising outcomes, and many analysts from within and without government have limited confidence that governments will get it right or do what is best. Governments can do great good, but they can also do great harm and damage the sectors they think they are assisting.

Dealing with policy issues: Pros and cons

In terms of policy effectiveness, governments are best equipped to deal with issues when they can be standardised or lend themselves to routine administration (such as taxation, entitlement provision, customs and quarantine, licences, passport control, etc.); they perform worst when they are faced with great complexity and uncertainty, non-routine problems, and unexpected events. Many important areas of public policy are more associated with the latter cluster of highly complex issues than the former routinised ones.

In addition to the limitations on government *per se*, we should also remember that we have multiple and competing governments in Australia, further complicating the picture. There are nine separate 'sovereign' governments in Australia, each with their own spheres of jurisdiction, constituencies and interests (and each with their own political oppositions). There are also 560 local jurisdictions with the closest relationships to the community at the ground level. These myriad jurisdictions continually interfere and encroach upon the policy responsibilities of the others in a fluid interface of 'contested federalism', sometimes labelled 'pragmatic federalism' (see Hollander and Patapan 2007). This makes any semblance of overall national coordination of a policy area difficult and protracted, and consistency is seen as a holy grail.

Australia is not alone in wrestling with these strategic, structural and implementation issues of governance. Globally, many other jurisdictions suffer from this same malaise. Europe is constantly wrestling with the competing demands of consistency versus diversity. America and Canada are similarly afflicted — with near-autonomous sub-national jurisdictions much more locally powerful than Australian states. New Zealand, with a unitary system of government, still has considerable local autonomy and discretion at the municipal level, especially in its provincial cities. Latin America has a long tradition of municipal and provincial government where regions can actively engage in public policy agendas relatively unconstrained by equity considerations.

To put it in a nutshell, public policy frameworks established by government can serve as initiators of change but also as impediments to change, with governments reacting, following, over-regulating, and seeking to control, but prevented from acting decisively. The relationship between policy settings and social change is a complex and often contradictory one, where governments can, at best, seek to facilitate change rather than lead and drive it. In many important ways, governments and their policies or laws provide the background context in which *other* drivers of change can take the initiative. Governments can provide some stability and continuities, offer certainties, guarantees, incentives, and impose penalties, which are important bedrocks to a modern functioning economy and society. They can mitigate sovereign risk by abiding by the rule of law, preserving institutional integrity, treating cases fairly and equally, providing some assurances of respect that are fundamental to social and economic planning, personal and group commitments, honouring ongoing agreements, purchases and investments, and so on. There is a fundamental role for government in regulating markets, especially in 'thin' markets and social areas (moving into the future, this may be more inter-jurisdictional and involve hybrid/voluntary forms, with government providing regulatory frameworks supplemented by self-regulation and conduct monitoring — health, professions, media, education, sport, advertising, consumer issues).

Yet we frequently overestimate the capacity of governments to plan strategically and achieve their intended objectives. As a comparatively 'statist' society, many Australians generally prefer to view governments as contributing to the 'solution' benignly and constructively — it is our domestic *Weltanschauung*. But governments often disappoint, perhaps because they cannot find or settle upon a given solution, (or, if one is found, because they cannot impose that solution on its constituents), and sometimes they cannot even win agreement about what the nature of the problem is. Governments have a great theoretical or normative potentiality for doing good and assisting good governance. Yet they often shirk their responsibilities to drive appropriate policy responses, offering second- or third-best compromises with predictable flaws. There are many possible reasons for this. They may not know what to do in a given circumstance, or find it hard to work out a practical solution amid all the competing pressures, or maybe they announce a solution but then find it impossible to agree on a course of action and stick with it. They may be too timid or reticent, too swayed by expedient politics, or too torn between competing alternatives. Sometimes governments may 'think' they know what they want to change in policy terms but be unable to carry it off and impose or facilitate their solution. Or they may be blocked by other powerful socio-economic forces and prevented from acting. The famous US policy analyst Peter Hall (1993) offers some persuasive scenarios explaining the various configurations governments find themselves in when confronted with dimensions of policy change. He argued that first order, second order and third order changes arise in ascending order from routine adjustments (first order) to changes in policy instruments (second order), to changing goals (third order), with each magnitude of change attracting different intensities of political contestation.

So, what's wrong with existing government and the public provision they provide?

In order to consider future reforms and improvements in the quality of governance and public policy outcomes, we need to examine more carefully the core attributes and capacities of existing government provision and the respective policy frames on which they rely. Governments have considerable baggage and bring past path dependencies to bear on current and future problems. Internally, governments have gradually changed from being traditional command hierarchies with limited responsibilities to broader institutional actors negotiating with policy networks, navigating complex relations with stakeholders, breeding interdependencies and engaging in shared responsibilities, but they *still* seek to operate in traditional command ways as if the landscape has not altered substantially (whether intentionally or by default). It is a modern conundrum that is sometimes difficult to fathom. In many social and economic sectors, as will be discussed below, governments feel that they have to collaborate in order to provide services (co-produce, co-design, co-deliver, etc.), but have not acquired the necessary skills and capabilities to be able to do so successfully and effectively, and their bureaucratic and traditional accountabilities may act as a gravitational pull against such endeavours.

Critiques of government as an institutional entity, and especially of its capacities to deliver effective policy, tend to commence with the observation that it is shaped by democratically elected governments (party regimes), but then focus on the limiting cultures and perverse incentives it operates with, in addition to the traditional ways in which public provision and public policies are structured and managed. A brief critique of the present state of Australian government is likely to include the following elements.

First, our governments are subservient to the political cycle. They are dominated by short-term calculations and are reactive and responsive to immediate electoral pressures. Governments tend to regard citizens as 'immediate bounded rationalists', interested primarily in instant gratification rather than long-term planning and preparation for future contingencies. Voters are thought to have a short attention span and politicians continually pander to it. At the same time, governments find it hard to interest the electorate in long-term issues and do not tend to invest much time or leadership acumen in educating or strategically directing policy issues of greater scope.

Second, governments are motivated and incentivised by popularity in ways that erode resilience and sustainability. Their concern with popularity limits their horizons and attention spans and reinforces the imperatives to surrender to the 24/7 media cycle. They rarely act deliberately in ways that threaten to erode populism or will make them deeply unpopular. This proclivity to seek popularity and be well-liked places a straitjacket around the kinds of issues governments are willing to address or engage with, including any possible solutions than can be considered and implemented. For example, constantly increasing the aged pension according to movements in average male earnings from generic taxation (consolidated revenue) is very popular among this older, welfare-dependent constituency, but does not particularly help provide sustainable incomes for growing numbers of older Australians into the future.

Third, majoritarian political systems are usually adversarial in political and policy terms. Successive governments can unpick the reforms of their predecessors. The 'winner takes all' philosophy is problematic for good policy development, and there is little effort invested in building consensus with opponents or rival political entities. There are many areas of wasted policy legacies — policies discontinued, dismantled, aborted, undermined, or entirely reconfigured. Adversarial systems tend to build distrust and scepticism of government and temporary policy solutions.

Fourth, in considering policy options, governments generally tend to be overly cautious and risk-averse. They are expedient and prone to back-sliding, especially if they meet resistance and the going gets tough (recent examples include the much mooted emissions trading scheme, the mining super profits tax, and the issue of substantial tax reform).

Fifth, many parts of the public sector have insufficient or inadequate capacities to perform the things asked of them. Jurisdictions are inward-looking, self-regarding and self-referential. Departments and agencies remain too insular, risk-averse, complacent, hide-bound and unwilling to embrace transformational change. Enduring bureaucratic norms and hierarchical authorities prevail in administrative systems, often working to narrow ministerial agendas, nervous of offending the political echelons, and staffed by those interested in time-serving rather than entrepreneurial activity. Agencies still tend to comply in perfunctory ways when reporting their activities or performances. Recruitment patterns have made public services more diverse and representative of the community, but because they still operate on conventions of a career service, flexibility and responsiveness have arguably been reduced in some sectors.

Sixth, governments have gradually denuded most of their internal organic research capacities and much of their policy capacities (collective memory, operational knowledge, technical capacities). They are left to search various external sources of research for policy-relevant works (for example, universities, think tanks, consultants, other jurisdictions, and even consulting Google). But these administrators may not have the analytical capacities to make the best choices when confronted with raw data, predigested options, or a range of alternatives.

Seventh, governments suffer from declining trust in public institutions and community disaffection. Despite appealing to populism, there are mounting arguments worldwide that many advanced democracies suffer from the malaise of 'democratic deficits' — which can exacerbate disaffection, alienation, social exclusion, de-legitimacy, political protests and social unrest — and a widespread perception that the political system increasingly represents and serves a narrow set of interests. If this leads to people disengaging from society and public life, then governments face greater problems trying to re-engage with these disaffected or marginalised cohorts. Cleavages marked by welfare dependency, regionalism, race or ethnicity may further exacerbate these issues.

Is cultural transformation necessary for the public sector?

Many of the impediments that afflict our current public bureaucracies and public providers are not insurmountable or unsolvable. But they will require governments to undertake various systemic transformations of structure, substance and process. Systemic changes will need to be made to the political regime, a movement away from command-driven cultures based on ministerial responsibility to empowering cultures based on learning and improvement. Public sector cultures of risk avoidance and blame-shifting are likely to be superseded with cultures of capacity-building and achievement-orientation, with policy workers more willing to explore other approaches to getting results, such as experimental policy-making. Traditional, narrow notions of public accountability (based on punitive rule-subservience and negative sanctions based on 'gotcha' logics) will need to be replaced by performance answerabilities and more generous reward and incentive structures for success. Within the administrative systems of policy-making, this will require something of a revolution in managerial thinking, capacity-calibration and organisational learning. This, in turn, will impact on many of the standard operating procedures and administrative routines of the entire public sector, such as organisational design incorporating networks; more externally focused management practices; more scope for outsourcing, working with partnerships and developing hybrid delivery systems; greater emphasis on stakeholders, recipients and clients, and the management of relationships with civil society; wider recruitment processes and lateral hiring of staff; more diverse career development trajectories; more outward-bound staff training and executive development; and performance review and management conceived of as outcome and impact assessments.

The Public Sector Research Centre, a private sector think-tank sponsored by the accounting firm PricewaterhouseCoopers, has recently identified a future set of different cultural and operational norms for government and our patterns of governance (Public Sector Research Centre 2013). It sees a broad set of transformations with the old statist/public administrative modes of government giving way and being superseded by new roles and relationships, new organisational norms and characteristics, new ways of organising and reviewing services, and new ways of incorporating the community as co-designers and co-producers of services. While improving policy and implementation effectiveness, some of these transformations may be undoubtedly more costly in the short-term (and run counter to current fiscal pressures), although in the longer-term greater benefits may eventually flow to the community. Its projections can be summarised as follows:

Old governments moving from:	New governance moving to:	Explanatory comment
Citizens under control	Citizens in control	Decentred, empowering citizens and community with meaningful control
Governing for citizens	Governing with citizens	Two-way interdependency and multiple initiations of policy and delivery systems
Organisational silos with discrete responsibilities	Organisation networks with multiple shared responsibilities	Porous agencies, working through/with others, shared responsibilities
Public sector organisations as big, all-in-one behemoths	Public sector organisations as small, flexible purpose-driven entities	Breakdown of autarky and monopoly, and replacement by customised and differently constituted agents
Government as service provider	Governments as service facilitator/broker/commissioning agent	Different role for governments and more subtle points of facilitation/intervention
Government owning inputs and processes	Governments and citizens owning outcomes	Greater community discretion and outcome setting, replacing governments calling all the shots

Old governments moving from:	New governance moving to:	Explanatory comment
Measuring outputs (activities and busyness indicators)	Measuring outcomes and intended impacts qualitatively	Substantive quantitative and quality evaluations by and for the community
Forced cooperation based on enforcement	Mutual collaboration based on trust	Self-organising relationships for mutual benefit
Trust in the 'strong, decisive leader'	Trust in each other and co-producers, the 'servant leader'	Governments performing coordinating role rather than directing role

This chart can be interpreted in at least two ways. It can be understood as suggesting that older styles of organisational management will be *replaced* by newer styles and cultures, or it can be interpreted as anticipating that newer styles of management will *co-exist* with older styles, supplementing each other and producing new synergies. Many will argue that there will always be some role for traditional hierarchic forms of administration and standardised delivery chains. But inevitably the newer cultures of governance and administration will challenge and erode the principles of traditional administration in the search for different outcomes.

Speaking from today's vantage point, despite these predictions of major transformational change (the supposed future 'nirvana'), governments are clearly a long way off such root-and-branch recalibrations. There is much talk of new governance models, but less actual progress on the ground. Somewhat contradictorily, there may be ample evidence to suggest that there has been some clawing back of more flexible and experimental managing styles in order to restore traditional accountabilities. Complacency still has its adherents, and some traditional public administrators (especially ministers) would still consider these transformational imperatives and opportunities as subversive cultures threatening old style administration. Hence, when looking across the entire public sector — from schools to hospitals, from central to line agencies, and from regulatory to delivery agencies — large parts of the existing public sector are not 'transformation ready' in the terms outlined above.

Government still retains resilience and some comparative advantages, but recalibration is necessary to progress in the future

Governments remain resourceful actors with a plethora of potentially powerful policy instruments and command powers at their disposal (including expenditures and program funding, taxation and fines, authorisations and enforcement powers, tax expenditures or concessions, legislation and regulations, direct provision and ownership, indirect provision and contractual engagement, and educational, promotional and marketing campaigns). These instruments are mostly deployed in immediate policy delivery rather than in anticipating future long-term needs, although there are successful examples of longer-term planning (such as superannuation, and educational completion targets at Year 12 and tertiary levels). Australian governments tend to use and deploy an ad hoc mix of instruments and powers, not necessarily optimising their effectiveness or impact. For instance, governments across the federal–state divide are not generally good at identifying key intervention points — identifying which instruments at their disposal will be most effective to use and which can make the greatest desired impact.

Governments can create the conditions upon which we are able to plan and anticipate future needs and constraints. This is a facilitating role, bringing expertise and needs together. To date, governments have not necessarily been good at this role and many of their formal attempts have become politicised, ineffective or were soon overtaken by events (for example, the Commission for the Future in 1980s, EPAC in the 1980s, the 2020 Summit of 2008, many state government future planning scenarios, the 'Big Australia' debates, and future workforce projection exercises variously produced by Commonwealth agencies). Long-term planning may be one area where governments can fulfil an essential role in bringing various players and voices together while mediating the longer-term public interest.

As the initiators of major strategic planning exercises, governments need to build in more adaptability and agility to future policy stances. There are good techniques for environmental scanning and scenario building/projection testing. Governments should produce projections and intended plans (budgets, employment estimates and housing forecasts, etc.) as a *range* of most likely forecasts (based on variable assumptions and calculations), not as artificially definitive numbers producing linear trends. At present, many of these documents are produced to make governments look good rather than to provide realistic assessments of projected circumstances.

Governments accordingly have a responsibility in agenda-setting, defining the issues we ought to be talking about and wrestling with solutions and options (a form of social 'mind-setting'). Traditional institutions that *could* play this role (for example, various parliaments and parliamentary committees, government departments, university research centres, and think tanks) have often been disappointing or episodic in their attention, so we tend to rely on specialised bodies with defined mandates (for example, Productivity Commission, Climate Commission/Council, the Inter-Generational Report exercise, the former Indicative Council, the Australian Institute of Health and Welfare), but most of these relate solely to economic, fiscal or population issues. There is scope to broaden these commission-type bodies to provide greater strategic direction, but the problem will always be the question over their substantive connection to existing policy-making processes and the priorities of the government of the day. On future agendas, governments need to relax their 'control' urges and allow different players to make different cases — encouraging radically different scenarios to be thought through and evaluated (through peer review processes directed at learning, not necessarily formal performance reporting). For example, in Australia with its vast land mass, we might like to encourage our states and regions to go in different directions and adopt different scenarios in order to evaluate their respective effectiveness in anticipating future needs.

Governments are becoming far more technologically sophisticated. The 'technology can transform government' movement is very strong in countries such as the US, Canada, Europe, and Singapore. The same is true in the areas of e-health, educational access and online delivery, one-entry portals, social media, and 'open government', where the bounds of public authority are porous and deliberations take place through joint collaborations. Having said that, while the promise of tech-enabled governance is clearly conceivable, the actual achievements to date have been generally disappointing.

Governments need to invest in consensual approaches where decisions are enriched by different voices and perspectives, and can stand the test of time. They need to promote community-wide dialogues over problems, issues and directions, bringing the various political parties to the table and moving towards shared objectives and outcomes. We need to develop notions of shared ownership of problems and their proposed solutions, while allowing scope for some diversity of options.

Governments need to facilitate change by welcoming greater experimental governance (see Charles Sabel's works on this — Sabel and Zeitlin 2010; see also Albury 2011), learning by doing, and greater autonomy for frontline deliverers/ providers/teachers/trainers in many policy areas: social disadvantage, schooling, technical education, higher education, and job-readiness. Experiments with behavioural economics (as is occurring in NSW at present in relation to job-readiness and employability) are worth monitoring and developing where they are effective. Experimentation and innovation are likely to require a greater role for professionally trained people with relevant technical and specialist skills (in delivering services in areas of health, education, social policy and welfare).

In operational terms, governments will face many workforce challenges in their own sphere of employment and engagement of myriad human resources (including contractual provision, greater reliance on part-time and casual workers, and volunteers). They will need to be 'faster' in responding to changing needs and developments, and as a result they will require flatter organisational structures, more streamlined capacities, more agile abilities, and more technological capabilities. There is much scope for closer engagement with the community and non-government actors through co-design procedures, co-delivery, co-production and the techniques of behavioural economics — if only governments were prepared to accept that they will inevitably have to share the risks and rewards and open up policy processes to a wider range of inputs.

On the one hand, governments can potentially do many things well and achieve intended outcomes for the economy and society, on the other hand, they can also do great damage through neglect, unwise decisions, or relying on inappropriate policy settings. They are less sensitive to the perverse consequences of their actions and inactions and rarely anticipate the unintended consequences of their policy frameworks or adjustments. In such circumstances, governments should be more prepared to experiment and explore alternative options in policy planning (for example, through random trials, customised experimentation, and alternative scenarios), realising that they are unlikely ever to know all the answers into the future, but still have some real capacities and technical abilities to assist social and economic development through better analysis and coordination.

The present volume of essays in reform options

The present volume of essays brings together a number of reflections and reform options from practitioners, researchers and analysts interested in improved governance. Some essays canvass particular ideas, such as Chris Eccles's focus on reforming trust in government, or Daniel Stewart's examination of the value of freedom of information laws to improve scrutiny of government performance. Other essays highlight continual areas of concern in underperformance and suggest better ways forward, such as Ian Marsh's analysis of the dysfunctionality of new public management when confronted with complex social problems and multiple disadvantage in regional Indigenous communities, Patricia Gerald's assessment of how 'follow the money' audit reforms should be conducted to produce the best results, and John Wanna's critical review of the history of euphemistic budget reforms while governments have largely shunned much-needed remedies to resource management. Other essays explore the analytical findings from previous episodes of successful reform, trying to generalise the lessons from success while at the same time pondering the question of why reform trajectories tend to stagnate unless they receive continual prodding and encouragement. In this latter category is the essay by Wendy Jarvie and Trish Mercer on educational reform in literacy at the turn of the last century, and Jeffrey Harwood's and John Phillimore's analysis of the achievements of cooperative federalism as evidenced by the national competition reforms. These essays point to areas for further development and improvement. None will contribute the last word on the topic, but all make considered contributions to meeting the reform challenges.

Part one of this book clusters together essays directed to examining systemic accountabilities, including central oversight and management of the core public service; parliamentary oversight of the public service; the benefit of transparency in improving government performance; the imperatives of further reform to our budgetary systems; and the effects of the limitations on parliamentarism on the prospects for good governance. In the last essay in this section, Harshan Kumarasingham and John Power appraise 'constrained parliamentarism' across the New Zealand and Australian contexts, concluding that historical, institutional, and electoral differences have resulted in far stronger constraints on executive power in Australia than its neighbour. The main message in each of these contributions is that we ought to be able to undertake periodic systemic reviews of the effectiveness of the system and its inherent limitations or institutional design problems.

In part two, the focus shifts to addressing the question of how policy processes can be improved to improve actual results and social impacts. Evert Lindquist and John Wanna re-emphasise the importance of implementation processes and their contributions to quality governance, as well as offering applied advice to policymakers in reviewing implementation. Jeffrey Harwood, John Phillimore and Patricia Gerald reflect on substantive improvements to policy outcomes driven through intergovernmental relations. Ian Marsh surveys a litany of poorly designed Indigenous programs that failed to deliver intended outcomes, and suggests better policy processes to improve Indigenous well-being. John Butcher explores the increasingly protracted relations between governments and the organisations representing the 'not-for-profit' sector, and considers the origins and value of formal 'compacts' that guide the quality and effectiveness of their policy relationships. Finally, Wendy Jarvie and Trish Mercer dissect the difficulties in prosecuting policy change in a highly contested policy sector with powerful stakeholders and interest groups. They centre their account on the importance of finding a champion of policy change with sufficient policy vision and political fortitude to overcome resistance and see reform through to fruition.

Each of the succeeding 11 chapters in this volume has some connection with the Australia and New Zealand School of Government (ANZSOG). Some were specifically commissioned research exercises, some were written for other purposes by ANZSOG-associated staff and have been included in this collection, others were presented at ANZSOG events and later polished for publication here. The collection bears close inspection from practitioners and researchers alike, and should make a valuable and long-lasting contribution to the ongoing reform of government in Australia.

References

Albury, D. 2011, 'Creating the Conditions for Radical Public Service Innovation', *Australian Journal of Public Administration* 70(3), pp. 227–235.

Hall, P. 1993, 'Policy Paradigms, Social Learning and the State: The case of economic policy-making in Britain', *Comparative Politics* 25, pp. 275–296.

Hollander, R. and H. Patapan 2007, 'Pragmatic Federalism: Australian federalism from Hawke to Howard', *Australian Journal of Public Administration* 66(3), pp. 280–297.

Public Sector Research Centre 2013. *The Future of Government*, PricewaterhouseCoopers, Sydney. Available at: http://www.pwc.com/en_gx/gx/psrc/publications/assets/pwc_future_of_government_pdf.pdf.

Sabel, C. and J. Zeitlin 2010. *Experimentalist Governance in the European Union*, Oxford University Press, Oxford.

Tingle, L. 2012. 'Great Expectations: Government, entitlement and an angry nation', *Quarterly Essay* 46, Black Inc., Melbourne.

Part I. Systemic Accountabilities

2. Restoring Trust in Government[1]

Chris Eccles

The topic of my chapter, restoring trust in government, has universal application to public administration and is central to many of the fundamental challenges facing government and its institutions. Accordingly, I want to address a number of key areas where we, as public servants, have the ability to both influence and initiate the process of restoring trust in government, more particularly, through the way we work with the citizens of New South Wales, a trust in and of the public sector.

We have all heard phrases such as 'I'm from the government and I'm here to help', and 'the cheque is in the mail'. These phrases have entered the lexicon as classic statements of counter-intuition, with the implication of cynicism and mistrust. But has it always been thus with trust?

To begin, let me provide some context. Various surveys and studies have found that, since the mid-1960s, public trust in government and political institutions has been decreasing in virtually all of the advanced industrialised democracies (Dalton and Wattenburg 2000). Research conducted using both series of the World Values Survey conducted in the early 1980s (1981–84) and the early 1990s (1990–93) provides substantial support for theories that focus on the performance of governments and political institutions to explain citizens' declining confidence in them (see http://www.worldvaluessurvey.org).

A 2005 survey of Canadian citizens found that the degree to which citizens trust government is dependent upon a number of factors (ICCS 2005). The survey found that citizen trust and confidence is promoted when public organisations provide:

- good leadership and management (50–65 per cent impact);
- equal and ethical treatment (10–15 per cent impact);
- quality services (10–20 per cent impact); and
- services that meet citizens' and community needs (10–25 per cent impact).

These measures do not, however, account for declining confidence related to how well a government is able to manage the economy. Many studies have found that citizens have less trust in governments that cannot generate economic growth, create jobs, and competently deliver social services (Nye 1997). Conversely,

---

1 This paper was written in 2011 when Chris Eccles was Director General of the NSW Department of Premier and Cabinet.

governments that can bring about economic growth, create jobs, provide access to education, and deliver services in an easy and transparent manner are more trusted (Fiorina 1978; Mackuen et al. 1992).

The most extensive evidence on public trust in government comes from the United States and its American National Election Studies data series (see http://www.electionstudies.org/). Early readings from the late 1950s revealed a largely supportive public with most people believing that:

- one could trust government to do the right thing;
- there were few dishonest people in government;
- most officials knew what they were doing; and,
- government was run for the benefit of all.

These positive feelings were relatively unchanged until the mid-1960s, and then declined sharply. For example, in 1964, 75 per cent of the American public believed they could trust their government to do the right thing most of the time, by 1995 only 15 per cent did so. Closer to home, New Zealand studies reflect a similar trend. In 1985, 8.5 per cent of New Zealanders had a great deal of confidence in their government, but by 1998 this had fallen to 2.5 per cent (State Services Commission 2002).

A study conducted in the United States using empirical evidence contends that the pervasiveness of the trend across advanced industrial democracies cannot be explained simply on the basis of government performance. This is especially so as the latter half of the twentieth century was a time of generally improving standards of living, characterised by rising affluence, expanding education, and improved social opportunities for most citizens.

Whilst there are national explanations for the drop in trust in government (in the case of the US, for example, the Vietnam War, Watergate, and the Lewinsky scandal), it is unreasonable to assume that a simultaneous decline of trust over the past 40 or more years throughout the advanced industrial democracies is purely coincidental. This prompts one to look beyond specific national conditions and take account of factors that are broadly affecting the advanced industrial democracies as a group. This then leads us to conclude that general forces of social change are affecting these nations, including Australia for which there is no nation-specific empirical, longitudinal data.

The changes, described as a 'social modernisation', are transforming the relationship between the citizen and the state. Scepticism of the political process has also grown more rapidly among the young and better-educated, with the new style of politics represented by less deference to authority, more assertive styles of action, and higher expectations for the democratic process

(Inglehart 1990; Dalton 2004). It is suggested that changing citizen values and expectations have created a new political Zeitgeist, which stimulates greater scepticism of government (Dalton 2005).

Globalisation, a greater interconnectedness through information and communications technology, and increased advocacy of non-government organisations have also contributed to making citizens more aware of their rights and therefore more demanding of their governments. Recent events in North Africa and the Middle East have made this dramatically apparent.

A literature review produced for the 'Seventh Global Forum on Reinventing Government' explored the theme of building trust in government and concluded that expectations of citizens vis-à-vis their governments and political representatives in the era of globalisation had changed with the possible emergence of a new civic culture:

> The new civic culture cherishes trust for itself ... demands sincerity and truthfulness in the words and deeds of representatives ... It wants to be able to monitor government performance much more closely than before ... [and suggests that] governments today would be better off applying programs and policies that enhance trust in government directly ... rendering politics more transparent and dispersing the power of political decision-making to foster accountability (Blind 2006).

Partially prompted by popular dissatisfaction with the governing process, contemporary democracies have implemented reforms to expand access, increase transparency, and improve accountability of government.

Political and social parameters are also at play, with political scandals, seemingly frequent findings of corruption, and the sometimes disproportionate focus of the media on these issues contributing to the decline of trust in government institutions and political leaders. However, these events tend only to reinforce the (generally poor) impressions of government already held by an increasingly cynical public.

Governments here have clearly recognised the importance of addressing the issue of trust. As opposition leader, former NSW Premier Barry O'Farrell made it clear in a speech to the Institute of Chartered Secretaries Australia that the NSW Liberals and Nationals were resolved to restoring trust in public institutions, and to 'unite the public sector, individuals and communities, and elected representatives in a network of trust' (O'Farrell 2010a). A number of initiatives that are currently being pursued in NSW are testimony to this commitment: the establishment of a Public Service Commission; legislation embedding new public sector values and an ethical framework; the strengthening of whistleblower protections; the imminent appointment of a Customer Service Commissioner; and the creation of Infrastructure NSW. I will return to these initiatives later.

How can the public sector meet the challenge of restoring trust and better meeting citizens' needs? As the literature reveals, there are various dimensions to the construct of trust and numerous factors that serve as a basis for understanding citizens' declining trust in government. In recognition of this, the OECD refers to the implementation of the so-called 'ITARI principle' as the basis for trust-building and performance improvements in the public sector (OECD 2009). The five components that comprise the ITARI principle will not be unfamiliar: integrity, transparency, accountability, responsiveness, and inclusiveness.

In order to ensure that we are able to act in an inclusive manner when dealing with citizens, community, and stakeholders, the public sector needs to address the critical challenge of increasing transparency in how decisions are made and implemented. This can be achieved by paving new ways to increase citizen and stakeholder participation and engagement in formulating public services and products. Facilitating a greater involvement and engagement with and amongst stakeholders is critical to assisting government delivers on the expectations of citizens.

A 'network of trust': Interventions designed to connect government and stakeholders

Critical to the way government interacts with key stakeholders — public servants, citizens and communities — is the creation of the 'network of trust' referred to by the NSW Premier in his speech to the Institute of Chartered Secretaries Australia. The vision is fourfold: for citizens to be able to trust public institutions and to defend their interests; for politicians and ministers to be able to trust that the public service will give them objective, high quality and fearless advice; for public servants to trust government to do what it says; and for public servants to be valued by government and citizens for their integrity, impartiality and expertise.

Key to facilitating a new vision of government–stakeholder interactions based on a mutual trust are a number of initiatives currently being pursued by the NSW government.

The new Public Service Commission will work with public servants and public sector workers as stakeholders, to restore and maintain the highest levels of integrity, impartiality, ability, accountability and leadership. It will also explore ways in which the public sector can develop its people through enhanced mobility, whether via exchanges between departments, agencies and other jurisdictions or secondments with the private and community sectors. A key challenge will be to ensure that the public sector workforce has the capabilities and technical skills to deliver efficient and effective services into the future.

A Customer Service Commissioner will work to ensure that government interactions with the citizens of NSW meet the needs of citizens. The then Premier Barry O'Farrell (2010b), in a pre-election address to the Committee for Economic Development Australia on 12 November 2010, indicated that the purpose of the commissioner is to:

- bring the interest of public service customers and the defence of public value and public interest right to the heart of decision-making;
- develop practical and sustainable ways to give government's customers the value and results they deserve; and,
- ensure customer-centred services are a strategic priority for government, with ministers to be the champions of the 'customer' within their portfolios.

The Premier further identified five customer service principles that provide a framework for implementing this new direction:

- making customer focus a leadership issue;
- simplifying government;
- redesigning public service delivery to suit people, not bureaucracies;
- devolving authority to people, communities and frontline staff; and
- measuring results and ensuring accountability.

A third body, Infrastructure NSW, has been established in legislation to work with the private sector to deliver coordinated infrastructure planning across the whole of government using the most efficient and effective funding mechanisms available, to deliver the best results possible. It will be responsible for preparing a 20-year 'State Infrastructure Strategy' for NSW, along with detailed five-year infrastructure plans that will set out the details of projects, sequencing and funding arrangements in the forward estimates of the NSW budget. The *intention* of the government in establishing this body is to ensure independent — non-political — infrastructure decision-making. The *impact* of Infrastructure NSW will be to bring private sector expertise to bear in this decision-making.

The need for a more outward-looking public sector

Giving more than lip service to the notion of putting citizens first means, in one sense, that the public sector must look beyond itself for developing solutions to public problems. We need to both understand and acknowledge that the public sector does not hold all the answers and, by extension, does not necessarily have the expertise, capacity and resources to meet the ever-evolving needs and expectations of citizens. The custom and practice — dare I say, 'culture' — of introspection is, I believe, the single greatest risk to the relevance and effectiveness of the public sector.

We must also ensure that we engage with communities and stakeholders so as to achieve sustainable, citizen-focused outcomes when developing and implementing policies or service delivery solutions. Furthermore, blindly following rules and processes risks creating 'solutions' that simply address internal control parameters and/or that align with 'conventional wisdoms'.

An outward-looking public sector will establish a dialogue with communities of interest to ensure priorities are appropriate and approaches sound. It will also encourage members of the wider community to more actively contribute to service delivery improvements, policy and program development, and to make progress in areas that rely more on public choices than on government interventions (such as saving water and lowering obesity levels).

Government will need to be open to feedback and actively engage with communities about decisions that concern the services to be provided and how they are funded, and remain open to new ways of providing services.

Embracing new approaches to improving the quality of policy advice and service delivery outcomes

Participatory approaches and requirements

If the trust of citizens is a prerequisite for the efficient functioning of government, we need to address the critical challenge of increasing transparency in how decisions are made and implemented by paving new ways to increase citizen and stakeholder participation and engagement.

Stakeholder engagement, a common activity across government, is a key component in effective service delivery. I need to emphasise that it is not an exercise in managing stakeholder expectations. Governments have become experts in stakeholder management. I am as guilty as the next senior public service manager of past laziness in the identification of stakeholders around a given issue (often falling back to the litany of usual suspects: the Business Council of Australia, Australian Industry Group, Australian Chamber of Commerce and Industry, and Australian Council of Trade Unions), and then attentiveness to the cosmetics of engagement while seeking to control, manage and/or minimise their actual impact.

A more productive way to conceptualise stakeholder engagement is to break it down into five broad categories of participatory approaches viewed along a continuum, starting with low-level engagement and leading to high-level partnering characterised by shared ownership and accountability. The participatory approaches on this 'engagement continuum' are defined as follows:

- Networking: a low level of engagement characterised by information exchange about strategies and activities;
- Coordination: structured consultation on strategies or activities to influence outcomes;
- Cooperation: formal involvement in the development of outcomes;
- Collaboration: similar to cooperation, except that this phase signals changes in the way stakeholders behave when working together; and
- Partnering: shared accountability for the product and in the achievement of the goals set.

Importantly, the model of the engagement continuum I have described imposes a discipline by requiring a forensic assessment of the exact relationship proposed for each stakeholder group and the level of reciprocity that can be expected from government in the relationship.

Too often, government defaults to the language of partnership — and thereby sets expectations around that promised engagement — when something different is intended. A more diligent and honest approach avoids pain on both sides by recognising that different levels of participation are acceptable and more or less desirable depending upon the characteristics of the policy process and the goals being pursued. In addition, each participatory approach will require a different design, using a new combination of tools and methodologies, much like the way that each participatory initiative contains a unique mix of people and institutions.

To return to rules and process fixation, misguided attempts to strictly standardise and replicate protocols, in line with conventional scientific practice, can also undermine the participatory process. To illustrate, there is a view that some of the frameworks that were successfully applied to the management of the multitude of projects that were undertaken in the lead up to the Sydney Olympic Games, and which were then retained post-Olympics, have had some longer-term unintended consequences. The nature of the Sydney Olympic Games projects (particularly in terms of arrangements like public–private partnerships), their scale (in terms of the magnitude of the work required), size (in terms of budget and other necessary resourcing), and the tight delivery time frames, together with the public scrutiny they received, demanded a specific and necessarily rigorous response in terms of the probity frameworks that were applied.

However, these highly engineered probity frameworks continue to be used today as a one-size-fits-all approach to risk management. Rather than pursue good outcomes, is it possible that the application of the pre-existing probity frameworks, through no better reason than a preoccupation with process, has created barriers to the fomenting of new ideas, stifled opportunity for innovation and resulted in reluctance on the part of the business community to effectively engage with the public sector and vice versa? Those from outside government who have confronted our approaches to unsolicited infrastructure proposals and tendering generally might be forgiven for thinking so.

I hasten to add that I am not advocating the dismantling of probity frameworks or the casting aside of risk management methodologies, but rather that they be fit for purpose, taking account of the value, complexity and sensitivity of the initiative or project being pursued. We should be reminded that the goal of risk management is not the total elimination of risk, but an approach aimed at effectively identifying and assessing risk with a view to mitigating its potential impact. Risk management frameworks, much like engagement strategies, need to be developed so that they are fit for purpose.

Sir David Normington, appointed to oversee public appointments and the civil service code and recruitment in the UK, criticised the recruitment code of practice as too 'process-driven … too complex, over-regulated', and 'too prescribed and specific'. He said that 'it is time for people to stop leaning on the rules', because 'if you are concentrating on stopping things you tend to forget that you are also there to enable'. He also made the point in this context that people need to start engaging their brains. I would like to think that this means looking for 'new ideas that work'. If this also means providing the public service with the authority, competence and tools to align probity and risk requirements with legitimate public service innovation and experimentation, then so be it.

Participation, as I have outlined, allows the community opportunity to contribute ideas and expertise to the solving of problems. Participation, in all of its forms, improves the effectiveness of government by encouraging partnerships and cooperation within and across levels of government, and between the government and private institutions.

Co-production and market design: Working towards citizen-centric solutions

The concepts of co-production, co-creation and market design have evolved from a similar footing; they each involve taking a citizen-centric approach to policy development and program delivery. It is no longer adequate for government to be just the rule-setter and service-provider. Government needs a restless value-seeking imagination that constantly searches out ways to create public value (Benington and Moore 2011).

Co-production is an active but voluntary behaviour by a citizen which is conjoint with government activity and which creates value in the form of outputs or outcomes. Support for co-production processes is central to the design policies that encourage, enable or educate citizens to make choices that contribute to wider public goals.

Co-production is not about offloading the delivery of services to the community to reduce spending; rather, it is defined by:

- Joint development of policy and service delivery to realise shared strategic outcomes;
- The community as co-architects in the design of policies and programs that concern them and their resources;
- Citizen participation and involvement in government activities; and
- Collaboration between the state and the citizen in the production of socially desired outcomes.

The aim is to mobilise the additional productive capabilities of citizens to complement service delivery in areas of public concern — volunteers of the rural fire service, for example, 'produce' emergency responses, but also assist, or 'co-produce', with respect to educating property owners of the need to undertake fire prevention or mitigation work. Citizens sorting their household waste to facilitate recycling are also engaged in co-production.

Market design builds further on the principles of co-production in that it adds elements of devolved government — where funding is provided to non-government entities for goods/services — and co-regulation — where the regulatory role is shared between government and industry.

Concluding observations

Introducing new participatory approaches where we must engage with citizens, and apply citizen-centric research and design thinking, can be challenging. According to Christian Bason of Denmark's MindLab, three myths in particular characterise the involvement of citizens in these types of processes (see Bason 2013).

First, there is the fear of 'citizen dictators': by involving citizens or business representatives explicitly, as public servants we might be devolving our decision-making authority. The purpose of involvement is not to ask citizens which ideas they prefer, but to explore which ideas are likely to work.

Second, citizen involvement requires too many resources: it will take too long and it will be too expensive. Energy and resources are necessary for citizen involvement, but consider the alternative: what does it cost to develop supposedly 'expert' solutions behind a desk, 'roll them out', and then realise, based on citizens' complaints, rising service costs and political fall-out, that the solution doesn't work? Citizen involvement is a cost-effective means of ensuring that new solutions really do meet users' needs, and that they hit the target in terms of service improvements and better outcomes.

Third, citizen involvement creates unrealistic expectations: now that we have generated these new ideas together, don't citizens expect something to happen? Most citizens and business owners understand that in a political system, especially in a democracy, there is no guarantee that just because a group of public servants think that an idea is a good one it will be judged so by top management or by politicians. It is therefore necessary to clarify expectations — that we would take the process and their input seriously — and report to them what, if any, ideas we would continue to work on.

We should nevertheless be encouraged in this endeavour, as it is evident that there is an enormous appetite for engagement in the business and non-government sectors, and, critically, a real and genuine willingness to make a contribution to NSW's enhanced performance. This was made clear to me soon after commencing my role here in NSW, when, at the invitation of former premier Nick Greiner, I was invited to an informal gathering of 20 or so influential people drawn from the business world, university, community and cultural sectors, and past mandarins from the bureaucracy. They shared their aspirations for NSW, their frustration at the generally closed and introverted nature of the public sector, and their enthusiasm to be involved in what they characterised as the rejuvenation of the state.

In considering how the NSW public service can push through this open door and take systematic advantage of the knowledge and experience held by people similar to those I met from outside government, I am working with Dr Michael Spence, Vice Chancellor at the University of Sydney, to convene forums that bring together senior public servants, academic, business and community leaders to talk about opening lines of engagement and explore ideas for unleashing the potential of our external partners (using the term in its true sense). From this will emerge a specific course of action for *how* the public service will move from introversion to extroversion. We have permission from this government to engage. It is now for us to make it happen.

To conclude, I am not so naive as to believe that the phrase, 'I am from the government and I am here to help', will ever again be accepted at face value. But I am confident that initiatives such as the NSW Public Service Commission, Infrastructure NSW, the Customer Service Commission, and the external leaders engagement exercise will go some considerable way to creating the foundations on which that trust can be built. To underscore these initiatives, I suggest we reword the phrase to say: 'I am from the government and I need — and want — *your* help'.

References

Bason, C. 2013, 'Engaging Citizens in Policy Innovation: Benefitting public policy from the design inputs of citizens and stakeholders as experts', in E. Lindquist, S. Vincent and J. Wanna (eds) *Putting Citizens First: Engagement in policy and service delivery for the 21st century*, ANU E Press, Canberra.

Benington, J. and M. Moore 2011, *Public Value, Theory and Practice*, Palgrave Macmillan, New York.

Blind, P. K. 2006, 'Building Trust in Government in the Twenty-First Century: Review of literature and emerging issues'. Available at: http://unpan1.un.org/intradoc/groups/public/documents/un/unpan025062.pdf.

Dalton, J. and M. Wattenburg (eds) 2000, *Parties Without Partisans: Political change in advanced industrial democracies*, Oxford University Press, Oxford.

Dalton, R. 2004, *Democratic Challenges, Democratic Choices: The erosion of political support in advanced industrial democracies*, Oxford University Press, Oxford.

Dalton, R. 2005, 'The Social Transformation of Trust in Government', *International Review of Sociology* 15(1), pp. 133–154.

Fiorina, M. P. 1978, 'Economic Retrospective Voting in American National Elections: A micro-analysis', *American Journal of Political Science* 22(2), pp. 426–443.

ICCS (Institute for Citizen-Centred Service) 2005, 'Factors Promoting Trust in Public Organization: Canadian Research' (Citizen Survey Data Analysis, N=7000), in *Citizens First 4*.

Inglehart, R. 1990, *Culture Shift*, Princeton University Press, Princeton.

Mackuen, M. B., R. S. Erikson and J. A. Stimson 1992, 'Peasants or Bankers?: The American electorate and the US economy', *American Political Science Review* 86(3), pp. 597–611.

Nye, J. 1997, 'Introduction: The decline of confidence in government', in J. Nye, S. Joseph, P. D. Zelikow and D. C. King (eds), *Why People Don't Trust Government?* Harvard University Press, Cambridge, pp. 1–19.

O'Farrell, B. 2010a, 'Starting the Change to Strengthen Professionalism in Public Sector Governance', address to the Institute of Chartered Secretaries Australia, 12 October 2010.

O'Farrell, B. 2010b, 'Starting the Change: Transforming customer service in NSW, address to Committee for Economic Development Australia, 12 November 2010.

OECD (Organisation for Economic Cooperation and Development) 2009, 'The Financial and Economic Crisis – Impact on E-Government in OECD countries', OECD paper to the 5th Ministerial E-Government Conference, 19–20 November 2009.

State Services Commission 2002, 'Declining Government Performance? Why Citizens Don't Trust Government'. Available at: http://www.ssc.govt.nz/node/4190.

3. Parliamentary Scrutiny of the Australian Public Service

Derek Drinkwater

Introduction

After a century of industrialisation and urbanisation, and a commensurate rise in state power, Australia is experiencing 'a major reconceptualisation of the role of government' (Nethercote 2003, p. 12). The need for Parliament to address such change had arisen as early as 1950, when Professor Wolfgang Friedmann called for 'a re-consideration of the problem of parliamentary control' over the increasingly pervasive activity and influence of governments (Friedmann 1950, p. 27). Ambitious initiatives to this end were introduced in the 1960s, with the past three decades witnessing the growth of a complex 'web of parliamentary scrutiny' of all aspects of governance, especially public administration (Cole 1980, p. 174). Today, Parliament's capacity to scrutinise the performance of ministers and public servants outside the chamber is of a similar order to its legislative power. This is a welcome development, which provides opportunities for identifying ministerial neglect and bureaucratic maladministration. It is also important in reducing their incidence. As Walter Bagehot put it: 'All checks are valuable, not in proportion to the vices which they discover, but in proportion to the vices which they prevent' (Bagehot 1974, p. 42). The purpose of this chapter is to determine whether this web has been as effective as its designers intended in ensuring the accountability to Parliament of Australia's main non-political institution of government, the Australian public service (APS) (the Commonwealth public service (CPS) 1901–73 when it received its present name).

The vehicles for enhanced scrutiny introduced from the early 1970s — expanded parliamentary committee arrangements, improved financial and auditing practices, more rigorous budget reporting procedures — transformed the means of evaluating public administration at the federal level. The earliest manifestation of parliamentary scrutiny of public service operations occurred in the Senate and the House of Representatives after federation in 1901. With some exceptions — chiefly, the activities of two parliamentary joint statutory committees — the Joint Committee on Public Accounts and Audit (1913–32, 1952–2011) and Public Works (1913–2011), only a modest degree of committee scrutiny took place during Parliament's first six decades. Wide-ranging scrutiny by committees across the whole spectrum of government activity did not become commonplace until the creation of a formidable Senate committee system in 1970. This event 'revolutionised the Parliament as a whole' (Reid and Forrest 1989, p. 375).

The importance accorded to the work of the Auditor-General, and to the requirement that departments and other Commonwealth agencies report annually on their activities to Parliament, fluctuated last century. It was only during the 1980s that these became major elements in parliamentary scrutiny. Government's growing complexity from the late 1960s also spawned new administrative machinery and relationships whose implications for governance are only now seriously emerging (and demanding to be addressed). Some of these raise questions central to scrutiny. They include the position of ministerial staff in Australian government–APS interchange; the obligations and responsibilities of public servants and ministerial advisers, especially in relation to parliamentary committees; and the increased exposure of APS employees to scrutiny in an atmosphere in which they, even more than ministerial staff and politicians, are called upon increasingly to shoulder accountability responsibilities that would previously have been borne by their ministerial chiefs.

Parliamentary scrutiny is more than 'the assertion of the supremacy of Parliament over the Executive Government in money matters' (Odgers 1979, p. 23). Ideally, its remit extends to monitoring administrative efficiency and influencing spending priorities and policies (HRSCE 1979, p. 11). As Stanley Bach has argued, 'if the process of scrutiny of legislation or administration did not change policy outcomes from time to time, it would serve no serious governmental function' (Bach 2003, p. 154). There are now 'numerous structures, processes and systems' which facilitate financial and administrative scrutiny (Baxter 2003, p. 65). Parliamentary scrutiny, like accountability, has become multidimensional, 'not a "thing" in itself, but a set of relationships through which political and bureaucratic actors must account for their integrity and their performance' (Stewart 2002, p. 69).

The advent of a Senate committee system and the House of Representatives Standing Committee on Expenditure (1976) strengthened scrutiny but did not displace the traditional apparatus of oversight and control. The problem remained of how best to bring information before Parliament in ways that would assist Senators and MPs to exercise their investigatory authority over standards of administrative performance and government financial management. In the mid-1970s this prompted the authors of one major review of public administration to call for improvements and refinements to Parliament's scrutiny function in several areas. This chapter examines these in turn: the chamber vehicles of Question Time (or Questions without Notice), Questions on Notice, and Matters of Public Importance (these counting as one category); committee activity; the work of the Australian National Audit Office (ANAO); budget evaluation and appropriation processes; and the accountability of ministerial advisers and public servants within the framework of parliamentary privilege (RCAGA 1976, pp. 108–113).

However, throughout the 1970s and 1980s it became clear that, although Parliament was no 'cipher in the sphere of public accountability', it still faced many obstacles in achieving 'the smallest kinetic effect upon the Public Service' (Reid 1981, p. 133). One commentator, in proffering reasons for this, complained that 'parliament's scrutiny of government administration has been hindered by secrecy, public service anonymity, limited resources and the burgeoning of inscrutable statutory bodies' (Indyk 1980, p. 93). Two decades on, it remained generally accepted that the Senate's 'key role' of scrutiny continued to be essential to a healthy Australian democracy (Faulkner 2003, p. 4). Much the same can be said of the House of Representatives, although its contribution to this process is often underestimated. Simplistic diagnoses based on portrayals of the Senate as Saint George and the executive (buttressed by the House of Representatives) as the dragon to be slain do little to improve public and specialist understanding of the situation. More detailed examination of the parliamentary record would assist in addressing such misconceptions. Initial research of this kind suggests that, today's high volume of parliamentary business notwithstanding, Australians could be better served by their elected representatives, whose primary tasks include ensuring more effective scrutiny of the APS.

In Australia (as in a number of other parliamentary democracies) such trends are adversely affecting the main institutions of governance, namely, the Parliament and the APS (Mulgan 2003, p. 57). The solution to this problem lies in understanding its deep-seated origins, rather than in resorting to the well-rehearsed mantra of the executive as the chief impediment to a degree of parliamentary scrutiny worthy of the name. It is also to be found in better methods of evaluating and assessing public administration in the federal sphere. An important basis for such innovation would be more trenchant research into the parliamentary sources themselves in understanding past developments, testing widely held hypotheses, and developing new approaches. While such calls are made periodically (usually in relation to estimates activity) (Uhr 1990, p. 83), the paucity of detailed studies of parliamentary history renders this a recurring problem. However, recognition of the need for intensive and sustained inquiry into parliamentary scrutiny is growing. A persuasive call to this effect was made by Colleen Lewis and Ken Coghill in their article, 'Surveying Research on Parliament and Parliamentary Oversight of the Public Sector' (Lewis and Coghill 2005).

Since the then Howard government achieved an (admittedly narrow) Senate majority following the 9 October 2004 general election, there has been an increase in discussions about parliamentary oversight procedures. The implications of this for parliamentary scrutiny of the APS have been the subject of considerable debate. Some Senators and MPs have maintained that the machinery of scrutiny in both houses remains as effective as ever. Others are much less sanguine, pointing to a notable decline in the number of sitting days (the Senate during the 41st Parliament had the then lowest number of sitting days for 50 years, the starting point of a trend of significantly lower allocated sitting days for the Senate); the deleterious effects of departmental restructuring on the Senate estimates process (for instance, difficulties in adequately examining the activities of the Department of Human Services which, for estimates purposes, for some time were spread across the Department of Finance and Administration and other agencies); an increasing tendency for the government to resort to classifying material as 'commercial-in-confidence' in order to avoid or delay providing information on APS administration; fewer so-called 'spillover' days for debate; and growing, deliberately imposed time and resources constraints on the consideration of legislation (National Institute for Governance 2005a).

The Rudd-led Australian Labor Party (ALP) government elected in 2007 was slow to act on parliamentary reform. However, in 2010, the first hung Parliament since 1941 forced the ALP and Coalition parties to implement meaningful parliamentary reform, most notably to Question Time due to the pressure of independent MPs. The independent MPs insisted on securing an agreement on parliamentary reform before any agreement on forming a government. As a result, changes to the standing orders, Question Time, House of Representatives committees and Private Members' Bills were negotiated and agreed to by both the ALP and Coalition parties. While the changes to parliamentary scrutiny procedures in the standing orders have been implemented, the spirit of the reforms were almost immediately abandoned as the Coalition reneged on much of the 'in principle' reforms outlined in 'Agreement for a Better Parliament: Parliamentary reform' (House of Representatives 2010). This fact is reflected in the continuing poor behaviour of MPs during Question Time and the institution's enduring low standing in the community. In this context it is difficult to assess the reform's long-term impact on the Parliament.

The role of Question Time, Questions on Notice, and Matters of Public Importance in legislative scrutiny

Question Time and committee activity are the best known features of the parliamentary machinery. According to received specialist and public opinion, Question Time is the one most abused by Senators and MPs. This is a longstanding concern. Even parliamentarians have variously described Question Time (the period set down for Questions without Notice) as a 'propaganda forum', a 'blood sport' and 'an absolute farce' (CPD (Commonwealth Parliamentary Debates) Senate, 9 September 1971, p. 583; 25 October 1973, p. 1451; 21 May 1990, p. 608). The most frequently aired complaint concerns the 'Dorothy Dixer' — a prearranged question addressed to the Prime Minister or a Minister by a government MP in order to show the administration in a favourable light (CPD, House of Representatives, 22 April 1971, pp. 1864–1865; 14 March 1973, pp. 538, 546; 13 October 1983, pp. 1702–1703).

Question Time has long been a point of debate and anxiety for parliamentarians, academics and citizens. Previously, the customary length of Question Time (approximately 45 minutes) was often criticised as being too short; yet parliamentarians repeatedly resisted proposals to extend its length beyond 45 minutes (CPD, Senate, 25 October 1972, pp. 1883–1889). Criticism of governments who curtail Question Time for perceived political purposes is invariably severe. In October 1993, for example, one Senator protested against the Prime Minister's decision the day before to terminate Question Time (in the House of Representatives) after only 25 minutes, allegedly to save the Minister for Finance further political embarrassment (CPD, 6 October 1993, p. 1727). More infamous still was the conclusion of Question Time after a single question by Prime Minster Julia Gillard following a failed attempt to censure the Prime Minister and the government by the leader of the opposition (CPD, House of Representatives, 24 August 2011, p. 9216). The practice of ministers reading prepared (and lengthy) answers to questions, which absorbs valuable time and reduces opportunities for participation by non-ministers, has regularly been deplored (CPD, House of Representatives, 1 May 1963, p. 926; 18 October 1983, pp. 1811–1812; 17 October 1991, p. 2174). Another common objection relates to the absence or inadequacy of procedures designed to prevent evasive replies to questions (CPD, Senate, 24 May 1972, p. 2025).

The degeneration of Question Time into a set-piece opportunity for tactical stroke and counter-stroke, in which replies to questions are constantly turned into matters for debate, has frequently drawn comment (CPD, Senate, 11 October 1973, p. 1155; 13 November 1990, pp. 3970–3971). In 1990, one opposition Senator insisted that, although some latitude for delay in protecting the government by such means was acceptable, when this became regular and systematic the situation was untenable (CPD, Senate, 21 May 1990, p. 608). Nevertheless, little improvement in Senators' or MPs' behaviour followed during the 1990s, or in the wake of the 2010 reforms.

Some prime ministers (and a long-serving party leader, W. G. Hayden) have put forward ambitious reform proposals for Question Time. Prime Minister E. G. Whitlam advocated changes to the Standing Orders whereby Senate ministers could be rostered to answer Questions without Notice in the House of Representatives (and vice versa) (CPD, House of Representatives, 30 August 1973, p. 632). On 25 February 1982, his successor as party leader, Bill Hayden, proposed that the following six-part motion be referred to the Standing Orders Committee (it was so referred, though the matters were never implemented):

The standing orders and practices which govern the conduct of Question Time, taking particular account of:

1. The definition of relevancy in answers to questions and the setting out of criteria to define relevancy in accordance with legal definition.

2. Length of answers to be subject to a time limit.

3. The need for clearer definition in the standing orders about the practice in relation to supplementary questions.

4. Senators who are ministers to attend the house to answer questions.

5. The appropriateness of setting down specified sitting days as days on which questions will be directed to ministers about particular departments.

6. Question Time to be a minimum of 45 minutes (CPD, House of Representatives, 25 February 1982, pp. 595–598).

Other suggested changes have included the proposal that Question Time continue each day until 28 questions are asked and answered (CPD, House of Representatives, 27 September 1993, p. 1158).

A survey of the Commonwealth Parliamentary Debates for both houses between 1964 and 2010 reveals Senators and MPs to have had a recurring interest in certain aspects of APS operations. All were frequently the subject of Questions without Notice. They included (principally) the size and costs of running the organisation; the recruitment and training of staff (from in-service training to cadetships to graduate programs); the employment of people with disability; the recruitment and development of Indigenous Australians; the role, numbers and level of seniority of women and the elimination of discrimination against them (from the abolition of the 'marriage bar' to the implementation of the 'equal pay for equal work' principle to affirmative action initiatives); public sector leave provisions and superannuation arrangements; the health of employees (for example, the high incidence of tenosynovitis and repetitive strain injury during the mid-1980s); public servants' membership of and/or dealings with trade unions; the freedom of expression allowed to public sector staff; the part played by ministerial advisers in APS–executive interaction (an issue first raised seriously in 1973); the activities and influence of the Public Service Board (abolished in 1987) and, later, those of the Department of the Prime Minister and Cabinet; the annual reports of departments and other government agencies; financial management reforms (notably, the changes introduced from the early 1980s); the new structures and practices consequent upon public service devolution in the late 1990s; and the steady growth in office automation culminating in the dominance of the internet and IT technologies over administrative processes and research methodologies.

Judgements regarding the role of Question Time in legislative scrutiny have been remarkably similar over the years. While Ken Baxter over-optimistically calls it 'a lethal weapon in the armoury of good governance' (Baxter 2003, p. 65), G. S. Reid and Martyn Forrest's description of it as 'a device for executive advantage in both houses' (Reid and Forrest 1989, p. 367) better reflects majority opinion on the subject. Hansard transcripts, committee report recommendations, and political party platforms of the 1990s and early 2000s, point to continuing concerns.

This has been the case in each house. Between 1989 and 1992, for example, 6,814 Questions without Notice were asked in the Senate and 2,595 in the House of Representatives. The latter's Standing Committee on Procedure, in its report 'About Time' (HRSCP 1993), sought to counter the decline in the number of questions being asked during Question Time. The Committee observed that the average number of questions put on each occasion had almost halved between 1976 and 1992 (from 19.3 to 10.8), despite the longer Question Time (a maximum of 62.8 minutes compared with a minimum of 48.5 minutes). By 1993, both figures had fallen further — 10.6 questions during a period of 48.2 minutes. The committee's suggested solution was a longer Question Time and the requirement that a minimum number of questions be asked. However, it concluded that procedural reform alone would not be enough; a different approach was needed by the government and the opposition to the issue of Questions without Notice (HRSCP 1993, pp. xi, 2, 21). In April 2007, the ALP promised that, if successful at the forthcoming election, it would require the attendance of all ministers during Question Time and ensure that all questions were properly answered (ALP 2007, p. 180). However, the commitment the party made in 2004 (in its 'Machinery of Government' policy) to work for a better Parliament–executive balance through Question Time reform was not part of its 2007 policy agenda (Latham and Faulkner 2004, p. 9).

Not surprisingly, the Liberal–National Party Coalition government argued that there was no need for reform, the Prime Minister, John Howard, defending his administration's approach to Question Time in comparison with that of his two ALP predecessors, R. J. L. ('Bob') Hawke and Paul Keating. He described the institution of Question Time, not as a courtesy extended to the House by the executive, but as an essential element of executive accountability to Parliament. 'In the end', Howard emphasised, 'the real determinant of the accountability of a government and of a prime minister is their willingness to front up here day after day to answer questions' (CPD, House of Representatives, 27 June 2002, p. 4602).

During the 13 years of the Hawke and Keating administrations (between March 1983 and March 1996), 9,248 questions (an average of 711 questions annually) were asked during Question Time in the House of Representatives, and 19,646 questions in the Senate (an annual average of 1,511 questions). Between the Howard government's election in March 1996 and November 2007 — a parliamentary period of 12 years — 14,150 Questions without Notice were asked in the House of Representatives (an average of 1,179 annually), and a total of 15,211 in the Senate (a yearly average of 1,170 questions). Since 1983, on the basis of the average number of questions asked each year, scrutiny during Question Time has clearly been more vigorous in the Senate under ALP governments and more marked in the House of Representatives under Coalition governments.[1] Although, in terms of the number of questions asked, Senate Question Time needs to become more robust in comparison with the years 1983–96, these findings provide a revealing contrast to the prevalent perception of a weak House of Representatives Question Time system under constant attack from the executive.

Changes since 2007

The election of the Rudd ALP government on 24 November 2007 resulted in modest reforms of Question Time in the Senate. In September 2008, the Senate Standing Committee on Procedure proposed changes to the nature of Question Time:

1. All primary questions to be placed on a Question Time Notice Paper by 11 am.

2. Up to 6 supplementary questions following each primary question.

3. Up to 2 minutes for an answer to each primary or supplementary question.

4. Answers to be directly relevant to each question.

The effect of these changes would have resulted in government agencies spending less time preparing briefs for questions that may arise during Questions without Notice. Moreover, these changes would have also facilitated greater engagement across the chamber and between multiple parties. However, these bold reforms

---

1 In only nine years during 1964–2011 did the number of questions asked in the House of Representatives exceed the number asked in the Senate (1964, 1965, 1966, 1967, 1969, 2005, 2006, 2007 and 2008).

were not adopted by the Senate. Instead, as outlined by the Senate Standing Committee on Procedure in its third report, the upper chamber held a two-week trial of the following during the last two sitting weeks of 2008:

1. no notice to be given of questions, as at present;

2. primary questions to be limited to one minute and the answers to them to two minutes;

3. two supplementary questions to be allowed to the questioner;

4. supplementary questions and the answers to them to be limited to one minute each;

5. answers to be required to be directly relevant to each question, as in the original proposal.

As Senator Faulkner outlined, the effect of these changes was ultimately rather cosmetic, increasing the total amount of time for the questioner by one minute and reducing the time for answers by one minute (CPD, Senate, 13 November 2008, pp. 26–27). These temporary procedures have not been adopted permanently, but were extended three times and are still in effect at the time of writing.

In the House of Representatives, the election of the first hung parliament since 1941 forced the issue of parliamentary reform upon all major parties. The independent MPs, spearheaded by Rob Oakeshott, negotiated an overhaul of parliamentary standing orders and procedures before agreeing to support either party to form a government (House of Representatives 2010). The reforms were aimed at making changes to the standing orders of the House of Representatives; they also sought to change the culture of parliamentary procedure. Three of the reforms called for by Bill Hayden were addressed or implemented. On 29 September 2010, amendments to the standing orders were introduced, placing formal time limits on questions of 45 seconds and four minutes for answers. On 8 February 2012, the time limits were further reduced on questions to 30 seconds and on answers to three minutes (CPD, House of Representatives, 8 February 2012, pp. 10–11). While a definition of 'relevancy' was not included in the parliamentary reforms, the standing orders were amended such that answers 'must be directly relevant to the question', and that 'a point of order regarding relevance may be taken only once in response to each answer' (CPD, House of Representatives, 29 September 2011, p. 123).

Additionally, the agreement called for the opposition to be given the opportunity to ask one supplementary question during each Question Time. While the provision for supplementary questions already existed within the standing orders, the privilege had not been used since 1998. The reforms provided the opportunity for the reinterpretation of this privilege and this process has continued with the introduction of an opportunity for a second supplementary question in 2012, on a trial basis. Finally, the agreement called for Question Time to end no later than 3.30 pm, thereby allowing time for 20 questions to be answered (House of Representatives 2010). The implementation of an outer time limit could be interpreted as a reaction against the former Prime Minister Kevin Rudd's regular practice of allowing Question Time to continue beyond 3.30 pm and even past 4 pm. On the other hand, Question Time has twice ended after only one question was asked (CPD, House of Representatives, 24 August 2011, p. 9216; 24 November 2011, p. 2011). While there has been criticism of these short Question Times, no minimum question threshold or time limit has been raised in the Parliament.

After more than a year in operation, the reforms to parliamentary procedures have produced modest improvements. The changes to time limits on Questions without Notice have modestly reduced the length of questions only by seconds. The changes have been made more successful by reducing the length of answers by ministers to government questions from an average of four minutes and 52 seconds to two minutes and 23 seconds. The opposition has made good use of the opportunity to ask supplementary questions, asking 64 supplementary questions in the period until October 2011 (Parliamentary Library 2011, p. 6). However, since these statistics were recorded in 2011, the opposition has on only five occasions not asked supplementary questions during Question Times (Parliamentary Library 2011, p. 9). Enforcing relevance remains a vexed problem, ultimately relying on the willingness of the Speaker to enforce a ruling. Yet, Speaker Peter Slipper took the unprecedented step of removing the call from Prime Minister Julia Gillard after several warnings of failing to be relevant (CPD, House of Representatives, 28 February 2012, pp. 1–2). However, Speaker Slipper's stance arose as a result of the finely balanced numbers of the minority Parliament and because it suited the political position of the government. It is unlikely that future speakers, conventionally supplied by the government, would have this capacity and security in their position to assert their will over ministers and prime ministers.

Nevertheless, commentators continue to lament the supposedly parlous state of Question Time. Coghill attributes this chiefly to the 'ridiculous' rules governing its operation and to ministers' prolonged 'preambles' to answers. He stigmatises this development as a 'peculiarly Australian problem', and proposes amended procedures designed to ensure that questions are answered, except where the national interest may be adversely affected (such a determination to be made by the presiding officer of the house concerned, namely, the President of the Senate or the Speaker of the House of Representatives, respectively). In addition, in instances where the Minister is genuinely unable to reply, the question could be placed on notice or answered by means of a ministerial statement (Coghill 2002).

Initiatives aimed at improving Question Time by making it longer, by increasing the number of questions asked daily, or by enhancing the quality of replies, collectively or individually, promise useful reform — but only if the executive has the will to embrace them. Clearly, however, while finer points such as the duration of Question Time and the length of questions are important, the first challenge is to increase the number of genuine questions (and answers) in both houses and, by doing so, to improve their efficacy as legislative scrutiny tools. This could be achieved through more definitive presiding officer rulings over the nature and content of questions — such rulings to derive their very real authority from the standing orders.

The best way forward almost certainly lies in implementing the remainder of the 1982 Hayden reform proposals and in ensuring that they are observed. Among the most effective means of achieving this would be to reshape the offices of President and Speaker so as to give them greater powers over the conduct of Question Time (as in Britain, in the case of the Speaker). Some of Hayden's recommendations have been in place in the British House of Commons for many years. These include the assignment of certain days on which MPs can question the staff of specific departments of state about their activities; provision for 'Cross-Cutting Questions' (a practice inaugurated in January 2003) whereby a number of ministers attend to answer questions on a topic encompassing the responsibilities of several government departments (a reform prompted by the 'cross-cutting' focus of 'joined-up government', which has strong resonances in Australia as 'whole of government'); and a separate Prime Minister's Question Time, whose existence eases pressure on the main Question Time.

The role of the presiding officers (notably, the independent Speaker of the House of Commons in the British context), in the Australian Parliament, if such reform were to be seriously contemplated here, cannot be overstated. In Britain, '[t]he Speaker controls the pace of Question Time', and he (or she) has the power 'to check a Member or Minister who is either too lengthy or is using Question Time as an opportunity for debate' (HCIO 2005, p. 5). The outcome is a Question Time that, through its provision for 'oral questions', serves well the interests of parliamentary scrutiny of government and public administration. Another significant factor in the effective functioning of the British Question Time machinery is the regular scrutiny of the parliamentary questions apparatus by Parliament itself. Since the Second World War — in contrast to Australian practice (though this is changing) — the subject has been investigated by British parliamentary select committees on 13 occasions (in 1946, 1958, 1965, 1970, 1972, 1976, 1990, 1993, 1994, 1995, 1997, 2002 and 2005). Since the election of the hung Parliament, the then speaker Harry Jenkins initiated some informal changes to increase the institution's independence, such as promising not to interact with his ALP colleagues until after the house had risen on Thursday evenings. However, these changes were self-imposed and, as a result of their uncodified nature, were able to be abandoned by any future speaker.

Table 1: Questions without Notice 1964–2011 (number asked annually)

	Senate	House of Representatives
1964	999	1,557
1965	803	1,796
1966	687	1,056
1967	1,063	1,164
1968	1,408	1,298
1969	158	905
1970	1,903	1,187
1971	2,439	1,218
1972	1,886	1,024
1973	2,625	1,219
1974	1,750	782
1975	1,884	956
1976	2,429	1,447
1977	1,954	1,021
1978	1,983	1,098
1979	2,008	1,033
1980	1,487	762
1981	1,758	943
1982	1,663	709
1983	1,263	597
1984	1,238	591
1985	1,424	734
1986	1,669	934
1987	1,507	900
1988	1,384	715
1989	1,903	665
1990	1,305	453
1991	1,893	861
1992	1,713	616
1993	1,181	429
1994	1,702	890
1995	1,464	863
1996	1,469	1,127
1997	1,757	1,482
1998	1,176	998

	Senate	House of Representatives
1999	1,671	1,370
2000	1,572	1,353
2001	1,050	927
2002	1,236	1,220
2003	1,333	1,194
2004	1,030	1,008
2005	1,069	1,274
2006	1,111	1,293
2007	737	904
2008	1,050	1,290
2009	1,368	1,187
2010	1,052	948
2011	1,453	882

Source: *Commonwealth Parliamentary Debates.*

Questions on Notice

Parliamentarians' areas of interest in APS administration from 1964 to 2011 as reflected in Questions on Notice were similar to those for Questions without Notice. In the 1960s, rarely did a Minister decline to provide an answer to a Question on Notice on the ground that the time and work involved in preparing a response would unwarrantably burden departmental staff. However, such a reply became more and more common during the 1970s and 1980s. Prime Minister William McMahon reminded MPs in August 1971 that 'the resources of Ministers and departments are not unlimited and, notwithstanding the importance of providing the Parliament with the information it seeks, there are competing demands' (CPD, House of Representatives, 26 August 1971, p. 798).

The leader of the government in the Senate, Sir John Carrick, was similarly direct in October 1982: 'I am not prepared to authorise the large diversion of resources in Departments which would be needed to answer [the Senator's] question in the terms asked.'

Nevertheless, as was common practice in such instances, he offered a compromise in the interests of scrutiny: 'If the honourable senator would like to rephrase his question so as to refer to a shorter period of time and to focus more precisely on his area of interest, Ministers will consider what assistance can be given' (CPD, Senate, 27 October 1982, p. 1927).

With the expansion of the APS and the wider public sector throughout the 1990s and early 2000s, Questions on Notice underwent a number of changes. Increasingly, many such questions took on an 'analytical' rather than a merely 'informational' character. The following inquiry (from 1991) is a good example:

Australian Public Service

(Question No. 740)

Are members of the Australian Public Service (APS) who are seconded to the staff of Ministers and Members of Parliament not denied the right to pursue their careers when they return to the APS?

Does existing legislation protect the rights of public servants who have worked on the personal staff of Members from all parties and whose characters have been impugned? (CPD, House of Representatives, 13 May 1991, p. 3616).

Putting aside the fact that departmental–ministerial/parliamentary staff interchange was largely an uncontroversial issue in earlier times (as distinct from the role of ministerial advisers) it is unlikely that such a question would previously have been coined in such subjective terms. Formerly, even questions seeking information to be used for a 'political' purpose, were couched more in terms of an information-seeking request.

Many have also become complex, focusing on the minutiae of governance in a few key areas such as staff numbers, program implementation and audit, the composition and make-up of ministerial adviser teams, outsourcing, and performance management (of both APS employees and organisations). Whereas previously, ministers and/or leaders of the government in each house had almost invariably refused to provide replies that would unjustifiably strain departmental resources, they were now promising to do so in respect of the most detailed questions, whether informational or analytical (see, for example, 'Australian Taxation Office: Staff' (No. 991), CPD, 17 February 2000, pp. 13860–13864). By 2005, the provision of replies on this scale had become a growing burden on employees, one which was hampering their capacity as policymakers and service providers to the extent that it was identified publicly as a serious issue by the then secretary of the Department of the Prime Minister and Cabinet, Dr Peter Shergold (2005).

Paradoxically, while the average number of questions placed on notice between 2000 and 2004 in each house did not rise significantly compared with that for the years 1970 to 2000, the delays in providing answers to questions (4, 6, 12 and even 18 months) is further evidence of this problem (CPD, House of Representatives, 13 March 2000, pp. 14, 437; 6 September 2000, pp. 20,

272–274). Such delays or 'slippage' had occurred occasionally in the past, with one MP recommending the adoption of the then House of Commons procedure requiring that all Questions on Notice ('written questions') be answered within one week of their being put on the Notice Paper (CPD, House of Representatives, 16 March 1971, p. 890). However, the situation did not improve, prompting Dr Shergold (as we have seen) to call for some relief for the beleaguered APS in August 2005.

Table 2: Questions on Notice 1964–2011

	Senate		House of Representatives	
	Total questions	Annual average	Total questions	Annual average
1964–69	-	-	4,907	818
1970–79	9,002	900	22,025	2,202
1980–89	8,780	878	16,992	1,699
1990–99	8,266	826	9,271	927
2000–11	13,197	1,199	6,017	1,203
Total/average	**39,245**	**957**	**67,350**	**1,432**

Source: *Commonwealth Parliamentary Debates.*

Following their peak in 2005, Questions on Notice were sustained at high levels in both the House of Representatives and the Senate until the demise of the Howard government in 2007. And, while the number of Questions on Notice in the Senate has remained fairly stable since the change of government, in the House of Representatives the number of Questions on Notice has collapsed dramatically. In the House of Representatives, the average time in which to obtain an answer to a Question on Notice in 2007–08 was 207 days before the change of government; after this it was only 26 days. The results were similar in the Senate: previously it had taken 115 days to provide an answer to Questions on Notice, and this improved to 55 days after the change in government (CPD, Senate, 13 November 2008, p. 26). There is little doubt that the Question on Notice, as it is presently perceived and framed, will remain a valuable tool of legislative scrutiny. Yet, it is clear that some refinement of the scope and degree of detail of many questions is urgently needed (the number does not present a problem — it is excessive in neither house). This could be arrived at through executive–opposition front bench agreement on the need for such reform and/or (as with Questions without Notice) the provision of greater powers to the presiding officers to assess the content and purpose of questions and to ensure that they are answered by a certain date (the British no longer have a parliamentary rule requiring this: HCIO 2005, p. 11). Only then, perhaps, will this growing problem be satisfactorily addressed.

Table 3: Questions on Notice 1964–2011 (number asked daily)

	Senate	House of Representatives
1964	-	814
1965	-	714
1966	-	654
1967	-	752
1968	-	1,072
1969	-	901
1970	817	2,269
1971	969	2,682
1972	757	1,626
1973	607	1,683
1974	560	2,875
1975	677	1,534
1976	1,658	1,870
1977	642	2,221
1978	1,116	3,126
1979	1,199	2,139
1980	1,137	1,694
1981	1,443	3,347
1982	1,700	2,214
1983	647	1,002
1984	587	910
1985	762	3,115
1986	818	1,876
1987	399	1,180
1988	589	876
1989	698	778
1990	423	507
1991	1,221	753
1992	896	927
1993	957	826
1994	970	1,044
1995	783	961
1996	373	1,159
1997	641	1,446
1998	568	861
1999	1,434	787
2000	1,392	1,132
2001	675	713
2002	1,054	1,281

	Senate	House of Representatives
2003	1,439	1,604
2004	1,000	1,287
2005	1,149	2,522
2006	1,497	2,358
2007	527	1,046
2008	1,210	554
2009	1,304	616
2010	837	421
2011	1,113	621

Source: *Commonwealth Parliamentary Debates*.

The Matter of Public Importance

The Matter of Public Importance (MPI) continues to be underrated as a tool of scrutiny by students of politics and public administration alike. As one academic commentator expresses the traditional view of MPIs: 'An MPI debate is really only an invitation to comment on a "matter for discussion", with no vote taken, as would be the case in a censure motion.' He concludes that, 'The parliamentary discussion is simply timed out. But it is a useful opposition tactic for getting arguments and evidence on the public record' (Uhr 2005, p. 11).

However, an analysis of the parliamentary record between 1964 and 2011 indicates the picture to be less clear-cut. The MPI, under this or earlier names,[2] has been employed to highlight significant gaps in public policy or issues in need of sustained attention. Prominent, early examples of this include those dealing with 'Equal Pay for Equal Work' (CPD, House of Representatives, 1 May 1962, pp. 1741–1753), 'Public Service', (CPD, House of Representatives, 14 May 1963, pp. 1288–1300); 'Commonwealth Public Service Annual Leave and Employment Conditions' (CPD, House of Representatives, 4 March 1970, pp. 54–60, 13 May 1970, pp. 2049–2063); 'Government Contracts' (CPD, House of Representatives, 8 March 1973, pp. 362–376); and, in the Senate (where it is employed far less than in the lower house), 'Review of Commonwealth Functions' (the alleged inadequacy and deleterious community effects of this review) (CPD, Senate, 11 November 1981, pp. 2018–2021). In contrast to earlier decades, several MPIs (in 1993 and 2003–04 in particular, relating to one minister's financial

---

2 Throughout this period, the term MPI was generally employed in the House of Representatives. In the Senate, the term Matter of Urgency (MoU) was used instead of MPI between 1963 and 1977, both MPI and MoU being employed interchangeably in 1978 and 1979. Since 1980, an MPI has been identified in the Senate independently of an MoU and a Matter of Public Interest (MoPI).

practices and the issue of APS politicisation, respectively) have raised awareness (among Senators and MPs, at least) of the MPI as a scrutiny vehicle (they will be examined in greater detail later).

Since 1990, the MPI has become a more common feature of parliamentary business in both houses. As well as the predictable interest in policy matters (mainly economic and foreign), ministerial decisions and public sector performance, there is a strong concern with the health of the institutions of governance and public administration. Major examples include 'Government Financial Management' (especially 'the process of government': CPD, Senate, 24 August 1990, pp. 2184–2204); 'Department of Social Security: Administration' ('The continuing failure of the Minister for Social Security to address the multitude of administrative problems currently besetting his Department': CPD, Senate, 11 October 1990, pp. 2921–2945); 'APS Politicisation' ('The growing politicisation of the public service, and attempts by the Government to withhold important information from parliament through doctoring and withholding reports': CPD, Senate, 12 August 2003, pp. 13343–13357); and 'APS Politicisation' ('That the Senate expresses its deep concern at the continuing politicisation of the public sector by the Howard Government': CPD, Senate, 25 March 2004, pp. 21986–22006). The MPI is now an established tool for such scrutiny in Senate deliberations.

Among notable House of Representatives examples are those dealing with damage to public confidence in the government's stewardship of public administration: 'The Operation of the Australian Loan Council' (CPD, House of Representatives, 3 November 1992, p. 2394; 4 November 1992, p. 2574; 5 November 1992, pp. 2748–2758); 'Australian Quarantine and Inspection Service' ('The government's failure to reform both the efficiency and culture of the Australian Quarantine and Inspection Service which is hampering Australia's competitiveness in world markets': CPD, House of Representatives, 16 December 1993, p. 4240); 'Commonwealth Financial Management' ('The government's failure to prudently manage the Commonwealth's finances': CPD, House of Representatives, 8 November 2000, pp. 22442–22453)[3]; and, 'Howard Government: Denigration of Government Institutions' ('The persistent failure of the Government to be accountable and to tell the truth, denigrating in the process institutions fundamental to Australian democracy, including the public service, the defence forces, the Parliament and the courts': CPD, House of Representatives, 21 March 2002, pp. 1921–1922).

---

3   One of the issues emphasised here was the 'radical decentralisation' of responsibility under the provisions of the *Financial Management and Accountability Act 1997,* which had — it was argued — contributed to a significant decline in Department of Finance and Administration supervision of departments engaging in foreign exchange related transactions.

The insistence of Senators and MPs that the MPI process be properly observed and the procedure's forensic nature, breadth, depth and coverage (especially since 1990) attest to the status they accord it (and to its effectiveness) as a vehicle of scrutiny. The opposition leader, E. G. Whitlam, in March 1970 was at pains to stress that, so far that year, the opposition had raised five MPIs, and each time the debate was gagged after one speaker from each side had spoken. He pointed out that in 1969 the average number of speakers had been four and, between 1960 and 1970, no fewer than three speakers on each side spoke on MPIs (CPD, House of Representatives, 18 March 1970, p. 561). Thirty years later, Dr Andrew Theophanous referred to this continuing problem as constituting, if not an abuse of procedure, then certainly a regrettable practice, when he argued that time be allocated to enable independent MPs to speak on MPIs and the Business of the House not be brought on precipitately, thus precluding them from speaking (CPD, House of Representatives, 6 September 2000, p. 20272). No doubt this premature curtailing of the MPI process in order to stifle or smother debate (amounting to attempted strangulation at birth in the cases of the Australian Loan Council and the Australian Quarantine and Inspection Service) and marked 'Denigration of Government Inspections' in other cases restricts scrutiny.

As a result of the reforms to parliamentary standing orders in September 2010, three substantive changes were made to MPIs. First, they increased the amount of time allowed for discussion to one hour and 30 minutes. This would permit the proposer and the next speaker to speak for 15 minutes and any following speakers for 10 minutes (CPD, House of Representatives, 29 September 2011, p. 117). Second, MPIs are now discussed directly after Question Time, thereby raising their prominence. Third, the agreement also outlined the principle that there should be a proportionate share of time for MPIs in order that all non-government members would have adequate time allotted (House of Representatives 2010, p. 4). However, additional changes would further improve the situation. For example, standing orders could be altered to make it mandatory for a minimum of four Senators and MPs to speak for a specified minimum length of time on each MPI. Notwithstanding this problem, the MPI remains a more estimable tool for scrutiny by the non-government parties (its main purpose anyway) than is often supposed. Few better examples of this can be found than the 'Community Grants' or so-called 'Sports Rorts Affair' of late 1993, which was pursued vigorously via the MPI process (the result being a ministerial resignation and the implementation of improved accountability processes earlier recommended by the Auditor-General). Two influential MPIs were involved here: 'Community Grants' ('The failure of administration in the Department of the Arts, Sport, the Environment and Territories as exemplified by the blatant misuse of taxpayers' money for political purposes': CPD, House of Representatives, 17 November 1993, pp. 3018–3027), and 'Community

Grants' ('The failure of the Minister for the Environment, Sport and Territories to adequately respond to the efficiency audit of the Auditor-General on the community cultural, recreational and sporting facilities program': CPD, House of Representatives, 22 November 1993, p. 3288).

The number of MPIs being raised in each house is another issue requiring attention. Since 1964, in every year except four (1983, 1984, 1989, 2011) the number of MPIs raised in the House of Representatives has been almost, and often more than, double that in the Senate (a total of 1,841 in the lower house as against 626 in the Senate). Clearly, further procedural reform (again, by means of standing orders) is needed to resuscitate the MPI as a vehicle for scrutiny in the upper house. The figures underline the need starkly: Senate MPIs 1997–2011, 152; House of Representatives MPIs 1997–2011, 664. The MPI has certainly proved itself a useful tool of scrutiny, and it is true that, as one former Senate Deputy President and MP put it, the MPI process offers the opposition and smaller parties 'very fair opportunities to put their point of view' (Hamer 2004, p. 294). Nevertheless, the MPI (particularly in the Senate) could clearly be rendered a sharper tool by addressing the issues of MPI debate gagging and the small numbers of Senate MPIs.

Table 4: Matters of Public Importance 1964–2011 (number raised annually)

	Senate	House of Representatives
1964	4	11
1965	3	6
1966	3	5
1967	9	12
1968	1	10
1969	6	28
1970	10	22
1971	12	23
1972	5	21
1973	6	18
1974	3	32
1975	3	26
1976	9	47
1977	16	48
1978	16	56
1979	25	52
1980	28	33
1981	31	51
1982	32	46
1983	23	42

	Senate	House of Representatives
1984	23	41
1985	26	57
1986	14	71
1987	14	65
1988	22	47
1989	31	44
1990	14	31
1991	14	46
1992	13	45
1993	3	17
1994	23	47
1995	20	40
1996	12	37
1997	3	52
1998	8	30
1999	9	45
2000	2	50
2001	4	35
2002	3	43
2003	8	45
2004	5	46
2005	14	51
2006	9	50
2007	5	39
2008	9	44
2009	20	45
2010	21	40
2011	32	49

Source: *Commonwealth Parliamentary Debates*.

Committees of the Parliament

Committees are the best known features of the parliamentary scrutiny machinery.

The *Sydney Morning Herald* of 20 June 2005 contained the findings of a survey of 46 Senate inquiries undertaken since 1996, most of whose major recommendations, according to survey authors Gerard Ryle and Lisa Pryor, have been largely ignored (Ryle and Pryor 2005). At first sight, figures for inquiry duration, number of report recommendations and estimated cost of these investigations make the Senate committee system appear to some degree to be a luxury of governance. While a relatively easy picture to create, this is in many respects misleading. The wide-ranging nature of Senate (and House of Representatives) committee inquiries, even if the majority of their findings are not implemented, still makes committees an influential tool of scrutiny. Although many committee recommendations are integrated into legislation and APS practice, it should be recognised that few governments have the capacity to reshape what are frequently complex spheres of governance by enshrining into public policy the numerous recommendations made by committees (some reports contain almost 100 recommendations). Politics and public administration essentially are exercises in reconciling resources with the most suitable avenue of policy; in this instance, to criticise governments for not implementing recommendations on such a scale never (or highly unlikely ever to have been) realisable anyway, is a superficial criticism that takes little account of the political or administrative challenges of governance.

It is perhaps also necessary to arrive at a more balanced view than that usually advanced in relation to recent committee work. As one Senator put it in December 2005 on the subject of committee activity since the government began to exercise its Senate majority (from 1 July of that year): 'we have seen the number of committee references that have been agreed to halved and, correspondingly, the number of committee references opposed doubled. That shows another example of the significant amount of scrutiny that has been prevented' (CPD, 8 December 2005, pp. 133–134).

He went on to protest against the government's refusal 'to allow scrutiny of basic broad policy matters', notably, by means of frequent use of the 'gag' or 'guillotine' in order to prevent or limit debate on proposed committee references. Yet, he called for a sense of perspective in discussions of this and related matters:

> I think it is important that we try to put a bit of a brake on this continual 'tit-for-tat' and dragging back through *Hansards* of the last 20 years, because none of us have totally clean hands here. We all know that guillotine motions can be justified. Every party in this place … voted for guillotines at various times.

This seems a useful plea for more measured commentary on developments in both houses.

Since the reforms to parliamentary procedure in 2010, the House of Representatives committees have undergone somewhat of a revival. The changes to the committee system outlined in clause 10 of the agreement (House of Representatives 2010, p. 6) and implemented through the standing orders (20 October 2010) were:

1. Reducing the number of committees from 12 to nine;

2. Reducing the number of committee members to seven;

3. Increasing the number of supplementary members from two to four thereby allowing greater participation of parliamentary members in committee business;

4. Stipulating that the Joint Committee of Public Accounts and Audit be chaired by non-government members;

5. Allowing the selection committee to refer controversial bills for further scrutiny by the relevant standing or joint committee;

6. Encouraging faster response times by government by requiring a ministerial explanation to the house if government responses are not received within six months; and

7. Enabling committee chairs and deputy chairs to make statements in the house about new inquiries during private members' business time.

The reduction in the number of standing committees was effectively cancelled out by the increase in the number of joint standing and select committees, having a negligible effect on the workload of Senators and MPs. As yet it is difficult to determine the effectiveness of the six-month time frame for government responses to reports. The time limit has elapsed for 14 reports, of which nine have since received a government response. As a result of the reforms, 67 out of 300 bills considered were referred by the Selection Committee for further scrutiny, comprising about one-fifth of government business. This compares favourably with the period 1994–2010 when only 16 bills underwent further investigation by house committees. In addition, the number of amendments made to bills based on committee recommendations has lead the House Standing Committee on Procedure to consider this reform a success.

Australian National Audit Office (Auditor-General)

The *Audit Act 1901* regulated the Auditor-General's first period of activity (1901–97), during which (in accordance with the legislation) he concentrated almost entirely on financial audit processes and financial accountability in a narrowly prescribed sense. Since 1998, under the terms of the *Auditor-General Act 1997*, audit goals and a greater emphasis on enhancing public sector efficiency have been the chief focus of the ANAO. An independent auditor, responsible for scrutiny of the Auditor-General's office itself, was appointed in May 1979. During the years under review here (1964–2011), with the exception of the first 'efficiency audit', this situation endured until 1983–84 when efficiency audits of APS operations and performance became an established part of ANAO activity (they remained so, along with the project audit — instituted in 1991 — until 1995). Since then the dominant form of audit has been the performance audit (formerly known as an audit report). Since 1998, the ANAO has devised a number of other types of audit: the assurance and control assessment audit; the business support process audit; the compliance assessment audit; the financial control and administration audit; and, the financial statement(s) audit. The ANAO's internet pages, which are among the most accessible and detailed of any Australian government (or associated) body, and the *Indexes to Papers Presented to Parliament,* contain an informative (and definitive) listing of all of its reports.

Its numerous important publications (many of which produce findings with implications for the whole field of public administration rather than for just the issue or agency under investigation) include 'Survey of Internal Audit in the Commonwealth Public Sector' (ANAO 1990); 'Accountability off the Rails — National Rail Corporation Limited: Erosion of Accountability to the Parliament' (ANAO 1991a); 'Implementation of Purchasing Reforms in the Australian Public Service' (ANAO 1991b); 'Financial Management: Department of Veterans' Affairs' (ANAO 1995); 'The Administration of the Australian National Training Authority' (ANAO 1996); 'Survey of Fraud Control Arrangements in APS Agencies' (ANAO 2000); 'Recordkeeping' (ANAO 2002); 'Absence Management in the Australian Public Service' (ANAO 2003a); 'Administration of Staff Employed under the *Members of Parliament (Staff) Act 1984*: Department of Finance and Administration' (ANAO 2003b); 'Annual Performance Reporting' (ANAO 2003c); and 'Performance Management in the Australian Public Service' (ANAO 2004b).

The 1997 legislation and consequential amendments to the *Public Accounts Committee Act 1951,* which also involved a change of name for the committee to Joint Committee of Public Accounts and Audit (JCPAA), marked a transfer from the executive to the Parliament of independent audit scrutiny (by the JCPAA) of government and the APS. The act also ensured that, henceforth, the Auditor-General would be more independent of both the executive and the Parliament by virtue of the considerable powers given to the JCPAA. Two parliamentary officers summed up the new arrangements in May 2001 as follows:

> The Auditor-General, by conducting financial and performance audits of Commonwealth agencies provides the technical expertise and detailed scrutiny necessary for the effective evaluation of public service performance. Parliament depends on the Auditor-General's reports as a basis for further public inquiries.
>
> By strengthening the independence of the Auditor-General and his office from the Executive and enhancing the role of Parliament in relation to the Auditor-General as both guardian and client, Parliament has gained

some crucial extra weighting in the ever changing dynamic of checks and balances that pervade Australian democracy (Kerley and Harris 2001, pp. 11–12).

The year 1997 ushered in 'a new legislative era' for the Auditor-General's activities, which saw routine financial auditing eclipsed (or at least matched) by auditing intended to 'add value and improve public administration' (Wanna, Ryan and Ng 2001, pp. 288, 295). The Royal Commission on Australian Government Administration's 1976 call for 'a renewed vitality' for the audit function (in the form of a wider and sharper reporting brief and a parliamentary committee with greater powers) had clearly been answered (RCAGA 1976, p. 375). Yet the ANAO further sought to improve APS accountability, not only through 'an integrated audit approach' (Barrett 2004, p. 8), but also by advancing public sector practice via initiatives such as 'Better Practice Guides'. These are designed to translate ideas and procedures of proven success in some organisations to other parts of the public sector. Thirty-three such guides were produced between June 1996 and December 2011 covering areas like 'Audit Committees' (July 1997) and 'Managing Parliamentary Workflow' (April 2003). They play 'a desirable and valuable role in supporting improved public administration' (Coghill 2004, p. 6).

A retired Auditor-General has referred to a number of challenges facing the ANAO. Towards the end of his tenure, the question of lower funding resulting from projected budget cuts and the potential threat this constituted to the ANAO's capacity to discharge its duties prompted him to express his concerns in a letter to the Prime Minister in early 2005 (Lewis 2005, pp. 1–2). This could be addressed by achieving a better balance between what appears to be a possible overemphasis on detailed reporting, and examinations of general trends, namely, less micro and more macro evaluation (the APS Senior Executive Service, for example, has been the subject of several micro but few — and then not at all recent — macro reviews). Another issue he identified related to how the organisation could 'strike the right balance of audit activity across the public service to fulfil [its] statutory obligations, while meeting the particular demands of Parliament and individual agencies. The key to this outcome is understanding the Parliament's priorities and the business/functional imperatives of agencies that are creating a need for audit examination' (Barrett 2004, pp. 2–3, 8).

The authors of the ANAO history may have had something like this in mind when they wrote, three years earlier, that 'the tyranny of Parliament over the auditor-general could be equally as threatening to the independence of the office as the tyranny of the executive' (Wanna, Ryan and Ng 2001, p. 289). Fortunately, there are no signs of this happening and the 1997 reforms must be judged a success. The Auditor-General's role in Australian governance continues to be 'a moderating one', with the ANAO acting as 'a unifying influence, improving interconnectedness by strengthening the influence of values of openness and transparency' (Coghill 2004, p. 7).

The ANAO could partly address its limited funding by redirecting existing funding to more broad-ranging audits and through a reduced emphasis on what might be termed micro auditing. This would entail a smaller focus on the minutiae of administration in the case of the APS. A combination of these approaches may well provide a workable and successful future model for the ANAO. It could, for example, undertake fewer micro audits (ANAO 2005b) and more macro audits (ANAO 2005a). The former could profitably be less detailed and time- and resource-consuming, and the latter focused more on the enunciation for the whole APS of general principles and guidance tools absorbed from ANAO experience.

Table 5: 'Audit' reports of the Auditor-General 1989–90 to 2010–11 (number tabled/presented)

1989–90	29
1990–91	34
1991–92	53
1992–93	38
1993–94	44
1994–95	31
1995–96	33
1996–97	40
1997–98	50
1998–99	49
1999–2000	52
2000–01	54
2001–02	67
2002–03	63
2003 – 04	59
2004 – 05	59
2005 – 06	51
2006 – 07	53
2007 – 08	46
2008 – 09	48
2009 – 10	50
2010 – 11	57

Source: Australian National Audit Office.

Budget evaluation and appropriation processes

The Commonwealth financial scrutiny framework, specifically the budget and appropriation machinery, was transformed between 1964 and the early 2000s. Although public accountability now emanates (as it did a generation ago) from a single 'source of initiative' — the Parliament (Reid 1981, p. 133) — the financial scrutiny apparatus has become more complex and been reshaped by greater community pressure for better services, as well as the accountability requirements generated by expanded and more intricate government outsourcing and procurement arrangements. Both the formal political expression of this change (for example, administrative law) and its informal manifestations (for instance, adroit and systematic use of the media by individuals, organisations and interest groups) have produced greater accountability demands on ministers and the APS, and increased the need for improved financial structures and practices to underpin their activities (O'Faircheallaigh, Wanna and Weller 1999, pp. 296–297).

Given its importance to sound governance, the issue of the effectiveness of the financial accountability structures and processes remains a central one. L. J. Hume, writing in June 1963, warned of the danger that' in the Commonwealth Parliament the work of scrutiny will become wholly ineffective, and that the annual financial routine will degenerate into a ritual' (Hume 1963, p. 165).

The financial documents debated by Parliament, he stressed, focused too much on 'certain technical details of the government's book-keeping' instead of on 'the broad economic impact and implications of programmes' (Hume 1963, pp. 165, 166). Despite such well-argued calls (which were prescient about what would come to pass 20 years on), reform in this area was minor during the 1960s and 1970s — with the notable exception of the appointment of Senate Estimates Committees (1970), which were given the power to examine government expenditure via systematic questioning of departmental staff.

After conducting a wide-ranging analysis of how things stood in the early and mid-1960s, one student of the subject concluded:

> Efficiency of the Commonwealth public service occupies only a minor place in the considerations of the Commonwealth Parliament. Parliament's interest in public service efficiency is determined partly by concern with its own prestige; partly by political considerations derived from party or public or electoral attitudes. Only in the former does Parliament tend to act as a unit with party differences submerged; here there is evidence of a 'parliamentary' attitude. In the latter the main concern is with political issues, with questions on administration subordinate (Holzheimer 1973, p. 249).

By 1976, the Royal Commission on Australian Government Administration had become convinced that the establishment of a forward estimates process was essential to sound Commonwealth financial management. Such reform would be 'central to the task of rational coordination of policies as well as the efficient use of resources' (RCAGA 1976, p. 357). The 1980s were to witness far-reaching changes which reshaped parliamentary financial scrutiny of APS operations; indeed, they altered the whole landscape of government financial management. The main initiatives were:

- *Review of Commonwealth Administration*: J. Reid, January 1983 — emphasis on the importance of APS and governmental financial accountability and management;
- *Financial Management Improvement Program — Diagnostic Study*: Public Service Board and Department of Finance, February 1984 — promotes the practice of 'program budgeting' which is introduced later that decade;
- *Budget Reform — A Statement of the Government's Achievements and Intentions in Reforming Australian Government Financial Administration*: Department of Finance, April 1984 — recommends that better methods of identifying and establishing budget priorities be devised; and
- Efficiency Audit created to enhance APS financial functions: September 1986 (Verspaandonk and Holland 2003).

The 1990s saw an even more significant series of reforms:

- *Financial Management and Accountability Act 1997* (FMA Act) — introduced responsibilities for agency heads in areas such as fraud (s. 45), the establishment of an audit committee (s. 46), debt recovery (s. 47), record-keeping (s. 48) and providing the Auditor-General with financial statements in the required form (s. 49); and
- *Commonwealth Authorities and Companies Act 1997* (CAC Act) — introduced a single set of core reporting and auditing requirements for the directors of Commonwealth authorities and companies that are separate legal entities established for a public purpose (and which are entitled to hold money in their own right).

The remaining key budget and appropriation accountability mechanisms under the FMA Act are FMA regulations, FMA delegations, chief executive's instructions, FMA orders, financial statement orders, and the 'Commonwealth Procurement Guidelines' (of which more later).

The need to ensure greater scrutiny of government contracting resulted in the Senate Order of 20 June 2001, which required ministers to table, twice yearly, letters of advice that agencies they administered under the FMA Act had placed on the internet lists of current contracts (to the value of $100,000 or more) into which these agencies had entered. The Auditor-General provides regular reports on this process (twice annually until December 2003 and once a year since then: ANAO 2004c, p. 21; Holland 2003). Documentation relating to maintaining the confidentiality of commercial information in connection with contracting and procurement activities is contained in the Department of Finance and Administration's publications, the 'Commonwealth Procurement Guidelines' (Finance and Administration 2004) and 'Confidentiality of Contractors' Commercial Information' (Finance and Administration 2003).

The wider budget framework comprises a number of elements. They are annual appropriations, special appropriations, special accounts, the Australian government budget, a charter of budget honesty (introduced in 1998), the pre-election economic and fiscal outlook, an annual final budget outcome report, and monthly consolidated financial statements for the Government (APSC 2005a, pp. 61–73).

Australia's federal budget and appropriation arrangements are generally performing well. The reforms introduced in the 1980s and 1990s, which sought to reduce the emphasis on compliance and increase that on performance, have been successful. These include:

- The publication of the forward estimates in the interests of greater transparency;
- The introduction of program budgeting, which requires the outlining of program budgets and targets, and also that all appropriations related to that objective be certified;
- The establishment of aggregate controls, such as efficiency dividends, and identification and reporting against efficiency and effectiveness indicators; and
- The implementation (for the first time in the 1999–2000 budget) of an integrated framework of accrual budgeting, accounting and reporting, one that specifies outcomes and outputs.

Accrual accounting, which requires items to be brought to account and included in the financial statements as they are earned or incurred, rather than as they are received or paid, made it necessary for agencies to redevelop what had formerly been cash-based financial management and reporting systems (APSC 2003, pp. 93–95, 98–99).

What, then, can be said in conclusion about the present system, and how it might be refined or improved? There has been a marked change for the better in procurement and contract management activity following the introduction of the 'Commonwealth Procurement Guidelines', the Department of Finance and Administration's financial guidance document on contractors' commercial information, and the Senate Contracts Order, and a significant decline in the incidence of confidentiality provisions in contracts. Nevertheless, the ALP insisted in 2004 on the need for independent, credible and public benchmarks against which outsourcing and contracting proposals could more profitably be assessed (Latham and Emerson 2004, p. 4). While the ANAO found in 2004, after an audit of five medium-sized FMA Act agencies (including the Department of the Treasury), that 'generally, agencies had developed adequate control structures for the application of financial delegations for the expenditure of public monies', it was clear that 'such delegations were not always being managed in accordance with relevant legislation' (ANAO 2004a).

Interestingly, in an echo of L. J. Hume's 1963 concern with the format and contents of the financial documentation, one of the pillars of the new financial framework has been the subject of considerable debate — the Portfolio Budget Statements (PBS) themselves. In its third report on the structure and contents of the PBS (in 2000), the Senate Finance and Public Administration Legislation Committee concluded that, in view of the divergence of opinion about the proper purpose of the estimates process, 'the PBS are inevitably compromise documents'. Their make-up was not always proving helpful in 'the formulating of questions on input and process' and they were certainly not for the 'uninitiated'. But the committee could find nothing wrong in principle with the PBS layout, advising (especially senior) APS staff to familiarise themselves more with PBS introductory material and the whole subject of public sector budgeting in an attempt to enhance their understanding of the PBS process. The committee also recommended that Senate legislation committees report on the adequacy of the PBS provided to them for each set of hearings (SFPALC 2000, pp. 3–4, 39, 42).

One Senator, however (speaking in the same year), was less indulgent towards the PBS. He described it (and the Portfolio Additional Estimates Statement) as being replete with jargon, often difficult to read (indeed, sometimes unreadable), hard to follow from one year to the next because of radical format changes, and much in need of an 'English translation' or the assistance offered by a 'Guide to the Galaxy', as it appeared to him that the document could not have been put together by someone on this planet (Hogg 2001, p. 169).

Another major criticism of today's financial accountability arrangements was voiced in November 2004 by D. W. Challen:

Since the introduction of accrual budgeting in 1999, the Commonwealth government has presented two sets of budget to Parliament, and they report substantially different figures for almost every item. As a consequence, Parliament is hopelessly confused. One set of budget is based on Australian Accounting Standards formulated for [private sector] business applications while the other is prepared according to the Government Capital Finance Statistics standards of [the] IMF [International Monetary Fund] (Challen 2004).

Challen went on to argue that weaknesses exist in the present public sector reporting framework, particularly in relation to meeting the information needs of users; urged that the objectives and associated qualitative characteristics of public sector financial reporting should be more carefully articulated; referred to the problems which have arisen from applying the for-profit concept of financial control to the public sector; and recommended that a more appropriate definition of a government reporting entity be arrived at (Challen 2004, p. 2 and *passim*).

Since 1964, Australian governments of all political hues have gone to considerable trouble (especially from the early 1980s onwards) to ensure greater financial accountability for their activities. In this they have been ably assisted by the APS and the wider public sector. At present, it cannot be said that the demands of the financial framework are an impediment to sound government and efficient public administration. However, it is probably salutary to remember that 'accountability is not an unqualified good to be maximised at all costs. It must always be subject to reasonable limits in the light of other conflicting values, including practicality and cost' (Mulgan 2003, p. 236).

The institutions and requirements of financial management scrutiny as they relate to APS operations are, as argued earlier, basically sound. However, another aspect of financial accountability, which affects but is not germane to public sector activities, continues to raise concerns. It relates to 'special appropriations' (more accurately, 'standing appropriations'). These provisions permit governments to appropriate money from the Consolidated Revenue Fund; such amounts are often unspecified and for no fixed duration. In the words of one Senator: 'The significance of standing appropriations from an accountability perspective is that, once they have been enacted, the expenditure they involve does not require regular parliamentary approval and therefore escapes parliamentary control' (Murray 2005, p. 2).

The number of these (and the amounts involved) has risen markedly since federation: from 10 per cent in 1910 to 56 per cent in 1970, to over 80 per cent of all present Commonwealth government expenditure (the UK figure is 25 per cent). While the Australian Parliament undertakes no specific scrutiny of the many bills containing special appropriations, the Senate nevertheless possesses the power to remove or restrict the provisions in legislation for standing appropriations if it deems them inappropriate for the purposes of their proposed enactment (Murray 2005, p. 3). The Senate Standing Committee on the Scrutiny of Bills would be well-placed to undertake the task of examining all existing legislation and identifying where such provisions exist. The Senate could then determine which to retain and which to abolish (a course of action that would, of course, require the government's imprimatur). Thereafter, the Scrutiny of Bills Committee might assume this as one of its regular responsibilities.

Accountability to parliamentary inquiry: Ministerial advisers and public servants

The role of 'special' or 'ministerial' advisers in Australian governance, in particular their accountability to Parliament, emerged as a major issue during the early 1970s when the number of such appointments rose markedly in comparison with those of former decades. The implications of this trend and the main concerns to which it still gives rise were expressed by Senator John Carrick (then an opposition frontbencher) in May 1973:

> People have been insinuated between the Minister and his departmental head as buffers, as indeed protectors, to prevent the department from giving its authentic and responsible view to the Minister. The special advisers are apparently immune. The advice that they give does not have to be recorded; it does not have to be documented; it is not capable in general terms of being examined by the public. I ask that in future the special advisers be present, along with the departmental officers at Estimates Committee hearings and that they be made available for examination through the Minister just as are departmental officers.

> The test of the system is simple. If it is true ... that the idea of the Senate Estimates Committee is, through the Ministers, to be able to draw out of the departmental officers the facts, the thinking of the departments, to get a participatory democracy between members of the Public Service and this Parliament, then the Government of the day cannot have any alibi for preventing the special advisers being brought into the open and being subject to scrutiny (CPD, Senate, 31 May 1973, pp. 2147–2148).

None of these questions has been seriously addressed, especially concerns about the accountability of ministerial staff, by any government since then, despite a regular stream of Questions on Notice requesting details of the growing numbers, conditions of employment, salaries and other entitlements of such staff. Since the passing of the *Members of Parliament (Staff) Act 1984*, the total number of those employed under this legislation has risen from some 700 to 1,200, with ministerial staff numbers themselves standing in mid-2004 at approximately 400 (Latham and Faulkner 2004, p. 7). The Royal Commission on Australian Government Administration, as early as the mid-1970s, found there to be 'a lack of clarity in the division of responsibility between ministers and officials' (RCAGA 1976, p. 54). The debate has widened much since then with the longstanding focus on accountability recently being matched by a recognition of the need to set out clearly the respective roles of advisers and public servants. One MP identified this issue in 1981, arguing that the accountability dilemma for ministers, the APS and its staff centred on the complexity of its functions. This often resulted in ministers being placed in a position of 'ministerial answerability' rather than 'ministerial accountability'. The solution to this problem, he concluded, was a better definition of accountability requirements for department heads and senior APS employees which would assist ministers to be truly 'accountable' and not just 'answerable' (Aldred 1981, pp. 76–77). Yet, in the words of one Public Service Board chairman, as the 1980s advanced, public servants (even with their minister present) were finding themselves increasingly in the spotlight (Cole 1981, p. 123). As early as 1982, one commentator was speculating that public examination of APS staff at estimates and other committee hearings could allow poorly performing ministers to escape appropriate scrutiny (Uhr 1982, p. 37). A set of guidelines aimed at clarifying the position of public servants in such proceedings was tabled in Parliament in August 1984. It was later revised to take account of the Senate Parliamentary Privilege Resolutions of 25 February 1988 (Senate, Table Office 1988, p. 3; Prime Minister and Cabinet 1989).

By 1996, some observers were complaining of 'the increasing "direct" accountability of public servants to Parliament' — that, more and more, senior public servants at the table, rather than ministers, were being required to answer questions and explain decisions, and to do so to an unprecedented degree (Halligan, Mackintosh and Watson 1996, pp. 62–63). Some senior parliamentary officers, however, regarded this very differently, seeing it as merely another evolutionary step in scrutiny to which the APS leaders would need to become accustomed. In 2001, reflecting that '[t]he advent of broad-based committee systems in both the Senate and House of Representatives, has led to scrutiny being extended generally from Ministers to public servants', they emphasised that '[s]crutiny can be better exercised by committee members directing questions requiring in depth or detailed answers to public servants who may be more familiar with such details than Ministers' (Kerley and Harris 2001, p. 9).

Similarly, Max Trenorden stressed at this time that the traditional doctrine of accountability (the Westminster conception of a single chain of accountability via a minister) was essentially no longer valid, and that there now existed different levels and degrees of accountability following the landmark public service devolution and decentralisation of the late 1990s. However, as an MP himself, he acknowledged the difficulty confronting politicians in drawing the line when questioning public servants before committees, as they are increasingly involved in policy development and its review. Finding a balance between the accountability of public servants for administration and the political responsibility of ministers in the greatly altered public policy arena of the early 2000s will not be easy. An initiative that could assist in this is a revised set of guidelines governing public sector employees' appearance before committees in an attempt to better define their roles and responsibilities while at the same time (by means of reform of the standing orders) placing the main burden to respond to committee scrutiny on the shoulders of the minister (Trenorden 2001, p. 98; Holland 2002).

Despite the direction offered to advisers in the Prime Minister's *Guide on Key Elements of Ministerial Responsibility* and the *Members of Parliament (Staff) Act 1984*, the issue of the conduct of ministerial advisers continues to raise questions. The Senate Select Committee on a Certain Maritime Incident, which reported in August 2002 (see especially the section on 'Accountability and Ministerial Advisers', SSCCMI 2002, pp. 173–187) identified 'a serious accountability vacuum at the level of ministers' offices'. The fact that it had been denied access to the relevant key ministerial staff during its inquiry caused the select committee serious concern and led it to recommend a number of reforms to existing arrangements. These included the formulation of a code of conduct to better regulate the activities and ensure the greater accountability of such staff.

The inquiry prompted considerable debate about the ministerial staff system during 2003. Anne Tiernan and Patrick Weller, while acknowledging that the edifice had developed into 'an important political institution', nevertheless identified five important deficiencies in it: the system had outgrown the arrangements designed originally to support and control it; the framework was based on an outdated set of myths and assumptions; the absence of a clear and shared understanding of the respective roles of ministerial staff and public servants was undermining the quality of APS advice and support to ministers; a number of partisan practices had developed around the system which was reducing general and specialist knowledge of its structure and operations; and the critical weakness of present practices centred on the issue of the accountability of ministers for the conduct and performance of ministerial staff, and the overall lack of accountability of staff themselves. 'Ministerial staff', they concluded, 'are the black hole of the executive — unaccountable in theory as well as practice' (Tiernan and Weller 2003, pp. 3, 9, and *passim*).

Dr Michael Keating has suggested that a new stage in accountability has been reached; just as public servants are now accountable for their advice and actions more broadly than to their minister alone, ministerial advisers must also be subject to a formal accountability regime which fully reflects their new roles and responsibilities in government, and particularly in executive–APS interaction (Keating 2003, pp. 92–93). Ambitious prescriptions to this end have been put forward by both academic authorities and a parliamentary committee. Anne

Tiernan and Patrick Weller advocate greater transparency through mandatory reporting about central elements of the system, improved monitoring of its performance, and devising clearer lines of responsibility for such staff (Tiernan and Weller 2003, p. 10). Megan Kimber, speaking in late 2004, called for a fresh setting out of the functions of and relationships between ministers, their staff and public servants (Kimber 2004). A welcome publication in this area is the Australian Public Service Commission's *Supporting Ministers, Upholding the Values* (APSC 2006).

The most ambitious recommended reforms, however, remain those put forward by the Senate Finance and Public Administration References Committee report on 'Staff employed under the *Members of Parliament (Staff) Act 1984*' (SFPARC 2003b). The Committee called, *inter alia*, for the government to make ministerial staff available to appear before parliamentary committees in certain (specified) circumstances; recommended that the government, in consultation with the Parliament, provide a framework for the appearance of such staff; argued that the Act be restructured so as to better define the different categories of ministerial office employment; called for improved record-keeping practices within ministers' offices; recommended that a code of conduct for ministerial staff be devised and implemented, with such a code for non-ministerial staff employed under the act to follow; and insisted on the need for better training of staff (SFPARC 2003b, pp. xix–xxiv). Similar calls appeared in the ALP's August 2004 machinery of government statement (Latham and Faulkner 2004, p. 7). In government, Senator John Faulkner tabled 'Code of Conduct for Ministerial Staff' on 26 June 2008. The code contained 21 clauses. Some of the obligations outlined included that all ministerial staff should declare any gifts or hospitality; have no other outside employment; be aware of the APS code of conduct; acknowledge that they do not have the power to direct APS staff or make decisions; and not knowingly provide false information (Special Minister of State 2008). Yet, the code did not require ministerial staff to be directly accountable or answer questions before Parliament. Indeed the subject continues to provoke contrasting interpretation. In 2002, the Clerk of the Senate, for example, rejected the claim that either in practice or in law, ministerial staff cannot be summoned to appear as witnesses before parliamentary committees because they have immunity from such calls arising from the immunity of their ministers (Evans 2002, p. 137). Yet, the Clerk of the House of Representatives asserts that ministers and/or their staff should not be called upon to appear before a house (or one of its committees) of which the Minister is not a member because this would constitute an infringement of privilege (Harris 2002, pp. 105–106).

It is still largely the case (as it was in 1989) that '[t]he duty of the public servant is to assist ministers to fulfil their accountability obligations by providing full and accurate information to the Parliament about the factual and technical background to policies and their administration' (Prime Minister and Cabinet 1989, p. 1). However, it cannot be denied that in doing so, and in their dealings with ministers, ministerial staff and parliamentary committees, public sector employees are now confronted with a more complex and demanding set of challenges than in the late 1980s. That having been said, the APS of today is much more aware of the need to reflect on questions of accountability and, as it has shown, to work with the government of the day (as well as academic and non-academic commentators) in developing processes designed to better address scrutiny demands.

The role of ministerial advisers and other such staff in APS–executive interaction has for some years received systematic attention in the Australian Public Service Commission's annual 'State of the Service' report. The detailed synopsis it contains of APS staff relationships with ministerial offices suggests a generally harmonious set of relationships (APSC 2005b, pp. 34–43). The main foundations of this seem to be trust and clarity about what is required of public servants in such interchange. The APS values and code of conduct have provided (and continue to provide) a solid basis for the former. In March 2006, in order to strengthen the latter, the Australian Public Service Commission (APSC) released *Supporting Ministers, Upholding the Values*.

Conclusion

Almost certainly the best way forward for parliamentary scrutiny inside the two houses lies in implementing the remainder of the 1982 Hayden reform proposals and in ensuring that they are observed. Among the most effective means of achieving this would be to reshape the offices of President and Speaker so as to give them greater powers over the conduct of Question Time (as in Britain, in the case of the Speaker). The three legislative (or chamber) scrutiny vehicles examined in this chapter (Questions without Notice, Questions on Notice and Matters of Public Importance) are clearly in need of some further reform. The administration of the current wave of reforms since September 2010 demonstrates that the extent and success of such change will depend largely on the preparedness of the executive and the opposition front bench to collaborate in devising and abiding by in good faith initiatives aimed at providing the presiding officers with greater real authority over parliamentary proceedings. Overseas experience shows that these vehicles would then function more effectively, resulting in improved parliamentary oversight of the public sector. Parliament's committees must also display a greater willingness to investigate all aspects of APS operations. Some improvement has occurred with the revitalisation of the House of Representatives committee system.

However, further gains could be made as trends in this area indicate that such scrutiny is neither broad-ranging enough nor based on the recognition that investigations of key features of public administration should be conducted regularly so as to better discern trends and devise improvements in processes and practices. Even in instances where encouraging work of this kind is begun, it is often not carried through. The Senate Finance and Public Administration References Committee reference, 'Australian Public Service Employment Matters' (28 June 1999), for example, was not readopted on 21 March 2002, despite the production of one valuable report on the subject entitled 'Australian Workplace Agreements' (SFPARC 2000). The question of the degree to which committee report recommendations and findings are being noted by public servants is also relevant. While the practice whereby the government of the day provides formal and detailed responses to report recommendations remains central to effective public administration, another opportunity exists in this context for APS employees to enhance their policy and administrative skills, one suggested recently by the British House of Commons Public Administration Select Committee. In its report, 'Government by Inquiry' (UKPSCPA 2005), it extended the conception and well-established practice of government response regarding implementation or non-implementation of recommendations to one concerned with public sector learning, namely, measures designed to ensure that the lessons of committee inquiries are better absorbed by public servants in order to improve their capability.

Scope exists, too, for the ANAO to undertake more review and follow-up inquiries and to revisit areas of APS administration, such as the structure, role and functioning of the Senior Executive Service. The proliferating number of separate bodies in the Australian government (which ebbs and flows around the 1,000 mark) reinforces the need to build on the reforms emanating from the Uhrig Report (2004) on Australian Government statutory authority governance, and to preserve and strengthen the present budget accountability and financial management arrangements governing APS operations. Despite the undoubted challenges they pose for the long-dominant, traditional Westminster model of governance, which has had considerable difficulty absorbing them, Australia (like Britain) appears to have accepted that '[g]overnment cannot be fully explained without reference to special advisers' (Blick 2004, p. 314). More importantly, perhaps, politicians, public servants and commentators (academic and non-academic) seem to have acknowledged that, the need for a finer definition of the special adviser system's principles and practice notwithstanding, the APS and the ministerial adviser have separate (albeit important and complementary) contributions to make to sound governance — contributions which need not conflict or adversely affect public sector efficiency or good government.

The shortcomings of Australia's parliamentary scrutiny arrangements as they relate to APS administration, which have been explored in this chapter, should not obscure the real possibilities that exist for change; nor should they overshadow the strengths of the present system and the impressive repository of existing Australian practice and ideas that is available to be drawn on in pursuing fruitful reform. Much can also be learned from the political and public administration experience and scholarship of other parliamentary democracies. Successful constitutional change depends greatly on a historical perspective (University of London, School of Advanced Study/History of Parliament Trust 2005). The same can be said of attempts to reform the government sector. The 'Effective Scrutiny' project at the School of Public Policy's Constitution Unit at University College, London, for example, has produced valuable research and political blueprints for improving scrutiny based on both historical research and analyses of present administrative practice. Some of its findings would undoubtedly be applicable in Australia. The British diplomat and writer on international affairs, Sir Harold Nicolson, a civil servant of 20 years' standing, regarded the civil service as a stable and essential anchor of governance. It was, he proclaimed, nothing less than 'the flywheel of the state', a body whose continuity and flexibility as an 'organism' rather than a 'machine' made it an immensely useful instrument of governance (Nicolson 1940, p. 4; 1950, p. 787). The Australian public service, like its British counterpart, faces constant challenges. Nevertheless, there is no reason to doubt its capacity to respond positively to and to benefit from the essentially sound apparatus of parliamentary scrutiny to which it is now and will continue to be subject.

References

Aldons, M. 2000, 'Rating the Effectiveness of Parliamentary Committee Reports: The methodology', *Legislative Studies* (15)1, pp. 22–33.

Aldons, M. 2001, 'Rating the Effectiveness of Committee Reports: Some examples', *Australasian Parliamentary Review* (16)1, pp. 52–61.

Aldons, M. 2003, 'Evaluating Parliamentary Committees: Light at the end of the tunnel?', *Australasian Parliamentary Review* 18(1), pp. 79–95.

Aldred, K. 1981, 'Accountability to the Parliament by the Executive and the Public Service: The view from the Parliament', in *Government Expenditure and Accountability: The Relationship between the Parliament and the Public Service in the 1980s,* Joint Committee of Public Accounts Seminar, 16 May 1980, AGPS, Canberra, pp. 74–81.

ALP (Australian Labor Party) 2004, ALP Platform.

ALP 2007, ALP Platform.

ANAO (Australian National Audit Office) 1990, 'Survey of Internal Audit in the Commonwealth Public Sector', Audit Report No. 6, (PP141/1990), AGPS, Canberra.

ANAO 1991a, 'Accountability off the Rails — National Rail Corporation Limited: Erosion of accountability to the Parliament', Audit Report No. 16, (PP308/1991), AGPS, Canberra.

ANAO 1991b, 'Implementation of Purchasing Reforms in the Australian Public Service', Audit Report No. 3, (PP185/1991), AGPS, Canberra.

ANAO 1995, 'Financial Management: Department of Veterans' Affairs', Performance Audit Report No. 7, (PP287/1995), AGPS, Canberra.

ANAO 1996, 'The Administration of the Australian National Training Authority', Performance Audit Report No. 2, (PP98/1996), AGPS, Canberra.

ANAO 2000, 'Survey of Fraud Control Arrangements in APS Agencies', Performance Audit Report No. 47, (PP122/2000), AGPS, Canberra.

ANAO 2002, 'Recordkeeping', Assurance and Control Assessment Audit Report No. 45, (PP250/2002), ANAO, Canberra.

ANAO 2003a, 'Absence Management in the Australian Public Service', Performance Audit Report No. 52, (PP126/2003), ANAO, Canberra.

ANAO 2003b, 'Administration of Staff Employed under the *Members of Parliament (Staff) Act 1984*: Department of Finance and Administration', Performance Audit Report No. 15, (PP410/2003), ANAO, Canberra.

ANAO 2003c, 'Annual Performance Reporting', Performance Audit Report No. 11, (PP342/2003), ANAO, Canberra.

ANAO 2004a, 'Financial Delegations for the Expenditure of Public Monies in FMA Agencies', Business Support Process Audit Report No. 42, (PP/2004), ANAO, Canberra.

ANAO 2004b, 'Performance Management in the Australian Public Service', Performance Audit Report No. 6, (PP/2004), ANAO, Canberra.

ANAO 2004c, 'The Senate Order for Departmental and Agency Contracts (Calendar Year 2003 Compliance)', Business Support Process Audit Report No. 10, (PP/2004), ANAO, Canberra.

ANAO 2005a, 'A Financial Management Framework to Support Managers in the Department of Health and Ageing', Performance Audit Report No. 5, (PP/2005), ANAO, Canberra.

ANAO 2005b, 'The Management and Processing of Leave', Performance Audit Report No. 16, (PP/2005), ANAO, Canberra.

APSC (Australian Public Service Commission) 2003, 'The Australian Experience of Public Sector Reform', APSC, Canberra.

APSC 2005a, 'Foundations of Governance in the Australian Public Service', APSC, Canberra.

APSC 2005b, 'State of the Service Report 2004–05', APSC, Canberra.

APSC 2006, 'Supporting Ministers, Upholding the Values', APSC, Canberra.

Bach, S. 2003, *Platypus and Parliament: The Australian Senate in theory and practice*, Department of the Senate, Canberra.

Bagehot, W. 1974, 'The Non-Legislative Functions of Parliament', in N. St John-Stevas (ed.), *Collected Works*, Vol. 6, *The Economist*, London, pp. 41–45.

Barrett, P. 2004, 'Profiling the ANAO', Address to the 2004 Program for Officials of South-East Asian Parliaments, The Australian National University. Available at: http://www.anao.gov.au/~/media/Uploads/Documents/address_to_the_2004_program_for_officials_of_south%20east_asian_parliaments1.pdf.

Baxter, K. 2003, 'Governance and the Public Sector', in *Current Issues in Public Sector Governance*, University of Canberra, Canberra, pp. 57–67.

Blick, A. 2004, *People Who Live in the Dark*, Politico's, London.

Bungey, M. H. 1979, 'The Role and Responsibilities of the Public Works Committee', in *Financial Administration: Parliamentary Scrutiny*, Joint Committee of Public Accounts Seminar, 1 June 1979, Commonwealth Parliament, Canberra, pp. 47–57.

Cairns, K. M. 1979, 'Parliamentary Scrutiny: The practice', in *Financial Administration: Parliamentary Scrutiny*, Joint Committee of Public Accounts Seminar, 1 June 1979, Commonwealth Parliament, Canberra, pp. 32–47.

Challen, D. W. 2004, 'Towards a Single Set of Accounting Standards for the Public Sector', CPA Public Sector Congress Annual Research Lecture, 17 November.

Coates, J. 1990, 'A Finance and Public Administration Perspective: Complementing the estimates scrutiny process', in *Parliamentary Workshop on Senate Estimates Scrutiny of Government Finance and Expenditure*, Canberra, 17 October 1989, Papers on Parliament No. 6, March, pp. 20–26.

Coghill, K. 2002, 'Question Time: Questionable questioning with few answers', Democratic Audit of Australia, Swinburne University of Technology. Available at: http://apo.org.au/research/question-time-questionable-questioning-few-answers.

Coghill, K. 2004, 'Auditing the Independence of the Auditor-General', Paper presented to the Political Science Program, Research School of Social Sciences, The Australian National University, 11 February. Available at: http://www.researchgate.net/publication/237601993_AUDITING_THE_INDEPENDENCE_OF_THE_AUDITOR-GENERAL.

Cole, R. W. 1980, 'Responsible Government and the Public Service', in P. Weller and D. Jaensch (eds), *Responsible Government in Australia*, Drummond Publishing, Richmond, pp. 168–177.

Cole, R. W. 1981, 'Accountability to the Parliament by the Executive and the Public Service: Alternative perspectives', in *Government Expenditure and Accountability: The relationship between the Parliament and the public service in the 1980s*, Joint Committee of Public Accounts Seminar, 16 May 1980, AGPS, Canberra, pp. 117–126.

Coleman, P. 1982, 'Parliament and the Administration in New South Wales and the Commonwealth', in J. R. Nethercote (ed.), *Parliament and Bureaucracy: Parliamentary scrutiny of administration: Prospects and problems in the 1980s*, Hale & Iremonger, Sydney, pp. 93–100.

Connolly, D. M. 1979a, 'Opening Remarks', in *Financial Administration: Parliamentary scrutiny*, Joint Committee of Public Accounts Seminar, 1 June, Commonwealth Parliament, Canberra, pp. 1–12.

Connolly, D. M. 1979b, 'The Role and Responsibilities of the Public Accounts Committee', in *Financial Administration: Parliamentary scrutiny*, Joint Committee of Public Accounts Seminar, 1 June, Commonwealth Parliament, Canberra, pp. 76–87.

Davey, R. C. 1959, *The Public Accounts Committee: Management Problems in Finance Branches*, Public Service Board, Canberra.

Evans, G. 1982, 'Scrutiny of the Executive by Parliamentary Committees', in J. R. Nethercote (ed.), *Parliament and Bureaucracy: Parliamentary scrutiny of administration: Prospects and problems in the 1980s*, Hale & Iremonger, Sydney, pp.78–93.

Evans, H. 2002, 'The Parliamentary Power of Inquiry: Any limitations?', *Australasian Parliamentary Review* 17(2), pp. 131–140.

Faulkner, J. 2003, 'Balancing Government Effectiveness with Oversight and Scrutiny', Address to the Sydney Institute, 30 September. Available at: http://australianpolitics.com/news/2003/09/03-09-30b.shtml.

Finance and Administration, Department of 2002 'Commonwealth Procurement Guidelines and Best Practice Guidance', February 2002.

Finance and Administration, Department of 2003, 'Confidentiality of Contractors' Commercial Information', February 2003.

Finance and Administration, Department of 2004, 'Commonwealth Procurement Guidelines', December 2004.

Financial Management Guidance Publication No. 3.

Fraser, J. 2005, 'Questions Farce-Tracked', *The Australian*, 10 August.

Friedmann, W. 1950, *Principles of Australian Administrative Law*, Melbourne University Press, Carlton.

Halligan, J., I. Mackintosh and H. Watson, 1996, *The Australian Public Service: The view from the top*, Coopers & Lybrand and the Centre for Research in Public Sector Management, University of Canberra, Canberra.

Hamer, D. 2004, *Can Responsible Government Survive in Australia?*, 2nd ed., Department of the Senate, Canberra.

Hancock, I. 2004, *The V.I.P. Affair, 1966–67: The causes, course and consequences of a ministerial and public service cover-up*, Australasian Study of Parliament Group, Canberra.

Harris, I. 2002, 'Rights and Obligations of a Legislature in a Federal, Bicameral System', *Australasian Parliamentary Review* 17(2), pp. 97–111.

HCIO (House of Commons Information Office) 2005, 'Parliamentary Questions', Factsheet P1 Procedure Series.

Hogg, J. 2001, 'Senate Estimates Committees', *Australasian Parliamentary Review* 16(2), pp. 167–173.

Holland, I. 2002, 'Accountability of Ministerial Staff?', Research Paper No. 19, 2001–02, Department of the Parliamentary Library, Canberra.

Holland, I. 2003, 'Is There Adequate Parliamentary Scrutiny of Government Contracts?', Department of the Parliamentary Library Research Note No. 38. Available at: http://parlinfo.aph.gov.au/parlInfo/search/display/display.w3p;query=Id%3A%22library%2Fprspub%2F6XF96%22.

Holzheimer, R. 1973, *Parliamentary Influence on the Efficiency of the Commonwealth Public Service, 1960–1964*, The Royal Institute of Public Administration (Queensland Group), Brisbane.

House of Representatives 2010, 'Agreement for a Better Parliament: Parliamentary reform'. Available at: http://parlinfo.aph.gov.au/parlInfo/download/library/jrnart/640272/upload_binary/640272.pdf;fileType=application%2Fpdf#search=%22library/jrnart/640272%22.

House of Representatives, Standing Committee on Economics, Finance and Public Administration 2003, 'Review of the Reserve Bank of Australia Annual Report 2002', (PP 404/2003), Commonwealth of Australia, Canberra.

HRSCE (House of Representatives, Standing Committee on Expenditure) 1979, 'Parliament and Public Expenditure', AGPS, Canberra.

HRSCP (House of Representatives, Standing Committee on Procedure) 1993, 'About Time: Bills, questions and working hours', AGPS, Canberra.

House of Representatives 2011, 'Interim Report No. 1: Monitoring and review of procedural changes implemented in the 43rd Parliament', AGPS, Canberra.

House of Representatives 2012, 'Interim Report No. 3: The effectiveness of reforms to the House committee system', AGPS, Canberra.

House of Representatives *Practice 1981*, J. A. Pettifer (ed.), AGPS, Canberra.

House of Representatives *Practice 1997*, 3rd ed., L. M. Barlin (ed.), AGPS, Canberra.

House of Representatives *Practice 2001*, 4th ed., I. C. Harris (ed.), Department of the House of Representatives, Canberra.

House of Representatives *Practice 2005*, 5th ed., I. C. Harris (ed.), Department of the House of Representatives, Canberra.

Hume, L. J. 1963, 'Parliamentary Scrutiny and the Financial Documents', *Public Administration* 22(2), pp. 165–178.

Indyk, M. 1980, 'Making Government Responsible: The role of parliamentary committees', in P. Weller and D. Jaensch (eds), *Responsible Government in Australia*, Drummond Publishing, Richmond, pp. 93–110.

Joint Committee on the Parliamentary Committee System 1976, 'A New Parliamentary Committee System', AGPS, Canberra.

Joint Committee on War Expenditure 1941, 'First Progress Report', Commonwealth Parliament.

Joint Select Committee on Public Accounts 1932, 'Report', Commonwealth Parliament.

Keating, M. 2003, 'In the Wake of "A Certain Maritime Incident": Ministerial advisers, departments and accountability', *Australian Journal of Public Administration* 62(3), pp. 92–98.

Keating, M. 2004, 'Developments in Australian Democracy and the Public Service', Address to 'Parliament, the People and the Public Service', Symposium of the Association of Professional Executives of the Public Service of Canada, Ottawa, October.

Kerley, M. and I. Harris 2001, 'Parliamentary Checks on the Executive', Address to the 'Commonwealth Workshop on Accountability, Scrutiny and Oversight', Canberra, 23–25 May.

Kimber, M. 2004, 'Ministerial Advisers: Guardians or usurpers of responsible government?', Paper presented to the Australasian Political Studies Association Conference, Adelaide, 29 September–1 October. Available at: http://www.adelaide.edu.au/apsa/docs_papers/Aust%20Pol/Kimber.pdf.

Langmore, J. 1996, 'Parliamentarians, Econocrats, and the People', in J. Disney and J. R. Nethercote (eds), *The House on Capital Hill: Parliament, politics and power in the national capital*, The Federation Press, Annandale, pp. 81–105.

Latham, M. and C. Emerson 2004, 'A Truly Independent Public Service'. Policy announcement: Australian Labor Party.

Latham, M. and J. Faulkner 2004, 'Machinery of Government: The Labor approach'. Policy announcement: Australian Labor Party.

Lewis, C. and K. Coghill 2005, 'Surveying Research on Parliament and Parliamentary Oversight of the Public Sector', *Australian Journal of Public Administration* 64(1), pp. 62–68.

Lewis, S. 2005, 'Auditor Plea to PM on Cuts', *The Australian*, 8 March.

Mackey, T. C. 1979, 'The Role and Responsibilities of the Senate Standing Committee on Finance and Government Operations', in *Financial Administration: Parliamentary scrutiny*, Joint Committee of Public Accounts Seminar, 1 June 1979, Commonwealth Parliament, Canberra, pp. 87–97.

Marsh, I. 2004, 'Time's Up for Party Politics', *The Australian Financial Review*, 26 November.

Morrison, Croxford, Chambers & Associates, 'Dealing With and/or Appearing before Parliamentary Committees', Kingston, ACT.

Mulgan, R. 2003, *Holding Power to Account: Accountability in modern democracies*, Palgrave Macmillan, Basingstoke.

Murray, A. 2005, 'Will Government Control of the Senate Change its Relationship with the Public Service?', Paper presented at the National Institute for Governance Seminar, 'Public Sector Governance and the Senate', Parliament House, Canberra, 9 November.

National Institute for Governance 2005a, 'Public Sector Governance and the Senate', Seminar, Parliament House, Canberra, 9 November.

National Institute for Governance 2005b, 'Trust in the Public Sector', Seminar, Old Parliament House, Canberra, 4 August.

Nethercote, J. R. 2003, 'Australian Public Administration in Perspective', in *The Australian Experience of Public Sector Reform*, APSC, Canberra, pp. 11–21.

Nicolson, H. 1940, BBC Home Service Broadcast (Transcript), 18 December, p. 4.

Nicolson, H. 1950, 'Marginal Comment', *The Spectator*, 9 June.

Odgers, J. R. 1979, 'Parliamentary Scrutiny: The theory', in *Financial Administration: Parliamentary scrutiny*, Joint Committee of Public Accounts Seminar, 1 June, Commonwealth Parliament, Canberra, pp. 23–32.

Odgers, J. R. 2001, *Odgers' Australian Senate Practice*, 10th ed., H. Evans (ed.), Department of the Senate, Canberra.

O'Faircheallaigh, C., J. Wanna and P. Weller 1999, *Public Sector Management in Australia: New challenges, new directions*, 2nd ed., Macmillan, South Yarra.

Parliamentary Joint Committee of Public Accounts 1993, 'The Midford Paramount Case and Related Matters', Report No. 325 (PP 491/1992), AGPS, Canberra.

Parliamentary Library 1995, 'Accrual Accounting: A cultural change', Report No. 338 (PP 182/1995), AGPS, Canberra.

Parliamentary Library 2011, 'Commonwealth Parliament: The first year', Department of Parliamentary Services, Canberra.

Parliamentary Joint Committee of Public Accounts and Audit 2000, 'Contract Management in the Australian Public Service', Report No. 379 (PP 456/2000), Commonwealth of Australia, Canberra.

Parliamentary Joint Committee of Public Accounts and Audit 2003a, 'Annual Report 2002–2003', Report No. 397 (PP 400/2003), Commonwealth of Australia, Canberra.

Parliamentary Joint Committee of Public Accounts and Audit 2003b, 'Review of Australia's Quarantine Function', Report No. 394 (PP 30/2003), Commonwealth of Australia, Canberra.

Parliamentary Joint Committee on Native Title and the Aboriginal and Torres Strait Islander Land Fund 2003, 'Effectiveness of the National Native Title Tribunal', (PP 434/2003), Department of the Senate, Canberra.

Prime Minister and Cabinet, Department of the 1989, 'Government Guidelines for Official Witnesses before Parliamentary Committees and Related Matters', Department of Prime Minister and Cabinet, Canberra.

RCAGA (Royal Commission on Australian Government Administration) 1976, 'Report', Chairman: H. C. Coombs, AGPS, Canberra.

Reid, G. S. 1981, 'Accountability to the Parliament by the Executive and the Public Service: An alternative view', in *Government Expenditure and Accountability: The Relationship between the Parliament and the public service in the 1980s*, Joint Committee of Public Accounts Seminar, 16 May 1980, AGPS, Canberra, pp. 126–136.

Reid, G. S. and M. Forrest 1989, *Australia's Commonwealth Parliament 1901–1988: Ten perspectives*, Melbourne University Press, Carlton.

Ryle, G. and L. Pryor 2005, 'The Inquiries that were Ignored', *Sydney Morning Herald*, 20 June.

Senate n.d., 'Procedures to be Observed by Senate Committees for the Protection of Witnesses'. Available at: http://www.aph.gov.au/Parliamentary_Business/ Committees/Senate/Procedures_to_be_observed.

Senate 1990, 'Senate Legislative and General Purpose Standing Committees: The first twenty years 1970–1990,' Senate Committee Office, Canberra. Available at: http://www.aph.gov.au/Parliamentary_Business/Committees/Senate/ Significant_Reports/first20years/contents.

Senate 2001, 'Consolidated Register of Senate Committee Reports (1970–2004)', Senate Committee Office, Canberra.

Senate, Table Office, 1988, 'Parliamentary Privilege: Resolutions agreed to by the Senate on 25 February 1988', Senate Table Office, Canberra.

Senate Committee of Privileges 1999, 'Parliamentary Privilege: Precedents, procedures and practice in the Australian Senate 1966–1999: 76th Report', (PP / 1999), Department of the Senate, Canberra.

Senate Committee of Privileges 2002, 'Parliamentary Privilege: Precedents, procedures and practice in the Australian Senate 1996–2002: 107th Report', (PP 345/2002), Department of the Senate, Canberra.

Senate Legal and Constitutional Legislation Committee 2003, 'Senate Legislation Committees: Reports on the examination of annual reports: March 2003', (PP 56/2003), Department of the Senate, Canberra.

Senate Legal and Constitutional References Committee 2002, 'Inquiry into the Outsourcing of the Australian Customs Service's Information Technology', (PP 265/2002), Department of the Senate, Canberra.

Senate Select Committee on the Functions, Powers and Operation of the Australian Loan Council 1993, 'Third Report', (PP 449/1993), Department of the Senate, Canberra.

Senate Standing Committee on Finance and Public Administration 1988, 'Non-Statutory Bodies: Further report' (PP 110/1988), AGPS, Canberra.

Senate Standing Committee on Finance and Public Administration 1989a, 'The Timeliness and Quality of Annual Reports', (PP 468/1989), AGPS, Canberra.

Senate Standing Committee on Finance and Public Administration 1989b, 'Government Companies and their Reporting Requirements', (PP 398/1989), AGPS, Canberra.

Senate Standing Committee on Finance and Public Administration 1990a, 'The Development of the Senior Executive Service', (PP 206/1990), AGPS, Canberra.

Senate Standing Committee on Finance and Public Administration 1990b, 'The Development of the Senior Executive Service: Performance Based Pay', (PP 3/1990), AGPS, Canberra.

Senate Standing Committee on Finance and Public Administration 1992, 'Management and Operations of the Department of Foreign Affairs and Trade', (PP 525/1992), Department of the Senate, Canberra.

Senate Standing Committee on Finance and Public Administration 1993, 'Performance Pay' (PP 432/1993), Department of the Senate, Canberra.

SFPALC (Senate Finance and Public Administration Legislation Committee) 2000, 'The Format of the Portfolio Budget Statements: Third report', Department of the Senate, Canberra.

SFPALC 2003, 'Senate Legislation Committees: Reports on the examination of annual reports: September 2003', (PP 267/2003), Department of the Senate, Canberra.

SFPARC 1995a, 'Property Management in the Australian Public Service', (PP 150/1995), Department of the Senate, Canberra.

SFPARC 1995b, 'Service Delivery … by the Australian Public Service', (PP 15/1996), AGPS, Canberra.

SFPARC 2000, 'Australian Public Service Employment Matters: First report: Australian workplace agreements' (PP/2000), Department of the Senate, Canberra.

SFPARC 2003a, 'Recruitment and Training in the Australian Public Service (APS)', (PP 200/2003), Department of the Senate, Canberra.

SFPARC 2003b, 'Staff Employed under the *Members of Parliament (Staff) Act 1984*', (PP/2003), Department of the Senate, Canberra.

Shergold, P. 2004, '"Lackeys, Careerists, Political Stooges"?: Personal reflections on the current status of public service leadership', *Australian Journal of Political Science* (63)4, pp. 3–13.

Shergold, P. 2005, Address to National Institute for Governance Seminar, 'Trust in the Public Sector', Old Parliament House, Canberra, 4 August.

Special Minister of State 2008, 'Code of Conduct for Ministerial Staff'. Available at: http://www.smos.gov.au/media/code_of_conduct.html.

SSCCMI (Senate Select Committee on a Certain Maritime Incident) 2002, 'Report', (PP 498/2002), Department of the Senate, Canberra.

Stewart, J. 2002, 'Public Sector Management', in J. Summers, D. Woodward and A. Parkin (eds), *Government, Politics, Power and Policy in Australia*, 7th ed., Longman, Frenchs Forest, pp. 67–89.

Tiernan, A. and P. Weller 2003, 'Ministerial Staff: A need for transparency and accountability?', Submission to the Senate Finance and Public Administration References Committee Inquiry into Members of Parliament Staff (MoPS).

Available at: http://www.google.com.au/url?q=http://aphnew.aph.gov.au/ binaries/senate/committee/fapa_ctte/completed_inquiries/2002-04/mops/ submissions/sub04.doc&sa=U&ei=eDsJVJrWGYu8ugTh9oBg&ved=0CBQQ FjAA&sig2=Y2SJnUmn-TU6XrJDj8qCCw&usg=AFQjCNHaVdQcAXCTtpG LQQ4FoB3BscSmMQ.

Tingle, L. 2004, 'Lobbyists Learn to Deal with the New Deck', *The Australian Financial Review*, 11 November.

Trenorden, M. 2001, 'Public Sector Attitudes to Parliamentary Committees: A chairman's view', *Australasian Parliamentary Review* 16(2), pp. 97–101.

Uhr, J. 1982, 'Parliament and Public Administration', in J. R. Nethercote (ed.), *Parliament and Bureaucracy: Parliamentary scrutiny of administration: Prospects and problems in the 1980s*, Hale & Iremonger, Sydney, pp. 26–67.

Uhr, J. 1990, 'Public Expenditure and Parliamentary Accountability: The debatable role of Senate estimates committees', in *Parliamentary Workshop on Senate Estimates Scrutiny of Government Finance and Expenditure*, Canberra, 17 October 1989, *Papers on Parliament* No. 6, March, pp. 79–113.

Uhr, J. 2005, 'Gaita-aid', *Australian Book Review* 270, p. 11.

UKPSCPA (United Kingdom Parliament, Select Committee on Public Administration) 2005, 'Government by Inquiry', (HC 51–I), 3 February.

University of London, School of Advanced Study/History of Parliament Trust 2005, 'What are Senates for?', University College, London, School of Public Policy, The Constitution Unit. Documentation on 27 May 2005 conference held at the Senate House, University of London.

Verspaandonk, R. and I. Holland 2003, 'Changes in the Australian Public Service 1975–2003'. Available at: http://parlinfo.aph.gov.au/parlInfo/search/ display/display.w3p;query=Id%3A%22library%2Fprspub%2F1CI96%22.

Wanna, J., C. Ryan and C. Ng 2001, *From Accounting to Accountability: A centenary history of the Australian National Audit Office*, Allen & Unwin, Crows Nest.

4. Assessing Access to Information in Australia: The impact of freedom of information laws on the scrutiny and operation of the Commonwealth government

Daniel Stewart

When the first freedom of information (FOI) legislation was introduced in Australia, its basic objectives were said to be 'simple' (The Freedom of Information Bill 1978, second reading speech, Senator P. D. Durack, 9 June 1978):[1] to make public the structure, functions and rules applied by government, and entitle members of the public to access government documents unless there are special reasons not to. Over 30 years later, the introduction of the 'most significant overhaul of the *Freedom of Information Act 1982* (Cth) (the FOI Act) since its commencement' referred to the same basic objectives, attempting to 'deliver more effective and efficient access to government information and promote a culture of disclosure across government' (Freedom of Information Amendment (Reform) Bill 2009, second reading speech, Anthony Byrne MP, Parliamentary Secretary to the Prime Minister, Parliamentary Debates, 26 November 2009). This chapter explores the development, interpretation and operation of the FOI Act over the intervening 30 years. It examines the role of the FOI Act within the broader legal framework regulating access to government information to assess its impact on government policy at the Commonwealth level. It suggests that achieving the objectives of the FOI Act has proven anything but simple.

The Australian Freedom of Information Bill 1978 was the first of its sort introduced in a Westminster-style democracy.[2] By the time it was enacted, Australia's contemporaries in Canada and New Zealand had also passed similar legislation. Other countries, including the UK, have since passed legislation emboldened by these early examples, and there has been a recent explosion of laws intended to provide access to government information in over 76 countries around the world (Ackerman and Sanoval-Ballesteros 2006, p. 86; Worthy 2010,

---

1   Unusually the second reading speech was not read out in Parliament but merely incorporated into Hansard prior to the parliamentary recess. The rush to have it introduced in this way in an attempt to quicken its passage proved pointless, however. See the discussion of the history of the *Freedom of Information Act 1982* (Cth) below.

2   Note that the Swedish Freedom of the Press Act 1766 is usually referred to as the first FOI legislation that inspired the United States 1966 legislation: see Lamble 2002.

pp. 561–582). However, despite this proliferation of access to information laws, our understanding of their impact is still developing (Worthy and Hazell 2010, p. 352).

Much of the assessment of the impact of government disclosure laws attempts a comparative evaluation of various elements or decisions made under FOI legislation. These comparisons are often based on high level indicators or aggregated data, often supplied by government agencies charged with administering or championing the Act, and suffer from ensuring the collection and aggregation of data are sufficiently rigorous and coordinated.[3] Descriptive summaries of the presence of various exogenously valued features within legislation are contrasted with other studies attempting to compare the practical operation of access laws through lodgement of standardised requests. Some groups have also focused on the utility of access laws to their specific interests, particularly journalists (Worthy 2010, p. 562). Questions arise as to the objective value of the criteria used as the basis of the comparison (see Hazell, Worthy and Glover 2010, pp. 51–52).

The operation of access laws also presents other important impediments to evaluation. Access to information laws, perhaps more than comparable forms of regulation, 'do not operate in a vacuum' (Julnes and Holzer 2001, p. 696). The political context in which the access laws operate can have significant effects on the operation of reform initiatives. The attitude or culture of government agencies can make a significant difference. The goals of access laws are often vague, generalised or uncertain, making assessment inherently subjective or incommensurate. Perhaps most importantly, where those goals relate to democratic ideals or enhancing societal governance generally, they are profoundly impacted by the operation of institutions at the legislative, government, judicial or electoral level (Julnes and Holzer 2001, p. 696; see also Moynihan and Pandey 2004, p. 431).

Any assessment of the impact of access laws involves reference to the objects or justifications for such laws. Justifications for greater access to government information include both consequentialist and deontological approaches. Exposure of government information is claimed to provide greater accountability and encourages better decision-making. Greater transparency in the decision-making process establishes responsibility for the decision, requires disclosure of the considerations involved in the decision and increases the range of interests consulted. Requiring access encourages efficiencies in record-keeping and information gathering processes, improving the responsiveness of consultation and enabling correction of incorrect or incomplete information. Transparency can also encourage greater institutional legitimacy or trust, preventing corruption and

---

3 See, for example, the admission that the list of bodies subject to the FOI Act collected in the 2010 Annual Report is contributed by individual departments and is not authoritative: O'Connor 2010, p. 132.

reducing rent-seeking, reducing costs associated with establishing or enforcing agreements or encouraging compliance and generally allowing for more effective implementation of public policies (Ackerman and Sanoval-Ballesteros 2006, p. 92).

Access to government information can also facilitate effective business practices. It has been suggested that

> [c]ommercial users are, in many countries, one of the most significant user groups. Public bodies hold a vast amount of information of all kinds, much of which relates to economic matters and which can be very useful for business. A right to information helps promote a fluid information flow between government and the business sector, maximising the potential for synergies. This is an important benefit of the right to information legislation, and helps answer the concerns of some governments about the cost of implementing such legislation (Mendel 2008, pp. 4–5).

Many of the consequentialist arguments above can relate generally to transparency in its various manifestations, in both the public and private sectors. However, justifications for transparency of government information in particular often relate to the contribution to participatory democracy. Participation at any level of the democratic process requires access to and an understanding of information about the activities of government. Engagement with the political process beyond exercising voting rights requires an awareness of the impact of government decisions and the interests they reflect. The ability to access, respond to and augment information utilised in the decision-making process in turn raises the level of political debate and more informed decision-making (Hazell, Worthy and Glover 2010, p. 87).

The rise of access to information laws has also been linked with its acceptance as an integral element of freedom of speech and as part of a general right to information. Such rights are based on realising our potential as citizens in a democratic society. For example, Mark Bovens suggests that information rights such as access to information

> concern first and foremost the social functioning of citizens, not only in relation to the public authorities, but also in their mutual relations and their relations with private legal entities. Information rights should be part of the civil rights chapter of constitutions, together with the other individual rights (Bovens 2002, p. 327).

With the right to information comes the correlative responsibility to participate in holding government to account (Roberts 2001, p. 243). Thus access to information is justified not just through the instrumental effects on the various participants in government, but in defining and enhancing the relationship between government and citizen (see also Rosanvallon 2008, p. 1).

The objects of the FOI Act were based on recommendations of the Senate Standing Committee for Legal and Constitutional Affairs into the first FOI Bill in 1979. They identified three specific justifications for freedom of information laws:

> With certain national security exemptions ... we believe that every individual has a right to know what information is held in government records about him [sic] personally ... Second, we believe that when government is more open to public scrutiny, it in fact becomes more accountable ... The accountability of the government to the electorate, and indeed to each individual elector, is the corner-stone of democracy, and unless people are provided with sufficient information accountability disappears ... Thirdly, we believe that if people are adequately informed, and have access to information, this in turn will lead to an increasing level of public participation in the processes of policy making and government itself ... Unless information is available to people other than those professionally in the service of government, then the idea of citizens participating in a significant and effective way in the process of policy making is set at nought (SSCLCA 1979).

Thus even though these justifications focus on the instrumental effects of FOI laws they recognise the reciprocal nature of the obligations imposed, focusing not just on the accountability of government but also the importance of greater participation of individuals in the policy process.

The objects clause originally inserted as s.3 of the FOI Act only partially addressed these justifications. The object of the FOI Act was 'to extend as far as possible the right of the Australian community to access to information in the possession of the [Commonwealth] Government'. It then referred to three ways this was to be achieved: by 'making available to the public information about the operations of departments and public authorities'; 'creating a general right of access to information in documentary form in the possession of Ministers, departments and public authorities, limited only by exceptions and exemptions necessary for the protection of essential public interests and the private and business affairs of persons'; and 'creating a right to bring about the amendment of records containing personal information that is incomplete, incorrect, out of date or misleading'. Subsection 3(2) then suggested:

> It is the intention of the Parliament that the provisions of this Act shall be interpreted so as to further the object set out in subsection (1) and that any discretions conferred by this Act shall be exercised as far as possible so as to facilitate and promote, promptly and at the lowest reasonable cost, the disclosure of information.

The objects clause therefore recognised the general rights of access and amendment but without reference to the accountability and participation these rights are expected to achieve. It wasn't until the recent 2010 amendments (*Freedom of Information Amendment (Reform) Act 2010* (Cth)) that the reciprocal operation of the FOI Act is recognised in its objects with an explicit statement:

s.3(2) The Parliament intends, by these objects, to promote Australia's representative democracy by contributing towards the following:

(a) increasing public participation in Government processes, with a view to promoting better-informed decision-making;

(b) increasing scrutiny, discussion, comment and review of the Government's activities.

The recent amendments also include 'recognition that information held by the Government is to be managed for public purposes, and is a national resource'.[4] Thus the objects of the amended FOI Act recognise the value that access to government information has in improving the relationship between government and individual and making greater utilisation of government information possible.

This chapter considers how effective the FOI Act has been in attaining these stated and unstated objectives. It attempts to describe the development and operation of the FOI Act, outlining the application of the major provisions of the legislation and the basis for calls for their reform. It explores the various tensions within the legislation, including the need to encouraging disclosure generally without entrenching the means for restriction of access; recognising the role of the public service as agents both of the government and the public generally; protecting the interest of the individual in the context of the collective benefits of disclosure; and balancing the long- and short-term costs and benefits of any access regime. Beyond these inherent tensions, however, this chapter also considers whether there might indeed be a more fundamental concern over the introduction and operation of the FOI Act: the focus in the FOI Act on providing a right to access to government information reinforces the separation between government and individual rather than enhancing the engagement of both in the process of policy-making.

Part I of this chapter reviews the development of the legal and political context in which the FOI was conceived and enacted, and how that context has continued to develop. Examining the legal framework of access to government information more broadly allows a consideration of the role of the FOI Act, both in the gaps it attempts to fill and the influence on the operation of that framework as a whole.

---

4 *Freedom of Information Amendment (Reform) Act 2010* (Cth) introduced what is now s.3(3) of the FOI Act.

Part I seeks to establish three propositions: existing legal restrictions motivated or encouraged resistance to the introduction of the FOI Act; introduction of the FOI Act did not have a significant effect on the development of other elements of the legal regulation of disclosure and may arguably have hindered further development; and any discussion of the impact of the FOI Act on government policy-making has to consider the legal and political context in which that reform took place.

Part II examines the history and operation of the FOI Act, in particular the impact that the utilisation of the exemptions to disclosure have had on achieving the objects of the FOI Act. It examines the way in which concerns over the impact of the FOI Act on conventions of responsible government manifested in a continuing reluctance to embrace the pro-disclosure culture that the FOI Act was seeking to achieve, and in particular the extent to which questions of deference to the judgement of the executive on the impact on the effective working of government undermined the potential contribution of the FOI Act.

Part III examines the role of the FOI Act in protecting the interests of individuals and organisations. It considers the operation of the FOI Act in facilitating access to personal information and the interaction with privacy concerns. It also considers the protection of confidential and business information. The role the FOI Act played in enhancing the trust in government commercial dealings and the impact that had on the scrutiny and enhancement of broader policy objectives is also discussed.

The final part of this chapter looks at other elements of the recent reforms to the FOI Act to consider their antecedents and possible effect on the ongoing impact of the FOI Act. In particular, it looks at the imposition of charges for access to government information and the inherent evaluation of costs and benefits such charges represent. It is suggested that some elements of that reform have the potential to substantially renew the relationship between government and citizen in the policy-making process, but concerns continue over the ability to carry out such a renewal given the history and operation of the FOI Act.

Part I: The legal context of access to government information

Breaking down government secrecy?

In the final months of 2010, Wikileaks, 'a non-profit media organization dedicated to bringing important news and information to the public',[5] released over 250,000 US diplomatic cables to five respected international news organisations

---

5   As described on the Wikileaks website, which is located on varying servers, including http://213.251.145.96/.

— *New York Times, The Guardian, Der Spiegel, Le Monde* and *El Pais* (see Benkler 2011, pp. 1–2). Those news organisations then helped sift through and publish a selection of cables, often in redacted form, with simultaneous release on the Wikileaks website. They continued to be released in stages. The release drew immediate calls for action to be taken to seek to prevent or discourage the release of what was claimed to be classified, highly sensitive or damaging material (BBC News 2010; Shane 2010; see also Benkler 2011). However, the consequences from the release have so far been less dramatic. As US Secretary of Defense Gates predicted at a Pentagon press briefing on the day of the release:

> Now, I've heard the impact of these releases on our foreign policy described as a meltdown, as a game-changer, and so on. I think — I think those descriptions are fairly significantly overwrought. The fact is, governments deal with the United States because it's in their interest ... They will continue to work with us. We will continue to share sensitive information with one another. Is this embarrassing? Yes. Is it awkward? Yes. Consequences for U.S. foreign policy? I think fairly modest (US Department of Defence 2010).

A similar scenario, although on a smaller scale, had played out in Australia some 30 years earlier. An initial distribution of some 662 copies of a 437-page book reproducing diplomatic memoranda, assessments, briefings and cables had resulted in the purchase of less than 100 copies before an injunction was obtained to prevent further sales. Copies had been sold to the Commonwealth government as well as the Indonesian and US embassies. Copies of some of the cables were to be serialised in *The Age* newspaper. Again, the main concern was perhaps what the fact of release — rather than the actual content of the documents — might mean for the relationship between Australia and the relevant countries concerned. As the secretary of the Department of Foreign Affairs suggested: 'It is much more likely to facilitate our future relations if the government has been seen to try its utmost to prevent that [disclosure] happening' (*Commonwealth v John Fairfax & Sons* (1980) 147 CLR 39 at 46).

An *ex parte* interim injunction was granted by Mason J in the High Court at 12.45 am on Saturday 8 November 1980, after the Commonwealth had become aware of the intended publication of the book and partial serialisation in *The Age* later that morning. It was too late to prevent distribution of an early edition of some 60,000 copies of the newspaper, or to prevent early sales of the book. In *Commonwealth v John Fairfax & Sons*, the Commonwealth government was successful in continuing the interim injunctions. However, the impact of the judgement was to significantly alter the ability of the government to keep secrets.

Mason J confirmed that protection of government material as confidential in Australia involved three elements: that the material to be protected was confidential in quality rather than public knowledge; that it was imparted in circumstances that imported an obligation of confidence; and that there will be unauthorised use of that information to the detriment of the party communicating it (*Commonwealth v Fairfax* (1980) 147 CLR 39 at 51 citing *Coco v A.N. Clark (Engineers) Ltd* [1969] R.P.C. 41 at 47). However, the detriment to be shown before the government could claim protection was significantly different to that of a private citizen:

> The equitable principle [of breach of confidence] has been fashioned to protect the personal, private and proprietary interests of the citizen, not to protect the very different interests of the executive government. It acts, or is supposed to act, not according to standards of private interest, but in the public interest. This is not to say that equity will not protect information in the hands of the government, but it is to say that when equity protects government information it will look at the matter through different spectacles.

> It may be a sufficient detriment to the citizen that disclosure of information relating to his affairs will expose his actions to public discussion and criticism. But it can scarcely be a relevant detriment to the government that publication of material concerning its actions will merely expose it to public discussion and criticism. It is unacceptable in our democratic society that there should be a restraint on the publication of information relating to government when the only vice of that information is that it enables the public to discuss, review and criticise government action.

> Accordingly, the court will determine the government's claim to confidentiality by reference to the public interest. Unless disclosure is likely to injure the public interest, it will not be protected.

> The court will not prevent the publication of information which merely throws light on the past workings of government, even if it be not public property, so long as it does not prejudice the community in other respects. Then disclosure will itself serve the public interest in keeping the community informed and in promoting discussion of public affairs. If, however, it appears that disclosure will be inimical to the public interest because national security, relations with foreign countries, or the ordinary business of government will be prejudiced, disclosure will be restrained. There will be cases in which the conflicting considerations will be finely balanced, where it is difficult to decide whether the public's interest in knowing and in expressing its opinion, outweighs the need to protect confidentiality.

In relation to the documents in question in that case, Mason J was not willing to accept that publication would prejudice national security, except perhaps in the limited sense that other countries might be less willing to provide information on a confidential basis (*Commonwealth v Fairfax* (1980) 147 CLR 39 at 51 citing *Coco v A.N. Clark (Engineers) Ltd* [1969] R.P.C. 41 at 53). Security classification, particularly in the absence of evidence as to the basis and currency of the classification, was not sufficient to demonstrate the requisite detriment. In any event, any impact on Australia's foreign relations had already substantially occurred due to the early sale of copies of the book to foreign governments. Mason J therefore established that there must be an identified impact on the public interest before government secrecy would be protected.[6]

Recognition of the public interest in disclosure of government information had been recognised two years earlier in the case of *Sankey v Whitlam* ((1978) 142 CLR 1). Former Prime Minister Gough Whitlam and members of his cabinet had been accused of a criminal conspiracy relating to their conduct in office, namely the borrowing of $4 billion without approval by the states, allegedly on the premise that they misrepresented the loans as being for temporary purposes where that was known not to be the case. As part of committal proceedings, cabinet papers and other official documents were subpoenaed and objections were raised over whether they were protected from disclosure in evidence by 'Crown', or 'public interest', privilege. It had been more or less accepted before this case that 'a certified claim by a minister to a court that the disclosure of documents would be injurious to the public interest would ordinarily be accepted by the court' (McMillan 2000, pp. 26–27). However, in *Sankey v Whitlam* the various judges of the High Court held that it was for the court to weigh up the competing public interests for and against disclosure in each case, irrespective of whether the claim for privilege was due to the contents of the documents in question or the claim they belonged to a class which in the public interest ought not to be disclosed. As Acting Chief Justice Gibbs suggested:

> The fundamental and governing principle is that documents in the class may be withheld from production only when this is necessary in the public interest. In a particular case the court must balance the general desirability that documents of that kind should not be disclosed against the need to produce them in the interests of justice. The court will of course examine the question with especial care, giving full weight to the reasons for preserving the secrecy of documents of this class, but it will not treat all such documents as entitled to the same measure of

---

6 The role of the court in assessing whether the Australian public interest in publication overrides the interest in preserving government confidentiality was endorsed by the majority of the High Court in *Attorney-General (UK) v Heinemann Publishers Australia Pty Ltd* ('Spycatcher case') [1988] HCA 25; (1988) 165 CLR 30 at [32]; see also *Attorney-General (UK) v Heinemann Publishers Pty Ltd* (1987) 10 NSWLR 86.

protection — the extent of protection required will depend to some extent on the general subject matter with which the documents are concerned. If a strong case has been made out for the production of the documents, and the court concludes that their disclosure would not really be detrimental to the public interest, an order for production will be made (*Sankey v Williams* (1978) 142 CLR 1 at 43).[7]

The various members of the court recognised that the public interest in withholding documents may have various elements, including protection of national security or relations with foreign governments. Many were sceptical of broad claims that release of documents of a particular class would impede the candour of advice given to ministers or in the formulation of policy (see *Sankey v Williams*, Gibbs ACJ at 40, Stephen J at 62–3, Mason J at 97). Instead, importance was placed on preserving the basis on which information is provided to government where disclosure to others would impair confidence in the government and its effective working.

Disclosure of Cabinet papers would therefore generally depend on the content and context, recognising the currency of the information and the broader impacts disclosure may have. But the inner deliberations of Cabinet and who-argued-what may be protected where disclosure would undermine the doctrine of joint responsibility essential to Cabinet's institutional integrity (*Sankey v Williams* Gibbs ACJ at 41-2, Mason J at 97-98). Importantly, anticipating the arguments accepted in *Commonwealth v Fairfax*, confidentiality of Cabinet meetings was not of itself sufficient to prevent disclosure. Later cases have drawn on this aspect of the case to emphasise that reference to the public interest in disclosure applied even to government holding of private information when that was provided to the government in supposed confidence (McMillan 2000, pp. 27–30). Thus in *Jacobsen v Rogers* ((1995) 182 CLR 572 at 590) it was stated:

> Confidential information of a business character required to be given by a statute which prohibits the disclosure of the information and protects it from production to a court would appear to present a particularly strong case for immunity. Nevertheless, even where the private right to confidentiality is of some magnitude and its preservation is in itself in the public interest, it must be weighed against the public interest in disclosure for the purposes of the investigation and prosecution of the offences in question (*Jacobsen v Rogers* (1995) 182 CLR 572 at 592 citing *Sankey v Whitlam* (1978) 142 CLR 1 at 60–62).

---

7   See also Mason J at 96: 'In determining this question the court, though it will give weight to the Minister's opinion that the documents should not be produced, is entitled to inspect the documents and form its own conclusion upon the question whether the public interest will be better served by production or non-production.'

Together, *Sankey v Whitlam* and *Commonwealth v Fairfax* represent a crucial turning point in the legal protection of government secrecy.[8] However, they represented cases lost by prime ministers and governments who had themselves played instrumental roles in advocating for and introducing FOI legislation. In some ways, *Sankey* and *Fairfax* also represented high points in the case against secrecy, with subsequent developments in public interest privilege and government confidentiality continuing to apply the principles and qualifications set out in those cases without apparent attempts to further expand openness in government.

Lack of authority to disclose government information

While the publishers were successful in restricting claims of government confidentiality in *Commonwealth v Fairfax*, this was not enough to lift the injunction and allow publication of the book. The case also considered two other claims for protecting government information: breach of the *Crimes Act 1914* (Cth) and breach of the *Copyright Act 1968* (Cth). The government was successful in continuing the injunction to restrain breach of copyright. Neither the concerns over the public interest that limited breach of confidentiality in government information in openness of government nor acknowledgement that publication, albeit limited, had already taken place, was sufficient to bring the impending publication within the fair dealing defences to copyright infringement. Fair dealing encompasses criticism or review, but that was unlikely to be successfully argued at any subsequent final hearing of the claim due to the lack of consent to the publication of previously unpublished (in the sense of publicly available) documents, and the lack of significant commentary on the government material. Similarly, the fair dealing exception of reporting the news was unlikely to apply to the subject matter of many of the papers; it would be the publishing of the papers that would create, rather than report on, the news in question. Mason J was prepared to speculate whether the publishing of unpublished works might be considered fair 'as against a government merely because that dealing promotes public knowledge and public discussion of government action' (*Commonwealth v Fairfax* (1980) 147 CLR 39 at 55). Similarly, Mason J acknowledged that a defence against copyright infringement might exist where publication would protect the community from destruction, damage or harm, but extending this to publication of material which discloses no clear illegality would 'break new ground' (*Commonwealth v Fairfax* (1980) 147 CLR 39 at 57). An injunction was therefore granted to prevent publication in breach of copyright until the final hearing of the matter.

---

8   For example, SSCCLA 1979, p. 59 suggested that the judgements in *Sankey* 'have challenged, or even undermined, many ideas that were previously held (and are reflected in the [Freedom of Information Bill 1978]) about the relationship between government and the courts'.

Mason J's speculations about extending the exceptions or defences to copyright infringement were not tested in a final hearing. There has been no significant clarification of the position since then, with doubts still remaining over whether the government occupies any special position in relation to unpublished works or public interest defences to infringement (see *Collier Constructions Pty Ltd v Foskett Pty Ltd* (1990) 19 IPR 44; Stewart, Grifffith and Bannister 2010, [8.51]–[8.520]). Reviews of government ownership and use of copyright have made a number of recommendations calling for limits on that use (see, for example, CLRC 2005), but it remains a matter for individual departments or the approach taken with individual documents (see, for example, Attorney-General's Department 2010).[9]

The other element of the *Commonwealth v Fairfax* decision was the claims relating to potential breach of the *Crimes Act 1914* (Cth). Section 79 of the Crimes Act creates, among other things, offences for communicating, retaining or receiving information with the intention of prejudicing the security or defence of the Commonwealth. Mason J held that this provision was not enforceable through an injunction to supplement the rights of the Commonwealth to enforce copyright or confidentiality (see *Commonwealth v Fairfax* (1980) 147 CLR 39 at 50). He did not speculate whether the requisite elements of the offence might be made out in the circumstances of that case.[10]

It is also an offence under s.70 of the Crimes Act, then as now, for Commonwealth officers to publish or communicate any information or documents that come into their knowledge or possession by virtue of being a Commonwealth officer unless they have lawful authority. This is subject to imprisonment for up to two years. Section 70 has been the basis of a number of convictions for disclosure of government information, the most recent that of Allan Kessing for the disclosure to *The Australian* newspaper of security risks at Sydney airport which had come into his possession as a Commonwealth customs officer (*Kessing v R* [2008] NSWCCA 310). Reforms to whistleblowing protection at the Commonwealth level have been proposed but, at the time of writing, legislation is yet to be introduced (Brown 2011).[11]

---

9   That statement expresses support for use of a creative commons licence permitting reproduction provided attribution of government ownership is made, but this is not compulsory and is in many cases merely treated as a default position subject to variation as warranted in the circumstances of the individual agreement or document.

10   Section 79 has since been augmented by s.91.1 of the Criminal Code which makes it an offence for a person to communicate information concerning the security or defence of the Commonwealth or another country to a foreign country or organisation with the intention of prejudicing the security or defence of the Commonwealth, or of giving an advantage to another country's security or defence. An article, record or document which is made, obtained, recorded, retained, forged, possessed or otherwise dealt with in contravention of this Part of the Criminal Code is forfeited to the Commonwealth. It is a defence if the information is lawfully publicly available.

11   For a general discussion of the state of whistleblowing in Australia see Brown and Latimer 2011, pp. 137–157. Note that s.16 of the *Public Service Act1999* (Cth) now states:

The offence under s.70 of the Crimes Act is complemented by regulations under the *Commonwealth Public Service Act 1902* (Cth). Up until 1974, there were strict limitations on the authority of public servants to engage in public comment on matters of administration or information of which they had official knowledge. At the time of *Commonwealth v Fairfax* the regulations still required that information concerning public business, the contents of official papers or any matter of which an officer has knowledge officially could only be disclosed in the course of a public servants official duties or with express approval. That general restriction continued until 2006 when it was replaced with regulations prohibiting disclosure of information connected with public service employment where it is confidential or 'it is reasonably foreseeable that that disclosure could be prejudicial to the effective working of government, including the formulation of implementation of policies or programs' (Reg 2.1 Public Service Regulations 1999 (Cth)).

Changes to the regulations relating to disclosure of information followed the declaration in *Bennett v President, Human Rights and Equal Opportunity Commission* ([2003] FCA 1433) that the previous version was unconstitutional. Bennett was dismissed from his job at the Customs Department on grounds relating to his public comment as a union representative on general staffing issues. Finn J drew on the constitutionally enshrined freedom of political communication that had been developed by the High Court in the early 1990s (see *Nationwide News v Wills* (1992) 177 CLR 1; *Australian Capital Television v Commonwealth* (1992) 177 CLR 106). Under that freedom, any law that burdens the freedom of public servants to disseminate information or communicate government and political matters was subject to the test of validity formulated in *Lange v Australian Broadcasting Corporation* ((1997) 189 CLR 520 at 567):

> When a law of a State or federal Parliament or a Territory legislature is alleged to infringe the requirement of freedom of communication imposed by ss 7, 24, 64 or 128 of the Constitution, two questions must be answered before the validity of the law can be determined. First, does the law effectively burden freedom of communication about government or political matters either in its terms, operation or effect. Second, if the law effectively burdens that freedom, is the law reasonably appropriate and adapted to serve a legitimate end the fulfilment of which is compatible with the maintenance of the constitutionally prescribed

---

A person performing functions in or for an Agency must not victimise, or discriminate against, an APS employee because the APS employee has reported breaches (or alleged breaches) of the Code of Conduct to:

(a) the Commissioner or a person authorised for the purposes of this section by the Commissioner; (b) the Merit Protection Commissioner or a person authorised for the purposes of this section by the Merit Protection Commissioner; or (c) an Agency Head or a person authorised for the purposes of this section by an Agency Head.

system of representative and responsible government and the procedure prescribed by s 128 for submitting a proposed amendment of the Constitution to the informed decision of the people ...

The first part of this test was described by McHugh J in *Levy v Victoria* ((1997) 189 CLR 579 at 622; see also *John Fairfax Publications Pty Ltd v Attorney-General (NSW)* (2000) 181 ALR 694 per Spigelman CJ):

> The freedom protected by the Constitution is not, however, a freedom to communicate. It is a freedom from laws that effectively prevent the members of the Australian community from communicating with each other about political and government matters relevant to the system of representative and responsible government provided for by the Constitution. Unlike the Constitution of the United States, our Constitution does not create rights of communication. It gives immunity from the operation of laws that inhibit a right or privilege to communicate political and government matters. But, as *Lange* shows, that right or privilege must exist under the general law.

The application of that freedom in the context of disclosure of government information requires recognition of the legitimate interests of the government. Finn J recognised that the complexity, and need, of maintaining public confidence, and the diversity of circumstances in which public officials may disclose information, suggested a variety of legitimate interests may need to be accommodated in any regulation of disclosure. Those legitimate interests included possible restrictions on partisan political activity to preserve the impartiality, neutrality and loyalty of its public service, or restrictions to maintain the effective working or efficient operation of government. In the case of regulations preventing disclosure of 'information about public business or anything of which the employee has official knowledge', Finn J stated:

> The dimensions of the control it imposes impedes quite unreasonably the possible flow of information to the community — information which, without possibly prejudicing the interests of the Commonwealth, could only serve to enlarge the public's knowledge and understanding of the operation, practices and policies of executive government (*Bennett v President, Human Rights and Equal Opportunity Commission* [2003] FCA 1433 at [99]).

In invalidating the regulations, Finn J rejected an argument that the regulations relied on the exercise of discretion in granting authority which would be exercised in the same way as determinations to release information under the FOI Act. Finn J considered the reliance on discretion unreasonably compromises the implied freedom of political communication by turning it into a dispensation and possibly resulting in at least the appearance of censorship (*Bennett v President, Human Rights and Equal Opportunity Commission* [2003] FCA 1433 at [103]). Therefore regulations restricting the authority of public servants to disclose information had to reflect a more considered balance between the competing interests at stake.

Administrative law developments

The case of *Commonwealth v Fairfax* indicates that although there was growing judicial recognition of the public interest in disclosure of government information there remained considerable legislative restrictions on that disclosure. The operation of the Copyright Act and Crimes Act provided considerable scope to discourage the disclosure of government information by providing ministers and departments with considerable discretion over what information may be publicly released. These restrictions continued to operate after the introduction of the FOI Act, with substantial reform only now being considered (see ALRC 2010).

There were, however, a number of other legislative reforms that preceded the introduction of the FOI that had important implications for openness of government. In 1971, the report of the Commonwealth Administrative Review Committee, or Kerr Committee (CARC 1971), tabled its findings. Appointed under limited terms of reference to update some of the technical or anachronistic elements of review of administrative decisions, the report presented a plan for a 'new administrative law'. Two subsequent committees (Bland Committee 1973; Ellicott Committee 1973) further developed that plan and led to the introduction of three important elements of the current administrative law system. The *Administrative Appeals Tribunal Act 1975* (Cth) established the Administrative Appeals Tribunal (AAT) to undertake merits review of a wide range of government decision and the Administrative Review Council to perform an advisory role. The *Ombudsman Act 1976* (Cth) established the Ombudsman's Office to handle complaints and investigate concerns over maladministration. The *Administrative Decisions (Judicial Review) Act 1977* (Cth) (ADJR Act) was introduced to simplify and extend the jurisdiction of the Federal Court to review the lawfulness of Commonwealth administrative decision. Importantly, however, '[e]ach of those Acts also affirmed the existence of a new legal right, that a person aggrieved by a decision should be entitled upon request to be given a written statement of the reasons for the decision' (McMillan 2000, p. 3, citing *Administrative Appeals Tribunal Act 1975* (Cth) s. 28; *Ombudsman Act 1976* (Cth) s. 15(2)(e); and *Administrative Decisions (Judicial Review) Act 1977* (Cth) s. 13).

The new administrative law package, particularly the ADJR Act, has had a substantial impact in providing an alternative to the common law system of judicial review described by the Kerr Report as 'technical and complex and in need of reform, simplification and legislative statement' (CARC 1971, [21]). However, the common law system remains an essential element of Australia's administrative law system. Its constitutional entrenchment has led to increasing recourse to common law judicial review as the limitations of legislative provision of review rights have been exposed (see, for example, Spigelman 2010). Some commentary has suggested that the ADJR Act may even have had a stultifying effect on the continued development of that common law system (Aronson 2005).

An essential element of that common law review — procedural fairness — requires that an individual be informed of the basis for any decision which affects them in a direct and immediate way. After the decision in *Kioa v West* ((1985) 159 CLR 550), any administrative decision which singled out an individual in a way distinct from the community at large had to be accompanied by notice of the case to be met, including any credible, relevant and significant information that may be adverse to the interests of the individual, or be invalid and of no legal effect. The range of interests protected by procedural fairness expanded considerably after *Kioa*, with commercial and personal interests and even procedural expectations requiring disclosure prior to being affected (see *Re Minister for Immigration and Multicultural Affairs; Ex parte Lam* (2003) 214 CLR 1).[12] It meant that even material submitted to the government in confidence may have to be submitted, in substance at least, in the course of making decisions to which it might relate (*VEAL v Minister for Immigration and Multicultural and Indigenous Affairs* (2005) 225 CLR 88). Procedural fairness has not, however, extended to an obligation to provide reasons in making a decision (*Public Service Board (NSW) v Osmond* (1986) 159 CLR 656), something that remains subject only to legislative prescription despite the clear benefit in understanding the elements of the decisions made against them (see Cane and McDonald 2008, p. 145, fn 129).

Parliamentary access

The final frontier of access to government information, however, has been, surprisingly, the ability of Parliament to require the provision of information. Since *Sankey v Whitlam* it has been maintained that the rights of Parliament to require disclosure is at least as great as the judicial arm of government. In *Egan v Willis* ((1998) 195 CLR 424) the High Court held that the NSW Legislative Council could hold a Council member in contempt for failing to produce documents as directed. The Court relied on the principle of responsible government, including the responsibility of the government to the upper house of Parliament. The Court stated that:

---

12   For a general discussion of the expansion of Natural Justice see Cane and McDonald 2008.

In Australia, s. 75(v) of the Constitution and judicial review of administrative action under federal and State law, together with freedom of information legislation, supplement the operation of responsible government in this respect (*Egan v Willis* (1998) 195 CLR 424 per Gaudron, Gummow and Hayne JJ; see McMillan 2000).

In a continuation of the dispute, the NSW Court of Appeal held in *Egan v Chadwick* ((1999) 46 NSWLR 563) that, like the Court in *Sankey v Whitlam,* the Council could determine claims of legal professional or public interest privilege, subject only to constitutional principles such as the maintenance of Cabinet confidentiality.

Numerous questions remain about the role of Parliament and the courts in enforcing parliamentary access to government information. Despite continued criticism by Senate and parliamentary committees over refusals by ministers and their staff to provide information, recourse continues to be political rather than punitive or judicial in nature (McMillan 2000, p. 30).

Conclusions

This part has attempted to outline the general legal framework affecting access to government information. It has suggested that the legal context in which the FOI Act was introduced was one of increasing judicial recognition of the public interest in disclosure of government information. Limitations on public interest privilege and government confidentiality, together with enhanced procedural fairness rights to participation, significantly limited the ability of government to restrict information from individuals singled out by administrative action. Legislation introduced in the new administrative law reforms of the 1970s also gave individuals considerable scope to have decisions that affected them as individuals reviewed and amended. The introduction of the FOI Act was not the only legal development that contributed to increased access to government information, and any assessment of its impact should be considered in this light.

However, the capacity of the courts to affect change in the conventions of government control of information utilised in the working of government was limited. There was little scope to encourage the capacity of government disclosure to enhance the legitimacy and effectiveness of government regulation, or to enhance the relationship between government and the public generally. That recognition had to come from within government itself.

Part II: Operation of the Act: In whose public interest?

In the second Garran Oration — the first having been given by Sir Robert Garran the year earlier — the Prime Minister, Malcolm Fraser, spoke on the theme of responsible government: 'Those who make government policy and control its implementation should be responsible and accountable for the performance of their trust' (Fraser 1978, p. 22). Beyond effective and democratic electoral and parliamentary machinery, responsible government for Fraser had two fundamental requirements:

> First, people and Parliament must have the knowledge required to pass judgment on the government. Secondly, the ministers and government must themselves be in control of public policy so that those who the Parliament and people can call to account are indeed those responsible. To the extent that responsibility is diffused beyond that elected government — other than by legislative intent — to that extent is effective, popular control diminished. These two conditions for effective responsibility in government are complementary, but there are also areas where they compete.
>
> The clearest area of competition is the appropriate extent of confidentiality in government. Too much secrecy inhibits people's capacity to judge the government's performance. A complete absence of privacy in our system, where advisers must be capable of advising governments of different political complexions, inhibits the frank and open discussion between ministers and between ministers and officials which is critical to effective government and ministerial control (Fraser 1978, p. 2).

Three years later, these words would be repeated (Hansard, Senator Puplick, Wednesday 8 April 1981, p. 1257) during the second reading speeches for the Freedom of Information Bill 1981 (Cth), an amended version of which would finally become law a year later. The tension between too much and too little secrecy has dogged the FOI Act since before its introduction. Concerns about the effect access will have on the working of government have continued to shape the boundaries of access to information ever since.

Under Fraser's prescription of responsible government, the role of the public servant was to act as the agent of the elected government. This requires a relationship of confidence and impartiality between senior administrators and government, and between public officials and the public. The role of the public service was not just to administer the executive function of government, but also to contribute to the formulation of new policy, and to facilitate public consultation both to encourage new ideas and to test the understanding and reaction to proposals developed by government. The recognition of the political nature of some senior public service positions led the Fraser government to reduce the security of tenure of such appointments (*Public Service Amendment (First Division Officers) Act 1981* (Cth)), a trend that continued with new managerialism and corporatisation of the government services as the FOI Act matured (see, for example, Kettl 2000, p. 7). It perhaps merely reinforced the perception that the relationship of trust and confidence extended from the public service to the government of the day rather than the public generally.

This part looks at how the structure and interpretation of the FOI Act arguably helped promote a culture of secrecy within government at a time when other legal and social developments were shifting towards greater openness. It examines the role that notions of ministerial responsibility and the relationship between Parliament, ministers and their departments has had on the development and operation of the FOI Act. It begins by setting out the basic elements of FOI legislation and the objections that were raised against its introduction. It then considers the interpretation of various elements of the legislation, in particular the objects clause, the public interest test in the exemption of documents relating to internal deliberations and the impact of conclusive certificates on the role of external review. It concludes that concerns over responsible government, and the role of the public service within that construction, has restricted the development of the FOI Act and its ability to meet its objectives of enhancing the relationship between the government and the public at large.

The Introduction of the Freedom of Information Bill 1978

Despite its promises on the eve of election (Australian Labor Party 1972; see Terrill 1998, p. 94), the Whitlam government was unable to pass freedom of information legislation. Efforts to release departmental reports met with considerable resistance within the bureaucracy, advice to ministers more so. Whitlam wrote of his government that it had 'devoted many hours of discussion to freedom of information legislation but not sufficient to overcome the resistance of its most senior and respected public service advisors' (Whitlam 1985, p. 621; see Terrill 2000, p. 99). An interdepartmental committee established to draft FOI legislation reported that FOI was 'extremely complex with far reaching implications' (Terrill 2000, p. 106). They offered no justifications in favour of the introduction of FOI legislation and expressed an intention that such legislation merely codifies rather than expands access. The change in government led to the establishment of a second interdepartmental committee. Prior to its report, however, the Royal Commission on Australian Government Administration had included a highly detailed draft bill and explanatory memorandum among its appendices and helped spur increased public pressure for reform (RCAGA 1976, 10.7.20). In June 1978, the Freedom of Information Bill 1978 was introduced into Parliament largely based on the second interdepartmental committee report.

The FOI Bill 1978 established many of the most important elements that continue to characterise the FOI Act. The most important of these features relating to access to government documents is set out below.[13]

Right of access

Under the FOI Act, every person has a legally enforceable right to obtain access to Commonwealth agency documents and official documents of a Minister, other than exempt documents. This was amended in 1991 to make it clear that this right of access was not affected by the reasons for seeking access.[14] Importantly, access was not dependant on demonstrating any special interest in or need for the document in question.

Application process

The basic procedure for accessing documents involved requests in writing to the agency or Minister. Agencies were obliged to assist in framing a suitable request and to direct the request to the appropriate agency or minister. There were time limits (originally 60 days but soon reduced to 30 days) on the agency or Minister to make a decision about the request. Access can be either to a copy of the document or being allowed to inspect it. Reasons have to be given if the request for access is refused wholly or in part. Fees for the application, search and retrieval of documents and deciding whether to grant access were set out in regulations.

Exemptions

Access to a document could only be denied on a ground set out in the legislation. Grounds for denying access included where providing access would 'interfere unreasonably with the operations of the agency or performance by the Minister of [their] functions' (s.13(3) FOI Bill 1978).[15] However the main grounds for refusing access related to classification as an exempt document. These fell into three main groups (see Creyke and McMillan 2009, p. 1198):

---

13   For a discussion of the elements of the Act relating to access and correction of personal information and proactive disclosure of information see Parts III and IV of this chapter.
14   Though note that the applicant's reasons may be relevant to being declared vexatious and prevented from making further requests: see *John Ford and Child Support Registrar* [2007] AATA 1242; 45 AAR 166 affirmed by the Federal Court in *Ford v Child Support Registrar* [2009] FCA 328.
15   Note that these provisions have undergone numerous revisions. See below under the discussion about document handling processes in Part IV.

- Exemptions to protect the workings of government — these included interests such as national security, defence, and international relations; Commonwealth–state relations; the national economy; law enforcement and the protection of public safety; and the financial, property and staff management interests of government. It also covered the processes of government including Cabinet deliberations and the internal deliberative processes involved with the functions of an agency or Minister.[16]

- Exemptions to protect third party interests — these included confidential informants; personal affairs of any person; material obtained in confidence; or trade secrets, business, commercial or financial information.

- Exemptions to uphold other recognised legal interests — these included information which other legislation required be kept secret; and documents subject to legal professional privilege. Enactment and subsequent amendment removed exemptions based on 'public interest' privilege and added documents whose disclosure would constitute a contempt of Parliament of a court; certain documents relating to companies and securities legislation; and electoral rolls and related documents.

These exemptions were often subject to further qualification. For example, refusing to disclose Commonwealth financial, property or staff management information required a 'substantial adverse effect' (ss. 39 and 40 FOI Bill 1978).[17] Importantly, internal working documents were only exempt if the disclosure would be 'contrary to the public interest' and the AAT was restricted under the bill from reviewing that conclusion (see s.37(4) FOI Bill 1978). Some exemptions, such as Cabinet documents, internal working documents or documents relating to security, defence, and foreign affairs, were also further protected by the issue of 'conclusive certificates', which restricted the capacity of the other bodies to call into question the basis of the exemption. The 1978 Bill, for example, prevented the AAT from reviewing the decision to give the certificate or the existence of proper grounds for the giving of the certificate. These provisions were generally amended in the 1982 legislation to restrict the AAT to whether there existed reasonable grounds for the respective claims. Amendments in 1983 gave the Minister, after the tribunal had found that there were no reasonable grounds for the certificate, the option to revoke the certificate or to give notice that the certificate will not be revoked to both the applicant and each house of Parliament (see Freedom of Information Amendment Act 1983 (Cth) which inserted s.58A).

---

16 Note that subsequent amendments separated out the exemption relating to Commonwealth–State relations (s.33A) and added exemption for documents that might affect the conduct of tests, examinations or audits (s.40) or discloses unfinished research (s.43A). Recent amendments have further consolidated the exemptions. For a recent discussion of how exemptions relating to Commonwealth–state relations, foreign governments and law enforcement might be interpreted by the AAT: see *Maksimovic and Commonwealth Director of Public Prosecutions and Anor* [2009] AATA 700 (11 September 2009).
17 See further the discussion in Part III below.

Agencies and the Minister retained discretion to provide access to documents even though they may be exempt. The Act was not 'intended to prevent or discourage Ministers and agencies from publishing or giving access to documents (including exempt documents) otherwise than as required by this Act, where they can properly do so or are required by law to do so' (s.12 FOI Bill 1978; s.14 FOI Act 1982). There was also provision to redact documents, i.e. to delete parts of the documents that fall within an exemption.

Access to external review

One of the key elements of the FOI Bill was the provision for external review by the then newly formed Administrative Appeals Tribunal. The tribunal is generally able to engage in merits review of the decision to refuse or defer access, exercising the powers of the decision-maker within the agency or the minister to consider the nature of the documents sought,[18] the elements of proposed exemptions and the reasons for and against disclosure. The tribunal, unless restricted by a conclusive certificate, is able to exercise all the powers and discretions conferred on the original decision maker, and may affirm, vary or substitute a new decision for that under review or refer the matter back for reconsideration. There is an onus on the agency or Minister to justify their decision to refuse a request for access. Unlike agencies or ministers however, the tribunal cannot grant access to exempt documents. The conclusive certificate described above ultimately restricts the scope of the tribunal's review. Other decisions under the FOI Act, such as imposing or declining to waive charges or correct personal records, are also generally subject to review by the tribunal.

The FOI Bill also made provision for decisions by agencies, but not ministers, to be reviewed internally (s.54 FOI Act 1982). Seeking internal review was necessary before going to the tribunal. There was also recognition of the role the Ombudsman might play in investigating complaints, particularly about delay, and the relationship with tribunal review. The FOI Act 1982 clarified the scope for the Ombudsman to investigate complaints about actions taken by agencies relating to an access request prior to any tribunal hearing being sought (s.57 FOI Act 1982).[19]

Enactment of the Freedom of Information Act 1982: Objections

It took almost four years after the introduction of the Freedom of Information Bill 1978 (the FOI Bill) before legislative expression of the so-called simple

---

18   Note that there are restrictions on the capacity of the AAT to access the documents in some circumstances.
19   For further discussion of the proposed role of the Ombudsman see the discussion in Part IV below.

principles of open government were accepted in the *Freedom of Information Act 1982* (Cth). Upon its introduction, the FOI Bill was criticised for its apparent restrictive approach to access to government information. The ability of ministers to issue certificates establishing conclusively the grounds on which access to documents could be denied, the lack of retrospective effect of the act, the breadth of the exemptions and the delays it permitted all seemed to provide the public servants with the ability to control the release of information (Terrill 1998, p. 91). The Senate Standing Committee on Constitutional and Legal Affairs, after an extensive inquiry with over 168 submissions and 129 witnesses, recommended that the legislation be substantially amended in an attempt to provide greater external scrutiny of any denial of access under the Bill. The government substantially rejected these recommendations in making only limited amendments to the Bill. Criticisms of the Bill largely continued. Further amendments to the cct the following year by the then new Australian Labor Party government did little to alleviate the concerns (*Freedom of Information Amendment Act 1983* (Cth)).

Opposition to the Bill highlighted several areas of concern, including the resource and administrative burdens of complying with access requests, the protection it affords to suppliers of information to government and how compliance would be monitored or enforced (see SSCLCA 1979, p. 21).[20] Concern from within the public service, however, focused on the compatibility of FOI legislation with the Westminster system of government in Australia. The Senate Standing Committee on Constitutional and Legal Affairs reported concerns from the highest levels of the public service about the fundamental attack the legislation represented (SSCLCA 1979, p. 34). Access to government information could erode both the collective responsibility of Cabinet and individual responsibility of ministers for the actions of their department. It would distort the political neutrality and hence loyalty and efficiency of the public service, and remove their anonymity. It would, in other words, present scrutiny of the deliberations and discord within government or the executive at the expense of scrutiny of the outcomes achieved.

The Senate Standing Committee presented the impact of freedom of information on responsible government in a different light. Exceptions to the legislation would preserve the confidentiality of Cabinet deliberations, individual views of ministers and the secrecy of advice tendered to Cabinet (SSCLCA 1979, p. 39). The practice of ministerial responsibility for the actions of their department bore little relationship with the theory — indeed, ministerial responsibility may be revitalised as ministers were required to answer for more of the activities and administrative decisions of their departments (SSCLCA 1979, p. 43). No longer would a minister access details going to the proper and efficient working of the

---

20 For further discussion of these issues see Part III.

departments under their responsibility at a time of their choosing. While the loyalty of public servants to government, of whatever persuasion, was important, the increasing influence and delegation of authority to the executive means that the public service should be more open to scrutiny and more accountable for its actions, both to Parliament and the public at large (SSCLCA 1979, p. 47–48). The exposure of the views of public servants may well change the nature of the advice provided, but for the better, particularly if it encourages public servants to join in public debate. As the Senate Standing Committee stated:

> It is in the interests of ministers themselves to expose the advice of their officials to public scrutiny so as to improve the quality of that advice and ensure that all possible options have been canvassed. Freedom of information legislation can be in the interest of the public servants and government agencies whose processes are opened up to public gaze too, for it will lead to more adequate public recognition of the effectiveness of the public service. Greater exposure of government agencies to scrutiny can be expected in the longer term to result in a reduction in the level of suspicion and distrust surrounding relations between some government and non-government agencies ...

> What has happened, in short, is that critics have got things the wrong way around. It is not that freedom of information will change our governmental system; it is rather that our changing governmental system is contributing to pressures for freedom of information legislation. A Freedom of Information Act is indeed one way to make government adaptable, flexible and effective (SSCLCA 1979, p. 26–27).

Of particular concern to the Senate Standing Committee was the ability to seek external review of decisions under the proposed FOI Act. The 'unnecessarily restricted jurisdiction of the Administrative Appeals Tribunal' was seen as a 'major inadequacy' (SSCLCA 1979, p. 286). Any special relationship between Parliament, ministers and public servants would 'only require that some, not all, documents of political significance ... be protected, and it would not follow that ministers, or senior public servants, alone should decide conclusively what documents bear upon that relationship' (SSCLCA 1979, p. 286) The Senate Committee acknowledged the AAT may properly be restricted by conclusive certificates from determining the public interest in disclosing documents relating to defence, national security, international relations and Cabinet and Executive Council documents. However, review of other exemptions should not be limited by the issue of conclusive certificates. As the Senate Committee suggested:

> There is no justification for such a system tailored to the convenience of ministers and senior officials in a Freedom of Information Bill that

purports to be enacted for the benefit of, and to confer rights of access upon, members of the public. This can only confirm the opinion of some critics that the bill is dedicated to preserving the doctrine of executive autocracy (SSCLCA 1979, p. 180).

As mentioned above, the FOI Bill excluded the AAT from reviewing whether disclosure of an internal working document would be contrary to the public interest. The Senate committee had accepted the exemption relating to internal working documents 'reluctantly' (SSCLCA 1979, p. 218) and mainly due to the public interest criterion allowing all relevant interests to be considered and weighed. It was considered 'naïve to expect that a phrase such as "public interest" can be administered properly by public servants, who clearly have an interest in non-disclosure' (SSCLCA 1979, p. 221). The court in *Sankey v Whitlam* ((1978) 142 CLR 1) had demonstrated its capacity to balance the competing public interests involved, and the courts would be involved with decisions to refuse access through judicial review of the grounds of refusal anyway. Importantly, a neutral tribunal standing outside the system would best allow for the development and change in emphasis that must necessarily occur in such a broad exemption (SSCLCA 1979, p. 223).[21] It would permit 'a natural growth in the ideas about the way in which government should relate to the community. The public interest in any situation will not require a fixed result. The result would vary from time to time, depending on many factors' (SSCLCA 1979, p. 222).

The Senate committee recommended that the AAT have the power to review whether disclosure of an internal working document would be contrary to the public interest. The government rejected this recommendation, responding that the 'proper place to challenge a decision not to release a document which is judged would substantially impair the proper and effective working of government was parliament' (see Government Response to the recommendations of the Report by the Senate Standing Committee on Constitutional and Legal Affairs on the Freedom of Information Bill, Hansard, 11 September 1980, p. 803). However, there were changes to the FOI Bill that partially met the committee's concerns. The AAT was given the power to review decisions relating to internal working documents, but conclusive certificates could still be issued in relation to such documents that limited review of the public interest to whether there existed reasonable grounds for such a claim. As we shall see below, this has had a considerable impact on limiting the scope for development of public interest grounds for disclosure.

Few of the other substantive recommendations of the Senate Standing Committee were adopted in the revised Freedom of Information Bill 1981 that, after minor

---

21   This sentiment was repeated in (SSCLCA 1987, [11.17]).

amendment, was enacted and came into operation in 1982.[22] There were only a limited number of substantive amendments of the legislation leading up to the most recent amendments. The change in government in 1983 brought with it changes to the FOI Act to provide a greater right to documents created before the enactment of the FOI Act, shift the ability to review decisions back to the AAT as originally intended, particularly in relation to conclusive certificates, and gradually reduce the time limits for compliance from 60 to 30 days (*Freedom of Information Amendment Act 1983* (Cth)). In 1986, application and decision-making fees were introduced and search and retrieval fees were increased in a move towards greater cost recovery (*Freedom of Information Laws Amendment Act 1986* (Cth)). Agency reporting obligations were also increased. In 1988, amendments were made reflecting the introduction of the *Privacy Act 1988* (Cth), and in 1991 there was some clarification and simplification of the procedures and operation of the act as well as a widening of the ability to refuse access due to the diversion of agency resources involved (*Freedom of Information Amendment Act 1991* (Cth)). Each of these amendments did little to alter the basic structure and operation of the act and if anything they reflect increased resistance to the disclosure of government information.[23]

The importance of the Senate Standing Committee conclusions goes well beyond the amendments to the original bill or legislation. As this chapter will discuss, they have provided the basis for many of the subsequent reviews and calls for substantive reform of the FOI Act. However, with the benefit of hindsight there are perhaps two main concerns that might be suggested. The first is that the Senate Standing Committee made various observations about the changing governmental system but only considered the value or implications of those changes to the extent they suggested a basis for greater openness in government. They fail to engage with the extent passage of the FOI Act might itself encourage further change and the implications that may have. Secondly, they are based on the assumption that the implementation of the FOI Act will accord with the committee's expectations, which in turn relies on the acceptance by those implementing the act of the value of greater openness in government that underpin those expectations. In other words, the positive impacts of the FOI Act which underpinned the committee's conclusions depend on how the FOI Act is interpreted and implemented. As we shall see in the following discussion, the practical operation of the FOI Act suggests that the concerns of public servants about the effects of the FOI Act may not have been so easily displaced.

---

22 Perhaps the most important not already discussed was the inclusion of the ability to amend personal records which is discussed below in Part III.

23 For a general discussion of the various amendments to the FOI Act see Paterson 2005.

Interpretation and operation of the FOI Act: The public interest in disclosure

One recommendation of the Senate Standing Committee was the inclusion of an objects clause in the FOI Act. As discussed above, the object of the FOI Act was described as extending as far as possible the right of the Australian community to access information in the possession of the government (FOI Act s.3(1)).[24] It also attempted to encourage a pro-disclosure 'leaning' of the act, so that interpretation of its provisions or exercise of the discretions it conferred was further that object and encourage disclosure (FOI Act s.3(2)). However, despite that explicit intention, any 'leaning' had limited effect (see Bayne and Robinson 1995, p. 114). Early decisions interpreting the provisions of the act cautioned against constructing provisions providing access generously while taking a narrow construction of exemptions which permitted information to be withheld: 'The rights of access and the exemptions are designed to give a correct balance of the competing public interests involved' (*News Corporation Ltd v National Companies and Securities Commission* (1984) 1 FCR 64 at 66 per Bowen CJ and Fisher J). By 1987 Burchett J stated:

> ... it is too late to regard [the objects clause] as introducing any bias into construction of the exemptions in the Freedom of Information Act. They are as much part of the Act as s11, which confers a right to access expressly subject to them and as a right relating to documents other than those which are exempt (*Arnold v Queensland* (1987) 73 ALR 607 at 626 per Burchett J; see generally Creyke and McMillan 2009, p. 1212).

It is this literal approach to the balance set out in the FOI Act that is reflected in the reasoning adopted in the influential AAT decision of *Re Howard and the Treasurer of the Commonwealth of Australia* ((1985) 7 ALD 626; [1985] AATA 100).

John Howard, the then deputy leader of the opposition, lodged an FOI request in July 1984 for documents provided by the Treasury to the Australian Council of Trade Unions (ACTU) Task Force during the bargaining over the 1984–85 Budget as part of the accord agreement reached between the Australian Labor Party and ACTU with respect to matters of economic policy. The Treasurer, Paul Keating, issued a conclusive certificate certifying that there were documents that met that request that were exempt as internal working documents, i.e. they 'would disclose matter ... relating to ... the deliberative processes involved in the functions of an agency or Minister or the Government of the Commonwealth' (s.36(1)(a) FOI Act). The issue of the certificate meant that the AAT was restricted to whether there 'exist reasonable grounds for the claim that the disclosure of the document would be contrary to the public interest' (s.58(5) FOI Act).

---

24   FOI Act s.3(1).

President Davies of the AAT referred to various decisions restricting the ambit of internal working documents. The ordinary meaning of deliberation involved the weighing up or evaluation of the competing arguments or considerations that may have a bearing upon the exercise of the agency's functions. The exemption does not include purely factual material (s.36(5) FOI Act), reports of scientific or technical experts (s.36(6)(a)), statements of reasons for adjudicative decisions (s.36(6)(c)) or documents that have to be disclosed before a decision is made prejudicial to an individual's interest (s.36(2)), but might include the collection and exchange of facts involved in providing advice, opinion or recommendation. There was also no need for the material to relate to policy formation or be considered as part of the ultimate policy decisions of government (see *Re Howard*, [8]–[15]).

In considering when the public interest would prevent disclosure, previous tribunal decisions had relied on 'public interest' privilege case including *Sankey v Whitlam* in concluding that the exemptions for internal working documents protected the integrity and viability of the decision-making process within government. They are designed to encourage debate within government, protect the public from confusion, maintain the integrity of the decision-making process itself by confirming that officials are judged by what they decide rather than what they considered before making up their minds (*Re Howard* at [18] citing *Re Murtagh and Commissioner of Taxation* (1984) 6 ALD 112 at 121–122), and prevent 'ill-informed or captious public or political criticism' by those 'ready to criticise without adequate knowledge of the background and perhaps with some axe to grind' (*Re Howard* at [19] quoting from Lord Reid in *Conway v Rimmer* (1968) AC 910 at 952, as approved in *Sankey v Whitlam*). Therefore, while 'the whole of the circumstances must be examined including any public benefit perceived in the disclosure of the documents sought' (*Re Howard*, [20]), Davies J was able to suggest general guides relating to disclosure of internal working documents:

(a) the higher the office of the persons between whom the communications pass and the more sensitive the issues involved in the communication, the more likely it will be that the communication should not be disclosed;

(b) disclosure of communications made in the course of the development and subsequent promulgation of policy tends not to be in the public interest;

(c) disclosure which will inhibit frankness and candour in future pre-decisional communications is likely to be contrary to the public interest;

(d) disclosure, which will lead to confusion and unnecessary debate resulting from disclosure of possibilities considered, tends not to be in the public interest;

(e) disclosure of documents which do not fairly disclose the reasons for a decision subsequently taken may be unfair to a decision-maker and may prejudice the integrity of the decision-making process (*Re Howard*, [20]).

The documents sought in *Re Howard* fell within these guides. Although they related to an agreement which placed the ACTU in a privileged position, Davies J did not accept that the government in forming a budget could not consult on a confidential basis with individual organisations. There were therefore no particular circumstances that favour disclosure (*Re Howard*, [24]–[27]). Falling within the guides set out by Davies J was therefore sufficient to shift the persuasive burden to establishing a separate reason for disclosure that offset the impact of disclosing internal working documents of this nature.

The guides set out by Davies J have been subject to considerable criticism, both academic and in decisions of the AAT (for example, *Re Rae and Minister for State for Aboriginal* Affairs (1988) 16 ALD 709; SSCLCA 1987, 11.7–13). They were not intended to be definitive — as Davies J suggested after setting out the guides:

> The FOI Act has been in operation since 1 December 1982. As was said in [previous AAT decisions] the Tribunal has not yet received evidence that disclosure under the FOI Act has in fact led to a diminishment in appropriate candour and frankness between officers. As time goes by, experience will be gained of the operation of the Act. The extent to which disclosure of internal working documents is in the public interest will more clearly emerge. Presently, there must often be an element of conjecture in a decision as to the public interest. Weight must be given to the object of the FOI Act (*Re Howard*, [21]).

However, the emphasis on the public interest in non-disclosure, expressed in general and non-tangible terms, has arguably enabled reliance on the guides to excuse non-disclosure at the expense of demonstrating actual harm. The criteria suggest the possibility of class exemptions without regard to the content of the documents subject to the disclosure request and the injury to the public interest likely to result from their release. Protection of policy documents would seem contrary to the objects of the Act, protecting the public from confusion and unnecessary debate seems 'elitist and paternalistic' (*Eccleston and Department of Family Services and Aboriginal and Islander Affairs* (1993) 1 QAR 60 at 137 per F N Albeitz (Information Commissioner); see Creyke and McMillan 2009, pp. 1221–1224). The impact on candour and frankness in particular has been rejected by more recent AAT decisions that have emphasised the need for concrete evidence of how the release of the documents would impair the efficient and effective performance of government functions (for example, *Re Cleary and Dept of the Treasury* (1993) 31 ALD 214; McKinnon and Secretary, Department of Prime Minister and Cabinet [2007] AATA 1969).

However, the *Re Howard* criteria continued to be adopted and adapted by decision-makers in refusing access. In 2002, Mr McKinnon, the FOI Editor of *The Australian Newspaper,* made two FOI requests: for '[r]eports, reviews or evaluations completed in [2002] detailing the extent and impact of bracket creep and its impact on revenue collection of income tax', and '[d]ocuments relating to any review/report or evaluation completed on the First Home [Owners] Scheme[25] in the last two years' (see *McKinnon v Secretary, Department of Treasury* (2006) 228 CLR 423 at [30]–[31] per Hayne J). Access to most of the documents that fell within these requests was denied on grounds that clearly echoed many of the criteria adopted in *Re Howard.* They included: 'Officers of the Government should be able to communicate directly, freely and confidentially', and 'in written form what they would otherwise do orally, in circumstances where any oral communications would remain confidential'; '[t]he release of material would tend to be misleading or confusing in view of its provisional nature'; 'cannot be put into context because of the absence of any explanation of the variables used or assumptions relied on'; not 'fairly disclose the final position reached'; and use 'technical terms and jargon' without 'sufficient information for an uninformed audience to interpret them correctly and reasonably' (quoted in *McKinnon v Secretary, Department of Treasury* (2006) 228 CLR 423 at [34] per Hayne J).

Each of these public interest grounds was accepted as reasonably open by the original AAT decision in *McKinnon* of President Downes J. The High Court did not have to explicitly consider the public interest grounds relied on by the government, but all the judgements emphasised the contestable normative assessment involved in determining where the public interest might lie in relation to any particular document. The joint judgement of Callinan and Heydon JJ suggested that ongoing sensitivity, the difficulty of placing information into context, and lack of trust in the public to understand the technicalities and jargon used, or concern over a lack of balance in the way the documents would be reported were not in themselves likely to be reasonable grounds on which the public interest of non-disclosure would be justified. However, jeopardy to candour and desirability of written communications, the tentativeness of matters and recommendations yet to be settled which might mislead the public,[26]

---

25   A scheme subsidising the purchase of a first home regardless of income.

26   See also:

> The release of the material would tend to be misleading or confusing in view of its provisional nature, as it may be taken wrongly to represent a final position (which it was not intended to do) and ultimately may not have been used or have been overtaken by subsequent events or further drafts (*McKinnon* at 228 CLR 423 at 450 [80] per Callinan and Heydon JJ)

Hayne J also suggests:

> In the case of those particular documents, the relevant grounds for the claim were grounds asserting that release of the material shown in the documents had 'the potential to lead to confusion and to mislead the public'. The appellant did not assert that this could not constitute a reasonable ground for the claim that had been made (*McKinnon* at 228 CLR 423 at 448 [70]).

and the threat to responsible government of revealing documents prepared for responding to questions in Parliament were all considered possibly reasonable justifications for non-disclosure (*McKinnon* 228 CLR 423 at 446–447).

Conclusive certificates

The issue to be decided in *McKinnon* involved the role of the AAT in reviewing non-disclosure decisions where a conclusive certificate has been issued. In such a case the AAT is not tasked with determining whether disclosure of the documents in question would be contrary to the public interest, but only with whether the documents come within the description of the exemption (for example, are indeed 'internal working documents') and, if so, 'whether there exist reasonable grounds for the claim that the disclosure of the document would be contrary to the public interest' (s.58(5) FOI Act). In the decision of the Full Court of the Federal Court leading to the High Court Appeal, the majority had rejected an argument about whether assessing reasonableness required considering factors both in favour of and against disclosure. For example, Tamberlin J had suggested that 'if there is a ground that is not irrational, absurd or ridiculous for a claim that the [desirability of preserving intra-government communications prior to making a decision] ... would not be served by disclosure, then that alone is sufficient' (see the description of the Full Federal Court decision in *McKinnon* (2006) 228 CLR 423; at 432 [14] per Gleeson and Kirby J; 443 [54] per Hayne J; and 468 [131] per Callinan and Heydon JJ).

The minority of Gleeson CJ and Kirby J held that the approach of the Full Federal Court was wrong in law. The reasonableness of any ground can't be based only on the existence of a relevant consideration in favour of non-disclosure. It must be based on all relevant considerations that have a rational bearing on the claim (*McKinnon* (2006) 228 CLR 423 at 430–431 [12]). Callinan and Heydon JJ, by contrast, focused on the wording of the FOI Act rather than the correctness of the Full Federal Court's approach. They held that the AAT's role did not involve any balancing exercise between competing reasons. One reasonable ground for the claim disclosure, they continued, is if it is contrary to the public interest, even if there are other grounds going the other way (*McKinnon* (2006) 228 CLR 423 at 468 [131]). Hayne J agreed with the orders of Callinan and Heydon JJ, but he took a slightly different approach. He stated that 'the tribunal's task is to decide whether the conclusion expressed in the certificate (that disclosure of particular documents would be contrary to the public interest) can be supported by logical arguments which, taken together, are reasonably open to be adopted and which, if adopted, would support the conclusion expressed in the certificate' (*McKinnon* (2006) 228 CLR 423 at 444 [56]–[57]).

The difficulty confronted by the court and by the AAT in determining its role in the presence of conclusive certificates comes arguably from the conflation of possibly distinct tasks. A claim that disclosure of a document would harm the public interest in the candour of policy advice, for example, requires an assessment of whether that is a reasonable claim in relation to the particular document in question which requires considering the probative evidence on whether release of that document would have the harm identified; whether the harm identified does indeed go to the broader public interest recognised by the FOI Act rather than the interests of any other individuals or institutions; and how the effect on the public interest of denying release of the document compares to the impacts on the public interest if the document was released. It is arguable that all judges in *McKinnon* recognised the need to evaluate evidence both in favour and against the impact on the public interest identified by the Minister; it is not enough for the AAT to merely consider whether there are arguments in favour of withholding disclosure being in the public interest. However, the role of the AAT is not asked its view on where the public interest might lie but merely whether there are reasonable grounds to accept the judgement of the minister in relation to each of the distinct elements of that question.

This commonality between the various judgements in *McKinnon* was accepted in the AAT decision of *McKinnon and Secretary, Department of Prime Minister and Cabinet* ([2007] AATA 1969). Once again the FOI Editor from *The Australian* newspaper faced a conclusive certificate refusing access to internal working documents, this time in relation to documents held by the Department of Prime Minister and Cabinet relating to options that had been considered for industrial reform in the previous 12 months or that related to particular consequences of industrial relations reform. Deputy President Forgie rejected various grounds for the conclusive certificate because either the documents in question did not relate to what might be a reasonable ground or that there was a lack of evidence that the particular documents would contribute to the harm identified.[27] There wasn't a sufficient link made between the need for an apolitical public service and the confidentiality of high level policy advice. As Forgie D.P. suggested, '[w]hy is it that the APS can only behave as a professional and apolitical body if its work in giving high level advice is kept out of the public arena?' (*McKinnon* (2007) AATA 1969 at [160]) . There was no reasonable basis for concluding that the advice of senior officials would be confused for final decisions taken by the

---

27 Various documents were also identified as Cabinet in confidence and claimed as exempt under s.34 as documents submitted to or part of the deliberative processes of Cabinet. Forgie D.P. held that while there are 'reasonable grounds for concluding that disclosure of documents in the nature of Cabinet documents … protected from disclosure under the FOI Act by s.34 would be contrary to the public interest [the documents in question] are not of that nature. The evidence does not support a finding that their disclosure would compromise the confidentiality of Cabinet deliberations and so the notion of collective responsibility of Cabinet' (*McKinnon* (2007) AATA 1969 at [152]).

government, or that the public would conclude that decisions were taken on the basis of the incomplete information set out in individual documents (*McKinnon* (2007) AATA 1969 at [157]–[158]).

Forgie D.P. also rejected as unreasonable the claims that disclosure would impair the frankness of advice, encourage oral rather than written advice which would impair understanding and assimilation of relevant material, and restrict accurate written records of decision-making processes. She pointed to the provisions of the *Public Service Act 1999*, written directions by the AAPS commissioner provided under that Act and various other materials that set out requirements for written records to be kept. As she suggested:

> The APS must ensure that it has reporting arrangements in place to give account of each agency's performance and its effective, efficient and ethical use of resources. That must be underpinned by existence and maintenance of good recordkeeping systems. These are not simply standards to aspire but statutory requirements framed in terms of the APS Values and the Directions made under them (*McKinnon* (2007) AATA 1969 at [162]).

However, Forgie D.P. accepted that the disclosure of tentative options put forward during the development of policy options might reasonably not be in the public interest. As he put it, various grounds in the conclusive certificates were based on the claims that 'the government of the day is accountable to the Australian community for what its policy is in a particular area and for what it has included in a particular Bill submitted to Parliament. It is not in the public interest to require it to explain what it considered and what it rejected' (*McKinnon* (2007) AATA 1969 at [153]).

There may be various arguments about why disclosure of the options considered and rejected, whether the views of interest groups or ministerial advisors or APS officers were preferred and the quality of the advice given might all appropriately be the subject of public scrutiny. However, the limited role of the AAT was to consider the reasonableness of the ground in the then current circumstances.

Those circumstances are that matters relating to workplace relations law are very topical and the subject of much debate. It is not, however, in the interests of the efficient use of resources that a government should be required to disclose options and opinions to which it had, or might have had, regard in formulating its final position. The public's scrutiny of a government policy or of a particular piece of legislation is not advanced by the government's explanation of why it did or did not adopt a particular option:

The government is currently accountable in the context of the workplace relations for its acts and omissions regarding the workplace relations law that has been enacted and not for amendments to that law that it may enact in the future (*McKinnon* (2007) AATA 1969 at [155]–[156]).

The two *McKinnon* decisions made clear that the role of the AAT in reviewing the issue of conclusive certificates did not extend to substituting its view of the impact of the public interest of withholding disclosure. It was a reasonable argument that withholding direct access to the deliberative process could be justified due to the accountability provided by public exposure of the results of that deliberative process and the possible detriment to its candour and efficiency. Thus the public interest protected under the FOI Act was able to be restricted by a view that the benefits of direct access to the deliberative process were outweighed by its costs. It was subject to the view of the Minister as to impact of disclosure on the particular policy in question, rather than the broader impact on policy-making, or government, in general.

Reform

In its 1987 report on the 'Operation and Administration of the Freedom of Information Legislation', the Senate Standing Committee on Legal and Constitutional Affairs concluded that many of the concerns that had been raised about the protection and promotion of frank policy advice and criticism had been unfounded. They did, however, express concern at the guides set out in *Re Howard* and their adoption in subsequent cases. In particular, they stated:

> The Committee acknowledges that documents relating to policy proposals considered but not adopted can be used to attempt to confuse and mislead the public. But the Committee considers that such attempts, if made, will be exposed. The process of doing so will lead to a better public understanding of the policy formation process (SSCLCA 1987, p. 168).

The 'Open Government' review by the Australian Law Reform Commission (ALRC) and Administrative Review Council (ARC) also emphasised the changing nature of the public interest and how it depended upon the application of amorphous, subjective criteria to the circumstances of each situation (ALRC, ARC 1995, pp. 95–96 at [8.13]). They recommended that the public interest not be defined, but that it should be made clear that factors such as embarrassment to government should be irrelevant (ALRC, ARC 1995, Recommendation 37 at 96). However, it has only been in the recent amendments to the act that these recommendations have been accepted. The most recent reforms to the FOI Act have picked up on this in leaving the public interest undefined, but setting out irrelevant factors as well as factors favouring access. Whether access to the document could result in embarrassment to the Commonwealth government or cause loss of confidence in the Commonwealth government; access to the document could result in a person misinterpreting or misunderstanding the document; the author of the document is of high seniority in the agency to which the request for access to the document was made; or access to the document could result in confusion or unnecessary debate can no longer be used as in determining the public interest in withholding a document from release (s.11B FOI Act).[28] The result of these amendments is that many of the *Re Howard* factors are no longer relevant when considering the public interest served by withholding a document from release.[29]

The concerns over conclusive certificates have also been the subject of various calls for reform. The 1987 Senate Standing Committee report recommended retaining conclusive certificates. This was based on what they considered the restrained use of such certificates and the accountability of ministers to Parliament if they decline to abide by a decision of the AAT. The Senate Standing Committee, referring only to the use of certificates to that point, suggested that placing greater review powers with the AAT risked undermining ministerial responsibility (SSCLCA 1987, p. 147).

The Senate Standing Committee did recommend, however, the addition of requirements to inform Parliament of the issue of conclusive certificates. There has never been any requirement under the FOI Act to disclose publicly the numbers of conclusive certificates issued. Despite this, the Senate Standing Committee was able to report that there had been 'only' 55 conclusive certificates issued between 1 December 1982 and 30 June 1986, 21 of which were issued by Treasury prior to a change in internal procedures (SSCLCA 1987, p. 145). The only other figures available seem to be estimates of between 12 and 14 conclusive certificates issued between 1996 and 2006 (see Costello, Treasurer 2007; Parliamentary Library 2008). The ALRC agreed that the use of conclusive certificates should be disclosed, but went further in recommending that they be only for a limited duration and calling for the abolition of conclusive certificates in relation to Commonwealth–state relations and internal working documents (ALRC, ARC 1995, p. 117). Other commentators also called for their abolition. As Rick Snell suggested:

> The existence of such certificates leaves the Act exposed to changes
> in political will and bureaucratic commitment to the principles and

---

28 The 'factors favouring access' are if disclosure of the document would promote the objects of the Act; inform debate on a matter of public importance; promote effective oversight of public expenditure; or allow a person to access his or her own personal information.

29 The recent amendments also make the public interest test more significant by applying it to all of what are termed conditionally exempt documents. The public interest test is therefore applicable to all the categories of exemption except those relating to national security, defence or international relations, Cabinet documents, prejudicing law enforcement or public safety, or to which secrecy provisions apply.

objectives of the legislation … The current restraint in the use of these certificates is not cause to allow the damaging potential of this mechanism to go unchecked (Snell 2004, p. 9).

The decision of the High Court in *McKinnon* also highlighted, however, the restricted role of the tribunal and the potential manipulation of the certificate process. The *Freedom of Information (Removal of Conclusive Certificates and Other Measures) Act 2009* (Cth) abolished conclusive certificates and replaced them with some procedural protections for what may be considered sensitive material relating to national security, defence or international relations and denying access to documents from seven listed security agencies.[30]

Conclusions

Recent reforms have continued the gradual development of our understanding of the 'public interest' for the purposes of the FOI Act. Of the five guides set out in *Re Howard* relating to access to the deliberative process, recent reform has left only two: concern over impeding frankness and candour, and disclosure of documents which do not reveal the reasons for a decision subsequently taken, and even these are judged by reference to the particular documents in question rather than available as a general claim. In many ways this reflects the discussion played out in the courts in decisions like *Sankey v Whitlam* and *Commonwealth v Fairfax* in the cases of public interest privilege and government confidentiality. However, the role of responsible government continues to be referenced. Recognition that government accountability is aimed at those responsible for the decisions of government has led to importance being given to the collective responsibility of Cabinet and the ability to protect the role of the public service in the provision of advice. This has allowed concerns over the importance of the role of the public service in influencing policy decisions to encourage restrictions on public disclosure of that role.

As the Senate Standing Committee suggested, there is a need to allow for the continuing development of our understanding of the public interest and the balance to be struck between disclosure and withholding access. However, that development has come slowly, and the concerns over use of conclusive certificates has demonstrated continuing resistance within the public service, at least within some departments at senior levels, over promoting disclosure at the possible expense of the involvement of the department in policy setting. Recent amendments to the FOI Act reflect long-held concerns over the ability of the government to interpret the public interest in disclosure unduly narrowly,

---

30 These include the Australian Secret Intelligence Service, Australian Security Intelligence Organisation, Inspector-General of Intelligence and Security, Office of National Assessments, Defence Imagery and Geospatial Organisation, Defence Intelligence Organisation, and the Defence Signals Directorate.

restricting access to politically sensitive documents and eroding insight into the policy development process. However, the amendments still reflect a view that access to government information — particularly relating to the deliberative process — may impede rather than enhance the government policy-making process. The role of the FOI Act in encouraging accountability of that process rather than just its product is still to develop.

Part III: FOI and non-government interests

On 7 September 2010, Prime Minister Julia Gillard announced that an agreement had been reached with two independents returning the Labor party to government. The process of agreement, she stated, had resulted in 'more openness, transparency and reform in how we conduct our Parliament and the business of government than at any other time in modern Australian politics ... let's draw back the curtains and let the sun shine in' (*The Age* 2010).

Crucial to that agreement was the Labor Party's commitment to the National Broadband Network (NBN). The NBN, built in partnership with the private sector, will reportedly be the single largest nation-building infrastructure project in Australian history (Prime Minister, Treasurer, Minister for Finance and Minister for Broadband 2009). In April 2009, it was announced that it would be built and operated by NBN Co, a company incorporated under the *Corporations Act 2001* (Cth). Initially this company would be a wholly owned Government Business Enterprise (GBE), but it has been established with eventual private ownership in mind. As a GBE it will be subject to various forms of accountability and governance requirements in addition to those applicable to incorporated bodies: it has to release annual statements of intent, keep its shareholder ministers informed of financially significant events, and is subject to review by the Auditor-General for example. But as an incorporated body it would not be subject to many other forms of accountability that apply to the public sector, including the *Freedom of Information Act 1982* (Cth).[31]

Two months after the Prime Minister's statements about openness, the Senate was demanding access to various documents relating to NBN Co, including release of its business plan, which had been provided to the government in line with commitments under the *Commonwealth Authorities and Companies Act 1997* (Cth) (Riley 2010). Under that Act and associated guidelines (Department of Finance and Deregulation 1997), GBEs like NBN Co are generally subject to governance and accountability requirements that echo those in the private sector, except that their reporting and other obligations are generally to the government. In

---

31   See *Crowe and NBN Co Ltd* [2011] AICmr 1 (25 January 2011), the first decision of the newly created office of FOI Commissioner, affirming that NBN Co is not an entity that is subject to the FOI Act.

the case of NBN Co, for example, it is the ministerial shareholders who receive reports and hold management to account. While there is an obligation to publicly release a GBE's statements of intent (see Department of Finance and Deregulation 1997, [2.5]–[2.7]), other important reporting requirements may not be available to public scrutiny. Only documents that relate to the affairs of an agency or department of state are accessible under the FOI Act. Where a GBE is not covered by the FOI Act, not even the actions of government in holding the GBE to account are subject to scrutiny under the FOI Act.

A summary business plan was eventually released as part of a compromise deal with independents to get crucial legislation considered by the Senate, but not until various claims had been made about the importance of maintaining the confidentiality of documents going before Cabinet, and the potential confusion arising from the various options outlined in the plan depending on pending determinations by other government agencies.[32] However, only a summary rather than full plan was released to address concerns over the commercial sensitivity of information in the complete plan, including commercial-in-confidence material gained from third parties and details about current and upcoming tender processes (Wilson 2010). The complete business plan was released a month later (itnews 2010).

In January the following year, realisation that NBN Co was not subject to the FOI Act was acknowledged by the Prime Minister as 'the ordinary operation of the Freedom of Information Act' (Massola 2011). However, enactment of legislation relating to access arrangements for the NBN[33] included amendments to the FOI Act to explicitly bring NBN Co under its scope, but also exempted NBN Co in relation to documents in respect of its commercial activities.[34] In putting forward the amendments, Greens MP Adam Bandt suggested that the public had a 'legitimate interest' in 'one of the largest sums of public money invested in one of the largest infrastructure projects in our history':

> The Greens are not prepared to see the continuation of a long-term trend of gradually corporatising government services and then claiming information is commercial-in-confidence. That trend has to be rolled

---

32 In this case the Australian Competition and Consumer Commission on competition concerns with the plan: see Grattan and Yeates 2010.

33 See Telecommunications Legislation Amendment (National Broadband Network Measures—Access Arrangements) Bill 2011 (Cth), which passed both houses on 28 March 2011, but as of 12 April 2011 had not yet received royal assent.

34 Which is further defined as (a) activities carried on by NBN Co on a commercial basis; or (b) activities, carried on by NBN Co, that may reasonably be expected in the foreseeable future to be carried on by NBN Co on a commercial basis (see clauses 121 and 122 of the Telecommunications Legislation Amendment (National Broadband Network Measures—Access Arrangements) Bill 2011 (Cth)).

back and [NBN Co] is the place to start. We also believe that maximum transparency is in fact the best way to build public confidence in the NBN (OpenAustralia 2011).

The opposition, however, did not support the amendment, suggesting that, as a business, all of the activities of NBN Co would be conducted on a commercial basis (OpenAustralia 2011).

As part of the amendment, there was to be a review of the operation of the FOI Act relating to documents of NBN Co within 12 months (National Broadband Network Companies Bill 2011 (Cth) s.100A and s.3).[35] Assurances were given that the review would consider issues raised in the case of *Commonwealth v Fairfax*, and whether to 'tighten FOI rules to prevent documents being withheld on the basis of "confidentiality" unless it was proven their release would be a "real detriment" to the Government or to NBN Co's commercial operations' (Crozier 2011).[36]

The issues surrounding the application of the FOI Act to companies like NBN Co highlights the role the FOI Act plays in the relationship between government and other organisations and individuals. This section will describe the range of agencies and other entities subject to the FOI Act. It will consider how individual interests, of both a commercial and private nature, are protected under the FOI Act and how the FOI Act continues to rely on the distinction between public and private interests despite their interdependence in the development and implementation of public policy.

Subject to the FOI Act

One of the basic functions of the FOI Act is to provide a right of access to non-exempt documents in the possession of an agency or, in some circumstances, ministers. 'Documents' in turn is very broadly defined to include any method of recording information, including electronically (s.4(1) and s.17 FOI Act). There is only limited scope to require the production of information not already recorded and available to the agency.[37]

An 'agency' is defined in the Act as:

- a department of the Australian public service; or

---

35 The review was announced on 16 April 2012, to be completed by 30 June 2012 (Roxon 2012).

36 Note however that the terms of reference for the review do not include any such reference. See Attorney-General's Department 2012.

37 Note that s.17 of the FOI Act refers to producing documents of discrete records held on computers. This might include running a search term through a database and providing access to the result. The Act deems access to information in this way as a separate document, but it does perhaps involve reducing information not otherwise distinctly available into documentary form.

- a 'prescribed authority', which includes unincorporated bodies established under legislation for a public purpose and, where declared in the regulation, other bodies established by the government or over which the government is in a position to exercise control.

Incorporated bodies such as NBN Co are therefore not generally subject to the FOI Act unless prescribed in regulations. Official documents of ministers are documents that are or used to be in the Minister's possession, that can be accessed by the Minister, and which relates to the affairs of an agency (s.4(1) FOI Act). Not all documents in the possession of ministers in their official capacity are subject to the FOI Act; documents relating to the activities of non-agencies such as incorporated bodies are not subject to the right of access under the FOI Act.

Agencies may also be excluded from the operation of the FOI Act in respect of some or all of their activities (s.7 and Schedule 2 FOI Act). Thus bodies set out in Part I of Schedule 2 are exempt entirely,[38] in Part II in relation to specified documents[39] and in Part III in respect of their commercial activities.[40] References to commercial activities in Schedule 2 means activities carried on by an agency on a commercial basis, or foreseeably might be carried on in the future on a commercial basis, in competition with private bodies (s.7(3) FOI Act). Broad interpretations by the AAT have meant that a wide range of activities are potentially captured by this exemption.[41] An agency and Minister is also exempt in relation to documents, or summaries or extracts of such documents, which originated or are received from various named security agencies, or relate to defence intelligence or restricted technology (see ss.7(2A), 7(2B) and 7(2C)).

There is no clear principled basis that has been used in exempting a body or certain of its documents from the operation of the FOI Act. The ALRC and ARC, in its 'Open Government Report', initially proposed repealing the exclusion of bodies entirely on the basis that the exemptions provide sufficient protection (ALRC, ARC 1995, p. 215). They were convinced, however, that alternative

---

38   This currently includes agencies such as Aboriginal Land Councils and Land Trusts, Auditor-General, Australian Government Solicitor and various security and defence agencies. Previously, GBEs such as the Commonwealth Bank (prior to its privatisation) were also listed.

39   This currently includes Australian Broadcasting Corporation, in relation to its program material and its datacasting content; Australian Postal Corporation, in relation to documents in respect of its commercial activities; Medicare Australia, in relation to documents in respect of its commercial activities; Reserve Bank of Australia, in relation to documents in respect of its banking operations (including individual open market operations and foreign exchange dealings) and in respect of exchange control matters; Australian Statistician, in relation to documents containing information collected under the *Census and Statistics Act 1905*; and Qantas and Telstra were also listed prior to privatisation.

40   This includes body corporates established under the *Dairy Produce Act 1986* (Cth), or *Primary Industries and Energy Research and Development Act 1989* (Cth).

41   See, for example, *Australian Postal Corporation v Johnston* [2007] FCA 386, where listings of licensed post offices maintained by Australia Post were held to be exempt from disclosure as included under Schedule 2. See also *Bell and Commonwealth Scientific and Research Organisation (CSIRO)* [2007] AATA 1569; (2007) 96 ALD 450 for a discussion of the relevant case law.

forms of accountability and the probable exemption of vast majority of their documents justified the exclusion of the security agencies. GBEs, similarly, should not be prescribed authorities and hence excluded from the act if they are 'engaged predominantly in commercial activities in a competitive market' (ALRC, ARC 1995, p. 216). Those not so engaged in a competitive market should be subject to the FOI Act and the general operation of its exemptions without being listed in Schedule 2. The exemption relating to business and commercial affairs should clearly apply to documents that contain information about the competitive commercial activities of agencies (ALRC, ARC 1995, p. 141).[42] These recommendations were not, however, adopted in the most recent reforms to the FOI Act, and the controversy over the treatment of NBN Co perhaps highlights the continuing need for this issue to be addressed.

The commercialised state

Concern over the FOI Act's coverage of the commercial activities of government agencies is just one concern over a trend towards greater commercialisation of government activities in general since its introduction in 1982. Renewed emphasis on the efficiency and effectiveness of government was accompanied by a shift to a 'managerialism' or 'new public management' philosophy, emphasising cost-effectiveness, service quality and organisational performance.[43] Attempts to expose public services to competition, contestability and market-based mechanisms led to increased use of a range of tools including 'deregulation, commercialisation, corporatisation, public sector down sizing, outsourcing of services and privatisation' (Taggart 1997, pp. 1–2). Accompanying this shift has been concern over the applicability and persistence of public sector forms of accountability (Mulgan 2003). Exclusions of public bodies from the ambit of accountability mechanisms like the FOI Act, or limitations on their exposure, have been questioned given the seemingly increasing reliance on private sector forms of governance and contracting as a means of regulation (Parker and Braithwaite 2003, pp. 119–145). As Finn suggests:

> The always fuzzy line between public and private has been reconstructed since freedom of information (FoI) legislation first appeared in Australia ... the commercial relations between government, business and the broader community have been fundamentally reshaped (Finn 2003, p. 60).

At a broader level, the emphasis on market mechanisms and privatisation of government services has brought with it recognition of a broad range of

---

42 This has since been accepted by the Courts. See, for example, *Secretary, Dept of Workplace Relations & Small Business v The Staff Development & Training Centre Pty Ltd* [2001] FCA 1375.
43 On the changing philosophies of the Australian public sector see Wilenski 1988. On new public management generally see Hood 1991.

regulatory mechanisms that can help enhance the achievement of public policy goals. A range of methods was available to the government, often in conjunction with the private sector, to help achieve its public policy — or at least political — aims. Creating and influencing markets, transactional regulation through contract or grant, regulation of structural elements like underlying standards, codes or architecture, and a range of informational regulation ranging from requiring disclosure to performance indicators, ratings or education were added to more traditional command and control mechanisms like requiring licences or approval (Freiburg 2010, p. 85). Most provided for an increased role for government in gathering and processing information.

This has meant that a significant proportion of the information generated and held by the reconfigured government is commercial in nature (see Paterson 2004, p. 321). That information can relate to the commercial activities of government itself, to contractual arrangements entered into with private bodies for the delivery of government services, to the activities and governance arrangements of organisations that government has some interest it, or have been provided in the course of some regulatory scheme in which government plays a supervisory or enforcement role. Finally, that information can be provided during the policy-making process, with the submission of commercial information used to influence the policy setting process or to contribute to a finding and recommendation of a government body.[44] Each of these avenues for the generation and collection of commercial information encompasses an incredibly broad range of circumstances and regulatory or public policy objectives.

Excluding access to commercial information may therefore have a significant impact on the achievement of those objectives. To the extent to which FOI obligations modify market mechanisms they may reduce the competitive benefits to be gained or have other unintended effects. Potential release of commercial information may increase the risks and hence costs associated with doing business with government, or reduce the incentives to be forthcoming in providing information. However, excluding such information from disclosure where it plays an increasingly important role in the way government is conducted may significantly undermine achieving the objectives of the FOI Act. Adequately scrutinising the conditions in and performance under government contracts, the effectiveness of the market design in achieving its regulatory aims, and the influence of regulatory capture or interest group pressures may all depend on access to documents that necessarily include commercial information of a public or private nature.

---

44   John McMillan has argued that in some ways the availability of access to information has led to non-government organisations asserting a right to set the agenda, propose options or veto proposals: McMillan 2002, p. 30.

The FOI Act attempts to balance these considerations in a number of ways. As discussed above, the FOI Act is focused on agency documents and there are general exclusions available for some bodies because of their commercial nature or documents relating to their commercial activities. There are also a number of specific exemptions relating to commercial affairs available both to government and non-government bodies to prevent release of documents. Under the 'reverse FOI' procedure (see ss.27 and 27A FOI Act), before release of a document containing information concerning a person's or organisation's private or commercial affairs, they must be given an opportunity to make submissions in support of it coming within the personal or business affair exemptions. These submissions must then be considered in deciding whether to grant access to the document, and if access is to be provided, an opportunity must then be given for proceedings to be brought in the AAT arguing that the exemption should apply.

Up until the recent amendments a document could be withheld as exempt in a commercial context if:

- its disclosure was prohibited under other legislation;[45]
- it disclosed trade secrets or information having commercial value that could be diminished if revealed (s.43(1)(a) and (b));
- its disclosure would found an action for breach of confidence (s.45); or
- it disclosed other information about a person's business or professional affairs or an organisation's[46] commercial or financial affairs which, if disclosed, could unreasonably adversely affect them or 'could reasonably be expected to prejudice the future supply of information to the Commonwealth' (s.43(1)(c)).

These provisions therefore recognise that commercial interests can be implicated in a request for disclosure of information in a number of ways. Disclosure can affect the intrinsic value of the information itself, the commercial activities of the party providing the information, or the relationship between the government and providers of information. The document being requested can also have originated in three arguably distinct situations: disclosure of information to government, either under compulsion or voluntarily; generated by government itself as part of its commercial affairs; or it relates to government contracts and other commercial affairs (see Paterson 2004, pp. 325–329).

The exemptions to disclosure for commercial information involve the same concern with balancing the effect of disclosure on the commercial interests of businesses and organisations (including the government itself) against the public interest in that information being known. Disclosure may undermine the public policy objective sought through the creation or collection of commercial

---

45 Either legislation specified in Schedule 3 or which expressly applied the FOI Act exemption: s.38.
46 Including government authorities.

information, including greater efficiency or effectiveness through use of a market mechanism or correction of a market failure. Alternatively, the information disclosed may be sufficiently distinct from the activities of government, placing the party disclosing the information at a competitive disadvantage, or devalue intellectual property rights. As Gurry has suggested, in discussing both commercial and private information provided to government:

> By limiting the use which the State may make of this information to the discharge of the function for which it is received, the law assures citizens that their confidences will not be abused for reasons of extraneous political expedience and provides a framework of trust conducive to the candid disclosure necessitated by the relation of the modern State and its citizens (Gurry 1984, p. 18).

However, the protection against disclosure of commercial information is not absolute. Where disclosure would defeat the regulatory objective of a legislative scheme, there can be explicit provision for non-disclosure of the relevant information. Otherwise, information about business or commercial affairs supplied to the government is protected only to the extent disclosure would reasonably affect them or unreasonably jeopardise trust, for example. The reference to reasonableness has allowed incorporation of elements of the public interest, including other factors for and against disclosure, in recognition that merely relating to the commercial affairs of a body is not sufficient in itself to justify withholding the information (ALRC, ARC 1995, [10.31]).

Information of intrinsic value independent of its use by government is separately protected but only if it can be shown that value would be diminished or it otherwise can be considered a trade secret. The AAT has confirmed that the value of information to a private body is treated differently to that held by the government. For example, in *Secretary, Dept of Workplace Relations & Small Business v The Staff Development & Training Centre Pty Ltd* ([2001] FCA 1375) the tribunal emphasised that 'information must have value to the [agency] in respect of those of its activities which can be said to bear a commercial, as opposed to an administrative or governmental character' (*Secretary, Dept of Workplace Relations & Small Business v The Staff Development & Training Centre Pty Ltd* [2001] FCA 1375, [28]), and stated that

> there is a distinction between government functions and trading or commercial functions and that that distinction holds true even though government may deliver its governmental functions to interested members of the public in a commercial format, for example, by 'outsourcing' them to private service providers (*Secretary, Dept of Workplace Relations & Small Business v The Staff Development & Training Centre Pty Ltd* [2001] FCA 1375, [26]).

Information disclosed in confidence to the government is also protected from disclosure under the FOI Act, but only if it would found an action in breach of confidence (s.45 FOI Act). The courts, drawing on *Commonwealth v Fairfax*, have confirmed that where information is supplied to, as well as generated by government, determining whether there has been a breach of confidence involves a consideration of the public interest in disclosure (see *Smith Kline & French Laboratories (Australia) Ltd v Sec, Dept of Community Services and Health* (1991) 28 FCR 291; 20 IPR 643). But the question of whether information provided to government is confidential doesn't just depend on the intention of the private or government party. It will also be affected by how subsequent use or disclosure of the information serves the legitimate interests of the public purpose that underlies the agency's authority (*Smith Kline & French Laboratories (Australia) Ltd v Sec, Dept of Community Services and Health* (1991) 28 FCR 291; 20 IPR 643).

Reform of the protection of commercial information

Despite the various limitations on the exemptions of commercial information from disclosure, the exemptions have been subject to considerable criticism over the extent they may operate to limit scrutiny of the commercial activities of government. Unlike the exemptions dealing with the internal workings of government, these exemptions affect not only the process and deliberations underlining particular public policy choices but also the evaluation of the outcomes of those choices. Protecting the commercial interests of parties dealing with government may prevent scrutiny of the extent to which the public policy objectives have been achieved. The mere fact that information is commercial in nature, or discloses information about the identity or participation of organisations in commercial dealings with the government, should not, in itself, be protected. Similarly, the mere fact that contracts include confidentiality clauses may merely indicate an intention to prevent public scrutiny of the terms of the contract. The exemptions from disclosure may provide the incentive for agencies to use provisions designed to protect third parties to instead protect the terms of the agreement, or government interpretation and enforcement of them, from scrutiny (see Paterson 2004, p. 328). As Frieberg has suggested,

> public costs are often unknown or uncalculated, while private costs tend to be regarded as commercially confidential. For a proper evaluation and comparison of costs to take place, both the public and private sectors will need to make their bottom lines, if not their calculations, more transparent. In the absence of valid comparisons, the process of contractualisation will continue to be based on ideology rather than economics (Frieberg 2010).

Continuing concern over the expenditure of public funds through contractual arrangements involving confidentiality provisions led the Senate to adopt a continuing order requiring government agencies[47] to list on their websites various details of all contracts with a value over $100,000, including whether there are any confidentiality requirements. Agencies have to also provide reasons for the confidentiality. The Commonwealth Auditor-General reports to the Senate each year on the possible inappropriate use of confidentiality provisions in government contracts (Senate Order for Departmental and Agency Contracts; see also Department of Finance and Deregulation n.d.). There has been a significant decline in the reported use of confidentiality provisions, from around 24 per cent to 10 per cent, since the introduction of the order (see ANAO 2003, p. 13).[48] The Auditor-General recently concluded there remained 'scope for improvement' in agencies understanding and application of the guidelines in order to assess whether particular contract provisions should be confidential (ANAO 2003, p. 13).

The recent amendments to the FOI Act have, however, sought to extend access to documents relating to the performance of government contracts. In so doing, the amendments have largely adopted recommendations in the 1995 'Open Government Report' (ALRC, ARC 1995, [15.8]–[15.15])[49] and the ARC report on 'The Contracting Out of Government Services' (Administrative Review Council 1998). The amendments allow requests for access to documents held by non-government parties who provide services under a contract. The services have to be in connection with that agency's functions or powers, and not merely provide services to the agency in question. Agencies are required to include provisions in the contracts to ensure they will be provided with documents held by the contracted service providers upon request from the agency after the agency receives an FOI request (s.6C FOI Act). An agency may not disclose the document under the FOI request if an exemption applies, or if all reasonable steps have been taken to obtain the document under the contractual provisions but the document has not been provided to the agency (s.24A FOI Act). This new amendment reflects what might be considered good practice in respect of monitoring the performance of contracted obligations. It emphasises that the agency retains responsibility for supervision of the contract, and that any

---

47   Defined as an agency within the meaning of the *Financial Management and Accountability Act 1997* (Cth) — generally bodies that owe direct financial reporting and accountability requirements as part of the Commonwealth government.

48   In 2009 there were 41,937 contracts for goods and services totalling $165 billion. Of these, 4,084 contracts were reported as containing confidentiality provisions. Of the 150 contracts examined, 14 per cent incorrectly included confidentiality provisions and 51 per cent were incorrectly listed as containing confidentiality provisions, thus restricting their access by the Senate and public.

49   The proposal is tied to recommendation 99 of the 'Open Government Report', which was concerned with 'the trend towards government contracting with private sector bodies to provide services to the community' on the basis that it 'poses a potential threat to the government accountability and openness'.

request for documents is done within the contractual framework. It means, however, that documents cannot be obtained from non-government parties outside of the contractual context.

The recent amendments also clarified how the public interest test applied to those exemptions dealing with commercial concerns. Trade secrets and other valuable information and information provided in confidence remain unconditionally exempt, but documents disclosing business or commercial affairs that might reasonably adversely affect those affairs or prejudice the future supply of information to the government must be disclosed unless their disclosure is contrary to the public interest (ss.47G and 11A FOI Act). While the impact of these clarifications is still uncertain, it may be relevant that some of the cases referred to in Part II, concerning exemptions relating to internal working documents, placed less importance on the public interest in accessing submissions and other documents relating to consultation with non-government organisations. For example, in *McKinnon and Secretary, Department of Prime Minister and Cabinet* ([2007] AATA 1969) it was suggested by Forgie D.P.:

> Those consulting with government are not subject to the same statutory standards as those working within the [Australian Public Service relating to record keeping]. It may be that, in particular circumstances, their candour and frankness would be inhibited. Deliberations and consultations that occur as part of the decision-making process are a different matter and are, in my view, more properly considered in the context of separating the pre-decisional deliberations from the post-decision deliberations and the principle that government is accountable for what is has done, or has omitted to do, in implementing a particular policy but is not accountable for what was put to it or considered by it and rejected (*McKinnon and Secretary, Department of Prime Minister and Cabinet* [2007] AATA 1969, [174]).

It may be that the courts will continue to allow withholding of documentation involving commercial information received from non-government parties. Therefore the recent amendments enhance the focus of the FOI Act on subjecting the performance of government to scrutiny but they also retain considerable scope for the government to enter into and maintain contractual and other commercial operations largely exempt from such scrutiny.

Private information

In 1991, the objects clause in the FOI Act was amended to include 'creating a right to bring about the amendment of records containing personal information that is incomplete, incorrect, out of date or misleading' (s.3(1)(c) FOI Act). It was inserted on the recommendation of the Senate Standing Committee on Legal and

Constitutional Affairs 1987 report on the Freedom of Information Act (SSCLCA 1987, pp. 35–36). Its inclusion is a compromise to address the perceived divergence between the general objects of the FOI Act and the provisions of Part V of the Act, which provided for a general right to amend records relating to an individual's personal affairs. The Senate Standing Committee actually recommended that Part V be removed from the FOI Act and placed in legislation dealing directly with privacy concerns. The *Privacy Act 1988* (Cth) was enacted in the year following the Senate Standing Committee's report, regulating the collection, storage, security, access, correction, use and disclosure of personal information. It required government agencies take reasonable steps to ensure that personal information records are correct, relevant, up to date, complete and not misleading. Access and amendment of personal information remains a part of the FOI Act, however.[50]

Amendment of personal records in Part V was originally included in the FOI Act 1982 only after a Senate amendment was accepted (*Hansard* (Senate) 8 April 1981, p. 1239; 29 May 1981, p. 2364; see ALRC, ARC 1995, p. 56). The Senate Standing Committee 1979 report (SSCLCA 1979) had anticipated that access to personal records was likely to be a significant proportion of access requests. In the absence of any legislative protection of privacy the Committee recommended that there should also be an ability to correct personal records where they are inaccurate, out of date, contain irrelevant information or are otherwise misleading (SSCLCA 1979, pp. 264–265). Calls to repeal the provisions after the enactment of the *Privacy Act 1988* (Cth) have not been accepted. For example, the ALRC and ARC, in the 1995 'Open Government Report', initially proposed removing the correction provisions from the FOI Act (ALRC, ARC 1995, [5.17]). This would have the advantages of removing the overlap and possible inconsistency between the Privacy and FOI Acts and only having one process for amendment of personal records. However, it was concluded that these did not clearly outweigh the disadvantages of the complexity of dealing with 'mixed' requests for both personal and non-personal information, the replication of procedures and exemptions in the Privacy Act and diversion of the privacy commissioner's resources. Importantly, the ALRC and ARC report accepted that access and amendment of personal information 'are as much matters of government accountability and openness as privacy and should, therefore, remain within the FOI Act' (ALRC, ARC 1995, p. 56).

By providing access and amendment of personal records the FOI Act provides a mechanism to scrutinise not only the accuracy of those records, but also the process and systems developed to collect and use the information in question. It helps to ensure that the design of those systems accord with the intended public policy objectives, and that the benefits outweigh the impact on personal

---

50   Note, however, that the recent reforms included altering the objects clause to once again remove explicit reference to access and amendment of personal records: see s.3 FOI Act 1982 as amended Act no.139, 2010.

privacy concerns. It therefore potentially goes beyond the privacy requirements of making only authorised and consented use of personal information, as well as providing a means to scrutinise compliance with other administrative law and FOI Act requirements to disclose the basis on which decisions are made to the detriment of a person's interests, especially when those decisions are made on the basis of considerations personal to an individual. Access to personal records also ensures that record-keeping practices are subject to scrutiny of sort, allowing the FOI Act to augment good record-keeping requirements in other legislation and as implicitly encouraged through FOI access requirements.[51]

Under the FOI Act, a person can request either an amendment or an annotation of records they have lawfully obtained containing their personal information (s.48 FOI Act). The agency has discretion to amend or annotate the record; though to the extent practicable they should not obliterate the previous text of the record (s.50 FOI Act). If the agency declines to amend the record then they must annotate the record with any statement provided by the person who is the subject of the record (s.51A FOI Act). Refusals to amend or annotate, or delays in responding to requests, are generally reviewable by internal and merits review, and now through the Information Commissioner. The amendment provisions have caused some concerns over the ability of applicants to essentially rewrite findings of fact or conclusions as to matters that are subject to disputes in other forums or under other regulatory schemes (see generally Creyke and McMillan 2009, pp. 1200–1201).

The relationship between the FOI Act and privacy concerns are also reflected in the exemptions for disclosure of personal information. Apart from the protection of information disclosed in confidence discussed above, the FOI Act also exempts unreasonable disclosure of personal information about any person (s.47F FOI Act 1982 (as amended Act no.139, 2010), previously s.41).[52] Again, the reference to reasonableness has been held to incorporate a public interest test (for example, *Colakovski v AOTC* (1991) 100 ALR 111). The *Privacy Act 1988* also provides limitations on the release of personal information to another person, but this is not generally subject to public interest considerations. The recent reform of the FOI Act has made it clear that unreasonable disclosure of personal information involves consideration of the extent the information is publicly known, the person was known to be associated with matters dealt with in the document, and whether there are other public sources of the information. It is also now clear that documents containing personal information are to be released unless that would be contrary to the public interest, so that factors favouring release of

---

51 See further the discussion in Part IV below.
52 Note there is provision to release information provided by a qualified person (medical practitioner, psychologist, counsellor, etc.) to another qualified person if it appears to the agency or Minister that disclosure might otherwise be detrimental to the applicant's physical or mental health or well-being.

the documents are also to be considered as well as those favouring withholding access (s.47F, s.11A and s.11B). Like the commercial information exceptions listed above, the 'reverse FOI' provisions apply to provide a person whose personal information is contained in requested documents and who might reasonably wish to contend that the document is therefore exempt, an opportunity to make submissions or to seek review of any decision to grant access before access is in fact provided (s.27A FOI Act 1982 as amended).

Personal information can include the names and other information of public servants whose duties were associated with requested documents. It was acknowledged in the 'Open Government' review that '[t]he disclosure of personal information of public servants as it relates to the performance of their duties for the government does not unduly threaten personal privacy and reflects the democratic objectives of FOI' (ALRC, ARC 1995, p. 131, quoting the Privacy Commissioner *DP Submission 81*). This was, however, subject to situations where harassment or personal security could be threatened or where information related to investigations into conduct affecting fellow public servants. The public interest test has to incorporate these considerations so as to ensure that the traditional anonymity of public servants is removed in favour of subjecting the bureaucracy to scrutiny (ALRC, ARC 1995, p. 131).

Similarly, the identity of persons who have made allegations that another person is involved in some form of wrongdoing may be withheld on a number of grounds, such as law enforcement, adversely affecting the operations of agencies, or breach of confidence as well as personal information. Other administrative law obligations may require the identity or substantial content of the allegations to be disclosed[53] and the FOI Act doesn't prevent a breach of those obligations resulting in the invalidity of the administrative decision in question.

Conclusions

The FOI Act attempts to balance the interests of both government and non-government organisations, recognising that these are interrelated in the development and institution of policy. However, there has been a concern that the interests of non-government parties are unduly elevated, particularly in the application of exemptions to disclosure. There is too much discretion given to government agencies to either claim confidentiality or seek exemptions to preserve their own interests rather than those of the non-government organisation involved. Dealing with disclosure of non-government information involves balancing difficult and potentially incommensurate factors when identifying

---

53   For example, obligations of natural justice require disclosure of information which may be credible, relevant and significant to an adverse effect on a person's interests: see *VEAL v Minister for Immigration and Multicultural and Indigenous Affairs* (2005) 225 CLR 88.

where the public interest may lie. Separation of the elements of the public interest favouring disclosure from general concerns over the accountability of non-government organisations and their role in public activities remains difficult but crucial to the effective operation of the FOI Act.

Part IV: Developing a culture of disclosure

Two days before the release of the 1980 federal budget, Journalist Laurie Oakes disclosed details of a draft (see Blenkin 2011) of the budget speech on national television. The source of the 'leaked' draft has never been revealed. It proved highly embarrassing to the then Treasurer, John Howard, and led to the Prime Minister, Malcolm Fraser, declaring that at least his office 'was not going to play that game [of leaking to advance a person or policy], ever' (see Skeketee 2011). So-called 'authorised leaking', however, has become a matter of course, particularly in relation to budget material, with speculation about impending budget measures being selectively released on a confidential basis to journalists in the hope of gauging and affecting public reaction to the official policy. As Laurie Oaks himself, perhaps not surprisingly, suggested many years later, 'leaks, and whistleblowers, are essential to a proper democratic system' (Oakes 2005; see Brown 2007, pp. 19–28). As Sir Humphrey in *Yes Minister* suggests, '[t]he ship of state ... is the only ship that leaks from the top' (Wikipedia n.d.).

Leaking, or whistleblowing, to an external agency, and particularly to the media, is a relatively extreme demonstration of the independence of the public service or individual members of government.[54] The extent of that independence — to whom the duties of the public service are owed — lies at the heart of the role of FOI in enhancing government policy development. Peter Shergold, then Secretary to the Department of Prime Minister and Cabinet, expressed it in this way:

> Of course the Australian Public Service needs to be accountable for the way it plays its role. It is — more than ever before. The Westminster tradition has evolved considerably in the last thirty years: there is now much greater scrutiny of public service decision-making than in the past through Parliamentary committees, the Audit Office, and the Ombudsman; through legislation which, within limits set by Parliament, provides freedom of information to the public; and the opportunity, through an extended panoply of administrative law, for citizens to have decisions reviewed. There is now a network of integrity which did not exist 30 years ago.

---

54 For a discussion of whistleblowing in the Australian context see Brown 2008.

Yet confidentiality remains a fundamental requisite of democratic decision-making. A public service that cannot provide its frank advice in confidence will rapidly lose its ability to influence. No government will willingly involve officials in decision-making if they fear that the written advice, or an account of its oral discussion, will end up in the newspapers if the government's judgment is not accepted. Those who leak the deliberations of government (as opposed to those who whistleblow on corruption), undermine democratic process. They erode the trust between government and public administration that lies at the heart of good governance. They diminish the opportunity for public servants to inform and influence policy and, conversely, reduce the willingness of government to seek the broadest range of advice from across the administration. They undermine whole of government approaches. It is for that reason that I protect the confidentiality of ministerial decision-making just as zealously as journalists protect the confidentiality of their informants (Shergold 2006).

But there are concerns over the public service acting merely as agents for the government. In 2006, Andrew Podger, reflecting on his 37 years in the public service, including his roles as Secretary of the Department of Health and Ageing, and Public Service Commissioner, criticised what he termed the overly responsive nature of some elements of the public service. As he suggested then, greater emphasis should be given to the public services 'obligations of professionalism, impartiality, being apolitical and complying at all times with the law: the obligations that imply a degree of independence notwithstanding our need to be responsive' (see Grattan 2005).

Podger was particularly concerned at the public service's role in an incident in the lead up to the 2001 general election where it was alleged that children of asylum seekers were being deliberately thrown into the water to enhance their chances of being allowed to enter Australia. The subsequent 'Senate Select Committee for an Inquiry into a Certain Maritime Incident' reported that the minister involved, Peter Reith, made 'a number of misleading statements, implying that the published photographs and a video supported the original report that children had been thrown overboard well after he had received definitive advice to the contrary' (SSCICMI 2002, p. xxiv).

The Senate Select Committee summarised their conclusions by pointing to a number of factors that contributed to the false reports, including 'genuine miscommunication or misunderstanding, inattention … and deliberate deception motivated by political expedience' (SSCICMI 2002, p. xxii). But also important 'was avoidance of responsibility, a public service culture of responsiveness and perhaps over-responsiveness to the political needs of ministers' (SSCICMI 2002, p. xxii). This and other instances of over-responsiveness suggested that 'some senior public servants are too concerned to please and serve partisan government interests by failing to keep proper notes, destroying diaries and ratcheting up security classification of documents' (Public Service Informant, July 2005, as quoted by Timmins 2006).

The different views about the role of the public service reflect continuing appreciation of the importance of the relationships between government and the public in the development and implementation of public policy. So-called 'authorised leaking of proposals' to assist with formal delivery recognises that engaging with media, stakeholders and the broader community can play an important role in both policy development and delivery. A public service that acts to support the government of the day can play an important role in both reducing political risks but also, ultimately, enhancing the effectiveness of government by greater engagement with the public at large.

In the latest review of Commonwealth administration, 'Ahead of the Game: Blueprint for the reform of Australian government administration', the relationship between ministers and the public service is described as a 'partnership to develop policy and implement government programs and services' (Department of the Prime Minister and Cabinet n.d.). The report sets out a 'vision for the future' including:

> An APS that captures ideas and expertise through the transformative effect of technology by:
>
> • Citizens directly communicating their views and expertise to government through multiple channels, including Web 2.0 approaches (for example, online policy forums and blogs);
> • Greater disclosure of public sector data and mechanisms to access the data so that citizens can use the data to create helpful information for all, in line with privacy and secrecy principles; and
> • Citizens become active participants involved in government, rather than being passive recipients of services and policies (Department of the Prime Minister and Cabinet n.d., p. 38).

This recommendation was complemented by the release of a separate report from a taskforce established to examine the role of technology in facilitating interaction with government. In 'Engaged: Getting on with government 2.0', the taskforce suggested that new collaborative technologies associated with the internet promised 'new tools for public servants to engage and respond to the community' (Government 2.0 Taskforce 2009, p. x). Embracing these possibilities, however, required

> [l]eadership, and policy and governance changes ... to shift public sector culture and practice to make government information more accessible

and usable, make government more consultative, participatory and transparent, build a culture of online innovation within Government, and to promote collaboration across agencies (Government 2.0 Taskforce 2009, p. x).

It requires changing the approach to government information, from a resource for government to 'a national resource that should be managed for public purposes' (Government 2.0 Taskforce 2009, p. x).

Together, these recommendations have been supported by the government through a 'Declaration of Open Government' based on principles of informing, engaging with and participation of the public (Department of Finance and Deregulation 2008). Mirroring developments in the US (http://www.data.gov/) and the UK (http://data.gov.uk/), the government has established a website gateway to accessing government datasets (http://data.gov.au/), and released guides as to the ways in which information is released to encourage access and reuse by the public (Australian Government n.d.). The recommendations are also reflected in recent reform of the FOI Act that now includes among its objects to provide the community with access to information held by the Commonwealth government, an intention 'by these objects, to increase recognition that information held by the Government is to be managed for public purposes, and is a national resource' (s.3(3) FOI Act 1982).

As the other parts of this chapter have suggested, these sentiments are not new. The original principles of the FOI Bill 1978 reflected the same objectives to both provide a right of access but also to encourage the proactive disclosure of government information. But there has been a shift in the nature and function of that information. As the first annual report on the operation of the FOI Act 1982 suggests, the FOI Act 'requires information about the operations of Commonwealth agencies to be made publicly available, particularly rules and practices affecting members of the public in their dealings with those agencies' (Attorney-General's Department 1983). Proactive disclosure of information held and generated by government may extend beyond informing the individual about how decisions about their interests are going to be made to informing the public more broadly.

This section examines the obligations of proactive disclosure in the FOI Act 1982. It looks at the limited nature of that disclosure when compared to developments in administrative law more generally. It then considers the extent to which proactive disclosure has been affected by considerations of resource constraint, including the impact on document handling and retrieval and the ability to recoup costs of FOI obligations, as well as the role of the Ombudsman or other government agencies in encouraging a pro-disclosure culture. It then considers the recent introduction of the Office of the Information Commissioner and the important role it will play in both encouraging proactive disclosure and enhancing government information processes more generally.

Publication of certain documents and information

Part II of the FOI Act, headed 'Publication of certain documents and information', was described by the 1979 Senate Standing Committee as 'one of the least known and publicised parts of the [FOI Bill 1978], but in our view one of the most important' (SSCLCA 1979, p. 87). It provides for:

- the publication of an annual statement of the general organisation and functions of an agency, particularly decision-making powers affecting members of the public; how the public can participate in policy development or administration, what documents are already or customarily made available to the public, how physical access to documents can be obtained and the procedures and contacts for making an FOI application (s.8 FOI Act 1982);

- making available to the public documents which are used by the agency in making decisions that affect rights, privileges or benefits, obligations, penalties or other detriments; including rules, guidelines or practices relating to the administration or enforcement of legislative or executive schemes; and at least once a year compiling a list of such documents (s.9 FOI Act 1982); and states that

- a person can't be prejudiced where a rule, guideline or practice is not made available or listed; provided the person was not otherwise aware of the rule, guideline or practice that should have been available or listed, and they could have avoided being prejudicially affected if they had known about it (s.10 FOI Act 1982).

These sections were the subject of considerable scrutiny during the enactment of the FOI Act. Amendments to the original Bill went beyond the recommendations by the 1979 Senate Standing Committee in some respects, particularly the provision for a lack of prejudice if the required 'hidden law' of the agency was not made publicly available. However, the provisions have never perhaps taken on the importance envisaged by the Senate Standing Committee.

The ALRC and ARC 'Open Government Report' suggested that the main aim of the provisions was to provide the public with guidance about the information held by the government, primarily to assist the formulation of access requests. However, the information disclosed under the provisions 'was not easily accessible and is rarely used' (ALRC, ARC 1995, p. 81). The internet being very much in its infancy,[55] the report recommended access be expanded beyond the regional offices of the Australian Archives to Australian Government Publishing Service shops, public libraries and branches of the relevant agency. Availability of the information needed to be better publicised. Compliance with the provisions was patchy and there was a need to monitor and enforce compliance through establishment of an FOI Commissioner.

Subsequent reviews of the operation of the provisions have confirmed their limited effect. The report by the Australian National Audit Office (ANAO) on 'Administration of Freedom of Information Requests' (ANAO 2003) found that only half of the agencies required to provide details of documents used to make decisions that affect the public in 2002–03 had done so, and only 31 per cent of the lists of such documents was current. There were no processes to actively follow up on lapsed statements (ANAO 2003, p. 40). However, the ANAO recommended that the amendment of the provisions be considered to provide for disclosure through an agency's website. In the 2006 'Scrutinising Government' report, the Ombudsman reached a similar, if not quite as extensive, conclusion about lack of compliance with Part II requirements (Commonwealth Ombudsman 2006, p. 15).

There has also been almost no case law on the interpretation and operation of the provision (see, for example, *Duncan v Chief Executive Officer, Centrelink* [2008] FCA 56). The few places where access was available, the uncertain definition of the information to be published, and a focus on rules and practices that might have an effect on individual interests all limited awareness of the availability and usefulness of the FOI requirements. Importantly developments in other areas of administrative law, in particular natural justice requirements, generally placed more extensive obligations for disclosure of how decisions affecting individual interests would be made. For example, natural justice obligations do not generally depend upon showing how any prejudice arising from the non-publication of the information may have been avoided. There was also considerable disparity between agencies as to how willing they were to adapt to the publication and information facilities of the internet. Agencies involved with high volume decision-making on an individual level were responding to a number of factors other than FOI requirements to embrace the information provision facilities the internet provides, including the need to reduce costs, remove duplication of services, improve 'client' satisfaction and reduce complaints (ALRC, ARC 1995, [7.7]–[7.8]).

---

55 The 'Open Government Report' mentions the recent establishment of a server at the National Library that could be used to provide access to government files.

Recent amendments

The recent amendments to the FOI Act include extensive reform of Part II. The new Information Publication Scheme (IPS) is intended to transform the FOI framework 'from one that is reactive to individual requests for documents, to one that also relies more heavily on agency driven publication of information' (OAIC n.d.). The IPS requires agencies[56] to disclose a broader range of information and encourages further proactive, and more accessible, disclosure of government information. An agency must have a plan stating what information it will proactively disclose, and how and to whom it will disclose it. Agencies continue to have an obligation to disclose their structural and organisational details, including decision-making powers affecting members of the public, how the public can comment on policy proposals, and other relevant contact information. Information in documents to which the agency routinely gives access in response to FOI requests or in response to requests from Parliament are also required to be disclosed in the IPS, although not if it is subject to exceptions (s.8C FOI Act) including personal and business information personal to those making an FOI request (see s.8(2)(g)(i), (ii) FOI Act). Information about how decisions affecting individuals are made is now included in a broader 'operational information' category, including all information which assists the agency perform its functions affecting members of the public.[57] Each agency IPS entry is required to be 'accurate, up-to-date and complete' (s.8B FOI Act).

Agencies are also required to consider the objects of the FOI Act and guidelines issued by the Information Commissioner when complying with IPS requirements (s.9A FOI Act). The Information Commissioner reviews the operation of the IPS, including investigating compliance, either after receiving a complaint or on its own motion (s.8F FOI Act). Results of that review will be provided in the Information Commissioner's annual reports. There are no direct enforcement measures provided, however, with the commissioner having limited compulsory powers in relation to the conduct of the investigation (see sections 79ff). Similar to prior to the amendments, a failure to list 'operational information' on the IPS can't prejudice an individual whose interests are affected by a decision assisted by that information, but only where the prejudicial affect could have been avoided if the information was known (s.10 FOI Act).

---

56   Note the IPS does not apply to ministers and their offices.

57   Section 8A(1) FOI Act includes '[t]he agency's rules, guidelines, practices and precedents relating to … decisions and recommendations'. The Office of the Australian Information Commissioner Guidelines state that operational information does not encompass information including policy analysis; hypothetical discussion; case study and culpability reports; audit and evaluation reports on the operation of a government program; and case management recording procedures (see OAIC n.d., [13.97]). However, such information may be published proactively or when subject to a FOI request.

Agencies are also able to publish other information as part of the IPS (s.8(4) FOI Act) and are of course not precluded by the FOI Act from publishing information generally, including information that could be withheld as exempted from disclosure if the subject of an FOI request (s.3A FOI Act).[58] The Office of the Australian Information Commissioner (OAIC) guidelines point out that agencies are required to explain in their agency plan 'the steps they will take to review their information holdings and identify information that may be suitable for publication' (OAIC n.d., [913.107]). They suggest that agencies should have regard to the interests of clients and stakeholders, general community interest, public demand, assistance in dealing with the agency, promotion of agency accountability or public understanding, whether the information is in an appropriate format to be accessible and reusable,[59] whether it needs revising or updating and whether there are privacy or security concerns (OAIC n.d., [13.109]). The discretion as to what additional information to release and where to release it remains with the agency however.

Disclosure logs

The recent amendments to the FOI Act also require both agencies and ministers to publicly release information in a disclosure log that has been released in response to an FOI request. Prior to this amendment, the FOI Act did not make explicit provision for the general release of information. Such forms of disclosure have, however, always been available. The exemptions to disclosure in the FOI Act provide a basis to withhold publication, but don't generally prevent disclosure where not otherwise prevented by other legislation or obligations of confidentiality. Release of documents in response to an FOI request has been, in effect, to the world at large, although in practice it was often up to the recipient of the information to release the information more broadly. The new disclosure log requirements formalise this aspect and provide for increased access to the information that has become publicly available.

Agencies and ministers must now publish, on their websites, lists of information released in response to an FOI request for documents held by the agency or Minister and either provide access, direct links or other details on how the information may be obtained (s.11C FOI Act). The information must be published within 10 working days of the grant of access to the FOI applicant.[60] There have been concerns raised by media organisations that this reduces their incentive

---

58   Note the discussion relating to general secrecy provisions under other legislation and the Public Service Act in Part 1 above.

59   Further reference is given to the publication on www.data.gov.au and the checklist available at www.finance.gov.au/e-government/better-practice-and-collaboration/better-practice-checklists/index.html.

60   There are no specific requirements as to how long the information must remain accessible, but archiving the information or making it available on request would meet the requirements under the FOI Act for access. See (OAIC n.d., [14.42]).

to make requests and pay the resultant fees if the information is going to be released publicly (see, for example, Australia's Right to Know Coalition 2011; Sear 2011). The Information Commissioner has recommended that maintaining trust and cooperation between agencies and FOI applicants, both in respect of particular agencies and the climate of efficient processing of FOI in the future, be considered in deciding how soon to publish released information on disclosure logs. Fees or charges might be waived, particularly where the information is released and published at the same time. The format to be adopted by the disclosure logs are not set out in the legislation, but OAIC guidelines refer to various government policies and standards to help ensure the documents are easy to locate and access (OAIC n.d., [14.50]), including by all members of the public (see the discussion in the guidelines about accessibility standards, OAIC n.d., [14.59]–[14.61]).

Personal, business, commercial, financial, professional affairs or other information of a kind determined by the Information Commissioner can be withheld from inclusion on the disclosure log where that would be 'unreasonable'. Generally this means that the disclosure logs won't include information about persons or businesses that also made the request. Releasing documents including the name of the agency official mentioned in connection with their duties would not be unreasonable. Note that these provisions mean that the decision to list a document on the disclosure log is separate and generally distinct from the decision to release the document. Procedures for informing a person or organisation whose information is included in released information do not apply to listing on disclosure logs, through the OAIC guidelines recommend including information about potential inclusion on disclosure logs in any 'reverse FOI' procedure (OAIC n.d., [14.19]).

Role of the Information Commissioner

The 1979 Senate Standing Committee review of the FOI Bill 1978, after summarising its recommended changes to the Bill, pointed out that '[l]egislation of course is one thing; its effective operation can be entirely another' (SSCLCA 1979, p. 30). While the committee expressed its hope that agencies would cooperate in the spirit of the legislation, it was 'essential that the operation of freedom of information legislation be kept under constant review' (SSCLCA 1979, p. 30). There was a need not only in monitoring and review of the operation of the Act and the balance of competing interests it represented, but also in mediating between agencies, individuals and the broader public interest. A body was needed to act as conciliator in disputes between agencies or ministers and individuals, counsel or assist individuals before the AAT in appropriate cases, and, going beyond enforcement of rights and obligations under the Act, to also provide advice and criticism to other departments.

The Senate Standing Committee recommended that these functions be split. A department directly headed by a Minister directly responsible, and answerable on a regular basis, to Parliament would have 'administrative responsibility for monitoring compliance with [FOI requirements] and of systematically reporting as to the extent to which agencies had fulfilled their obligations' (SSCLCA 1979, p. 305). The Attorney-General's Department was selected for this purpose. The close comparability of the other required functions with the 'general administrative role performed by the Ombudsman', and the resource benefits of not having to establish a separate bureaucracy meant that the Ombudsman's Office was preferred to the establishment of an at least formally separate Information Commissioner (SSCLCA 1979, p. 306). The Senate Committee felt that the powers of the Ombudsman's Office would need to be expanded to ensure that it could adequately fulfil these additional functions under the FOI Act.[61]

Much of this role of the Ombudsman, along with the role of monitor and rapporteur, was realised by enactment of the FOI Act and its 1983 amendments. However, resource constraints in the mid-1980s led to the general monitoring and reporting roles being shifted to the Attorney-General's Department (*Freedom of Information Amendment Act 1991* (Cth), based on the recommendations of the Parliament of Australia; SSCLCA 1987).[62] The Ombudsman's Office was therefore left with its general powers under the *Ombudsman Act 1976* (Cth) to investigate administrative actions of government agencies, including FOI matters, either upon compliant or on its own motion. Decisions of ministers and relating to public sector employment remained outside its jurisdiction. The FOI Act provided for some additional powers and limits in relation to matters appealed to the AAT or correction of records (see ss.56–57 FOI Act prior to 1 November 2011). Thus the Ombudsman was able to 'investigate complaints about agency decisions to deny or grant limited access to documents, the amount of fees and other charges ... delays in responding to requests or other administrative processes, and the adequacy and clarity of reasons for decisions' (Commonwealth Ombudsman 2006, pp. 3–4). This role reflected the more general role of the Ombudsman in 'ensuring agencies implement sound document management procedures, provide clear and accessible information, and are open and responsive to complaints about issues to do with access to information' (Commonwealth Ombudsman 2006, p. 4).

Despite these synergies between the Ombudsman's broader role and its role under the FOI Act, concerns remained (Commonwealth Ombudsman 2006, p. 5). The ALRC and ARC 'Open Government Report' considered that 'many of the

---

61   For example, to allow it to review decisions by Ministers under the FOI Act and to investigate complaints while an appeal to the AAT was pending, as well as having a role in AAT proceedings.

62   Responsibility for administration of the FOI Act, and the general monitoring and reporting requirements, has at times resided with the Department of Prime Minister and Cabinet, but is now back with the Attorney-General's department.

shortcomings of the [then] current operation and effectiveness of the Act can be attributed to this lack of a constant, independent monitor of and advocate for FOI' (ALRC, ARC 1995, pp. 61–62). They considered the most effective means of improving administration of the FOI Act would be the appointment of an FOI Commissioner. The commissioner would, on the basis of regular audits, monitor compliance with and administration of the act; promote the act; provide advice, assistance and facilitation to agencies and the public; provide legislative policy advice; and participate in broader information policy (ALRC, ARC 1995, pp. 63–69).

Importantly, however, the report recommended that the commissioner not be given investigatory powers to form a view as to the correctness of specific actions or decisions under the act, and no determinative powers to review an agencies FOI decision (ALRC, ARC 1995, pp. 69–70). The AAT would remain the sole reviewer of FOI decisions. The report considered that providing the commissioner with determinative powers would be incompatible with its role in developing guidelines, providing advice to agencies and, particularly, facilitating requests for disclosure. Conflicts of interest or erosion of the perception of independence could arise. Merits review was available by going to the AAT, and any criticisms of the practices of the AAT could be rectified without having to provide for another form of merits review (ALRC, ARC 1995, p. 70).

Additional reviews of the FOI Act by the Commonwealth Ombudsman in 1999 (Commonwealth Ombudsman 1999) and the Senate Legal and Constitutional Legislation Committee 2001 (SLCLC 2001) also encouraged the establishment of an FOI Commissioner, either as an independent body or, given resourcing constraints, as a specialised unit within the Ombudsman's Office. The 2004 review by the ANAO emphasised the lack of any government agency with responsibility to ensure general compliance with the FOI Act or to identify improvements both to the operation of the act or information collected (ANAO 2003, [2.30]). The ANAO recommended the Attorney-General's Department take a more active role in monitoring agency compliance (ANAO 2003, [2.29]). The most recent review of the Commonwealth Ombudsman in 2006 reiterated the need to establish a statutory FOI commissioner 'who would play an active role in publicising the legislation's existence, monitor compliance with its provisions and promote its effective operation' (Commonwealth Ombudsman 2006, p. 33).

Election commitments by the Labor party to reform FOI legislation in the lead up to the 2007 election included the establishment of an Office of the Information Commissioner and establishment of various statutory office holders to act along with the Privacy Commissioner to provide a 'clearing house for complaints, oversight, advice and reporting of freedom of information and privacy matters'

(Rudd and Ludwig 2007, p. 6). These reforms were instituted by the *Freedom of Information Amendment (Reform) Act 2010* (Cth) and the *Australian Information Commissioner Act 2010* (Cth).

Delays

The most common complaint to the Ombudsman about the operation of the FOI Act related to delays in the processing of FOI requests (Commonwealth Ombudsman 2006). In general, an agency has 30 days to respond to an FOI request. If the request concerns a state government or another business or person requiring a 'reverse FOI' consultation the time limit can be extended to up to 60 days. The time limit can be extended for the time waiting for the applicant to respond to a notification about likely charges involved with the processing of their request. The Ombudsman's own motion investigations into administration of the FOI Act in 1999 and 2006 both concluded that there was, in general, excessive delays in responding to FOI requests, though these varied considerably between agencies. Alarmingly, the Ombudsman suggested that this was not just the result of the nature of the FOI requests or the allocation and efficient use of resources within the agency. As the 1999 'Needs to Know' report suggested,

> the investigation also identified a more pervasive malaise in the administration of FOI: a growing culture of indifference or resentment towards the disclosure of information, ailing standards of training and development and a profound lack of understanding of or commitment to the ethos and purpose of the legislation. It appeared that, although the FOI Act had wrought some change in the culture of public administration, its goals had been imperfectly achieved. Many of the early FOI practitioners were advocates of open government, but had, over time, been replaced by staff who had grown up in a very different environment, with FOI just one of a number of competing demands on agency time and resources (Commonwealth Ombudsman 1999).

In the 2006 'Scrutinising Government' report, the situation had perhaps improved, but the complaints received by the Ombudsman, albeit a relatively small proportion of the total number of FOI requests (Commonwealth Ombudsman 2006, p. 9),[63] still indicated that agencies were failing to allocate adequate resources, had developed a culture of 'compliant but protracted processing of FOI requests' (Commonwealth Ombudsman 2006, p. 15), and that 'good FOI administration is of dwindling importance, in some agencies at least' (Commonwealth Ombudsman

---

63   For example, in 2004 there were 275 complaints arising out of over 39,265 FOI requests.

2006, p. 28). 'Moreover, there are proportionally more "other-than-personal" FOI requests taking more than 60 days to process than is the case for personal FOI requests' (Commonwealth Ombudsman 2006, p. 18).[64]

The recent amendments to the FOI Act provide for complaints to be investigated by the new Information Commissioner, or the Ombudsman where that is considered appropriate (where the complaint is part of a wider grievance about the agency, for example). The commissioner has powers similar to the ombudsman to make inquiries, obtain information from any person or inspect relevant documents, including exempt documents (see ss.79–82 FOI Act as amended). There is no formal power to compel agencies to resolve the complaint, however the commissioner can require the agency to provide particulars of any action it will take in response to the investigation (s.89 FOI Act as amended) and can then report to the relevant minister's and have the report tabled in Parliament. Like the Ombudsman, the Information Commissioner is only able to investigate complaints against agencies and not ministers (OAIC n.d.), [11.6]).

Reviews

The recent reforms go beyond the many recommendations for the creation of an Information Commissioner by giving that office the function of reviewing FOI decisions along with the other functions envisaged by the various recommendations. Applicants unhappy with the response to their request for access to documents can seek review by the Information Commissioner. It is intended that this will provide 'a simple, expedient and cost efficient system for external merits review', based mainly on the submissions and papers provided by the parties, rather than through formal hearings (Explanatory Memorandum, Freedom of Information Amendment (Reform) Bill 2010, p. 32). The commissioner can affirm, vary or set aside the original decision relating to access and substitute a new decision (s.55K FOI Act). Applicants who disagree with the Information Commissioner's decision can apply to the AAT for review (s.57A FOI Act). The commissioner can also refuse to review a matter and refer the review to the AAT where, for example, the commissioner has played a role in the dispute or it would more effectively resolve the dispute to do so (s.54W FOI Act). Importantly, in any review by the commissioner, the agency or Minister who made the initial decision relating to access to a document has to justify the position they took; there is no onus on the applicant to establish that the document should be released or the conditions of that release (s.55D FOI Act as amended). The commissioner is given various powers in relation to gaining access to documents and agencies have an obligation to assist the commissioner in carrying out the review (see generally Part VII FOI Act as amended).

---

64   In 2003–04, the respective proportions were in the order of 17 per cent and 12 per cent respectively.

There is no cost to the applicant for review by the commissioner,[65] and the intended informality of proceedings may also help to keep costs low, but there will remain considerable time and resource costs involved. It is unclear whether interposing a hopefully more cost efficient review by the commissioner before an appeal to the AAT will reduce the total costs of reviews. The concerns of the ALRC and ARC about the conferral of a review function on the commissioner remain: potential confusion about sources of review; potential delays before a final decision can be obtained given right of the agency or minister to appeal to the AAT; and potential conflict between the objectives of facilitating reform within agencies and acting as arbiter of disputes between agencies and individuals disgruntled with agency decisions. The role of the commissioner in working with agencies in relation to record-keeping, developing processes and policies in relation to proactive release of documents, and dealing with complaints through a process of investigation and reconciliation all require a considerable degree of goodwill between agencies and the commission. It will be a difficult balance to maintain that goodwill, particularly given the resistance of some agencies and the considerable resource costs they may be faced with, while also sitting in judgement of the response of agencies to access requests.

As John McMillan, now the Information Commissioner, commented on the 20-year anniversary of the enactment of the FOI Act, '[t]he cost to government of administering FOI requests poses an unresolvable dilemma' (McMillan 2002, p. 23). Responding to access requests imposes administrative burdens that divert resources from other activities. 'On the other hand, the success or failure of an FOI scheme can hinge on the issue of costs … A high-costs regime can be used by government to deter requests and to corrode the spirit of an FOI Act' (McMillan 2002, p. 23).

In the first annual report on the operation of the FOI Act, it was stated:

> It is not intended that the costs incurred under the Act should be offset by any revenue generating mechanism to recover costs. The Act does not seek, by means of the scheme of charges for access, to recover the full costs of meeting [FOI] requests. Most significantly, the Act provides that charges cannot be made for time spent in examining a document with a view to deciding whether the document contains exempt matter (Attorney-General's Department 1983, p. 143).

This view reflected the concern of the Senate Standing Committee's 1979 report that charges for decision-making time might be applied inconsistently or depend on the commitment to openness: 'It hardly seems fair or just, in a Bill designed to confer rights of access, that an agency's charges are inversely related to its commitment to the philosophy underlying the Bill' (SSCLCA 1987, [11.22]).

---

65   Appeals to the AAT will involve an application fee of $777 as at 1 March 2011.

Within three years (see *Freedom of Information Law Amendment Act 1986* (Cth)), however, there was an application fee of $30 and internal review charges, increases in the hourly charges for search and retrieval and, perhaps most significantly, a 'decision-making fee' of $20 per hour for time spent by public servants in deciding whether to release information (Ardagh 1987, p. 22). There were exemptions for persons seeking personal income maintenance information — for example, information about pensions, government allowances, etc. — and the ability to waive most fees requiring the agency or Minister to take into account 'whether the giving of access is in the general public interest or a substantial section of the public'.[66] The introduction of these charges were widely criticised: they went against the stated intention of the government not to introduce such charges; they would be a deterrent against lodging applications, particularly by those seeking policy information in the broader public interest; and they encouraged inefficient document handling and decision-making processes under the act (see, for example, Ardagh 1987, p. 23). It has been observed that the 1986 charges marked a turning point in the operation of the FOI Act, encouraging usage of the act to be dominated by access to personal records (McMillan 2002, pp. 23–24).

Even after the increase, the charges paid under the act were far exceeded by the estimated costs of complying with the FOI Act. For example, in 2009–10, $211.612 was collected in fees for initial and internal review applications, amounting to 41 per cent of total FOI revenue. Agencies notified a total of $3,177,732 in charges to applications, but through the exercise of their discretion to reduce or waive fees collected only $305,178, or 10 per cent, of those charges. The total amount of fees and charges, however, only represented 1.9 per cent of the total costs reported in the annual report for the operation of the FOI Act (O'Connor, B., Minister for Privacy and Freedom of Information 2010). Over the 30 years of the FOI, reported fees and charges represent only 2.08 per cent of the estimated total costs of administering the FOI Act (OAIC 2012, p. 5).

---

66 Section 30A FOI Act allowed the agency or Minister to remit the fee for any reason, including that payment of the fee would cause financial hardship or giving of access in the general public interest or in the interest of a substantial section of the public. This section was abolished in the recent amendments and replaced by s.29(5) which makes it clear that in deciding whether to reduce or not impose the charge the Minister must take into account the same two factors. The Information Commissioner is also now able to review decisions relating to reducing the charges imposed.

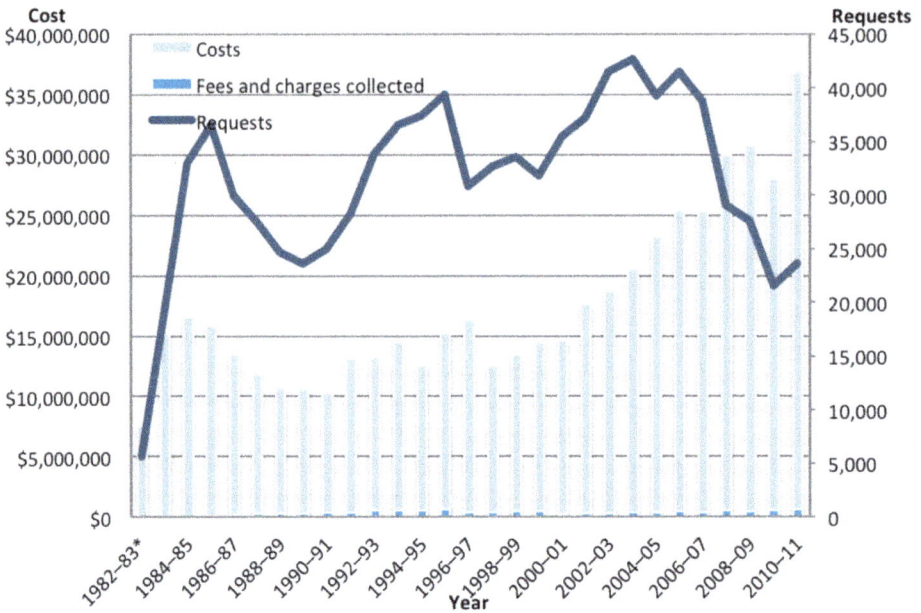

Figure 1: Costs and charges in relation to FOI requests

Source: OAIC 2012, p. 20.[67]

The costs of administering the FOI Act are generally based on the percentages of staff time reportedly allocated to complying with the requirements under the Act. There is considerable variation in the costs per request between agencies[68] and, as Figure 1 suggests, an increase in the raw figures over time despite a general decrease in requests in recent years. The high number of requests for personal information received by some agencies, the resources otherwise available to some agencies, and the level of interest in particular developments in any year all play a role. As the 1987 Senate Committee report suggested:

> The introduction of the FOI Act formed part of a trend towards increasing openness in government. In turn, the Act has had an impact upon that trend. Some of the material released under the FOI Act would have been released even in the absence of the legislation. The Committee has no method of determining what proportion of FOI access requests are

---

67   Note that there was a change 'from using the average of the salary levels of the three agencies recording the highest total FOI costs in pre-2006–07 FOI annual reports to using Australian public service base salary median figures, and the inclusion of Senior Executive Service salary costs since 2006–07, means that tables, charts and appendices in FOI annual reports that contain pre-2006–07 salary cost components are not strictly comparable with their post-2005–06 equivalents' (Annual Report p. 21).

68   For example, in 2009–10 there were 11 agencies with an average cost per request received greater than $10,000.

for such material. But the proportion, at least in the area of applicants seeking access to personal or personnel files, would appear to be high (SSCLCA 1987, p. 15).

The report points out that calculating total and average costs of compliance with the FOI Act depends on many agency-specific factors, including the approach taken to providing access outside of the FOI Act, allocation of resources to complying with the FOI Act rather than general document and information handling procedures, and approaches to initial and internal decision-making (SSCLCA 1987, p. 15). Some material released, such as the disclosure of internal manuals, may also have benefits to the agency beyond compliance with the FOI Act. The committee noted, however, that the costs of the FOI Act extended beyond that reported by agencies, to include costs to information providers, costs of the tribunal and court systems to resolve FOI disputes, opportunity costs of the resources allocated to FOI matters, and possible costs of 'threatened or actual reduction in information flow to [the Commonwealth]' due to the possible disincentives created through the FOI Act (SSCLCA 1987, p. 28). Though the published information about costs must be 'treated with some caution', the committee was prepared to assume that the omissions and deficiencies could 'cancel each other out' (SSCLCA 1987, p. 33).

Against those costs the committee attempted to compare the (admittedly unquantifiable) benefits of the legislation. They described how some agencies had reported greater awareness of the need for objectivity in dealing with the public, improved quality of decision-making, improved communications with and understanding of clients, improved efficiency of records management and greater public awareness of the role of the agency (SSCLCA 1987, p. 19). Disclosure under the FOI Act could lead to changing what would otherwise have been a 'poor decision', benefits to news reporting, assistance in claiming personal, business or professional benefits provided by the government, and increased certainty over how access was provided all potentially involved considerable benefits to the recipients of the information and the public at large. The committee concluded that the benefits of FOI were considerable, but that attention had to continue to be paid to the costs of the operation and administration of the FOI Act (SSCLCA 1987, p. 33).

The 2010 amendments to the FOI Act altered the fee structure again. All application fees, including fees for internal review, have been abolished. There are no costs to access your personal information. In line with a greater emphasis on reducing delays in the processing of requests, all charges will be waived if a statutory timeframe is not met (*Freedom of Information Amendment (Reform) Act 2010* (Cth)). The introduction of the IPS and disclosure logs are also intended to reduce the number and nature of individual requests (OAIC n.d., [13.65] and [14.4]). Finally, the role of the Information Commissioner in developing government information policy, including the role of government information as a national resource, will include information handling and processing reforms.

The fee structure was subject to review a little over a year after its amendment, with the OAIC recommending significant changes to the charges framework (OAIC 2012). The review is based on the role of government in meeting a substantial part of the costs of what it terms a democratic right, but seeks to use charges as an incentive to moderate unmanageable requests and simplify access processes even further. The review makes 10 recommendations, including various ways to simplify the types and calculation of charges and circumstances for waiver of charges, but there are perhaps two main aspects to the suggested changes.

The first suggested change comes from recognition that there are many, largely informal, ways in which information is provided on request. Agencies would be encouraged to more clearly identify these administrative access schemes on the agency's website where information that is open to release under the FOI Act could be obtained largely free of charge. Anyone not satisfied with the response to a request under the administrative access scheme could then make a formal request under the FOI Act. Bypassing the administrative access scheme by making a request under the FOI Act for information that could have been obtained under the access scheme will lead to an application fee being imposed (OAIC 2012, pp. 59–60).

The second suggested change stems from a concern that some agencies face a substantial administrative burden in handling large and complex requests, particularly where access under the FOI Act is being used as a substitute for other forms of access (such as the discovery process in litigation, see OAIC 2012, pp. 69–70). Under the FOI Act, agencies can refuse a request if satisfied that it would 'substantially and unreasonably divert the resources of the agency from its other operations' (ss.24 and 24AA FOI Act).[69] Before refusing the request, the agency has to consult with the applicant about possibly revising the request (s.24B FOI Act). It has been emphasised that this discretion to refuse access on the basis of resource costs can only be used in strict circumstances, and not merely because of the costs of inefficient record-keeping or the number of documents potentially in issue (OAIC n.d., 'FOI Guidelines', [3.47]). However, agencies have regarded the discretion as imprecise or indeterminate and have preferred to rely on the setting of high fees to encourage further discussion about the scope of requests (OAIC 2012, p. 69). The review therefore suggests

---

69 Note that agencies can treat multiple requests for the same documents or relating to the same subject matter as a single request (s.24(2) FOI Act).

that greater certainty be introduced through the imposition of a cap of 40 hours on the processing time for a request before it can be refused (OAIC 2012, pp. 68–70).

Conclusions

As John McMillan has suggested, 'the fee scale alone will not hold the balance between the democratic potential of FOI and the cost to government' (McMillan 2002, p. 24): much depends on the attitude of the agency to the request. Any objective to promote disclosure of information at the lowest reasonable cost

> can only be realised fully if in the administration of the Act there is a recognition (and quantification, roughly speaking) of all the intangibles that bear upon the true 'cost' of an FOI request: the democratic principles that underpin the FOI Act, the public interest purpose (if any) to which the requested information may be put, the reasonableness (or otherwise) of the agency and an applicant consulting about or shaping the request, and whether the resource burden of a particular request is attributable more to the unsatisfactory nature of file management or FOI processing in an agency than to the nature of the request (McMillan 2002, p. 25).

The recent amendments reflect this concern with information management. The expanded role of proactive disclosure under the IPS, and assisting access through disclosure logs both are instances of the increased emphasis on information management. As the amended objects clause now states, information held by the government is to be managed for public purposes, and is a national resource (s.3(3) FOI Act). The emphasis on ready release of information is further emphasised in the review of FOI charges suggestions to further encourage informal access regimes and place caps on processing time.

In many ways this emphasis on information management may facilitate the change of culture that is seen as essential to fulfilling the objectives of the FOI Act. Reducing the costs associated with fulfilling FOI requests while enhancing the means by which an agency can communicate with the public provides an added incentive to facilitate access generally. However, the emphasis on information management may serve to only highlight the distinctive treatment of personal or non-sensitive requests and those that have the potential to be embarrassing to the government.

Conclusion: The impact of FOI?

In May 1980, federal Cabinet met to decide on the government's response to the Senate Standing Committee's report on the Freedom of Information Bill. It was a meeting which would shape FOI laws in Australia for the next three decades. Before Cabinet was a submission reporting on the views of the most influential government departments. They all opposed extending disclosure beyond the limited amount already provided for by the FOI Bill 1978.[70]

The Finance Department, led by Ian Castles, was concerned about the significant cost implications of the Bill, and was opposed 'as a matter of principle, to the proposal to appoint a "Referee"' (the AAT). Treasury, through its Secretary John Stone, warned that 'Ministers should be left in no doubt whatsoever as to the cost and resource implications'. With Finance, they suggested that 'the final decision on whether to release confidential commercial information should rest with the suppliers', who would 'be the best judge of whether its release would be harmful to [their] own commercial interests'. For the Department of Prime Minister and Cabinet, the Bill as it stood already represented 'a major innovation, with significant though unquantifiable costs and major administrative difficulties'. Appointing an external referee to review claims to exemption would 'add an unnecessary new layer of review to the existing mechanisms' and any appeal should rest with the Minister. The chairman of the Public Service Board commented that 'Ministers might find this a suitable occasion to review the whole subject'.

They were right, and wrong, about the implications of the FOI Act. Costs and resource implications would indeed continue to influence the operation of the FOI Act. Commercial concerns under the act would continue and incorporate those of the private individual. However their concern that an external referee would threaten the role of government departments in our system of ministerial responsibility is less apparent. As the 1987 Senate Standing Committee report would suggest, any concern about loss of candour or the quality of advice had diminished with the realisation that, 'as a result of the way courts and the tribunal have interpreted the FOI Act, public servants have become increasingly confident that the Act provides sufficient protection' (SSCLCA 1987, [2.71]).

The FOI Act has generally been credited with significantly enhancing the openness and transparency of government.

---

70 See Cabinet Submission No. 3938: Freedom of Information Bill 1978 — report of Senate Standing Committee on Constitutional and Legal Affairs — Related to Decision No. 11134, 11653, 12437, 11185(Ad Hoc), 11610(Ad Hoc), 11623, 11632(Ad Hoc) part of series A12909, 1980, pp. 77–80. Available at http://recordsearch.naa.gov.au/scripts/Imagine.asp?B=30484359.

There can be no doubt that Australian government today is considerably more open than it was when FOI laws were first considered during the later part of the 1970s. Freedom of information has both been part of, and underpinned, broader changes. These have included changes in doctrines of public law that have brought it more into line with the traditional openness of courts, changes in the framework and practices of government, and more complex philosophies of government. The fact that freedom of information makes disclosure possible and that disclosure may be politically embarrassing means that governments now need to think more carefully about the consequences of their actions. At the same time, it has increased community awareness about government actions and made the community more demanding of explanations about situations touching on probity and propriety in government (Paterson 2005).

The ALRC and ARC 'Open Government Report' states that the enactment of the FOI Act in 1982 brought about a 'fundamental change in the law in Australia relating to access to government-held information and challenged the boundaries of government secrecy' (ALRC, ARC 1995, p. 11). The FOI Act

> has had a marked impact on the way agencies make decision and the way they record information. Along with other elements of the administrative law package, the FOI Act has focused decision-makers' minds on the need to base information on relevant factors and to record the decision making process. The knowledge that decisions and processes are open to scrutiny, including under the FOI Act, imposes a constant discipline on the public sector (ALRC, ARC 1995, pp. 15–16).

But the report then suggests that the 'assessment is not entirely positive … There is a perception … that the Act is not achieving its objectives' (ALRC, ARC 1995, pp. 15–16). Subsequent reviews have confirmed the impression that the FOI may work well in facilitating access to personal information, but not so well in providing access to policy-related information (Commonwealth Ombudsman 2006, p. 1).

The Commonwealth government is clearly much more open than at the time FOI legislation was being considered. The role of the FOI Act, however, remains difficult to isolate. The trend towards openness was already evident as the FOI Act was being introduced — indeed it was an important part of the acceptance of the obligations the FOI Act imposed. Courts had already cast doubt on any presumption of the government-determined need for secrecy, and other administrative law amendments, both in legislation and by the courts, soon had a profound influence on decisions affecting individual interests. Recognition of the constitutional protection of representative government followed, although it never reached the point of securing any right to government disclosure in the absence of statutory provision.

However, the application and interpretation of the FOI Act arguably did not follow that judicial trend. Emphasis on the need for balance reflected in the structure and drafting of the FOI Act conferred extensive discretion on agencies and ministers to withhold information from disclosure. Concerns over the impact of disclosure on the internal deliberations of government extended exceptions and justified certificates preventing disclosure. The uncertain and intangible public interest in disclosure was subjected to the concerns of those charged with administering the Act.

Government has continued to evolve. Emphasis on the commercial concerns both of and in relationship with government was reflected in the FOI Act's protection of those interests. The inherent tension between privacy interests and open disclosure was increasingly tightened one way through the introduction of legislative protection and a statutory agency devoted to monitoring, enforcement and encouragement of privacy interests.

An officer to champion greater openness in government has come only with the most recent reforms to the FOI Act. Up until now, access to government information has largely come at the initiative of the individual, primarily through seeking information personal to them or the organisations they represent. Proactive disclosure has been limited along with systematic attempts to improve the document and information handling of government. Delays in responding to requests and providing information, attitudes to the application of exemptions, and the imposition of, albeit largely potential, charges and fees have all contributed to discourage the pursuit of information in the public interest. It remains to be seen whether the current emphasis on proactive disclosure and efficient access will bring with it a heightened willingness to disclose sensitive or embarrassing material.

The theme common to much of the discussion in this chapter has been the effect of the FOI Act on the relationship between government, the public service, and the public. The impact of government disclosure laws depend on the political and constitutional climate in which they operate. At the Commonwealth level, concerns over the impact of FOI legislation on our system of responsible government have continued to be raised by those subjected to FOI obligations. Subjecting agencies to individual scrutiny distinguishes their role in policy development and implementation, multiplying avenues and opportunities for allocating responsibility. Perhaps, in the process, this increased separation between agencies and their ministers serves to reduce the influence of those agencies and the public service in general, affecting their role in the policy making process and the effectiveness in turn of the FOI Act in holding that process to account. The potential operation of the FOI Act has therefore been resisted as agencies side with ministers in the competition with the public over access to the inner workings of government. Information, instead of being a resource available to all in an effort to generate and improve policy, remains used as currency to gain or maintain political favour.

The recent amendments to the FOI Act in many ways reflect recommendations made before the FOI Act was first enacted. They reflect the view that greater disclosure of government information has the potential to enhance the discussion among all participants in the policy-making process, which in turn places responsibility on all of those participants to make use of that information appropriately. It remains to be seen whether the amendments go far enough for the FOI Act to realise this potential.

References

Ackerman, J. and I. Sanoval-Ballesteros 2006, 'The Global Explosion of Freedom of Information Laws', *AdministrativeLaw Review* 58.

Administrative Review Council 1998, 'The Contracting Out of Government Services', Report No. 42. Available at: http://www.arc.ag.gov.au/Publications/ Reports/Pages/Reportfiles/ReportNo42.aspx.

The Age 2010, 'Transcript of Julia Gillard's Announcement', 7 September 2010. Available at: http://m.theage.com.au/federal-election/transcript-of-julia-gillards-announcement-20100907-14zhs.html.

Ardagh, A. 1987, 'The Walls of Secrecy are Going Up Again', *Legal Service Bulletin* 12. ,

Aronson, M. 2005, 'Is the ADJR Act Hampering the Development of Australian Administrative Law?' *Australian Journal of Administrative Law* 12.

Attorney-General's Department 1983, 'Annual Report on the Operation of the Freedom of Information Act 1982 for the period 1 December 1982 to 30 June 1983', AGPS.

Attorney-General's Department 2010, 'Intellectual Property Principles for Australian Government Agencies'. Available at: http://www.ag.gov.au/www/ agd/agd.nsf/Page/Copyright_CommonwealthCopyrightAdministration_ StatementofIPPrinciplesforAustralianGovernmentAgencies.

Attorney-General's Department 2012, 'Review of NBN Compliance with FOI', 16 April 2012. Available at: http://www.ag.gov.au/Consultationsreformsandreviews/Pages/Review-of-NBN-compliance-with-FOI.aspx.

Australian Government n.d., 'Publishing Public Sector Information'. Available at: http://webguide.gov.au/.

Australian Labor Party 1972, 'It's Time', speech by the Leader of the Opposition, 13 November 1972.

Australia's Right to Know Coalition 2011, 'Response to the Discussion Paper: Disclosure Logs, Office of the Australian Information Commissioner', 28 March 2011.

ALRC (Australian Law Reform Commission) 2010, 'Secrecy Laws and Open Government in Australia', Report No. 112, 17 September.

ALRC, ARC (Australian Law Reform Commission, Administrative Review Council) 1995, 'Open Government: A review of the federal Freedom of Information Act 1982', Report No. 77.

ANAO (Australian National Audit Office) 2003, 'Audit Report No. 57, 2003–2004: Administration of freedom of information requests'.

Bayne, P. and K. Rubenstein 1995, 'The Objects of the Freedom of Information (FOI) Acts and their Interpretation', *Australian Journal of Administrative Law,* 2.

BBC News 2010, 'US Embassy Cables: The background', 29 November 2010. Available at: http://www.bbc.co.uk/news/world-us-canada-11862320.

Benkler, Y. 2011, 'A Free Irresponsible Press: Wikileaks and the battle over the soul of the networked fourth estate'. Available at: http://benkler.org/Benkler_Wikileaks_current.pdf.

Bland Committee 1973, 'Final Report of the Committee on Administrative Discretions', Parliamentary Paper No. 316.

Blenkin, M. 2011, 'How 1980 Marked a Turning Point to Reform', *The Age*, 1 January 2011. Available at: http://news.theage.com.au/breaking-news-national/how-1980-marked-a-turning-point-to-reform-20110101-19c70.html.

Bovens, M. 2002, 'Information Rights: Citizenship in the information society' *Journal of Political Philosophy* 10.

Brown, A. J. 2007, 'Privacy and Public Interest Disclosures: When is it reasonable to protect whistleblowing to the media?', *Privacy Law Bulletin* 4.

Brown, A. J. (ed) 2008, *Whistleblowing in the Australian Public Sector: Enhancing the theory and practice of internal witness management in public sector organisations*, ANU E Press, Canberra.

Brown, A. J. 2011, 'Courage Needed to Protect Whistleblowers', *The Australian*, 24 June 2011. Available at: http://www.theaustralian.com.au/business/legal-affairs/courage-needed-to-protect-whistleblowers/story-e6frg986-1226080859231.

Brown, A. and P. Latimer 2011, 'Whistleblower Legislation in Australia: Analysis and reform', in M. Arszulowicz and W. W. Gasparski (eds), *Whistleblowing: In defence of proper action*, Transaction, New Brunswick.

Cane, P. and L. McDonald 2008, *Principles of Administrative Law: Legal regulation of governance*, Oxford University Press, Oxford.

CARC (Commonwealth Administrative Review Committee) 1971, 'Report', Parliamentary Paper No. 144.

CLRC (Copyright Law Reform Commission) 2005, 'Crown Copyright Report'.

Commonwealth Ombudsman 1999, '"Needs to Know": Report on the investigation of administration of FOI in Commonwealth agencies'.

Commonwealth Ombudsman 2006, '"Scrutinising Government": Administration of the Freedom of Information Act 1982 in Australian government agencies', March.

Costello P., Treasurer 2007, 'Questions in Writing: Freedom of Information', House of Representatives, *Debates*, 20 March 2007.

Creyke, R. and J. McMillan (eds) 1998, *The Kerr Vision of Australian Administrative Law: At the twenty-five year mark*, Centre for International and Public Law, ANU, Canberra.

Creyke, R. and J. McMillan 2009, *Control of Government Action: Text, cases and commentary,* 2nd ed., Lexis Nexis Butterworths, Chatswood.

Crozier, R. 2011, 'Greens Win NBN Co FOI Review', *itnews*, 25 March 2011. Available at: http://www.itnews.com.au/News/252354,greens-win-nbn-co-foi-review.aspx.

Department of Finance and Deregulation n.d., 'Listing of Contract Details on the Internet (Meeting the Senate Order on Departmental and Agency Contracts): Financial management guide 8'.

Department of Finance and Deregulation 1997, 'Governance Arrangements for Commonwealth Government Business Enterprises'.

Department of Finance and Deregulation 2008, 'Declaration of Open Government'. Available at: http://www.finance.gov.au/e-government/ strategy-and-governance/gov2/declaration-of-open-government.html.

Department of the Prime Minister and Cabinet n.d., 'Ahead of the Game: Blueprint for reform of Australian government administration'. Available at: http://www.dpmc.gov.au/publications/aga_reform/aga_reform_blueprint/ index.cfm#blueprint.

Ellicott Committee 1973, 'Report of the Committee of Review of Prerogative Writ Procedure', Parliamentary Paper No. 56.

Finn, C. 2003, 'Rethinking Commercial Confidentiality in the Decade of Competition Policy', *Freedom of Information Review* 106.

Fraser, J. M. 1978, 'Responsibility in Government' *Australian Journal of Public Administration* 37.

Freiberg, A. 2010, *The Tools of Regulation*, Federation Press, Sydney.

Grattan, M. 2005, 'Yes, Minister: Your will is my command', *The Age*, 6 July 2005. Available at: http://www.theage.com.au/news/michelle-grattan/yes-minister-your-will-is-my-command/2005/07/05/1120329444456.html.

Grattan, M. and C. Yeates 2010, 'Xenophon Deal advances NBN', *The Age*, 25 November 2010. Available at: http://www.theage.com.au/technology/ technology-news/xenophon-deal-advances-nbn-20101124-187e8.html.

Government 2.0 Taskforce 2009, 'Engage: Getting on with government 2.0'. Available at: http://www.finance.gov.au/publications/gov20taskforcereport/ index.html.

Gurry, F. 1984, *Breach of Confidence*, Oxford University Press, Oxford.

Hazell, R., B. Worthy and M. Glover 2010, *The Impact of of the Freedom of Information Act on Central Government in the UK: Does FOI work?*, Palgrave MacMillan, Basingstroke.

Hood, C. 1991, 'A Public Management for all seasons?', *Public Administration* 69(1).

itnews 2010, 'The NBN Co Business plan at a glance', 20 December 2010. Available at: http://www.itnews.com.au/News/242325,the-nbn-co-business-plan-at-a-glance.aspx.

Julnes, P. and M. Holzer 2001, 'Promoting the Utilization of Performance Measures in Public Organizations: An empirical study of factors affecting adoption and implementation', *Public Administration Review,* 61(6).

Kettl, D. F. 2000, 'Public Administration at the Millennium: The state of the field', *Journal of Public Administration Research and Theory* 10.

Lamble, S. 2002, 'Freedom of Information: A Finnish clergyman's gift to democracy', *Freedom of Information Review* 97.

Massola, J. 2011, 'Julia Gillard Backs FOI Exemption for Taxpayer Funded NBN', *The Australian*, 18 January 2011. Available at: http://www.theaustralian.com.au/national-affairs/julia-gillard-backs-foi-exemption-for-taxpayer-funded-nbn/story-fn59niix-1225990173260.

McMillan, J. 2000, 'Parliament and Administrative Law', Research Paper No. 13, 2000–01, Department of the Parliamentary Library.

McMillan, J. 2002, 'Twenty Years of Open Government: What have we learnt?', Inaugural Professorial Address: Administrative Law, ANU, 4 March.

Mendel, T. 2008, *Freedom of Information: A comparative legal survey*, 2nd ed. UNESCO, Paris.

Moynihan, D. P. and S. K. Pandey 2004, 'Testing How Management Matters in an Era of Government by Performance Management', *Journal of Public Administration Research and Theory,* 15(3), pp. 421–439.

Mulgan, R. 2003, *Holding Power to Account: Accountability in modern democracies*, Palgrave MacMillan, Basingstroke.

OAIC (Office of the Australian Information Commissioner) n.d., 'FOI Guidelines'. Available at: http://www.oaic.gov.au/publications/guidelines.html.

OAIC 2012, 'Review of Charges under the Freedom of Information Act 1982'.

Oakes, L. 2005, 'Pillars of Democracy Depend on Leaks', *The Bulletin/National Nine News*, 24 August 2005.

O'Connor, B., Minister for Privacy and Freedom of Information 2010, 'Freedom of Information Act 1982: Annual Report 2009–2010'.

OpenAustralia 2011, 'House debates: Tuesday, 1 March 2011: Telecommunications Legislation Amendment (National Broadband Network Measures — Access Arrangements) Bill 2010: Consideration in Detail'. Available at: http://www.openaustralia.org/debate/?id=2011-03-01.77.1.

Parker, C. and J. Braithwaite 2003, 'Regulation', in P. Cane and M. Tushnet (eds), *The Oxford Handbook of Legal Studies,* Oxford University Press, Oxford.

Parliamentary Library 2008, 'Bills Digest: Freedom of Information (Removal of Conclusive Certificates and Other Measures) Bill 2008'. Available at: http://www.aph.gov.au/library/pubs/bd/2008-09/09bd105.htm#_ftn10.

Paterson, M. 2004, 'Commercial in Confidence and Public Accountability: Achieving a new balance in the contract state', *Australian Business Law Review* 32.

Paterson, M. 2005, *Freedom of Information and Privacy in Australia: Government and information access in the modern state*, Lexis Nexis Butterworths, Chatswood.

Prime Minister, Treasurer, Minister for Finance and Minister for Broadband 2009, 'New National Broadband Network', Press release, 7 April 2009.

Riley, J. 2010, 'Conroy survives Gag; Mr X, Fielding on side', *IT Wire*, 18 November 2010. Available at: http://www.itwire.com/it-policy-news/government-tech-policy/43299-conroy-survives-gag-mr-x-fielding-on-side.

Roberts, A. 2001, 'Structural Pluralism and the Right to Information', *University of Toronto Law Journal* 51.

Rosanvallon, P. 2008, *Counter Democracy: Politics in an age of distrust*, Cambridge University Press, Cambridge.

Roxon N. 2012, 'Review of NBN Compliance with FOI', Media Release, 16 April 2012. Available at: http://www.attorneygeneral.gov.au/media-releases/pages/2012/second%20quarter/16-april-2012---review-of-nbn-compliance-with-foi.aspx.

RCAGA (Royal Commission on Australian Government Administration) 1976, 'Report', Chairman: H. C. Coombs, AGPS, Canberra.

Rudd, K. and J. Ludwig 2007, 'Government Information: Restoring trust and integrity', Policy Document, October 2007.

Sear, J. 2011, 'Restricting Freedom of Information Revelations', *Crikey*, 11 April 2011. Available at: http://blogs.crikey.com.au/purepoison/2011/04/11/restricting-freedom-of-information-revelations/.

Shane, S. 2010, 'Keeping Secrets Wikisafe', New York Times, 11 December 2010.

Shergold, P. 2006. 'Pride in the Public Service', speech delivered at the National Press Club, Canberra, 15 February 2006. Available at: http://www.pmc.gov.au/speeches/shergold/pride_in_public_service_2006-02-15.cfm.

Skeketee, M. 2011. 'How Laurie Oakes Trumped John Howard', *The Australian*, 1 January 2011. Available at: http://www.theaustralian.com.au/in-depth/cabinet-papers/how-laurie-oakes-trumped-john-howard/story-fn7f6f9t-1225979649015.

SLCLC (Senate Legal and Constitutional Legislation Committee) 2001, 'Enquiry into the Freedom of Information Amendment (Open Government) Bill 2000', April 2001.

Snell, R. 2004, 'Conclusive or Ministerial certificates: An almost invisible blight on FOI practice', *Freedom of Information Review* 109.

Spigelman, J. 2010, 'The Centrality of Jurisdictional Error', *Public Law Review* 21.

SSCICMI (Senate Select Committee for an Inquiry into a Certain Maritime Incident) 2002, 'A Certain Maritime Incident'. Available at: http://www.aph.gov.au/Parliamentary_Business/Committees/Senate_Committees?url=maritime_incident_ctte/report/index.htm.

SSCLCA (Senate Standing Committee on Legal and Constitutional Affairs) 1979, 'Freedom of Information: Report by the Senate Standing Committee on Constitutional and Legal Affairs on the Freedom of Information Bill 1978, and aspects of the Archives Bill 1978'.

SSCLCA 1987, 'Freedom of Information Act 1982: Report on the operation and administration of the Freedom of Information Legislation'.

Stewart, A., P. Griffith and J. Bannister 2010, *Intellectual Property in Australia*, 4th ed., Lexis Nexis Butterworths, Chatswood.

Taggart M. 1997, 'The Province of Administrative Law Determined?', in M. Taggart (ed.), *The Province of Administrative Law*, Hart Publishing, Oxford.

Terrill, G. 1998, 'The Rise and Decline of FOI in Australia', in G. Terrill and A. McDonald (eds), *Open Government*, Macmillan Press, London.

Terrill, G. 2000, *Secrecy and Openness: The federal government from Menzies to Whitlam and beyond*, Melbourne University Press, Melbourne.

Timmins, P. 2006, 'No Paper Trail if Possilbe', 5 February. Available at: http://foi-privacy.blogspot.com.au/2006/02/no-paper-trail-if-possilbe.html#.VBuAjyg4Z4g.

US Department of Defence 2010, 'DOD News Briefing with Secretary Gates and Adm. Mullen from the Pentagon', 30 November 2010. Available at: http://www.defense.gov/transcripts/transcript.aspx?transcriptid=4728.

Whitlam, G. 1985, *The Whitlam Government, 1972–1975*, Penguin Books, Ringwood.

Wilson, L. 2010, 'NBN Study "Highly Sensitive"', *The Australian*, 20 November 2010. Available at: http://www.theaustralian.com.au/news/nation/nbn-study-highly-sensitive/story-e6frg6nf-1225956833353.

Wikipedia n.d., 'The Bed of Nails (Yes Minister)'. Available at: http://en.wikipedia.org/wiki/The_Bed_of_Nails_(Yes_Minister).

Wilenski, P. 1988, *Public Power and Public Administration*, Hale & Iremonger in association with the Royal Australian Institute of Public Administration, Sydney.

Worthy, B. 2010, 'More Open But Not More Trusted?: The effect of the Freedom of Information Act 2000 on the United Kingdom central government', *Governance* 23.

Worthy, B. and R. Hazell 2010, 'Assessing the Performance of Freedom of Information', *Government Information Quarterly* 27.

5. Through a Glass Darkly: The vicissitudes of budgetary reform in Australia

John Wanna

Introduction

The budgeting of public resources is supposedly one of the most crucial tools in public governance. Budgets and the associated allocation and management of financial resources are a fundamental source of power to governments — and money invariably lies at the heart of almost all public policy decisions and activities, as Peter Walsh (1995) once argued. It provides governments with their wherewithal, their real authority and the ability to achieve their aims. Ostensibly, budgets allow governments to plan and fund their priorities, to resource existing commitments, to reduce allocations to less preferred activities, or change the tax-benefit trade-off between citizens and government (Wildavsky and Caiden 2004). This is the theory, but practice is very different and much more complicated.

Budgets are multiple things to multiple constituencies; they serve many purposes and functions across government and between government and the community. Their functions include economic management and macroeconomic policy, sustaining public finances, fiscal policy, revenue functions, investment intentions, expenses, allocative functions, technical efficiency, performance evaluation and accountability review (see Wanna et al. 2003, pp. xxix–xxx). These functions are not necessarily complementary, consistent or cumulative. Hence, unlike private choice, public budgeting is a complex, repetitive set of collective choices about resources and provisions various governments consider society needs (some of which relate to given 'mandates' but other choices no one can remember making), and then accounting for these choices and decisions.

Budgets have long been a traditional ritual of modern government. They are a major undertaking of government, performed annually. They are political exercises as much as administrative exercises. Our governments invest a great deal of time, resources and political capital in putting the annual budget together and selling it. They take great pride in their successful delivery and reception in Parliament, and with the media, interest groups and wider community. They are frustrated and perplexed when budgets flop or receive a less than rapturous ovation from stakeholders and critics. Budgets are also a routine confidence issue and governments can themselves fall if their budgets are rejected or deferred.

But, for the purposes of this chapter, it should be recognised that budgets are also hard to put together and there may be little scope for flexibility in the overall budget. They are massive in scope; there are many competing demands; there are many stakeholders and recipients involved; they often defy orderliness or tidiness; they defy planning logics and mathematical rationalities. They are notoriously difficult to compile and keep together. There are masses of information to be assembled, weighed, evaluated and used as foundations for other calculations and projections. They are constantly buffeted by events, changing perceptions and shifting interpretations. They simultaneously look backwards and forwards — governing from behind to meet the challenges of the future.

Budgets and budget formation are also highly secretive and undertaken away from the glare of publicity (see Heclo and Wildavsky 1974; Wanna et al. 2003, p. xxxiii). They involve back room processes and decisions, internal rules and conventions, ways of doing things that are not disclosed. Rules are changed periodically often to disadvantage certain claimant groups or agencies. Ministers may 'see' only a thin veneer of the budget — generally those elements that concern them or for which they have personally lobbied. We, the public, generally see but the tip of the iceberg and have to guess what goes on under the surface. Furthermore, budgets are supposedly an accountability device, transparent and open to scrutiny and requiring legislative authorisation (as a form of control on executive government). Yet, budgets are presented in ways that differ markedly from the ways they were put together. It is as if we have two separate processes or logics of action that hardly interrelate with each other. As will be argued, despite claims of greater openness, this lack of clarity and transparency remains a major problem. The political executive likes to keep the legislature guessing, at arm's length and one or two steps behind the action. There are problems with the alignment of data and activities, figures and results; it is hard to identify or distinguish 'old money' from 'new money', offsets from new programs, and how changed preferences for reporting activities vary from previous years.

Once budgets are consolidated and formally presented they are judged by the community, the media, money markets, commentators, lobbyists, and the government's political opponents. There is a tendency here to see success in the form of projected surpluses — the notion that government can pay for itself rather than that government is using its funds wisely. So surpluses (especially year-on-year), as Australian treasurers are fond of saying, indicate we are managing well and practicing sound financial management. Like George Orwell's farm animals, governments seem to bleat 'one surplus good, two surpluses better'.

But are we managing well? Does the existence of a surplus necessarily mean that we are following best practice budgetary and financial management? The Howard government's finance minister, Senator Nick Minchin, in his opening address to the senior budget officials (OECD) meeting in Sydney June 2006 (Minchin 2006), implied that this was the only measure for judging budgetary performance — as he unfavourably compared state budget deficits with federal surpluses. This may not be the most appropriate indicator of success (nor a fair comparison). Moreover, the budgetary system under the Howard government did not really experience adverse economic circumstances and so was not tested. After 1997, the Howard government enjoyed high economic growth and a mining boom; it did not face significant fiscal pressures and presided over massive year after year spending increases only surpassed by even more massive revenue receipts (see Wanna et al. 2000, p. 258–269; Laurie and McDonald 2008). Arguably, the reluctance to seriously reform the tax side of the budget equation means that taxation revenues give the appearance of good budgetary practice, without it necessarily being so.

In this chapter, I explore briefly the imperatives for budgetary reform and comment on where they came from. I then trace and explain the particular trajectory followed in Australia and note the vicissitudes of budget reform over time. I do not attempt a comprehensive detailed overview of budget reform, as I have undertaken that in other publications (Wanna et al. 2000; O'Faircheallaigh et al. 1999; and Wanna et al. 2003, and later in Wanna et al. 2010). Rather, I will pick out some of the key successes that have improved our management of public finance, after which I indicate a few weaknesses and deficiencies in our current system — highlighting the problems associated with the present outcomes framework. I explore some dead ends and dry gullies we once went up before deserting them. Then I raise some problems with our present practices of budgetary reporting and accountability. Finally, I offer a series of propositions from my research to perhaps challenge preconceptions about the overall nature of budgetary reform.

Background: Traditional budgets and the imperatives for budgetary reform

Conventional wisdom, and much of the relevant academic literature over the twentieth century asserted that traditional budgets and internal budgetary processes were conservative, incremental and risk-averse (Wildavsky 1964). They locked in governments and gave them limited scope for reallocation. They were often beyond political control or influence and, over the post-war era, expenditures grew less according to political preferences than to internal logics of growth and augmentation. International comparative analyses of expenditure increases over this period highlight the consistency of growth patterns within distinct national clusters (Scandinavian, Anglo-American and Continental European: see Castles 1999). Ministers often played a relatively insignificant role in the process except for the presentational functions and events (for example, introducing the budget to the legislature, or selling it afterwards). Many cabinets were not involved in setting aggregate budgetary frameworks or informed about decisions in detail. Because most of the new policy decisions and commitments feeding into a collective budget were made on the basis of comparing the relative merits of rival bids, budgetary processes had to find ways to reduce or mitigate political conflict through the proliferation of rules, disciplines and timelines (see Wildavsky 1964). Budgeting became acknowledged as an annual repetitive cycle where adjustments were made at the margin.

So, as a means of rationing claims from 'spender' departments, budgeting was undertaken largely in secret using bilateral negotiations or side deals. A semblance of control over the process — often interpreted as exercising power over the public purse — gave budget guardians such as treasuries or finance departments the illusion of power. They performed the role of devil's advocates, but were often outplayed or outmanoeuvred by spending agencies who regularly overspent their allocations. The command-post mentality of central budget agencies fitted only with a budgetary system based on input allocations within a punitive administrative culture, which was increasingly seen as dysfunctional to modern governance (Schick 2001; Wanna et al. 2003). Moreover, the role performed by central guardians was reactive rather than strategic, and generally prevented or restrained governments from doing the things their component parts had proposed.

Such input-driven systems remained largely unchallenged until the economic and fiscal crises of the 1970s and 1980s, when governments presided over large and repeated deficits, and debt levels rose because of structural budgetary imbalances. Compounding resource problems saw governments gradually take a closer interest in both their fiscal policy settings and internal budgetary processes (Keating 1990; Keating and Holmes 1990; Keating and Dixon 1989). New governments proposed various half-baked or speculative suggestions for budgetary reform, often not worked out in detail (see ALP 1983; Australian Government 1984), or issued persuasive arguments on the need for substantial reform (for example, New Zealand Treasury 1984). If politicians were to be held accountable for the consequences of poor budgeting outcomes, then they and their senior advisers felt they ought to exert greater influence over crucial aspects of government budgeting, including aggregate-setting and discretion over the allocation of the 'base' and new money/new policy proposals.

Governments began a process of containing expenditure growth, targeting spending, using co-payment and user-charging devices to ration and direct resource public provision. The early methods were fairly crude, blunt and limited in their effectiveness. The Fraser governments (1975–83) attempted budget control through arbitrary top-down ceiling controls, clawbacks and across-the-board cuts. The subsequent Hawke (1983–91) and Keating (1991–96) governments forced managers to manage within prescribed resource limits set over the medium term, thereby bringing aggregate budgets under control (see Wanna et al. 2000). By the mid-to-late-1980s governments had made the difficult transition from consecutive high deficits in final budget outcomes to annual surpluses often exceeding budgetary forecasts. Budgets and financial management in the modern expansive state had been brought under administrative control possibly for the first time since the parsimonious nineteenth-century era of small government liberalism.

This is probably the most significant single achievement of modern budgetary reform and the associated adoption of sophisticated information technology systems. Governments, if they so desired, now had the capabilities to be able to bring their budgets under control and into balance. But as the years 1990–92 showed, and then again in the global financial crisis after 2008, public budgets were not recession proof; a point that is still evident in many OECD nations such as the US, the UK, Ireland and most of southern Europe.

There were many budgetary and financial management adaptations that were regarded as successful and which have proved useful in improving resource utilisation. We should acknowledge these and give credit — as I will later turn to highlight some deficiencies in the present systems. Successful innovations have included:

- A consolidated budgetary process allowing the comparative merits of budgetary proposals to be judged and argued out with a consolidated reporting of budget measures;
- A strong Expenditure Review Committee (ERC) of Cabinet with senior guardian ministers able to impose discipline over the budget process;
- The 'medium-term economic framework' (MTEF) that sits on the formally documented 'fiscal strategy statement';
- One-line operating budgets providing greater flexibility with departmental expenditures and expenses;
- Full cost budgeting on an independent accrual accounting basis, providing systematic recognition for assets and liabilities as well as revenue and expenses;
- A tighter focus on core public sector activities (moving out of Government Business Enterprises, and other entities) through privatisation of functions

not fitting the current role of government and restructured corporate governance arrangements to improve accountability for the remaining government functions;

- Greater attention to a results-based orientation in public finance in the formulation process, in-year operations and with budget reporting;

- Offsets and matching saving requirements from bidding departments have provided, on occasion, a test of priority and seriousness of budget submissions;

- Asset recognition, asset management and property leasing across government.

Australia and New Zealand were soon regarded as leaders in the field. Many of the budgetary and IT reforms practiced here were taken up internationally as other countries adopted improved practices in their own jurisdictions. Considerable policy transfer occurred especially across the OECD (see Wanna et al. 2010); some simply through information exchange about local innovations; some through the direct importation, copying and adaptation of innovations developed elsewhere; some through the dissemination of endorsed practices (best practice principles) by the OECD and IMF (for example, OECD 2001; and by the Senior Budgetary Officials meetings, OECD 2004; IMF 1999); and some through the bullying of donor financial institutions anxious to proliferate their notions of good governance structures to local polities before releasing funds. In addition, legions of consultants, former budgetary officials and occasional academics cruised the world proselytising the merits of various reform initiatives (usually ones with which they had been personally associated, but thereafter presented as frozen snapshots in time rather than intermediate stages in a longer evolution of change).

The transfer of budgetary rules and procedures has included legislative instruments (for example, the *Fiscal Responsibility Act 1994* of New Zealand was later replicated in Australia in the *Charter of Budget Honesty Act 1998*, and adapted almost simultaneously by various state governments too: see Wanna 2006). It has included the uptake of substantive *innovations* (for example, one-line budgets, MTEF, centrally imposed aggregate spending limits, Cabinet budget review committees, and the consolidated running costs arrangements, many of which were exported from Australia and New Zealand to countries such as the Netherlands, Canada, Denmark and Ireland, as well as many smaller Asian and Pacific nations). In addition, improved accounting techniques have received international acceptance (such as internationally recognised standards, accrual budgeting systems). Not all countries achieved similar rates of progress. There was much cultural and institutional adaptation, and there still remains much diversity in country-specific arrangements. However, a significant group of OECD nations now operate much more sophisticated budgetary systems with far greater control over the total budget.

Explaining Australia's ad hoc trajectory of budgetary reform

Australia's trajectory or path dependency in budget reform was far from linear and planned. It was not programmatic or designed according to an overall template or blueprint. There was no rational design, no calculated schedule or intended agenda of reform. Nevertheless, governments and their central budget agencies have generally insisted budget reform was rational, planned, linear, always anticipated, and a process of progressive consolidation — when often it was nothing of the sort. The Department of Finance was once renowned for saying there were never 'problems' overseeing the budget process, just 'challenges'.

The process of reform was piecemeal and staccato, where the consequences or change are often unintended and unforeseen. As such, various reforming governments from Fraser to Hawke and Keating to Howard embarked upon a meandering journey of budget reform. The journey was associated with changing circumstances and technical possibilities as well as by changing considerations — getting control of expenditures, consolidating operating budgets, identifying programs and sponsoring program management, separating 'program' costs from running costs, using various costing methodologies, and the use of market delivery mechanisms.

The process was ad hoc, but not totally random. Instead, some broad principles and directions can be traced that shaped the government's thinking. These broad principles followed rather than led the unfolding path of experimentation. Over time, governments endorsed the principles of devolution and devolved responsibilities, of a results-based focus in spending allocations. There were disputes and disagreements along the way between advocates of rival directions — especially between 'central controllers' and 'devolved managers'. In the process many players and agencies suffered identity crises — what were they doing, why, how, what value did they add to the process (this included agencies such as the Treasury, Finance, the Auditor-General, and even Parliament). As victors and survivors get to write history, the eventual winners were able to rationalise the sustainable components of the process much later (see Management Advisory Board 1997; Department of Finance and Administration 1998). They then insisted that the successful reforms *had been intended* from the outset, that they *knew they would work*, were *augmented and extended* when successful, and then *documented* and if necessary *legitimised* through changed legislation or budget rules. Myth was built on myth, and was disseminated internationally through the OECD and senior budget officials meetings (see Chan et al. 2002).

Elsewhere I have clustered the surviving reforms under six headings to indicate the different trajectories and objectives of many of the reform experiments (O'Faircheallaigh et al. 1999). These headings are:

- Political and ministerial reforms — for example, ERC, approving fiscal targets, political discipline, spending rounds consolidated to specific windows;
- Budgetary and technical reforms — for example, consolidation of running costs, one-line budgets, outcome budgeting, various incentive arrangements with agencies;
- Managerial and systems reforms — for example, program management, business plans, management information systems;
- Program evaluation reforms — for example, evaluation processes, compulsory evaluations, performance audits, benchmarking, triple bottom line reporting;
- Market-based and contract management — for example, competitive tendering, outsourcing; and
- Accounting and reporting reforms — for example, accrual budgeting, improved integrated reporting, financials and non-financials.

In the struggle for the hearts and minds of the reform movement, the so-called 'managerialists' won the day (those seeking not to reduce the state but to make it perform better and deliver more efficient and effective services). So, Australia took on a pragmatic, managerialist-inspired approach to budgetary reform, accompanying an expansionist Commonwealth government with galloping expenditures and expanding policy horizons (Laurie and McDonald 2008). The new legions of public managers became the specific focus and essence of the changes. Australia's budget reform trajectory consciously and unconsciously privileged the managers. Managerial incentives became central to the character of reform and its momentum. It also became highly path-dependent. In many ways Australia's ad hoc trajectory was a 'provider-led' reform strategy — driven by champions in central agencies (with a few supporters out in line agencies) who argued the case that program managers should be given more operational discretion. Put differently, the program managers captured the reform process, implying that the 'providers' rather than the 'principals' ran the show — distinctly unlike the New Zealand trajectory. Australia is an example of bureaucratic capture of budget reform.

The path of reform was clearly not neo-liberal in character (and it is a misdiagnosis to see it in such terms as some have) but dedicatedly managerialist — oriented around 'doing more', 'making managers manage', improving 'value for money' (Keating 1989). It gave executives resource latitude within a managerialist-driven system. The presumption was that the spenders and program managers would manage their budgets better and more conservatively if allowed to do so

— and using the potentialities of devolved financial management most program managers were able to come in under budget so that agencies were able to carry forward funds year after year. Under new public management and then accrual budgeting in an 'outcomes framework', spenders needed to exercise their own guardian roles and 'behave' within the negotiated resource limits (see Kelly and Wanna 2001). While constraints were important, managers were given flexibility to manage within program structures, and told to identify outputs and results.

By omission or contrast, Australia's reform path gave less emphasis to other factors such as accountability, performance, 'policy integrity' or policy effectiveness. We can contrast the Australian trajectory with those found in other nations that have undertaken budgetary reform. Canada placed more focus on policy integrity, policy priorities and policy rationing. New Zealand centred its approach on ministers purchasing outputs from managers. The UK placed emphasis on systematic administrative reviews of spending and later on combined outputs (joined up initiatives). The Netherlands emphasised the central withdrawal from social services and the devolution of service delivery to regional and municipal governments.

In Australia, management instruments and budgetary instruments were blended and overlaid upon each other. Resource allocation shifted from a historical fascination with 'front-end' analysis (preoccupied solely with input data and detailed spending amounts on itemised units), to an MTEF oriented towards results (outcomes and/or outputs) with considerable devolution of resource usage to operational management, and eventually the full costs of services acknowledged in budget allocations (a performance and activity focus).

Importantly, Australia's promotion of budgetary reform was often the initial catalyst and main driver of wider public sector reform and improvements in public management. Indeed, some would argue that budgetary reform has significantly biased the nature of new public management especially in the Anglo-American nations, giving a strong resource-orientation to the reforms (Wanna et al. 2000, Chapter 12; Halligan 2004). Thus, management reforms, business plans, citizens charters, outsourcing, the streamlining of industrial relations, and human resource management reforms were often premised or built on the foundations of budgetary reform. Some would further argue that budgetary orientations and practices drove policy choices especially in the 1980s and mid-1990s — when portfolios and agencies were allowed to reallocate internally and clawbacks such as the efficiency dividend encouraged agencies to invent new policy bids to replenish their operating budgets.

To some extent Australia's managerialist trajectory hit a brick wall when a budgetary 'outcomes/outputs framework' was superimposed over the system. This was introduced in 1999–2000 as a blanket-like framework that supposed it could be applied equally to all parts of the public sector. Initially, the outcomes framework was welcomed and received a positive reception (by Cabinet, many individual agencies, by parliamentary committees and the Auditor-General). There was much hype about the integrated and interlocking nature of the 'backward mapping' decision process — going from desired outcomes to deliverable outputs to budget allocations — or at least in theory (see Chan et al. 2002). But many of these promises led to disappointment (see Tanner 2006 for the ALP's 'Operation Sunlight' proposals).

Problems with the outcomes framework and budget processes

To date, it is clear there are a number of fundamental problems that have arisen with our reforms.

First, the reforms have been aimed at better internal resource utilisation by operational managers rather than at strategic allocations or allocative efficiency at the whole of government level. We can ask a series of questions here: to what extent does the budget process allow governments to undertake strategic thinking and implement chosen strategies, especially the possibilities for strategic decision-making/action by governments over policy issues of concern to them? Are budget processes aligned with the government's strategic directions and leadership style?

There is an empirical question as to how far strategic considerations can be addressed through the budget process, and this varies from jurisdiction to jurisdiction. Across the OECD (especially in the parliamentary democracies) we can detect various ways in which political actors (ministers and especially prime ministers) have sought to enhance their involvement in budget decision-making, usually to increase their influence beyond merely ratifying decisions taken elsewhere. Cabinets and senior financial ministers are more involved in determining the initial framing decisions concerning budget aggregates and underlying assumptions (for example, the prudential budgeting used by Canada, Sweden's expenditure envelopes, or Australia's medium-term strategy with budget aggregates and forward estimates). Some nations have enhanced the power of ministers to determine new policy initiatives on specific spending cabinet committees (for example, Canada's twin cabinet policy committees for economics and social policy). Governments have also driven major cutting exercises or deep review into base spending areas or targeted areas for cutbacks

(Australia in the mid-1980s, then in 1996–97 and then after the election of the Rudd government in 2007–08; Canada in 1995–96 with the 'program review' exercise).[1]

Although results-related in format, the Australian 'outcomes framework' has significant problems that have hardly been addressed since its introduction in 1999. The main exception was the opposition Labor Party's 'Operation Sunlight' document (Tanner 2006), which provided a critical review. But most of its recommendations were not implemented. Cynics would argue that allocation to 'outcomes' is a disguise and that in reality it is a glorified framework for *base budgeting at the agency level*. Budgetary systems that protect the base budget of agencies ('base-plus' budgeting) are relatively impervious to major changes in strategic direction from the centre. Moreover, the emphasis on outcomes has arguably distracted attention away from analysing the ongoing activities of government. It may be possible for some decentralised strategic realignment to be exercised *within* agencies or departments providing they have the discretion, scope and capacity to move resources without unduly restrictive rules operating from the centre or having to curtail/downsize essential services. Without large surpluses, base budgeting (including standing appropriations and non-discretionary spending) is likely to account for up to 95 per cent of available resources in the budget round, especially if jurisdictions have large intergovernmental responsibilities and recurrent spending commitments (for example, sub-national jurisdictions).

Related to the budgetary process, and feeding in at critical moments, is the increasing use of politically articulated 'top-down' strategic priorities, which are essentially forms of policy rationing. In Australia, a small group of very senior ministers participate in an annual two-day retreat (the 'senior ministers' review') in late November to determine key government priorities (usually three to four key priorities) for the upcoming budgetary formulation round (commencing December to March). The Prime Minister then writes out to all Cabinet and other ministers informing them of the priorities to be used in framing the forthcoming budget. Other policy issues not on the senior ministers' list have less chance of winning ERC approval in the process.

Prime ministers have further enhanced their discretion over the budget process by imposing greater personal determination over spending initiatives (which can be used either for strategic or expedient purposes). Prime ministerial preferences, formulated perhaps with input from advisers in their private office or department, can predetermine agendas or set key priorities without input from Cabinet colleagues, or be decisive in determining final spending items (and

---

1   See Appendix 1 at the end of this chapter discussing what a more strategic budget process would look like and what kind of decisions it might contain.

the timing of them). The Commonwealth's $10 billion Murray-Darling Basin water initiative, announced in January 2007, was a case in point (see the critique by the then Treasury Secretary, Ken Henry 2007). The personal preferences of Prime Minister John Howard were increasingly imposed throughout his long tenure prior to and through the senior ministers' review. This process is backed by charter letters and annual performance letters from the Prime Minister to ministers and departmental heads that provide explicit details on government expectations of the portfolio, policy priorities and strategic issues.

But these windows for strategic interventions by senior politicians do not achieve much if the politicians themselves do not choose to be strategic or avail themselves of the opportunity. The Australian Cabinet has progressively downsized the amount of business going to Cabinet (reducing the detailed workload), ostensibly to allow Cabinet to focus on the important issues to the government as a whole. Some Cabinet meetings have been given over to 'strategic Cabinet days' at which a senior minister will brief Cabinet on a selected policy topic (usually without accompanying briefing documents or associated paperwork, and with PowerPoint presentations the preferred mode of address) and no routine matters are presented. In standard Cabinet meetings a proportion of time can also be set aside for strategic discussions. These developments are meant to provide Cabinet with ample opportunities to debate issues without officials and without mountains of paperwork to digest.

However, while some of these events have been regarded as valuable sessions, others have degenerated into pep-talks, rallying speeches, discussions of political tactics or to mulling over the most recent opinion poll results. Hence, simply allowing ministers more time to consider strategic issues as part of the processes of collective responsibility does not mean that they will *think* or *behave* strategically. There are many criticisms of government remaining reactive and preferring expedient or short-term adjustments in policy settings.

A former head of the South Australian Cabinet office, Adam Graycar, recently argued that strategic initiatives were often not addressed through the budget process but instead dealt with on the side by 'passing the hat around'. He found that

> colleagues in line agencies are so very tightly constrained financially that they cannot see beyond their core business and agency boundaries. They have very little financial flexibility, and Treasury bureaucrats in our jurisdiction, like their counterparts in other jurisdictions, have acculturated into knowing the price of everything and the value of nothing … The budget process is a mightily inefficient process of being barely accountable for funds previously allocated, or fighting ferociously for crumbs with which to fund new programs or respond to

cost pressures. If a new proposal involves contributions from, or benefits to multiple agencies, then we have a process not unlike passing the hat around for funds (Graycar 2007, p. 13; see also Graycar and McCann 2012).

Second, outcomes and objectives are only loosely related to the resource appropriation process or performance reporting process. Outcomes are expressed at a high level of abstraction, often as vague composite expressions. Some are inspirational 'feel-good' phrases under which almost anything can fall or be counted. Some provide a grand edifice under which relatively mundane activities are found (for example, the Department of Finance's 'Efficient Functioning of Parliament' which provides drivers for the car fleet and the checking of parliamentary receipts and entitlements). This problem has been identified by the Australian National Audit Office (ANAO) and some parliamentary committees on a number of occasions but little has been done to rectify the concerns (see Senate Standing Committee on Finance and Public Administration 2007). The ANAO has warned agencies to express their outcomes with 'sufficient specificity' to ensure that they are meaningful. Yet departments continue to produce many woolly or platitudinous statements of intent in their portfolio budget statements:

- Efficient Functioning Parliament (Department of Finance and Administration);
- Strong and Resilient Communities (Department of Families, Community Services and Indigenous Affairs);
- Families and Children have Choices and Opportunities (Department of Families, Community Services and Indigenous Affairs);
- Higher Productivity, Higher Pay Workplaces — previously Higher Productivity, Higher Wages (Department of Employment and Workplace Relations);
- Assisting Regions to Manage their own Futures (Department of Transport and Regional Services); and
- Public Understanding in Australia and Overseas of Australia's Foreign and Trade Policy and a Positive Image of Australia (Department of Foreign Affairs and Trade).

Many of these are clearly omnibus outcomes in that contributions to the outcome could come from many sources, agencies, policies, events and circumstances. Many agencies across government may make contributions to such intentions (for example, climate change, productivity, or a sustainable economy). It is a myth that all outcomes are conveniently located in one agency (or even one division of one agency) even if other agencies may assist in the delivery of particular outputs (for example, Centrelink assisting with the Department of Families, Community Services and Indigenous Affairs' family payments). Across the Commonwealth, one division of a department will nominally have sole responsibility for one outcome — which could be highly systemic or generic in character, when in reality the agency only makes a small contribution to the desired outcome. This insistence on outcomes each *located within one agency* is a budget rule of convenience for the central agencies not a reflection of the world of public policy.

There have been criticisms of the degree to which outcomes are changed or subjected to revision — with approximately 20 per cent of agency outcomes experiencing some changes over the past few years. But as the ANAO (2006) has pointed out, while some change may be justified, changes to outcome statements erode the capacity of external scrutineers to follow budget activity and performance over time. At present, agencies are required to provide explanations of the changed formulation from year to year and translation maps to allow comparative scrutiny in portfolio budget statements, but the changes are rarely (if ever) challenged or even discussed by Parliament. The only significant challenge to outcome descriptions in recent years, though ultimately impotent, has come through the *Combet v Commonwealth* High Court challenge, which examined the validity of certain advertising expenditure under the 'higher pay, higher productivity' outcome for the Department of Employment and Workplace Relations. By a margin of five to two, the court found that outcomes were a legal form of appropriation under which diverse items of spending could be made; in essence, the court backed executive privilege in this instance (and argued it was not the role of the courts to decide what was government policy and it was better for parliament to decide such matters). But it could take a different view in the future and force subsequent governments to specify their spending more precisely (as the two dissenting judges implied).

In performance management and reporting, secretaries, executives and program managers have direct incentives to deliver on budget or within budget — even under-budget, but certainly not over-budget — rather than seeking to maximise outcomes. At the state level, the enormous problems with child safety that were historically swept under the carpet indicates a history of low resource priority, and that managers were more interested in managing within their resource constraints than addressing the policy problem. There are also criticisms that many areas of public policy breed increased dependencies — and that the bureaucracy and delivery agencies are often complicit in this — rather than lessening dependencies (for example, middle-class welfare, rental or wage supplementation schemes). This is especially pronounced in the social, community and health sectors, the childcare industry, and of certain client types — such as families, farmers, and the disabled.

It is also dubious whether the outcomes framework really applies to central agencies that either have coordination functions or process functions that do not easily fit a results-based framework. Arguably, the imposition of a one-size-fits-all 'outcome framework' that may suit sectoral or client-based agencies does not apply as well to central agencies (Australian Public Service Commission, Attorney-General's Department, Prime Minister and Cabinet, Treasury, Finance) and most of the foreign affairs and national security organisations — or any other entities without tangible outputs (and some agencies do report that they have no outputs or only have loose output groups). Their activities are principally internal advice, policy analysis and review, and corporate governance. As one Treasury official said, most of the activity under the outcome statement 'sound macro-economic environment' involved Treasury preventing silly schemes and crackpot ideas from being advanced or accepted, especially from ministers — sometimes even their own minister — and from various sectional interests (see Wanna 2011). The outcome 'sound macroeconomic environment' in reality consists of Treasury providing policy advice, analysis and forecasting to the government. It was also hard to demonstrate effectiveness in performance terms, especially if Treasury had prevented bad policy advice going through.

Taking these criticisms together, there is an accepted mythical or fictional dimension to the 'outcomes framework'. Most of the budget is not allocated by outcomes, even though it can be presented as if it were. Most funding and allocative decisions are not based on the priority of the outcome to government, but on the organisational units that have been swept under that particular outcome label for presentational purposes. By some estimates, less than 7 per cent of the budget is formalised according to notions of outcomes — the rest by standing appropriations and departmental items (the old running costs system). After years in operation, many agencies do not appear to have structured their organisations around the outcomes framework, but instead prefer to structure their operations according to activities, business groups or organisational entities. There are questions of how far these generic indicators of government priorities are integrated into the real operations of government agencies (see ANAO 2006). As the Labor Party argued in 'Operation Sunlight' while it was in opposition, many outcomes and the documents relating to them are 'virtually meaningless' and 'open slather for political pork-barrelling' (Tanner 2006).

As Allen Schick (2007) said on a visit to Australia, 'why does Australia persist with a budgetary system that no one believes is working?' In his own inimical way he was highlighting the apparent contrast between the formal rules and the practical reality. Another senior public servant not from a budget agency claimed that one of the present-day major challenges for government was 'how to make the outcomes and outputs framework work — especially when there were claims it would turn the world around, and it hasn't'. The next big budgetary debate in Australia should address the issue of whether to enhance the outcomes–outputs framework or to replace it with an alternative system.

Elsewhere in the budget processes, some key institutions, such as the ERC, may now have outlived their principal usefulness. This high-level budget review committee can trace its antecedents back to 1975, but has been accused by senior officials across government of distorting policy-making and impeding good decision-making. It can often discourage agencies from making submissions for fear of losing resources under the operations of the offsets requirements — having offsets confiscated as cuts but not gaining acceptance for the new proposal. Agencies have learnt to bypass ERC or to game the system by massaging the types and levels of funds for which they apply (one or two big items or 'majors' or lots of 'minors'). Defence and national security proposals now bypass ERC entirely and go through their own budgetary evaluation process (the national security committee of Cabinet) which is not linked to the ERC process but has its own aggregate limits imposed by Cabinet. ERC was once the lynchpin of collective decision-making premised on assessing *all* policy *comparatively* at one point in time in the budget cycle. Other agencies have now resorted to using other political tactics to secure resources outside the formal budgetary process (strong ministers, exceptional cases, infrastructure needs, regional priorities, etc.) where they stand greater chances of success and can circumvent the normal budgetary rules.

With Labor again coming back into government after winning the 24 November 2007 election, they had the opportunity to fundamentally review the budget framework and the internal budgetary processes. 'Operation Sunlight' had promised a range of reforms (to disclosure and reporting, tightening the outcomes framework, etc.) and the new Finance Minister, Lindsay Tanner (2008), committed the government to a phased-in series of reform initiatives (16 in total), and invited the former Australian Democrat Senator Andrew Murray to conduct a forensic review of budgetary accountabilities (Murray 2008). But no sooner had these intentions been announced than the global financial crisis hit Australia and the government's enthusiasm for reform evaporated.

Dead ends, dry gullies and unintended consequences

As mentioned earlier, budget reformers and central budget agencies often paint a glorious triumphal picture of the reform journey. However, on a day-to-day basis, reform ideas often occurred spontaneously in different parts of the system. System changes could occur unexpectedly or as an unintended by-product of some other change. Assessments of what can be attempted or achieved has often meant that second- or third-best alternatives were explored and trialled. Some changes appear now to have been almost random experiments. Looking back, there have been many procedures and budget rules adopted as leaps of faith or with great hopes, but which have been quietly disposed and denied when they are no longer found appropriate. I will mention a few of these below.

Portfolio budgets emerged in the 1980s as a result of aiming to implement program budgeting. Program budgeting was never adopted (although some new measures on the margins may have received direct program allocations). Instead, Australia chose to budget for portfolios, as Pat Barrett (1988) has argued, and within that envelope of funds the various ministers and agencies could have various program structures and move funds between them over time (allowing fungibility). The myth of introducing program budgeting was partly maintained as the Department of Finance consolidated running costs into one-line appropriations — but not on a program by program basis — hence agencies had no program budget *per se*, but consolidated running costs they could apply across whatever program, business lines or corporate structures they chose. For around a decade Finance pretended it could distinguish between 'program costs' and 'running costs' and keep the two separate, but prior to the accruals framework these two labels tended to overlap or be substitutes for each other. Some agencies creatively gamed the new rules. The ABC, for instance, argued that because it made TV 'programs' all its costs were therefore program costs — and so not subject to the efficiency dividend — it claimed not to have any 'running costs'.

Although Australia did not deliberately plan to install portfolio budgeting, it worked at the political and administrative level. Yet once accrual budgeting was adopted in 1999–2000, the government (perhaps unintentionally) sacrificed portfolio budgets in favour of agency-based budgets, which has reduced flexibility and increased silo thinking. A clear unintended consequence of accruals was the compartmentalisation of agencies as single budget agencies, in essence dealing with the central budget agency directly. The techniques or ideology behind accruals meant that entities had to be directly responsible for the control and management of their resources; hence the way financial resources were identified and recorded by accountants at an agency level shaped the distribution of resources. This process of compartmentalisation was underscored by the *1997 FMA* and *CAC Acts*, which held the head of agency or CEO to account as the accountable officer for financial resources. A further unintended consequence was that, under accruals, agencies were effectively given non-lapsing appropriations which, if not spent within the approved year, could be spent in the future for the purpose identified in the appropriation — leaving some to question the constitutional legitimacy of this practice.

In 2000–01, the government committed itself with much fanfare to pricing reviews as a way of improving the efficiency of cost structures in government (see Kelly and Wanna 2004). Despite the problem of identifying prices when so much of what the government did had no market price or was not subjected to market disciplines, the government persevered with this innovation. Pilot studies of agencies were undertaken before more widespread pricing reviews were attempted, but the results were disappointing. There were two main findings that appeared: there was much arguing about what constituted 'price' or what methodologies were appropriate to calculate this figure; and it was not clear that much had been achieved in terms of useful information. The only possible exception being that the only price comparisons which could be made with any rigour were for common services and activities such as human resources, finance, and parliamentary services. Pricing reviews were quietly dropped as both guardian and spending departments realised their limitations or futility.

In 1996–97 the Howard government formally embraced the purchaser–provider model for service delivery and outsourced provision based on tight contracts (National Commission of Audit 1996). It viewed this as a way to contain costs, allow devolved forms of delivery (sometimes using different or competing delivery modes), and being able to hold providers to account for results. There was also some discussion of offloading responsibilities, and perhaps even some component of accountability (although the Auditor-General consistently argued that accountabilities could not be 'outsourced'). After the major debacle with the compulsory outsourcing of IT in the late 1990s — when two Cabinet decisions contradicted each other, one to go ahead and the other to delay — the Howard government downplayed its enthusiasm for adopting the purchaser–provider split as a panacea for all government services. Instead, the Commonwealth spoke of funder–provider relations and grant-based assistance schemes where the aim was not to 'purchase' a service entirely using contracts, but contribute to desired outcomes in the community (for example, support of childcare centres, family support programs, etc.). The Commonwealth does not accept sole responsible for the final activity but makes funding contributions or subsidies available to those providing the service. Some of these funder–provider schemes operated through the states (for example, programs for health and housing, the disabled and homeless), and states for their part have largely refrained from participating in these programs as contractual providers. In the community sector, many of these non-government 'providers' are not-for-profit organisations that deliver a range of existing services, not necessarily only those that receive federal contributions. Faced with such difficulties, the Commonwealth generally abandoned the purchaser–provider model except in the area of employment services where the Department of Employment and Workplace Relations has attempted to make the model work through private-for-profit providers and corporate arms of voluntary organisations.

Vouchers were also mooted as a way to empower clients and citizens and re-route funding through the end-users rather than the organisational deliverers. Health and education were proposed as the major sectors where such 'buyers-choice' schemes could be trialled. A former education minister, David Kemp, tried in vain to shift educational funding to the recipients rather than to institutional providers. But after a decade virtually no voucher schemes have been introduced — although some quasi-schemes involving limited portability have been used (for example, postgraduate scholarships for graduates that go where the student elects rather than being allocated to a particular university, or childcare subsidies or rebates paid to the parent rather than the centre). Again, discussion of voucher-driven funding models has largely abated.

Evaluation has long been the holy grail of the managerialists, many of whom were anxious to show value for money and establish systematic methods of improving policy design and undertaking policy learning. Various schemes have been implemented, none of which has been continued after an initial experimental phase. We have seen a succession of evaluation exercises since the 1970s: joint management reviews, program reviews, appropriateness reviews ordered by Cabinet, compulsory schedules of three- and five-year evaluation reviews, lapsing program reviews, and more recently strategic or cluster reviews. All imposed large investments of resources (especially time), not necessarily to much effect. Many of the evaluation schemes relied on the reviewing agency doing the review or being centrally involved in it, which then undermined the credibility of the findings. Other reviews were used tactically to try to justify more resources for a program in subsequent budget rounds. Each form of evaluation, with the exception of the Auditor-General's efficiency or performance audits (which do not quite fulfil the same function), was terminated, usually within a short period of being announced. Lapsing reviews, for instance, were discontinued when the volume of work for agencies after about three years was so great they could not justify the effort involved. Program lapsing reviews were replaced by cluster reviews of related services as programs came up for renewal. It will be interesting to see whether they fare better than their predecessors. The sorry history of repeated attempts to introduce workable and effective evaluation processes has moved many senior officials to question why policy evaluation has never got off the ground in Australia.

Other dead ends and dry gullies have included:

- the experiment with agency banking undertaken in 1999, but reversed later so that the Department of Finance could practice better cash management;
- the capital use charge initially set at 11–12 per cent (on a base of 6 per cent plus risk margin), with agencies funded for capital at the outset of the budget year but then charged for their capital usage at the end of the year (allowing

them to keep any 'savings'), recommended by accountants — the measure did not prove any assistance in the management of assets and tended to remain an accounting exercise;

- the experiment with devolving the construction of expenditure estimates to line agencies has been gradually reined in by Finance following a succession of missed accuracy targets (revenue estimates have been even more off target) — agencies still input the raw data but Finance now has the final say on what the estimates will be;

- devolved procurement was meant to enable agencies to arrange and control the costs of their own procurement, but the policy was recentralised under new guidelines issued in 2005.

The travails of budgetary reporting: Distorting the glass darkly

Budget documentation is ostensibly produced for accountability and scrutiny purposes, but arguably has now been overshadowed by marketing and presentational considerations. Governments are judged on their budgets by many diverse audiences, so the baroqueness of budget presentation is now assured. Governments have long used budgets to gild the lily, disguise realities, and convey favourable impressions.

Despite the *Charter of Budget Honesty* (which required more integrated reporting but which still has many problems: see Wanna 2006), budget documentation is now more confusing, and in certain respects less informative and non-transparent. Allan Barton (2006) once calculated that up to nine different measures of budget balance or outcome can be found in budget documentation, and treasurers tend to hop backwards and forwards to their preferred sets of figures. So, from year to year we have seen various treasurers talking about the fiscal balance, the underlying cash balance, the headline balance and the size of the surplus to GDP. The most wanton disregard for accuracy and disclosure came with the Coalition government's deliberate non-counting of the GST revenues in the Commonwealth accounts (instigated by Treasurer Peter Costello), despite the Australian Bureau of Statistics (ABS) and Auditor-General both arguing these revenues should be included. By not including the GST all manner of falsehoods were perpetrated, especially when calculating comparative spending patterns, such as the magnitude of Commonwealth revenues to GDP, the size of the Commonwealth government in OECD material, comparative expenditures across governments, and internal proportions of spending which are distorted because a large chunk of transfers to the states are not included. This tax was not counted largely because the former Treasurer had earlier promised to cut

Commonwealth outlays from the levels reached under Keating (from 27 per cent to 23 per cent); discounting one-sixth of the budget was his way of giving the illusion the Commonwealth had shrunk since 1996 (see Wanna et al. 2000, p. 258). It also avoided any impression that the Commonwealth tax per capita had increased during the life of the Coalition's tenure in government. The exclusion of the GST was made solely at the insistence of the former Treasurer while the incoming Rudd government announced its intention to reverse this stance and recalculate expenses from 2000, which it promptly did. Such sophistry over the GST did not prevent the previous government occasionally threatening to put 'conditions on GST transfers' if states do not comply with some federal wish or dictate. So, in spite of the sentiments expressed in the *Charter of Budget Honesty*, the government could well be open to charges of giving deliberate misinformation or partial reporting.

In relation specifically to the reports required by the charter, the legislation was introduced with good intentions but was corrupted by political circumstance and occasionally sidelined. The government made political mileage about its commitment to look at long-term demographic impacts to the budget. Yet in 2001–02 as the intergenerational report was due, the government became bogged down in the detail and had to pull material together at short notice (the statement seemed to have been overlooked). Treasury produced the first report without involving other research units across government such as the ABS. The second report was produced in-house, led by a Treasury team. Circumstances have also seen various financial reports politicised, such as when Peter Costello released a separate Mid-Year Economic and Fiscal Outlook (MYEFO) report, which he claimed was 'more accurate' the day before his department released the real one, and then refused to discuss the departmental report. The process of costing election commitments is at present hopelessly compromised meaning the provisions of the Act — which could be beneficial to parties in the lead up to the election — are largely made ineffective (for example, evaded, delayed or used simply in costing 'saving' measures). The release of the 2007 MYEFO in October 2007 was slightly early, suiting the government's election timing — and half the report was a detailed exposition of the Howard government's intended tax cuts for the period up to 2010 — and subverting the intent of the report, which was to be a mid-year progress report on actual movements since the last budget. Such examples indicate governments are motivated to use these reports expediently as a convenient vehicle for their own political purposes.

The preference for reporting against a selected results-based format has come at the cost of detailed input information and detailed activity information. Whereas many large private corporations collect detailed information on the bases of both results and input costs, and report on key changes continuously, governments have now scaled back their presentation of input data, relying on annual accrual financial statements to tell the financial story. Despite parliamentary committees recommending greater program information to go with other budgetary documentation (for example, in portfolio budget statements) the government has steadfastly refused to provide this information, claiming it would only add levels of confusion to the available documentation. Finance already collects much of this input and program information, but the Howard government chose not to release it. Labor committed itself to producing greater input transparency and program performance data on coming to office, but it remains to be seen whether it would honour such commitments.

The usefulness of budget information to readers, inside and outside of Parliament, is also open to debate. Understanding of accrual financial information requires a basic technical accounting knowledge, which does not come naturally to politicians and lay commentators. For example, the implications of asset sales on net worth and future earning capacity get barely any attention compared with the consequences of increased receipts for surplus cash available to be used.

There is still a huge asymmetry in the annual budget presentation. Governments almost exclusively give prominence to new initiatives and priorities announced through their budgetary parameters, providing little new information on ongoing measures and commitments other than forward estimates. Some agencies in their annual reports do provide informative details and highlight innovations in their base budget activities — but often 12–15 months after the event. The attention given to special appropriations, which lock-in over 80 per cent of total Commonwealth expenditure each budget, is almost insignificant compared with the detailed information on departmental outputs, which comprise around 15 per cent of annual expenses.

There are some other small, simple issues that have reduced transparency for no apparent reason. The government now chooses not to produce historical graphs of functional outlays/expenses — as it did prior to 1999 — which showed comparative spending data in a sectoral area over time. Such 10–15 year graphs allowed readers to observe what patterns were unfolding, where blow-outs were occurring, where tightening or deprioritisation had been made, and which functions were declining in importance. For a while, no functional data was presented at all, but after some parliamentary feedback an annual table has been included in the budget, but only with that year's functional expenses shown (but at a high level of functionality).

For a couple of years in the 1980s, the government also courageously produced 'offset savings' graphs, showing the offsets 'captured', the recycling of money, and how much offsets contributed to new policy proposals. They then terminated this experiment. In 1996 the Howard government produced a report 'Meeting Our Commitments', which listed the magnitude of the various savings measures across government, and where the savings were made, but the government never repeated this exercise. Readers have to search through individual agency portfolio additional estimates statements for records of savings. But even this information is often unsatisfying, as it frequently records book transfers associated with reductions in estimates rather than true savings.

Performance claims by agencies are not usually audited or subject to independent scrutiny (although some could be taken up in performance audits). Many outcomes cannot be closely tied to performance indictors or even to definable outputs. Yet governments do not externally report performance against programs that would give Parliament a good indication of actual performance in agencies. In terms of reporting, the outcomes framework assumes the Commonwealth does things and delivers directly, when in fact it often does not. Agencies process benefits and other transfers according to conditions set by Parliament, provide grants and co-fund activities performed by others, or make contributions to services (health, housing, childcare, environmental management, family income maintenance, etc.). The effectiveness and efficiency of government spending in these activities is virtually impossible to measure in a meaningful way and cannot easily be attributed to the Commonwealth. Line agencies are often aware of this problem, but the issue has not fully crystalised at the centre of government.

In budgetary reporting we have frequently changed the formal requirements and added the emphasis on reporting impact intentions (perhaps for the better), but we have a long way to go to find an appropriate balance of disclosure and provide meaningful information.

Some key propositions and observations from Australia's trajectory of reform

Looking back on the trajectory of reform over the past 30–40 years, the following propositions are apparent.

First, governments seem quickly to run out of steam in undertaking budgetary reform. Three to five years seems to be the norm for reform — in the government's first and perhaps second terms especially. They can criticise their predecessors and inherited systems, they have their own new agendas and priorities, and they have enthusiasm as a new government to make changes. They then tire of the reform commitment, are satisfied with their handiwork, and will not allow or contemplate further changes. Two good examples will suffice: the Hawke government (1983–91) introduced most of its budget reform between 1984 and 1987, after which it held the system in place with some gradual adaptations;

the Howard government (1996–2007) introduced its accrual-based outcomes/ outputs framework in 1999 and then largely left the framework unchanged since implementing it. This suggests budget reform itself has a life cycle: conception, development, implementation and consolidation followed by stagnation.

Second, contrary to the allure of 'strategic budgeting', budgets tend to drive policy (not vice-versa), or, put alternatively, form and process drives strategy. The enshrinement of agency-level base budgeting within the outcomes framework further limits the potentiality of budgets to be strategic. If we want to achieve greater strategic direction, we may need to change the way we budget first. There are other models from which we can draw; we may need to strengthen and redesign the 'challenge function', where existing programs are systematically challenged in regard to their continued relevance and effectiveness; we may need to reconsider ways to achieve greater levels of reallocation (including with transfers and entitlements); or we may need to readdress the incentive structures and dependencies between governments and citizens.

Third, at the same time as we have reformed budgeting — especially on the expenditure side, focusing more and more on the smaller discretionary component — so the budget itself has become less important to the economy (and, arguably, to governments and the policy process). Much of the budget works on auto-pilot (consumer price adjustments to programs, bracket-creep with income tax, depreciation schedules, pension and benefit adjustments, etc.). We have structured budget processes to remove the scope for discretion. Surplus funds have been moved into special accounts and quarantined funds (such as the Future Fund, Education Fund and Infrastructure Fund) where discretion is limited. The budget is heavily geared towards transfer payments and citizen entitlements governed by standing appropriations. Governments themselves often recognise this — that is why so much of political presentation on budget day is take up with tax cuts, distractions, proposed future funds or foundations.

Fourth, while much of the Australian budget reform trajectory aimed to consolidate a formerly fragmented set of processes, the system has begun to re-fragment. We set out to prevent cabinets making decisions without costings, without Treasury analysis, and without being able to make assessments of comparative worth of projects and programs. Hence, we consolidated budgetary processes, designed specially tailored Cabinet processes, and argued for annual consolidation and prevention of out-of-budget spending wherever possible. We sought control and we largely achieved it. Then budgets began to be more about 'facilitation' and we relaxed the tightness in process — much of it deliberately. This occasionally comes back to haunt us (for example, the 2007 water announcement of $10 billion, which was not costed or authorised by Cabinet). We have gone through a roller coaster from fragmentation, to control and consolidation, to re-fragmentation. Relaxed controls appear to have suited the political style of the day especially in a post-9/11 security context. But the fragmentation of decision-making comes at a price to the detriment of good governance and strategic leadership.

Fifth, relationships between budgets and performance are difficult and problematic. It is hard to combine or integrate these without avoiding unwanted consequences, perverse or distorting incentives, gaming or capture. While governments constantly talk of relating and integrating performance to budget allocations, they have found it difficult to do in practice. Maybe we should keep these two functions separate and discrete while concentrating on finding better ways to have dialogue between them. We have a long way to go here.

Sixth, we need to appreciate that budget processes not only provide possibilities and scope for governments to do things, but also impose restraints on what governments can do and how they do it. There will always be a tension between these competing forces — the desire for efficiency and effectiveness versus integrity and accountability. These are not the same things, and there is little evidence that they are conflating under new public management or outsourced forms of delivery.

Seventh and finally, although governments talk about the benefits of whole-of-government approaches and meeting priorities together, ministers are still risk averse about interdepartmental collaboration. Budgets allocate to silos, and accrual budgeting has unintentionally made the situation worse, not better. We need to find ways to resource whole-of-government initiatives that give these items the high priority that governments claim.

Appendix 1: What would a 'strategic budget' look like, and who can play the strategic role?

If budgets serve as routine planning instruments, to what extent are they capable of being strategic or of enhancing strategic decision-making? This question raises the age-old public finance issue of effective collective choice between competing alternatives — guns or butter, war or peace, productivity versus lifestyle choices. It also raises the issue of how far resources can be reallocated, and whether inherited allocations remain strategic or need to be changed.

In more recent times, this conundrum has been depicted as the search for the holy grail of 'strategic budgeting' — theoretically conceived notions of strategic decisions leading budgetary allocations, and policy leading financial decisions.

What, then, might a strategic budget look like? How are the terms 'budgeting' and 'strategic decision-making' linked, or how can they be linked? What would be the perceived benefits of a strategic budget process? The term 'strategy' is much over-used, and has many different meanings and interpretations. For politicians, 'strategy' often translates into 'popular', 'successful', 'winning options'. Ministers may only have broad and amorphous notions of strategic directions (ideas, priorities, immediate goals) that need to be integrated with operational concerns. For administrators, words such as 'consistency', 'direction' and 'integration' often come to the fore. In most cases, bureaucrats become concerned with strategic direction, meaning that 'strategy' is often a bureaucratic discourse — part of preparing themselves to be responsive to political/government priorities.

Officials generally consider a strategic budget — or a strategic-driven budget process — as a blueprint or coherent overall plan, making sense of resource determinations and providing unambiguous direction. To many, it would ideally include the following characteristics:

- clear directions and articulation of objectives and priorities;
- policy decisions drive the finances and allocative efficiencies;
- the focus is on the budget in total not on the margins;
- governments look to longer-term time frames and anticipatory planning in relation to future expected demands;
- more reliable information on results and outcomes achieved;
- indications of relative success are acknowledged and maintained; and
- the processes of budget-setting align with the government's strategy.

This is not the system of budgeting we see today in Australia, although elements can be detected in the present practices.

References

ALP (Australian Labor Party) 1983, 'Labor and Quality of Government'.

ANAO (Australian National Audit Office) 2006, 'Application of the Outcomes and Outputs Framework', Audit Report No. 23, 2006–07.

Australian Government 1984, 'Budgetary Reform', AGPS, Canberra.

Barrett, P. 1988, 'Emerging Management and Budgetary Issues: The view from the centre', *Canberra Bulletin of Public Administration* 54.

Barton, A. 2006, 'Sense and Nonsense in Government Accrual Accounting and Budgetary Systems', in B. S. Grewal and M. Kumnick (eds), *Engaging the New World: Responses to the knowledge economy*, Melbourne University Press, Melbourne.

Castles, F. 1999, *Comparative Public Policy: Patterns of post-war transformation*, Edward Elgar, Cheltenham.

Chan, M., M. Nizette, L. La Rance, C. Broughton and D. Russell 2002. 'Australia', *OECD Journal on Budgeting*.

Department of Finance and Administration 1998, 'Specifying Outcomes and Outputs: Implementing the Commonwealth's accrual-based outcomes and outputs framework'.

Di Francesco, M. 1998, 'The Measure of Policy?: Evaluating the evaluation strategy as an instrument for budgetary control', *Australian Journal of Public Administration* 57(1), pp. 33–48.

Graycar, A. 2007, 'Central Agencies: Leadership or treading on toes', *Public Administration Today* 12.

Graycar, A. and B. McCann 2012, 'Implementation: Making hard work of something simple', *Australian Journal of Public Administration* 71(3).

Halligan, J. 2004, 'The Australian Public Service: Redefining boundaries', in J. Halligan (ed.), *Civil Service Systems in Anglo-American Countries*, Edward Elgar, Cheltenham.

Heclo, H. and A. Wildavsky 1974, *The Private Government of Public Money*, Macmillan, London.

Henry, K. 2007, 'Treasury's Effectiveness in the Current Environment', speech to Treasury staff, 14th March.

IMF 1999, 'Code of Good Practices on Fiscal Transparency'.

Keating, M. 1989, 'Quo Vadis?: Challenges of public administration', *Australian Journal of Public Administration* 48(2).

Keating, M. 1990, 'The Processes of Commonwealth Budgetary Control', in J. Forster and J. Wanna (eds), *Budgetary Management and Control*, Macmillan, Melbourne.

Keating, M. and G. Dixon 1989, *Making Economic Policy in Australia, 1983–1988*, Longman Cheshire, Melbourne.

Keating, M. and M. Holmes 1990, 'Australia's Budgetary and Financial Management Reforms', *Governance* 3(2).

Kelly, J. and J. Wanna 2001, 'Are Wildavsky's Guardians and Spenders Still Relevant?: New public management and the politics of government budgeting', in L. Jones, J. Guthrie and P. Steane (eds), *Learning From International Public Management Reform*, Elsevier Science, Amsterdam.

Kelly, J. and J. Wanna 2004, 'Crashing Through with Accrual-Output Price Budgeting in Australia', *American Review of Public Administration* 34(1).

Laurie, K. and J. McDonald 2008, 'A Perspective on Trends in Australian Government Spending', Commonwealth Treasury, Canberra.

Management Advisory Board 1997, 'Beyond Bean-Counting: Effective financial management in the APS — 1998 and beyond', Management Advisory Board, Canberra.

Minchin, N. 2006, Speech to the 27th Annual Meeting of Senior Budget Officials of the OECD, Sydney, 5th June.

Murray, A. 2008, 'A Review of Operation Sunlight: Overhauling budgetary transparency', Report to the Finance Minister, Andrew Murray, June.

National Commission of Audit 1996, 'Report of the Commission', AGPS, Canberra.

New Zealand Treasury 1984, 'Economic Management', Wellington.

OECD 2001, 'OECD Best Practices for Budget Transparency', May, Paris.

OECD 2004, 'Senior Budget Officials Newsletter', February.

O'Faircheallaigh, C., J. Wanna and P. Weller 1999, *Public Sector Management in Australia: New challenges, new directions*, Macmillan, Melbourne.

Parliament of Australia 1995, 'Financial Reporting for the Commonwealth: Towards greater transparency and accountability', Joint Committee of Public Accounts, November.

Parliament of Australia 1998, 'Charter of Budget Honesty Bill 1996', Bills Digest No. 142 1997–98.

Schick, A. 2001, 'The Changing Role of the Central Budget Office', *OECD Journal on Budgeting* 1(1).

Schick, A. 2002, 'Does Budgeting Have a Future?', *OECD Journal on Budgeting* 2(2).

Schick, A. 2007, Presentation to ANZSOG Seminar: Public Budgeting, ANU, Canberra.

Senate Standing Committee on Finance and Public Administration 2007, 'Transparency and Accountability of Commonwealth Public Funding and Expenditure', Commonwealth of Australia, March.

Tanner, L. 2006, 'Operation Sunlight: Enhancing budget transparency', ALP, Canberra.

Tanner, L. 2008, 'A List of Labor's Proposed Reforms', email to David Uren, *The Australian* from Finance Minister, 14 April.

Walsh, P. 1995, *Confessions of a Failed Finance Minister*, Random House, Sydney.

Wanna, J. 2006, 'Between a Rock and a Hard Place: The nonsense of Australia's Charter of Budget Honesty Act 1998', paper delivered to the Australasian Political Studies Association conference, Newcastle.

Wanna, J. 2011, 'Treasury and Economic Policy: Beyond the dismal science', *Australian Journal of Public Administration* 70(4), pp. 347–364.

Wanna, J., L. Jensen and J. de Vries (eds) 2003, *Controlling Public Expenditure*, Edward Elgar, Cheltenham.

Wanna, J., L. Jensen and J. de Vries (eds) 2010, *The Reality of Budgetary Reform in the OECD Nations*, Edward Elgar, Cheltenham.

Wanna, J., J. Kelly and J. Forster 2000, *Managing Public Expenditure in Australia*, Allen & Unwin, Sydney.

Wildavsky, A. 1964, *The New Politics of the Budgetary Process*, Pearson Longman, New York.

Wildavsky, A. and N. Caiden 2004, *The New Politics of the Budgetary Process*, 5th ed., Pearson Longman, New York.

6. Constrained Parliamentarism: Australia and New Zealand compared[1]

Harshan Kumarasingham and John Power

Introduction

It has been an eternal quest to limit the powers of the executive. In the 'new Westminsters'[2] of the Commonwealth, the Montesquieuan model of separation of powers was theoretically influential and yet practically avoided, as in the UK. Aside from the US and Westminster models, Bruce Ackerman has argued of a third model of democratic governance in the wake of the Second World War: constrained parliamentarism. This model sits between the presidentialist American form of Montesquieu and the parliamentary sovereignty that affords the British executive a near elective dictatorship. Constrained parliamentarism 'rejects the US separation between executive and legislature and grants broad powers to the governmental coalition that gains parliamentary support. It rejects Westminster by insulating sensitive functions from political control' (Ackerman 2007). This framework of Ackerman's has mainly been confined to public law scholars.[3] Applying this model to the field of comparative politics, Power has examined this both theoretically and through the example of Australia (Power 2010, 2012), which placed the earlier writings of Ackerman (2000) at its centre. Recently, we have also used this approach on New Zealand (Kumarasingham and Power 2013). In the penultimate section of this chapter, we briefly consider the reasons why we — unlike virtually all other students of comparative governance — have found Ackerman so central. This consideration may open some new perspectives on comparative studies of regimes. According to Ackerman, there are 'three legitimating ideals' informing his approach to constrained parliamentarism:

> The first ideal is democracy. In one way or another, separation [of branches of governance] may serve (or hinder) the project of popular self-government. The second ideal is professional competence. Democratic laws

---

1   The New Zealand sections of this chapter are drawn from our article, Kumarasingham and Power 2013.
2   This term was used by Kumarasingham 2010a and 2013 to describe states that had taken the Westminster system and adapted it from Britain.
3   A recent examination found that all but four of 69 references to the Ackerman essay were in law journals.

remain purely symbolic unless courts and bureaucracies can implement them in a relatively impartial way. The third ideal is the protection and enhancement of fundamental rights (Ackerman 2000, p. 640)

Ackerman then goes on to consider a number of institutional specifics that he contended best furthered these legitimating ideals; eight were already in existence in some regimes around the world.

In seeking to employ this framework in the development of a theory of fiducial governance, Power has adapted and modified it. In particular, he has shaped a different approach to strategic constitutional reform issues. In this chapter, we step back to consider an important question in the comparative study of governance: the assessment of the regimes of Australia and New Zealand in the context of the original Ackerman framework. For our project, it is important to ask which of these regimes conforms more closely to the ideals of constrained parliamentarism?

Australia and New Zealand compared

Australia and New Zealand, in creating their own states, evoked Britain and transplanted the system they knew best: the Westminster System (Patapan, Wanna and Weller 2005). This legacy was critical for executive power. The legacy of Royal Prerogatives travelled to the Antipodes also for the use of the local executive. Power became just as centralised as Westminster with few institutional restraints and the focus clearly on the executive. Dissipation of power was neither sought nor encouraged.

> Royal tradition helps to explain other characteristics. It is hierarchical; participants look to the leadership for guidance and assume a degree of authority: not quite the Stuart version of divine right, but sometimes a level of obeisance that comes close. Prime ministers can appoint; prime ministers can fire. Power is centralised; it may have moved from the monarch to the prime minister or cabinet, but power-sharing comes hard even within the traditions of collective government (Rhodes, Wanna and Weller 2009, p. 49).

This bequest meant that in new Westminsters such as Australia and New Zealand, there was a 'legacy of vague accountabilities and fertile ground for Executive dominance' (Kumarasingham 2013). Australasian adaptions also meant both states are distinct not only from Britain, but from each other. However, New Zealand and Australia have enough resemblances at the executive level of the 'first among equals' variety perennially to draw attention to the substantial powers of the centre operating in a well-established parliamentary environment. In the

Westminster tradition, conventions surround these executives with flexibility and opacity, which promotes expectations and evasions of how power should and should not be used. It is in this context that we compare and assess these two Australasian countries.

With the the six features shared by the two regimes shown first, the eight enacted institutional specifics identified by Ackerman are:

- parliamentary democracy;
- professional public service;
- independent judiciary;
- securing human rights;
- integrity of major institutions;
- serial referenda;
- federal structure; and
- strong upper house.

On any mechanistic assessment, Australia would clearly conform more closely to the constrained parliamentarism institutional specifics, for it has a federal system, and most of its jurisdictions possess bicameral legislatures. However — and the raising of this question challenges one of the key premises of the Ackerman approach — does this mean that the legitimating ideals are therefore more fully realised in Australia than in New Zealand? Whatever our answer to this first question, we go on at the end of this chapter to consider the use of the modified Ackerman framework for the comparative study of governance regimes. We do this by comparing it with the very different framework proposed by the Canadian scholar Alan Siaroff, in his impressive work, *Comparing Political Regimes* (2009).

In approaching these questions, we shall naturally build on the work already done on Australia. In particular, we shall rely on Power's use of the recent work of Sawer et al., *Australia: The state of democracy* (2009), for on most of the Ackerman specifics they provide instructive assessments of the strengths and weaknesses of the Australian regime. In what follows, we shall provide summaries of the treatment of each of the eight institutional specifics in the Power monograph. As we proceed down the list, we shall make some comparisons with the New Zealand experience on each institutional specific.

Parliamentary democracy

Reviewing the comprehensive listings by Sawer et al. of the 27 strengths and 32 weaknesses of the Australian system, Power has focused on the ways in which long-established interests have continued to be still largely unchallenged. He attributed this dominance primarily to the heavy constraints imposed by the nation's constitution. In contrast, governing elites in New Zealand have been less heavily constrained in adapting to changing times. Thus there has been, in recent years, much stronger representation of women in Parliament in New Zealand than in Australia (Siaroff 2009, p. 165), and indigenous minorities have also enjoyed stronger representation. One important benchmark for estimating the strength of the legislature is the relative strength of its committee systems (Halligan, Miller and Power 2007). While in recent years there has been a considerable strengthening of the influence of committees in the Australian Parliament, the influence of their New Zealand counterparts remains stronger.

New Zealand's adoption of the mixed member proportional (MMP) electoral system in time for the 1996 general election changed the nature of its democracy. The two-party system and with it the majoritarian manner of politics, which had been the mainstay of much of modern New Zealand politics, was replaced by a proportional system that emphasised representation and multiparty coalition. MMP ushered in new conventions of democracy (Palmer and Palmer 2004). Not only did new parties come into the Parliament, but also more women, Maori, ethnic groups and political viewpoints. After decades of one party cabinets, the governing elites had to contend with making coalition agreements beyond their party and often without pre-election agreements. However, the executive itself in 'its day-to-day functioning has changed relatively little', nor has MMP altered the principal fact that in New Zealand 'executive power is [still] concentrated in a Cabinet that is founded, in general, upon convention, not law' (Boston and Bullock 2009). Indeed, the Key Cabinets from 2008 to the present have been like the cabinets of first past the post (FPP) days in having only one party represented, since the support party ministers sit outside Cabinet. The multi-party governing arrangements that have characterised the post-FPP era, whether labelled or typified as coalitions or minority governments with outside support, has not altered the formal powers of the executive and MMP has not provided any new institutional constraints upon it. The New Zealand regime adopted the German MMP electoral system without importing the other aspects of German polity, which provide 'veto players' or constraints on the executive and institutions, such as its Constitutional Court, federal system, European Union, written constitution, and the Bundestag's power of 'constructive' votes of no-confidence (Helms 2000). New Zealand's institutional closet remains bare compared to the German constitutional structure whose electoral system it chose to emulate.

Professional public service

In attempting to explain the steady politicisation of Australian public services in recent decades, Power attributed considerable importance to the disappearance of senior collegial bodies (such as public service boards). Without these traditionally important constraints, the offices of public service commissioners have been marginalised in modern managerialist times.

The public service reforms of the mid-1980s in New Zealand were arguably the most radical in the Commonwealth (Prebble 2010). Some of those reforms were the separation of the government's trading interests from its non-commercial activities (establishing state-owned enterprises, in sectors from rail to telecommunications, required to return dividends to the Crown), the restructuring of departments to a smaller, more market-orientated design where roles such as policy and operations were split, the introduction of output budgeting, and the reallocation of responsibility of employment decisions from a central public service commission to the heads of departments (now called chief executives). The chief executives themselves were now placed on short-term contracts and employed by the statutory State Services Commissioner, but were free to employ their own staff. These structural reforms have not been without controversy, with many public servants losing their jobs due to the restructuring and privatisation. However, most commentators contend that the public service is now 'more efficient and performance orientated'. Like Australia, the public service has been forced to surrender its monopoly of providing advice to ministers with use of consultants and advisors increasing by creating 'contestability in the market for policy advice' (Shaw 2006). These developments have caused one seasoned commentator to ask whether the public service is still capable of looking after the longer-term public interest (James 2009). Indeed, with the campaign to reduce public expenditure in the public services, there is a rumour that even the institution designed to represent and guard the interest of professional public service, the State Services Commission, could itself face abolition as some of its functions have already been transferred elsewhere (*Dominion Post*, 31 May 2011).

Independent judiciary

In the words of a former Chief Justice of the High Court (of Australia), the Court has 'an uneasy and ill-defined relationship with the other arms of government' (Mason in Patapan 2000, p. viii). The principal reason for this unsatisfactory state of affairs has been the court's clear recognition in recent years of the political dimension of much of its work. By discarding the apolitical mask, the Court has, of course, laid itself open to the claims of the underprivileged, as was most recently illustrated in the November 2010 decision (*Plaintiffs M61 and M69 of 2010 v Commonwealth of Australia*), which drove a large hole in the Commonwealth's border protection arrangements. (It is difficult to believe that the New Zealand judiciary would be so assertive vis-à-vis its political executive). The discarding of one orthodoxy has, however, not yet been followed by a coherent statement of the nature and boundaries of the form of politics with which the judiciary is now grappling. In the absence of such an understanding, we find that some attorneys-general are now refusing to play the traditional roles of defenders of the judiciary when they face political attack.

New Zealand's judiciary also has a difficult relationship with the executive. In 2003, the government ended appeals to the London-based Privy Council without a referendum and established the Supreme Court as the highest appellate court. The government has openly quarrelled with the Supreme Court, especially over questions about Indigenous land rights and prison policy. In recent years the Supreme Court has consistently been told to 'stick to the bench'. New Zealand attorneys-general and other related ministers have openly criticised the judiciary in Parliament and the press. This was especially apparent with the controversy surrounding the *Seabed and Foreshore Act 2004* (Stockley 2006). As Chief Justice Dame Sian Elias recently commented, 'In New Zealand the independence of the judiciary from other sources of state power is fragile.' Unlike the UK, Canada and Australia, administrative autonomy is not held by the judges, but by the executive through the Ministry of Justice (Elias 2011).

Securing human rights

In Australia, as elsewhere in many regimes in the British Commonwealth (including the UK and New Zealand), discourse on this topic in recent years has been dominated by the 'charter' approach (for a recent important example, see Australian Human Rights Commission 2009). In regimes adopting this approach (which in Australia have included Victoria and the Australian Capital Territory), the ultimate formal sovereignty of the Parliament is not questioned. However, the judiciary is empowered to refer back to the Parliament and the government any conflicts it might perceive between statutorily recognised human rights, on the one hand, and measures in proposed legislation, on the other. In such cases, it is then up to the Parliament to determine what to do. One defect in all the current charter arrangements has been noted by Power (2010, pp. 39–40). Although they are all supposed to stimulate greater dialogue between the branches of government, there has been a lack of a suitable collegial body through which such dialogue could be conducted. The councils of state proposed by Power would supply such a suitable institutional site (Power 2010, pp. 52 ff.).

For New Zealand, the 1840 Treaty of Waitangi holds a central symbolic and political place in the human rights of the nation. This treaty between Maori and the Crown was initially viewed by a nineteenth-century Chief Justice as a 'simple nullity' and it is still denied general effect by a single statute and does not have any overriding effect. However, it has moral force and is given specific legal effect in particular pieces of legislation. The Treaty is also used by the Waitangi Tribunal in its recommendations on claims against the Crown and to aid the interpretation of statutes in the courts. Former President of the Court of Appeal Lord Cooke of Thorndon ruled in 1993 that 'the Treaty created an enduring relationship of a fiduciary nature akin to partnership. Each party [Maori and Crown] accepting a positive duty to act in good faith, fairly, reasonably, and honourably towards each other'. Cooke referred to it as 'simply the most important document in New Zealand's history', a far cry from the opinions of his predecessors on the New Zealand bench. Though it is not entrenched, it is a strong influence and the 'Cabinet Manual' requires Cabinet papers to identify any implications of proposed policies in terms of the Treaty and executive proposals for legislation must demonstrate their consistency with Treaty principles (Palmer and Palmer 2004, pp. 336–348).

Along with the Treaty of Waitangi, New Zealand has placed high importance on human rights since it helped draft the UN Declaration on Human Rights in 1948. The human rights commissioners are appointed by the Governor-General on the advice of the Minister of Justice and report to the Prime Minister over New Zealand's compliance with international human rights legislation. The Human Rights Commission also monitors and makes inquiries into infringements of human rights and often makes public statements on such issues. New Zealand has always believed it has led the world in human rights, with its status as the first country to legislate for women to vote, the introduction of old age pensions in the 1890s, and, as a recent report made by New Zealand to the United Nations on Human Rights states, 'The idea that everyone deserves an equal opportunity in life — "a fair go" — is an important part of New Zealand's national identity and approach to human rights on the international stage' (New Zealand National Universal Periodic Review 2010).

Integrity of major institutions

The starting point for any discussion under this heading must be the important National Integrity Systems Assessment report, which has called for each Australian jurisdiction to create a 'non-partisan' governance review council to coordinate the activities of the several bodies now concerned with issues of institutional integrity. It has also stressed the need for these councils to gain 'institutional champions' (Griffith University Institute for Ethics, Governance and Law and Transparency International 2005, p. 61; see also Head et al. 2008), and it is hard to see how political leaders could not be prominent among these champions.

The obvious place to start a search for such champions is the list of institutions provided by the report's mapping exercise. Here we encounter a most surprising omission, for there is no acknowledgement of the integrity role that is being played, or could be played, by the head of state. Both former Governor-General

Paul Hasluck, who introduced important innovations in this area, and former Victorian Governor Richard McGarvie, who emerged a few years ago as the latest champion of the Hasluck approach (McGarvie 1999), are ignored.

New Zealand's 1982 *Official Information Act* has been successful in promoting transparency and availability of information from the bureaucracy. Indeed, New Zealand has the enviable title of being the least corrupt country in the world (Transparency International 2013) and its public service has high standards of political neutrality in the Westminster tradition. However, institutions that administer the country are often weak against the powers of the executive. New Zealand's compact and centralised institutions are dominated by the executive. The head of state, House of Representatives, judiciary and other limited state institutions are either unable or unwilling to provide strong scrutiny of the executive. This has been shown throughout New Zealand history.

This occasionally elicits concern, with examples such as the *Environment Act* passed in May 2010, which sacked elected Environment Canterbury councillors and replaced them with government-appointed ones and delayed new elections until at least 2013 (*The Press*, 30 March 2010), or the September 2010 *Canterbury Earthquake Response and Recovery Act* which in the wake of earthquakes in the region gave the executive massive power to intervene by Order-in-Council, which cannot be challenged by the courts (New Zealand Law Society 2010). However, as part of the 2008 Confidence and Supply Agreement between the Maori and National parties, these actors have recently begun moves to establish a framework for the 'Consideration of Constitutional Issues' to examine New Zealand's constitutional arrangements, especially concerning the Treaty of Waitangi (Office of the Deputy Prime Minister of New Zealand 2010). How much this makes any progress for constitutional analysis or reform remains to be seen as the 2004–05 all party Constitutional Arrangements Committee had a similar brief, but achieved little.

Referenda

The Australian Constitution has proven extremely difficult to change, with only eight proposals (of 44) being approved in referenda during more than a century. It is now more than a decade since any referendum was put to the people. Australia is thus far away from Ackerman's preferred state — where the citizenry would regularly be accorded the opportunity to vote on major issues. Few commentators have considered the possibility that it has been the party system that has been responsible for many of the negative votes. While it has been widely recognised that bipartisan agreement has been a necessary prerequisite for success, few have pondered the implications of the observation of former Prime Minister John Howard that often even the securing of such agreement might be counterproductive, in that the citizenry might have well-founded suspicions that anything that the major parties agreed on might well serve their shared interests rather than the public interest. Clearly, any reforms that improved the fiducial standing of the party system could improve the chances of referendum success, as would regular referendum experience for the citizenry.

Constitutional change in New Zealand is easier than overseas and has far fewer hurdles to surmount than Australia. However, this has not meant that referenda have been carriers of change to the New Zealand regime. Indeed, with the very notable exception of MMP, all the major constitutional changes to New Zealand's regime over the past 60 years have been delivered by the governing elite to the people without referenda. Referenda have been sporadic in New Zealand. Part of the reason for this is that unlike Australia, for example, there is no requirement to hold referenda on particular issues. Since 1993, New Zealanders have been able to initiate their own referenda and there have been almost 40 such citizen-initiated petitions. However, a successful petition needs the signatures of 10 per cent of the electorate, and only three petitions have satisfied this requirement and come to vote. In conjunction with the November 2011 general election, the New Zealand electorate was asked in a referendum whether to retain MMP. Almost 58 per cent of the voters favoured the retention of MMP. As stipulated by the *Electoral Referendum Act* (2010), the Electoral Commission held its own independent review of MMP. However, this review's findings, presented in October 2012, predictably did not advocate major institutional reforms, but instead provided suggestions for technical changes within the existing institutional framework (New Zealand Electoral Commission 2012).

Federal structure

The most recent review of the condition of Australian federalism (Fenna 2009, p. 155) concluded that there was little compelling reason to support the continuation of the system, for there 'has been the apparent absence of any sociological basis for divided jurisdiction in this country'. It could be, however, that there are other reasons — such as improvement in the quality of governance through a regime of serial referenda — that could still be persuasive. The best of the students of modern Australian federalism, Brian Galligan, has attempted to show how strong popular involvement has imparted republican legitimacy to the system.

Galligan searchingly uncovered and criticised a number of the premises that had long dominated thinking about the Australian constitutional system. His great accomplishment is to demonstrate that all the various proponents of responsible government have paid insufficient attention to the considerable constraints that have been placed on all our governments and their constituent branches by our federal constitutional framework. These constraints are, in Galligan's view (1995, p. 14), appropriate and legitimate, because federation entailed a 'transformative act of the Australian people'. In this respect, he is aligning himself with one of the two traditions that have dominated Australia's 'dual constitutional culture': the federal (which Galligan favours), and parliamentary responsible government (Galligan 1995, p. 50). However, the blocking of full parliamentary responsible government carries considerable costs. As Sawer et al. (2009, p. 295) have recently observed: 'The system creates subnational "veto points" that can obstruct policy which a national government has been elected to enact and hence frustrates "the will of the people".'

This leads us to a problem: whether the contemporary citizenry will be satisfied that it has participated sufficiently in the shaping of the Australian constitutional framework for it to be accorded full democratic legitimacy. Unlike Galligan, who has been quite content to contend that the necessary constitutional legitimation was achieved in Australia in the one founding moment more than a century ago, Ackerman (2007, p. 1800) explicitly considers the implications of long lapses in time: 'It is one thing for South Africans or Germans to follow a constitution handed down a decade, or a half-century, ago; quite another for Americans to cling to an antique text that fails to mark any of the nation's recent achievements.'

The issues raised by Galligan and others on the Australian state are interesting when compared with New Zealand. Martin (2001) has convincingly demonstrated that the federal movement enjoyed much stronger support from colonial political leaders in Australia than in New Zealand. New Zealand is unitary, unicameral, and continues with an unwritten constitution (Levine 2004). Because of the absence of the above, New Zealand lacks any sub-national 'veto points' that can frustrate 'the will of the people'. Again, unlike Australia, there are limited avenues for the 'will of the people' to be expressed other than at triennial national elections. New Zealand's parliamentary responsible government is not responsible in a deliberative democracy way, as there are few forums other than the executive dominated single house chamber for this to occur, and minimal conventions on consultation on policy and constitutional matters. Two recent events in local government demonstrate the centralising and unitary favouring nature of the New Zealand regime. From November 2010, Auckland became a 'super city' with the elimination of the regional council and the dis-establishment of seven city and district councils to make one powerful unitary 'super council' — the largest in Australasia (Royal Commission on Auckland Governance 2009). Perhaps this could make Auckland a sub-national veto point, but if so this will be at central government behest. The propensity for central interference was also seen in May 2010 when the elected Environment Canterbury councillors were sacked using legislation passed under urgency. The council members were replaced by government-appointed ones and new elections were delayed until at least 2013, after disputes continued over Canterbury's water management (*The Press*, 30 March 2010).

Strong upper house

Bicameralism does not sit easily with Westminster regimes, but is nonetheless common in them. As the Abbe Sieyes observed long ago, if the governing party controls the upper house, much of what that house does is superfluous. If, on the other hand, the government of the day does not control the upper house, much of what it does will be obstructive (Uhr 2008, p. 13).[4] Upper houses retain their attractiveness, however, for the more consensually-minded democrats, for in most jurisdictions they have shown greater readiness than their lower house colleagues to become involved in policy development through committee activity (Halligan et al. 2007). In modern democratic times, the balance of power has shifted towards lower houses in most bicameral regimes. In the Australian states, for example, most upper houses have lost much of their blocking powers. Contemporary theorising has also followed this trend; thus Ackerman's framework of constrained parliamentarianism envisages an upper house with only 'half' powers.

Although Ackerman (2000, pp. 671 ff.) gives some consideration to federalism as one of the constraints in his framework, he does so in a curiously limited way. His discussion of federalism is devoted almost totally to the ways in which it can shape upper houses at the national level. In his advocacy of German-style 'half-house' upper houses, he gives insufficient attention to the optimal balance that should be struck between the powers of an upper house, on the one hand, and its effectiveness, on the other. The Australian experience suggests that a 'half-house' upper house might not be powerful enough to be properly effective and that greater powers might therefore be desirable, even though these powers might occasionally be misused. In addition, Ackerman's focus on the relation between federalism and his preferred 'one-and-a-half' legislature raises a serious problem that he does not consider. Upper houses in federal systems are more likely to be in serious political conflict with their lower houses than are upper houses in unitary systems (Tsebelis and Money 1997, p. 212).

There have been strong voices expressing a view contrary to that of Ackerman — that accountability should weigh more heavily than democracy. Consider, for example, some of the arguments recently advanced in the revealingly entitled volume *Restraining Elective Dictatorship: The upper house solution.*

---

4 An innovation in Singapore has shown how the review function so often associated with upper houses might in a unicameral regime be discharged by another institution — in the case of Singapore, none other than a directly elected presidency: see Tan 1997.

In the opening chapter of the volume, the editors make the important point that 'an institution with its own democratic credentials constitutes a far more substantial accountability hurdle than any creation of ordinary statute law' (Prasser et al. 2008, p. 6). They do not, however, go beyond the Parliament in their search for appropriate democratic mechanisms for holding the executive to account. Like the contributors that follow them, they do not directly address the problem caused by rigid party discipline. Instead, they seem to assume that the benefits of having an upper house that lacks a government majority will always outweigh the costs.

The Legislative Council of New Zealand was abolished in 1951 with alarming ease and was never replaced, though there have been several attempts to replace it. In its near 100 years of existence the non-elected Legislative Council did little to improve accountability or scrutiny of the executive (Jackson 1972; Kumarasingham 2010a). However, there have been numerous attempts and ideas first to reform and then to replace the Legislative Council; over 60 years on, the idea still has a few embers burning. The interest in bicameralism in New Zealand is in whether it could improve the institutional and deliberative performance of the state and act as a check on the executive, which still retains its hegemony despite MMP. Arguably many of the most controversial constitutional episodes since the abolition of the upper house could have been slowed at the very least with a renovated upper house in place. An upper house could have provided greater deliberation and accountability of such controversial events as the divisive 1951 waterfront strike and the government's draconian response to it, the divisive social policies and economic autarky of Muldoon, and the radical privatisation under the fourth Labour government, which were often enacted without electoral mandate (Kumarasingham 2010a and 2010b; Aroney and Thomas 2012).

Palmer and others have argued that select committees are New Zealand's answer to any need of an upper house (Palmer and Palmer 2004). The 1985 reforms designed to strengthen their powers and extend their jurisdiction were introduced to toughen the legislature's power to hold the executive accountable. Though MMP has changed the complexion of the committees so that more parties are represented, they are still simulacrums of parliamentary strength and therefore executive influence. Indeed, the Key government (and similar moves happened under Clark) has even appointed a Minister to head a select committee showing the limits of their democratic parliamentary ability to resist executive instruction let alone being able to robustly scrutinise and hold the executive to account.

Excursus? Two approaches to the comparative study of regimes: Ackerman and Siaroff compared

At first glance, the work of Siaroff (2009) appears to be closer than Ackerman (2000) to the central purposes of our governance project. He attends more closely to contemporary head of state functions. Indeed, his identification of the 13 regimes where the head of state plays a corrective role is a valuable update of earlier work that he had done.[5] Which brings us to the issue flagged at the outset: why has the Ackerman framework proven to be especially relevant to our concerns? In order to address this important question, we shall introduce a comparison of Ackerman with a more 'mainstream' student of comparative governance – Siaroff (2009). In his impressive work, *Comparing Political Regimes* (which, like all other mainstream works, ignores Ackerman), Siaroff suggests an original way of comparing New Zealand and Australia:

Table 1: Electoral System Centralism versus Localism

		Electoral system and election centralism *versus* localism	
		Lower	Higher
Supermajoritarianism	Higher	Australia	
	Lower		New Zealand

Source: Adapted from Siaroff 2009, Figure 8.1.

While this table strikingly suggests strong differences between the two regimes, we remain unsure of its heuristic standing. What, if anything, is the significance of Australia sharing a cell with Canada, Colombia, Comoros, India, Madagascar, Mauritania, Mexico, Micronesia, Palau, and the United States? What is the significance of New Zealand sharing a cell with Andorra, Estonia, Finland, Lesotho, Mauritius, Samoa, and San Marino?

---

5   On his reading of this earlier work — Siaroff 2003 — Power had nominated only six such 'corrective' regimes where the heads of state played roles similar to that had been developed in Australia by Governor-General Hasluck (1979). The fuller list now supplied by Siaroff provides ample opportunities for the investigation of the ways in which heads of state around the world have managed the 'dual mandate' problem that has so vexed many Australian republicans: Power 2008. All 13 of the regimes identified are 'semi-presidential' — Elgie 2004; Elgie and Moestrup 2007, 2008 — i.e. they have a directly elected head of state confronting a head of government enjoying the confidence of the legislature: Bulgaria*, Croatia, Ireland*, Lithuania*, Macedonia*, Mongolia, Poland*, Portugal, Romania*, Taiwan, Timor–Leste, Turkey (whose head of state will first be directly elected only in 2014), and the Ukraine. (NB: those marked with * are those earlier selected by Power).

Of rather more interest in the current context is Siaroff's understanding of 'supermajoritarianism', for it represents a rather mechanical expression of Ackerman's constraints. We can most conveniently see this if we list the seven variables that Siaroff uses to construct his index of supermajoritarianism:

- existence of sub-national governments of some power;
- bicameralism in the national legislature;
- judicial review of legislation;
- office of head of state with some power;
- referenda;
- consociational democracy; and
- difficulty of amending the constitution.

This brief comparison indicates a conclusion that at first glance does not seem all that striking: the approaches of differing students of comparative governance are heavily shaped by their purposes. Siaroff's work is aimed at deepening our understanding of the key variables that underpin differing levels of performance of modern regimes. Ackerman, on the other hand, is more tightly focused on the openings for institutional reform offered by differing regimes. It is for this reason that we have found the Ackerman framework more useful for our project, for we are ultimately concerned with constitutional reform. While this concluding observation about differing purposes leading to different approaches and choices might seem commonplace enough, it is one that is seldom explicitly advanced in writings on comparative governance. It is time that it was.

Conclusion

This chapter strongly suggests that the concept of constraint is more nuanced and complex than we had thought when we began composing it. Conventionally, 'constraint' is typically used as a virtual synonym with 'restraint'. In order to correct this unduly negative conception, Power, following Ackerman, has contended that many constraints are better conceptualised as limits that support as they restrain. In our explorations, however, we have come to a somewhat different conclusion, for the nature of constraints varies considerably from one context to another. In general, constraints on executive power have been heavier and more rigid in Australia than in New Zealand, and are so experienced by members of political executives. Nothing constrains a political executive more heavily than the embedding of other political interests in long-established institutional structures (for example, those of a federal system).

In a unitary system such as New Zealand's, the constraints may be less heavy, but nonetheless substantial, if only because they have been more freely chosen. Since the Second World War, New Zealand has probably provided more instructive reform lessons that any other nation. From the abolition of the upper house of Parliament by a conservative government in the 1950s, through the most radical restructuring of the public service by a Labour government in the 1980s, to the sweeping overhaul of its electoral system in the 1990s, New Zealand displayed an unquenchable thirst for reform. Unlike the Westminster regime from which it derived, it lacked a set of established constraints on executive power that had evolved over many centuries. Unlike the other 'dominions', it came to lack many of the other institutional constraints — federalism, bicameralism, and a written constitution — that had helped them compensate for the absence of many of these historical constraints. These changes bore heavily on the constraints operating on the national political executive. In some ways, these new patterns of constraint were more demanding of the political executive than were those operating on its counterpart across the Tasman.

This suggests that the main value of the framework of constrained parliamentarism is not that of facilitating comparisons between regimes, but rather that of providing some benchmarks for the systematic tracing of the overall constraining pattern in each regime. Australia and New Zealand need such benchmarks to meaningfully test the health of their democracy.

References

Ackerman, B. 2000, 'The New Separation of Powers', *Harvard Law Review* 113(3), pp. 633–729.

Ackerman, B. 2007, 'Meritocracy v. Democracy', *London Review of Books* 29(5).

Aroney, N. and S. Thomas 2012, 'A House Divided: Does MMP make an upper house unnecessary for New Zealand?', *New Zealand Law Review* 403.

Australian Human Rights Commission 2009, 'National Human Rights Consultation Report', Australian Human Rights Commission, Canberra.

Boston, J. and D. Bullock 2009, 'Experiments in Executive Government under MMP in New Zealand: Contrasting approaches to multi-party governance', *New Zealand Journal of Public and International Law* 7(1), pp 39–76.

Elias, D. S. 2011, 'Fundamentals: A constitutional conversation', *Waikato Law Review* 19, p 8

Elgie, R. (ed.) 2004, *Semi-Presidentialism in Europe*, Oxford University Press, Oxford.

Elgie, R. and S. Moestrup (eds) 2007, *Semi-Presidentialism Outside Europe: A comparative study*, Routledge, London.

Elgie, R. and S. Moestrup (eds) 2008, *Semi-Presidentialism in Central and Eastern Europe*, Palgrave Macmillan, Basingstoke.

Fenna, A. 2009, 'Federalism', in R. A. W. Rhodes (ed.), *The Australian Study of Politics*, Palgrave Macmillan, Basingstoke, pp. 146–159.

Galligan, B. 1995, *A Federal Republic: Australia's constitutional system of government*, Cambridge University Press, Cambridge.

Griffith University Institute for Ethics, Governance and Law and Transparency International 2005, *Chaos or Coherence: Strengths, opportunities and challenges for Australia's integrity systems*, NISA, Brisbane.

Halligan, J., R. Miller and J. Power 2007, *Parliament in the Twenty-First Century: Institutional reform and emerging roles*, Melbourne University Press, Carlton.

Hasluck, Paul 1979, *The Office of the Governor-General*, Melbourne University Press, Carlton South.

Head, B. W., A. J. Brown and C. Connors (eds) 2008, *Promoting Integrity: Evaluating and improving public institutions*, Farnham, Ashgate.

Helms, L. (ed.) 2000, *Institutions and Institutional Change in the Federal Republic of Germany*, London, Macmillan.

High Court of Australia 2010, *Plaintiff M61/2010E v Commonwealth of Australia; Plaintiff M69/2010 v Commonwealth of Australia*, 272 ALR 14.

Jackson, W. K. 1972, *The New Zealand Legislative Council: A study of the establishment, failure and abolition of an Upper House*, University of Otago Press, Dunedin.

James, C. 2009, 'Who Guards the Guardians?', address to the New Zealand Institute of Public Administration.

Kumarasingham, H. 2010a, *Onward with Executive Power: Lessons from New Zealand 1947–57*, Victoria University of Wellington/Institute of Policy Studies, Wellington.

Kumarasingham, H. 2010b, 'What if New Zealand had Reintroduced an Upper House?' in S. Levine (ed.), *New Zealand as it Might Have Been 2*, Victoria University of Wellington Press, Wellington, pp. 253–270.

Kumarasingham, H. 2013, 'Exporting Executive Accountability? Westminster Legacies of Executive Power', *Parliamentary Affairs*, 66(3), pp. 579–596.

Kumarasingham, H. and J. Power 2013, 'Constrained Parliamentarism in the New Zealand Regime', *Commonwealth & Comparative Politics* 51(2), pp. 234–253.

Levine, S. 2004, 'Parliamentary Democracy in New Zealand', *Parliamentary Affairs* 57(3), pp. 646–665.

McGarvie, R. 1999, *Democracy: Choosing Australia's republic*, Melbourne University Press, Carlton.

Martin, G. (ed.) 2001, *Australia New Zealand and Federation 1883–1901*, Menzies Centre for Australian Studies, Kings College, London.

New Zealand Electoral Commission 2012, 'Report of the Electoral Commission on the Review of the MMP Voting System', Wellington.

New Zealand Law Society 2010, Press Release on Canterbury Earthquake and Responses Act, 29 September.

New Zealand National Universal Periodic Review 2010, 'National Report submitted in Accordance with Paragraph 15(a) of the Annex to Human Rights Council resolution 5/1' Wellington.

Office of the Deputy Prime Minister of New Zealand 2010, 'Consideration of Constitutional Issues', Wellington.

Palmer, G. and M. Palmer 2004, *Bridled Power: New Zealand's constitution and government*, 4th ed., Oxford University Press, Melbourne.

Patapan, H. 2000, *Judging Democracy: The new politics of the High Court of Australia*, Cambridge University Press, Cambridge.

Patapan, H., J. Wanna and P. Weller (eds) 2005, *Westminster Legacies: Democracy and responsible government in Asia and the Pacific*, UNSW Press, Sydney.

Power, J. 2010, *Fiducial Governance: An Australian republic for the new millennium*, ANU E Press, Canberra.

Power, J. 2012, 'Fiducial Governance: Heads of state and monitory branches', *Administration and Society* 44(1), pp. 30–63.

Prasser, S., J. R. Nethercote and N. Aroney 2008, 'Upper Houses and the Problem of Elective Dictatorship', in N. Aroney, S. Prasser and J. R. Nethercote (eds), *Restraining Elective Dictatorship: The upper house solution?*, University of Western Australia Press, Crawley, pp. 1–8.

Prebble, M. 2010, *With Respect: Parliamentarians, officials and judges too*, Victoria University of Wellington/Institute of Policy Studies, Wellington.

Rhodes, R. A. W., J. Wanna and P. Weller 2009, *Comparing Westminster*, Oxford University Press, Oxford.

Royal Commission on Auckland Governance 2009, 'Report to the Governor-General', Wellington.

Sawer, M., N. Abjorensen and P. Larkin (2009) *Australia: The state of democracy*, The Federation Press, Sydney.

Shaw, R. 2006, 'Consultants and Advisors' and 'The Public Service' in R. Miller (ed.), *New Zealand Government and Politics*, Oxford University Press, Melbourne, pp. 257–285.

Siaroff, A. 2003, 'Comparative Presidencies: The inadequacy of the presidential, semi-presidential and parliamentary distinction', *European Journal of Political Research* 42(3), pp. 287–312.

Siaroff, A. 2009, *Comparing Political Regimes: A thematic introduction to comparative politics*, 2nd ed., University of Toronto Press, Toronto.

Stockley, A. 2006, 'Judiciary and Courts', in R. Miller (ed.), *New Zealand Government and Politics*, Oxford University Press, Melbourne, pp. 145–160.

Tan, K. 1997, 'The Election of a President in a Parliamentary System: Choosing a pedigree or a hybrid?', in K. Tan and L. P. Er (eds), *Managing Political Change in Singapore: The elected presidency*. Routledge, London.

Transparency International 2013, 'Corruption Perception Index 2013'. Available at: http://www.transparency.org/cpi2013/results.

Tsebelis, G. and J. Money 1997, *Bicameralism*, Cambridge University Press, Cambridge.

Uhr, J. 2008, 'Bicameralism and Democratic Deliberation', in N. Aroney, S. Prasser and J. R. Nethercote (eds), *Restraining Elective Dictatorship: The upper house solution?*, University of Western Australia Press, Crawley, pp. 11–27.

Part II. Policy Processes

7. Is Implementation Only About Policy Execution?: Advice for public sector leaders from the literature

Evert Lindquist and John Wanna

Introduction

We were asked to undertake a review of the literature on policy implementation, delivering policy reform, and organisation change and to explore the implications for public sector leaders charged with implementing public policy in fluid, often turbulent, environments. The goal was to inform a short, accessible guide for public sector leaders (State Services Authority 2011). The research questions animating that review (with some adaptation) were as follows:

- How is the operating environment of the public sector distinctive with respect to the challenges of implementation?
- How should public sector leaders anticipate the need for policy reform and understand implications for their agencies, which may or may not have been involved in the design and implementation of the reforms?
- How do public sector agency leaders work with governments and other public organisations to anchor reform? What leadership strategies and organisational capabilities are needed?
- What are key success factors associated with successful implementation and how do public sector agency leaders know when reform has stuck? What are the indicators and metrics for assessing performance for implementation?
- Why do reforms and implementation become derailed or lose momentum?

The volume and breadth of the policy implementation, policy reform and organisational change literature make it impossible, given our space constraints, to systematically review all of the contributions and provide detailed account of debates and insights. The purpose of this chapter is to provide a more detailed and accessible account of the literature on policy implementation, delivering policy reform, and organisation change, as well as to develop an integrating framework. It also seeks to identify concepts and theoretical frameworks approaches that will be useful to public sector executives seeking to anticipate, implement and anchor government commitments in ever-changing environments, including shifting and emerging new government priorities, and to mobilise their organisations to maintain focus and be agile.

There are several themes we would like to foreshadow. First, strategies and advice on anchoring policy implementation should directly acknowledge the conditions of generalised overload of the governance systems, the shifting attention spans of governments, the rapidly evolving environment of public agencies, the multiple demands on agencies, and the inherent complexity of most policy problems. All of these factors point to the need for anticipatory, focused and strategic agency leadership. Second, effective implementation for any agency — regardless of the nature of the reform initiative or how central the agency was in its design and implementation — requires clarity of mandate and reasonable expectations, sufficient capability for carrying out responsibilities, and recognition that implementation is an administrative and political challenge requiring ongoing engagement with ministers, stakeholders, and other public agencies, often associated with other levels of government. Third, a huge tension inherent in delivering policy reform is the need for public sector leaders to strike the right balance between implementing (or imposing) a given strategic reform versus leaving scope for learning and adjustment in the face of unknown and/or changing conditions for implementing organisations.

The literature on policy implementation: An overview

The literature on policy implementation, which emerged during the 1970s and gained a great deal of recognition because of Pressman and Wildavsky's seminal *Implementation: How great expectations in washington are dashed in Oakland, or why it's amazing that federal programs work at all* (1973). However, Pressman and Wildavsky's contribution, though a landmark, was part of burgeoning scholarly interest across several countries about why policy plans failed to meet their stated objectives. Moreover, this work was only one stream of writing on policy development, policy and program evaluation, knowledge and research utilisation, policy termination, etc. It was part of the policy movement that included establishing policy schools at universities and policy analysis and research units in government. The policy implementation literature was seen as exploring *one phase* of the larger policy cycle, which has always considered the implications of one phase for others and transcended artificial boundaries (for example, Hogwood and Gunn 1984; Bridgman and Davis 2000; Pal 1997).

The literature on policy implementation is vast; there have been a succession of books (for example, Pressman and Wildavsky 1973; Bardach 1977; Van Horn 1979; Nakamura and Smallwood 1980; Williams 1980; Williams et al. 1982; Mazmanian and Sabatier 1983; Goggin et al. 1990; Hill and Hupe 2009), collections and special issues (for example, Mazmanian and Sabatier 1981; Williams 1982; Ingram and Mann 1980; Palumbo and Calista 1990; Schofield and

Sausman 2004; Honig 2006a), and hundreds of articles and chapters following the explosion of literature during the 1970s and 1980s. Moreover, many of the ideas reflect and build on broader insights permeating the policy-making and public management literature. An extensive set of references is provided at the end of this chapter (for more, see Hill and Hupe 2009; Goggin et al. 1990).

To begin with, however, a few preliminary observations are in order. First, since the early 1970s contributors have grappled with how to deal with 'wicked problems' even though that nomenclature only recently came into common use (the term emerged with Rittel and Webber 1973). Second, the implementation literature has always had a practical orientation (that is, providing advice to political and administrative leaders alike), even though it can be theoretically and empirically informed in sophisticated ways — that said, its focus has been on chronicling how implementation worked and whether policy and program goals were achieved and, if not, explaining why not. Much of the literature is more evaluative than managerially inclined. Overviews of the trajectory of the literature can be found in numerous sources (Hill and Hupe 2009; Winter 2003; May 2003; O'Toole 2003; Meyers and Vorsanger 2003) and in almost every article.

Finally, over the decades there has been considerable navel-gazing about the state of the literature on policy implementation (for example, Hjern 1982; Hill 1997; Lester et al. 1987; Lester and Goggin 1998; Winter 1999; deLeon 1999a, 1999b; Schneider 1999; Lester 2000; Kettunen 2000; Meier 1999; Potoski 2001; Goggin et al. 1990; O'Toole 1986, 2000, 2004; Barrett 2004; Scofield 2001, 2004; etc.). One claim surfacing in the late 1990s was that the literature had lost momentum, but Saetren (2005) and this chapter shows quite the opposite; there is more writing on aspects of implementation in a greater variety of journals, with diverse themes taken up in different ways, under different labels, and often in distinct substantive fields (for example, education, health, etc.).

The early trajectory of the policy implementation literature

The earliest contributions to the literature opened up the field by pointing to the gap between policy goals and results (for example, Pressman and Wildavsky 1973). In particular, there was considerable interest in how policies and programs legislated at the national or federal level of government might not have achieved the hoped-for results on the ground, and how they could take shape in very different ways in different sub-national and local jurisdictions. Interestingly, even though the terminology of 'wicked problems' and 'service-delivery networks' were not invoked at the time, a review of the literature quickly shows that most of the writing of the 1970s and 1980s were indeed about national government programs seeking to address tough social and other challenges, and often sought to do so in collaboration with state-level governments and non-profit and other providers. By the late 1990s and early 2000s, of course, scholars and practitioners alike developed an interest in the notion of policy and service-delivery networks, and this language permeates modern implementation studies and discourse.

All accounts found in the implementation literature acknowledge that early contributions rapidly divided into two broad streams and orientations:

- *Top-down perspectives* and analysis seeking to explain why policy did not have its intended effects in terms of outcomes or exploring better ways to implement policy as designed. Hill and Hupe (2009) suggest that the exemplars of the top-down approaches include Pressman and Wildavsky (1973), Van Meter and Van Horn (1975), Bardach (1977), Mazmanian and Sabatier (1981), and Hogwood and Gunn (1984). In this stream of literature, policy outcomes that differed from those intended were seen as failures, distortions, evidence of lack of willingness of staff in field operations, legislative interference, other levels of governments, and third-party providers to comply with central policy edicts. In addition to seeking to identify the causes of divergence from intended policy, such writing was dedicated to finding better ways for central authorities to anticipate implementation challenges and the behaviours of delivering agents, to better coordinate implementation activities within and across governments, and to identify better tools and instruments for achieving policy goals and objectives. This writing, usually examining US programs (but not always), often explored implementation issues for the national government in the context of federalism, working with state and local governments and non-profit and for-profit organisations to deliver programs.

- *Bottom-up perspectives* on implementation seeking to explain why outcomes diverged from policy intentions by studying the behaviour of actors in the implementation chain: field staff and in other government and delivery organisations (either dysfunction or better-than-designed approaches). Seminal studies explored the reactions of implicated organisations and staff (Van Meter and Van Horn 1975), the reactions of overloaded street-level bureaucrats (Weatherly and Lipsky 1977; Lipsky 1980), the behaviour of individuals, groups, and organisations reacting in organisational and political ways to central plans (Hjern 1982; Ingram 1977), the under-specification and often poorly communicated policies and subsequent interpretation by staff and others (Yanow 1993), and the natural effects of ambiguity, diverging interests, bargaining and negotiation (Matland 1995; Barrett 2004).

These emphases and divisions in the literature persist to this day, notwithstanding efforts to integrate the two perspectives. Many practitioners and scholars continue to seek to find better ways to execute or measure the impact of policy as originally defined in legislation, while others are more interested in the dynamics of implementation, exploring issues from the vantage point of implementation agents such as regional field offices, frontline staff, non-government delivery organisations, and clients.

Interestingly, at an early point these analytic streams were heavily informed by organisation theory (for example, Van Meter and Van Horn 1975; Elmore 1979; Berman 1978; Barrett and Fudge 1981; Montjoy and O'Toole 1979; O'Toole and Montjoy 1984) and this continues to this day (for example, Honig 2006a, 2006b). This takes the load off this chapter to review the literature on organisational theory, behaviour, change, and development, because many insights have long been factored into implementation analysis, albeit in varying ways. Their insights remain salient for policy practitioners and agency heads to this day.

Integrative implementation frameworks: Top-down/bottom-up

While the top-down and bottom-up perspectives remain distinct traditions and themes in the policy implementation literature, there were early efforts to develop comprehensive and integrative theories and frameworks. These contributions recognised that the top-down and bottom-up perspectives each identified important variables and issues. Some of these contributions include the following:

- *Backwards-mapping*: Elmore's (1979) seminal contribution focused on why and how policy designers should engage in backwards-mapping when undertaking top-down design to anticipate frontline dynamics and behaviours. He suggests that it is important to maximise discretion for managers closer to where policy is delivered. This perspective goes beyond the 'chain-of-steps' approach of Pressman and Wildavsky (1973) or the guerrilla tactics implied by Bardach's *Implementation Game* (1977). Elmore sees policy as partially emergent, and implementation likely requiring bargaining and negotiation, and asks whether policies as conceived anticipate the behaviour of frontline staff.

- *Contingency and implementation*: Berman (1978, 1980) suggests that policy implementation strategies differ depending on the scope of change, degree of technical certainty, degree of consensus, amount of coordination required, and the stability of environment. For the purposes of analysis, he set out two very different implementation strategies — programmed versus adaptive — with the former better specified and more about compliance in tightly coupled systems, and the latter less defined, more emergent in loosely coupled systems, and shaped relatively more further into the process and from the bottom-up. Neither is innately superior; their efficacy depends on the circumstances.

- *Ambiguity and conflict*: Like Berman (1978), Matland (1995) sought to reconcile top-down and bottom-up perspectives with a contingency approach by suggesting that different implementation styles are effective for different contexts. His much-cited typology identified four distinct styles and contexts: *administrative,* for low ambiguity and conflict environments; *political,* for high conflict and low ambiguity situations; *experimental,* for low conflict and high ambiguity contexts; and *symbolic* implementation when ambiguity and conflict are high.

- *Embracing complexity*: Mazmanian and Sabatier (1983) drew on Sabatier (1986) to develop a sophisticated integrative framework, embracing all of the top-down and bottom-up factors identified in the literature. It included all as variables that might influence and condition the implementation process (see Diagrams 1 (p. 215) and 2 (p. 216)). They note that implementation can be evaluated from many different vantage points: the centre, periphery and target groups (Mazmanian and Sabatier 1983, p. 11). However, their work ultimately used enacted legislation as a point of departure and sought to explain why policies do not succeed and the circumstances under which they can be better specified to achieve desired goals.

- *Interdependence and task requirements*: O'Toole and Montjoy (1984) drew on organisation theory to analyse different potential patterns in 'interorganisational policy implementation'. Informed by the seminal work of Thompson (1967), this approach elegantly considers the different kinds of interdependence among organisations flowing from the nature of the policy, the distribution of authorities, and task requirements. It is congruent with bottom-up approaches focusing on implementing entities, and the need to collaborate across agencies (Bardach 1997) and with frontline officials and service delivery entities.

- *Exchange and bargaining*: Stoker (1989) offers an 'implementation regime' framework designed to embrace top-down features and concerns (central authority seeking compliance, despite the challenge of complexity and securing intended objectives in federal systems) with bottom-up (competing values, diffuse authority, and likely bargaining and conflict resolution among the middle and frontline organisations, and clients). Policy implementation is cast as an exchange process where value can be added by different actors, and does not presume that all politics is completed in design phase. Moreover, the process deals with unanticipated or insufficiently acknowledged matters, and sees implementation as a bargaining game and local participants as problem-solvers. The framework anticipates a dynamic and evolutionary approach from initiation to routinisation to reformulation. Ultimately, Stoker sought to show how broader governance regimes as rules and norms condition these dynamics and produce accommodation, and broaden our notions of how cooperating can be secured and what constitutes 'performance'.

- *Information and incentives*: Goggin et al. (1990) set out a dynamic model of implementation which they call a 'communications' model of intergovernmental policy implementation. This taps not only into cybernetic models, but also multi-level institutions, and includes variables pertaining to inducements, constraints, resources, federal and state ecological capacity, feedback from actors to policy authorities, and outcomes. Ultimately, though, this approach is about ascertaining the effectiveness of different policies across sectors and jurisdictions, and is less about developing a better strategic or managerial approach. The framework is intended to inform more systematic social science research on implementation, whereas Mazmanian and Sabatier (1983) sought to speak to scholarly and practitioner audiences.

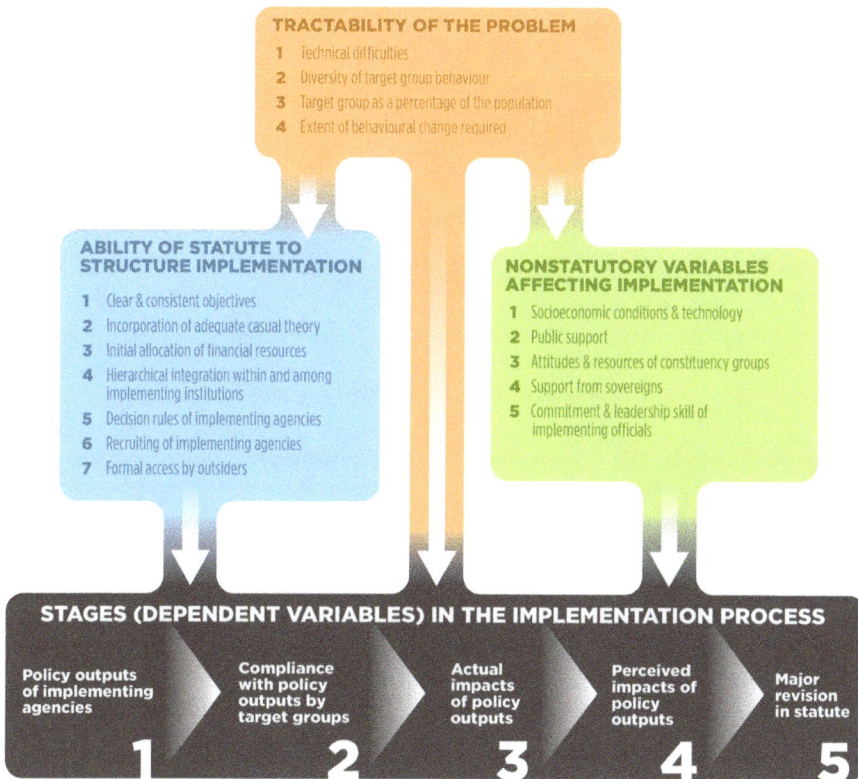

Diagram 1: Variables involved in the implementation process

Source: Adapted from Mazmanian and Sabatier 1983.

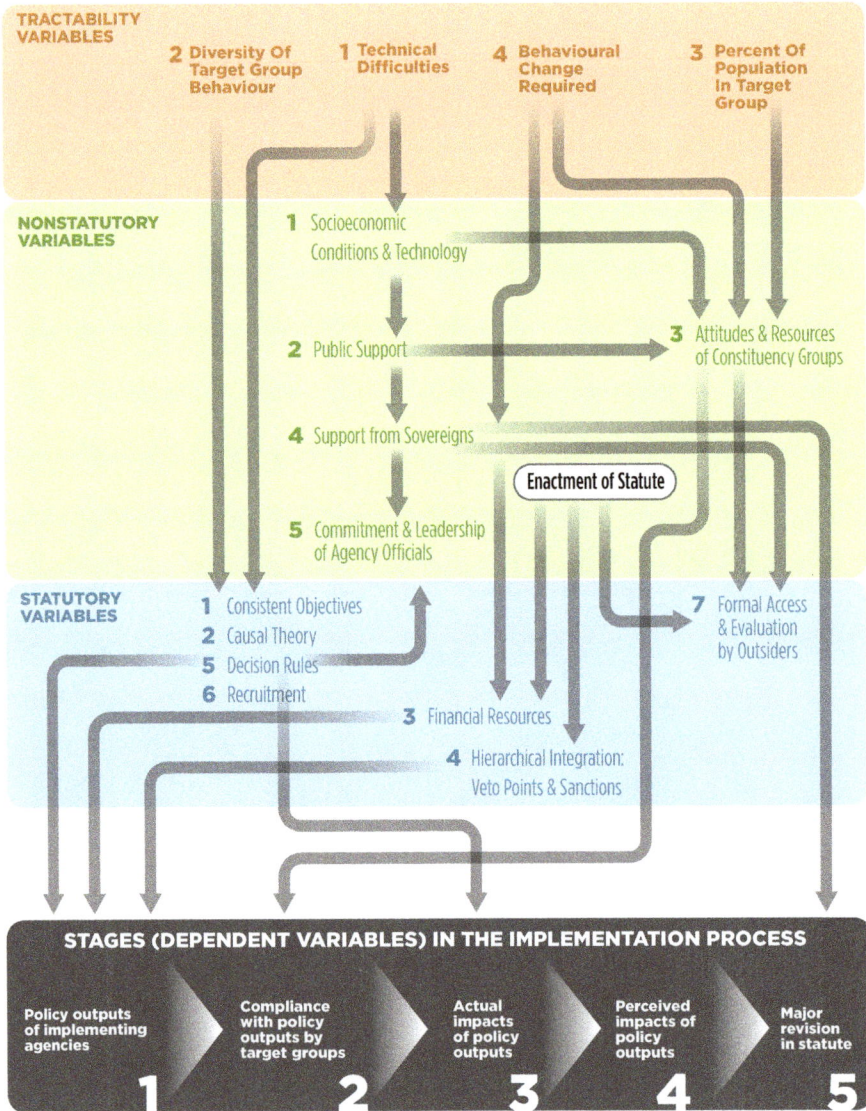

TRACTABILITY VARIABLES

2 Diversity Of Target Group Behaviour
1 Technical Difficulties
4 Behavioural Change Required
3 Percent Of Population In Target Group

NONSTATUTORY VARIABLES

1 Socioeconomic Conditions & Technology
2 Public Support
3 Attitudes & Resources of Constituency Groups
4 Support from Sovereigns
Enactment of Statute
5 Commitment & Leadership of Agency Officials

STATUTORY VARIABLES

1 Consistent Objectives
2 Causal Theory
5 Decision Rules
6 Recruitment
7 Formal Access & Evaluation by Outsiders
3 Financial Resources
4 Hierarchical Integration: Veto Points & Sanctions

STAGES (DEPENDENT VARIABLES) IN THE IMPLEMENTATION PROCESS

Policy outputs of implementing agencies **1**
Compliance with policy outputs by target groups **2**
Actual impacts of policy outputs **3**
Perceived impacts of policy outputs **4**
Major revision in statute **5**

Diagram 2: Variables and stages affecting the implementation of a statute

Source: Adapted from Mazmanian and Sabatier 1983.

These efforts to integrate and acknowledge that designing effective policy and implementation strategies requires understanding the nature of a policy, its broader political history and environment, its complexity, and the organisational and broader environment. There is no one best way to implement. Successful implementation strategies are contingent, and will differ across policies, domains, and jurisdictions. As Berman (1978), Mazmanian and Sabatier (1981), and Matland (1995) suggest, these strategies and observed behaviours might vary with respect to the level of analysis and over time. Importantly, an implication of Stoker (1989) is that a policy may be underspecified, whether by design or not, for the implementation challenges at hand.

Another form of integration, similar to Goggin et al. (1990), can be found in a wide range of systematic efforts under the labels of 'evaluations', 'trials and pilots' and 'quasi-experiments' which, in different ways, seek to measure and account for variation in the performance and efficacy of policies. These empirical and data-rich (big-N) studies also started to emerge and gather steam as part of the evaluation stream in the policy analysis movement in the 1960s and 1970s. We do not have the space here to review such studies, but a review of Lynn et al. (2001), Ingraham and Lynn (2004), and the *Journal of Policy Analysis and Management* over the last 10 years will quickly provide a sense of this perspective. In order to account for differing performance, investigators specify indicators similar to many of the factors and variables considered important to implementation researchers, including resources, actors, constraints, incentives, time, etc. However, the ultimate focus differs; the emphasis in these studies is on accounting for and explaining performance, whereas implementation studies have typically sought to understand strategies and capacities. Indeed, often pilots and trials were put in place to avoid full 'testing' by rolling out a large-scale, national policy intervention.

Recent developments in the policy implementation literature

The implementation literature has continued to grow and branch out during the 1990s and early 2000s (Saetren 2005). The best single source for an overview of the scholarly literature is the second edition of Hill's and Hupe's (2009) comprehensive monograph, which is targeted for researchers rather than practitioners. Here we will briefly describe the ways in which the literature has deepened, some of which has involved levering insights from related streams of literature:

- *Increasing use of more sophisticated concepts and methodologies for better recognising and analysing the broader organisational networks that emerge or are encountered as governments seek to deliver policy and services*: There is better appreciation of different kinds of networks, network dynamics, the reality of multiple goals and interests, the extent to which governments might directly or indirectly shape networks, and how they might work in more productive and collaborative approaches (O'Toole et al. 1997; Klijn and Teisman 1997). Other contributions have shed light on the work of intermediary organisations, not directly in the chain of government hierarchy, but supporting policy authorities, line bureaucracies, and delivery agents (for example, Honig 2004a).

- *Greater use of principal-agent, public choice, and game-theory perspectives to sharpen insights, testable propositions, and empirical studies on policy implementation*: This reflects broader analytic trends in the social sciences, public administration, and political science. It might be thought that such frameworks would tend to focus primarily on the issues having to do with compliance, coordination, and performance (or many of the themes associated with top-down issues), but game theory has also been used to model more dynamic features and behaviour in networked contexts, driven by incentives, rules, the availability of information, monitoring capability, etc. (for example, Klijn and Teisman 1997; Goggin et al. 1990).

- *Increased interest in the merits and implications of choosing a mix of policy instruments in order to navigate networks and challenging implementation environments*: Scholars have recognised that implementation often involves working with networks, requiring better appreciation of indirect and direct strategies working at the organisational and network levels, in potentially more collaborative environments (de Bruijn and ten Heuvelhof 1997; Howlett 1991, 2005). This in turn requires new forms of leadership, skill and knowledge in government and public administration organisations. Howlett (2005) drew attention to policy and implementation styles, referring to the repertoires and cultures of dominant coalitions, including government agencies and other key interests, in particular policy sectors. Such styles should be understood if they are to be navigated, altered or overcome.

- *Increased awareness of whole-of-government, cross-government, horizontal, and multi-level governance environments of implementation*: Like the increased awareness of instrument-mix and networked environments, this work suggests broader perspectives on how to approach policy design and implementation strategies, including coordination and mutual adjustment strategies across departments and agencies, and levels of government to better achieve desired outcomes (Management Advisory Committee 2004; Howlett 2005).

- *Fostering inter-organisational collaboration*: This has long been an important theme in the implementation literature (for example, Van Meter and Van Horn 1975; O'Toole and Montjoy 1984; O'Toole 2003). More recently, it has been explored with respect to the extent of trust and goal congruence as pre-conditions (Lundin 2007a, 2007b). This work recognises that, in networked contexts, cooperative and adaptive strategies will be required to address tensions arising from competing values and interests (Cline 2000). At a more micro-level, there has been increasing acknowledgement of the importance of getting agencies to work together (Bardach 1997), emerging from early analysis of implementation games (Bardach 1977). Bardach's recent work is called 'craftsmanship theory', dedicated to exploring the conditions for bottom-up and lateral collaboration and leadership across agencies, even after top-down announcements.

- *Anticipation and collaboration as a strategy for adapting to multi-level, dynamic implementation environments*: Complexity and 'wicked problems' are inherent features of many implementation challenges (otherwise it would be relatively straight-forward to proceed with a top-down, programmed strategy), along with ambiguity and value-conflict. Mazmanian and Sabatier (1983) tackled this head on, providing scenarios for leaders to consider when designing strategies (see next section for more detail). Exworthy and Powell (2004) tapped into agenda-setting models to point out that, adopting and implementing policies in the congested state are not only a matter of waiting for the right windows opening across a central government, but also eventually at the local level across delivery agencies, which must collaborate with each other. This presumes that a reasonably good chain of relationships, resources, and incentives extend from the centre of government to regional operations of departments working at the local level.

- *Examining how implementing agents get informed, interpret and build skill for the policies they are to implement*: Hill (2003) reviews how street-level bureaucrats access 'implementation resources' (ideas, skills, practices, rationale, etc.), contractors, academics, entrepreneurs, foundations, trade journals, and professional associations to interpret policy intentions, ascertain appropriate organisation behaviours, and identify new theories and skills to guide practice. Honig (2004a, 2004b) analyses how intermediary organisations — which she refers to as the 'new middle management' but which stands outside the implementation chain — can serve both policy authorities and implementing agents provide such resources, including policy-specific and system knowledge. Schofield (2004) refers to the challenge of managers interpreting and operationalising policy as 'learned implementation' (see Diagrams 1 (p. 215) and 2 (p. 216)), which can increase motivation and commitment. Spillaine et al. (2002) and Yanow (1993) analyse this as a sense-making and meaning-making activity by individuals, groups, and organisations. Kelman (2005) shows how administrative leaders can identify and unleash 'reform coalitions' from within organisations to implement new policy regimes.

- *Closer examination of various organisational capabilities to guide implementation at the centre of government*: This writing reviews efforts to build capabilities for oversight such as tracking systems, project management, cabinet implementation units, problem-solving teams, and gateway reviews for major projects (Lindquist 2006; Barber 2007; Marsh and Fawcett 2010). Honig (2003, 2006b) considers how central administration offices facilitate implementation of educational policy reforms. These can be seen as more modern efforts to shape and fix implementation games (Bardach 1977).

- *If implementation can be viewed as part of the democratic governance process, it is legitimate that various interests work hard to reshape policy to meet the needs of groups and communities*: Congruent with the adaptation perspective, this possibility was recognised as high-conflict implementation situations by writers such as Matland (1995). DeLeon and deLeon (2002) suggest that a 'consensual theory of implementation' should be developed and, as we discuss below, Patashnik (2008) sees implementation as the next and sustained round of political and policy debate. To some extent, their approach seeks to explicitly recognise and bring politicians back into implementation analysis.

These newer concepts and perspectives have not turned the implementation literature on its head, but sharpen the analysis of many of the themes, issues and strategies it has long broached. As we see later, many have relevance for the kind of advice that would be relevant for public sector agency leaders.

Recent literature on delivering sustainable policy reform

There has been growing interest in the topic of delivering policy reform that is durable; many of the themes in this literature overlap heavily with the traditional implementation literature, but it is more explicitly political in that it seeks to understand how reforms get anchored and this usually involves political mobilisation and strategies. Barber (2007) and Lindquist (2006) have explored these themes with respect to creating bureaucratic capacities at the centre of government to monitor the progress of government priorities, to fix problems as they arise, and to drive change. Here the focus is more on making good on government priorities.

The writing that has gained most attention and animated a recent ANZSOG conference comes from the work of Erik Patashnik (2003; 2008). While Patashnik relies heavily on the implementation literature, he considers broadly how implementation works at the political level as opposed to the organisational or managerial levels. His work presumes, as does that of deLeon and deLeon (2002) and Matland (1995), that policy implementation often proceeds in contested and conflict-ridden domains, and that concerted political mobilisation is essential for ensuring policy durability and success. It picks up themes found early on in the implementation literature (Bardach 1977) that the implementation phase essentially provides another opportunity to undermine, re-make or elaborate an approved policy. Seen this way, implementation is just another forum for policy contestation. By means of comparing several different cases, Patashnik considers how political and administrative leaders blocked efforts by groups opposed to new policy regimes and prevent political erosion of those policies, how they established and mobilised new coalitions of interests in support of the new policy frameworks, and made accommodations to galvanise those interests. An important contribution of this work is that it points to the time horizons required for policy implementation, noting that administrative strategies and tactics cannot likely proceed and succeed without significant political support.

Interestingly, Patashnik's analysis has an important precursor in the implementation literature: Mazmanian and Sabatier (1983) identified implementation scenarios that took into account distinct political and economic contexts, and explicitly acknowledge the time horizons involved when attempting to secure change. It is a more dynamic and strategic way to understand Matland's (1995) analysis (see Diagram 3, next page). In short, Patashnik (2008) provides some case studies to complement these early insights. Crosby (1996) provides similar perspectives on what it takes to anchor structural-adjustment regimes in developing countries, which involves not only mobilising organisational capabilities and political support, but also leadership, new perspectives, skills and time.

There has also emerged work on 'policy execution' in the consulting world (Eggers and O'Leary 2009), invoking terminology from the early days of the literature (Van Meter and Van Horn 1975). This work definitely elicits more attention than policy implementation and is a direct response to the notion that government and public sector organisations often find it difficult to (but must) follow-through on the commitments they have made, and must find contemporary ways to do so. Indeed, the Eggers and the Barber contributions represent a huge strand of for-profit and consulting expertise seeking to bring private-sector techniques and perspectives into the government sector. This work does not contribute much from a conceptual or empirical perspective, and the terminology belies the notion that the challenges are, in fact, quite complex, and require the mobilisation of resources, multiple partners, networks, and learning — themes long in the scholarly and applied literature.

However, Lindquist and Wanna (2011) point to limitations of the 'delivering policy reform' and 'policy execution' perspectives. These perspectives seek to maintain the integrity of original policy designs and consider the ongoing political and administrative effort required to anchor policy over many years in complex institutional environments, the politics for political and administrative leaders of fighting or neutralising interests seeking to undermine the policy reforms, and explore balancing the need to modify reforms so they work better and anchoring the reforms with fidelity to original intentions. Similar to the 'compliance' perspective found in the early implementation literature, the original policy goals are taken as given, and implementation seeks to deliver and execute them, with implication that they are a government priority and require central monitoring and oversight, and thus are infused with a 'performance' orientation.

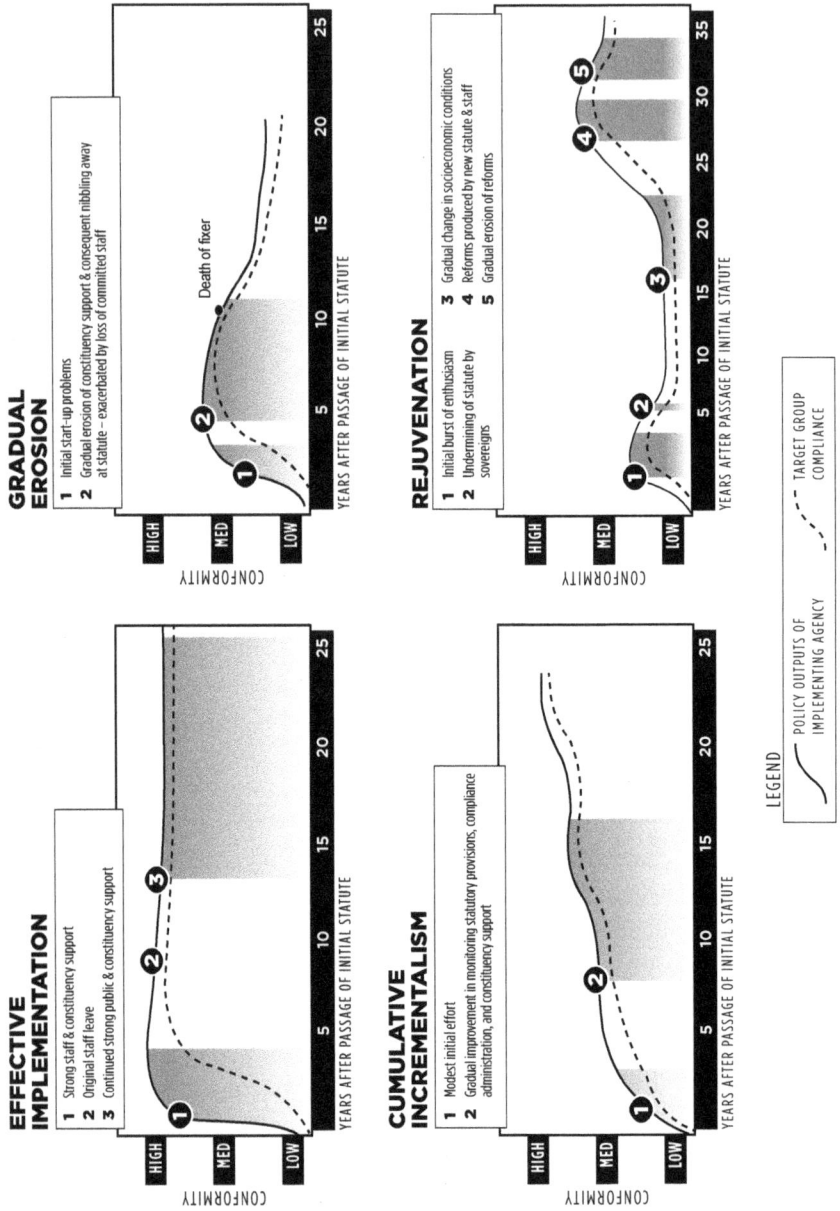

Diagram 3: How policy outputs and target-group compliance conform with statutory objectives over time: Four scenarios

Source: Adapted from Mazmanian and Sabatier 1983.

These perspectives, however, presume that the logic and theory behind the policy reforms is correct, and that the necessary organisational capabilities are ready, and that the environment remains congruent for its implementation. If these conditions are not met, the policy will have to be adjusted and even reformulated, placing us squarely back into the realm of the adaptive and learning perspectives on implementation. The key tension here concerns the extent to which policy reforms can be modified without losing their integrity and momentum. Indeed, one could envision a tipping point where policies have been anchored, but can be modified in a positive manner without returning to the previous regimes considered to be unproductive or unfair.

Policy implementation: The organisational dimension

There is a huge literature on organisations and organisational change, most of which focuses on corporate sector and for-profit organisations, where the aim is to increase profitability, meet market and customer needs, etc. Most of this literature, unlike what we have reviewed above, is not focused on public organisations and the complex and fluid environments in which they work (although it does consider the challenge of working in evolving and increasingly networked environments). Conversely, the literature has been heavily informed by organisation theory and change perspectives.

Our purpose here is to identify some key areas to consider how agency leaders of public organisations might anticipate and work towards anchoring policy reforms introduced by governments. We make a distinction between the external-strategic dimension, which is more complicated due to public governance dynamics and constraints, and the internal-strategic dimension, which takes leaders somewhat more squarely into the traditional parameters of the organisational change and development literature. Key themes to consider are as follows:

- *Executives must anticipate and prepare organisations for change*: This requires scanning and analysing policy and organisational environments, forging new alliances, adopting new technologies, preparing executive colleagues for new responsibilities that might come their way, recruiting at the apex and in critical areas elsewhere in the organisation with these considerations in mind, and communicating with staff and stakeholders (for example, Selznick 1957).

- *Executives must assess how organisational culture fits with implementation tasks*: Leaders should have a nuanced sense of the nature and source of the culture(s) in their organisation, and which parts may most resist versus be capable of taking on new tasks and responsibilities (Wilson 1989). They must ascertain whether new capabilities or units are required for new roles and responsibilities (for example, cope with crisis, adopt new technology, work with clients or partners in a fundamentally different way, deliver higher probity/accountability, etc.).

- *Executives must identify new values, meaning, and narratives*: The arrival of a new policy often requires that executives understand them as potentially bringing in new values, meanings and priorities, which implies consciously and proactively striking new balances among existing and new values, and developing new language and frames — the process of sense-making — not only for communicating the nature of the new challenges but also linking them to previous understandings and meanings (Barnard 1938; Selznick 1957). Moreover, this needs to be considered not only for the executive's organisation but also the larger network of organisations involved in the implementation.

- *New tasks require different expertise and relationships*: New policies usually require different or new task structures and ways of doing work, new and different mixes of professional expertise, and imply different task environments in the sense of different organisations to link with inside and outside the organisation (Thompson 1967; Wilson 1989). Agency leaders need to have a fine-grained sense of how specific task environments will shift for implicated units in their organisations, how this will affect more general balances struck across the organisation, and the extent to which this will affect the organisation's sense of mission and culture, whether new understandings and frames need to be developed.

- *New tasks could imply structural change and new repertoires*: Taking on new tasks goes beyond thinking about new leadership and capabilities in a public organisation. It may also have structural and process implications. As new units are established around new tasks and to instil new values, frames, and culture, structural change may be required in the larger organisation in order to ensure coordination inside and outside the organisation, despite the upheaval and human and other costs of proceeding, and work and decision-making may have to proceed in different ways. This needs to be anticipated, monitored, and changed if required.

- *Embedding change is hard work*: The challenge of anchoring or embedding change with respect to incentives, work practices, cultures, and monitoring is an enduring theme in the organisational change literature (Kotter 1990, 1996), and is no less important for policy implementation. Agency leaders must carefully consider the internal incentives for staff to work in new ways and potentially with different partners. Again, this points to assessing the extent to which there is a need for professional development, new recruitment mixes for leaders and core staff alike, and whether monitoring and performance systems are aligned with the new and/or expanded objectives of the organisation.

- *Internal change is as important as external change*: Typically, agency heads are more focused on external challenges and contingencies, leaving managers and frontline staff to work through implementing strategies. However, the greater the change flowing from policy implementation (breadth and amount of departure from current practice), the more demand there will be for significant organisational change, requiring that leaders have greater strategic engagement with staff and encouraging creative thinking on their part, and, of course, the stakes for dealing with the external environment will be raised considerably. This suggests that leaders need to balance how they allocate their time and strategic effort, since both dimensions are critical for success.

- *Leading organisations in networks*: Much of the traditional organisational change literature has focused on how leaders can change the values, capabilities and focus of staff. However, in recent years this has been greatly complicated by many organisations having to work in very different ways as a result of new technology, new economic realities, and new expectations of clients and external environments. Increasingly, leaders and their organisations must learn how to work in partnerships, and collaborative and networked arrangements as a matter of course, and sometimes under stress and in fluid environments. This requires finding leaders with the right expertise who are comfortable with working in more collaborative ways.

- *Banking on change*: Leaders seeking to implement policies and programs must anticipate continual change, arising from not only the evolution of ongoing initiatives but also the arrival of other priorities, such as additional policies to implement, the adoption of new technologies and reporting systems, and the inevitable calls for restraint. The key challenge here is how to maintain engagement, motivation, and strategic focus in the organisation to bed down policy initiatives in the midst of competing priorities and potential turmoil.

There are vast streams of literature on the topics enumerated above, and we cannot do justice to the evolution of thinking in those areas. What is important about the themes and topics identified above is that they bring an *organisational dimension* to the policy implementation challenges which are the focus of this paper, and which need to be brought to bear on the strategic considerations for agency heads as they prepare themselves and their organisations for moving forward.

Pulling it all together: Implications for public sector leaders

This section distils implications from the literature in order to answer the research questions identified in the introduction of this chapter. We have supplemented them with some other questions we think are pertinent to the goals underpinning the literature review.

How is the public sector operating environment unique?

Both the policy implementation and the policy reform literature study the challenge of converting adopted public policy and government intentions into workable, sustainable programs and achieving intended results. Like the new public management reforms of the late-1980s and 1990s, the policy execution and organisational change literature often seeks to draw lessons from the private sector, but are often simplistic because the public sector environment is more complex and challenging. Figure 1 (opposite) provides a long list of the distinctive features of government responsibilities and associated challenges when attempting to implement new policies.

This list shows that implementing policy in a public sector environment promises to be challenging, and the literature has always understood it as such. We believe that there is little that the public sector can learn from the private sector in this regard. Yes, it would be wonderful to have clear goals, strong and enduring political support, well-aligned stakeholder and service-delivery networks, fully capable lead agencies and partners willing to collaborate, and reasonably stable environments, including funding; but it is difficult to imagine counting on this in a public-sector context. Moreover, new governance challenges have emerged; more fluid political and funding environments, and more attentive media and critics. However, good leaders should be aware of these challenges and, in light of the considerable writing and experience with implementation, presumably be better prepared about how to plan and strategise in the face of them.

How should public sector agency leaders anticipate and prepare for reform?

This question is interesting because most observers *presume* that executive leaders of departments and agencies were informed of policy reforms and involved in their design. But these can be heroic assumptions for two reasons: a secretary or chief executive may *not* have been in the policy design and approval loop, and not privy to all of the considerations and balances that informed the decisions; and a secretary or chief executive may be new to the position or the

- Governments are typically the custodians (or agents of last resort) of many difficult or wicked problems (homelessness, poverty, crime, health, etc.).
- Policy interventions to these problems often involve working with multiple and often reluctant partners, including different levels of governments and organisations in different sectors. Often these 'partners' actively resisted the adopted policy and/or have other priorities.
- In addition to the general challenge of overload, the attention of political leadership will likely shift due to crisis and other pressing challenges, so securing the government and ministerial engagement for seeing a newly adopted public policy through may be difficult.
- State governments are often recipients of Commonwealth policy initiatives (and may have shaped them through negotiations of some sort) and may have different visions, priorities and preferred approaches to implementing policy.
- State governments and agencies will be the enacting authorities for policies, seeking to deliver policies and programs with one or more department or agency and their regional operations, and often with local governments, non-profit/community groups, and contractors.
- The accountability environment for implementing public sector agencies is unforgiving, with the 24-hour news cycle and the scrutiny of opposition parties and a variety of audit and monitoring agencies, which ensures that delays, oversights, and mistakes can quickly become front-page news and comprise the reputation of governments.
- Despite announced plans of the Commonwealth and state governments, the availability of resources or even political agreements cannot always be counted upon due to factors and considerations beyond the policy to be implemented, suggesting that agency leaders should be prepared for different scenarios and to adapt.
- Beyond the matters of resourcing and political agreements, the structure of incentives and the oversight regime confronting all actors in the delivery chain, including state governments, is critical to ensuring take-up and degree of success.
- The amount of technical and cultural shift inherent in new policy regimes, the lead times for implementation, the number and capabilities of key stakeholders, the nature and quality of reform coalitions, and the readiness and centrality of a lead or supporting agencies vary considerably across policy initiatives creating distinct policy and administrative challenges.
- The extent of political interest of governments in anchoring a reform beyond adoption, the willingness and capabilities of reform opponents to resist, and the skill and adroitness of agency heads in working with political leaders and other stakeholders to further implementation.

Figure 1: Policy and implementation challenges for government

appointment may have been announced as part of the policy reform or in the wake of it. In either case, the agency head needs to quickly learn of the rationale, expectations, and nuances behind the decision, including the extent to which other levels of government and potential service providers were informed and perhaps had expectations about their roles, resourcing, flexibility, etc.

Public sector leaders, particularly those new to their responsibilities, need to fully understand the origins of the policy, including the needs, pressures, and the politics that led to its enactment. Moreover, they also need to appreciate the range of actors implied in the upstream of policy development and the downstream of implementation, their interests, capabilities, and ability to block and further the policy as originally designed. They need to understand the role of their agency in the firmament of actors involved with implementing the policy, as well as its sources of power, influence, and leverage. Much depends, of course, whether an agency was a policy-taker or policymaker in the upstream of the policy development, and whether it will be an implementation lead or contributor in the downstream.

The literature on organisations and change has long suggested that leaders — whether of private or public organisations — should be scanning environments for threats and opportunities, and preparing their organisations for change. This implies developing anticipatory repertoires such as strategic planning and environmental scanning, and open-minded and alert leadership. In a public sector context, this would also include regular communication with political leaders and agency-head colleagues, awareness of what comparator sectors and agencies have been experiencing in other jurisdictions, and monitoring stakeholder, client and citizen needs and satisfaction.

Why do reforms become derailed or lose momentum?

Implementing significant reforms can take several years, and sometimes even decades, for all the foundational elements to put in place, secured, and made sustainable. Two critical questions, however, are: is the reform yet another in a long line of reforms on an overloaded agenda, or if it is a top priority of a government performance-monitoring from the centre?; and, can political attention be sustained at the implementation phase, increasing momentum and the room for manoeuvre for agency leaders as they seek to implement a policy reform? In some cases, reform proposals are driven by politicians (ministers) while in others reforms are often sponsored by agency leaders and or other significant stakeholders (for example, tariff reform).

These questions are important because as has long been apparent from the literature, there is no shortage of factors which could undermine the implementation of a policy. Figure 2 (opposite) provides a long list of the factors working to undermine implementation of policy reforms. Despite this depressingly long list of negative dynamics and possibilities, many policies and substantial programs and reforms do get enacted, flowing from good leadership and no small amount of foresight, creativity, and good fortune (Patashnik 2008; Lindquist, Vincent and Wanna 2011). We turn to these factors next.

How do public sector agency leaders make reform stick?

If a policy is well-designed and properly resourced, and the environment congruent with expectations inherent in the design, then it is possible for a programmed solution to be implemented and made to stick — otherwise there

- Unclear or inconsistent policy designs, including poor choice of instruments.
- Under-specification of a new policy variously in order to secure approval, because not enough was known about how things work, or it was understood there will be 'learning-by-doing'.
- Insufficient recognition of the inherent complexity not only of the problem seeking to be remedied but also of the solution arrived at as a 'public policy' (i.e. making the policy work is more complex than imagined at the design phase).
- Value conflicts and interest conflicts, impossibility of securing consensus, agreement on means and ends, and how to evaluate outcomes.
- Insufficient anticipation of implementation challenges, including the motivations and power of intermediary organisations and street-level bureaucrats, and the incentives and resources required to engage, mobilise and influence them as well as the policy's target groups.
- Insufficient political and administrative leadership assigned for implementing the policy reform. Unrealistic expectations built into the theory informing the policy, the outcomes that could be reasonably achieved with the instruments and resources at hand, and — to the extent that the policy adoption involved 'emulation' — the extent to which similar cultural conditions exist.
- Shrewd political and other interests actively seeking to undermine adopted policies. Insufficient mobilisation of reform champions among beneficiaries as well as insufficient awareness or strategies for dealing with interests benefitting from the previous policy regime.
- Whether intentionally or not, public and other organisations in the implementation chain which either inadvertently or systematically bend (and sometimes re-formulate) the adopted policy into repertoires consistent with prior programs, organisational capabilities, and values.
- Agency leaders have insufficient repertoires for collaboration and for anchoring change (new work patterns, incentives, value balances, frames, etc.).
- Inability to identify new external partners and/or work in new ways in order to achieve the objectives inherent in the policy reforms.
- Insufficient monitoring or delayed feedback on the activities of agents in the delivery and oversight chain to inform timely adjustment and learning.
- Growing awareness that a reform may be unworkable, along with insufficient ability or interest to make needed adjustments in the policy framework and/or implementation arrangements.
- Growing attention of the media and political opponents about implementation gaps, whether the policy was proceeding as originally planned or in a more emergent manner.
- Insufficient recruitment and evolution in relevant professional repertoires, skills and perceptions over time, and insufficient awareness of the rationale and requirements of the new policy.
- Insufficient repertoires for monitoring and assessing progress, sharing that information with partners, political leaders, and others in favour of the new policy regime.
- Lead implementing agencies are given other government priorities or crises to manage, government interest in securing reform dissipates, and turnover in top executive leadership.
- The sponsoring environment continually shifts (including new government priorities, budget and other constraints), complemented by insufficiently anticipatory, adaptive, and creative leadership, which, in turn, leads to strategic and operational overload.

Figure 2: Factors working to undermine implementation of policy reforms

will be many adjustments along the way. Even Patashnik's (2003) 'policy reform' stream of thinking sees that successful implementation requires ongoing political attention, administrative adaptation, and likely modest re-shaping of the original policy. It has to be acknowledged that sometimes policies as enacted, for a variety of reasons, need to be significantly changed or even dropped. Rather than enumerate a list opposite the points identified in Figure 2, we instead make some broad points.

First, the literature indicates that policy gets shaped and reshaped at all phases of the policy cycle. Accordingly, implementation can be seen not just as a matter of finding strategies to enact a policy, but also an opportunity to refine or improve what otherwise could have been a broad or imperfect policy through more detailed planning, design, and learning from different approaches to implementation across a system or region. Implementation can be seen as an opportunity for policy adjustment or policy elaboration, even if others see this as program design and implementation. It requires recognising the extent of ambiguity in the policy as announced (and what needs to be further specified, negotiated or learned about), the extent of political conflict, and what operational skills and cultures must shift inside and outside pertinent public agencies.

In short, it is only in certain circumstances that agency leadership can simply be about securing approvals and authorities. It is far more likely that implementation leadership will be about operationalising, elaborating and specifying broader policy goals, securing necessary resources for implementation, assembling the right capabilities and educating implementers down the line and in the field, as well as collaborating, negotiating, and forming the productive administrative coalitions with other agencies, levels of government, and non-government partners, including non-profit, community and for-profit entities. Indeed, the great tension emerging from the literature is the need for leaders to be goal-oriented but contingent, knowing when to drive forward and execute, and when to compromise, adapt, and perhaps achieve goals in ways different than originally imagined. With these broader considerations in mind, Figure 3 (opposite) identifies more specific lessons for keeping reforms on track and anchored.

A crucial insight from the literature is that policy implementation is not simply a strategic management and administration activity, it also involves political management — good leaders shrewdly engage stakeholders, build and support coalitions in support of reforms, and engage political masters at the right time. It is about continuously maintaining, galvanising and mobilising support for reforms inside and outside agencies.

- Negotiate and work with political leaders to elicit ongoing support for implementing initiatives.

- Keep ministers informed of progress and identify how they might make strategic contributions as required, even if not a top government or ministerial priority.

- Map the full range of implicated interests, networks and coalitions at play.

- Find ways to strengthen entities that will benefit from and support reform implementation.

- Forge strong working relationships with agencies across levels of government to build and strengthen a reform coalition, and institute regular opportunities for reporting and strategising.

- Develop realistic time frames for anchoring reforms (two years or a decade) to manage internal and external expectations, and focus energies on foundational elements of reforms.

- Understand current incentives/disincentives and develop a new incentive structure appropriate to the implemented policy.

- Steadily recruit the right leaders and technical expertise in the agency and the broader implementing network.

- Ensure sufficient implementation resources to support administrative and delivery staff.

- If required, institute sufficient structural change at appropriate junctures, but otherwise rely on good communications, temporary task force and coordination structures.

- Develop a strategic approach to communications: ensure two-way channels with staff, external coalitions, delivery partners, and sponsors in government; encourage feedback and monitoring; and institute repertoires for informing the broader public about progress.

- Develop robust, focused and relevant reporting systems that recognise the emergent and evolutionary quality of most implementation initiatives.

- Institute staff engagement and client satisfaction feedback capabilities and repertoires, and ensure timely collection of data.

- Design reporting systems to inform future evaluations and assessments of the performance of implemented policies, whether planned or emergent.

Figure 3: Keeping policy implementation on track: Repertoires for agency leaders

How do public sector agency leaders know when implementation has succeeded?

Implementation is often a moveable feast, with plans and objectives evolving in response to political and other external circumstances, as well as from learning and change. Furthermore, gauging whether a policy reform has achieved intended outcomes and new thresholds of performance is different from assessing whether a reform-as-enacted stuck, for better or worse. With these caveats, several indicators inferred from the literature are displayed in Figure 4.

- Information and feedback is regularly obtained from key stakeholders and beneficiaries of the new policy, and the emerging regime reflects stakeholder input on making it more workable.

- Ability to demonstrate progress even if the causal link between the policy as implemented and the outcomes are unclear or contested, as well as respect for meeting project management targets, understanding the limits of policy approach, and what accounts for differences.

- Trust and shared expectations were built with collaborating departments, agencies, delivery agents, and intermediary organisations.

- Expectations about what could be accomplished with the implemented policy and available resources were met, even if issues have been identified, and political leaders and the public are aware what the reforms have achieved.

- Key stakeholders who opposed the reforms see key objectives and some of their concerns are met, and that other stakeholders, agencies, and delivery agents have coalesced around the reform.

- The right agency leaders and managers were put in place to institutionalise the reforms as programs, and the next generation of leaders selected and recruited based on the new model.

- Changes are embedded into repertoires; new recruits know little about what was previously done — it is no longer relevant or a festering matter.

- The reforms are not only insulated from legislative unpacking and relatively immune to end-runs through other policies and regulatory decisions.

- Success is recognised internally and sought-after by other jurisdictions.

- The leaders who guided change among the agencies in the implementation network move on to take up new challenges and opportunities.

- New thresholds of performance are met (for example, speed, consistency, tailoring, fewer backlogs), but ministers, executives and stakeholders take up issues within the new policy framework.

Figure 4: How might agency leaders know policy implementation has succeeded?

That said, aside from a 'performance' perspective (timelines met and outcomes achieved, usually under a programmed implementation scenario), the literature does not have definitive views on what might constitute success when implementation becomes increasingly emergent, negotiated, and adaptive. Moreover, these notions of success may vary across initiatives and the extent to which there are real gaps in anticipated and touted performance with respect to costs, outputs and outcomes.

Other lessons from the policy implementation and reform literature

There is no need to repeat the many lessons from the implementation literature for agency heads to consider. Successful executive leadership during any kind of policy implementation will be about differing degrees of responsibility for achieving success, balancing competing demands in an evolving environment, and preparing a dynamic reality and different scenarios. With this in mind, we want to step back and consider two significant lessons.

First, when attempting to understand implementation (and develop a strategic posture), much depends on one's vantage point. The literature does a good, if not bewildering job considering the different actors involved in implementation: politician, executive, middle manager, frontline delivery staff, recipients (citizens, communities, etc.), or observer (scholar, evaluator, etc.). Not only are these equally legitimate and material perspectives, those designing and implementing policy should seriously consider the other levels of analysis in order to better design policy, anticipate how to coordinate implementation, and work with inevitable frontline dynamics of other actors.

A second implication is that, when making assessments and drawing lessons for designing better policy and for strategic leadership, much depends on the specific policy domain (transportation systems, energy, disability, water distribution, etc.) and the governance context (country, state, local/community, network). This greatly affects the distribution of power, how decisions get made, where capabilities are distributed, and the specific roles for different public organisations as well as the strategic challenges confronting agency heads. An important implication is that agency leaders would do well to put themselves in the strategic shoes of other leaders, when making assessments and attempting to develop strategic decisions to guide implementation.

Conclusion: An integrative, strategic framework for leaders

There is no shortage of frameworks in the policy implementation literature, but most were developed for analytic purposes rather than for informing strategic leadership. That said, the implications of the literature for strategic leadership are numerous. Indeed, it identifies so many variables, factors, and perspectives on implementation that it would be easy to develop a lengthy checklist of all the things that should be aligned and done in order for a policy implementation to be successful (see, for example, the checklists in Bridgman and Davis 2000, chapters 10 and 13).

We caution against relying on the checklist approach. Such checklists do not anticipate the different kinds of policies that need to be implemented, the different contexts in which policies get implemented, nor the extent to which evolving environments can directly and indirectly pose new and anticipated challenges. Though the literature does an excellent job in identifying the great range of actors which might be implicated in an implementation (ministers, executives, middle managers, frontline bureaucrats, intermediary organisations, counterparts in other governments, contractors, community groups, interest groups, etc.), there is little focus on the challenges of *specific* public organisational leaders (other than those actually driving the change) and their executive teams, how they might support ministers and governments, nor how strategic priorities might vary across these agency leadership teams depending on the role they play in particular implementation firmaments.

Rather than develop another checklist, it is better to develop a framework that is more strategic and assists agency heads to survey contexts, identify emerging policy and implementation initiatives, and assess the preparedness of their agencies and networks to further impending change. It must acknowledge the extent to which circumstances and challenges can vary across enacted policies. Much of what makes for good policy implementation and organisational change is well-known, but varies considerably in lesson-drawing for public sector leaders with respect to:

- *specific situational contexts* — crisis-driven, central government priority driving a mandate, a central invention or policy developed closely with implementing agencies, etc.;

- *scale of policy interventions* — broader interventions imply more agencies, external partners, and possibly levels of government, etc. — which implies different roles for different agencies and different combinations of partners and other organisations to contend with;

- *fluidity of political and policy environment* — new and changing priorities, crises — which requires thinking in scenario-based and multiple-level (political and administrative) terms;

- *centrality of an executive's organisation to implementing and realising the interventions* — acting as a partner to many other organisations during implementation is very different from acting as a lead implementation agency;

- *extent of alignment of an agency's core capabilities for the implementation tasks at hand*, and the extent to which new capabilities, repertoires, and relationships have to be built in order to implement and embed a new policy and delivery regime;

- *extent of policy coherence and an implementation plan understood by different stakeholders*, which is different from a policy that is flawed in terms of logic or not well thought out, or deliberately underspecified, and which requires more flexibility, learning, and emergence in implementation;

- *extent to which implementation partners know and have worked with each other*, the amount of trust, and the extent to which implementation resources independent of specific agencies might be available to tap into; and

- *extent to which the time frames envisioned for successfully implementing and anchoring new policies are understood* — three months, two years, a decade?

These variables, when combined, produce considerably different strategic fields in which executives might attempt to move forward with an implementation checklist.

A strategic implementation framework should focus on key strategic moments for agency heads, encouraging them and their executive teams to ask the right questions. Although Berman (1980, 1978) suggested three phases — mobilisation, implementation, and institutionalisation — given that agency heads need to learn about the genesis of new policies, and that they will need adjustment reconsideration at some point, the following five phases might be worth considering: (1) understanding a policy's genesis; (2) planning and mobilising for implementation; (3) implementation as strategy and management; (4) institutionalisation (embedding); and (5) appraising policy regimes. What would make a framework organised around these phases interesting and productive is that the strategic context for every implementation is unique and usually evolving. Such a framework should contain questions probing the understanding of agency heads about whether the policy as originally conceived is working, whether new capabilities and relationships need to be developed, whether new strategies and tactics are required in light of evolving environments or learning about the real incentives and behaviours of delivery agents and target groups, and what strategies are required to deal with interests seeking to undermine the new policy regime.

All of this should be generally distilled into a *visual organising framework* that identifies all of the key variables and considerations broached in the literature review, organised around the phases identified above. Distinct questions and pointers could be dealt with under each phase, as well as how particular themes (for example, handling the politics of interests, changing environments, motivating staff and agents, working with partners, monitoring and performance, etc.) might evolve across the phases. Each phase would contain its own scoping SWOT-type questions (strengths, weaknesses, opportunities and threats) and call on executives to adopt a different strategic focus in the service of the broader implementation.

References

Barber, M. 2007, *Instruction to Deliver: Tony Blair, public services and the challenge of achieving targets*, Politicos, London.

Bardach, E. 1977, *The Implementation Game: What happens after a bill becomes law*, MIT Press, Cambridge.

Bardach, E. 1997, *Getting Agencies to Work Together: The practice and theory of managerial craftsmanship*, Brookings Institution, Washington, DC.

Barnard, C. 1938, *The Functions of the Executive*, Harvard University Press, Boston.

Barrett, S. M. 2004, 'Implementation Studies: Time for a revival?: Personal reflections on 20 years of implementation studies', *Public Administration* 82(2), pp. 249–262.

Barrett, S. and C. Fudge (eds) 1981, *Policy and Action*, Methuen, London.

Berman, P. 1978, 'Macro- and Micro-Implementation', *Public Policy* 26, pp. 165–179.

Berman, P. 1980, 'Thinking about Programmed and Adaptive Implementation: Matching strategies to situations', in H. Ingram and D. Mann (eds), *Why Policies Succeed or Fail*, Sage, Beverly Hills, pp. 205–227.

Bridgman, P. and G. Davis 2000, 'Implementation' and 'Checklists for Policy Development', in *The Australian Policy Handbook*, 2nd ed., Allen & Unwin, Crows Nest.

Cline, K. D. 2000, 'Defining the Implementation Problem: Organizational management versus cooperation', *Journal of Public Administration Research and Theory* 10(3), pp. 551–571.

Crosby, B. L. 1996, 'Policy implementation: The organizational challenge', *World Development* 24(9), pp. 1403–1415.

de Bruijn, J. A. and E. F. ten Heuvelhof 1997, 'Instruments for Network Management', in W. J. M. Kickert, E.-H. Klijn, and J. F. M. Koppenjan (eds), *Managing Complex Networks: Strategies for the public sector*, Sage, London, pp. 119–136.

deLeon, P. 1999a, 'Cold Comfort Indeed', *Policy Currents* 8(4), pp. 5–8.

deLeon, P. 1999b, 'The Missing Link Revisited: Contemporary implementation research', *Policy Studies Review* 16, pp. 311–338.

deLeon, P. and L. deLeon 2002, 'What Ever Happened to Policy Implementation', *Journal of Public Administration Research and Theory* 12(4), pp. 467–492.

Eggers, W. D. and J. O'Leary 2009, *If We Can Put a Man on the Moon …: Getting big things done in government*, Harvard Business School Press, Boston.

Elmore, R. F. 1979, 'Backward Mapping: Implementation research and policy decisions', *Political Science Quarterly* 94(4), pp. 601–616.

Exworthy, M. and M. Powell 2004, 'Big Windows and Little Windows: Implementation in the "congested state"', *Public Administration* 82(2), pp. 263–281.

Goggin, M. L., A. Bowman, J. Lester, and L. O'Toole 1990, *Implementation Theory and Practice: Toward a third generation*, Scott Foresman, Little, Brown, Glenview.

Hill, H. C. 2003, 'Understanding Implementation: Street-level bureaucrats' resources for reform', *Journal of Public Administration Research and Theory* 13(3), pp. 265–282.

Hill, M. 1997, 'Implementation Theory: Yesterday's issue?' *Policy and Politics* 25(4), pp. 375–385.

Hill, M. and P. Hupe 2009, *Implementing Public Policy: An introduction to the study of operational governance*, 2nd ed., Sage, London.

Hjern, B. 1982, 'Implementation Research: The link gone missing', *Journal of Public Policy* 2(3), pp. 301–308.

Hogwood, B. W. and L. Gunn 1984, *Policy Analysis for the Real World*, Oxford University Press, Oxford.

Honig, M. I. 2003, 'Building Policy from Practice: Central office administrators' roles and capacity in collaborative educational policy implementation', *Educational Administration Quarterly* 39(3), pp. 292–338.

Honig, M. I. 2004a, 'The New Middle Management: Intermediary organizations in education policy implementation', *Educational Evaluation and Policy Analysis* 26(1), pp. 65–87.

Honig, M. I. 2004b, 'Where's The "Up" in Bottom-Up Reform?', *Educational Policy* 18(4), pp. 527–561.

Honig, M. I. 2006a, 'Complexity and Policy Implementation: Challenges and opportunities for the field' in M. I. Honig (ed.), *New Directions in Education Policy Implementation: Confronting complexity*, State University of New York Press, Albany, pp. 1–23.

Honig, M. I. 2006b, 'Street-Level Bureaucracy Revisited: Frontline district central-office administrators as boundary spanners in educational policy implementation', *Educational Evaluation and Policy Analysis* (28)4, pp. 357–383.

Howlett, M. 1991, 'Policy Instruments, Policy Styles, and Policy Implementation: National approaches to theories of instrument choice', *Policy Studies Journal* 19(2), pp. 1–21.

Howlett, M. 2005, 'What is a Policy Instrument?: Tools, mixes, and implementation styles', in P. Eliadas, M. Hill and M. Howlett (eds), *Designing Government: From instruments to governance*, McGill-Queen's University Press, Montreal and Kingston, pp. 31–50.

Ingraham, P. W. and L. E. Lynn, Jr. (eds) 2004, *The Art of Governance: Analyzing management and administration*, Georgetown University Press, Washington, DC.

Ingram, H. 1977, 'Policy Implementation Through Bargaining: The case of federal grants-in-aid', *Public Policy* 25, pp. 499–526.

Ingram, H. and D. Mann (eds) 1980, *Why Policies Succeed or Fail*, Sage, New York.

Kelman, S. 2005, *Unleashing Change: A study of organizational renewal in government*, Brookings Institution, Washington, DC.

Kettunen, P. 2000, 'Implementation Approach: The political scientist's perspective', *Policy Currents* 10:1–2, pp. 3–5.

Klijn, E. H. and G. R. Teisman 1997, 'Strategies and Games in Networks', in W. J. M. Kickert, E.-H. Klijn, and J. F. M. Koppenjan (eds), *Managing Complex Networks: Strategies for the public sector*, Sage, London, pp. 98–118.

Kotter, J. P. 1990, 'What Leaders Really Do', *Harvard Business Review*, pp. 103–111.

Kotter, J. P. 1996, *Leading Change*, Harvard Business Press, Boston.

Lester, J. P., A. M. O'Bowman, M. G. Goggin, and L. J. O'Toole, Jr. 1987, 'Public Policy Implementation: Evolution of the field and agenda for future research', *Policy Studies Review* 7(1), pp. 200–216.

Lester, J. P., and M. L. Goggin 1998, 'Back to the Future: The rediscovery of implementation studies', *Policy Currents* 8, pp. 1–9.

Lester, J. P. 2000, 'Back to the Future in Implementation Research: A response', *Policy Currents* 10(1–2), pp. 2–5.

Lindquist, E. A. 2006, 'Organizing for Policy Implementation: The emergence and role of implementation units in policy design and oversight', *Journal of Comparative Policy Analysis* 8(4), pp. 311–324.

Lindquist, E. A. and J. Wanna 2011, 'Delivering Policy Reform: Making it happen, making it stick', in E. A. Lindquist, S. Vincent and J. Wanna (eds), *Delivering Policy Reform: Anchoring significant reforms in turbulent times*, ANU E Press, Canberra.

Lindquist, E. A., S. Vincent and J. Wanna (eds) 2011, *Delivering Policy Reform: Anchoring significant reforms in turbulent times*, ANU E Press, Canberra.

Lipsky, M. 1980, *Street-Level Bureaucrats: The dilemmas of individuals in public services*, Russell Sage Foundation, New York.

Lundin, M. 2007a, 'When Does Cooperation Improve Policy Implementation?', *Policy Studies Journal* 35(4), pp. 629–652.

Lundin, M. 2007b, 'Explaining Cooperation: How resource interdependence, goal congruence, and trust affect joint actions in policy implementation', *Journal of Public Administration Research and Theory* 17(4), pp. 651–672.

Lynn, Jr., L. E., C. J. Heinrich and C. J. Hill 2001, *Improving Governance: A new logic for empirical research*, Georgetown University Press, Washington, DC.

Management Advisory Committee 2004, 'Connecting Government: Whole of government responses to Australia's priority challenges', Australian Public Service Commission, Canberra.

Marsh, D. and P. Fawcett 2012, 'Policy Transfer and Policy Success: The case of the gateway review process', *Government and Opposition* 47(2), pp. 162–185.

Matland, R. E. 1995, 'Synthesizing the Implementation Literature: The ambiguity-conflict model of policy implementation', *Journal of Public Administration Research and Theory* 5(2), pp. 145–174.

May, P. J. 2003, 'Policy Design and Implementation', in B. Guy Peters and J. Pierre (eds), *Handbook of Public Administration*, Sage, London, pp. 223–233.

Mazmanian, D. A. and P. A. Sabatier (eds) 1981, *Effective Policy Implementation*, Heath, Lexington.

Mazmanian, D. A. and P. A. Sabatier 1983, *Implementation and Public Policy*, Scott, Forseman, Glenview.

Meier, K. 1999, 'Are We Sure That Lasswell Did it This Way?: Lester Goggin and implementation research', *Policy Currents* 9(1), pp. 5–8.

Meyers, M. K., and S. Vorsanger 2003, 'Street-Level Bureaucrats and the Implementation of Public Policy', in B. Guy Peters and J. Pierre (eds), *Handbook of Public Administration*, Sage, London, pp. 245–255.

Montjoy, R. S. and L. O'Toole Jr. 1979, 'Toward a Theory of Policy Implementation: An organizational perspective', *Public Administration Review* 39(5), pp. 465–476.

Nakamura, R. T. and F. Smallwood 1980, *The Politics of Policy Implementation*, St. Martin's, New York.

O'Toole, Jr., L. J. 2000, 'Research on Policy Implementation: Assessment and Prospect', *Journal of Public Administration Research and Theory* 10(2), pp. 263–288.

O'Toole, Jr., L. J. 2003, 'Interorganizational Relations in Implementation', in B. Guy Peters and J. Pierre (eds), *Handbook of Public Administration*, Sage, London, pp. 234–244.

O'Toole, Jr., L. J. 2004, 'The Theory-Practice Issue in Policy Implementation Research', *Public Administration* 82(2), pp. 309–329.

O'Toole, Jr., L. J., K. I. Hanf and P. L. Hupe 1997, 'Managing Implementation Processes in Networks', in W. J. M. Kickert, E.-H. Klijn, and J. F. M. Koppenjan (eds), *Managing Complex Networks: Strategies for the public sector*, Sage, London, pp. 137–151.

O'Toole, Jr., L. J. and R. S. Montjoy 1984, 'Interorganizational Policy Implementation: A theoretical perspective', *Public Administration Review* 44(6), pp. 491–503.

Pal, L. A. 1997, *Beyond Policy Analysis: Public issue management in turbulent times*, Nelson, Scarborough.

Palumbo, D. J., and D. J. Calista (eds) 1990, *Implementation and the Policy Process: Opening up the black box,* Greenwood, New York.

Patashnik, E. M. 2003, 'After the Public Interest Prevails: The political sustainability of policy reform', *Governance* 16(2), pp. 203–234.

Patashnik, E. M. 2008, *Reforms at Risk: What happens after major policy changes are enacted*, Princeton University Press, Princeton.

Potoski, M. 2001, 'Implementation, Uncertainty and the Policy Sciences', *Policy Currents* 11(1–2), pp. 2–5, 283–308.

Pressman, J. L., and A. Wildavsky 1973, *Implementation: How great expectations in Washington are dashed in Oakland, or why it's amazing that federal programs work at all*, University of California Press, Berkeley.

Rittel, H. W. J. and M. M. Webber 1973, 'Dilemmas in a General Theory of Planning', *Policy Sciences* 4, pp. 155–169.

Sabatier, P. A. 1986, 'Top-Down and Bottom-Up Approaches to Implementation Research: A critical analysis and suggested synthesis', *Journal of Public Policy* 6(1), pp. 21–48.

Saetren, H. 2005, 'Facts and Myths about Research on Public Policy Implementation: Out-of-fashion, allegedly dead, but still very much alive and relevant', *Policy Studies Journal* 33(4), pp. 559–582.

Schofield, J. 2001, 'Time for a Revival? Public Policy Implementation: A review of the literature and agenda for future research', *International Journal of Management Review* 3(3), pp. 245–263.

Schofield, J. 2004, 'A Model of Learned Implementation', *Public Administration* 82(2), pp. 283–308.

Schofield, J. and C. Sausman 2004, 'Symposium on Implementing Public Policy: Learning from theory and practice: Introduction', *Public Administration* 82(2), pp. 235–248.

Schneider, A. 1999, 'Terminator? What, Me?: Some thoughts about the study of policy implementation', *Policy Currents* 9(1), pp. 1–5.

Selznick, P. 1957, *Leadership in Administration: A sociological perspective*, University of California Press, Berkeley.

Spillaine, J. P., B. J. Reiser and T. Reimer 2002, 'Policy Implementation and Cognition: Reframing and refocusing implementation research', *Review of Educational Research* 72(3), pp. 387–431.

State Services Authority 2011, 'Making Public Policy Stick: Policy implementation literature report', State Government of Victoria State Services Authority, Melbourne. Available at: http://www.ssa.vic.gov.au/images/stories/product_files/862_making%20public%20policy%20stick.PDF.

Stoker, R. P. 1989, 'A Regime Framework for Implementation Analysis: Cooperation and reconciliation of federalist imperatives', *Policy Studies Review* 9(1), pp. 29–49.

Thompson, J. D. 1967, *Organizations in Action*, McGraw-Hill, New York.

Van Horn, C. E. 1979, *Policy Implementation in the Federal System*, Heath, Lexington.

Van Meter, D. S. and C. E. Van Horn 1975, 'The Policy Implementation Process: A conceptual framework', *Administration and Society* 6(4), pp. 445–488.

Weatherly, R. and M. Lipsky 1977, 'Street-Level Bureaucrats and Institutional Innovation: Implementing special education reform', *Harvard Educational Review* 47(2), pp. 171–197.

Williams, W. et al. 1982, *Studying Implementation: Methodological and administrative issues*, Chatham House, Chatham.

Williams, W. 1980, *The Implementation Perspective: A guide for managing social service delivery programs*, University of California Press, Berkeley.

Wilson, J. Q. 1989, *Bureaucracy*, Basic Books, New York.

Winter, S. C. 1999, 'New Directions for Implementation Research', *Policy Currents* 8(4), pp. 1–5.

Winter, S. C. 2003, 'Implementation Perspectives: Status and reconsideration', in B. G. Peters and J. Pierre (eds), *Handbook of Public Administration*, Sage, London, pp. 212–222.

Yanow, D. 1993, 'The Communication of Policy Meanings: Implementation as Interpretation and Text', *Policy Sciences* 26(1), pp. 41–61.

8. National Competition Policy and Cooperative Federalism

Jeffrey Harwood and John Phillimore

Introduction

The National Competition Policy (NCP) is widely regarded as one of Australia's most successful examples of cooperative federalism. Through the Council of Australian Governments (COAG), the Commonwealth, states and territories agreed in 1995 to implement a set of microeconomic reforms focused on removing impediments to equal competition between public and private businesses and creating competitive pricing and regulatory mechanisms for utility services and road transport. In return for the successful implementation of the reform package, the Commonwealth transferred payments to the states and territories. The NCP was subsequently commended as an economic success by the Productivity Commission (2005). However, whether it should be regarded as a successful example of cooperative federalism is a matter deserving further consideration.

For some, the NCP comprised soundly based policy goals and realised worthwhile microeconomic reforms that states and territories would not otherwise have achieved (see, for example, Banks 2005; Productivity Commission 2005; Sims 1999; Thomas 1996). However, there are some critical views that the nature and implementation of the NCP favoured the Commonwealth, threatened community service obligations, did not take into sufficient account regional needs and failed to achieve the environmental benefits envisaged to flow on from more efficient markets, especially in the case of rural water schemes (see, for example, Butler 1996; Boswell 1996; Carver 1996; Fenna 2007; Hollander 2006; Hollander and Curran 2001).

This chapter evaluates the NCP as an example of cooperative federalism. After providing an account of the way the NCP came into being, was implemented and evolved, we consider the competing interpretations. In assessing those propositions, we draw upon discussions with six senior policy officers from various agencies in four states who were responsible for its implementation, and from the National Competition Council (NCC). A close reading of NCP documents further enlightens our evaluation. Our conclusion is that while in many respects a good example of Australian governments working together, the NCP was ultimately too coercive in its application to constitute an entirely successful example of cooperative federalism.

The National Competition Policy

The decision by COAG (COAG 1995a, 1995b) to implement the NCP was the culmination of an economic reform process that began with the floating of the Australian dollar in 1983. This was followed by further deregulation of financial markets and a series of sectoral plans designed to promote industrial development and locally manufactured exports. Tariffs were subsequently lowered in the motor vehicle, textile, clothing and footwear, and telecommunications sectors. While these reforms were intended to make the private sector more competitive, less attention was being paid to the public sector. Following the release of the National Competition Policy Review Report (Hilmer et al. 1993), however, attention shifted to the structural reform of government utilities, regulatory and pricing frameworks, and the extent to which government legislation supported or undermined competition. The solution, it was argued, was the application of market-based policy instruments to the public sector.

As Painter (1998, pp. 81–89) has explained in detail, the resulting NCP was forged through both conflict and cooperation. The then Prime Minister, Paul Keating, was anxious to implement Hilmer's proposed reforms and was prepared to impose these upon the states. On the other hand, the states were arguably in their strongest position vis-à-vis the Commonwealth. The NCP called for the reform of government business enterprises, notably the network utilities; however, these were state government instrumentalities and the Commonwealth needed the states' cooperation for such reforms to proceed. Although the High Court had not stopped the Commonwealth from encroaching upon the states' traditional policy jurisdictions, it had been reluctant to intervene in support of the Commonwealth in matters affecting the institutional governance of the states. The states were in an unusually strong position.

The states, though, were prepared to cooperate with the Commonwealth. Importantly, from the states' perspective, the NCP would not directly expand Commonwealth powers. Moreover, most states had Liberal-led governments at the time that had already initiated microeconomic reforms within their jurisdictions (Painter 1998, p. 82).[1] In this respect, there was policy convergence between state and Commonwealth central agencies — what Painter (1998, p. 83) referred to as the 'central agency club' — in which the focus was on achieving certain economic outcomes, rather than following federal principles. The outcome was a compromise, with the Commonwealth agreeing to the states being responsible for implementing the NCP in return for payments upon

---

1 For most of the negotiations over the NCP in 1994–1995, only the Commonwealth, Queensland and the Australian Capital Territory had Labor governments. However, just before the intergovernmental agreements were signed at the April 1995 COAG meeting, a Liberal government took office in the Australian Capital Territory (February) and the Labor Party won government in New South Wales (March).

meeting particular policy milestones (Painter 1988, pp. 88–89). Furthermore, membership of the two institutions created to administer the NCP — the NCC and the Australian Competition and Consumer Commission (ACCC) — would require the majority approval of the states and territories. By accepting the need for national uniformity under the NCP and the use of template legislation to achieve this objective, the states relinquished their legislative sovereignty. Hence, at the fifth COAG meeting, held in Canberra on 11 April 1995, the respective parties signed the three intergovernmental agreements that provided the foundation of the NCP.

The institutional components

The NCP comprised three intergovernmental agreements (IGAs) and an Act of the Commonwealth Parliament. First, by signing the Competition Principles Agreement 1995 (NCC 1998), the respective governments agreed to:

- implement the concept of 'competitive neutrality', such that private and government businesses could compete equally;

- establish mechanisms that prevented government business enterprises from exploiting their monopolies;

- the structural reform of public monopolies;

- rationalise the regulatory and pricing frameworks of water, gas and electricity utilities, along with the road transport sector;

- establish a national access regime designed to facilitate sharing of 'essential infrastructure' among competing businesses; and

- amend laws that hinder competition, except in cases found to be in the public interest.

The second IGA was the Conduct Code Agreement 1995 (NCC 1998), which required the amendment and use of the *Trade Practices Act 1974* to prevent anti-competitive behaviour by government and unincorporated businesses.

Third, the Agreement to Implement the National Competition Policy and Related Reforms (Implementation Agreement) 1995 (NCC 1998) specified an arrangement whereby the Commonwealth would compensate the states and territories some of the costs of implementing the NCP. The Commonwealth agreed to maintain the per capita financial assistance grants to the states and territories and provide competition payments upon satisfactory progress in implementing NCP reforms. This was intended to reflect the fact that, although the benefits of greater competition flow on to the community in general, the direct fiscal benefits tend to flow to the Commonwealth in the form of increased taxation revenue. In addition, the states would lose dividend income from their public utilities (which could be substantial and which, moreover, could be tapped at will). It was estimated that the competition payments would cost the Commonwealth $4.2 billion (in 1994–95 prices) over the nine years of the policy (COAG 1995b, 1995c).

The final component of the NCP was the *Competition Policy Reform Act 1995* (Commonwealth of Australia 1995), which established the NCC under the *Trade Practices Act 1974*. Part IIA of the *Trade Practices Act* established the NCC with a Council President and maximum of four councillors serving terms of no more than five years. (Initially, the councillors were jointly appointed by the Commonwealth, states and territories for a period of three years, and supported by a secretariat of 12 officials, some of whom were on secondment from sub-national jurisdictions). As such, the NCC was a Commonwealth statutory body, whose role was to advise the Commonwealth, states and territories on (rather than implement) the NCP. The NCC was also responsible for assessing individual state and territory governments' progress in implementing the reforms, ascertaining whether they had made sufficient progress to receive their compensation payments, recommending to the Commonwealth Treasurer whether the respective governments should receive their competition payments and making available to the public information about the details and progress of the NCP.

The *Competition Policy Reform Act 1995* also established the ACCC under the *Trade Practices Act 1974*. Part II of the *Trade Practices Act 1974* made provision for a Commission Chairperson and any number of other commission members to have terms of up to five years. As in the case of the NCC, a majority of states and territories had to agree with appointments for them to be confirmed. The ACCC was made responsible for administering the *Trade Practices Act 1974*, informing businesses and consumers about their obligations and rights under the Act, and acting as an oversight body to identify cases of price fixing and market sharing and report these to the relevant authorities.

Implementation

National access regime

In accordance with the NCP, a national access regime was established, along with various industry specific access regimes. The ACCC was made responsible for administering the regime. Some of the industry regimes — for example, rail networks, ports and electricity distribution networks — came under the jurisdiction of state and territory legislation and were administered by the relevant state and territory oversight authorities.

Competitive neutrality

All states and territories implemented competitive neutrality principles to ensure that government and private businesses could compete on equal terms. Guidelines were published to inform the respective parties of their obligations and complaints handling offices were established. Independent oversight bodies were also established to monitor and regulate the prices set by monopoly providers. For example, the Economic Regulation Authority was established by the government of Western Australia in January 2004 to monitor that state's electricity, gas and water sectors, ensure that the respective access and pricing regimes are consistent with the relevant pieces of legislation, to promote and monitor the use of customer charters, and to carry out inquiries when required by the state government (ERA 2009).

Application of the *Trade Practices Act 1974*

In 1996, the Competition Code (Part XIA) was added to the *Trade Practices Act 1974*. This allowed the states and territories to incorporate a version of Part 4 of the Act, the Competition Code, to cover their jurisdictions. Consequently, state and territory governments, unincorporated bodies and government business enterprises were no longer exempt from engaging in anti-competitive practices (unless given permission to do so by the ACCC on grounds of public interest). The states and territories agreed to this and they passed the necessary legislation by July 1996 (Productivity Commission 2005, p. 13).

Legislative reforms

It was originally estimated that the review and reform of legislation deemed anti-competitive would be finished by 2000 in accordance with clause 5 of the Competition Principles Agreement. COAG subsequently extended the time of review to 30 June 2002. An additional 12 months was later granted by the NCC (2003, 4.1), but with the cautionary note:

> Review and/or reform activity that is incomplete or not consistent with NCP principles at June 2003 will be considered to not comply with NCP obligations. Where noncompliance is significant ... the Council is likely to make adverse recommendations on payments.

Table 1 sets out the annual payments made to the states and territories and the penalties imposed by the Commonwealth.

Table 1: Payments and penalties under the NCP

	1997-98		1998-99		1999-2000		2000-01		2001-02		2002-03		2003-04		2004-05		2005-06		Total	
	Pay-ments	Penal-ties	Pay-ments	Penal-ties	Pay-ments	Penal-ties	Pay-ments	Penal-ties	Pay-ments	Penal-ties	Pay-ments	Penal-ties	Pay-ments	Penal-ties	Pay-ments	Penal-ties	Pay-ments	Penal-ties	Pay-ments	Penal-ties
NSW	72.2	–	73.0	–	148.6	–	155.9	–	242.5	–	251.8	–	203.5	25.4	233.5	–	291.8	–	1672.8	25.4
Vic	52.9	–	53.6	–	109.2	–	114.7	–	179.6	–	182.4	–	178.7	–	201.9	–	187.7	–	1260.7	0
Qld	39.2	–	39.8	–	81.5	–	73.0	–	147.9	0.27	138.9	0.27	87.9	7.3	143.2	7.5	178.8	7.8	930.2	23.14
WA	20.7	–	21.1	–	43.2	–	45.5	–	71.1	–	72.0	–	33.6	14.9	53.6	15.4	66.9	23.8	427.7	54.1
SA	17.0	–	17.0	–	34.5	–	35.9	–	55.7	–	57.1	–	40.7	5.8	50.4	3.0	51.3	9.1	359.6	17.9
Tas	5.4	–	5.4	–	10.8	–	11.2	–	17.4	–	17.7	–	17.2	–	19.8	–	19.1	–	124.0	0
ACT	3.5	–	3.5	–	7.2	–	7.5	–	11.6	–	12.4	–	11.0	–	13.6	–	12.8	–	83.1	0
NT	2.2	–	2.2	–	4.5	–	4.5	–	7.6	–	7.5	–	5.9	–	8.5	0.4	8.0	–	50.9	0.4
Total	213.1	0	215.7	0	439.5	0	448.0	0	733.3	0.27	739.9	0.27	578.5	53.4	724.4	26.3	816.5	40.7	4909.0	120.94

Source: Payment figures are taken from Final Budget Outcome documents, penalty figures are taken from the Treasurer's media statements and NCC annual reports.

NB: Totals may not add up due to rounding.

Although an occasionally contentious component of the NCP, the legislative review and reform requirement was generally met. In 2001, the NCC decided to differentiate between priority and non-priority legislation. The former were seen to have a much greater impact upon competition so that their review and reform would provide the most benefit to the wider community. Thus, in assessing whether the progress of the individual states and territories was sufficient to recommend to the Treasurer that they receive their competition payments, completion of the priority legislation reviews was pivotal.

The NCC (2005, 9.6) subsequently recommended that the states and territories be penalised and they responded accordingly by finishing most of the reviews by 2005 (see Table 2).

Table 2: Completion rates of legislative reform (1995–2005)

Federal jurisdictions	Percentage of legislative reform completed (1995–2005)		
	Priority	Non-priority	Total
Australian Capital Territory	82	98	93
Commonwealth	64	89	78
New South Wales	88	94	91
Northern Territory	82	90	85
Queensland	85	92	87
South Australia	69	94	83
Tasmania	84	96	91
Victoria	84	91	88
Western Australia	55	77	68

Source: NCC 2005.

While the access regimes, competitive neutrality, the *Trade Practices Act 1974*, and the legislative reviews were implemented to improve competition in general, they were also applied more specifically to key infrastructure: water, gas, electricity and road transport.

Water

The so-called 'water reforms' agreed to as part of the NCP were intended to address the widely-held view that Australia's water industry was unsustainable and inefficient. It was agreed by COAG (1994a, 1994b) that overuse of urban and rural supplies and the environmental degradation of water supplies necessitated a package of reforms to address these issues. The package included institutional, pricing, investment, allocation, and trading reforms. The institutional reforms entailed corporatising water utilities by 1998, separating responsibility for resource management, standards, compliance and provision of services, and the establishment of integrated resource management mechanisms. It was also agreed to implement pricing reforms that comprised consumption-based pricing mechanisms, withdraw cross-subsidies where possible, and make transparent the subsidies that remain. Investment reforms were implemented to ensure that further infrastructure developments were environmentally acceptable and economically viable. Finally, it was agreed that water should be allocated on the basis of effect upon the environment, that land title and water rights should be detached, that entitlement be based upon 'ownership, volume, reliability, transferability and, if appropriate, quality', and trading in allocations and entitlements be introduced by 1998.

By the end of 2004, the states and territories had made substantial progress on the implementation of these reforms. Water utilities had been corporatised or, in the case of South Australia, contracted out to the private sector, and the service provision and regulatory divisions had been separated (Productivity Commission 2005, p. 27). Furthermore, all participants had passed legislation to separate land title from water entitlements, and established requirements for environmental assessments. The NCC (2003, p. xiv) attributed delays in reforms to the conflicting interests of the various stakeholders, and to the difficulty in reconciling 'the diversity of administrative and legislative environments across jurisdictions'.

Gas

Like the electricity industry, the gas industry was characterised by vertically integrated government monopolies, which strictly regulated gas suppliers (Productivity Commission 2005, pp. 23–24). Legislation controlled the distribution of gas both within and between states and territories. The states and territories successfully implemented the requisite reforms identified as essential for a competitive gas industry. These reforms included the separation of the transmission and distribution operations; rescinding legislation and regulations that prevented states and territories trading in gas; the institution of the National Gas Access Code to facilitate 'third party access to gas transmission and distribution pipelines'; the corporatisation of government gas authorities; and the introduction of fully competitive retail markets.

Electricity

Prior to the NCP, the Australian electricity market was highly regulated and dominated by government-owned and vertically integrated utilities that were bounded by state borders (Productivity Commission 2005, p. 21). Consequently, electricity prices were unnecessarily high and oversupply was the norm. The proposed solution was the creation in 1998 of a national electricity market, comprising all states and territories except Western Australia and the Northern Territory. The Productivity Commission (2005, p. 22) subsequently reported that most governments met their requirements. Certainly, all had established mechanisms to allow third party access to network infrastructure. The state-owned utilities, whether privatised, leased or corporatised, had been broken up into their constituent parts — generation, distribution, regulation and retail. Under this policy of vertical disaggregation, most large customers could choose their supplier, as could most domestic users.

However, a fully competitive national electricity market was not realised. The Productivity Commission (2005, p. 22) attributed this to insufficient grid interconnection, which meant that potential users were unable to access various suppliers; too few generators to stimulate competition upstream; price signals to residential users that were 'inflexible'; the existence of multiple regulators (that is, one in each sub-national jurisdiction); and a lack of competition in electricity generation.

Transport

The road transport industry had long been covered by the various rules and regulations of each sub-national jurisdiction (Productivity Commission 2005, p. 25). This imposed costs on users which were, in turn, passed onto consumers. The primary objectives of the NCP reforms were to reconcile the costs with heavy vehicle charges, and replace the various state and territory regimes with a national regulatory framework. It was envisaged that such a framework would include a national heavy vehicle registration scheme, agreement between the jurisdictions over the transporting of dangerous products, roadworthiness, driving hours and the regulation of oversized vehicles, and a mechanism to ensure compliance with the framework.

Apart from matters pertaining to licensing and registration, the states and territories had completed most of the proposed NCP transport reforms by the time of the 2005 assessment by the NCC (2005, 8.1). The NCC (2005, 8.2–5) noted that the Commonwealth had yet to pass legislation enabling a national heavy vehicle registration scheme, while the Australian Capital Territory was still deliberating over how to regulate the renewal of heavy vehicle registrations. Western Australia had two remaining reforms to address concerning the local introduction of the national drivers' licence classifications and the adoption of a single, nationally valid, drivers' licence, although the legislation for these was being debated in the Western Australian Parliament.

Other reforms

Although the NCP is notable for its application to public utilities and the road transport industry, it was applied to many other industries in ways that were sometimes resisted by stakeholders and the Commonwealth, state and territory governments, leading to sub-national governments being penalised financially under the NCP (see Table 2). Elements of the agriculture industry were especially opposed to reforms proposed under the NCP. For example, there was considerable opposition to the removal of the Australian Wheat Board's effective monopoly over wheat exports. Despite the NCC's call for the *Wheat Marketing Act 1989* to be revised or revoked, the Commonwealth refused to deregulate the wheat export industry. Likewise, the Western Australian government was steadfast in its refusal to deregulate potato marketing; unlike the Commonwealth, it was subsequently penalised a total of $7.5m.

The pharmacy sector was another that successfully avoided deregulation and evidenced the Commonwealth's 'flexibility' in applying COAG agreements in contrast to the NCC's 'literal' interpretations. The National Competition Policy Review of Pharmacy Regulation reported to COAG in 2000 and recommended that the states and territories be required to remove all restrictions on the number of pharmacies that could be owned by a single pharmacist, but also recommended that limits be placed on the number of pharmacies controlled by individual friendly societies within a jurisdiction. The first recommendation was supported by a COAG working group and accepted by COAG (NCC 2005, 19.9–10). The working group rejected the second recommendation and COAG accepted its counter-proposal that individual friendly societies be free to operate under the same conditions of ownership as pharmacists. In 2004, however, with every sub-national jurisdiction yet to completely deregulate pharmacy ownership, the Prime Minister informed each of the states and territories that they would not incur penalties provided they legislated minimum limits of ownership as stipulated by him. Nevertheless, the NCC (2005) still noted that by not deregulating the pharmacy industry, each sub-national government was failing to meet its obligations under the Competition Principles Agreement.

However, not all the states and territories felt the wrath of the NCC. Victoria, Tasmania and the Australian Capital Territory did not suffer permanent deductions as a consequence of adverse findings by the NCC. The other jurisdictions were penalised for a variety of reasons. Permanent deductions were applied to New South Wales for failing to deregulate rice marketing, liquor sales marketing, and the chicken meat industry. Queensland was penalised for failing to deregulate liquor sales marketing and making insufficient progress on water reforms. Western Australia was punished for failing to deregulate retail trading hours, liquor sales marketing and potato marketing, and for having outstanding legislation review items. South Australia was also penalised for having outstanding legislation review items, as well as failing to deregulate the chicken meat industry, liquor sales marketing, and barley marketing. Finally, the Northern Territory was subjected to permanent deductions for not deregulating liquor sales marketing.

NCP as an exemplar of cooperative federalism

The NCP is often promoted as an exemplar of collaborative federalism, an initiative that realised worthwhile reforms that states and territories would not otherwise have achieved. The Western Australia Chamber of Commerce and Industry, for example, described the NCP as 'one of the greatest achievements of cooperative federalism in recent years' (CCIWA 2007, p. 7). Typically, such views are expressed because of the economic outcomes that NCP has delivered, the positive role of the NCC as a purportedly neutral arbiter between the Commonwealth and the states and territories, and the use of incentive payments to encourage scheduled implementation of the NCP reforms.

Measurable economic success

First and foremost, the microeconomic reforms that the NCP brought about are widely seen as being in the national interest. In its report on the NCP, for example, the Productivity Commission (2005, p. 40) used the growth in multifactor productivity (MFP) — 'the efficiency with which both labour and capital inputs are used in production' — as its primary indicator of improved economic performance. The Productivity Commission (2005, p. 46) found that MFP in the telecommunications sector had evidenced an annual seven per cent increase from 1996–97 to 1999–2000, while MFP in the postal services sector had increased 3.5 per cent per annum over the period from 1992 to 2002. Overall, the Productivity Commission (2005, p. 35) estimated that the NCP has contributed a 'permanent increase' of at least 2.5 per cent in Australia's GDP.

Governance

Second, officers interviewed regarded the NCC as a fair and reasonable broker in its negotiations with the states and territories. They attributed this to the relative autonomy of the NCC, the professionalism of the officers involved and the mechanism through which the NCC operated, notably, the procedure by which the NCC forwarded a draft report to the states and territories, allowed them the opportunity to respond and, then, negotiate a deal with the NCC.

Reform funding

The incentive payments are almost universally regarded as being crucial to the successful implementation of the NCP. By enabling them to highlight the cost of not pursuing reforms, central agency ministers were able to win over their colleagues in Cabinet meetings. Moreover, local media publicised the potential loss of revenue and politicians had to justify delays in implementing NCP reforms. In this way, everybody could ascertain whether it was worth sacrificing the incentive payment to maintain the policy status quo. Western Australia's decision not to deregulate shopping hours, for example, could only be justified by the Western Australian government after holding a referendum.

Those who saw the NCP as a successful example of cooperative federalism emphasised the initial process and policy outcomes. For them, cooperation meant collaboration over policy formulation and a signed agreement. Success was measured in terms of achieving microeconomic reforms and improvements in economic productivity that could be associated with the reforms.

NCP as less-than-ideal cooperative federalism

Despite the praise lavished on the NCP as a positive example of cooperative federalism, it also received its share of criticism during and after its implementation. Although the NCP was premised upon agreement between the federal partners, some within the states and territories felt that it did not treat equally all levels of government, that the review process of the NCC was not sufficiently transparent, and that the demands to comply with the NCP threatened state autonomy.

Inequitable treatment

Perhaps the most consistent criticism was that the NCP framework did not hold the Commonwealth accountable for implementing reforms the same way it did the states (NCC 2004, p. 39; New South Wales Government 2004, pp. 18, 20). The objective of the payments mechanism under the NCP was to act as an incentive — albeit a negative incentive — to discourage inaction by the respective sub-levels of governments. However, the mechanism did not extend to include the Commonwealth, despite the fact that by the time that the NCC had completed its final assessment of legislative reviews, the Commonwealth had reviewed only 78 per cent of its legislation. This meant that some officials saw the NCC as a 'policeman' for the Commonwealth to cajole the states and territories into doing its bidding.

Lack of transparency

The review mechanism of the NCP reinforced the belief of some states that the NCC and the Commonwealth were working together to impose policy upon the states. The Victorian government (Victoria 2004, p. 15), for example, voiced its frustration that the NCP did not contain a formal process after the annual submission by the states. Although the states and territories could see and comment upon the draft report, they were not shown the recommendations. Furthermore, there was no logical framework for NCC decisions and its recommendations as to whether penalties should be applied.

The NCC (2004, p. 39) acknowledged that transparency was lacking in the reporting processes. It pointed out that it was not to blame: there was nothing requiring it to make its reviews public. It also explained that some reports were not released because they were unpopular with government. By making all reports public, governments would be compelled to follow processes and meet acceptable standards. Moreover, such reports needed to meet consultation standards that would be acceptable to stakeholders and the wider community.

State policy autonomy challenged

A more fundamental criticism of the NCP was that it was a national, rather than federal policy, which diminished the policy autonomy of the states and territories (Fenna 2007, pp. 189–190). Significant parts of the NCP, though — indeed, perhaps the bulk of the NCP — concerned collective goods whose boundaries in most respects do not exceed sub-national jurisdictions. Moreover, the inclusion of financial incentives undermined the idea of states and territories proceeding in a federal fashion, that is, in their own direction at their own speed. Thus, it could be said that the uniform national approach reflected a common view that this was the best policy approach to take, rather than any need for policy uniformity *per se* due to inter-jurisdictional inefficiencies.

The national electricity market provides an interesting example of this tension between national and federal policy. In this case, there were likely inter-jurisdictional spillover benefits of having a single regulator and market, rather than multiple regulators and markets. Although Western Australia and the Northern Territory were excluded from the new federal market, they were not excluded from the new national policy requirements. This is not to suggest that the disaggregation of Western Power, for example, was an inherently sub-optimal policy for Western Australia, rather that it was not a federal policy that had obvious spillovers or involvement with the other sub-national jurisdictions.

The Western Australian government found itself under considerable pressure to have the requisite legislation passed by the State Parliament, with the Treasurer (Hansard 2005) informing Parliament:

> We have already suffered a suspension of our competition policy payments of more than $11 million for 2004–05, and we would be facing a further suspension or deduction of competition policy payments of more than $11 million for this financial year. If we go past the decision on the competition policy payments this year, we lose any chance of getting back the suspension that was imposed last year and we would most likely lose the more than $11 million at stake this year.

The challenge that the NCP posed to the policy autonomy of the states and territories was further evidenced by the NCC's assessment of how the 'public benefit' clause was applied. Subclause 1(3) of the Competition Principles Agreement 1995 (NCC 1998) required that certain matters of 'public benefit' be 'taken into account' during policy and legislative reviews. These matters included:

- government legislation and policies relating to ecologically sustainable development;

- social welfare and equity considerations, including community service obligations;

- government legislation and policies relating to matters such as occupational health and safety, industrial relations and access and equity;

- economic and regional development, including employment and investment growth;

- the interests of consumers generally or of a class of consumers;

- the competitiveness of Australian business; and

- the efficient allocation of resources.

The states and territories understood the clause to mean that policies and legislation could be permitted to restrict competition if it was likely to undermine, for example, community service obligations. The NCC (1996), on the other hand, noted that the subclause did not state the weight that should be attributed to each matter, nor did it set out to explain to what extent sectoral interests should be prioritised over the interests of the entire community. Hence, the clause provided 'an aid to assist review rather than a mechanism for imposing blanket exemptions on reform' (NCC 1996, p. 6). Ultimately, the NCC settled upon subclause 5(1) of the Competition Principles Agreement 1995 for guidance, which stated:

> The guiding principle is that legislation (including acts, enactments, ordinances or regulations) should not restrict competition unless it can be demonstrated that:
>
> (a) the benefits of the restriction to the community as a whole outweigh the costs; and,
>
> (b) the objectives of the legislation can only be achieved by restricting competition.

The case of retail shopping hours in Western Australia is probably the most striking example of the NCC not accepting a state government's interpretation of the public benefit. Partial reform of trading hours was blocked in the conservative-controlled Legislative Council. The NCC (2002, 10.6–7) acknowledged this, but argued that Western Australia must still meet its NCP obligations. The NCC (2003, pp. xlii) subsequently recommended that the Western Australian government be penalised $7.52 million for not deregulating retail shopping hours. The Western Australian government sought to diffuse the issue by holding a referendum simultaneously with the 2005 state election. Following a resounding result from the public rejecting liberalisation (WAEC 2008), the Western Australian Treasurer wrote to the NCC: 'The letter advised that the Council, to conclude otherwise, would have to assume that it knows more than the public about Western Australia's public interest' (NCC 2005, 14.30). In its 2005 assessment, the NCC (2005, 14.30–31) countered:

> Clause 5 of the CPA … requires governments to remove restrictions on competition unless they can demonstrate that the restrictions are warranted — that is, that restricting competition benefits the community overall (being in the public interest) and that the restriction is necessary … Where a government introduces or retains competition restrictions, and this action was not reasonably drawn from the recommendations of a review, the Council looks for the government to provide a rigorous supporting case, including a demonstration of flaws in the review's analysis and reasoning. The Council considers that conducting a referendum does not absolve a government from its NCP legislation review obligations.

The NCC held firm and withheld the incentive payment.

A conceptual consideration

Although both sides present convincing cases about the merits and shortcomings of the NCP as an example of cooperative federalism, it appears that their assessments are focused primarily upon different stages of the policy process. The view that the NCP constituted a successful exercise in cooperative federalism is based upon how the NCP was formulated through intergovernmental relations and constituted in intergovernmental agreements. Certainly, the states, territories and the Commonwealth negotiated over the inclusion of competition payments and the use of template legislation. Officials in the national and sub-national central agencies worked together to prepare the legislation and agreements. Finally, the respective parties willingly signed the three agreements at a COAG meeting.

The view that the NCP was a less than successful example of cooperative federalism reflects a focus upon federal relations during its implementation. From this perspective, the states and territories assumed that the public interest clause would give them some leeway to address local political demands or to reflect local circumstances. Moreover, it was assumed that the process would be transparent and that they would be able to bargain with the Commonwealth if there were disputes over policy implementation. Instead, the lack of transparency in the deliberations over reform payments reinforced a lack of trust among the states and territories towards the Commonwealth.[2]

The works of Sawer (1977) and Painter (1998) — two leading Australian federalism scholars — suggest that the latter view has a stronger case. Over three decades ago, Sawer (1977, p. 6) proposed that cooperative federalism was evidenced by the following characteristics: 'each of the parties to the arrangement has a reasonable degree of autonomy, can bargain about the terms of cooperation, and at least if driven too hard, decline to cooperate'.

This is not to suggest that an absence of conflict between the participants is an essential element of cooperative federalism. On the contrary, it is unlikely that they will always agree. Governments will inevitably differ over values and interests, and will seek to position themselves favourably to achieve desired policy outcomes. As Painter (1998, p. 23) remarked,

---

2   Changes in government since April 1995 also exacerbated tensions between the Commonwealth and the state and territory governments over the NCP. Although a Liberal–National Coalition government was elected nationally in March 1996, at state level, Australian Labor Party governments were being elected (Tasmania in 1998, Victoria in 1999, Western Australia, the Northern Territory and the Australian Capital Territory in 2001, South Australia in 2002). Following the election of the Labor government in South Australia in March 2002, Australia faced the unique situation of having all states and territories with Labor governments with only the Commonwealth having a Coalition government. Hence, there was at least a perception that the Commonwealth Coalition government was adjudicating on the performance of state and territory Labor governments.

intergovernmental cooperation is tactical, and it is normally temporary because it coexists with competition and conflict (even within the same room). While voluntary, it can be induced and maintained by sanctions, such as the moral sanctions that develop from a 'culture of cooperation'. By definition, however, if the capacity to impose sanctions is too unevenly distributed, we more than likely have coercion …

It is reasonable to assert that the states and territories entered into the NCP voluntarily. This is consistently raised by officers who view the NCP as a positive example of cooperative federalism — the states and territories were not compelled to sign. Of course, if they did not sign, then they would forfeit the opportunity to receive payments forthcoming to the signatories. After all, the payments were provided as compensation for the cost of implementing the reforms.

It is important to note that although the NCP was based upon agreements freely entered into by the states and territories, the parties did not retain a 'reasonable degree of autonomy' and the 'capacity to impose sanctions' (or provide rewards, depending upon one's perspective) was skewed in favour of the Commonwealth. The decision by the NCC to withhold payments to Western Australia because of its refusal to deregulate trading hours was notable not just because it challenged the autonomy of that state's government to regulate trading hours, but also because it raised the point of who should define the 'public interest'. Clearly, the Western Australian electorate thought that the current regulatory arrangement was in their 'public interest'. The imposition of sanctions from Canberra following a state referendum is consistent with a coercive, rather than cooperative, form of federalism.

As only the Commonwealth could impose penalties, there was an imbalance in power relations that was inconsistent with Painter's notion of cooperation. As was explained above, the NCC acknowledged that the Commonwealth had not been as diligent as most of the states and territories in reviewing its legislation, but that it was unable to do anything about this except to make the public aware of this fact. Only the Commonwealth, through the NCC, could withhold the incentive payments on the grounds of unsatisfactory progress. This imbalance in power relations was further highlighted by the position of the Commonwealth Minister as the final judge on the matter. Certainly, the states and territories retained the right not to undertake every reform called for under the NCP, however, such a decision would draw sanctions more in keeping with coercive forms of federalism.

Ultimately, cooperative federalism as a concept is not meaningful unless it is applied to both the formulation and implementation stages of a policy. The NCP was defined as a policy response to perceived inefficiencies in the Australian economy and was continually justified and evaluated in these terms. Many policy officers, particularly from state central agencies, indicated that this was their prime concern — not federal relations. The implication for Australian federalism and cooperative federalism, in particular, was that the reform program took precedence over notions of cooperation between the federal partners; in effect, the ends justified the means. It could be argued that NCP had more in common with what has been termed 'pragmatic federalism' (Hollander and Patapan 2007).

Conclusion

While it was instrumental in advancing microeconomic reform, the National Competition Policy was far from a perfect example of cooperative federalism. On the one hand, it was based upon agreements entered into voluntarily by the Commonwealth, states and territories. On the other hand, the Commonwealth did not implement reforms as diligently as the states, some reforms were expensive to administer, and others imposed disproportionate hardships upon some communities and businesses. Contrary to its remit, the National Competition Council endeavoured to influence policy outcomes, rather than simply monitor implementation of NCP obligations. An examination of the NCP from the theoretical perspectives offered by Sawer and Painter reveal that it did not offer the states sufficient policy autonomy and bargaining power to fully constitute cooperative federalism. Nevertheless, it is still one of our best examples of how the federal partners can work together to achieve mutually desired outcomes.

References

Banks, G. 2005, 'Structural Reform Australian-Style: Lessons for others?', Presentation to the IMF, World Bank and OECD, May 2005. Available at: http://www.pc.gov.au/news-and-media/chairmans-speeches/gary-banks/cs20050601/cs20050601.pdf.

Boswell, R. 1996, 'The Implications of National Competition Policy', *Australian Journal of Public Administration* 55(2), pp. 79–82.

Butler, G. 1996, 'National Competition Policy: The downside', *Australian Journal of Public Administration* 55(2), pp. 104–106.

Carver, L. 1996. 'Consumers/Citizens and the National Competition Policy', *Australian Journal of Public Administration* 55(2), pp. 88–93.

Commonwealth of Australia 1995, *Competition Policy Reform Act 1995*. Available at: http://www.comlaw.gov.au/Details/C2004A04938.

COAG (Council of Australian Governments) 1994a, COAG Communiqué, 25 February. Available at: http://archive.coag.gov.au/coag_meeting_outcomes/1994-02-25/index.cfm.

COAG 1994b, 'Attachment A: Water resource policy'. Available at: http://archive.coag.gov.au/coag_meeting_outcomes/1994-02-25/docs/attachment_a.cfm.

COAG 1995a, COAG Communiqué, 11 April. Available at: http://archive.coag.gov.au/coag_meeting_outcomes/1995-04-11/index.cfm.

COAG 1995b, 'Attachment A: Agreement to implement the national competition policy and related reforms', 11 April. Available at: http://archive.coag.gov.au/coag_meeting_outcomes/1995-04-11/docs/attachment_a.cfm.

COAG 1995c, 'Attachment: Conditions of payments to the states', 11 April. Available at: http://archive.coag.gov.au/coag_meeting_outcomes/1995-04-11/docs/attachment_a_parta.cfm.

ERA (Economic Regulation Authority (Western Australia)) 2009, 'Strategic Plan 2008–10'. Available at: http://www.era.wa.gov.au/cproot/6704/2/20090325%20ERA%20Strategic%20Plan%202008-10.pdf.

Fenna, A. 2007, 'The Division of Powers in Australia: Subsidiarity and the single market', *Public Policy* 2(3), pp. 175–194.

Hansard (Western Australia), 2005, 'Business of the House (Assembly)', extract from Hansard, Thursday 22 September. Available at: http://www.parliament.wa.gov.au/Hansard/hansard.nsf/0/3410d49a9c1db017c8257570001285bf/$FILE/A37%20S1%2020050922%20p5928b-5930a.pdf.

Hilmer, F., M. Rayner and G. Taperell (The Independent Committee of Inquiry into a National Competition Policy) 1993, 'National Competition Policy'. Available at: http://www.ncc.gov.au/images/uploads/Hilmer-001.pdf.

Hollander, R. 2006, 'National Competition Policy, Regulatory Reform and Australian Federalism: Research and evaluation', *Australian Journal of Public Administration* 65(2), pp. 33–47.

Hollander, R. and G. Curran 2001, 'The Greening of the Grey: National competition policy', *Australian Journal of Public Administration* 60(3), pp. 42–55.

Hollander, R. and H. Patapan 2007, 'Pragmatic Federalism: Australian federalism from Hawke to Howard', *Australian Journal of Public Administration* 66(3), pp. 280–297.

NCC (National Competition Council) 1996, 'Considering the Public Interest under the National Competition Policy'. Available at: http://ncp.ncc.gov.au/docs/PIRePu-001.pdf.

NCC 1998, 'Compendium of National Competition Policy Agreements', 2nd ed. Available at: http://www.ncc.gov.au/images/uploads/PIAg-001.pdf.

NCC 2002, 'Assessment of Governments' Progress in Implementing the National Competition Policy and Related Reforms, Volume One: Assessment'. Available at: http://ncp.ncc.gov.au/docs/2002%20assessment.pdf.

NCC 2003, 'Assessment of Governments' Progress in Implementing the National Competition Policy and Related Reforms, Volume One: Overview of the national competition policy and related reforms'. Available at: http://ncp.ncc.gov.au/docs/2003%20assessment.pdf.

NCC 2004, 'Submission to the Productivity Commission Review of National Competition Policy Arrangements'. Available at: http://www.pc.gov.au/inquiries/completed/national-competition-policy/submissions/71/sub071.pdf.

NCC 2005, 'Assessment of Governments' Progress in Implementing the National Competition Policy and Related Reforms: 2005'. Available at: http://ncp.ncc.gov.au/docs/2005%20assessment.pdf.

New South Wales Government 2004, 'Productivity Commission Review of National Competition Policy Arrangements: NSW Government submission'. Available at: http://www.pc.gov.au/inquiries/completed/national-competition-policy/submissions/99/sub099.pdf.

Painter, M. 1998, *Collaborative Federalism: Economic Reform in the 1990s*, Cambridge University Press, Cambridge.

Productivity Commission 2005, 'Review of National Competition Policy Reforms', Productivity Commission Inquiry Report No. 33. Available at: http://www.pc.gov.au/inquiries/completed/national-competition-policy/report/ncp.pdf.

Sawer, G. 1977, *Federation Under Strain: Australia 1972–1975*. Melbourne University Press, Melbourne.

Sims, R. 1999, 'In Defence of Competition: The successful application of competition policy in NSW Rail', *Australian Journal of Public Administration* 58(4), pp. 96–104.

Thomas, C. 1996, 'Why National Competition Policy?', *Australian Journal of Public Administration* 55(2), pp. 100–103.

Victoria, State of 2004, 'Victorian Government Submission: Inquiry into national competition policy arrangements'. Available at: http://www.pc.gov.au/inquiries/completed/national-competition-policy/submissions/51/sub051.pdf.

WAEC (Western Australia Electoral Commission) 2008, 'Referendum Results'. Available at: http://www.elections.wa.gov.au/elections/referendums/past-referendums/sr2005.

9. The Malfunctions of New Public Management: A case study of governance in Indigenous affairs[1]

Ian Marsh

Indigenous policy presents in acute form a case study of challenges to present public administration practice. Successive governments have promised to reduce extreme disadvantage and to do this in conjunction with affected citizens.[2] But failures persist. In looking for explanations, Dr Peter Shergold (2006) has not only arraigned governance as a threshold cause but also set a high bar for its practice:

> I am aware that, for some fifteen years as a public administrator, too much of what I have done on behalf of government for the very best of motives has had the very worst of outcomes ... In my personal opinion three things need to be done ... We need to tailor government programs to the particular circumstances of discrete communities ... We must ensure that discretionary government expenditures are negotiated to goals that address local needs ... Community challenges are almost invariably holistic in their nature and require a variety of programs from all three tiers of government to be delivered in a coordinated whole of government manner.

---

1   This is an abridged version of a paper prepared for the Alice Springs think tank Remote Focus in 2011 as part of a review of governance in remote Australia. The original paper, 'The Evolution of Governance in Remote Australia: From centralised and top-down towards contextualised and collaborative approaches', and the final report, 'Fixing the Hole in Australia's Heartland', are both available at www.desertknowledge.com.au.

2 For example, a recent policy statement (Australian Government 2011) states: 'Genuine engagement with Aboriginal and Torres Strait Islander Australians is fundamental to our efforts to improve life outcomes and close the gap in the indigenous disadvantage ... A critical step in improving outcomes for Aboriginal and Torres Strait Islander Australians is for government agencies, service providers and contractors to engage them as valued stakeholders in the development, design, implementation, monitoring and evaluation of policies, programs, services and legislation that have an impact on them.' Also in November 2011, the Commonwealth released its 'Indigenous Economic Development Strategy' which states: 'Government cannot act alone. Success depends on working in partnership with indigenous leaders communities and individuals and with business, industry peak bodies and non-government organizations.' Writing in 2005, Peter Shergold, the former Secretary of DPMC and a primary author of the current framework, observed: 'We need to drive governance programs in the direction of connectedness. Programs need to be made more flexible, responsive to community needs and priorities and delivered in a holistic manner ... More importantly, there needs to be a delivery of programs in a seamless manner to local communities' (2006).

Such aspirations are echoed in more general terms in recent reports on broader public sector reform. At the federal level, such ideas figure prominently in the Moran Review (AGRGA 2010), and at a state level, in the Western Australian Economic Audit Committee Report (WAEAC 2009).

So how equipped is the Australian public service to meet such challenges? This chapter suggests there is a long way to go. Moreover, the central obstacles to their realisation lie in structural features that are keystones of new public management. Specifically:

- Governance arrangements are a threshold cause of policy failure in Indigenous affairs. As discussed later in detail, centralised protocols and siloed departments undercut local responsiveness. Reframed governance will not, of course, by itself solve the many problems of Indigenous disadvantage. That can ultimately only be achieved with the active involvement of the affected citizens. But this essential mobilisation is negated by the present governance framework and cannot be remedied within it.

- The challenge in designing new policies is a structural one. Local discretions in service delivery and decentralised governance designs are unattainable within the present protocols surrounding budgeting, siloed departments, human resources management and accountability arrangements. All these protocols need ultimately to be reworked if the circle is to be squared between local discretion, continuous improvement, and centralised accountability. Britain has begun to experiment in whole-of-government budgeting (NAO 2013). But ultimately the challenge goes deeper, perhaps ultimately to a framework that Charles Sabel has described as 'experimentalist governance' (for example, Sabel 2004; Sabel and Zeitlin 2011).

- The challenge in designing new policies is also a strategic one; a rethink from fundamentals is required (for example, Shergold 2013). This is first and foremost a challenge to imagination. A paradigm shift — one that challenges structurally embedded habits, practices, and approaches — will always be hard to accomplish. This is particularly hard in Australia's policy system which has few if any platforms that can host appropriate conversations and exchanges.

At the heart of this chapter is a simple claim: there is an imperative need to reframe governance. This composite concept recognises the essential interdependence between the formal apparatus of the state and its publics. The parties are engaged in a dynamic exchange, the opposite of directed, deferential, passive or paternalistic linkage. In achieving positive and sustainable outcomes, engagement has a primary rather than a secondary role.[3] Compounding this

---

3 For a sensitive discussion of the complexity of choice in an Indigenous context, particularly the tensions between individualist and collectivist patterns, see Rowse 2002, 2012.

challenge is the overlap of policy responsibilities between federal and state government. While present rhetoric gestures to the intergovernmental, systemic and contextual character of policy challenges, practice falls far short of stated ambitions.

Indigenous affairs display these difficulties in sharp relief. The following section explores the structural barriers which inhibit decentralised, whole-of-government practice. This is followed by a review of responses elsewhere to analogous challenges. The conclusion evaluates the challenge of grafting such approaches into Australian public administration.

What are the structural barriers to whole-of-government?

Two official Management Advisory Committee reports (2004, 2007) noted five changes in organisation and processes that were deemed essential to underpin whole-of-government practice:

1. substantial initial cross-agency/stakeholder agreement about the broad purposes to be pursued;

2. use of the outcomes budget framework to pool resources and to create appropriate accountability frameworks;

3. lead-agency staff empowered with sufficient authority to manage whole-of-government settings and to lead the engagement of local stakeholders;

4. empowering these same managers to engage with relevant individuals and interests; and

5. ensure the individuals engaged in these latter roles have the appropriate networking, collaboration and entrepreneurial skills.

How did this unfold in Indigenous affairs?

A first step involves assessment of the multitude and variety of programs that have been established to drive change in local communities. The 'Strategic Evaluation of Indigenous Programs' (Department of Finance 2010) offers the most recent comprehensive overview. It identified no less than 232 individual programs which in one way or another support Indigenous Australians. This report reviews these programs in the context of the various broad outcomes that the government has established. An earlier Australian National Audit Office (ANAO) report (2007) focused on the four primary departments: Department of Education and Science (DES), Department of Employment and Workplace Relations (DEWR), Department of Families, Community Services and Indigenous Affairs (FaCSIA), and Health and Ageing. This report identifies 94 programs, either mainstream or niche, that are relevant to Indigenous affairs. DES operates 15 Indigenous-specific programs and 43 mainstream programs that have Indigenous applications; DEWR operates 11 Indigenous-specific programs and the Job Network; FaCSIA operates six Indigenous-specific and six mainstream programs; Health and Ageing operates five Indigenous-specific programs and nine mainstream programs. To add to the complexity, many of these major programs have sub-components.

To coordinate funding, the federal government decided to establish Indigenous Coordinating Centres (ICCs) at a regional or area level. In practice, coordination can be achieved by one of two means: by brokering linkages between communities and programs; or by joining individual programs into a funding block, which is more demanding. Meantime, to test the model, trials at selected sites were introduced in 2003.

In a report on these trials, Gray (2006) explored the challenge of program management as perceived on-the-ground, in this particular case from Wadeye. The trial was intended to reduce the number of individual programs that local communities need to manage. In fact, in the course of the trial the number of relevant programs increased to 90. In another example, Dillon and Westbury (2007, p. 66) list the five Commonwealth programs that could be tapped to fund natural resource management on Indigenous land:

> An important and growing policy area where in recent years scores of Indigenous ranger programs have emerged across northern Australia focused on land and resource management. Program funding in this area comes from a diverse array of agencies: the National Heritage Trust, the Indigenous Protected Areas Program, CDEP, STEP and the ABA ... Programs vary in size from hundreds of millions (for example the CDEP or ARHP) to less than half a million (for example the Indigenous Children's Program).

With 39 per cent of the Indigenous population under 15, education is another critical area. The same authors note the array of programs relevant here:

> The national flagship programs include the Youth Allowance and Abstudy: the former is targeted at young people studying, undertaking training for Australian apprenticeship, looking for work, or sick; the latter at indigenous students. Over and above this, FaCSIA has four 'niche' programs which provide youth services of various kinds with a total national budget of $34.6 million and a client base of approximately

340 000 nationally. DEST has at least ten youth related Indigenous specific niche programs … the data on numbers of service providers suggests that the availability of these programs in remote Australia is very patchy … It is clear that across the national government there are a couple of hundred different programs potentially allocable to the circumstances of remote citizens. Access is a different matter entirely (Dillon and Westbury 2007, pp. 67–68).

Finally, they note the bewildering array of programs aimed at Indigenous housing:

The existence of concurrent state and national responsibilities means that in some areas programs are duplicated by each jurisdiction. Housing is a classic example where states, territories and national governments deliver both mainstream and Indigenous housing and housing related programs, and even within the national government there are a number of separate Indigenous housing programs (CHIP/NAHS, CHIP/AACAP, FHBH) all delivering housing and essential services at the community level, along with the Australian Regional Housing Programme which funds the states and territories to deliver housing at the community level (Dillon and Westbury 2007, p. 65).

The whole-of-government architecture was designed to ensure these programs are accessed by the citizens that they are intended to serve. How effective have these arrangements proven to be?

Whole-of-government architecture

Since whole-of-government arrangements were introduced in 2002, there have been at least nine reviews. The first four covered the initial COAG trials and the rest focused on subsequent developments. Seven were official or commissioned evaluations and the remainder were independent academic assessments: Urbis, Keys and Young 2006; Morgan Disney and Associates 2006; Gray and Sanders 2006; Gray 2006; ANAO 2007; KPMG 2007; Hunt 2007; FaHCSIA 2004; O'Flynn et al. 2011. All these reviews repeat points stressed in the Management Advisory Committee documents, namely that whole-of-government will not work without devolution of authority, funding, accountability and coordinated organisation. They also all found continuing and unresolved administrative difficulties.

As an introduction to these unresolved problems, consider the case of Mutitjulu, ironically the first community named in the Northern Territory Emergency Response (NTER). Before whole-of-government was conceived, this community tried, over more than a decade, to obtain for itself a new style of governance (Smith 2009). Its efforts foundered on immovable central structures. This story starts in 1991 when the Women's Council prepared a report highlighting concerns about 'controlling and caring for children'. A series of submissions and discussions followed. In 2000, the community council at Mutitjulu asked Centrelink, the Aboriginal and Torres Strait Islander Commission, and the then Department of Families and Community Services to work with it to develop a practical strategy to deal with welfare dependency and related family problems. Following a consultation, the Community Council itself proposed a Participation and Partnership Agreement. The departments did not respond. Why?

> First, the key departments would not support an 'All in' community model of welfare reform and would not support linking Youth Allowance with school attendance, even though these had been specifically requested by community members … Second, Centrelink and FACS would not countenance an indigenous community working with them to develop and implement locally-relevant breaching rules. Neither would they countenance a community organisation being provided with a delegation under the Social Security Act in order to do so … Third, entrenched inter-departmental turf wars in Canberra meant that the departments concerned were unable to negotiate a common position … And finally the Australian government was unable or unwilling to reform the chaotic state of its departmental program funding in order to streamline the pooled funding and grant reporting arrangements that would have been required … In late June 2007, the Australian government announced that Mutitjulu would be the first community into which it activates national emergency measures. It will do so unilaterally (Smith 2009, p. 6).

So far as coordination is concerned, we will see little has changed.

The findings of the various evaluations affirm that whole-of-government is confounded at the critical regional and ICC levels. The obstacles are structural, not contingent. Consider the two most recent reports, an official report conducted by KPMG (2007) and an independent report conducted by academics from The Australian National University and the University of Canberra (O'Flynn et al. 2011). The KPMG study involved a review of internal documents as well as interviews with 158 Australian and state government agency staff and 35 community organisations. The report compared the proclaimed objectives of the policy with the experience and observations of local staff. Despite six years' experience and at least eight preceding reviews, structural obstacles to joined-up work persisted. Here is a summary:

• Departmental silos persisted: Line agency staff presented to communities/ organisations as representative of their agency. Communities/organisations reported that they did not know who to talk to. ICC staff and line agency staff rarely visit communities together (p. 19).

- Funding protocols prevented discussion with applicants: Many line agency staff were unable to provide governance and financial management assistance to organisations due to probity issues relating to assessment of funding applications (p. 21).

- ICC managers lacked authority: Managers indicated that they did not have authority to gather agency staff support. Line agencies confirmed that their staff remained their direct responsibility (p. 23).

- Funding and reporting arrangements inhibited whole-of-government collaboration: Line agencies have different program guidelines, funding rounds and delegations, and different risk assessment protocols. In some cases this resulted in applications undergoing up to eight different risk assessments (p. 29). One ICC took over 12 months to negotiate and approve an SRA which was worth under $50,000 in funding (p. 32). One agency may apply more rigorous risk assessment for applications over $100,000, while another agency's more rigorous assessment only applies to applications over $150 000 (p.34).

- The problems are structural: 'The implementation of whole-of-government collaboration in ICCs is an area requiring significant improvements. Many of the issues that impede whole-of-government are structure and have little to do with ICC staff and management's willingness to collaborate' (pp. 10, 29).

The findings of the university-based study (O'Flynn et al. 2011) echo these conclusions, albeit in more graphic terms. This study was based on 48 field interviews covering staff at ICCs, state and regional offices, and in Canberra. It suggests that, despite the top-down whole-of-government effort, Mutitjulu's experience has not been transcended. Their conclusion is unequivocal: 'Due to entrenched barriers, which permeate the broader public service, ICCs have been a failed experiment.'

Like KPMG, O'Flynn et al. identify structural failings in the basic organisational design:

- No or limited assignment of authority to the ICC managers,
- An ad hoc approach to the representation of departments (which meant staff were withdrawn as cost pressures emerged);
- An under-investment in skills; and
- Inconsistent operating systems.

They cite the comments of ICC managers, first on their delegations of authority:

> I could not go out and direct another person to do something in this ICC ... because they're not from my agency. I could (only) ask, influence, beg (Executive Level, ICC: 248).

> Whole of government doesn't work ... when you've got all different agencies sitting in the one place, supposedly working together ... they're supposed to be all collaborating and telling each other what they're doing ... I'm telling you it doesn't work and I work in an ICC and I've been there since the day it started (Executive Level, ICC: 248).

> The fact that we're co-located with [Department A] and [Department B] and a couple of [Department C's] people is just window dressing. So there's no whole of government activity between them ... There's no practical program [or] whole of government approach (APS Level, ICC: 248).

The NTER Review also picked up these criticisms but this time from the perspective of the clients:

> There was extensive comment in communities about the lack of co-ordination across locally based professional staff. Between the GBMs, Community Employment Brokers and shire service managers, there is not a clear point of authority or coordination (p. 86).

A second set of unresolved governance issues arose from conflicting vertical and horizontal tensions which cut across in the administration of programs. According to O'Flynn et al.:

> The pervasiveness of a program focus and the silos that it creates were seen as impossible to combat even in a setting where there was physical co-location and strong endorsement from Ministers and Secretaries (2011: 249).

A third problematic element involved centralised decision-making. This aspiration also fell foul of more embedded administrative practices and requirements:

> The idea [was] for ICCs to have a pool of money that they could make decisions about. Well, in the great thing about being risk averse that was all centralised back in Canberra: ... useless basically. It just went against the whole thing about whole of government which is about sharing, devolving, not controlling everything, but taking responsibility and it's the same pattern. And that was a bit of its undoing, in fact because it was to give people the power to do the deal on the ground (Senior Executive Service, ICC, p. 249).

Most recently, under the 2009 National Partnership Agreements between the Commonwealth and the states, the same broad arrangements have been extended to coordinate the delivery of programs across jurisdictions. Six agreements have already been signed and others are foreshowed in relation to native title claims arrangements, remote infrastructure and healthy food. In general, the parties also commit to 'developing a co-ordinated approach', and 'enabling initiatives to be delivered in a manner appropriate to needs in particular locations'. To oversee the arrangements, a Coordinator-General based in Canberra was appointed in 2009. This position was abolished in 2014.

Accountabilities as a structural barrier to local effectiveness

Central accountability requirements create another barrier to on-the-ground effectiveness. Take health services. In the interests of enhancing local choice and control, the Aboriginal community controlled health services were established in the 1980s. Funding was later transferred to the Aboriginal and Torres Strait Islander Commission and grants were on a yearly basis, but with an expectation of continuance. The Commonwealth Department of Health assumed responsibility in 1995 and thereafter funding increased. The pattern of funding has since further evolved with most services now drawing support from several sources: a core operating grant from the Office for Aboriginal and Torres Strait Islander Health; state government health department grants; and by proposal driven niche-funding that could include broader social purposes.

Each funding source adopts its own application process, accountability framework and priorities. In an assessment of these arrangements, Lavoie et al. (2009, p. 6) note:

> Analyses conducted by the Victorian Department of Health suggests that the reporting and compliance burden is disproportionate compared to that imposed on other small and medium-size funded agencies.

For example, Aboriginal agencies receiving on average $2 million were accountable for between 26–30 activities. Non-governmental organisations typically received total funding of $10 million for the same array of activities. This study also found that agencies can be required to produce up to 59 separate reports for 13 programs. This boosts transaction costs disproportionately. Further, in a small service, disentangling the daily time allocation of a single staff member between varieties of programs can be wholly artificial. Finally, a 12-month funding cycle makes the recruitment of staff precarious.

These multiple accountabilities and the associated burden of transaction costs have persisted despite having figured so strongly in other evaluations. This suggests that the requirements derive from wider structural imperatives and cannot be excised without systemic change.

Consultation and the development of social capital

As noted at the outset, every official report since 2001 has emphasised the imperative of working with and through local communities (for example, Commonwealth Grants Commission 2001; Morgan Disney and Associates 2006; NTER Review 2008; Department of Finance 2010; Productivity Commission 2012). To illustrate the complexities that can arise, Edmunds (2010, p. 16) cites the negotiations over James Price Point, which involved Woodside and a proposed liquified natural gas development. Negotiations were conducted with the Kimberley Land Council, the organisation which had statutory responsibilities for consultation under the *Native Title Act*. The council had secured a consensus amongst key traditional owners. But a dissident group challenged these processes. Edmunds (2010, p. 16) comments:

> This is a common situation and one that traditional law could once have dealt with. However, it fits uneasily into contemporary decision making, raising a crucial question about how much, and whose consent is needed for informed consent.

If this is one dimension of the issue, another is the quixotic (from the perspective of local communities) behaviour of their governmental interlocutors. Take the NTER, which banned sales of alcohol on Aboriginal land. According to Marian Brady, a specialist in alcohol use in Indigenous communities:

> The (political grandstanding associated with the NTER) was a little strange considering that most Aboriginal land in the Territory was already dry. There were already 107 general restricted areas, all on Aboriginal land and all in non–urban areas except for one town camp in Alice Springs ... the alcohol recommendations in the *Little Children are Sacred* report ... are designed to work with and enhance the NTs existing legislative structure ... the Intervention measures unhelpfully cut across them (cited in Edmunds 2010, p. 19).

Another example involved the impact of the NTER at Wadeye, an early trial site:

> When a crisis erupted at the Wadeye trial site ... the Commonwealth government resorted to a more coercive approach characteristic of hierarchical or contract government ... It has chosen not to develop housing through the legitimately elected Thamururr Regional Council, with whom it signed the COAG trial agreement thereby by-passing and potentially undermining the very indigenous governance structure it partnered with only four years ago, and to which it remains formally committed in the NT bilateral agreement (Hunt 2007, p. 167).

Smith (2009) describes the proposed governance arrangements for the West Arnhem Shire that were developed slowly and after protracted negotiations that had begun in 2004. Their purpose was to plan implementation of a new local government shire covering the entire region. Following protracted on-the-ground negotiations over three years, which progressively built support amongst relevant groups and communities, a new governance structure had been settled. In 2007, the Intervention aborted these arrangements, leaving behind a frustrated and cynical local community.

According to the ANAO, in 2007, 75 per cent of 257 managers surveyed responded positively to the statement: 'The Indigenous Affairs Arrangements (IAAs) have encouraged consultation with indigenous communities at the local and regional levels.' How effective were these conversations from the perspective of their interlocutors? The on-the-ground evidence is not positive. For example, in May 2010, DEEWR and FaHCSIA issued a draft Indigenous economic strategy. Submissions were invited and consultations held with Indigenous communities throughout Australia. The following are the reporter's notes on the consultations held in various remote centres in November 2010. In Alice Springs, for example:

> Approximately 22 (indigenous) participants attended the workshop ... People participated in both the questions and answer session and the table discussions but there was widespread criticism of the relevance of the Indigenous Economic Development Strategy to remote areas and the likelihood of anything changing on the ground ... There are no economic foundations in remote communities and this needs to be acknowledged ... There was widespread criticism that the strategy was homogenising and represented an urban western model ... (it) needs to respond to the different circumstances, opportunities, economies and drivers in remote regional areas...There are so many economic strategies around that people are blasé about 'just another plan' ... The gap between the strategy and what is happening on the ground is very wide ... There is a different sort of economy operating in remote areas. It's not just a matter of transferring these into real jobs, they are real jobs but not recognised as such.

The report records analogous sentiments from participants in all the other consultations sites covering Broome, Cairns, Port Lincoln and Karratha. Here is one more observation from Karratha:

> Real engagement means listening to indigenous people and not just telling them ... previous feedback for policy development over the years has been ignored. There is no apparent correlation between what the Australian government proposes and what indigenous people want ... Different communities have different needs and opportunities.

The overall funding framework

At a material level, W. H. Stanner's indictment of the 'great Australian silence' in relation to Indigenous Australians is reflected in the legacy of past policy failures:

> The list would include in no particular order, the pre-existing failure of educational outcomes, which lead to a largely non-literate indigenous citizenry, extreme housing shortages for personnel required to deliver government funded programmes and service across remote Australia; poor law enforcement and less than optimal levels of intellectual capital within government agencies relevant to remote service delivery ... The combined absence of social and physical infrastructure means that there is nothing for governments to graft mainstream services onto as happens elsewhere. Government appear to discount or underestimate the importance of a pre-existing network of social, physical governance and business infrastructure ... (Dillon and Westbury 2007, p. 59).

One important source of equality in services for Australians is the periodic determinations of the Commonwealth Grants Commission (CGrC). Via complex metrics, the CGrC attempts to equalise funding for service provision around Australia. But there are several problems. First, determinations are based on average or mainstream needs. There are no special provisions or allowances for remedying acute backlogs such as those that exist in remote Australia. These were comprehensively documented by the CGrC in its 2001 report.

Second, while the Commission grants money on the basis of an assessment of needs in particular areas like housing, transport etc., there is no requirement for governments to spend their allocations in these areas. The states and territories are free to spend as they choose. Indeed, the states and territories may also use the existence of special Commonwealth programs as a ground for reducing their own allocations to Indigenous services.

There is no mechanism to check that funds are spent in line with the principles behind their allocation. A significant proportion of the funds allocated by both the CGrC and the Commonwealth to the Northern Territory are in recognition of the special needs of Indigenous Australians. According to a Northern Territory Council of Social Services analysis of the 2008 Northern Territory budget:

> The spending priorities of the NT government exacerbate the differences in measures and senses of equality for low-income and disadvantaged people thereby contributing to the reduced life expectancy, poor health, violence and other differences that they are intended to address (NTCOSS 2008; see also *The Australian*, 24 October 2009).

Another issue concerns allocations to local government. These are determined on a per capita basis:

> The bizarre result is that jurisdictions like the Northern Territory with one sixth of the Australian land mass receive less in local government assistance than is notionally allocated to the population of Geelong (Dillon and Westbury 2007, p. 188).

Whole-of-government policy development: A case study of CDEP

Whole-of-government is difficult to achieve not just in on-the-ground delivery, but also in processes of cross-departmental policy development. Despite its popularity and considerable impact in remote Australia, at the same time as it is promulgating ambitious employment targets, the government is also curtailing the Community Development Employment Project (CDEP). At its peak, CDEP engaged some 40,000 people:

> From 2005, CDEP has been systematically dismantled ... Without much evidence, CDEP is being blamed for cost shifting by governments and for poor mainstream employment outcomes ... as CDEP is dismantled people will be given the choice of mainstream work or welfare, on the proviso that work might require migration from home communities ... This policy change fails to recognise Indigenous aspirations, cultures and life projects (Altman 2009, p. 8).

The specific situation of citizens in remote Australia has seemingly received short shrift. What is to be done in remote communities where there is zero conventional economic infrastructure? For example, to illustrate the effectiveness of CDEP, Altman describes the experience of the Kuninjku community in west Arnhem Land:

> For the majority of Aboriginal people in remote communities migration away from ancestral lands ... and from extended kin networks will be neither an aspiration nor a solution. This in turn suggests that key institutions like CDEP that are currently being dismantled will need to be retained (Altman 2009, p. 13).

He notes the specific contributions of CDEP to the Kuninjku economy: harvesting game for local consumption; producing art for sale in the national and global art market; and being employed in paid provision of environmental services.

A review of CDEP by the Department of Finance (2009) found that the scheme had very limited success in fulfilling its work readiness charter and that it was almost impossible to assess its community development contribution. It also noted these goals are likely to conflict. Altman's (2011) detailed evidence that the scheme had worked positively as an enabler of remote livelihood possibilities in the hybrid economy played no role in the finance assessment.

The changes to the CDEP scheme in the Northern Territory also indicate the difficulties government faces in managing policy development on a whole-of-government basis. The reductions in CDEP employment displaced populations from outstations and other settlements. But the scheme was run down without town camp capacities being augmented. Moreover, there was no development of new town-based employment opportunities and no or little opportunity for mainstream employment.

Beyond whole-of-government: Squaring the circle between central accountability and place-centred governance

The previous section catalogued the structural difficulties that have hampered realisation of whole-of-government aspirations. These include the relevance of local contexts; high and increasing transaction costs; a turn to micro-management; the confounding of freedom of action on the part of local staff; and, above all, the incompatibility between highly centralised organisational, HR and funding protocols and local discretions. In this respect, Australian experience matches that of other jurisdictions, which have tried whole-of-government and found it wanting. In search of remedies, a number of new or supplementary frameworks have been introduced to shift the locus of choice and decision away from highly centralised arrangements towards more localised contexts. This is reflected both in the 'Total Place' (HM Treasury and Department of Communities and Local Government 2010) initiatives in England and in the attention to place-based approaches in current OECD work. In both cases, the drastic cuts in public spending following the 2008 global financial crisis have coloured implementation (for example, Crowe 2011). Also relevant are 'learning-by-doing' approaches which offer a new accountability framework to reconcile national concerns with local initiative and freedom of action. Finally, imaginative 'place-based' developments, covering the provision of otherwise threatened local services and the realisation of efficiencies through collaboration between authorities at the local level, are also evident in Australia. These are detailed in a comprehensive report on local government in outback Queensland (Dollery and Johnson 2007). These varied governance designs are reviewed in turn. A concluding section explores the consistency of these approaches with recent official reviews of the public sector in Australia.

The 'Big Society' in Britain

The coalition government in Britain has sought to implement more decentralised governance arrangements via its 'Big Society' agenda.[4]

Decentralised governance represents a deliberate shift away from the top-down pattern which was common to both the Thatcher–Major and Blair–Brown governments. In particular, the Blair–Brown years were marked by substantially increased investment in the public sector and the development of arrangements to enhance central control, but in conjunction with whole-of-government delivery at the local level. Organisational arrangements to buttress central control and to drive service improvement included special units in the Cabinet office to facilitate strategy development and to drive program change. In addition, the performance framework was extended with a plethora of targets and measures. To facilitate joined-up working, joint funding agreements were also introduced. There is an extensive literature on all these developments (for example, Parker et al. 2010; Barber 2008; Marsh and Miller 2012, particularly chapters 3 and 4).

The profound limitations of this experience fanned interest in more radically decentralised approaches. An early move occurred in 2006 when the Lyons review of local government proposed attention to place-based approaches. In subsequent years, within and beyond government, attention to alternatives flourished. Think tanks have been important contributors to the emerging agenda (for example, Demos (Wind-Cowie 2010); Institute of Public Policy Research 2010; Institute for Government (Adonis and Sims 2011); New Economics Foundation (Coote 2010)). In addition, the House of Commons Public Administration Committee and the Communities and Local Government Committee have serially reviewed aspects of the new approach.[5]

The government has since taken several steps to advance its decentralising agenda, notably the establishment of its Whole Place Community Budgets Programme. This sought to shift the initiative in service design from central to place-based authorities. It sought to join up relevant central and local

---

4   Greg Clark (now a minister in the British government) wrote a book in 2003 which he describes as making the case that 'if central government is everywhere, then local government is nowhere' (Clark 2003).

5   A comprehensive list of House of Commons committee enquiries on community budgets and the 'Big Society' follows: Community Budgets (Communities Select Committee 2013); Integration across Government and Whole-Place Community Budgets (Public Accounts Committee 2013); Taking Forward Community Budgets (Communities SC 2012); Localisation Issues in welfare reform (Communities SC 2011); Mutual and Co-operative approaches to delivering local services (Communities SC 2012); Localism (Communities SC 2011); The Big Society (Public Admin Select Committee 2011); Further Report on The Big Society (Public Admin SC 20912); Citizens and public services (Public Admin SC 2013); Department of Communities and Local Government: Financial sustainability of local authorities (PAC 2013).

departments and agencies (and, where appropriate, NGOs and the private sector) to create proactive services that could be responsive to specific local or client circumstances and needs. The promise was greater impact at less cost.

Four English pilots have now been successfully completed. The program was administered by the Department of Communities and Local Government. In essence, this program brought together public and private sector bodies to develop new ways of delivering local services. It aimed to increase efficiency and improve service outcomes through more integrated service provision across multiple agencies. The project commenced in 2011 and local authorities were invited to apply to participate in the pilots.

The pilots involved joint project teams from central government and the relevant authorities. The teams first mapped highest cost services/categories and then sought to devise joined-up programs. This work was supported by five technical advisory sub-groups, each focusing on developing a methodology for a specific policy area: health and adult social care; criminal justice; families with complex needs; the economy; and education and early years. These groups identified sources of information on unit costs and outcomes and promoted consistency in assumptions.

The approach is described in detail in evidence to the Communities Select Committee (Localism HC 547, 7 June 2011), in an NAO report (2013) and also in a comprehensive report for the Local Government Association (2013).

The following is a brief sketch of each pilot:

West Cheshire: Total public service spends in the area in 2010–2011: £2.4 billion. A Public Services Board was established to provide overall strategic and managerial direction. The project united local authorities with four central departments (Health, Justice, Education, and Home Office). Collaboration was developed around five themes: starting well (early intervention in complex families); working well (local economic growth, work ready individuals); living well (community empowerment, safer communities, affordable housing); ageing well (home services); and smarter services (integrated asset management, poled customer insight, data sharing, strategic commissioning). Estimated savings: £56 million over five years.

Essex: Total public service spend in the area in 2010–2011: £12.8 billion. This involved 15 local authorities. An Executive Board was established. Collaboration was developed around four themes: families with complex needs; economic opportunity (focused on skills and infrastructure); community safety (reducing reoffending and domestic abuse); and health and well-being (focused on integrated commissioning). Estimated £414 million in net benefits over six years, comprising £127 million of cashable savings and £287 million of economic, social and fiscal benefits.

Greater Manchester: Total public service spend in the area in 2010–2011: £21 billion. The project involved 10 unitary authorities represented by the Greater Manchester Combined Authority. There were four themes: early years (school readiness, links to 'troubled families' work stream); worklessness; reducing reoffending (young people, women and repeat offenders); and integrated health and social care (dementia and psychiatric, drugs and alcohol, end-of-life, fit-for-work, acute conditions). £270 million of net savings over five years

West London Tri-borough: Total public service spend in the area in 2010–2011: £6 billion. Involved three London boroughs: Westminster, Kensington and Chelsea, Hammersmith and Fulham. Oversight through an established board. Themes included troubled and complex families; work and skills; health and social care; strategic coordination of infrastructure. Collaborative planning commenced in 2011 and involved shared library, adult social care, and children's services across three boroughs. This is to be extended to integration of public health functions and corporate services covering ICT and facilities. Estimated £70 million of net savings annually

The National Audit Office (NAO) assessment (NAO 2013) supported these initiatives. The report also highlighted the need to develop more robust, standardised measurement tools as experience accumulated. As a result of these experiments, more robust methodologies are being developed to measure savings and to allocate contributions, 'including financial incentives or funding arrangements that encourage partners to invest across organisational boundaries, particularly where reform takes longer to be financially viable' (NAO 2013, p. 10).

As might be expected, in a change on this scale the development of methodologies and protocols remains a work-in-progress — refined arrangements remain to be fully developed in a number of areas including:

- standardised information and information sharing protocols;
- a protocol concerning the sharing of savings, particularly where costs and benefits accrue to different agencies and/or over significantly different time periods;
- how incentives for participation can be maintained and strengthened over a program whose pay-offs are relatively long term; and
- how accountability structures might be reframed.

The NAO also commented: 'The anticipated savings from this initial exercise may appear modest compared with total public expenditure. However it is still early days ... Importantly, the current exercise focused on testing a new way of working rather than maximising the results over the short term' (NAO 2013, p. 24).

The program described above has involved methodologies for co-funding between departments and agencies, and has also shown how initial protocols might be developed surrounding accountability, HR assignments, and the sharing of returns.

But the enduring success of this approach also requires a public service culture that is open to innovation. This involves prioritising, as a subject for routine attention, continuous improvement via service design. Here the Cameron government has commissioned six independent bodies to constitute what it has termed 'What Works Institutes'. Their remit is exercised under the auspices of the Cabinet Office. Their role is to identify sectors of pressing social need and major public spending, where an evidence base exists but where this is either not synthesised authoritatively or where communication of findings is deficient. The aim is to aid strategic and operational development and day-to-day practice amongst at least three distinct groups:

- Commissioning staff: In areas where services are delivered by NGO or for-profit contracts, the institutes will assist those who commission services in informing their decisions on how best to spend public money;

- Service managers: In areas of direct service provision, the institutes will assist public services managers in establishing how best to deliver public services and how to improve their service; and,

- Policy managers: In policy design, the institutes will assist departments in developing an informed view of what is and is not cost effective in public services.

The six centres cover: health and social care, education attainment, ageing better, local growth, crime reduction, and effective early intervention. Together these centres cover some £200 billion of public spending.

To ensure research outputs are utilised by government, a senior civil servant has been appointed as National Advisor to engage with ministers and other stakeholder groups. This officer is located in the Cabinet Office and reports to the Minister for Government Policy and the Chief Secretary to the Treasury.

Place-based approaches in recent OECD work

The extent and variety of place-based approaches in recent OECD studies indicate the emergent appeal of this framework. In the quest for sustainable economic development, jobs and the effective provision of public services, the establishment of context-specific capabilities are seen to be primary. They represent the next move in the development of public management. Place-based approaches are suggested for a variety of contexts including economic development and innovation, social development, city and rural development, unemployment, deprived areas, and high needs contexts. This is indicated in the following list of recent studies (with additional studies listed in the footnote):

- *Managing Accountability and Flexibility in Labour Market Policy* (2011)
- *Breaking out of Policy Silos: Doing more with less* (2010)
- *Strategies to Improve Rural Service Delivery* (2010)
- *Regions Matter: Economic Recovery, Innovation and Sustainable Growth* (2009)
- *How Regions Grow: Trends and Analysis* (2009)
- *Linking Regions and Central Government: Contracts for Regional Development* (2007)
- *Governing Regional Development Policy: The Use of Indicators* (2009)
- *Flexible Policy for More and Better Jobs* (2009)
- *Linking Regions and Central Government: Contracts for Regional Development (2007)*
- *The New Rural paradigm: Policies and Governance* (2006)[6]

One proposition is common to these reports: while it is paramount to get institutions right at the local or regional level, there is no one-size-fits-all solution. According to one OECD analyst:

> In many countries, the regional/central vertical governance gap is significant: the centre faces information gaps and the regions confront capacity gaps. Moreover, it makes little sense to speak of 'centralisation' or decentralisation in general – the details are always the key (Coleman 2010).

Historic, institutional and local characteristics should shape governance designs. For example, in relation to development, the emphasis is on differentiated

---

6   Delivering Local Development through a Comprehensive Approach to Strategy, System and Leadership: Highlighting the case of Derry–Londonderry, Northern Ireland (2011); New Approaches to Rural Policy: Lesson for around the world (2005); The New Rural Paradigm, Policies and Governance (2006); OECD Territorial Reviews: France (2006); Job Rich Growth: Strategies for local employment, skills development and social protection (2011); OECD Science, Technology and Industry Outlook (2010).

strategies and organisational designs which can detect and then exploit existing or potential niches or opportunities. Implicit in all of the foregoing is the key role of local engagement and empowerment.

In designing place-based arrangements, the OECD has developed two frameworks. The first sets out systematically the seven core dimensions of a governance system: information, capacity, funding, policy, administration, objectives and accountability (see Table 1). These individual elements are defined as follows (Chairbit 2011):

i. *An information gap* is characterised by information asymmetries between levels of government when designing, implementing and delivering public policies. Sometimes the information gap results from strategic behaviours of public actors who may prefer not to reveal too clearly their strengths and weaknesses, especially if allocation of responsibility is associated with conditional granting. However, it is often the case that the very information about territorial specificities is not perceived by the central decision maker whilst sub national actors may be ignorant about capital objectives and strategies.

ii. *The capacity challenge* arises when there is a lack of human knowledge or resources available to carry out tasks, regardless of the level of government (even if, in general sub national governments are considered to be suffering more from such difficulties than central government).

iii. *The fiscal gap* is represented by the difference between territorial revenues and the required expenditures to meet local responsibilities and implement appropriate development strategies. In a more dynamic perspective, fiscal difficulties also include mismatch between budget practices and policy needs: in the absence of multi-annual budget practices for example, local authorities may face uncertainty in engaging in appropriate spending, and/or face a lack of flexibility in spending despite its appropriateness in uncertain contexts. Too strict earmarking of grants may also impede appropriate fungibility of resources and limit ability to deliver adapted policies.

iv. *The policy challenge* results when line ministries take a purely vertical be implemented at the territorial level. By contrast, local authorities are best to customise complementarities between policy fields and concretise cross-sectional approaches. Limited coordination among line ministries may provoke a heavy administrative burden, different timing and agenda in managing correlated actions etc. It can even lead to strong inconsistencies when objectives of sectoral policymakers are contradictory.

v. *The administrative gap* occurs when the administrative scale for policy making, in terms of spending as well as strategic planning, is not in line with relevant functional areas. A very common case concerns municipal fragmentation which can lead jurisdictions to initiate ineffective public action by not benefitting from economies of scale. Some specific policies also require very specific and often naturally fixed, boundaries.

vi. *The active gap* refers to different rationalities from national and sub-national policymakers which create obstacles for adopting convergent strategies. Common examples arise from political and departmental purposes. Divergences across levels of government can be used for 'cornering' the debate instead of serving common purposes. A local mayor may prefer to serve constituents perceived aspirations instead of aligning decisions to national or state wide objectives which may be perceived as contradictory.

vii. *The accountability challenge* results from the difficulty to ensure transparency of practices across different constituencies and levels of government. It also concerns possible integrity challenges of policymakers involved in the management of public investment.

These 'gaps' together constitute the architecture that is essential for effective place designs. In the absence of appropriate arrangements in any one building block, the entire design of place governance is put at risk. In turn, this emphasises the significance of a diagnostic phase in which local conditions, needs and circumstances need to be clearly identified.

The second framework, 'Bridging Coordination and Capacity Gaps' (see Table 2), illustrates the approaches adopted in various states to overcome coordination and capacity gaps. A particular state might use various combinations of these instruments, depending on what it seeks to achieve through decentralisation and what coordination and capacity gaps are relevant. The key point again is the variety of approaches that are evident around OECD states and the specifically local character of any particular design.

Table 1: 'Mind the Gaps' – A tool for diagnosis

Administrative gap	'Mismatch' between functional areas and administrative boundaries = > **Need for instruments for reaching 'effective size'**
Information gap	Asymmetries of information (quantity, quality, type) between different stakeholders, either voluntary or not = > **Need for instruments for revealing & sharing information**
Policy gap	Sectoral fragmentation across ministries and agencies = > **Need for mechanisms to create multidimensional/ systemic approaches, and to exercise political leadership and commitment**
Capacity gap	Insufficient scientific, technical, infrastructural capacity of local actors = > **Need for instruments to build capacity**
Funding gap	Unstable or insufficient revenues undermining effective implementation of responsibilities at sub-national level or for crossing policies = > **Need for shared financing mechanisms**
Objective gap	Different rationalities creating obstacles for adopting convergent targets = > **Need for instruments to align objectives**
Accountability gap	Difficulty to ensure the transparency of practices across the different constituencies = > **Need for institutional quality instruments**
Bridge the coordination and capacity gaps	
Contracts	France, Italy, European Union, Canada
Performance Measurement & Transparent evaluation	Norway, United Kingdom, United States
Grants, co-funding agreements	All countries: general purpose grants v. earmarked, equalisation mechanisms
Strategic planning requirements, multi-annual budget	Along with investment contracts
Inter-municipal coordination	Mergers (Denmark, Japan) v. inter-municipal cooperation (Spain, France, Brazil, etc.)
Inter-sectoral collaboration	Finland, France …
Agencies	One ministry v. interministerial mechanisms United Kingdom, Canada, Chile
Experimentation policies	Sweden, United States, Finland
Legal mechanisms and standard settings	All countries, but more or less implemented
Citizens' participation	A question of degree
Private sector participation	From strategy design … to vested interest
Institutional capacity indicators	Italy for sub-national level

Source: Adapted from Charbit 2011.

A decentralised approach is reinforced in literatures on regional innovation systems to which we now turn.

EU 'learning-by-doing', experimentalist or pragmatist governance

The European Union (EU) is a complex multi-level governance design for which it is hard to find precedents. In areas where common action has been agreed, the diversity of approaches and structures between member states ruled out top-down or one-size-fits-all designs. So how could action be coordinated? In answering this latter question, the EU has introduced an approach which may have applications to coordinated action between and within levels of government in Australia, specifically in the context of remote Australia.

The EU approach replaces principal-agent designs with a 'learning-by-doing' or pragmatist one (Sabel and Zeitlin 2011). The former design continues to dominate public policy thinking in Australia. A central tenet of principal-agent theory is that the principal can determine desired outcomes in advance. Pre-determined performance metrics allow the principal to hold the agent accountable for outcomes, thus obviating shirking, opportunism and other deceptive behaviour on the part of the agent. This has been widely applied in public sector settings in Australia — in a variety of human services contracts, for example (see Marsh and Spies-Butcher 2009). But the diversity of conditions across the country has required adaptation. Hence in equalising comparisons the centre adds in a variety of qualifying factors that it considers appropriate. Influenced by this thinking, elaborate contractual, co-production, outsourcing and reporting structures have developed in a variety of fields (for example, surveyed in Productivity Commission 2010).

At least three basic features of human service (and other) contexts undercut advance determination of outcomes by a centrally located principal:

- *First, the knowledge guiding the decisions of both principals and agents is provisional*: both are operating with corrigible information and judgements. Unintended consequences, ambiguity and difference abound. It is impossible to devise programs from first principles that survive the effort to realise them. In the case of the principal, this involves judgements about attainable outcomes and, in the case of agents, this involves judgements about the practices most likely to enhance performance in the pursuit of these outcomes.

- *Second, providers have information that is essential to adapting performance outcomes for the overall system that recognise best practice*: the principal is setting outcomes that need to reconcile efficiency and quality in a way that minimises incentives for provider gamesmanship, creates incentives for efficiency and that does so in a way that also promotes quality services for clients. Any one of the outcomes is complex. Their achievement in combination is a daunting challenge. Only the providers have information that is relevant to making this latter judgement. The principal needs routine access to provider information in order to refine and develop her understanding of desired outcomes in the light of provider and client experience.

- *Third, providers' own knowledge of how to attain quality services for clients is varied and developing*: providers' own knowledge of how best to serve clients — and how best to establish organisational and governance routines that reinforce these outcomes — is itself corrigible and experimental. Different organisations will attain different outcomes and it will not be immediately apparent which represents the best achievement of not necessarily consistent purposes. Dynamic efficiency through the whole system thus requires the routine collection, assessment and dissemination of performance information amongst providers.

An 'experimentalist' or pragmatist approach represents an alternative to these architectures, but one that promises to shift exchanges from a primarily punitive to a primarily learning basis (Sabel 2004; Sabel and Zeitlin 2011). This builds on earlier work on continuous performance improvement and 'learning by doing' — an approach to dynamic efficiency that was developed by the Toyota Motor Company in its management of buyer–supplier relationships (Sabel 1992). Here is how this might be translated to public policy settings:

> General goals or designs are set provisionally by the highest level — parliament, a regulatory authority, or the relevant corporate executives … then the provisional goals are revised in the light of proposals by lower level units responsible for executing key aspects of the overall task (Sabel 2004, p. 11).

Sabel proposes to recast fundamentally the terms of the accountability relationship between principals and agents:

> Compliance or accountability in the principal agent sense of rule following is There are in effect no fixed rules, or, what comes to the same thing, a key rule is to continuously evaluate possible changes in the rules. *Accountability thus requires not comparison of performance to a goal or rule, but reason giving: actors in the new institutions are called upon to explain their use of the autonomy they are accorded in pursuing the corrigible goals* [emphasis mine]. These accounts enable evaluation of their choices in the light of explanations provided by actors in similar circumstances making different ones and vice versa.

Agents who fail to perform to best-practice levels are first given the chance to improve via an exchange of knowledge about their potential to improve: 'Repeated failure to respond, even with assistance, is, however, likely to bring about the dissolution of the offending unit' (Sabel 2004, p. 14). This broad approach has been widely tested in a variety of human services and other public policy settings in the US (Sabel and Simon 2010).

Pragmatist or experimental principles define an approach to the management of intergovernmental and purchaser–provider relations wholly different from the structure that is now dominant in federal and state jurisdictions. The alternative 'experimentalist' or pragmatist approach to system design builds on a broad structure of intergovernmental and purchaser–provider relationship, but places exchange in a context that emphasises learning by both parties.

Australian local government practice

The foregoing discussion focused on regions as the relevant spatial unit and involved governance models drawn from international practice. Parallel experiments and possibilities are also evident in Australian local government practice. The models that have been developed here have clear implications for imagining various possible forms of regional governance. These local government arrangements are comprehensively explored in a report of the collaborative practices of shires in remote Queensland (Dollery and Johnson 2007). The report documents the many imaginative responses of individual councils to preserve community amenities and to reconcile local responsiveness with efficient resource management and relationships with other levels of government. The focus of the report is the Remote Area Planning and Development Board which is a not-for-profit, Australian Securities and Investments Commission-listed company involving a collaboration of 11 councils in western Queensland. Its core concerns are transport, regional planning, capacity building, natural resource management, service development, technology and communications, development of sustainable industries, and investment attraction.

The report documents the many imaginative roles that are being undertaken by the individual councils to ensure community amenities are maintained at desired standards:

> In the absence of any other feasible service providers, local councils must provide a large range of essentials services. For instance, there are not many councils in Australia that provide the postal services (as in Barcoo and Ilfracombe); offer banking facilities (Blackall, Boulia, Tambo and Winton); a café (as in Boulia, Isisford and Winton); undertaker services (Barcoo, Blackall, Boulia, Ilfracombe and Tambo); real estate agency

activities (Diamentina); operate general stores (Ilfracombe and Isisford); provide freight services (Isisford); or operate the local newspaper (Blackall) … In addition, each council provides extensive support to the humorous community and sporting organisations in their boundaries (Dollery and Johnson 2007, p. 104).

Other services include:

Aramac Shire either directly or indirectly provides … a bakery, Home and Community Care programs, and a rural transaction centre. Similarly, Barcaldine Shire delivers a number of state government programs including rural family support, 60 and Better, Home Assist Secure and a HACC program … BARCO Shire Council provides the Jundah Post Office … the Council provides a bus service and a 4WD vehicle for the three schools in the Shire; the Council provided land for the Windorah Medical Clinic; it provided land for state community housing; it has undertaker services and provides burial services … Barcoo Shire has set up a bursary system for residents undertaking tertiary, diploma or trade qualifications … Blackall Shire assist its residents by providing an 'in-store' Westpac Bank facility in the Council office and it acts as a 'developer' baby providing an industrial estate as well as residential land for sale … [it] runs an extensive local economic development program … an airport (with 3 commercial flights a week); SBS radio transmission; youth development services, including employment initiatives (Dollery and Johnson 2007, p. 105–106).

Conclusion

The foregoing suggests the timeliness of a shift of governance towards more place-based spatial levels. This is the next logical step in the development of public sector governance. As noted at the outset, this is wholly consistent with the vision for public sector reform advanced in a number of recent official reports; for example, at the federal level, in the Moran Review (AGRGA 2010); and at a state level, in the Western Australian Economic Audit Committee Report (WAEAC 2009). This latter report specifically foreshadows the replacement of 'agencies operating in silos' with more decentralised citizen-focused arrangements. Both these reports underline the profound challenge to centralised processes, cultures and organisational and budgetary protocols that are involved in a further iteration of public sector reform. The evidence reviewed in the last section suggests governance designs are available — but, as British experience attests, the difficulties in translating aspirations into practice remain formidable. No less profound obstacles can be anticipated in Australia.

Indeed here they are compounded by intergovernmental considerations. On the other hand, both fiscal and political imperatives imply dictate a shift to citizen focused services. The demand for more proactive services that are and sensitive to context will not go away. In charting a new path, a first challenge is to imagination — there is another way.

References

Adonis, A. and S. Sims 2011, *Mayors and the Localism Bill,* Institute for Government, Carlton Gardens.

AGRGA (Advisory Group on Reform of Australian Government Administration) 2010, 'Ahead of the Game: Blueprint for the teform of Australian government administration'. Available at: http://www.dpmc.gov.au/publications/aga_reform/aga_reform_blueprint/docs/APS_reform_blueprint.pdf.

Altman, J. C. 2009, 'Beyond Closing the Gap: Valuing diversity in Indigenous Australia', CAEPR Working Paper No. 54. Available at: http://caepr.anu.edu.au/Publications/WP/2009WP54.php.

Altman, J. C. 2011, 'The Draft Indigenous Economic Strategy: A critical response', CAEPR Topical Issue No. 3. Available at: http://caepr.anu.edu.au/Publications/topical/2011TI3.php.

ANAO (Australian National Audit Office) 2007, 'Whole-of-Government Indigenous Service Delivery Arrangements', ANAO Audit Report No 10. Available at: http://www.anao.gov.au/Publications/Audit-Reports/2007-2008/Whole-of-Government-Indigenous-Service-Delivery-Arrangements.

Australian Government 2011, 'Engaging Today, Building Tomorrow: A framework for engaging with Aboriginal and Torres Strait Islander Australians.

Barber, M. 2008, *Instruction to Deliver: Fighting to transform Britain's public service*, 2nd ed., Methuen, London.

Communities and Local Government Select Committee 2011a, 'Localism', Third Report, 9 May. Available at: http://www.publications.parliament.uk/pa/cm201012/cmselect/cmcomloc/547/547.pdf.

Charbit, C. 2011, 'Governance of Public Policies in a Decentralised Contexts: The multi-level approach', OECD Regional Policy Development Working Paper 2011/04. Available at: http://www.oecd.org/governance/regional-policy/48724565.pdf.

Clark, G. 2003, *Total Politics: Labour's Command State,* Conservative Policy Unit, London.

Coleman, W. 2010, Presentation to Australian MPs, October, 2010.

Commonwealth Grants Commission 2001, 'Indigenous Funding Inquiry: Final report'. Available at: https://cgc.gov.au/index.php?option=com_content&view=article&id=53:2001-indigenous-funding-inquiry&catid=39&Itemid=160.

Coote, A. 2010, 'Cutting It: "The Big Society" and the new austerity', New Economics Foundation, London.

Crowe, J. 2011, 'The Government's Plans for Decentralisation and Localism: A progress report', *The Political Quarterly* 82(4), pp. 651–657.

Department of Finance 2009, 'Review of the CDEP Scheme'. Available at: http://www.anao.gov.au/~/media/Uploads/Documents/evaluation_of_the_community_development_employment_projects_(cdep)_program.pdf.

Department of Finance 2010, 'Strategic Review of Indigenous Expenditure'. Available at: http://www.finance.gov.au/sites/default/files/foi_10-27_strategic_review_indigenous_expenditure.pdf.

Dillon, M. and N. Westbury 2007, *Beyond Humbug: Transforming government engagement with Indigenous Australia*, Seaview Press, South Australia.

Dollery, B. and A. Johnson 2007, 'RAPAD (Remote Area Planning and Development Board) Report: Sustaining outback communities', University of New England, Armidale.

Dorf, L. and C. Sabel 1998, 'A Constitution of Democratic Experimentalism', *Columbia Law Review* 98, pp. 267–473.

Edmunds, M. 2010, *The Northern Territory Intervention and Human Rights: An anthropoligical perspective*, Whitlam Institute, University of Western Sydney, Bankstown.

FaHCSIA (Department of Families, Housing, Community Services and Indigenous Affairs) 2004, 'Evaluation of ICCs'. Available at: https://www.dss.gov.au/sites/default/files/documents/06_2012/icc_review_report_0.pdf.

Gray, B. 2006, 'COAG Trial Evaluation, Wadeye, Northern Territory', WJG and Associates. Available at: http://www.territorystories.nt.gov.au/handle/10070/143460.

Gray, W. and W. G. Sanders 2006, 'Views from the Top of the "Quiet Revolution": Secretarial perspectives on the new arrangements in Indigenous affairs', CAEPR Discussion Paper 282/2006. Available at: http://caepr.anu.edu.au/Publications/DP/2006DP282.php.

H. M. Treasury and the Department of Communities and Local Government 2010, 'Total Place: A Whole Area Approach to Public Services'. Available at: http://webarchive.nationalarchives.gov.uk/20130129110402/http:/www.hm-treasury.gov.uk/d/total_place_report.pdf.

Hunt, J. 2007, 'The Whole-of-Government Experiment in Indigenous Affairs: A question of governance capacity', *Public Policy* 2(2), pp. 155–174.

Institute of Public Policy Research 2010, 'Capable Communities: Towards citizen-powered public services', Institute of Public Policy Research, London.

KPMG 2007, 'Evaluation of Indigenous Coordination Centres. Available at: www.dss.gov.au/sites/default/files/documents/06_2012/icc_review_report_0.pdf.

Local Government Association 2013, 'A Guide to Whole Place Communicty Budgets'. Available at: http://www.local.gov.uk/community-budgets/-/journal_content/56/10180/3930626/ARTICLE.

Management Advisory Committee 2004, 'Connecting Government: Whole of government responses to Australia's priority challenges', Australian Public Service Commission, Canberra.

Management Advisory Committee 2007, 'Note for file: A report on recordkeeping in the Australian Public Service', Australian Public Service Commission, Canberra.

Marsh, I. and R. Miller 2012, *Democratic Decline and Democratic Renewal: Political change in Britain, Australia and New Zealand,* Cambridge University Press, Cambridge.

Marsh, I. and B. Spies-Butcher, 2009, 'Pragmatist and Neo-classical Policy Paradigms: Which is the best template for program design?', *Australian Journal of Public Administration* 68(3), pp. 239–255.

Morgan Disney and Associates 2006, *Synopsis Review of the COAG Trial Evaluation.* Available at: https://www.dss.gov.au/sites/default/files/documents/05_2012/coag_trials_overview.pdf.

NAO (National Audit Office) 'Case Study on Integration: Measuring the costs and benefits of whole-place community budgets'. Available at: http://www.nao.

org.uk/press-releases/department-for-communities-and-local-government-case-study-on-integration-measuring-the-costs-and-benefits-of-whole-place-community-budgets-2/.

NTCOSS (Northern Territory Council of Social Services) 2008, 'Submission to the Enquiry into Government Expenditure on Indigenous Affairs and Social Services in the Northern Territory'.

NTER Review (Northern Territory Emergency Response Review) 2008, Department of Families, Housing, Community Services and Indigenous Affairs, Canberra.

O'Flynn, J., F. Buick, D. Blackman and J. Halligan 2011, 'You Win Some, You Lose Some: Experiments with joined-up government', *International Journal of Public Administration* 34(4), pp. 244–254.

Parker, S., A. Paun, J. McClory and K. Blatchford 2010, *Shaping Up: A Whitehall for the future*, Institute for Government, London.

Productivity Commission 2010, 'Contribution of the Not-for-Profit Sector'. Available at: http://www.pc.gov.au/__data/assets/pdf_file/0003/94548/not-for-profit-report.pdf.

Productivity Commission 2012, 'Indigenous Expenditure Report' Steering Committee for the Review of Government Service Provision. Available at: http://www.pc.gov.au/gsp/ier.

Rowse, T. 2002, *Indigenous Futures, Choice and Development for Aboriginal and Islander Australia*, UNSW Press, Kensington.

Rowse, T. 2012, Rethinking Social Justice: From 'peoples' to 'populations', Aboriginal Studies Press, Canberra.

Sabel, C. 1992, 'Learning by Monitoring: The institutions of economic development', in L. Rodwin and D. Schon (eds) *Rethinking the Development Experience: Essays provoked by the work of Albert O. Hirschman*, The Brookings Institution, Washington.

Sabel, C. 2004, 'Beyond Principal-Agent Governance: Experimentalist organisation, learning and accountability', in E. R. Engelen and M. S. D. Ho (eds), *De Staat van de Democratie: Democratie voorbij de staat*, Amsterdam University Press, Amsterdam.

Sabel, C. and W. Simon 2010, 'Minimalism and Experimentalism in the Administrative State', *The Georgetown Law Review* 100, pp. 54–93.

Sabel, C. and J. Zeitlin 2011, 'Experimentalist Governance', in D. Levi-Faurr (ed.), *The Oxford Handbook of Governance,* Oxford University Press, Oxford.

Shergold, P. 2006, 'Indigenous Economic Opportunity: The role of the community and the individual', speech delivered to First Nations Economic Opportunity Conference, 19 July. Available at: http://www.google.com.au/url?q=http://www.ceo.wa.edu.au/listserver/cwac/doc00001.doc&sa=U&ei=C8QfVJDoJMbe8AX4xYIw&ved=0CBoQFjAB&sig2=RqytPYuXH648eJW16CA5dg&usg=AFQjCNEyzWndLLGxvE9ay761M6iVlxS10A.

Shergold, P. 2013, 'An Agenda for Reform of the Australian Public Service', in D. Markwell, R. Thompson and J. Leeser (eds), *State of the Nation: Aspects of Australian public policy,* Menzies Research Centre, Canberra.

Smith, D. 2009, 'From COAG to Coercion: A story of governance failure, success and opportunity in Australian Indigenous affairs', Paper presented to ANZSOG conference: Governing Through Collaboration: Managing Better Through Others, 28–29 June. Available at: http://caepr.anu.edu.au/others/governance/Occasional-papers-1190988000.php.

Urbis, Keys and Young 2006, 'Evaluation of the Murdi Paarki COAG Trials'. Available at: www.dss.gov.au/sites/default/files/documents/05_2012/coag_nsw.pdfWAEAC.

WAEAC (Western Australia Economic Audit Committee) 2009, 'Putting the Public First: Partnering with the community and business to deliver outcomes: Summary report'.

Wind-Cowie, M. 2010, *Civic Street: The big society in action,* Demos, London.

10. Australian Sub-National Compacts with the Not-For-Profit Sector: Pathways to cross-sector cooperation

John Butcher

Introduction

In this chapter we trace the history of formal policy frameworks for cross-sector cooperation in Australia's states and territories. Inspired by the original 'English' Compact, initiated by the Blair Labour government in 1998, the policy frameworks examined are intended to establish agreed rules of engagement between government (and its instrumentalities) and the not-for-profit (NFP) sector — especially those parts of the sector upon which government has become increasingly reliant for the delivery of public services.

Compacts represent an express acknowledgement by government of the contributions to social well-being made by civil society actors. They also embody the reciprocity implicit in the government–NFP sector relationship and are generally intended to act as a touchstone for agreed values, principles, attitudes and norms. To the extent that contemporary governments assert the intrinsic value of collaboration with non-state actors (O'Flynn and Wanna 2008) compacts offer symbolic proofs of a commitment to cross-sector partnership.

Most compacts also seek to alleviate the impact upon NFP service providers of externalities associated with government procurement and contracting processes that have tended to focus on the exchange of public funds for capability (service provision). Frequently cited as constraints on the capability and capacity of government's partners in the NFP sector are: high transaction costs; burdensome reporting; excessive prescription; failures to fund the true cost of service delivery; and operational uncertainty associated with short-term contracts (Productivity Commission 2010).

Here it must be noted that many NFP providers of contracted services reject the notion that they are merely contractors or agents. Rather, NFP organisations often see themselves as policy actors in their own right, with an implied mandate to represent constituencies of interest. NFP organisations are also repositories of expertise, knowledge and the custodians of stakeholder trust. So, in addition to exchanges of financial consideration for services rendered, contracting in the public services space involves exchanges of authority and legitimacy (Casey 2004).

Elson (2011, p. 137) observes that there have been few comparative analyses of framework agreements for cooperation at the sub-national level within the same country and this is certainly true of Australia, not least because the policy landscape is dynamic and still evolving. The analysis presented here is based upon extensive interviews undertaken between November 2010 and October 2011 with public officials, sector representatives and other policy actors in Australia's six states and the Australian Capital Territory. It is hoped that this work will make a useful contribution to both theory and praxis.

Compacts in Australia

In March 2010 the then Australian Prime Minister, Kevin Rudd, announced a national compact between the Commonwealth (federal) government and the country's NFP sector. The Commonwealth was a latecomer in this policy space (Butcher 2011, 2012; Butcher et al. 2012). For over two decades successive state and territory governments — most of them Labor governments — have looked to compacts to resolve the tensions and contradictions inherent in the contract state. This chapter tells the lesser-known story of these policy frameworks.

Between 2001 and 2012, compacts or compact-like policy frameworks have been actively considered in every Australian state and territory. Some have endured, some have fallen by the wayside, and others have failed to fully come to fruition. Some have enjoyed, and continue to enjoy a measure of success. Others have failed to earn the full confidence of stakeholders inside and outside government. The cross-sector policy frameworks implemented in each jurisdiction have differed in their scope, institutional arrangements and operational frameworks. Some were developed and agreed bilaterally between government and its NFP sector partners; others have taken the form of unilateral policy statements. Some purport to be whole of sector frameworks, while others are expressly focused on the health and social welfare sub-sectors.

In the discussion that follows, we consider the range of factors influencing the adoption of compacts as well as the factors contributing to their success and failure. Of course, it is not possible to examine each of the cases in detail in a chapter of this length. Nevertheless, the appendix at the end of the chapter provides a contextual snapshot of each state and territory.

Leading from below

Australia is a federal state in which the constitutional division of powers confers primary responsibility upon states and territories for the delivery of health and human services, housing and education (ACT 2000b, p. 6; Casey et al. 2008c, p. 4). As a result, state and territory governments have a significant policy and financial exposure to the NFP sector. The rapid expansion of Australia's NFP sector through the 1970s and 1980s was largely underwritten by increases in social expenditure by state and territory governments. Today, income from state and territory governments represents a significant share of the aggregate recurrent income for Australia's community sector organisations (ACOSS 2011).[1]

From the mid-1990s, state and territory governments have confronted the twin challenges of fiscal pressures and increasing demand for public services — including demands for greater choice in in relation to services and providers (Cook et al. 2012). In response, governments have sought — where politically and practically feasible — to ultilise non-state service providers in the NFP and for-profit sectors.

Human services account for a significant share of outsourced service delivery owing in part to the labour-intensive nature of these industries and the presumed lower cost structures prevailing in the NFP community services sector (Productivity Commission 2010, p. 249). Other advantages claimed for NFP service providers include greater nimbleness, responsiveness, acceptability to consumers and capacity for innovation (McDonald 1999; McDonald and Marston 2002).

Just as NFP service providers have become dependent upon government grants and contracts for a significant share of their income, so too state and territory governments have become dependent upon NFP service providers for the delivery of public policy and programs. Notwithstanding the interdependence of the public and NFP sectors, this is not a relationship of equals. A number of formal reviews have confirmed that NFP service providers often operate within significant constraints imposed by government policy, including high transaction costs, financial uncertainty, onerous reporting requirements, micro-management, excessive focus on inputs, and failure to fund the full cost of service delivery (Auditor-General 2000; PAEC 2002; QAO 2007; VAGO 2010).

These factors help to explain why formal cross-sector policy frameworks to support enhanced cooperation between government and the NFP sector emerged

---

1   State and territory governments also exercise regulatory functions in relation to the NFP sector. The regulatory environment in which NFP organisations operate has been characterised as consisting of 'uncoordinated regimes at the Commonwealth and state/territory levels' in which '[d]isparate reporting and other requirements add complexity and cost, especially for organisations operating in more than one jurisdiction' (Productivity Commission 2010, p. 113).

first in state and territory jurisdictions. However, it should also be noted that a compact between the Commonwealth government and the NFP sector was never in prospect at any time during the 11 years during which the centre-right Liberal–National Coalition governed nationally (Lyons 2001, 2002, 2003).

Compacts and Labor governments

As was the case federally, policy frameworks for cross-sector cooperation in states and territories (with only one exception, to be discussed later in this chapter) have been initiated by Labor administrations. In part this might be explained by the fact that the Australian Labor Party has strong historical and institutional associations with parts of what might be collectively termed 'civil society' (which includes the NFP sector), in particular the labour movement and progressive social movements. To the extent that centre-left political parties share values and constituencies with significant parts of the NFP sector, they might also exhibit a predisposition to enter into formal partnership frameworks based on an assumption that they and the sector are fellow travellers of a sort.

During the period of the Howard Coalition government (1996–2007) compacts with the NFP sector formed an important part of the policy palette in all Australian states and territories. During this period an especially antagonistic relationship prevailed between the federal government and parts of the NFP sector, particularly around the government's contracting practices and its intolerance of policy advocacy by the sector (Australia 2010; Productivity Commission 2010, pp. 309–310) — a situation that might have galvanised the sector to forge agreements with receptive state and territory Labor governments.

Process streams analysis

The adoption by state and territory governments of formal cross-sector policy frameworks exhibits features of policy transfer and/or policy convergence. Policy diffusion is evident where the preferred policy responses in one jurisdiction are systematically conditioned by prior choices made in others (Simmons et al. 2006, p. 787). The transmission between jurisdictions of public administration doctrines, such as those encompassed by new public management, are often thought of in these terms (Hood 1991; Common 1998; Halligan 2011). Policy convergence, on the other hand, is marked by a tendency for policy formulations to grow more alike in response to emerging problems (Drezner 2001). In other words, governments confronting similar problems might more or less independently come up with similar solutions.

That formal cross-sector policy frameworks in Australia's states and territories contain substantially similar provisions and language is indicative of direct policy transfer (in so far as it reflects conscious and deliberate policy borrowing). However, cross-sector policy frameworks have emerged at different times and their political and practical expression differs substantially between jurisdictions, which is strongly suggestive of policy convergence. Explaining the emergence of compacts requires an analytic frame that supports a contextual analysis of the historical, political and institutional factors affecting the ways in which policy problems are framed and the roles played by policy actors in enabling (or impeding) the implementation of solutions (Common 2010).

Process streams analysis offers a useful approach for framing a plausible explanatory narrative. In his seminal book, *Agendas, Alternatives and Public Policies* (first published in 1984), Kingdon posed the questions 'what makes an idea's time come?' and 'what makes people in and around government attend, at any given time, to some subjects and not to others?' (Kingdon 1995, p. 1). Kingdon observed that in the volatile marketplace of ideas and solutions some ideas never gain traction, others become prominent and then fade, and some 'achieve lasting high agenda status' (Kingdon 1995, p. 116).

Kingdon posits the existence of three major 'process streams': the *problem stream* (for example, the emergence of consensus about problems that require resolution, such as the unintended externalities associated with contracted service delivery); the *policy stream* (for example, communities of policy 'specialists' in which alternative solutions to problems are formulated and tested, such as formal cross-sector framework agreements); and the *politics stream* (for example, events or circumstances that influence political receptiveness to problems and solutions, including swings in public opinion, interest group pressures, elections, changes of government, or machinery of government changes).

Although the three streams operate largely independently, they come together at critical times. When they do, they can result in the opening of a 'policy window', which offers a time-limited opportunity for new policy ideas to be placed on the policy agenda. In Kingdon's words: 'A problem is recognised, a solution is available, the political climate makes the time right for change, and the constraints do not prohibit action' (Kingdon 1995, pp. 86–88).

However, the opening of a policy window is not alone sufficient to place a proposal on the policy agenda. In most cases this requires the intervention of policy entrepreneurs who seek to couple their preferred solutions to existing problems. Policy entrepreneurs are people who have the connections, knowledge, profile and personal qualities necessary to promote the coupling of their preferred solutions with existing policy problems (Kingdon 1995, pp. 166–169, 181–182).[2]

Whether compacts survive the tumult of political contestation and policy implementation can depend on their maintaining what Kingdon refers to as 'high agenda prominence' (Kingdon 1995, pp. 103, 198). This can be especially challenging in environments characterised by multiple policy domains and in which individual and collective policy actors have differing values, priorities and operational norms. Compacts can also be crowded off, or down the policy agenda as a result of political turbulence in the form of events such as a change in leadership (a frequent occurrence in Australian politics in recent years), the loss or turnover of key personnel (such as a CEO of a public sector agency or an influential thought leader in the NFP sector) or by other crises that serve to refocus and re-prioritise the attentions of policymakers and implementers.

A decline in agenda prominence can also occur when decision-makers conclude that once the policy has been announced their mission has been accomplished. Framework documents — such as compacts — that enunciate the purpose and means for cross-sector cooperation can be potent policy markers. However, the crafting of such a document is not an end in itself; it is only a beginning. Without an implementation strategy and follow-through the legitimacy of the initiative and the opportunity to have a positive impact is compromised (Almog-Bar and Zychlinski 2012). Other threats are institutional resistance (e.g. an effect of path dependence and isomorphism); disconnects between institutional narrative and organisational behaviour (Meyer and Rowan 1991); the failure to fully understand or accept the purpose of the policy framework; and unrealistic expectations (contributing to cynicism and a loss of legitimacy).

Relevance in Australia

Kingdon's process streams analysis offers a useful lens through which to view compacts and other forms of cross-sector agreement, but how might it apply in the Australian context?

First, in the problem stream, we have witnessed in Australia and elsewhere a broad consensus among policy practitioners and researchers about the range

---

2   Kingdon and other like-minded theorists (such as March and Olsen 2006) draw upon neo-institutionalist theory in their analysis of political and policy phenomena, bringing together strands of normative (institutional logics), rational choice (bounded rationality), and historical (path dependency) perspectives in a compelling synthesis. Kendall 2003, Brock 2008, Elson 2011, and Phillips 2003 each draw upon Kingdon in their analyses of compacts in the UK and Canada. Compacts might also be usefully examined through other lenses, including policy implementation (Elson 2006) or from a functional legal/administrative perspective (Bullain and Toftisova 2005).

of tensions, contradictions and externalities associated with the contract state. These include failures to fund the full cost of service delivery, burdensome reporting and compliance requirements, and the substitution of competitive behaviours for collegiality among NFP service providers.

Second, in the policy stream, we have observed since 1998 the emergence within various policy communities of energetic policy discourses concerned with cross-cutting or joined-up policy and implementation; social capital; public value; co-production; boundary-spanning, network and relational governance; and so on. Policy entrepreneurs within these same policy communities have at various times promoted compacts or similar frameworks as a means to realise cross-cutting policy aims.

Third, in the politics stream, Australia's two major political parties have both embraced the central tenets of new public management. It is sometimes observed by political commentators that the 'professionalisation' of politics in contemporary Australia and the efforts of the Australian Labor Party (ALP) and the Liberal Party of Australia to command the political middle ground has left few points of policy difference between the two major parties (Johnson 2011; Aitkin 2013). Clearly signalling those points of political and policy difference — particularly in times of political change — is an essential part of political marketing. For this reason alone, the idea of a formal framework document, rich in political symbolism, might have great appeal in light of the social democratic and corporatist traditions of the ALP — especially if the framework does not result in a significant impost on government.[3]

Australian cross-sector policy frameworks

The analysis presented here is based upon an extensive review of relevant primary documents and a more limited secondary literature. The primary literature is replete with policy documents, press releases, correspondence and reports (including parliamentary reports, reports by state audit offices and consultants). This literature is invaluable in reconstructing the policy histories of the relationship frameworks in each jurisdiction.

Insights drawn from the literature are corroborated by in-depth interviews conducted with senior public officials, senior NFP sector representatives and other elite policy actors in each jurisdiction (with the exception of the Northern Territory). In order to protect the confidentiality of interviewees, none are identified by name or organisation.

---

3   Similar observations have been offered in relation to the Canadian Accord (Canada 2001) by Phillips 2003 and Brock 2004, 2008.

Each of Australia's eight states and territories has explored the potential of formal relational frameworks between government and the community or voluntary sectors. Their form, content and implementation processes differ in each jurisdiction and sector confidence in state/territory frameworks is mixed — as is confidence in the effectiveness of compacts generally. It *is* difficult to neatly pigeonhole Australian state and territory policy frameworks. This is unsurprising given the complexity of the political and policy environments within which they arise, and the different perspectives and priorities brought to the table by the parties.

A variety of forms

The Australian Capital Territory (ACT) led the way in 2001 with what the government and the community sector proclaimed as 'the first Compact of its kind in Australia' (ACT 2001, p. 4). This first compact, initiated by a Liberal territory government, was subsequently adopted by a succeeding Labor government and remains an important touchstone for social policy in the ACT. The most recent framework agreement (at the time of writing) is the 2012 partnership agreement between the Tasmanian Department of Health and Human Services, the Department of Premier and Cabinet, and the community sector (Tasmania 2012). The Tasmanian agreement represents the culmination of an on-again/off-again conversation between government and the sector about a formal relationship framework begun in 1996 (personal communication 2011l; Tasmania 2012).

To date, three jurisdictions have implemented bilateral framework agreements between a state or territory government and groups representing broad coalitions of NFP organisations. These are the ACT (the 'Social Compact'), New South Wales (NSW, with 'Working Together for NSW') and Queensland (the 'Queensland Compact'). Of these, only the 'Social Compact' continues to have policy relevance — helped by the fact that Labor has governed continuously in the Territory since 2001.[4] By contrast, 'Working Together for NSW' had already declined in policy salience before the election of a Liberal–National Coalition state government in 2011. The 'Queensland Compact' — once considered an exemplar framework — was displaced by the election of a Liberal–National Party government in 2012.[5]

Cross-sector frameworks implemented in Victoria, South Australia and Tasmania have been more narrowly cast as agreements between state government departments — predominantly in the human services and community health

---

4 The next election will be held in October 2016.
5 It should be noted that neither 'Working Together for NSW' nor the 'Queensland Compact' were formally rescinded — as non-statutory instruments such a step is effectively moot.

domains — and relevant NFP sub-sectors. In this, they are more explicitly concerned to address the legacy of problems arising in the contractual relationships between governments and NFP service providers. In Victoria, a proposal for a bilateral compact between government and the NFP sector was rejected in favour of domain-level partnership agreements between government departments and related groupings of NFP organisations. The first of these domain-level partnership agreements commenced in 2002 between the Department of Human Services and 'health, housing and community service organisations'. This agreement was renewed in 2009 (in the form of a memorandum of understanding) and the model has since been extended to other policy domains such as early childhood development.

Although the language of some of these framework documents — such as the 'Queensland Compact' — suggests broad application to the whole-of-government and the whole-of-sector, for the most part they apply to the human services and community services sectors.[6] Although central agencies — for example, a premier's or chief minister's department — have had early involvement in the development of cross-sector frameworks in a number of jurisdictions (for example, in the ACT, New South Wales and Tasmania) in all cases the policy lead for these agreements resides primarily with line agencies with a policy lead in the human services domain.

Although all Australian jurisdictions have considered formal cross-sector policy frameworks, two — Western Australia (WA) and the Northern Territory (NT) — have followed a different path. In WA the 'Delivering Community Services in Partnership Policy' (Western Australia 2011b) is not an agreement, although it was co-developed by government central agencies, key line departments, and NFP sector representatives. The policy was endorsed by the state cabinet, is strongly championed by the Premier and enjoyed the strong support of community sector leaders. The Northern Territory commenced the development of a framework agreement in 2004–05, but later abandoned these efforts. There were signs in 2011 that the NT Labor government might revisit the idea of a formal cross-sector framework (Henderson 2011; NT Government 2011), however, any such development was forestalled by the election in 2012 of a majority Country Liberal Party government.

---

6   This can also include community-based human services provided within a health portfolio. In Australia, the terms 'community services sector' or simply 'community sector' are frequently used to denote that part of the NFP sector providing community-based human services.

Centre-left *versus* centre-right

With the exception of the ACT,[7] state and territory cross-sector policy frameworks were initiated under centre-left Labor governments — most during the period in which the centre-right Liberal–National Coalition governed nationally (1996–2007).

As long-standing state and territory Labor governments faltered under the weight of incumbency, frameworks for cross-sector cooperation were inherited by nominally conservative administrations. So far, five jurisdictions have elected centre-right governments: Western Australia in 2008, Victoria in 2010, New South Wales in 2011, and Queensland and the Northern Territory in 2012. Labor governments were narrowly returned in Tasmania and South Australia (SA) in 2010, and in the Australian Capital Territory in 2012 (in coalition with the ACT Greens).

Superficially, centre-left governments would appear to be the natural allies of the NFP sector. However, it has been observed by NFP policy actors in a number of jurisdictions that Labor governments often expect their NFP partners to be compliant, grateful, and to refrain from criticism. The following comment by a senior NFP sector official reflects a commonly expressed sentiment:

> For many peak bodies, sometimes there's a perception that Labor governments are 'friendly towards them', but in fact, in lots of instances Labor governments expect peak bodies to be friendly towards *them* …

> Oftentimes, governments — particularly modern Labor governments — have often misinterpreted that the place of peaks is to support them, and not to apply critical analysis and provide policy guidance from a point of independence (personal communication 2011c).

Another observed:

> I can remember people on the Left of the ALP in New South Wales [expressing] exactly that view, you know, 'you should be damn grateful we're in and do what we want' — that sort of view, and I think the Left of the ALP still suffers from that in that 'we're the repository of all the good policy ideas' and at the end of the day the public sector still knows how to do it best. Sorry, I don't think either of those things are true (personal communication 2011b).

---

7   In April 2001, the Liberal government of the Australian Capital Territory published 'Compact: Community partnership ACT Government: the first step', which was hailed as 'the first Compact of its kind in Australia': Australian Capital Territory 2001, p. 4. Following a change of government in November 2001, the incoming Labor administration effectively rebranded and reissued the document as the *Social Compact* (2004) but without materially altering its contents: ACT 2000b, 2001.

By contrast, Liberal–National governments can be more accepting of the legitimacy of NFP organisations as autonomous actors, particularly those embodying traditional liberal values of independence (from government), self-reliance and personal responsibility:

> Oftentimes Liberal governments — I mean genuine liberal governments — sometimes appreciate the place of advocacy in a much clearer and less emotional manner and as a result are sometimes able to have much clearer relationships with bodies like peak bodies, because they see their place and they understand what it is (personal communication 2011c).

No two succeeding Liberal–National administrations exhibit identical policy responses. In New South Wales and Victoria Liberal–National governments continued to steer a course already set in train by previous Labor administrations: whereas the Victorian Coalition government continued along the constructive policy track established by Labor, in New South Wales an already moribund compact was ignored by the incoming government. Similarly, Western Australia's Liberal government (first elected in 2008 and re-elected in 2012) has enlarged upon policy foundations built by the previous Labor government and, in so doing, revived a stagnant government–NFP sector relationship.

In 2011, the Western Australia government announced its 'Delivering Community Services in Partnership Policy' (2011b) together with significant new investments aimed at ensuring the viability and sustainability of NFP enterprises in particular sub-sectors (Western Australia 2011a). In contrast, the Queensland Liberal–National Party (LNP) government, elected in a landslide in 2012, focused on reducing state expenditure. The 'Queensland Compact' was set aside and its governance mechanisms discontinued. So-called 'gag clauses' were re-inserted in service provision agreements to debar organisations from advocating for policy change or even including links on their website to other sites that advocate for legislative change (Queensland Law Society 2012). The Queensland NFP sector responded cautiously to these changes — presumably to avoid antagonising a government aggressively pursuing a program of fiscal consolidation.

Policy windows and policy entrepreneurs

Formal policy frameworks for cross-sector cooperation have been initiated during times of political and structural change. From the early 1990s Australian governments have wrestled, collectively and individually, with the challenges of reforming and modernising the economy and public administration. Greater choice, competition and contestability in public service provision required major improvements in public sector efficiency, responsiveness and effectiveness. Australian governments at all levels increasingly arrived at the conclusion that state predominance in public infrastructure, public utilities and public services could not be sustained. Market-testing, the separation of purchaser and provider functions, outsourcing, privatisation and purchase-of-service contracting were the new watchwords of Australian governance.

By the late 1990s there emerged in the problem stream a broad critique of the limitations, contradictions and externalities associated with new public management (see Pusey 2008). Meanwhile, in the policy stream, policy alternatives centred on notions of joined-up governance and more pluralistic approaches to the realisation of government's policy aims began to be promoted by state and non-state policy actors. Some of these proved to be skilled policy entrepreneurs capable of shaping policy preferences within government and the NFP sector.

From 1996–2007 the centre-right Liberal–National Coalition governed nationally. This was a government dedicated (ostensibly) to reducing the size and reach of the state, in part by leveraging competitive markets. For much of this period the centre-left ALP governed in Australia's states and territories. Although they too realised the necessity of structural reform, state and territory governments were also attracted to Blairite third way discourses then shaping social policy in the United Kingdom — discourses not unnoticed by thought leaders in the NFP sector, some of whom looked to compacts as a bulwark against the adverse impacts of contracting.

Policy windows opened at different times, under different circumstances and with different results in Australian states and territories. All states and territories have at one time or another embarked on the development of a formal cross-sector policy framework. In a number of jurisdictions, however (NSW, WA, NT, Queensland) political turbulence in the form of leadership change, changes of government, structural change in the machinery of government and/or the departure of senior personnel (some of them the very policy entrepreneurs who caused compacts to be placed on the agenda in the first place) contributed to the *closing* of policy windows.

Policy initiation, implementation and practice

In some jurisdictions, central agencies and/or line departments have assumed the lead in top-down approaches to the development of cross-sector agreements, largely driven by a desire to resolve tensions arising in their contractual relationships with NFP service providers. Examples include South Australia (SA) and New South Wales. In others, the agreement-making process was initiated either by the sector itself in a bottom-up process (Queensland) or came about as the result of a bottom-up and top-down convergence of government and sector agendas (ACT, Tasmania, Victoria, WA).

Each of the state and territory frameworks contains mutualistic elements, such as statements about the respective roles and contributions of the parties; shared principles, aims and objectives; and the standards of conduct expected of government and the sector. There are also notable differences between jurisdictions in terms of the role played by central agencies; the presence (or absence) of influential champions; the establishment of effective governance structures (including reporting and evaluation requirements); the formulation of action plans; the application of dedicated resources; and the degree of vertical and horizontal integration with related policy frameworks.

These factors can be important determinants of success. Any failure to institutionally embed formal framework agreements heightens the risks of fragmentation, inconsistency, irrelevance and cynicism — leading ultimately to a loss of policy salience. Even those policy frameworks that have enjoyed strong support within the NFP and public sectors can falter at critical moments in the politics stream, such as a change in leadership or a change of government. As observed by a key policy actor in Queensland, 'there is no real way to future proof documentation that carries a previous Premier's and Minister's picture' (personal communication 2010d).

Policy impact

The practical impact of cross-sector policy frameworks is difficult to gauge. It has to be borne in mind that in many respects these are aspirational frameworks. A compact represents an idealised relationship; the behaviours and practices set out in a framework document will not necessarily be mirrored on the ground — at least not without investing effort in a process of managed change.

Examples of effective cross-sector policy frameworks are those operating in Victoria and WA. These are acknowledged by policy actors in the public and NFP sectors as having made a positive contribution to the quality and durability of the relationship between government and the human services sector. Both states also have dedicated units focused on issues of sustainability and capacity-building for the broader NFP sector (an Office for the Community Sector in Victoria, and a Community Engagement Unit in WA).

In both jurisdictions, governance structures have been established to guide implementation of the policy framework(s) and these exhibit a high degree of vertical and horizontal integration with allied policies. WA is notable in two respects: the government and the sector have eschewed a bilateral compact in favour of a comprehensive policy statement; and a centre-right government appears to have succeeded in negotiating a settlement with the sector where a centre-left government demonstrably failed.

In Queensland, a state Labor government and the NFP sector accepted the need for a new settlement that would reflect their mutual dependence and underpin needed reforms. At its inception in 2008 the 'Queensland Compact' was regarded as an exemplar and even informed the development of the 'National Compact'. Implementation was guided by an action plan (Queensland 2008) overseen by a Compact Governance Committee (CGovC). The CGovC, headed by an Independent Chair appointed directly by the Premier, reported annually on compact achievements (Queensland 2009, 2010).

Following the election in 2012 of the LNP government led by Premier Campbell Newman, the CGovC ceased to meet and the Independent Chair was not renewed. The 'Queensland Compact' was no longer on the policy radar and the new government elected not to publish an external review of the compact completed prior to the election. The experience of the 'Queensland Compact' serves to illustrate the potential transience of cross-sector policy frameworks and the importance of obtaining cross-party support for the aims and aspirations they embody.

The contrasting circumstances of the ACT, SA and NSW are also instructive.

In the years since its launch in 2004 the ACT's 'Social Compact' (ACT 2004) had declined in visibility and relevance. Accepting the need to revive and revitalise their relationship, the ACT government and the community sector undertook to refresh the framework and a revised 'Social Compact' was launched in 2012 (ACT 2012). The ACT government, in partnership with the community sector, subsequently initiated a Community Sector Development Program to develop the skills and capabilities of the sector leaders to meet the reform pressures facing their organisations (personal communication 2013).

In SA, the framework agreement between the state government and the health and community services sector, 'Stronger Together' (South Australia 2009), was built upon foundations established by an earlier partnership agreement, 'Common Ground' (South Australia 2004). Billed as a 'reinvigorated approach between the partners to pool resources, resolve problems and develop new and creative approaches to service provision', candid accounts of public officials and sector representatives suggest divergent perceptions of the framework's effectiveness. Although state government officials speak highly of the framework (personal communication 2011q) the assessment of a key policy actor in the NFP sector is far less positive (personal communication 2011c).

In NSW, a first-term Labor government placed a compact on the policy agenda as part of its platform for the 1999 state election. However, it was not until 2006 that the compact, 'Working Together for NSW' (NSW 2006), was finalised and launched — by which time the State Premier who had presided over its development, Bob Carr, had resigned. The long gestation of the agreement, together with the departure of key instigators in the public and NFP sectors, foreshadowed a fraught implementation process. By the time of the 2011 state election at which Labor lost government to the centre-right Liberal–National Coalition, 'Working Together for NSW' was widely acknowledged as a 'dead letter' — full of laudable words, but having had little discernable effect on the operations of government or the sector (Casey et al. 2008a; Dalton et al. 2008; Edgar and Lockie 2010; personal communication 2010a, 2010f, 2011b).

Australia's most recent cross-sector policy framework, the Tasmanian 'Partnership Agreement' between the Department of Human Services and Health, the Department of Premier and Cabinet and the community sector (Tasmania 2012) represents a policy coda to a decade-long conversation about the government–sector relationship. Relations between the NFP sector and government in the island state are generally cordial and constructive. Like the ACT, Tasmania is a small jurisdiction in terms of both population and geography, and exhibits considerable mobility within and between the public and NFP sectors — factors that act to reduce barriers to cooperation.

At the time of writing the NT is the only jurisdiction that has not implemented a formal cross-sector policy framework. In 2004–05 the NT Labor government led by Clare Martin initiated consultations with the NFP sector about a framework agreement. However, the policy window closed abruptly when, in June 2007, the federal government announced a sudden and dramatic incursion into Aboriginal affairs in the NT — the Northern Territory Emergency Response (NTER) (Sanders 2008). The NTER was broadly interpreted as a rebuke to the NT Labor government and represented a significant loss of political capital for the Chief Minister, who resigned in November 2007 (Murdoch and Holroyd 2007). By 2011, senior figures in the NT government appeared to be revisiting the possibility of a formal cross-sector policy framework (Henderson 2011; NT Government 2011). However, Labor's defeat at the 2012 general election once again saw the policy window close.

Table 1: Effectiveness of policy instruments

Framework documents exhibiting some effectiveness and durability		Framework documents exhibiting mixed effectiveness	
Delivering Community Services in Partnership 2011 (WA)	Memorandum of Understanding (MOU) 2009–12/Partnership Agreement 2010–14 (VIC)	Queensland Compact 2008	Social Compact 2004 and 2012 (ACT)
• Unilateral government policy statement co-developed with the sector • Policy lead shared by central agencies • Takes the place of former Labor government's 'Industry Plan' • Addresses practical structural reform agenda in relation to pricing, funding, red-tape, workforce and capacity-building • Oversight by Partnership Forum comprised of departmental and NFP representatives • Achieving a compact not a priority for sector	• Formal bilateral agreements between Victorian government line agencies (health and human services and early education) and relevant parts of the NFP sector • Policy lead resides with individual line agencies • Complementary but separate cross-sector initiatives (Office for the Community Sector, 2008) exist alongside agreements • MOU model well regarded by sector	• Bilateral agreement between state government and the Futures Forum on behalf of community services sector • Developed in response to sector mobilisation around the Community Services Sector Charter (2007) • Focus on structural reforms to improve the government-sector relationship and to build the capacity of the community services sector Policy lead resides with Department of Communities • Oversight by Compact Governance Committee (CGovC) • Independent Chair appointed by Premier (now lapsed) Reports annually on Action Plan approved by CGovC • Compact in abeyance following defeat of Bligh Labor government in 2012 state election	• A Statement of Understanding between government and the community sector • Focus mainly on human services • Policy lead resides with health and human services line agency • Oversight by Joint Implementation Group • Declining awareness and impact since 2004 Social Compact 'refreshed' in 2012

Source: Author's research.

Table 1: Effectiveness of policy instruments continued

Framework documents exhibiting minimal impact		Framework documents recently established/ not yet formalised	
Stronger Together 2009 (SA)	**Working Together 2006 (NSW)**	**Partnership Agreement 2012–15 (TAS)**	**Common Cause 2004/05 (NT)**
• Agreement between community services and health line agencies and relevant sub-sectors • Policy lead resides with line agency Initiated by the human services line agency as a mechanism to manage relationship with the sector • Little evidence of vertical and horizontal integration with complementary policy frameworks for social inclusion and volunteering • Evidence of disconnects in both awareness and application.	• Bilateral agreement between the state government and the Forum of Non-Government Agencies (FONGA) • Purpose was to strengthen working relationships between government and the sector • Focus mainly on human services and procurement relationship • Policy lead resides with human services line agency • Oversight by Joint Reference Group • Few attributable impacts • Low levels of awareness and perceived relevance • Policy widely regarded by sector and government agencies as a 'dead letter' • Liberal-National government elected in 2011 has re-focused on red tape reduction and social impact investment.	• Partnership Agreement between DHHS, DPAC and the Community Sector launched by Premier Laura Giddings in October 2012 • The Departments of Health and Human Services (DHHS) and Premier and Cabinet (DPAC) represent the government • Agreement is aligned with the National Compact and has whole-of-government implications. Governed by the Peaks' Network and Government Strategic Forum which will prepare an implementation plan outlining specific actions and measurable targets • The Forum will prepare an annual report and commission an independent review and evaluation at the end of the first two years	• No formal instrument for cooperation in place • An early attempt to develop a formal partnership framework (Common Cause, 2004/05) was abandoned, possibly as a result of leadership change (resignation of Chief Minister, Clare Martin) and the Commonwealth government's 2007 NTER • A 'conversation' about a 'social participation framework' initiated by Labor government shortly before the 2012 election. • Policy direction unclear following the formation of the Country Liberal Party government following the 2012 general election

Source: Author's research.

Discussion

The 'hollowing' of the state (Rhodes 2000, 2007; Di Francesco 2001) and the marketisation of social provision have deepened the mutual dependency between governments and the NFP sector; governments are increasingly dependent upon the NFP sector to deliver services, while NFP organisations are increasingly dependent upon government contracts for their income.[8] Dependence has also contributed to a blurring of the boundaries between the public and NFP sectors to the extent that the latter has come to resemble the 'shadow state' foreshadowed by Wolch (1990) a quarter of a century ago.

Network approaches to governance have long been argued to present advantages over hierarchy or market as a means of adapting, coordinating and safeguarding exchanges in the face of demand uncertainty and task complexity (Jones et al. 1997). However, the promotion of network governance as a means to overcome the traditional, hierarchical model of government is a relatively recent phenomenon (Eggers 2008, p. 23). So-called 'third way' policy formulations emphasising joined-up approaches to governance have indeed lent impetus to the pursuit of more collaborative forms of cross-sector engagement, especially in the pluralist mixed economy of social provision. Even so, the capacity for bureaucratic, cultural and operational rigidity in the public and NFP sectors to subvert the stated aims of formal cross-sector policy frameworks should not be underestimated.

Abiding by the spirit and letter of compacts can be problematic for both sectors. Not only do compacts have no legal force, they are also susceptible to haphazard implementation and waning commitment. Despite underpinning commitments partnership and collaboration, aligning operational practices with the rhetoric of compacts can be problematic. Compacts also raise difficult questions about the nature, role and composition of the NFP sector as well as questions about the legitimacy of representative organisations and their authority to speak on behalf of a broader sector. The NFP sector is, after all, a diverse, variegated and sometimes unruly political space.

Compacts also serve to highlight the difficulty of effecting institutional change. Public sector organisations sometimes exhibit a deep (and increasingly anachronistic) attachment to command and control notions of governance, even when they are patently dependent upon third parties for the implementation and delivery of programs and services (Shergold 2008). NFP organisations, on the other hand, sometimes appear to regard contractual compliance and reporting as both an affront to their cultural and operational autonomy and an unnecessary regulatory impost with no intrinsic value (Shergold 2008, p. 7).

---

8   The 'hollowing out' thesis advanced by Rhodes, Di Francesco and others describes a state that has moved beyond the logics of 'command and control' to a greater reliance on networks and 'diplomacy' (Rhodes 2007). The hollowed-out state is characterised by external dependence and internal fragmentation that both weaken the central organising capacity of the state and challenges the executive's ability to 'steer' (Rhodes 2000, p. 350; Di Francesco 2001, p. 106). Characteristic of the 'contracting state', hollowing out raises normative questions about both the role of the state and the ability of the state to influence the direction and coherence of policy and outcomes (Di Francesco 2001, pp. 104–106).

Curiously, there is little tangible evidence for the explicit adoption of policy learnings between states — even between states with Labor governments. The cases do suggest, however, that the rise and fall of compacts is closely associated with the opening — and closing — of policy windows occasioned by political events such as an impending, or recent elections, or changes in leadership. The cases also suggest that institutional neglect and complacency also contributes to a decline in the agenda prominence of cross-sector frameworks.

Conclusion

Do governments and the NFP sector need formal policy frameworks for cross-sector cooperation? Clearly, key policy actors in Australia's states and territories have at various times concluded that they do. It is also clear that faith in the potential of such frameworks to materially reshape the relationship between governments and the NFP sector is frequently challenged.

Compacts are intended to provide a roadmap for navigating a tricky political and policy terrain. In so doing, they have the potential to confront and challenge prevailing notions about the respective cultural and operational norms that shape the identity and modus operandi of the public and NFP sectors. Where compacts come into existence against an historical backdrop of cross-sector cooperation; where they demonstrate joint ownership and a commitment to a concrete program of meaningful actions; where they are guided by sound governance and exhibit vertical and horizontal policy integration, compacts can serve to provide a space in which governments and the NFP sector *can* work collaboratively in achieving shared aims.

It is important to not underestimate the difficulty of promoting compacts across the breadth and depth of the public and NFP sectors. Here it is important to reflect on the fact that a compact is a process not a paper: some stakeholders will have low expectations of a compact (which might result in low levels of commitment), and others will expect the compact to solve all their problems (thus creating the preconditions for disappointment and disengagement). Managing expectations is critical.

A compact is not a magic bullet. However, the continuing interest in codifying the terms of engagement between the public and NFP sectors suggests that, despite their limitations, compacts — or something like them — will continue to form a part of the policy toolkit.

Postscript

This paper was originally presented at the the Association for Research on Nonprofit Organizations and Voluntary Action (ARNOVA) Annual Conference in Toronto, in 2011. Although every effort has been made to bring the content up to date, the volatile nature of Australian politics makes this task difficult — if not impossible. The durability of compacts rests, as often as not, on the fortunes of government and the dominance at any given time of particular policy discourses. A change of government nationally in 2013 signalled abrupt changes in the direction of NFP policy in the federal sphere. It is too soon to tell whether the change of government in Tasmania (2014) will affect the tenor of the government/NFP relationship, and the implications of dramatic changes of government in Victoria (2014) and Queensland (2015) are as yet unknown. The imperative to reform and modernise the relationship between human services 'commissioners' and NFP providers was given added impetus by Peter Shergold, who was tasked to undertake a review by the Victorian government in 2013 (Shergold 2013). However, new funding modalities (via the National Disability Insurance Scheme) and experimental financial instruments (social impact bonds) have the potential to transform the foundations of that relationship and, perhaps, render compacts obsolete.

Appendix: A survey of Australian policy frameworks for cross-sector cooperation

Although compacts have been part of the policy mix in Australian states and territories for over a decade, there have been few comprehensive surveys of the state of play and relatively little has been published in peer reviewed journals (Brown and Ryan 2003; Butcher 2006, 2011; Casey and Dalton 2006; Pugh and Saggers 2007; Baulderstone 2008; Casey et al. 2008a, 2008b, 2008c; Dalton et al. 2008; Edgar and Lockie 2010).

The landscape of the NFP policy space is changeable: political events can crowd compacts off the policy agenda; portfolio or machinery of government changes can result in a loss of continuity and salience; new problems and new solutions seize the attention of policymakers; neglect and complacency can fatally compromise even best-intentioned policy ideas. So it is that, almost as soon as one attempts to compile a definitive account of the range of policy responses in the states and territories, the accretion of policy change renders some part of the account obsolete. Nevertheless, the brief sketches presented below offer a useful glimpse of the situation in Australia's states and territories as at the time of writing.

Vignette 1 — Australian Capital Territory: The social laboratory

The Australian Capital Territory has a population of approximately 367,000, the majority of which live in Canberra, the national capital. Self-government was granted to the ACT in 1988 and the ACT's Legislative Assembly exercises the normal functions of a state legislature as well as local government functions. The Assembly's 17 members are elected using a Hare-Clark proportional representative electoral system and, from the time of its first election in 1989, minority governments have been the norm in the ACT, apart from 2004–08 when Labor (which previously headed a minority government elected in 2001) formed the Territory's first majority government. Following elections in 2008 and 2012 Labor has governed in coalition with the ACT Greens.

The ACT has been described as a 'social laboratory' — often in association with Labor governments (Fischer 1984). The ACT led the way with Australia's first compact in 2001 (ACT 2001), just months before the launch of the Canadian Accord. This was not a Labor initiative, however. Rather, the first ACT compact commenced under a minority Liberal government led by Chief Minister Gary Humphries (2000–01).

In 2000, Humphries succeeded the previous Chief Minister Kate Carnell (1995–2000), following the latter's resignation in the face of a threatened no-confidence motion after a series of high-profile public scandals (Singleton 2001). That the Liberal government chose to pursue a compact was possibly motivated by a desire to ease long-standing tensions with the community sector ahead of the 2001 election (personal communication 2011a).

The 2001 compact continued to guide government policy after the election of a Labor minority government in 2001. It was republished in a revised edition in 2003 and was eventually replaced in 2004 with a rebadged and rebranded version of the previous government's compact. The new 'Social Compact' (ACT 2004) contained few material changes to the core provisions of the original. This is perhaps unsurprising given that in framing its pre-election budget, the previous Liberal government emphasised social spending in an attempt to outflank the centre-left Labor Party (Singleton 2001, pp. 587–588).

The impetus for the original compacts (Liberal and Labor) came from the Chief Minister's Department. Both the 'Social Compact' and an associated community sector funding policy were co-designed by public sector officials and government's community sector partners (personal communication 2011h, 2011i). However, a 'Functional Expenditure Review' undertaken in 2006 saw the policy lead transfer to the Department of Disability, Housing and Community Services which, by virtue of its share of contract and grants funding, was seen to have greater 'direct ownership of contracting policy' (personal communication 2011i).

Initially the 'Social Compact' stimulated interest in the NFP policy space and was seen to make a difference (personal communication 2011i). Although the sector acknowledged the compact's good intentions, it also expressed concern about a range of perceived problems with its operation (ACTCOSS 2008). Personnel changes, administrative reorganisations, and emerging processes also took a toll and the influence and visibility of the compact waned (personal communication 2011i).

In 2011 a Joint Community-Government Reference Group (established in 2004 to oversight the 'Social Compact' and the community sector funding policy) undertook a review of the 'Social Compact'. One official observed that as a small jurisdiction in which ministers and senior executives are quite accessible, 'we're well-placed to get it right and to connect and communicate effectively with our community partners' (personal communication 2011h).

A refreshed 'Social Compact' was launched in June 2012 (ACT 2012). The 'Social Compact' is intended to complement the Canberra Plan, the 'Canberra Social Plan' and policy governing community engagement. Officials acknowledge the ongoing challenge of maintaining the relevance of policy frameworks, particularly as the principles and behaviours they engender become woven into practice (personal communication 2011h). One official looks forward to the day when policy frameworks mandating respect, equity and acceptance of diversity are regarded as anachronistic because these attitudes and behaviours have become ingrained (personal communication 2011i).

Vignette 2 — South Australia: 'Stronger Together', or the weakest link?

South Australia's key relationship framework document, 'Stronger Together' (2009) forms one part of a suite of policy documents and institutional arrangements that, in the words of a key policy actor from the NFP sector: 'probably don't hang together as neatly and as easily as we would necessarily like them to' (personal communication 2011c). Although portrayed in some quarters as an example of a well-functioning framework agreement (Baulderstone 2006), the South Australian example is also offered as a cautionary tale of a framework agreement hampered by weak institutional arrangements and a low level of executive commitment (ACOSS 2008).

'Stronger Together' and its predecessor document, 'Common Ground' (South Australia, 2004), were initiatives of the former SA Departments of Families and Communities, and Health. Although the NFP sector participated in drafting both agreements, the sector harboured 'a level of cynicism about the capacity of the agreement to change the nature of the relationship in a really fundamental way' (personal communication 2011c). Interviews with elite policy actors in the NFP sector, line agencies of government and central agencies reveal important 'disconnects' in the way the parties think about the effectiveness of the framework document and the overall health of the relationship between government and the sector.

There is a view, widely shared in the sector, that framework documents such as 'Stronger Together' serve symbolic as opposed to practical purposes: 'over the years government has wanted some instruments that can be paraded in a public context' (personal communication 2011c). One key NFP policy actor admitted being 'very sceptical and cynical about any real intention on the part of the government to behave in a manner that would be consistent with the "Stronger Together" agreement' (personal communication 2011c). Barriers in gaining access to the responsible Minister coupled with a bureaucracy with little latitude to negotiate the parameters of public policy, serves to diminish 'Stronger Together' as a mechanism for promoting robust policy discussion (personal communication 2011c).

Conversely, officials in the SA government line agency primarily responsible for the administration of the agreement consider that, on the whole, peak organisations are 'very happy' with 'Stronger Together': 'there's a great sense of ownership around it … it gets referred to regularly within the Peaks Forum as a guide … it holds a certain amount of power' (personal communication 2011j). One official suggested that there was a 'healthy tension' in the cross-sector relationship, pointing out that attempts by public sector agencies to partner effectively with peak organisations are sometimes made difficult by matters beyond their direct control (such as resourcing) while peak organisations sometimes 'respectfully decline' to work with line agencies 'because they're mad with the government' (personal communication 2011j).

The relationship between government and the sector in South Australia has been observed to vary 'from sub-sector to sub-sector, and from personality to personality' (personal communication 2011c) and was described by one senior central agency official as 'patchy'. The same official conceded that 'some agencies and individuals within agencies are doing very well and in other circumstances that's not the case', adding: 'It would be unfair to say there's a poor relationship across the board — it would [be] wrong to say that — nor could you say there are no issues at all' (personal communication 2011k). It is noteworthy that strong cross-sector relationships appear to exist in policy domains not covered by 'Stronger Together', such as the arts (personal communication 2011p).

South Australian central agencies exercise no oversight of cross-sector relationship frameworks. Although line agency officials suggested that some level of central agency coordination might be welcome, the suggestion was dismissed by one central agency official who observed, 'those days are gone' (personal communication 2011k).

In smaller jurisdictions, such as South Australia, relationships between individuals often exert greater influence on the shape of the cross-sector discourse than official processes or institutional frameworks — both within and across domain boundaries, and between sector representatives and particular officials and/or ministers. This observation is echoed in other small jurisdictions such as the Australian Capital Territory and Tasmania.

Vignette 3 — Victoria: 'Horses for courses'

Reform to 'rationalise' the public sector reached its apotheosis in Victoria under the Liberal–National Coalition government led by Premier Jeff Kennett (1992–99) who 'eagerly embraced the neoliberal agenda of the economic policy think-tanks' (Economou 2006, p. 370). In 1992, the Coalition defeated a third-term Labor government mired in political crises. Asset sales, spending cuts, administrative consolidation and outsourcing formed the core of the new government's strategy, leading to Victoria being dubbed 'the contract state' (Alford and O'Neill 1994). In the process, the Victorian NFP sector, which has a long history of community engagement, was marginalised as a policy partner (personal communication 2011f, 2011n; Webster and Atkins 2011). The effect was a sector that was less collegial, faced greater uncertainty, and reported higher transaction costs and overheads flowing from the new contracting regime (personal communication 2011n). Even so, contracting did leverage service change and fresh thinking (personal communication 2011n).

The 1999 state election saw the Labor Party form a minority government. Premier Steve Bracks described his government as 'financially conservative and socially progressive' (Costar and Hayward 2005, p. 111). Labor made substantial investments in health, education and regional development, and 'did much to restore civility to public life after the divisiveness and sheer self-indulgence of Kennett's reign' (Dyrenfurth and Bongiorno 2011). The Bracks' government emphasised inclusivity (Hayward 2006) and advocated a partnership approach to human services delivery (PAEC 2002). Labor went on to win elections with working majorities in 2002 and 2006. A 2002 report found several problems associated with the complexity of service agreements for community, welfare and health services and pointed to work then occurring in overseas and Australian jurisdictions around the issue of formal partnership frameworks (PAEC 2002).

The Victorian community sector first advocated a compact as early as 2000 and most recently in 2006 (VCOSS 2006). Calls for a compact gained little traction, but the Premier's department offered strong support for achieving a better alignment between the Department of Human Services processes and the way community organisations work (personal communication 2011n). This led in 2002 to a partnership agreement between the Department of Human Services, the Victorian Council of Social Service, and the Victorian Health Care Association. The Partnership Agreement has been renewed periodically. Now in the form of a memorandum of understanding, the framework celebrates a strong, positive relationship based on trust, respect and collaboration and understanding (DHS 2009). However, its primary focus is streamlining funding arrangements and improving consistency (personal communication 2011f). Although parts of the sector have 'grumbled' from time to time, positive results have generated broad confidence in the DHS's — and the government's — commitment to the process (personal communication 2011f).

A compact is no longer a priority for the Victorian NFP sector, whose interests run more to practical matters such as pricing, funding and contracting arrangements, red tape reduction, data collection and workforce issues (personal communication 2011f). Reviews of NFP regulation (Victoria 2007a) and performance (Victoria 2007b) contributed to the establishment in 2008 of an Office for the Community Sector, initially within the Department of Planning and Community Development (now in the Department of Human Services). The Office for the Community Sector works with agencies and the sector to reduce compliance burdens, cut red tape, and strengthen sector capacity (personal communication 2011n). It has no role with respect to partnership agreements. The Bracks government also instituted a fixed price index mechanism that has worked 'remarkably well' over the last decade (personal communication 2011n).

The Victorian model of sector-specific frameworks begun under Labor continued under the Liberal–National Coalition government (personal communication 2011n); a trend confirmed in 2010 with a separate partnership agreement in the early childhood development domain (Victoria 2010). The Coalition government, elected with a slim majority in 2010, sought to distance itself from the Kennett legacy (personal communication 2011f). Furthermore, the Black Saturday bushfires of 2009 and the floods of 2011 highlighted the constraints under which community services operate and strengthened the government's resolve to 'do everything they can to make it easier for those organisations to deliver' (personal communication 2011n). The Andrews Labor government, elected in 2014, has undertaken to work in partnership with the sector, possibly building upon the Community Sector Reform Council established by the Napthine Coalition government.

Vignette 4 — Western Australia: Taking the road less travelled

The relationship between government and the NFP sector in Western Australia has been evolving over a long time. In 2004, the WA Labor government initiated an 'Industry Plan' for the non-government human services sector with three broad objectives: improving the relationship between government and the sector; ensuring the viability and sustainability of non-government human services; and building sector capacity (Western Australia 2004). The plan was complemented by a policy statement on funding and purchasing community services (Department of Premier and Cabinet 2002), and an indexation policy for non-government human services (Department of Premier and Cabinet 2004). Both measures were strongly influenced by an earlier WA Auditor-General report that found significant shortcomings with the contracting regime used to procure services from NFP service providers (Auditor-General 2000).

Once considered a possible precursor to a compact, the 'Industry Plan' faltered owing to a lack of central agency leadership (personal communication 2011o), inconsistent implementation (personal communication 2011o), and a failure to enforce the application of policy guidance by line agencies (personal communication 2011o, 2011g). As one central agency official commented:

> There had been great policies launched in the past but then implementation had failed. Line agencies had gone back to 'bad behaviours'. We've had standard templates and approaches but everyone had butchered them along the way (personal communication 2011o).

In 2008, the newly elected Liberal–National government established the Economic Audit Committee to conduct a wide-ranging audit of the efficiency and effectiveness of state government functions, including how government partners with the NFP sector to deliver community services (EAC 2009). Wishing to respond to the opportunities presented by an economic boom created by the State's mining industry, the new government initiated a change agenda built around a narrative of delivering better outcomes for Western Australians (personal communication 2011o). This provided a 'platform for engagement' between government and the sector (personal communication 2011g). A 'Partnership Forum', comprised of public and NFP sector leaders and chaired by the former Secretary of the Prime Minister's Department, Dr Peter Shergold, was established in mid-2010 to address issues relating to social innovation; the resolution of long-standing problems with contracting; and historic failures to fund the full cost of services delivered by the NFP sector (personal communication 2011o).

The 'Delivering Community Services in Partnership Policy', launched in July 2011, is the centrepiece of a suite of administrative and financial measures aimed at rebuilding government's relationship with the sector and placing the sector on a more sustainable footing (Western Australia 2011b). Although it is not a bilateral agreement, the policy was extensively co-produced by government officials and sector leaders. As one close observer remarked: 'WACOSS [Western Australian Council of Social Service] has been almost joined at the hip with [the Department of] Premier and Cabinet throughout this process and I think that has raised some concerns actually, as regards its potential to been seen as supping with the devil' (personal communication 2011o).

There is a broad consensus amongst sector representatives and public sector officials that Shergold played a critical role by building trust and understanding amongst the participants in the process. Even more important has been the hands-on role played by Premier Barnett, which has given added impetus and authority to the change agenda: 'To have a First Minister that is driving this across government is quite important … eighteen months in and he's still engaged in [the] process' (personal communication 2011o).

In its 2011–12 budget the state government committed $604 million over four years to help redress the gap between the level of funding provided in state contracts and the actual cost of service delivery and an additional $400 million for new services. One senior official suggested that there was genuine surprise in some quarters at the size of the spend: 'Only through actions can you demonstrate genuine listening and partnership' (personal communication 2011o). An ongoing challenge will be to sustain the momentum of change and the capacity of the sector to remain engaged in the policy and implementation process (personal communication 2011g).

Vignette 5 — Tasmania: The long conversation

The 2012 Tasmanian 'Partnership Agreement' between the Department of Health and Human Services, the Department of Premier and Cabinet, and the community sector represented the culmination of an on-again/off-again conversation about a formal relationship framework begun in 1996 (personal communication 2011l; Tasmania 2012). According to one official, the fact that the cross-sector relationship is mediated by a line agency is 'entirely problematic because it reduces the sector relationship essentially to a service delivery role', thereby reinforcing the emphasis on contracting and procurement (personal communication 2011m).

The extent of outsourced service provision in Tasmania has increased over time. With a population of 512,000 and a total land area of 68,401 square kilometres, Tasmania exhibits strong formal and informal connections both within the NFP sector and between the sector and government. The community sector is closely knit and there is a 'strong relationship' between the sector and government, based on 'a process of strong consultation in the way [government] forms its policies and the way it does its business' (personal communication 2011d). Tasmania's small size also serves to accentuate differences in the size and market-share of NFP service providers, ranging from those with a part-time executive officer supported by volunteers through to large employing organisations — a prime example being Anglicare, which delivers services 'across absolutely every conceivable part of the community sector' (personal communication 2011d).

Personal relationships between state and non-state policy actors are also important: 'We hold a lot of store in the development of personal relationships', says one sector informant (personal communication 2011d). 'Everybody *does* know everybody', said a senior official (personal communication 2011l). A downside is that cross-sector relationships are so often 'person dependent': 'a champion or a leader … moves on and then things go splat' (personal communication 2011e). Tasmanian ministers are highly accessible to the sector, and the Hare-Clark electoral system makes political compromise virtually unavoidable (Labor governed in Tasmania with the support of the Tasmanian Greens, two of whom were ministers in the government).

Partnership is an important theme in the State's political ecology: over recent years the Tasmanian government has entered into a number of partnership agreements with local councils and institutions such as the University of Tasmania. Social inclusion, social enterprise and place-based approaches have figured strongly as organising perspectives in Tasmanian social policy (personal communication 2011m). It can also be said that Tasmanian approaches reflect to some degree a diffusion of policy and praxis from the mainland, most noticeably from Victoria (personal communication 2011l, 2011m, 2011e).

At one time promoted within government as an indicator of success in forging effective cross-sector relationships (OCS 2009), by 2009 cross-sector discussions 'ran out of steam' (personal communication 2011l) — largely owing to personnel and structural changes in the Department of Health and Human Services (personal communication 2011d, 2011m).

In 2010, Peter Shergold was enlisted to help restart the conversation around a framework agreement (personal communication 2011l). Although initiated by the government, one official observed: 'I don't think the sector needed to be dragged kicking and screaming' (personal communication 2011m). The agreement 'very quickly became a joint enterprise', and, despite 'the normal suspicions that you would expect from the sector', key policy actors have reported high levels of good-will (personal communication 2011m).

A sector leader commented that 'there is a lot of hope resting on a partnership agreement', despite lingering cynicism within the sector (personal communication 2011e). The sector appears to accept the practical necessity for the policy lead to reside with the DHHS, nevertheless it is hoped that avenues will be found to eventually extend the footprint of the agreement to policy domains beyond traditional community services (personal communication 2011e). In the meantime, practical issues of workforce recruitment, retention and replacement are of primary concern (personal communication 2011l).

Vignette 6 — New South Wales: A long road to nowhere in particular

In New South Wales, the conversation leading to a formal policy framework around the government–sector relationship commenced in the mid-1990s (personal communication 2011b). As Australia's largest state, government agencies' operational and financial exposure to the NFP sector is enormous and has grown steadily as third party contracting grew in importance as a staple service delivery strategy.

The desire for a formalised relationship was driven by policies favouring greater competition in the procurement of public services (personal communication 2010a, 2011b). A difficult relationship between the sector and a State Coalition government (1988–95) was succeeded by an equally problematic relationship with a national Coalition government (1996–2007). The idea of a compact was largely 'sector driven', and a former Director of the New South Wales Council of Social Service, Gary Moore, played an early leading role (personal communication 2010f, a). Alarmed at the 'unfettered market change' that defined the mid-to-late-1990s, the sector (and Moore in particular) looked to the proposed 'English Compact' for inspiration (personal communication 2011b).

A window of opportunity for change opened in NSW with the election of a Labor government in 1995. The new Labor Premier, Bob Carr, was receptive to the sector's proposal for a formal relationship framework, although there is a lingering view in the sector that Carr was less interested in fundamental change than he was in political branding in the lead-up to the 1999 state election (Casey et al. 2008a; Edgar and Lockie 2010; personal communication 2010a, 2011b). Negotiations on a compact commenced in 2001 and were conducted on behalf of the sector by the Forum of Non-Government Agencies — a coalition of peak and service provider organisations — and on behalf of government by the NSW Premier's Department.

It is noteworthy that the compact was being actively developed during a turbulent period of significant change in the modus operandi of the public and NFP sectors (personal communication 2010a). To some extent, the parties looked to the compact to resolve problems it was not designed to address. For example, the bureaucracy looked to the compact to drive rationalisation within the sector, while the sector looked to the compact to resolve competitive pressures and tensions amongst provider organisations (personal communication 2010a). The compact was sometimes used in an adversarial way to confront and criticise government. One official remarked that parts of the sector see government agencies 'as the big bag of money in the room' while failing to reflect on their own obligations under the compact (personal communication 2010c).

'Working Together for New South Wales' was launched in 2006 by Premier Carr just months before he resigned from politics. It came to be regarded by the sector as narrowly instrumental and overly focused on funding agreements (personal communication 2010a). Although originally intended to apply across government, the bureaucracy concluded this was not feasible owing to cultural, operational and institutional differences between human services sub-sectors (personal communication 2010f). Weak institutional design, machinery-of-government changes, turnover of personnel, inconsistent representation and the loss of corporate memory all helped to undermine the legitimacy and relevance of the compact (personal communication 2010a).

Although there is no clear consensus on this point, it is possible that successive leadership changes in NSW contributed to the progressive marginalisation of 'Working Together'. The long gestation of the compact (1999–2006), coupled with personnel changes, also contributed to a loss of interest once it became policy (personal communication 2011b). With Carr's departure, suggested one observer, 'you almost immediately saw the Compact being put in the bottom drawer' (personal communication 2010a). 'Working Together' was virtually a 'dead letter' by the time of the Coalition victory at the 2011 state general election. The state government has not revisited the idea of a formal relationship framework although called upon to do so by the sector (NCOSS

2011). Government continues to liaise with the sector on new policy initiatives such as 'social benefit bonds' (Treasury (NSW) 2012). For its part, the Forum of Non-Government Agencies has elected to emulate its Queensland counterpart by largely appropriating the Community Services Charter developed by the Futures Forum (FONGA 2011).

Vignette 7 — Queensland: So near and yet so far

In Queensland, a decade of state Labor government went by without any significant moves by either government or the NFP sector towards a formal relationship framework. An early top-down policy overture in this direction, 'Engaging Queensland' (Department of Families 2003), focused primarily on supporting volunteering as opposed to engaging the non-government sector in issues of policy or funding generally.

In August 2007, the Futures Forum, a coalition of peak and service provider organisations, launched a Queensland Community Services Sector Charter, the purpose of which was to 'to define and communicate to other sectors of society (Government, business and community) what the community services sector is, and to raise awareness of its vital role and invaluable contribution to society' (Futures Forum 2007). The Futures Forum was a response both to tensions in the government-sector relationship and those inherent in a diverse and fragmented sector (personal communication 2010b).

In September 2007, the charismatic and populist Premier, Peter Beattie, retired in favour of his deputy, Anna Bligh. The charter and leadership change coincided with a report by the Queensland Auditor General that found an excessive focus on compliance in state agencies' management of funding to non-government organisations (QAO 2007) and an internal review of the Department of Communities. The latter resulted in the publication of the 'Framework for Investment in Human Services' (Queensland 2007) — 'the absolute precursor to the Queensland Compact' (personal communication 2010e).

These events provided the impetus for action on government–NFP sector relations. Through the Framework, five major human services agencies, together with the Treasury, sought to establish clear and agreed funding processes. Said one official, this was about 'government getting its house in order' (personal communication 2010e). The charter added weight to efforts to address observed problems with the relationship, and the Futures Forum became the key interlocutor with government. A Joint Working Group was formed to oversee consultations about a compact and an associated 'action plan' — the rationale being that a compact without an action plan is 'happy words and not a whole lot else' (personal communication 2010e).

The 2008 'Queensland Compact' became a touchstone for the 'National Compact'. A Compact Governance Committee (CGovC) was created (with a membership drawn from government and the sector) to which the Premier, whose personal political support was critical (personal communication, 2010b, 2010d, 2010e), appointed an 'Independent Chair'. The CGovC provided a 'safe and reliable forum for discussion' in which 'hard conversations' could occur and consensus reached about reform priorities (personal communication 2010d).

Although the Queensland Compact was extolled in some quarters as 'best practice' (personal communication 2010d), scepticism persisted amongst service providers who believed it constrained their capacity to maximise their interests. The dominant view, however, was one of cautious optimism: 'We knew, as it progressed, it was going to be a less than perfect vehicle but we felt, hey, it's going to be better than anything we've got, and there's no basis for these conversations at the moment, so why don't we have a go?' (personal communication 2010b).

The CGovC saw its role as moving a range of issues from being 'intractable' to 'just plain hard' (personal communication 2010d). The action plan developed to further the compact focused on concrete measures, process reforms and culture change. The CGovC, with secretariat support from the Department of Communities, gave the action plan a strong regional focus and reported annually against achievements.

A landslide defeat of the incumbent Labor government in the 2012 general election threw the compact into abeyance. The new government chose not to release an independent review of the compact, the CGovC was suspended and its independent chair was not reappointed. The Liberal–National Party (LNP) government focused on expenditure reductions and reimposed gag clauses in service procurement contracts. In 2015, the Queensland Council of Social Service (QCOSS) welcomed the formation of a minority Labor government as an 'opportunity to put the co-design and place-based solutions into action – with government, the community sector, community and the private sector working together to get the best possible outcomes for all Queenslanders'.

Vignette 8 — Northern Territory: A relationship framework stillborn

The Northern Territory does not, at present, have a formal policy framework for cross-sector cooperation. In 2005, the former Labor government led by Chief Minister Clare Martin (2001–07) engaged the firm RPR Consulting[9] to assist with the development of a partnership framework between the NT government

---

9 RPR Consulting was one of two consulting firms engaged by the ACT Government to assist in the development of the Territory's first compact in 2001 (ACT 2000a).

and the community sector. The consultant's final report, 'New Foundations', recommended the adoption of a 'Common Cause Charter' as a framework for future relationships between the government and community sectors. It also recommended the formation of a joint taskforce to steer the implementation of the proposed charter as well as the creation of a number of 'peak councils' (DCM 2004). By 2008, however, and despite initial good intentions, the taskforce had ceased to operate, leading to cynicism within the community sector (Casey et al. 2008c, p. 17; NTCOSS 2008).

Leadership change was a possible factor in the apparent abandonment of the process for developing a formal framework document in the NT. The then Chief Minister Clare Martin was the first female and the first Labor Chief Minister in the NT. Labor under Martin held a one-seat majority after the 2001 election and increased its majority in a landslide win at the 2005 election. The win might have provided added impetus for Martin's push for a new settlement with the sector.

In June 2007, the federal government led by John Howard, relying upon constitutional powers to override NT government jurisdiction in Aboriginal communities, announced the Northern Territory Emergency Response in response to the alarming prevalence of child sexual abuse in Aboriginal communities. The NT government's cooperation in the federal government's NTER was highly contentious. This was a show of political resolve on the part of the federal government in an election year. Although there was strident criticism of the NTER from a number of quarters, the federal government was on safe political ground: there was no political skin to be lost protecting Aboriginal children or in overriding a Labor government portrayed as failing to act on their behalf. Martin was surprised and seemingly unsettled by the move. The NT government was obliged to acquiesce and Martin's and Labor's credibility with the community sector was undermined.

Martin resigned suddenly in November 2007, citing the NTER as a factor (she was subsequently appointed as the Chair of the Australian Council of Social Service). At the 2008 NT election, Labor was returned with a one-seat majority under Martin's successor, Paul Henderson. The defection of a Labor MLA to the Country Liberal Party in 2009 led to a minority Labor government dependent upon the support of one independent MLA. Labor lost the 2012 general election, in part owing to a swing against it in Indigenous communities that comprise around 30 per cent of the NT population of 233,000.

It is likely that the NTER helped to push 'Common Cause' off the policy agenda. By 2011 there were signs of a possible reopening of the policy window, possibly influenced by the example of the National Compact. The former Chief Minister affirmed that 'building stronger relationships and creating opportunities to improve systems and support for non-government organisations' and 'reducing red tape' would be a priority of his government (Henderson 2011). In the area of child and family services, the NT Labor government called for '[t]he development of new partnerships with the non-government sector' (NT Government 2011). In mid-2012, Labor initiated a 'conversation' with Territorians about a 'social participation framework' that would clarify the respective roles of 'individuals, community groups, businesses, government agencies and non-government organisations' (DCM 2012).

Hot button social issues such as child protection, compulsory income management, substance abuse, domestic violence and youth justice dominate in the Territory. These issues disproportionately affect Indigenous communities, and policy responses must therefore take into account vast distances, small populations and geographically dispersed communities with complex needs. Political ructions in the territory have also offered distractions, such as when Chief Minister Terry Mills was controversially replaced as leader after only seven months in office while on an overseas trip and an abortive leadership coup was launched against his successor, Adam Giles, in 2015.

References

ACOSS (Australian Council of Social Service) 2008, 'National Compact Consultation: Final report'.

ACOSS 2011, 'Australian Community Sector Survey 2011', ACOSS Paper 173, Volume 1: National. Available at: http://acoss.org.au/images/uploads/ACSS_2011_Report_Volume_1_National.pdf.

ACT 2000a, 'An ACT Compact on Relationships Between the Government and Community Sectors: Background briefing', ACT Government Chief Minister's Department, Canberra, October.

ACT 2000b, 'Focusing Partnership — Building Community: Towards a compact of understanding between the ACT Government and community sector', Government of the Australian Capital Territory.

ACT 2001, 'Compact: Community partnership ACT Government: The first step', Chief Minister's Department, Community Policy Unit.

ACT 2004, 'The Social Compact: A partnership between the community sector and the ACT government', Australian Capital Territory Government, Deptartment of Urban Services.

ACT 2012, 'The Social Compact: A relationship framework between the ACT Government and community sector', Australian Capital Territory

Government, ACT Community Services Directorate. Available at: http://www.communityservices.act.gov.au/__data/assets/pdf_file/0009/130140/Social_Compact.pdf.

ACTCOSS (ACT Council of Social Service) 2008, 'Finding Solutions: Towards the long term viability of the ACT community sector'. Available at: http://www.actcoss.org.au/publications/Publications_2008/2108REP.pdf.

Aitkin, D. 2013, 'Labor and the Liberals: The real differences'. Available at: http://donaitkin.com/labor-and-the-liberals-the-real-differences/.

Alford, J. L. and D. O'Neill (eds) 1994, *The Contract State: Public manangement and the Kennett government,* Centre for Applied Social Research, Deakin University, Melbourne.

Almog-Bar, M. and E. Zychlinski 2012, 'A Façade of Collaboration', *Public Management Review* 14, pp. 795–814.

Auditor-General 2000, *A Means to an End: Contracting not-for-profit organisations for the delivery of community services*, Office of the Auditor-General, Western Australia.

Australia 2010, 'National Compact Between the Australian Government and the Third Sector', Consultation Report, Commonwealth of Australia, February.

Baulderstone, J. M. 2006, 'Changing Relationships Between the Public Sector and Community Service Organisations: Insights from the South Australian case', paper delivered to Public Policy Network Conference, Adelaide, South Australia.

Baulderstone, J. M. 2008, 'Changing Relationships Between the Public Sector and Community Service Organisations: Insights from the South Australian case', *Public Policy,* 3(1), pp. 1–16.

Brock, K. L. 2004, 'The Devil's in the Detail: The Chretien Legacy for the third sector', *Review of Constitutional Studies* 9, pp. 263–283.

Brock, K. L. 2008, 'Policy Windows and Policy Failures: Using Kingdon to explain the later life cycle of the voluntary sector initiative', paper delievered to Canadian Political Science Association meeting, University of British Columbia. Available at: http://www.cpsa-acsp.ca/papers-2008/Brock.pdf.

Brown, K. and N. Ryan 2003, 'Redefining Government–Community Relationships Through Service Agreements', *Contemporary Issues in Business and Government* 9, pp. 21–30.

Bullain, N. and R. Toftisova 2005, 'A Comparative Analysis of European Policies and Practices of NGO-Government Cooperation', *International Journal of Not-for-Profit Law* 7, pp. 64–112.

Butcher, J. 2006, 'Government, the Third Sector and the Rise of Social Capital', *Third Sector Review* 12, pp. 69–88.

Butcher, J. 2011, 'An Australian Compact with the Third Sector: Challenges and prospects', *Third Sector Review* 17, pp. 35–58.

Butcher, J. 2012, 'The National Compact: Civilising the relationship between government and the not-for-profit sector in Australia', in R. Laforest (ed.), *Government-Nonprofit Relations in Times of Recession,* McGill-Queen's University Press, Toronto.

Butcher, J., J. Casey and B. Dalton 2012, 'An Australian National Compact: Something old, something new?', *Nonprofit Policy Forum* 3(2).

Canada 2001, 'An Accord Between the Government of Canada and the Voluntary Sector', Government of Canada.

Casey, J. 2004, 'Third Sector Participation in the Policy Process: A framework for comparative analysis', *Policy and Politics* 32, pp. 241–257.

Casey, J. and B. Dalton 2006, 'The Best of Times, The Worst of Times: Community-sector advocacy in the age of compacts', *Australian Journal of Political Science* 41, pp. 23–38.

Casey, J., B. Dalton, R. Melville and J. Onyx 2008a, '"An Opportunity to Increase Positive Results" or "So Disappointing After So Much Energy"?: A case study on the long gestation of working together for NSW', Centre for Australian Community Organisations and Management Working Paper, University of Technology Sydney.

Casey, J., B. Dalton, J. Onyx and R. Melville 2008b, 'Advocacy in the Age of Compacts: Regulating government-community sector relations — International experiences', Centre for Australian Community Organisations and Management Working Paper No. 76, University of Technology Sydney.

Casey, J., B. Dalton, J. Onyx and R. Melville 2008c, 'Advocacy in the Age of Compacts: Regulating government–community sector relations in Australia', Centre for Australian Community Organisations and Management Working Paper No. 78, University of Technology Sydney.

Common, R. K. 1998, 'Convergence and Transfer: A review of the globalisation of new public management', *The International Journal of Public Sector Management* 11, pp. 440–450.

Common, R. K. 2010, 'When Policy Diffusion Does Not Lead to Policy Transfer: Explaining resistance to international learning in public management reform', paper delivered to 14th International Research Society for Public Management Conference, University of Berne.

Cook, B., V. Quirk and W. Mitchell 2012, *The Impact on Community Services of Staff and Service Reductions, Privatisation and Outsourcing of Public Services in Australian States*, Centre of Full Employment and Equity, University of Newcastle, Newcastle.

Costar, B. and D. Hayward 2005, 'Steve Bracks: Victoria's "nice guy" who won against the odds', in J. Wanna, J. and P. D. Williams (eds), *Yes Premier*, UNSW Press, Sydney.

Dalton, B., J. Casey, J. Onyx, R. Melville and F. Lockie 2008, 'Advocacy in the Age of Compacts: NSW community sector workers speak about their experiences', Centre for Australian Community Organisations and Management Working Paper, University of Technology Sydney.

DCM (Department of the Chief Minister) 2004, 'Common Cause Taskforce Terms of Reference: A partnership between the Northern Territory Government and the community', Government of the Northern Territory.

DCM 2012, 'Social Participation Framework', Government of the Northern Territory. Available at: http://www.dcm.nt.gov.au/strong_community/social_participation_framework.

Department of Premier and Cabinet 2002, 'Funding and Purchasing Community Services: A policy statement on a fresh approach to funding and purchasing relationships with not-for-profit sector', Western Australian Government.

Department of Premier and Cabinet 2004, 'Western Australian Government Indexation Policy for the Non-Government Human Services Sector', Western Australian Government.

DHS (Department of Human Services) 2002, 'Partnership Agreement: Partnership in practice', Government of Victoria.

DHS 2009, 'Memorandum of Understanding 2009 to 2012: Between the independent health, housing and community sector and the Department of Human Services', Government of Victoria.

Di Francesco, M. 2001, 'Process not Outcomes in New Public Management?: "Policy coherence" in Australian government', *The Drawing Board: An Australian Review of Public Affairs* 1, pp. 103–116.

Department of Families 2003, *Engaging Queensland: The Queensland Government Policy on Volunteering*, Department of Families, Brisbane.

Drezner, D. 2001, 'Globalization and Policy Convergence', *International Studies Review* 3, pp. 53–78.

Dyrenfurth, N. and F. Bongiorno 2011, *A Little History of the Australian Labor Party*, UNSW Press, Sydney.

EAC (Economic Audit Committee) 2009, 'Putting the Public First: Partnering with the community and business to deliver outcomes', Final Report.

Economou, N. 2006, 'Jeff Kennett: The larrikin metropolitan', in P. Strangio and B. J. Costar (eds), *The Victorian Premiers 1856–2006,* The Federation Press, Annandale.

Edgar, G. and F. Lockie 2010, 'Fair-Weather Friends: Why compacts fail non-government organisations', *International Journal of Sociology and Social Policy* 30, pp. 354–367.

Eggers, W. D. 2008, 'The Changing Nature of Government: Network governance, in J. O'Flynn and J. Wanna (eds), *Collaborative Governance A new era of public policy in Australia?,* ANU E Press, Canberra.

Elson, P. 2011, 'The Emergence of Structured Subnational Voluntary Sector_ Government Relationships in Canada: A historical institutional analysis', *Voluntary Sector Review* 2, pp. 135–155.

Fischer, K. F. 1984, *Canberra, Myths and Models: Forces at work in the formation of the Australian capital*, Institut für Asienkunde, Hamburg.

FONGA (Forum of Non-Government Agencies) 2011, 'The New South Wales Community Sector Charter', Council of Social Service of New South Wales, Sydney.

Futures Forum 2007, 'Queensland Community Services Sector Charter'. Available at: http://www.qcoss.org.au/sites/default/files/the-charter.pdf.

Halligan, J. 2011, 'NPM in Anglo-Saxon Countries', in T. Christensen and P. Lægreid (eds), *The Ashgate Research Companion to New Public Management,* Ashgate Publishing Co., Farnham, Surrey and Burlington.

Hayward, D. 2006, 'Steve Bracks: The quiet achiever', in P. Strangio and B. J. Costar (eds), *The Victorian Premiers 1856–2006,* The Federation Press, Annandale.

Henderson, P. 2011, 'Strengthening Relationships Between the Non Government Sector and Territory Government', Northern Territory Government. Available at: http://www.territorystories.nt.gov.au/bitstream/handle/10070/236981/Henderson-041111-Strengthening_relationships_between_the_non_government_sector_and_Territory_government.pdf.

Hood, C. 1991, 'A Public Management for all Seasons?', *Public Administration* 69, pp. 3–19.

Johnson, C. 2011, 'Gillard, Rudd and Labor Tradition', *Australian Journal of Politics and History* 57, pp. 562–579.

Jones, C., W. S. Hesterly and S. P. Borgatti 1997, 'A General Theory of Network Governance: Exchange conditions and social mechanisms', *The Academy of Management Review* 22, pp. 911–945.

Kendall, J. 2003, *The Voluntary Sector,* Routledge, London.

Kingdon, J. W. 1995, *Agendas, Alternatives, and Public Policies,* Longman, New York.

Lyons, M. 2001, 'Compacts Between Governments and the Voluntary Sector', paper delivered to conference 'Governance and Partnerships in the Third Sector: Reconciling Agendas for Change', Melbourne, 27 April. Available at: http://www.communitybuilders.nsw.gov.au/compacts.pdf.

Lyons, M. 2002, 'Institutional Prerequisites for Successful Compacts Between Governments and the Third Sector or Why a Compact is not yet possible in Australia', paper delivered to Sixth Australian and New Zealand Third Sector Research Conference, Auckland.

Lyons, M. 2003, 'Improving Government-Community Sector Relations', *The Journal of Contemporary Issues in Business and Government* 9, pp. 7–20.

March, J. G. and J. P. Olsen 2006, 'Elaborating the "New Institutionalism"', in R. A. W. Rhodes, S. Binder and B. Rockman (eds), *The Oxford Handbook of Political Institutions,* Oxford University Press, Oxford.

McDonald, C. 1999, 'The Third Sector in the Human Services: Rethinking its role', in I. O'Connor, J. Warburton and P. Smyth (eds), *Contemporary Perspectives on Social Work and the Human Services: Challenges and change,* Longman, Frenchs Forest.

McDonald, C. and G. Marston 2002, 'Fixing the Niche?: Rhetorics of the community sector in the neo-liberal welfare regime', *Just Policy* 27, 3–10.

Meyer, J. W. and B. Rowan 1991, 'Institutionalised Organisations: Formal structure as myth and ceremony', in W. W. Powell and P. J. DiMaggio (eds), *The New Institutionalism in Organizational Analysis,* University of Chicago Press, Chicago and London.

Murdoch, L. and J. Holroyd 2007, 'Clare Martin and Deputy Quit', *Sydney Morning Herald*, 26 November 2007.

NCOSS (NSW Council Of Social Service) 2011, 'NCOSS News', March. Available at: http://www.ncoss.org.au/vote1fairness/NCOSS-News-2011-election-issue.pdf.

NSW 2006, 'Working Together for NSW: An agreement between the NSW Government and NSW non-government human services organisations', NSW Department of Community Services and the Forum of Non-Government Agencies.

NT Government 2011, 'Safe Children, Bright Futures: Strategic Framework: The Northern Territory Government response to the report of the board of inquiry into the child protection system in the Northern Territory', Northern Territory Department of Children and Families.

NTCOSS (Northern Territory Council of Social Service) 2008, 'Annual Report'.

OCS (Office for the Community Sector) 2009, 'Office for the Community Sector Newsletter', Department of Health and Human Services, Hobart.

O'Flynn, J. and J. Wanna (eds) 2008, *Collaborative Governance: A new era of public policy in Australia?,* ANU E Press, Canberra.

PAEC (Public Accounts and Estimates Committee) 2002, 'Report on the Department of Human Services: Service agreements for community, health and welfare services', Parliament of Victoria.

Phillips, S. D. 2003, 'In Accordance: Canada's voluntary sector accord from idea to implementation', in K. L. Brock (ed.), *Delicate Dances: Public policy and the nonprofit sector,* McGill-Queen's University Press, Kingston.

Productivity Commission 2010, 'Contribution of the Not-for-Profit Sector'.

Pugh, J. and S. Saggers 2007, 'Cross-Sectoral Frameworks for Community Development in Western Australia', Centre for Social Research, Edith Cowan University. Available at: http://www.ecu.edu.au/__data/assets/pdf_file/0011/176735/CrossSector-Framework-CommDev-Nov2007.pdf.

Pusey, M. 2008, 'In the Wake of Economic Reform … New Prospects for Nation-Building?', in J. Butcher (ed.), *Australia Under Construction*, ANU E Press, Canberra.

QAO (Queensland Audit Office) 2007, 'Results of Performance Management Systems Audit of Management of Funding to Non-Government Organisations'. Available at: https://www.qao.qld.gov.au/files/file/Reports/2007%20Report%20No.%202.pdf.

Queensland 2007, 'Queensland Government Framework for Investment in Human Services', Queensland Government and the Futures Forum.

Queensland 2008, 'Compact Governance Committee Action Plan'. Available at: http://www.pc.gov.au/__data/assets/pdf_file/0013/90022/sub156-attachmentc.pdf.

Queensland 2009, 'The Queensland Compact: Annual Report 2009', Queensland Government and the Futures Forum.

Queensland 2010, 'The Queensland Compact Annual Report 2010', Queensland Government and the Futures Forum.

Queensland Government/Futures Forum 2008, 'The Queensland Compact: Towards a Fairer Queensland', Queensland Department of Communites, Child Safety and Disability Services.

Queensland Law Society 2012, 'Gag clauses concerning'. Available at: http://www.qls.com.au/About_QLS/News_media/Media_releases/Gag_clauses_concerning.

Rhodes, R. A. W. 2000, 'The Governance Narrative: Key Findings and Lessons from the ESRC's Whitehall Programme', *Public Administration* 78, pp. 345–363.

Rhodes, R. A. W. 2007, 'Understanding Governance: Ten years on', *Organisation Studies* 28, pp. 1243–1264.

Sanders, W. 2008, 'In the Name of Failure: A generational revolution in Indigenous affairs', in C. Aulich and R. Wettenhall (eds) *Howard's Fouth Government*, UNSW Press, Sydney.

Shergold, P. 2008, 'Contracting Out Government: Collaboration or control?' Neil Walker Memorial Lecture, Centre for Social Impact, University of New South Wales.

Shergold, P. 2013, 'Service Sector Reform: A roadmap for community and human services reform', Final report, Melbourne VIC, Department of

Human Services. Government of Victoria. Available at: http://www.dhs.vic.
gov.au/__data/assets/pdf_file/0004/850108/Service-sector-reform-roadmap-
report-shergold-2013.pdf. Accessed 23 September 2014 .

Simmons, B., F. Dobbin and G. Garrett 2006, 'Introduction: The international
diffusion of liberalism', *International Organization* 60, pp. 781–810.

Singleton, G. 2001, 'Political Chronicles: Australian Capital Territory — January
to June 2001', *Australian Journal of Politics and History* 47, pp. 585–593.

South Australia 2004, 'Common Ground', Department of Health and Department
for Families and Communities, Government of South Australia.

South Australia 2009, 'Stronger Together: An agreement between the State
Government of South Australia and the Health and Community Services
Sector', SA Health and the Department for Families and Communities,
Government of South Australia.

Tasmania 2012, 'Partnership Agreement between DHHS, DPAC and the
Community Sector 2012–2015', Department of Human Services and Health
and the Department of Premier and Cabinet, Government of Tasmania.

Treasury (NSW) 2012, 'Social Benefit Bonds Trial in NSW'. Available at: http://
www.treasury.nsw.gov.au/site_plan/social_benefit_bonds_trial_in_nsw_
FAQs.

VAGO (Victorian Auditor-General's Office) 2010, 'Partnering with the Community
Sector in Human Services and Health'. Available at: http://www.audit.vic.
gov.au/publications/2009-10/20100526-Community-Partnering-Full-Report.
pdf.

VCOSS (Victorian Council of Social Service) 2006, 'Building a Strong and a Fair
Community: Call to political parties 2006 Victorian State Election'. Available
at: http://vcoss.org.au/document/building-a-strong-and-fair-community-
call-to-political-parties-2006-victorian-state-election/.

Victoria 2007a, 'Review of Not-for-Profit Regulation Final Report', State Services
Authority. Available at: http://www.ssa.vic.gov.au/products/view-products/
review-of-not-for-profit-regulation.html.

Victoria 2007b, 'Stronger Community Organisations: Project report of the
steering committee', Department of Planning and Community Development,
Government of Victoria. Available at: http://www.vicsport.asn.au/
Association-Club-Support/SCOP/.

Victoria 2009, 'Partnership Agreement between the Victorian Department of Education and Early Childhood Development and the Municipal Association of Victoria', Department of Education and Early Childhood Development, Government of Victoria.

Victoria 2010, 'Partnership Agreement Between the Department of Education and Early Childhood Development and the Victorian Community Sector 2010–2014', Department of Education and Early Childhood Development, Government of Victoria.

Webster, M. and C. I. Atkins 2011, 'Jeff's Agenda', *Insight: Quarterly journal of the Victorian Council of Social Service*, pp. 13-15.

Western Australia 2004, 'Industry Plan for the Non-Government Human Services Sector', Government of Western Australia.

Western Australia 2011a, '2011-12 Budget Overview', Government of Western Australia.

Western Australia 2011b, 'Delivering Community Services in Partnership Policy: A policy to achieve better outcomes for Western Australians through the funding and contracting of community services', Department of Premier and Cabinet, Government of Western Australia.

Wolch, J. 1990, *The Shadow State: Government and voluntary sector in transition*, The Foundation Center, New York.

Personal Communications

Personal communication 2010a, interview by author with senior NFP policy actor NSW, Sydney NSW, 17 November 2010.

Personal communication 2010b, interview by author with senior NFP policy actor QLD, Brisbane QLD, 20 December 2010.

Personal communication 2010c, interview by author with senior state policy officer NSW, Sydney NSW, 18 November 2010.

Personal communication 2010d, interview by author with senior state policy officer QLD, Brisbane QLD, 20 December 2010.

Personal communication 2010e, interview by author with senior state policy officer QLD, Brisbane QLD, 22 November 2010.

Personal communication 2010f, interview by author with senior state policy officers NSW, Sydney NSW, 18 November 2010.

Personal communication 2011a, interview by author with senior NFP policy actor ACT, Canberra ACT, 1 April 2011.

Personal communication 2011b, interview by author with senior NFP policy actor NSW, Sydney NSW, 13 September 2011.

Personal communication 2011c, interview by author with senior NFP policy actor SA, Adelaide SA, 6 July 2011.

Personal communication 2011d, interview by author with senior NFP policy actor TAS, Hobart TAS, 3 October 2011.

Personal communication 2011e, interview by author with senior NFP policy actor TAS, Hobart TAS, 4 October 2011.

Personal communication 2011f, interview by author with senior NFP policy actor VIC, Canberra ACT, 15 April 2011.

Personal communication 2011g, interview by author with senior NFP policy actor WA, Perth WA, 4 July 2011.

Personal communication 2011h, interview by author with senior state policy officer ACT, Canberra ACT, 6 April 2011.

Personal communication 2011i, interview by author with senior state policy officer ACT, Canberra ACT, 31 April 2011.

Personal communication 2011j, interview by author with senior state policy officer SA, Adelaide SA, 7 July 2011.

Personal communication 2011k, interview by author with senior state policy officer SA, Adelaide SA, 21 July 2011.

Personal communication 2011l, interview by author with senior state policy officer TAS, Hobart TAS, 3 October 2011.

Personal communication 2011m, interview by author with senior state policy officer TAS, Hobart TAS, 4 October 2011.

Personal communication 2011n, interview by author with senior state policy officer VIC, Melbourne VIC, 18 April 2011.

Personal communication 2011o, interview by author with senior state policy officer WA, Perth WA, 5 July 2011.

Personal communication 2011p, interview by author with senior state policy officers NSW, Adelaide SA, 6 July 2011.

Personal communication 2011q, interview by author with senior state policy officers SA, Adelaide SA, 7 July 2011.

Personal communication 2013, meeting with senior government public officials ACT, 19 November 2013

11. Championing Change in a Highly Contested Policy Area: The literacy reforms of David Kemp, 1996–2001

Wendy Jarvie and Trish Mercer

When John Howard won a landslide victory over Paul Keating in March 1996, his junior Minister for Schools, Vocational Education and Training was David Kemp.[1] Portrayed by the media as a dry Liberal with conservative economic and social views, Kemp was a well-known political figure. His hands-on experience as a senior adviser in Malcolm Fraser's prime ministerial office in the late 1970s had been complemented by his time as a politics professor at Monash University, where he published a study of Australian politics which combined a theoretical analysis with his insider knowledge of Australian politics and government (Kemp 1988).

In the radical schooling reform agenda that Kemp would pursue, improved literacy attainment of Australian school children, particularly in their primary years, would represent a core element, if not the centrepiece. His approach displayed a singularity of purpose and a clear understanding of how to employ the push-pull levers of the Commonwealth's federal powers.[2] The Howard government, notwithstanding what has been seen as a traditional Liberal commitment to federalism, would become a strongly central government, partly attributable to the increasingly antagonistic Commonwealth/state environment — by 2002, all state and territory governments were Labor-controlled. Howard himself articulated his approach in terms of an 'aspirational nationalism' (Anderson and Parkin 2010, p. 97). In Liberal eyes, Commonwealth intervention in state policy areas was justified if it was supporting key Liberal objectives of individual decision-making and free markets (Kemp 2013). Indeed, Commonwealth Liberal intervention in education had long been manifest in schooling policy, beginning with Prime Minister Menzies' funding of science laboratories in schools in the 1960s.

Hollander and Patapan (2007) have labelled the defining characteristic of the Howard government and the preceding Hawke–Keating governments as 'pragmatic federalism', in that both tended to directly engage with pressing

---

1   David Kemp was promoted the following year to the portfolio ministry of Employment, Education and Training. This mega portfolio (DEETYA) was later reduced to Education, Training and Youth Affairs (DETYA) when Employment was established as a separate ministry with Industrial Relations.

2   While this paper will focus on Kemp's literacy reforms, numeracy improvement was also a key goal and was pursued concurrently.

problems without resort to larger theoretical concerns. While still influenced by ideas and values, it was the convergence of an identified problem with an opportunity for political engagement which served to create the window for a policy solution to emerge, and this tended to favour the Commonwealth over the states in policy outcomes (Hollander and Patapan 2007, pp. 280–281, 283–285). Kemp undoubtedly had a deep philosophical adherence to Liberal tenets and in his pursuit of literacy policy reform from 1996 was fully prepared to adopt an interventionist approach with state education systems. In bringing together the streams of problem, politics and policy, his approach appears to have been characterised by a pragmatic 'problem-defined and problem-driven' focus (Hollander and Patapan 2007, p. 291), which we will show was illustrated through the following features:

- First, his identification of an urgent literacy problem and his readiness to seize on the opportunities in government to capitalise on recent developments in educational and public policies;
- Secondly, the importance he attached to marshalling a supportive evidence base and communicating the literacy problem to a public audience, notwithstanding the contested nature of this evidence;
- Thirdly, the influence of the political environment in terms of the political backing he received for his reform focus, particularly from Prime Minister Howard, and the broader alignment with Howard's federalist ambitions and first- and second-term priorities;
- Fourthly, the deliberate carrot and stick tactics which he employed to secure the support, or at least reluctant acquiescence, of both government and non-government education sectors to his policy solutions; and
- Finally, the underpinning partnership between the Minister, his Chief of Staff and senior departmental officers which provided the administrative mobilisation to embed these policy solutions into a lasting reform agenda.

Kemp's approach, together with his department's focus on implementation, illustrates the importance of having both policy and administrative champions, particularly in such a contested policy area. In examining his literacy reforms, the authors have drawn on interviews with several key players: Kemp himself, senior Commonwealth education department bureaucrats, two state education department directors-general, and the researcher who was heavily involved in literacy assessment.[3]

---

3   While not taking any role in the literacy reforms, the authors worked at the Senior Executive Service level in Kemp's department during the early part of the period: Wendy Jarvie worked from 1997 to 1998 in Analysis and Evaluation Division; Trish Mercer briefly in the Schools area in 1996 before she became an Area Manager in Queensland. We are grateful to Bill Daniels (a former DEETYA senior officer and, from July 2001, Executive Director of the Independent Schools Council of Australia) who provided access to the minutes of the Board of Management meetings of the Council for 1996 to 2001, which provided useful insights into the perspectives of the Independent schools sector.

Positioning literacy as an urgent policy problem

Kemp's literacy agenda was based on his belief that individuals had to take responsibility for their own success, and that the role of education policy is to ensure that individuals have the right skills to achieve this (ABC 1999, pp. 3, 11). Since the early 1990s, he had been developing and articulating Liberal educational policy. In July 1991, speaking at the National Press Club as Shadow Minister for Education, he had asserted that 'no one area of national policy is more important for Australia to get right than education', and that gaining an internationally competitive edge in education was as important as acquiring such competitiveness in transport, communication or the waterfront (Kemp 1991).

By 1996, in the Coalition's election platform, this had crystallised into a commitment to work in a 'partnership approach' with the states on a National Literacy and Numeracy Strategy, including building a national database on literacy and numeracy standards in Australian schools (Liberals and Nationals Election Platform 1996, pp. 1, 3). In his early ministerial speeches, he drew attention to the social and economic costs of inadequate language and literacy skills (Kemp, Media Release: 'A National Literacy Goal', 21 June 1996); by the next year, he was hailing literacy as 'the key equity issue in education today' (Kemp, Media Release, 16 September 1997). This prioritising of literacy intrigued many media commentators, who began to describe him as a 'crusader' (Channel Nine 1999). Kemp himself nominated his motivation as having come from the feedback he had received in his early days as Minister from industry and 'from those who feel that their own literacy is not what it should be', and there was also the personal element of being the father of two young children (Kemp, Media Release, 5 September 1999; *The Australian*, 6 February 1999, p. 8).

In concentrating on literacy achievement, Kemp capitalised on recent developments in Australia and internationally. From the mid-1980s, interest in measuring the performance of students and of education systems through standardised literacy and numeracy testing had been increasing, particularly in countries such as the United Kingdom and United States. This standards-based agenda had itself been influenced by the broader global trend to reform public sector management and to increase accountability (Watson 2011, pp. 7–8). Within Australia, different state governments had begun to introduce standardised assessment testing of students in their education systems, notwithstanding strong opposition from the Australian Education Union (AEU) (Peach 1998, p. 8; *The Australian,* 6 August 1997, p. 11). The capability now existed, through psychometric measurement techniques, to enable the equating of state tests to derive national data. To capitalise on this, in 1995 the new and influential Report of Government Service Provision produced for the Council of Australian Governments had signalled strong interest in developing such nationally comparable data on student learning outcomes, although there was a pragmatic awareness that this would require a significant commitment from both Commonwealth and state governments to be implemented (Dowling 2008, p. 3; Steering Committee for Review of Commonwealth/State Service Provision 1995, pp. 199–201). In Kemp's early months, a first move in this direction was taken when senior education officials agreed in May to recommend to their ministers that literacy and numeracy benchmarks should be developed to indicate the student outcomes expected for particular years in schooling (Peach 1998, pp. 8–10). Kemp's reform focus on literacy and measurement was seen as being 'absolutely on the right track' by the influential directors-general of education in New South Wales (Ken Boston) and Victoria (Geoff Spring) (Boston 21 February 2013; Spring 25 March 2013).

Marshalling the evidence

As a new minister, Kemp sought to engage with key stakeholders such as the cross-sectoral Australian Primary Principals' Assocation (Kemp, Media Releases, 17 April 1996, 29 May 1996, 19 July 1996). As early as May, he had quietly sought the views of the peak independent schools body (National Independent Schools Council) as to 'reasonable accountability requirements' for national data collections on school and student performance (Board Minutes 10 May 1996).

This approach was an early indication of his determination, well before 'evidence-based policy' had acquired political currency, to collect an authoritative evidence base on current literacy and numeracy performance in order to galvanise public debate. The literacy agenda itself was hardly new: an emphasis on literacy policy and accompanying programs of assistance had been a recurring feature under the Hawke–Keating Labor governments through the 1990s (Harrington and McDonald 1999). But reliable data had not been available. Initially, Kemp relied on the higher end of estimates in a 1993 House of Representative Standing Committee on Employment, Education and Training report, that between 10 and 20 per cent of children finished school with literacy problems. He used this statistic in unveiling a 'Literacy Strategy', with five key steps, at the Australian College of Educators' Conference in June 1996 and foreshadowed that he would be seeking state and territory support for his fifth step, a national goal that every child leaving primary school should be able to read, write and spell at an appropriate level (Harrington and McDonald 1999, p. 6; Kemp Media Release 21 June 1996). This was indeed agreed as a national goal on 18 July at Kemp's first meeting of the Ministerial Council for Education, Employment, Training and Youth Affairs (MCEETYA). Ministers moreover agreed to support this goal through the development of common literacy benchmarks for Year 3 and Year 5 students and, importantly, the associated determination of levels of performance to be met in reading, writing and other essential aspects of literacy

(MCEECDYA, 17–18 July 1996). Thus at his first Commonwealth/state meeting, Kemp had achieved progress towards assessing not only student outcomes but also potentially the performance of the education systems themselves. He had also signalled a recurring political tactic of outing his agenda before discussion with his ministerial colleagues.

The cornerstone of Kemp's evidence base would be the first comprehensive literacy survey of Australian primary school children in 16 years — in April, he pledged support for this survey, commissioned as part of the Keating Labor government's 'Working Nation' reforms (Kemp, Media Release, 17 April 1996; Comber et al. 1998, pp. 18, 25). Conducted in August 1996 by the Australian Council for Educational Research (ACER) with support from the schooling systems, the unions and professional associations, the National School English Literacy Survey (hereafter the National Literacy Survey) involved nearly 7,500 children and an additional 800 Indigenous sample, at a cost to the Commonwealth of $2.6 million. This survey would establish reliable, national baseline data on the literary performance of children in Years 3 and 5 of schooling which would support the development of the national benchmarks agreed by MCEETYA in their July meeting (MCNSELS 1997, pp. 5, 250–252, 309).

Kemp, however, was not content to wait on the survey's results. In October 1996, in a major policy statement delivered at the Centre for Independent Studies, he drew on an ACER comparative analysis constructed from youth longitudinal surveys which indicated that, in 1995, 30 per cent of 14-year-old students did not have adequate basic literacy skills, as against 28 per cent in 1975. Describing this relatively small increase as 'alarming', he attributed these results to a 'cult of secrecy' which limited the ability of schools to improve student academic performance and challenged his state counterparts to publish their schools' academic results. Not surprisingly, Kemp's claims attracted considerable media interest and, concurrently, academic and union opposition to what they saw as his support for the introduction of school rankings and flawed analysis (Kemp, Media Release, 22 October 1996; *The Australian*, 22 October 1996, p. 1, 23 October 1996, p. 15, 24 October 1996, p. 10; Martin 1997, p. 9). Politically, however, this challenge could not be ignored, demonstrated by New South Wales premier Bob Carr's announcement that, given these 'very, very disturbing' figures, his state would consider widening a pilot project to test Year 7 literacy in 1997 (*The Australian*, 23 October 1996, p. 3).

On the eve of the next MCEETYA meeting on 14 March 1997, the Minister announced that he would be asking state education ministers to endorse a national literacy test for Year 3 students and that he would consider withholding schools funding if literacy levels failed to improve.[4] Notwithstanding hostile media reactions from several state ministers and the Liberal Premier of Western Australia, MCEETYA nevertheless agreed to the Commonwealth's proposal for a National Literacy and Numeracy Plan, including literacy and numeracy tests for both Year 3 and Year 5 students from 1998 — duly reported in *The Australian* as 'a historic agreement' between Commonwealth and state (with support also from the Catholic and independent school sectors). The states would continue to conduct their own tests with national benchmark data derived from their results. This was the first of a series of key MCEETYA meetings where Kemp arranged for either a ministerial-only session, or preceding dinner so that ministers could negotiate directly on this sensitive issue; having secured their agreement to a testing regime, he then retreated from his threat to tie federal funding to literacy improvement (*The Australian,* 12 March 1997, p. 3, 15 March 1997, p. 1; Dowling 2008, p. 4; MCEEDYA, 14 March 1997).[5] In contrast to such tough negotiations, Kemp's strategy with the non-government schools sector was more conciliatory, with separate discussions conducted by both the Minister and his key bureaucrats with Independent schools' representatives. The implications of national testing was a sensitive issue for the sector and in May 1997 they were only prepared to provide a holding response to Kemp's request for their support (National Independent Schools Council Board Minutes, 8 November 1996, 21 March 1997, 23 May 1997).

Publicising the evidence

As 1997 progressed, the political tensions in the schools sector continued to rise, highlighted at a forum on literacy in July to which Kemp invited 28 academic leaders. One of the documents for the day, entitled *Australian Literacies* and prepared by academic experts, directly challenged Kemp's position by stating unequivocally that there was 'no general literacy crisis in Australia' (Lo Bianco and Freebody 1997, p. xvi). Literacy had become a highly contested policy area and Kemp was viewed by many in the education community as having manufactured a literacy crisis and attached at least some of the blame to literacy teaching (Gill 1998; Martin 1997, pp. 8–10; Comber et al. 1998, pp. 18, 19). Early in 1998, an article by four prominent academics was published which closely analysed Kemp's public statements and compared the Howard education agenda with that of the former Labor government. The authors were dismissive of the

---

4 Kemp had supported his announcement by releasing yet another piece of ACER research, based on a five-year study of the education and career paths of 2,000 Australian teenagers, which demonstrated the disadvantage that young people without adequate literacy and numeracy faced in the education, training and labour market: Kemp, Media Release, 11 March 1997.

5 This ministerial-only meeting was reported in *The Australian* and both Dr Evan Arthur (then head of the Literacy and Special Programs Branch in DEETYA) and Dr Kemp have recalled that this was a deliberate tactic, as were the preceding ministerial dinners, to secure agreement to the Commonwealth's agenda: Arthur 2012; Kemp 2012.

various postwar 'literacy crises' that they saw as indicative of governments facing major social, economic and cultural change and discerned a deeper, more political motivation in Kemp's agenda: 'the current literacy crisis has been deployed to undermine community confidence in public schooling, and at the same time deflect attention and responsibility from material problems of poverty and youth unemployment' (Comber et al. 1998, pp. 19–27).[6] Although others were not so forceful in their criticisms of Kemp's literacy preoccupation, the views of Comber et al. on the negative aspects of testing were shared by many colleagues.[7]

This academic reaction had been stimulated at least in part by a media debate which played out in September 1997 following the simultaneous release by the Commonwealth of two reports on the results of the National Literacy Survey. The first, 'Mapping Literacy Achievement', was prepared by the Survey's Management Committee which included education system representatives, the unions and ACER. It was welcomed by the education community as a comprehensive map of literacy performance (MCNSELS 1997, pp. x, 3–4; Gill 1998, pp. 13–14). The main message was that the majority of students were achieving well, although there was a significant spread of achievement. Central to its approach was a comparison of student survey performance in relation to an indicative range of student achievement in which might lie the new draft MCEETYA benchmarking standards released in June and developed by a Benchmarking Task Force chaired by the Director-General of Education Queensland, Frank Peach. The conclusion in this report was that only six and four per cent of Year 3 students were performing below this draft benchmark range in writing and reading respectively, rising to 15 and 21 per cent for Year 5 students. According to the Commonwealth representative (Evan Arthur), however, the Management Committee had earlier commissioned ACER to develop a more precise mapping of the draft benchmarks against the survey's results, but had subsequently chosen to employ an indicative range in presenting these results (Arther 2011).[8]

---

6   This article was published in a book edited by Alan Reid, which focused on what was described as the contemporary debate about the survival of the public education system. Comber et al. 1998, p. 31, for example argued that 'literacy' was functioning as a metaphor for 'schooling' and specifically public schooling: Reid 1998, pp. xi, xiii.

7   In April 1997, 50 Victorian literacy experts (from peak bodies and universities) sent a letter to Kemp, arguing that the expenditure on national literacy testing would be better spent on teacher training and professional renewal: *The Australian*, 23 April 1997, p. 39. For other examples of opposition to testing, see *The Australian*, 20 July 1999, p. 6; 3 April 2000, p. 15; Professor Alan Luke and Dr Brian Comber quoted on ABC 1999, pp. 7, 8.

8   While the methodology employed was technically complex, the choice of an indicative range in presenting the results would appear to have overstated achievement, when ACER's methodological analysis (reported in Appendix 3) is examined more closely. The report compares achievement under the existing English curriculum profiles to the range expected in the draft benchmark standards. ACER reported that not all the students within the particular profile (Level 2 for both writing and reading in the case of Year 3 students) which contained the draft writing and reading benchmarks would have met the appropriate benchmark —

Such methodological reliance on an indicative range, not surprisingly, was anathema to Dr Kemp, who was determined to present a clear line (i.e. an exact score) in the survey results as to who was above or below the draft benchmarks; his recollection is that he was 'shocked' that 'nowhere was there any analysis that could tell the community how many students had sufficient literacy to allow them to continue education' (Kemp 2012). Geoff Masters has recalled that Kemp was very clear that the survey report would not be released until ACER had analysed the results in terms of what was an acceptable level of literacy performance. To this end, Masters and Margaret Forster of ACER developed what they described as 'clear performance standards in reading and writing' by utilising the draft benchmark standards to calculate a minimum score that would constitute a satisfactory performance for the student's age or year group. Under this approach, published as 'Literacy Standards in Australia', very different results were reported: 28 per cent of Year 3 and 33 per cent of Year 5 students did not meet the identified performance standards for writing; and 27 per cent of Year 3 and 29 per cent of Year 5 students did not meet the standards for reading. Girls met the standard more often than boys, but only a very low percentage of Indigenous students met them.[9]

These differing presentations of the survey's results would have been sufficient to ensure strong media interest and robust debate at the next MCEETYA meeting. However, Kemp's decision to air the findings on Channel Nine's *60 Minutes* current affairs program on 14 September 1997, some two days after he had provided 'Literacy Standards in Australia' to his ministerial colleagues, created what the AEU called 'Literacy Hysteria Week' and was later described as 'sensational [media] coverage', both electronic and print (Martin 1997, p. 8; *The Australian*, 6 February 1999, p. 8). The media focused on Kemp's portrayal of 'a serious literacy problem', with nearly one-third of primary children unable to read or write at an adequate standard, requiring urgent 'national co-operative effort' (Kemp, Media Release, 15 September 1997). Nearly two years later, the acrimonious response this had produced, particularly from state education ministers, was manifest on the ABC's *Four Corners* program (titled 'War of Words') with critics such as Phil Gude (the Victorian Liberal Education Minister) standing by his accusation at the time that Dr Kemp was 'deliberately and mischievously manipulating data to portray literacy at a perilous level' (ABC 1999, p. 7; Comber et al. 1998, pp. 3, 19). Peach, the bureaucrat heading the

---

for example, at least some of the 42 per cent of Year 3 students assessed at English Profile Level 2 would not have met the Year 3 draft reading benchmark range as this was located towards the upper end of this Level 2: MCNSELS 1997, pp. iv, vi, Appendix 3, 314–329.

9 ACER, for whom this was a very sensitive exercise in terms of reputational regard, were careful to report that it was the Minister who had asked for an exact score, in the belief that how schoolchildren were performing in relation to such a performance standard 'would be useful information for the Australian community': Masters and Forster 1997, pp. 10–12, 15, 19, 22; Kemp, Media Release, 15 September 1997; Masters 2012.

Benchmarking Taskforce, had noted pointedly in May 1998 at an educational conference that 'Literacy Standards in Australia' had 'caused considerable national concern by its use of what some argued were arbitrary and highly judgemental decisions' in attempting to align the survey's reading and writing results against the draft reading and writing benchmarks for Years 3 and 5 (Peach 1998, p. 13). Yet notwithstanding these strong criticisms, the statistics in 'Literacy Standards in Australia' would be cited not only by the media and other commentators but also in significant reports such as the Productivity Commission's Report on Government Services (*The Australian,* 22 September 1997, p. 1; SCRRCSSP 1998, p. 42; Argy 1998, pp. 120–121; Alloway and Gilbert 1998, pp. 249, 252).[10]

In an attempt to regain the initiative, state and territory ministers met without Kemp on 22 September and issued their own ten-point plan to advance previously agreed recommendations in the National Literacy and Numeracy Plan. Kemp, however, rejected out of hand the states' request for an additional $513 milllion in federal funding over the next four years (Peach, 1998, p. 13; *The Australian,* 22 September 1997, p. 1). By November, when Arthur briefed independent schools' representatives, there appears to have been bureaucratic agreement on key assessment details but there remained 'State ministerial concern about the public presentation of data' (National Independent Schools Council Board Minutes, 14 November 1997). The draft literacy benchmarks for children in Year 3 and Year 5 were finally approved by all education ministers in the following year and, significantly, included a line drawn across the range to represent satisfactory performance (MCEECDYA, 23 April 1998; Arthur 2011).

While Kemp earned the ire of many state education ministers and bureaucrats as well as academics for his political use of literacy data, it is nonetheless apparent that he devoted considerable resources and energy to accumulating an evidence base on literacy. Those who worked closely with him have remarked on this determination. Professor Masters has recalled how Kemp, with his social science training, 'was focused on evidence, he valued research and he wanted to use it' (Masters 2012). Indeed, John Roskom, his Chief of Staff from 1996 to 1998, described his boss as having a deep belief 'that his opponents, if provided with sufficient evidence, could be won over'.[11] Moreover, he was well able to analyse and interpret the highly technical detail associated with testing and benchmark

---

10   Kemp does not appear to have directly rebutted any of the criticisms of how he employed the survey data, but Frank Devine (a supportive journalist presumably briefed by Kemp's office) reported in late September that the analysis by ACER in regard to the survey results and the draft benchmarks had been done at the request of the management committee for the survey (the 'Harrington Committee') but had then been buried in the Appendix to 'Mapping Literacy Achievement': *The Australian,* 25 September 1997, p. 13.

11   Roskom made these comments when Kemp was retiring from federal politics in 2004: *The Age,* 17 July 2004. In a similar vein, Steve Sedgwick (the DEETYA and then DETYA Secretary at this time) has recalled how Dr Kemp would look to build the case publicly and then seek to make common cause with his state ministerial colleagues: Sedgwick 2012.

development — an asset he exploited in ministerial council meetings (Arthur 2012; Sedgwick 2012). It is an open question as to whether Kemp would have focused so strongly on evidence if it had not fitted his purpose. Certainly, by publicly releasing the separate report he had commissioned on the National Literacy Survey's results on a populist TV show, Kemp the politician fully intended to create controversy and a public debate which would promote his agenda of locking state ministers into support for a national testing and benchmark regime and presenting this as a Commonwealth driven initiative.

Getting the Commonwealth politics right

Kemp's preoccupation with evidence was not shared by his Prime Minister. Paul Kelly has depicted the Howard Cabinet as more often than not seeing 'the academy as unfavorably disposed towards its objectives' with Howard employing research and advice 'to realize his aims'.[12] In terms of the overarching directions of schooling policy, however, the Minister and Prime Minister were very closely aligned. The Howard government was more centralist than its predecessors and Kemp, while genuflecting to the primary responsibility for schooling held by the states, had defined a formative role for the Commonwealth. He saw this as based on the 'strong national interest in the educational outcomes of Australia's schools', manifested not only in the Commonwealth's significant funding contribution, but also through the indirect cost of 'school failure' borne through unemployment benefits and social programs (Kemp, Media Release, 21 April 1997).

In education, the broader political agenda favouring privatisation, competition and choice was manifested in the Howard government's user choice approach to funding of vocational education, and the introduction of performance-driven funding of higher education research.[13] In schools education it was evident in the removal of restrictions on the establishment of new private schools, emphasis on quality and performance standards and expansion of non-government school funding.[14] Howard articulated this focus in 2007 when he contended that quality in schooling 'demands choice, diversity, specialisation, transparency and competition.' Support for testing of students' knowledge and more transparency to empower parents were examples he cited of his 'traditional views' which he contrasted with the 'postmodernist values' of educational theorists and some Labor governments (*The Australian,* 16 May 2007, p. 14).

---

12 Kelly, as Editor-at-Large of *The Australian,* is a respected commentator on public policy. This was an address to the Institute of Public Administration's Council: Kelly 2006, p. 15.

13 See, for example, the White Paper on higher education research funding: Kemp 1999.

14 The non-government school funding policies of the Howard government are well described by Wilkinson et al. 2007, pp. 151–180 and Paul Kelly, *The Australian,* 16 May 2007, p. 14.

In 1999, the political significance of the literacy reforms was articulated publicly when *The Australian* labelled this as 'a Howard battlers' issue because the Howard battlers were missing out on literacy.[15] Given the extent to which the schooling reform priorities pursued by Kemp dovetailed with the Coalition's broader political agenda, it is unsurprising that Kemp was frequently reported as having the strong support of his Prime Minister and that Howard regularly praised Kemp's literacy reforms (see, for example, *The Australian*, 22 December 1997, p. 11, 6 February 1999, p. 8; AustralianPolitics.com 2001). Certainly Kemp's skill at selling the government's policies was seen by some of his opponents as responsible for his promotion to the Cabinet ministry of Employment, Education and Training in October 1997 (Martin 1997, p. 11).

Getting state agreement

Getting state agreement: The carrot

Aside from such marketing abilities, Kemp was determined to exert influence through all the avenues available to him as a federal minister. In his *Foundations for Australian Political Analysis,* he cited persuasion, grants and physical coercion as some of the most important social mechanisms for political strategies (Kemp 1988, p. 7). As a Minister, he was successful in quarantining schools' programs from the tough funding cuts in the early Costello budgets and in securing some additional funding commitments for literacy and numeracy initiatives. For example:

- The government's first budget, in August 1996, included an additional $45 million for a National Literacy and Numeracy Strategy;
- During 1997, there were targeted funding announcements, such as $7 million for literacy training for primary school teachers and $6.2 million for English as a second language tuition for Indigenous students; and,
- $1 million to establish an annual National Literacy Week was announced in March 1999, and later in the 1999 budget two significant 1998 election commitments were funded, with $47.1 million for literacy initiatives in middle schooling and $84 million for MCEETYA's National Literacy and Numeracy Plan (Kemp, Media Releases, 20 August 1996, 15 September 1997, 1 October 1997, 16 March 1999, 11 May 1999).

Such funding largesse was aimed as much at the diverse non-government school community as the government sector. Securing their agreement to

---

15   According to the reporter Catherine Armitage, this issue was discussed regularly at cabinet's employment subcommittee meetings: *The Australian,* 6 February 1999, p. 8.

come on board with national assessment testing of *all* students involved sensitive negotiations and was seen in the media as largely a *quid pro quo* for the substantial funding increases available for non-government schools under the revised socio-economic status recurrent funding arrangements (Channel Nine 1999).[16] However, the Commonwealth drew the line at meeting the very substantial costs for government and non-government systems in administering the new national tests, insisting that education authorities needed to reassess their funding priorities. Kemp was adamantly of the view that literacy and numeracy should be the 'first call on the education dollar' (*The Australian,* 12 March 1997, p. 3).[17]

Getting state agreement: The stick

In his study of Australian politics, Kemp had highlighted the Commonwealth's greater capacity in federal conflicts to extend its authority (Kemp 1988, p. 143). In office he worked to expand the Commonwealth's influence in the schooling sector, with education becoming a prominent example of the government's willingness to employ conditionality in Commonwealth grants as a vehicle to achieve policy priorities (Anderson and Parkin 2010, p. 101). During 1996 and 1997, Kemp had publicly advocated that individual schools should be required to publish their literacy performance results as a public accountability measure (*The Australian,* 24 October 1996, p. 10; Comber et al. 1998, p. 27: Kemp, Media Release, 21 April 1997). He was also willing to employ — or at least to threaten to employ — the Commonwealth's financial power as a lever to compel state and territory governments to implement his literacy standards. Having created a media furore in September 1997 with his *60 Minutes* appearance and the release of 'Literacy Standards in Australia' with its alarming statistics, Kemp almost immediately announced that the Commonwealth would impose a condition on future access to literacy program funding, thus enacting a threat he had raised earlier in the year — states and territories would be required to provide a detailed plan on how schools would ensure that their students were reading and writing adequately by the end of Year 3.[18]

These plans became a regular requirement for education systems to access Commonwealth literacy funding. By mid-1999, there was media speculation that Kemp was investigating how to extend this by linking individual school funding

---

16 Reflecting these sensitivities, Kemp's department reported in 1999 that all government and most non-government education authorities had participated in literacy benchmark exercises for Years 3 and 5: DETYA 1999.

17 Despite Kemp's views, later in 1997 there were discussions between DETYA and an Independent Schools representative concerning funding support for Independent schools, but this does not appear to have eventuated: National Independent Schools Council Board Minutes, 26 August 1997.

18 Notwithstanding Kemp's interest in ensuring that the literacy performance of individual schools was made public, the reporting agreed by MCEETYA was only at the state level (without even any differentiation by system): Kemp, Media Release, 16 September 1997.

to compliance with the literacy and numeracy benchmarks (*The Australian*, 19 July 1999, p. 4; 20 July 1999, p. 6). Throughout 2000, the independent schools sector was monitoring the strengthened accountability requirements as a 'major issue' for their schools, with concerns at the discretionary powers reserved for the Minister (National Independent Schools Council Board Minutes, 26 February, 26 May, 25 August, 6 October and 24 November 2000). Kemp may have been partially motivated by his exasperation at the delays in implementing MCEETYA's decisions from 1996–97 to develop and report progress against literacy and numeracy benchmarks for Year 3 and Year 5 students. There was a long and tortuous process of equating the different state and territory tests to enable national comparability; ministers only finally reached agreement in May 1999 that such tests needed to contain more common elements to achieve such comparability (*The Australian*, 3 May 1999, p. 17; 19 July 1999, p. 4). Finally, in early 2000, the first report (restricted to the Year 3 reading component) was released, with the results indicating that some 87 per cent of Australian Year 3 students had achieved the benchmark — such a striking improvement on the 1996 survey results that Professor Peter Freebody of Griffith University drily remarked that 'the latest round of *testing* seems to indicate either that [literacy levels] improved very dramatically in a very short period of time or that [Kemp's claim of a "literacy crisis"] was an overstatement' (ABC 1999, p. 7; *The Australian*, 17 March 2000, p. 15).[19] An alternative interpretation could be that the questions in the new benchmark testing had been 'dumbed down', given that ACER's Geoff Masters was publicly quoted as claiming that state educators were pressuring his experts to accept easier questions. Both Kemp and his state colleagues, however, were quick to deny that this was occurring (*The Australian*, 25 February 2000, p. 1).[20]

Later in 2000, Kemp secured an important amendment to the Schools States Grants legislation so that education authorities, to receive funding under the Commonwealth's literacy and numeracy program, would be required to report against performance measures and targets for literacy and numeracy. National reporting of state performance was now a legislated Commonwealth requirement — seen as an example of the Howard government's engagement in 'regulatory' federalism, under which funding access was conditional on state compliance with central policy demands (Vromen et al. 2009, p. 309). Some state ministers contended that Kemp had threatened them with the withdrawal of funds from low performing schools. Both the former directors-general that we interviewed recalled that the ministerial-only meetings were 'bunfights': Geoff Spring

---

19   Kemp himself had predicted in 1999 that the result would be in the low-to-mid-80s.

20   In January 2005, the *Sydney Morning Herald* reported that a dyslexic Year 3 student, who was in the bottom 17 per cent in the NSW Basic Skills test and was said to be two years behind his peers, nevertheless met the literacy benchmark for Year 3. In our interview in 2012, Kemp indicated that he now has doubts as to whether the process employed at the time to establish equivalences across the various state tests was highly accurate and effective: AUSPELD 2005, p. 3; Kemp 2012.

indicated that Kemp used his negotiating strengths 'to imply that funds were at risk if they didn't co-operate' (Spring 2013; Boston 2013). Nevertheless, Kemp was adamant when interviewed by the ABC in August 1999 that he had never threatened to withdraw funding and that his interest was in identifying schools so that they could be helped by the relevant state system.[21]

While state ministers resented his tactics, Kemp was often publicly regarded as having brought a sustained spotlight onto an important issue in school literacy (Argy 1998, pp. 120–121; *The Australian,* 6 February 1999, p. 8; Channel Nine 1999). Despite having ranged against him what the ABC *Four Corners* program described as a 'formidable array' of opponents from political, bureaucratic, academic and professional quarters, he was seen as having successfully corralled all of the states and territories into accepting an ongoing system of literacy testing and public reporting by engaging the weight of public opinion (ABC 1999, p. 7). During his time as Minister, virtually every MCEETYA meeting included resolutions on literacy and/or numeracy, as ministers worked through the complex issues involved in establishing national standards for the benchmarks and reporting framework and then progressively extending it to encompass both literacy and numeracy for schoolchildren in Years 3, 5 and 7 (and later 9).[22] By 2000, furthermore, the introduction of national testing had become a bipartisan issue, with federal Labor publicly declaring their support for such a regime (*The Australian,* 29 July 2000, p. 30).

The public service partnership: Administrative mobilisation

In implementing enduring policy reform, the importance of 'administrative mobilisation' is now recognised (Lindquist and Wanna 2011, p. 3). While Kemp may have won the political battle, the administrative task of developing the benchmarks and calibrating individual state and territory tests for national comparability was a hard slog over many years, engaging the attention of senior bureaucrats, their technical staff and external psychometric experts. Kemp's department (DEETYA and later DETYA) was initially slow to respond

---

21   This was aired on the *Four Corners* program in August 1999 and also in the media in the previous month. Clearly many in the education community were concerned that the Minister did intend to use his abilities to withhold funding. In 1997, Kemp had stated in a media release that if any state or territory did not provide an adequate detailed plan, 'the Federal Government would review how its funding could best be used to ensure each child's needs were met': ABC 1999, pp. 8–9; *The Australian,* 20 July 1999, p. 6; Kemp, Media Release, 16 September 1997.

22   Although Queensland, Victoria and Tasmania were initially of a similar political leaning, Kemp appeared to bring his agenda unilaterally to MCEETYA meetings, with the exception of his first meeting in 1996 when he joined with Bob Quinn (the Queensland minister) to bring a critical package of resolutions on literacy: Peach 1998, pp. 9–10.

to their Minister's interest in literacy, given the more hands-off role that the Commonwealth had tended to play in schooling. But, by mid-1996, a dedicated literacy team had been brought together, combining strategic policy skills, Commonwealth/state experience and literacy expertise.

The partnership which key departmental officers forged with Kemp and his key advisers was critical to the long term success of Kemp's agenda.[23] Kemp had a clear set of beliefs as to the respective roles of minister and public servants; in particular, he believed that ministers should control policy development, while the public service provided technical advice. In his 1988 book, Kemp had argued policy advice required 'a [political] value component' supplied by ministers and their staffers to complement the department's technical advice (Kemp 1988, pp. 309–10). The DEETYA secretary, Steve Sedgwick, considered that his Minister had a very clear view on how the department could support his agenda, reflected in the open and robust discussions which he and the relevant branch head Evan Arthur were able to have with Kemp and his Chief of Staff Roskom, as Kemp teased out his agenda and took advantage of political and administrative opportunities (Sedgwick 2012; Arthur 2012).

In supporting their Minister at ministerial council meetings, DEETYA/DETYA were known for their tightly organised approach to the MCEETYA processes and the associated meetings of chief education officers. Given the complex technical issues involved, the development of the benchmarks and reporting arrangements necessitated the establishment of a separate Benchmarking Task Force in which DEETYA officers played a more active role than they had taken previously. Moreover, as Bill Daniels (then in charge of the schools branches in DETYA) has recalled, Commonwealth/state bureaucratic interactions during the Kemp years were characterised by considerable antagonism given the political environment (Daniels 2013). The pressure of the constant negotiations, consultations and problem solving required within these various official forums was captured in Sedgwick's undoubtedly understated comment in the department's 2000–01 annual report that while the changes to a stronger accountability framework in schooling were usually pursued collaboratively in Commonwealth/state forums, this was 'not without times of tension and difficulty' (DETYA 2001). His counterpart in Queensland, Peach, had indeed sharply reminded an educators' conference in May 1998 that the Commonwealth had no delivery responsibilities in schooling, although he assured his audience that his Benchmarking Taskforce believed that 'a solution is possible and attainable [on the benchmarking exercise]' (Peach 1998, pp. 8, 15).

---

23 When Kemp first became Minister, the Secretary of the department was Sandy Hollway, who supported Kemp through the early critical years of his schooling reforms but left in 1997 to become the CEO of the Sydney Organising Committee for the Olympic Games.

The priority the department attached to the literacy agenda in its work program was reflected in the space devoted to recording progress on the literacy and numeracy benchmarks and associated initiatives in its annual reports each year. Literacy, for instance, featured continuously in the Secretary's report on the portfolio's major developments and achievements. Utilising the capacity under the new Literacy Program for national projects, the department commissioned and published a considerable body of research on literacy issues such as early childhood literacy development and the literacy development of boys (DETYA 2002, chapter 4, outcome 1; Harrington and McDonald 1999). To assist in communicating the Minister's agenda, the department took the further step of releasing departmental papers, such as:

- A discussion paper in October 1997 on the allocation of literacy grants (following Kemp's decision to require detailed literacy plans from systems); and

- In February 1998, a policy paper outlining the Commonwealth's literacy and numeracy policy principles and goals, associated funding strategies and particular areas of literacy disadvantage (Harrington and McDonald 1999; Peach 1998, p. 10).

Through these diverse activities, across the first and second terms of the Howard government, the department at both executive and officer level had clearly engaged very actively with their Minister's policy interest and had adapted to Kemp's particular ministerial style, the urgency of his time horizons and the highly technical nature of this policy issue. The close working relationship was recognised not only by Kemp, who has acknowledged the role of the department (and especially Dr Arthur's work) in the development of national testing as 'tremendously important', but also by state officials (Kemp 2012; Boston 2013).

Pragmatic federalism in action

This examination of David Kemp's literacy reforms has highlighted that, notwithstanding their roots in Liberal philosophy of individual advancement, a highly pragmatic approach was adopted by Kemp to drive them through. This pragmatic approach, in which the individual policy problem was given primacy over the theoretical formulation of the problem and potential remedy, has been discerned in the broader policy agendas of the Howard government (Hollander and Patapan 2007, pp. 290–291).

Table 1 summarises the features of Kemp's approach. His first step was to identify — or, as his opponents would have said, to construct — the literacy levels of primary school children as a significant public problem, beginning with his development of the opposition's election platform and manifested very early in his ministerial term by what was perceived publicly as his 'crusade' on literacy. In championing literacy standards as a major policy issue, he was assisted by an international and domestic environment which was increasingly supportive of standardised assessment and national reporting as the means of extending the accountability of teachers, schools and systems. Kemp brought a particular bent towards the acquisition of a supportive evidence base to underpin his agenda and to generate public debate; the planned National Literacy Survey of primary school children was a timely platform for this. His controversial decision to insist on presenting a clear line on the survey's results through a specially commissioned (second) report, and then to announce the results on a populist national television program in September 1997, powerfully cemented in the public mind that Australian schools were experiencing a 'literacy crisis'. In 't Hart's view, 'turning up the heat' on your political adversaries is 'a *sine qua non* of reformist leadership' and Kemp would presumably have endorsed this position ('t Hart 2011, p. 203).

Kemp believed that winning the public debate was crucial to achieving reform in a policy area with powerful interest groups. Although it alienated the education community, it ensured that state ministers could not hold out against his determination not only to establish national benchmarks for literacy and numeracy at critical years of schooling but to report nationally on performance by equating the results of their individual state tests. Unlike the health sector, where a deep evidence base demonstrating which interventions work has been carefully built up through bureaucratic and academic partnerships over several decades, evidence in the schools sector is a far more contested area and frequently challenged as politically motivated (see, for example, Vromen et al. 2009, pp. 17, 331, 335). While Kemp undoubtedly had a deep attachment to discovering and communicating the evidence on literacy attainment, which he believed had been kept from the public domain (Kemp 2012), his methods were seen by many not only as polarising and divisive but also as motivated by his underlying political agenda.

Table 1: Kemp's literacy reforms: Pragmatic federalism in action

Elements of reform approach	How Kemp pursued these
1. Positioning literacy as an urgent policy problem	a. Identified literacy standards as a priority in Opposition election platform b. Capitalised on national and international initiatives in standardised assessment c. Publicly 'crusaded' for literacy as a core skill for individual and for national productivity.
2. Marshalling and publicising the evidence	a. Built strong (but contested) evidence base, taking advantage of National Literacy Survey of primary schoolchildren (the first in 16 years) b. Ensured that the survey results clearly showed the proportion of children who were below the relevant benchmark, despite state objections and academic critics c. Used popular media to highlight 'alarming' results and win public debate.
3. Getting the Commonwealth politics right	a. Ensured his education agenda was politically aligned with government's and Prime Minister's priorities in terms of competition and choice agendas b. Positioned and 'sold' literacy reforms as in the 'national interest'
4. Getting state agreement — the carrot	a. Used evidence and persuasion in ministerial meetings, particularly ministerial-only sessions b. Secured additional Commonwealth funding for literacy and numeracy c. Cultivated non-government sector to ensure their involvement in national testing.
5. Getting state agreement — the stick	a. Imposed conditions on states for funding, e.g. detailed plans for literacy improvement b. 'Stalking horse' — made threats to withhold or tie literacy funds to literacy improvement c. Legislated as Commonwealth funding requirement for education systems to report literacy and numeracy performance.
6. The public service partnership	a. Held strong views on the minister's responsibility for policy development. b. Had a good working relationship with department — saw officers as administrative champions, and was comfortable with robust discussions c. The department, in turn, mobilised to prioritise literacy in its work program and Commonwealth/state negotiations.

Although Kemp initially operated 'below the radar' within the new Howard government in prosecuting such a determined agenda, his success in generating the pressure of public opinion for action on literacy also built his internal political capital, evidenced in his promotion to the senior ministry. Howard's public recognition of Kemp's achievements on the literacy agenda indicated the support Kemp acquired within the cabinet, and certainly his schooling reforms were seen as closely aligned with the government's adoption of choice and competition as two of its political mantras. For the Coalition, the public support for their schools agenda represented an electoral advantage, by eroding what had traditionally been seen as a core strength for Labor (Senior 2008, p. 221).

In the federal arena, Kemp was willing to employ the range of powers available to him as a Commonwealth minister, in order to secure state cooperation. He controlled the agenda by negotiating directly with his ministerial counterparts; there was at that stage no 'human capital' agenda within the Council of Australian Governments to buttress, or alternatively derail, his plans. His ability to understand both the research and technical aspects of literacy was a powerful asset in arguing the case in ministerial council meetings, particularly in ministerial-only meetings or dinners. On certain key issues, such as the decision to retain state tests, he made concessions, recognising, for example, that a fully national test 'was a step too far at that time' (Kemp 2012). He brought additional funding and a greatly heightened profile for school literacy to the negotiating table, which helped to build support from the non-government school sector. Conversely, Kemp put as much pressure as he could bring to bear on his state counterparts and on non-government school systems to agree to his strategies on literacy improvements, such as the legislated conditionality of providing an annual plan to access Commonwealth literacy program funding and annual reporting against performance targets. Although his department had not initiated the work on literacy, their role as administrative champions was vital, particularly in terms of their involvement in the technical detail underpinning the development of the literacy and numeracy benchmarks and the national equating of state test results. This served to maintain the momentum on national assessment, against resistance from state bureaucrats and ministers, for whom testing results were high stakes and a threat to their administrative or political capital.[24] If reforms involve 'wars not battles', this sustained attention to implementation was intrinsic to overcoming opposition to such systemic change ('t Hart 2011, p. 209).

Yet despite such sustained attention from Kemp and his department over more than five years, literacy reform remained an unfinished agenda when he left the portfolio in November 2001 (to move to the environment portfolio) and the public spotlight moved to other schooling issues. In November 2004, following his retirement from politics, he was quoted in *The Australian* as laying the blame at the door of state bureaucrats and teacher unions for this failure to maintain the momentum to lift literacy levels, exemplified in the extended delays by the states in publishing nationally the results of the literacy tests (*The Australian*, 18 November 2004, p. 11). It was not until 2008, under the leadership of Julia Gillard, Minister for Employment, Education and Workplace Relations and

---

24   The high stakes involved have been highlighted by Dr Bob Lingard and a visiting UK academic in 2010: Lingard 2009, pp. 13, 19; Robin Alexander quoted in SEEWRC 2010, p. 41.

Deputy Prime Minister in the new Rudd Labor government, that a fully national test (NAPLAN) was conducted, and this was followed by the establishment of a national body (the Australian Curriculum and Assessment Reporting Agency) and a national website, *My School*, which enabled comparative reporting on literacy and numeracy results at an individual school level. The national assessment regime has also catalysed other reforms — in Queensland, for example, the introduction of the benchmarks and national reporting impelled a major reconsideration of the educational disadvantage faced by its students in having one fewer year of compulsory schooling; Peter Beattie's Labor government finally took the step of adding this additional year, at least partly to enable parity in national reporting.

While Howard may have lauded Kemp's achievements in literacy reform at the time, he did not refer to this singular achievement in his subsequent autobiography.[25] While there has been broader acknowledgement of the profound impact (both positive and negative) of the introduction of national literacy and numeracy testing and reporting as an accountability tool through output measurement, Kemp's driving role has rarely been highlighted, despite the public recognition during his time as minister.[26] From his perspective as an educational assessment expert closely involved in national testing, Masters certainly regards the 'Kemp years' as 'pivotal' in the development of literacy and numeracy performance standards and reporting (Masters 2012). Arguably, the Minister (with assistance from his department) displayed what Lindquist and Wanna have described as the qualities for durable policy reform: 'anticipation, contingency planning, considerable prudential judgment and strategic leadership'.[27]

Epilogue

In July 1999, Kemp had predicted that the introduction of testing would 'establish a new benchmark ... against which the success of policies in future years is going to have to be measured' (ABC, 1999, p. 8). Yet notwithstanding

---

25   The ex-Prime Minister does not mention Kemp in his capacity as Education Minister, and the one schools policy of which he remains 'intensely proud' is the rapid expansion of independent schools charging low to moderate fees: Howard 2010, p. 243, 487.

26   In his 2008 article on school assessment, Steve Dowling recognised the profound impact of the introduction of testing in the late 1990s and acknowledged that Kemp was Education Minister at the time when national testing was introduced, although he did not directly describe his role in this reform. There has been some recent recognition that NAPLAN was built on the 'Howard government's initiative': see Bamford 2010; Dowling 2008, p. 3.

27   Educational policy-making tends to be critiqued by academic observers as 'messy' and 'ad hoc' or, alternatively, driven by hostile announcements without sufficient attention to implementation issues and risks: Lindquist and Wanna 2011, pp. 3, 11; Reid 1998, p. xi.

Kemp's spotlight on Australia's literacy achievements, the nation's performance as measured by the international benchmark of the OECD's Programme for International Student Assessment tests, declined between 2000 and 2009.[28]

The reasons for the decline are still being debated. One possibility is that the benchmarks created by the Commonwealth and states were set too low, producing little urgency for change in teaching and school management practices from either education bureaucracies or their ministers. It could also be that schools are not employing the most effective literacy strategies, or that other changes in the student population or school structure have offset the increased literacy focus. The most authoritative comment has come from a paper prepared for the panel conducting the Review of Funding for Schooling (the Gonski review), established by the Gillard Labor government. This found evidence that the decline in reading and mathematics was linked to the increased concentration of disadvantaged children in largely government schools. This change was, in turn, partly the result of other Kemp reforms which enabled parents to exercise choice in the school their children went to, the corresponding growth of the non-government school sector and a resulting loss of middle class children from the public system (Gonski et al. 2011, pp. 20–22).

If this is true, it would tend to suggest that, ironically, David Kemp's literacy reforms, as important as they were, were undermined by parental choice — the other key plank in his schooling reform agenda.

References

Alloway, N. and P. Gilbert 1998, 'Reading Literacy Test Data: Benchmarking success?', *The Australian Journal of Language and Literacy* 21(3).

Argy, F. 1998, *Australia at the Crossroads: Radical free market or progressive liberalism?*, Allen and Unwin, St Leonards.

ABC 1999, *Four Corners* transcript: 'War of the Words', 9 August. Available at: http://www.abc.net.au/4corners/stories/s44493.htm.

Anderson, G. and A. Parkin 2010, 'Federalism: A fork in the road?', in C. Aulich and M. Evans (eds), *The Rudd Government: Australian Commonwealth Administration 2007–10*, ANU E Press, Canberra.

Arthur, E. 2011, interview by Trish Mercer, 31 August 2011.

---

28   Hollander and Patapan highlight the risk that a pragmatic federal approach, especially where there are crisis driven policy formulations, can have unintended consequences: Hollander and Patapan 2007, p. 291.

Arthur, E. 2012, interview by Wendy Jarvie and Trish Mercer, 4 May 2012.

AUSPELD (The Australian Federation of SPELD Associations) 2005, 'Submission to the National Inquiry into the Teaching of Literacy'. Available at: http://auspeld.org.au/wp-content/uploads/2010/08/2005_auspeld_nat_inq.pdf.

Australianpolitics.com 2001, 'Election policy speech by John Howard', 28 October. Available at: http://australianpolitics.com/2000/10/28/john-howard-election-policy-speech.html.

Bamford, P. 2010, 'Teaching to the Test', 7 April. Available at: http://inside.org.au/teaching-to-the-test/.

Boston, K. 2013, Interview by Wendy Jarvie and Trish Mercer, 21 February 2013.

Channel Nine 1999, *Sunday* transcript, 13 June 1999. Available at: http://sgp1.paddington.ninemsn.com.au/sunday/political_transcripts/transcript_340.asp.

Comber, B., B. Green, B. Lingard and A. Luke 1998, 'Literacy Debates and Public Debates: A question of "crisis"?', in A. Reid (ed.), *Going Public: Education policy and public education in Australia*, Australian Curriculum Studies Association in association with the Centre for the Study of Public Education at the University of South Australia, Canberra.

Daniels, B. 2013, Interview by Trish Mercer, 3 April 2013.

DEETYA 2002, 'Annual Report'. Available at: http://www.dest.gov.au/portfolio_department/dest_information/publications_resources/profiles/deetya_annual_report.

DETYA (Department of Employment, Training and Youth Affairs) 1999, 'Annual Report'. Available at: http://www.voced.edu.au/content/ngv22140.

DETYA 2001, 'Annual Report'. Available at: http://www.voced.edu.au/content/ngv20768.

Dowling, A. 2008. *Output Measurement in Education, Policy Analysis and Program Evaluation*, Australian Council for Educational Research. Available at: http://research.acer.edu.au/policy_analysis_misc/2.

Gill, M. 1998, 'Who Set the Benchmarks?: Analysing the national literacy agenda', *English in Australia* 121. Available at: http://www.aate.org.au/documents/item/477.

Gonski, D., K. Boston, K. Greiner, C. Lawrence, B. Scales and P. Tannock 2011, 'Review of Funding for Schooling: Final report'. Available at: http://www. schoolfunding.gov.au/review.

Harrington, M. and S. McDonald 1999, *Literacy: A chronology of selected research and Commonwealth policy initiatives since 1975*, Parliamentary Library, Parliament of Australia, Canberra. Available at: http://aph.gov. au/parlinfo/download/library/prspub/QWJ06/upload_binary/qwj066. pdf;fileType=application/pdf.

Hollander, R. and H. Patapan 2007, 'Pragmatic Federalism: Australian federalism from Hawke to Howard', *The Australian Journal of Public Administration* 66(3).

Howard, J. 2010, *Lazarus Rising: A personal and political autobiography*, Harper Collins, Pymble.

Kelly, P. 2006, 'Re-Thinking Australian Governance: The Howard legacy', *Australian Journal of Public Administration* 65(1).

Kemp, D. A. 1988, *Foundations for Australian Political Analysis Politics and Authority*, Oxford University Press, South Melbourne.

Kemp, D. A. 1991, 'Mediocrity or Excellence', address to National Press Club, 3 July, recording held by National Library of Australia, Canberra.

Kemp, D. A. 'Media releases 1996–99', previously in Minister Archive on Commonwealth Department of Education, Science and Training (DEST) website.

Kemp, D. A. 1999, 'Knowledge and Innovation: A policy statement on research and research training', Department of Education, Training and Youth Affairs.

Kemp, D. A. 2012, interview by Wendy Jarvie and Trish Mercer, 6 August 2012.

Kemp, D. A. 2013, personal communication, 19 February 2013.

Liberals and Nationals Election Platform 1996, 'Schools and TAFE'. Available at: http://parlinfo.aph.gov.au/parlinfo/download/library/partypol/1279303.

Lindquist, E. and J. Wanna 2011, 'Delivering Policy Reform: Making it happen, making it stick', in E. Lindquist, S. Vincent and J. Wanna (eds), *Delivering Policy Reform: Anchoring significant reforms in turbulent times*, ANU E Press, Canberra.

Lingard, B. 2009, 'Testing Times: The need for new intelligent accountabilities for schooling', *QTU Professional Magazine*, November.

Lo Bianco, J. and P. Freebody 1997, *Australian Literacies: Informing national policy on literacy education*, Language Australia, Melbourne.

MCNSELS (Management Committee for the National School English Literacy Survey) 1997, 'Mapping Literacy Achievement Results of the 1996 National School English Literacy Survey', Commonwealth Department of Employment, Education, Training and Youth Affairs, Canberra.

Martin, R. 1997, 'Manufacturing the Literacy Crisis', *Australian Educator: The magazine of the Australian Education Union* 16.

Masters, G. 2012, Interview by Wendy Jarvie and Trish Mercer, 28 June 2012.

Masters, G. and Forster, M. 1997, 'Literacy Standards in Australia', Dept of Employment, Education, Training and Youth Affairs (DEETYA). Available at: http://research.acer.edu.au/cgi/viewcontent.cgi?article=1005&context=m onitoring_learning&sei-redir=1&referer=http%3A%2F%2Fwww.google. com.au%2Fsearch%3Fclient%3Dsafari%26rls%3Den%26q%3DLiteracy %2BStandards%2Bin%2BAustralia%25E2%2580%2599%2C%2Bin%2B Monitoring%2BLearning%26ie%3DUTF-8%26oe%3DUTF-8%26gfe_rd% 3Dcr%26ei%3DVOsgVObTGsiN8QenrYCgBw#search=%22Literacy%20 Standards%20Australia'%2C%20Monitoring%20Learning%22.

MCEECDYA (Ministerial Council for Education, Early Childhood Development and Youth Affairs) 1996–2001, 'Information Statements Released by Former Ministerial Councils', Ministerial Council for Education, Employment, Training and Youth Affairs. Available at: http://www.mceecdya.edu.au/ mceecdya/about_mceecdya,11318.html.

National Independent Schools Council Board Minutes, various dates. Independent Schools Council of Australia, Canberra.

Nous Group, Melbourne Graduate School of Education (MGSE) and National Institute of Labour Studies (NILS) 2011, 'Schooling Challenges and Opportunities: A report for the review of funding for schooling panel', August. Available at: http://www.Nousgroup.com.au/NILS/MGSE.

Peach, F. 1998, 'The National Literacy and Numeracy Strategies: Implications for educators', *Unicorn Journal of the Australian College of Educators*, 24(2), Special Issue: Literacy and Numeracy.

Reid, A. 1998, 'Preface', in A. Reid (ed.), *Going Public: Education policy and public education in Australia*, Australian Curriculum Studies Association in association with the Centre for the Study of Public Education at the University of South Australia, Canberra.

Sedgwick, S. 2012, interview by Wendy Jarvie and Trish Mercer, 3 August 2012.

SEEWRC (Senate Education, Employment and Workplace Relations Committee) 2010, 'Inquiry into Administration and Reporting of NAPLAN Testing', Parliament of Australia.

Senior, P. 2008, 'Liberal Party Policy Challenges', in P. Van Onselen (ed.), *Liberals and Power: The road ahead*, Melbourne University Press, Melbourne.

SCRRCSSP (Steering Committee for Review of Commonwealth/State Service Provision) 1998, 'Report on Government Service Provision', Commonwealth Government.

Spring, G. 2013, Interview by Wendy Jarvie and Trish Mercer, 25 March 2013.

't Hart, P. 2011, 'Epilogue: Rules for reformers', in E. Lindquist, S. Vincent and J. Wanna, *Delivering Policy Reform: Anchoring significant reforms in turbulent times*, ANU E Press, Canberra.

Vromen, A., K. Gelber and A. Gauja 2009, *Powerscape: Contemporary Australian politics*, Allen and Unwin, Crows Nest.

Watson, L. 2011, 'Federalism and Education Policy: The USA and Australia compared', paper presented to School of Business, University of New South Wales, Canberra, 19 May.

Wilkinson, I., B. Caldwell, R. Selleck, J. Harris and P. Dettman 2007, *A History of State Aid to Non-Government Schools in Australia*, Department of Education, Science and Training, Commonwealth of Australia, Canberra.

12. Cross-Jurisdictional Performance Audits: Impacts and options for the Australian National Audit Office

Patricia Gerald

'To attack the Auditor-General, is to seek to weaken the Parliament. To weaken the Parliament's ability to hold the executive to account is to attack and weaken the centrepiece of our defences against tyranny and corruption. It is an attack on the people itself.'
— *Former Commonwealth Auditor-General, John Taylor* (The Age, 5 December 1996, p. 17)

Introduction

The lack of auditing of Commonwealth transfers to states and territories in Australia has been described as a 'glaring gap' in the accountability of Commonwealth spending (Wanna and Podger 2009). Payments to the states and territories amounted to $97 billion in 2011–12, representing 25.7 per cent of total Commonwealth expenditure, a significant source of funding for services provided to Australians including education, health, and Indigenous programs (Australian Government 2012). Some of these transfers are unconditional, but many are conditional, with specific Commonwealth objectives or expected outcomes. In 2011–12, conditional transfers amounted to $49.9 billion (Australian Government 2012). Although the Commonwealth Parliament remains accountable for the efficient and effective spending of conditional funds by the recipient states and territories, according to the pre-agreed terms, the Commonwealth Auditor-General has not reviewed these transfers.

The governing legislation of the Commonwealth Auditor-General is regularly reviewed by the Joint Committee of Public Accounts and Audit (JCPAA), a parliamentary committee tasked with ensuring that audit legislation remains current, relevant and sufficient for the Auditor-General to carry out his mandate. The 2009 review, 'Inquiry into the *Auditor-General Act 1997*', highlighted gaps in accountability, particularly in areas of spending made by 'agents' of the Commonwealth: a private sector contractor, non-governmental organisation (NGO), government business enterprise (GBE), or other level of government, such as a state, territory or local government. The review resulted in several amendments to the Commonwealth *Auditor-General Act 1997*, including the addition of powers to allow the conduct of performance audits of these agents, referred to as 'Commonwealth Partners'. These powers often referred to as 'follow-the-money' provisions were awarded to the Auditor-General with the intent of addressing these gaps in accountability.

As the Commonwealth Auditor-General begins to conduct these audits, in the case of state and territory governments it will involve crossing jurisdictional and constitutional boundaries into areas traditionally accessed only by state and territory auditors-general. Such access could impact a variety of stakeholders and further strain an already tenuous Commonwealth–state relationship. The Commonwealth Auditor-General is wading into politically and administratively sensitive terrain.

This study examines the new provision allowing the Commonwealth Auditor-General to conduct audits of states and territories, referred to in this report as cross-jurisdictional performance audits (CJPAs), and seeks to answer two central research questions:

- How will the introduction of CJPAs of states and territories by the Commonwealth Auditor-General likely impact key stakeholders, including the Australian National Audit Office (ANAO)?
- How does this approach to inter-jurisdictional auditing compare to alternative approaches such as cooperative audits, both in Australia and internationally?

By identifying areas of impact, this investigation seeks to help the ANAO anticipate challenges to the introduction of CJPAs, promote discussion about alternatives, and develop options for optimal implementation.

This research is informed by a review of the literature on performance audit, an international scan of the mandates of other auditors-general, interviews with Australian auditors-general and other key individuals, and an online survey of national audit offices in other jurisdictions on their views on inter-jurisdictional auditing. Based on these findings, a summary of key stakeholder impacts is presented, including impacts on the ANAO's performance audit process, followed by a framework for comparing different approaches to inter-jurisdictional audit and options for implementation at the ANAO.

Background and context

This section provides necessary background about the Commonwealth Auditor-General and the events leading up to the current amendments.[1] First, it provides an overview of the role of the Auditor-General and performance audit at the

---

1 Information in this section was gathered from a variety of sources including gray literature, government and professional association websites, internet searches, news media, academic journals and books.

ANAO. It then outlines the current state of Commonwealth–state relations, with a specific focus on federal financial transfers and why they are a concern in terms of auditing and accountability. This is followed by a review of the amendment process and outcomes. The final part identifies the Auditor-General's key stakeholder relationships.

Accountability and the role of the Auditor-General

The Commonwealth Auditor-General is an independent officer of the legislature responsible to the federal Parliament for providing oversight of government operations and expenditures (see Figure 1). The Auditor-General supports accountability through the provision of financial, compliance and performance auditing services to Parliament and all federal public sector entities (ANAO 2011). Supported by the ANAO and broad access-to-information and premises powers under the *Auditor-General Act 1997*, the Auditor-General can identify areas for investigation and recommend improvements in public administration and service delivery (ANAO 2011). Despite the combined revenues and expenses of the General Government Sector of some $675 billion, the ANAO carries out its oversight duties with an annual budget of only $78m, or roughly 0.01 per cent of the total (McPhee 2011).

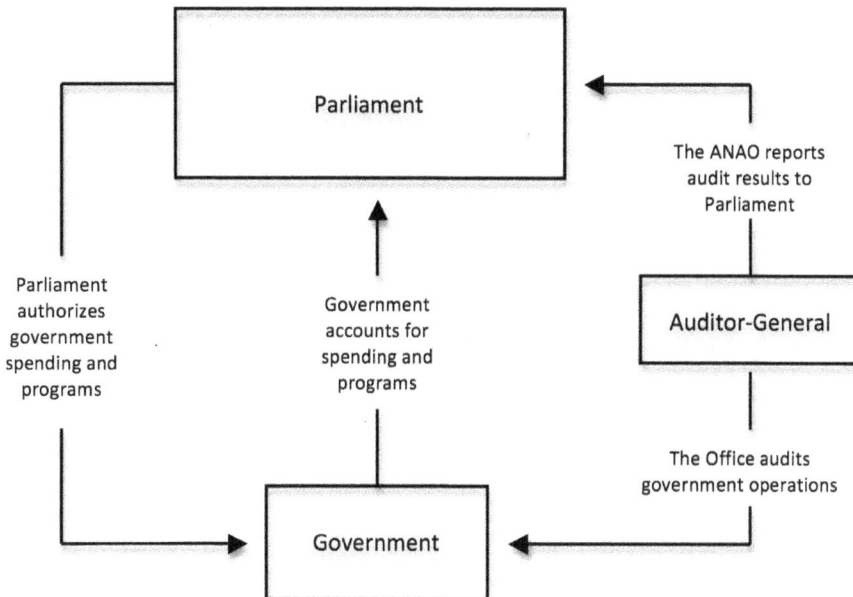

Figure 1: The role of the Auditor-General as an independent officer of the Parliament

Source: Adapted from Office of the Auditor-General of Canada 2007, p.4.

Performance audit

Until 1979, the Auditor-General provided oversight through traditional audit practices known as financial or attest audits, and, in some cases, through compliance audits. Over the years it became increasingly clear that a financial account of *how much* was spent did not tell an adequate story for accountability purposes as to *how well* money had been spent, or whether value for money had been achieved. Something was needed to assess the managers and departments responsible for making spending and operational decisions, especially in light of 'perceived concerns about wasteful use of money and other resources' (Wanna, Ryan and Ng 2001, pp. 206–207).

In 1979, the ANAO was given the authority to carry out 'efficiency audits', which marked the beginning of an entirely new role for the Auditor-General, and a major expansion in his work. It also led a fundamental change in the ANAO's relationship with stakeholders (Wanna, Ryan and Ng 2001, p. 203), particularly with the departments and agencies they audit, known as 'auditees'. No longer simply reviewing financial accounts, auditors would develop audit-specific performance criteria and assess management performance against those criteria. Some areas of the public sector resisted the new practices, which were seen as 'a threat to their operations, responsibilities and policy capabilities' (Wanna, Ryan and Ng 2001, p. 204). By 1997, new legislation renamed efficiency audits as 'performance audits' (see Figure 2), and today they represent about 40 per cent of the ANAO's overall spending (ANAO 2012b). Approximately 56 performance audits are conducted and tabled in Parliament each year.[2]

The Australian federal context

As in many federal nations, the relationship between the Commonwealth and state governments in Australia is often strained. Since the Commonwealth has few exclusive powers but is involved to a high degree in shared functions, grievances between the jurisdictions often stem out of conflicts over the Commonwealth's involvement in these areas that are constitutionally the responsibility of the states (see Twomey and Withers 2007). This is compounded by a vertical fiscal imbalance, which sees the Commonwealth centrally raising the majority of the tax revenue while the states, with limited revenue-raising capacity, are left with higher public expenditure demands that 'greatly exceed' their revenue-raising capacity (Quiggan 2005, p. 2). For example, Australian states do not have access to income tax revenues unlike many other federations (see Figure 3).

---

2   The number of performance audits undertaken can vary slightly from year to year.

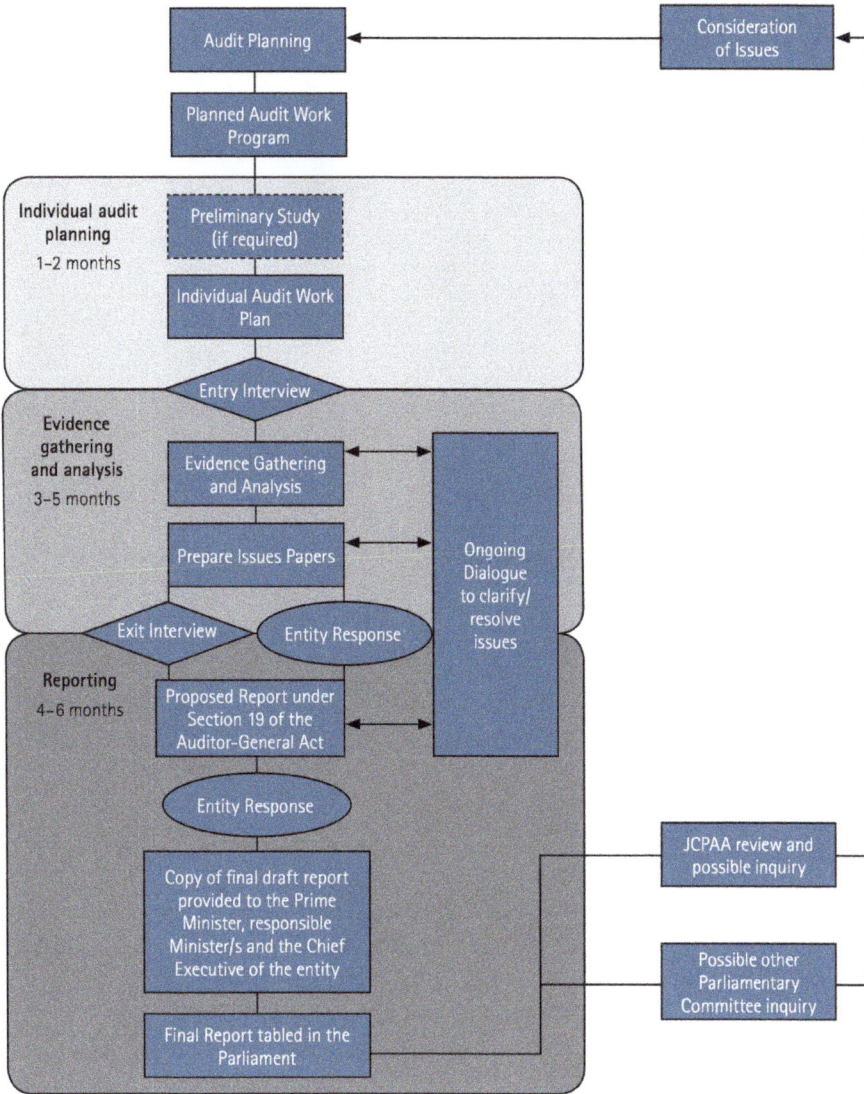

Figure 2: Standard performance audit process at the ANAO

Source: ANAO 2008, p. 5.

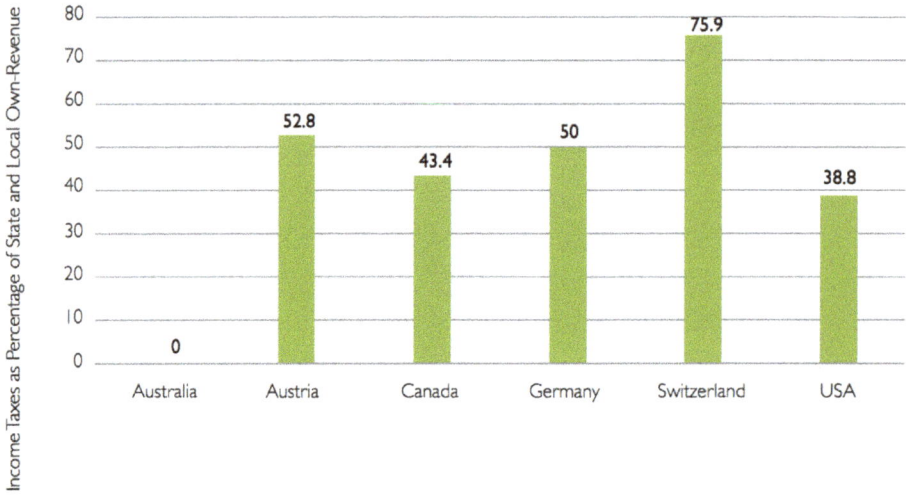

Figure 3: State government access to income taxes: Selected federations, 1965–2004

Source: Twomey and Withers 2007, p. 39.

To address this fiscal imbalance, states and territories in Australia are given significant annual financial support from the Commonwealth government, amounting to $97 billion in 2011–12, about 25.7 per cent of the Commonwealth's total expenditure (Australian Government 2012). In some cases, transfers can be as much as 60 per cent of a state's total revenue (Quiggan 2005). Not surprisingly, such dependence has increased the Commonwealth's power and influence (Fenna 2008), producing a federation more centralised than originally intended (Podger and Wanna 2012). Some critics refer to this dynamic as 'opportunistic federalism', whereby the Commonwealth, 'picks and chooses State issues upon which to intervene for political purposes' (Twomey and Withers 2007, p. 28), effectively rendering the states as service delivery agents of the Commonwealth.

In 2009, the Council of Australian Governments (COAG) introduced reforms to address vertical fiscal imbalance-related issues including a commitment by the Commonwealth to provide ongoing financial support for states' service delivery in three ways, including general revenue assistance, National Specific Purpose Payments (SPPs) and National Partnership Payments (NPPs). The latter two payments are considered to be conditional grants because they are attached to a set of Commonwealth objectives, outcomes, outputs and performance indicators. Although performance reporting associated with the SPPs and NPPs is managed by the COAG Reform Council and the COAG Standing Council on Federal

Financial Relations, prior to the 2011 amendments to the *Auditor-General Act 1997*, these payments were not subject to the oversight of the Commonwealth Auditor-General, nor by state level auditors.

Despite the financial framework reforms, federal financial transfers end up as services delivered by both jurisdictions. For example, responsibility for education services rests with the state governments, yet the Commonwealth makes contributions to education through its $9.7 billion National Schools SPP. Since SPPs are attached to national policy objectives, the Commonwealth government is responsible for attaining these objectives, yet the accountability attached to the Commonwealth portion of the funds rests with states for proper management and reporting to the Commonwealth as to how the funds were spent.

The JCPAA and the Inquiry into the Auditor-General Act 1997

In 2009, the *Inquiry into the Auditor-General Act 1997* (the Inquiry) was undertaken by the JCPAA. Representing the formal link between the Commonwealth Auditor-General and the Australian Parliament, the JCPAA is a parliamentary committee that informs the Auditor-General of the Parliament's audit priorities, recommends the resource levels for the ANAO (McPhee 2012), and regularly reviews the legislation to ensure it remains relevant in the modern public sector environment (ANAO 2012a). While the 2009 review was considered to be routine (eight years had passed since the previous one), its timing could not have been more opportune for the Auditor-General in light of the recent reforms to the federal financial relations framework.

One area the JCPAA was interested in reviewing was the Auditor-General's 'capacity to examine the financial and performance outcomes from Commonwealth investments in the private sector and Commonwealth grants made to State and local governments' (JCPAA 2010, p. xi).

Such access is often called 'follow-the-money' legislation, as it enables the auditors to follow the spending trail from end-to-end without being restricted once service delivery leaves the Commonwealth jurisdiction. References to 'follow-the-money' legislation often bundle together the ability to audit transfers to any third party or Commonwealth partner, including states and territories, private companies or NGOs. However, there is a significant difference between auditing contractors and auditing state and territory partners, and this issue figures prominently later on in this report.

In a submission to the Inquiry, the Institute of Public Administration of Australia made reference to the financial transfers to the states and territories, showing concern that 'the Commonwealth Auditor-General does not audit these programs against the agreed objectives, nor do state Auditors-General', and that 'states may report back on their claimed performance but the Commonwealth has no real check as to their validity and reliability,' (JCPAA 2010, p. 58). The Commonwealth Auditor-General confirmed the notion of the 'gap', explaining that the ANAO is 'constrained at the moment to look at state performance or the performance of grantees under [the] act, so it is a central issue' (McPhee 2010, p. 8). An issue further compounded by the recent reforms to the federal financial framework, which relaxed the Commonwealth prescriptions on state service delivery (JCPAA 2010).

To address the cross-jurisdictional issues in the JCPAA's terms of reference for the Inquiry, the ANAO identified options in order of potential impact and preference:

- Full access powers to audit states and territories in receipt of transfers 'in circumstances where there is a corresponding or reciprocal responsibility to deliver specified outcomes in accordance with agreed arrangements'.

- The same as above, but rather than amend the Auditor-General's legislation, the powers could be provided via separate legislation governing SPPs.

- Make it mandatory that SPP legislation and agreements include access provisions for the Auditor-General — something already occurring on an ad hoc basis.

- Explore 'further cooperation between the Auditor-General and the state and territory Auditors-General', the preferred option of other stakeholders, such as the Australian Council of Auditors-General and the Institute of Public Administration of Australia (ANAO 2009).

Further cooperation meant pursuing cooperative audits between the Commonwealth and state auditors-general to address issues of mutual concern, in this case the federal transfers. However, the cooperative audit approach did not receive much discussion by the JCPAA after ANAO flagged the secrecy and information sharing provisions in the Act, different audit office priorities, and the challenges with synching performance audit cycles with each other, making the timing of the phases difficult to align.

Resulting amendments and the new mandate

In their final report, the JCPAA recommended enhancements to the mandate of the Auditor-General, including the power to conduct cross-jurisdictional performance audits of states and territories. By December 2011, Parliament had endorsed several amendments to the Act, which represented 'the most significant enhancement of the auditor-general's mandate since the addition of efficiency audit powers in 1979' (INTOSAI 2012a). The new legislation allowed for the audit of 'Commonwealth partners', a term used to group together any recipient or contractor receiving money directly or indirectly from the Commonwealth for a particular purpose. This includes state and territory bodies, but, in these cases, an audit may only be conducted at the request of the JCPAA or the responsible Commonwealth minister. However, the Auditor-General can ask the JCPAA or the responsible minister to request such an audit (ANAO 2012a).

The Auditor-General will need to employ this new power in a way that develops its legitimacy. However, performance auditing is often a high-profile activity. It is unclear what plans exist for conducting cross-jurisdictional performance audits, and what reactions might emerge from the states, territories, and other stakeholders.

Summary of key stakeholder relationships

Although the Auditor-General and the ANAO derive credibility from their independence and objectivity, the development of meaningful relationships is also central to the execution of the mandate. Such relationships can help to promote the value of the Auditor-General and the ANAO to the public sector, which points to the need to manage expectations (Wanna, Ryan and Ng 2001). What follows reviews key stakeholder relationships, including potential new ones which might emerge with the introduction of CJPAs and possibly some form of cooperative auditing.

Parliament and the JCPAA

As part of its regular operations, the ANAO 'provides briefings to ministers, shadow ministers, parliamentary committees and their staff on audit reports tabled in the Parliament' (Barrett 2002, p. 35) making the Auditor-General's relationship with Parliament a critical activity of the audit office. Despite the emphasis on the significance of independence, the Auditor-General's objectives can only be fully met with the 'trust and respect of the Parliament' (Barrett 2002, p. 45). By extension, this notion of trust also holds true for the Auditor-General's relationship with the JCPAA. The JCPAA must determine the audit priorities of Parliament, advise the Auditor-General of those priorities, and review all reports tabled by the Auditor-General in each house of Parliament. The JCPAA oversees the operations, resources and external audit of the ANAO, reporting to both houses on matters relating the Auditor-General's functions and powers they believe require attention.

Auditees: Departments and agencies

A positive relationship with an auditee makes for a more efficient audit. Since 1995, the ANAO has considered auditees to be important stakeholders (Wanna, Ryan and Ng 2001). Cooperation is necessary and encouraged for building trust, adding value, maintaining credibility, and ultimately gaining 'genuine acceptance of [the ANAO's] recommendations' (Barrett 2002, p. 38).

Commonwealth-level departments and agencies could have a stake in the new CJPA process. Prior to CJPA access, performance audits were limited by restrictions to the assessment of Commonwealth level entities, and in the cases of transfers to states and territories, the ANAO could only comment on the performance of those Commonwealth entities in managing state and territory agents, and without access to state and territory files. The case for CJPAs flows from the idea of an end-to-end audit that includes access to the state and territory agencies as well as assessing management of services funded by the Commonwealth. CJPAs have the potential of revealing issues at the state and territory level which have not been seen and which could be detrimental to the Commonwealth departments as well as state and territorial governments.

Executive coordinators (central agencies): Treasury, Finance, Prime Minister and Cabinet

Wanna, Ryan and Ng (2001) describe the relationship between the Auditor-General and central agencies as one of ambivalence: they have a mutual interest in accountability, but the potential for exposure is a political risk. Risk is typically high because central agencies are 'active players with their own agendas and powers and have a major say in determining many of the circumstances under which the Audit Office operates' (Wanna, Ryan and Ng 2001, p. 247).

In the context of this report, the Commonwealth central agencies can be seen as having a vested interest in extending the powers of the Auditor-General in order to improve accountability for intergovernmental transfers, and, in particular, if they seek to shift the focus to the management and performance of states and territories.

Professional bodies and international associations

The ANAO maintains relationships with several domestic professional associations, including Chartered Practising Accountants Australia and the Institute of Chartered Accountants Australia, and makes contributions to developing accounting and auditing standards to the Australian Accounting Standards Board and the Auditing and Assurance Standards Board (ANAO 2012a).

The ANAO is also a member of several international and regional institutions, with the primary purposes of information sharing, training and development, and setting of international standards. The most important among these groups is the International Organisation of Supreme Audit Institutions (INTOSAI), represented by 170 Auditors-General around the world. The ANAO sits on the Global Working Group, Professional Standards Committee, Performance Audit Subcommittee, and Working Group on Environmental Auditing (ANAO 2012a). INTOSAI is a venue where offices can share ideas and promote better practices. The introduction of CJPAs could have an impact internationally if Australia is deemed an innovator in auditing of intergovernmental transfers.

Media, academics, commentators and the public

The media often plays a role in highlighting the ANAO's work. Although the ANAO maintains a public website containing its reports and better practice guides, the extent of media coverage depends on what is said in Parliament. The media can play a major role in shaping public perceptions about the quality of the programs and services of the Commonwealth, as well as those of academics and other commentators. Ultimately, the Auditor-General and the ANAO aim to improve public administration, and it is important to maintain links with the media and to the public. Academics and other sector specialists can also assist the Auditor-General (Lonsdale 2008), especially when there is a need for expertise in certain issue areas that is not available in-house.

The addition of CJPAs to the Auditor-General's mandate could influence the public. As voters, they elect different representatives to the Commonwealth and state and territory governments, creating two chains of accountability. Changing how accountability works or increasing transparency of operations could impact the public's perception of both levels of government and ultimately confidence in the political process, perceptions of the quality of public services, and even voting behaviour.

ANAO (internal relationships)

Internally, the Auditor-General has one stakeholder: ANAO staff. The Performance Audit Services Group will be the most impacted by the new legislation, but the entire office could also be influenced because a new set of program activities may affect resourcing, staff experience, planning, and timing of audits. The CJPA approach may affect the performance audit process at each of the stages.

New stakeholder relationships post-amendments

Figure 4 depicts the external stakeholder relationships that may arise at the state level if the Auditor-General moves forward with CJPAs and possibly cooperative audits.

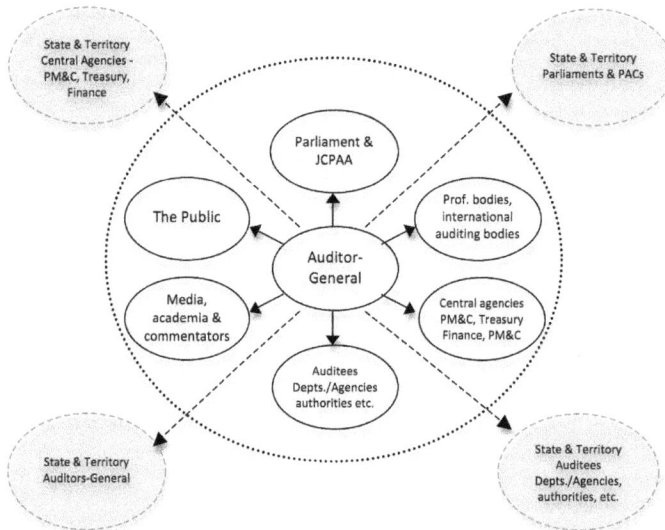

Figure 4: Anticipated stakeholder relationships of the Auditor-General during CJPAs

Source: Adapted from Wanna, Ryan and Ng 2001, p. 230.

State and territory auditors-general

All six states in Australia have Auditors-General, as do the Northern Territory and the Australian Capital Territory. Until recently, contact between these auditors-general has occurred primarily at the bi-annual meetings of the Australasian Council of Auditors-General.[3] The Commonwealth Auditor-General occasionally contacts auditors-general in other jurisdictions, but separate jurisdictional mandates and responsibility to different parliaments tends to discourage such contact.

The introduction of CJPAs and possible cooperative audits could significantly affect state and territory auditors-general. There could be an increase in time demands from the Commonwealth Auditor-General not only through consultation and information sharing, but because of the potential impacts on

---

3   The Australian Council of Auditors-General includes members from Fiji, New Zealand and Papua New Guinea.

their own performance audit programs. Commonwealth CJPAs may stir state and territory parliamentary interest in a topic not previously identified in their annual audit work programs. It is possible that the new legislation for CJPAs might force more interest by the state and territory auditors-general into cooperative audits in order to keep the Commonwealth Auditor-General out of their turf. Again, this would serve to shift state and territory audit priorities.

State and territory parliaments and PACs

Although state and territory parliaments and public accounts committees (PACs) may not be directly impacted by CJPAs, indirect impact may occur depending on the audit topic. If a CJPA has significant outcomes at the state and territory level, the respective parliaments might take notice and demand action or further investigation by state or territory governments or their respective auditors-general. CJPAs could also induce the state and territory auditors-general to pursue more cooperative audits with the Commonwealth Auditor-General, potentially diverting attention from previously identified state and territory audit priorities.

State and territory executive coordinators: Treasury, Finance, Premier and Cabinet

The states and territories are inextricably linked to the Commonwealth government, due to financial transfers. State governments have always had an interest in the accountability arrangements for intergovernmental transfers with respect to whether the Commonwealth was spending its own money efficiently and if it had 'handed over the due surpluses' (Wanna, Ryan and Ng 2001).

However, the introduction of CJPAs could change this relationship if the states and territories feel threatened by the new powers, particularly when audits leave them exposed or portrayed negatively. Mere access alone is enough to cause friction in light of historical mistrust between the states and territories and the Commonwealth, and explains the frequent references to sovereignty and constitutional rights when CJPAs were a prospect. Conversely, there is potential for positive outcomes for the states and territories from CJPAs in cases which might expose Commonwealth mismanagement or at best invite changes to the often-criticised restrictions and prescriptions placed on the transferred funds, which can result in perverse spending by the states and territories.

State and territory auditees: Departments and agencies

State and territory departments and agencies will be a new stakeholder for the ANAO, and sentiments could be similar to those of the executive and central agencies when conducting CJPAs. As Commonwealth auditors approach state and territory departments for information, it is unclear how they will be received. Will state and territorial audit offices be expected to give advice to the departments and agencies they ordinarily audit? Will these departments and agencies simply see the ANAO as another audit office? Another set of issues will arise once issues papers are shared for review and reports released to Parliament and the public for consideration. At the very least this raises critical issues about whether and how to foster trust in such potentially difficult terrain.

Literature review

The literature review focuses on academic and professional literature relating to the emergence, development, process, application and impacts of performance audit, including its various external influences and modern day challenges. Literature on the emerging use of cross-jurisdictional and cooperative approaches to performance audit is reviewed and a conceptual framework developed to illustrate how CJPAs might impact the standard performance audit process at the ANAO.

Origins and growth of performance audit

As recent as 2011, literature on performance auditing has been described as 'underdeveloped' (Furubo 2011), and much of what is available is often focused on the qualities it shares with the field of evaluation (Chelimsky 1985; Leeuw 1996; Pollitt and Summa 1996; Pollitt et al. 1999). While there is general acceptance that performance audit has drawn considerably from the field of evaluation, particularly in the development of its methods (Lonsdale et al. 2011), this has not precluded a broad discussion of performance audit as a unique practice.

Performance audit (known also as efficiency audit and value-for-money audit) first emerged the United States in the 1920s with the establishment of the General Accounting Office (later Government Accountability Office), who had been tasked with investigating and making recommendations to Congress on greater economy or efficiency in public expenditures (Budget and Accounting Act of 1921, Sec. 312(a), 42 Stat. 25). However, performance audit began to emerge more significantly in the 1970s as a distinct practice with statutory backing at audit offices around the world, including Canada, Australia, the United Kingdom, and parts of Western Europe and Scandinavia (Pollitt et al.

1999). From seemingly humble beginnings, contemporary performance audit now takes its place as a key area of the overall audit functions carried out by auditors-general (see Figure 5).

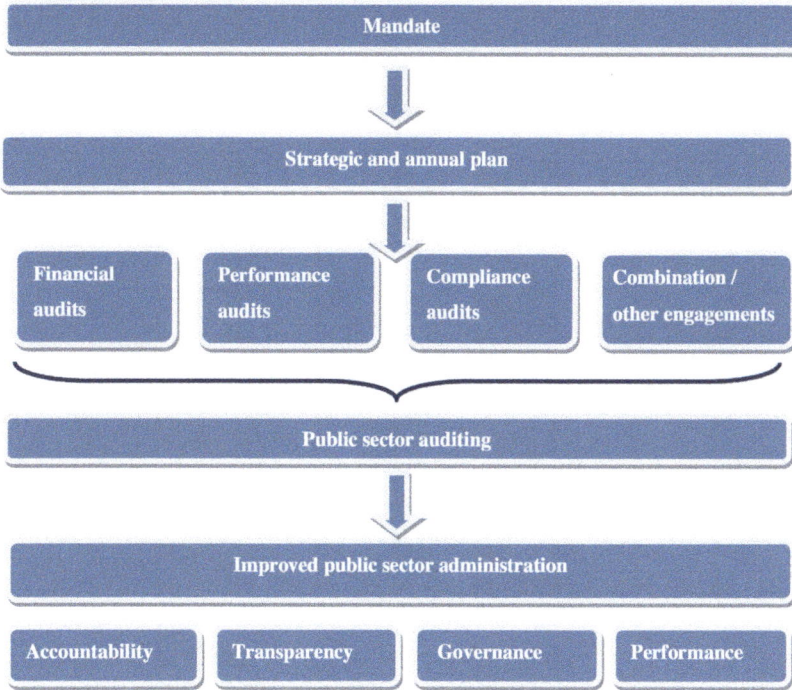

Figure 5: Role of performance audit in broader scope of activities conducted by supreme audit institutions (SAIs)

Source: INTOSAI 2012b, p. 8.

Performance audit and accountability

The notion of the inadequacy of traditional forms of audit (English and Guthrie 2000) and the subsequent emergence of performance audit, is widely recognised as a direct consequence of the widespread administrative reforms that swept across the public sector in the 1970s under 'new public management' (NPM) (see Aucoin 1990; Pollitt and Summa 1995; Leeuw 1996; English and Guthrie 2000; Gendron et al. 2007; Funnell and Wade 2012). As the reforms placed a new emphasis on 'leaner government, better service delivery, and more efficient and effective management of government programmes' (Funnell and Wade 2012, p. 435), the rules-based and process-driven routines of the past were gradually replaced with a more results-based accountability, focused on identifying desired outcomes, setting performance targets for the public service, and measuring the extent of achievement of those targets (Aucoin 1990; Hood 1991; Pollitt and Summa 1995).

Barzelay (1997, p. 235) saw the take-up of performance audit by external audit institutions as an action rationalised by NPM, while Power (1997, p. 7) suggested it represented a whole new system of values, which he referred to as the 'audit society'. Given their shared concern with efficiency and effectiveness of public spending, the strong links between NPM and performance audit are not that surprising, having been described by another author as a 'mutual co-dependency' (English and Skaerbaek 2007, p. 239).

The literature generally supports the notion that performance audits make a unique contribution to public sector accountability. For example, Pollitt (2006, p. 48) points to the ability of performance audit reports to 'command political attention', due in part to their mandatory review by parliamentary committees. Similarly, Lonsdale et al. (2011) sees performance audit reports as accountability mechanisms in their own right — the public availability of their reports offers citizens a rare window into the actual management of government operations. In Australia, Funnell (1996) and Funnell and Wade (2012, p. 447) have described performance audit as a 'source of institutional pressure, exerted on the Executive on behalf of the Parliament to account for the efficiency, effectiveness and economy with which it manages and uses public resources'.

Performance audit in practice

The academic and grey literature identifies two chief purposes of performance audit (Barzelay 1997; Pollitt and Summa 1996; Lonsdale 2000, INTOSAI 2012b). The first is to provide oversight and scrutiny of government spending, which links to the accountability and transparency aspects of governance. The second, a more recent development, is to improve public administration, or more specifically, the management practices of public sector managers.

The objectives of performance audit have been articulated in many ways, depending upon the supreme audit institution (SAI), its mandate, legislation, and resource capacity. Objectives for individual audits are usually expressed in one overall question or statement that the audit will address and can also include financial and compliance components. Auditing standards developed by INTOSAI (INTOSAI 2012b) set a baseline for the kinds of objectives an individual performance audit ought to have, including the three 'Es' often referred to by SAIs. These include an examination of one or more of the following assertions:

- *Economy* of activities in accordance with sound administrative principles and practices, and management policies. The principle of *economy* is about keeping the costs low. The resources used should be available in due time, in appropriate quantity and quality and at the best price.

- *Efficiency* of utilisation of human, financial and other resources, including examination of information systems, performance measures and monitoring arrangements, and procedures followed by audited entities for remedying identified deficiencies. The principle of *efficiency* is about getting the most from available resources. It is concerned with the relationship between resources employed, conditions given and results achieved, in terms of quantity, quality and timing of outputs or outcomes.

- *Effectiveness* of performance in relation to the achievement of the objectives of the audited entity, and the actual impact of activities compared with the intended impact. The principle of *effectiveness* is about meeting the objectives set. It is concerned with attaining the specific aims or objectives set and/or achieving the intended results. Where appropriate, the impact of the regulatory or institutional framework on the performance of the entity should also be taken into account (INTOSAI 2010, p. 2; INTOSAI 2012c, p.4).

Process and methods

Despite early views of performance audit as merely a technical discipline (Adams 1986), there has since been consistent attention paid to the variability and non-standardisation of performance audit in practice (Glynn 1985; Guthrie 1987; Hamburger 1989; Barzelay 1997; Pollitt et al. 1999). Hamburger (1989, p. 4) disagreed with the presumed objectivity of the technical performance audit, believing that, 'far from being a neutral, technical discipline, performance audit is what the auditors choose to make it'. Likewise, others have highlighted that the application of performance audit depends upon the context and the subject matter (Pugh 1987; Guthrie 1989), ultimately subject to influences of social and organisational factors (Guthrie 1989). More recently, the literature seems to have accepted this variability in application as a positive feature, referring to the benefits of its 'fluidity', 'malleability' and 'flexibility' (Jacobs 1998; Guthrie and Parker 1999), as what makes performance audit so unique (Justesen and Skaerbaek 2010; Funnell 2011; Kells 2011; Lonsdale et al. 2011). This flexibility in application is also supported in the contemporary professional literature, including implementation guidelines issued by INTOSAI (2004), which stipulate that

> performance auditing is complex investigatory work that requires flexibility, imagination and high levels of analytical skills. Streamlined procedures, methods and standards may in fact hamper the functioning and the progress of performance auditing. Consequently, standards — as well as quality assurance systems — that are too detailed should be avoided (p. 29).

Despite all the variations that may take place, there are some consistencies in practice. Many SAIs use the INTOSAI guidelines as their program foundation, followed by their individual system constraints, such as mandate and resourcing. The first step in a performance audit is the preliminary phase of topic selection. INTOSAI (2012c, p. 3) recommends that performance audit topics 'should aim to maximise the expected impact from the audit while taking into account audit capacities', which can be done by giving due regard to audit problem and or risk assessment and materiality of significance (including financial, social or political significance). Pollitt et al. (1999) identified five common selection factors: cost of the audit; the risk to public funds; coverage of the greater audit field; follow-up of earlier topics that had identified problems; and topics with high political attention.

Once topics have been approved, they go through roughly the same three phases: audit planning, conducting, and reporting (See Figure 6).

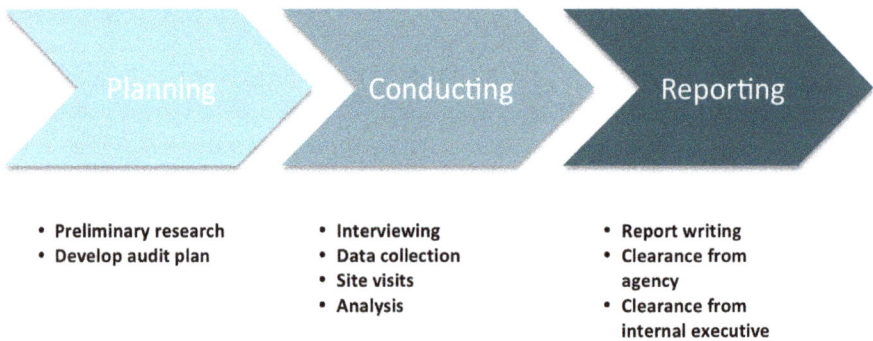

Planning	Conducting	Reporting
• Preliminary research • Develop audit plan	• Interviewing • Data collection • Site visits • Analysis	• Report writing • Clearance from agency • Clearance from internal executive

Figure 6: Typical phases of the performance audit process

Source: Adapted from various performance audit manuals in Canada, Australia, and the UK.

- *Audit planning*: The planning phase includes development of background information, risk assessment, possible evidence sources, feasibility, significance/materiality, objective, scope, methodology, resource requirements (including staff numbers and skill sets), estimated cost, and audit timeline.

- *Conducting*: The conducting phase consists of the collection and examination of the data sources as outlined in the planning phase. The nature and extent of audit evidence required for the audit is driven by the topic and the objective. Typically there is a variety of evidence collected — including physical, documentary, testimonial or analytical — the relevance of which should be explainable and justifiable. All findings and conclusions must be supported by audit evidence. Data is often sought from sources and stakeholders other than the auditee to provide a more complete picture. Analysis of all data collected also occurs in this phase.

- *Reporting*: The reporting phase involves the write up of the analysis conducted by the auditors. Each report is unique and they often vary considerably in scope and nature amongst SAIs. Reports include information about the objective of the audit, the methods, scope, criteria, data sources and findings. Findings make clear conclusions and if necessary include recommendations. All relevant viewpoints are to be considered and reported in a balanced fashion. Unless prohibited by their mandate, SAIs should always give the auditee the opportunity to comment on the audit finding, conclusions and recommendations — this process is often referred as the 'clearance process' (Sharma 2007; Lonsdale 2008) or as extending the principles of natural justice (INTOSAI 2010, p. 3–7).

Pressures and influences

The practice of performance audit does not happen in isolation. The process has both an influence on, and is influenced by the outside world. According to Lonsdale (2008) and others (Pollitt et al. 1999), these influences or pressures can have an effect on the actual conduct of the audit work. Pollitt and Summa (1999) have developed a conceptual model to represent how the basic performance audit process of an SAI is subject to various external influences, as well as to indicate how performance audit reports can make impacts on their greater operating environment (see Figure 7). Developments in public management outside of the audit environment can have impacts on how performance audits are organised internally. Likewise, recommendations from performance audit reports can result in changes in the management practices of public agencies or departments (Pollitt et al. 1999). Changes to any one element of this process can result in flow-on effects to any or all of the stakeholders involved.

Relationships

Several authors in the performance audit literature have referred to the conflicting demands placed on auditors by their various stakeholders. Put and Turksema (2011, p. 51) describe the role of an auditor as a constant 'balancing act between listening to stakeholders and safeguarding their independent position', while Wanna, Ryan and Ng (2001, p. 229) point to the inevitability that each of these stakeholders will have different expectations and perceptions of the auditors based upon the nature of each of these relationships. For the government bodies or auditees, the audit needs to be useful, and to be a learning experience for them. At the same time, Parliament is also considered a main client of most SAIs, and therefore their focus is 'much more on performance compliance and transparency, and where independent opinions are considered of prime importance' (Put and Turksema 2011, p. 52).

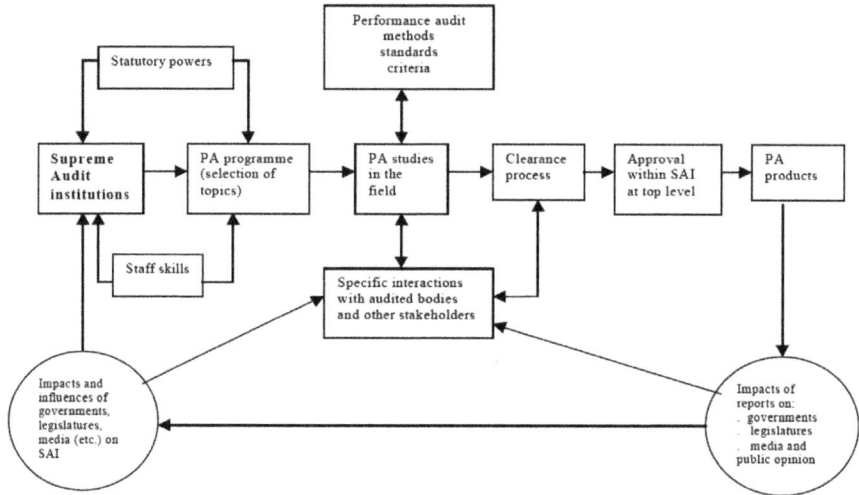

Figure 7: Influences on the performance audit process

Source: Pollitt and Summa 1999, p. 8.

The implications of poor stakeholder relationships in Australia have been long documented by Funnell (1998, 2003) and others (Taylor 1996; Guthrie and Parker 1999; English and Guthrie 2000; Lonsdale 2008), particularly with respect to attempts by the executive government in Australia to limit the intrusions of performance audit by 'attacking the reputations of auditors-general and their staff' (Funnell and Wade 2012). Funnell and Wade (2012) cite similar instances in other countries such as the UK and Canada, where their executives have attempted to undermine audit credibility through a variety of measures including:

> limiting their resources, challenging their mandates and denigrating the quality of individual reports, accusing the auditors of blinkered naivety which leads to incomplete findings, and an alleged tendency to encroach on policy issues (Funnell and Wade 2012, p. 439; see also Sutherland 2001).

The relationship between auditors and auditees is also well documented in the literature (Keen 1999; Morin 2001, 2008; Sharma 2007; Talbot and Wiggan 2010; Funnell and Wade 2012). Keen (1999, p. 522) highlighted the amount of negotiation required between auditor and auditee and the inevitability of their disagreement due to different belief systems and assumptions. Similarly, Morin (2001, p. 115) has observed the complexity of the relationship, 'where perceptions of reality outweigh reality itself, where power plays occur and where the reactions of both parties are quite unpredictable'. More recently, Funnell and Wade (2012) have summarised the 'persistent problems' between auditors and auditees at the ANAO over the years, and found that much of the tension results from a difference of interests and perceived value. Auditors have an interest in the 'survival and growth' of performance audit and believe in its ability to add value to public administration, while auditees tended to view the practice in a negative light, and question the credibility of the practice in an attempt to 'protect themselves and their agency' (Funnell and Wade 2012, p. 446). Despite some evidence of auditees responding with compromise, Funnel and Wade (2012, p. 447) document the 'overwhelmingly ... resistant forms of tactical behaviour ... especially those associated with the strategic responses of defiance and manipulation'.

Other external relationships include those with academics, consultants and specialists who provide the Auditor-General with sector specific or technical knowledge on some audits. Many audit agencies — including the Office of the Auditor General of Canada and the UK National Audit Office — access experts with reference or expert panels (Lonsdale 2008), perceived as playing a 'major part in the development of VFM [value for money] quality assurance processes' (Lonsdale 2008, p. 236). Academics, for example, often assist agencies in developing performance audit methods as well as in clarifying the links between evidence and conclusions (Lonsdale 2008).

Impacts

Clearly relationships play an important role in the performance audit process, and many SAIs have taken efforts to improve these relationships based upon the belief that they will result in more positive impacts. Often this is done through follow-up audits, where auditors check to see whether earlier recommendations were followed (Pollitt et al. 1999; van der Knaap 2011), but others take measures on the front-end of an audit to encourage uptake of the entire process. In Australia for example, the ANAO commits itself to a 'no surprises' approach to performance audits:

> The ANAO seeks to establish a relationship with entities and other parties such that there are 'no surprises' in the final audit report. This approach provides opportunities for entities and other parties to discuss the audit findings during the course of the audit. The benefit of this approach is to ensure that reports are accurate, evidence-based, balanced and fair. (ANAO 2012a, p. 8)

This approach has been further supported by a shift in focus from government waste and program failures — sometimes referred to as 'gotcha' audits — to reports focused on opportunities for learning and the promotion of better practices (Barrett 2011). Lonsdale (2000; Lonsdale et al. 2011) observed this shift in focus as a move towards the notion that performance audits ought to 'add value' to the greater world of public administration and management, by 'identifying better ways of doing things' (Lonsdale 2000). Part of this was accomplished by shifting the timing of performance audits from an almost exclusively *ex post* approach to one that included the commencement of audits *during* the implementation of programs, the idea being that early intervention would help identify better practices as the programs rolled out and result in better impacts. In addition, some SAIs now develop their audit recommendations so that lessons learned can have a broader application beyond the audited department, while others develop stand alone better practice guides, which provide generalised advice on range of topics affecting public sector managers.[4]

Empirical studies that measure impacts have long been highlighted as a deficiency in the performance audit literature by several authors, including Wilkins (1995), Lonsdale et al. (1999), Morin (2001, 2008), and Barrett (2011). As one Auditor-General in Australia has observed, 'it's the holy grail for us that we all try to work out. You can see things change, and for the better, but trying to measure it is very difficult'. Barrett (2011) has echoed this sentiment and places emphasis on the achievement of identifiable outcomes for performance audit as a better way to measure impacts.

---

4   For examples, refer to the ANAO website at www.anao.gov.au, the NAO website at www.nao.org.uk, or the GAO at www.gao.gov

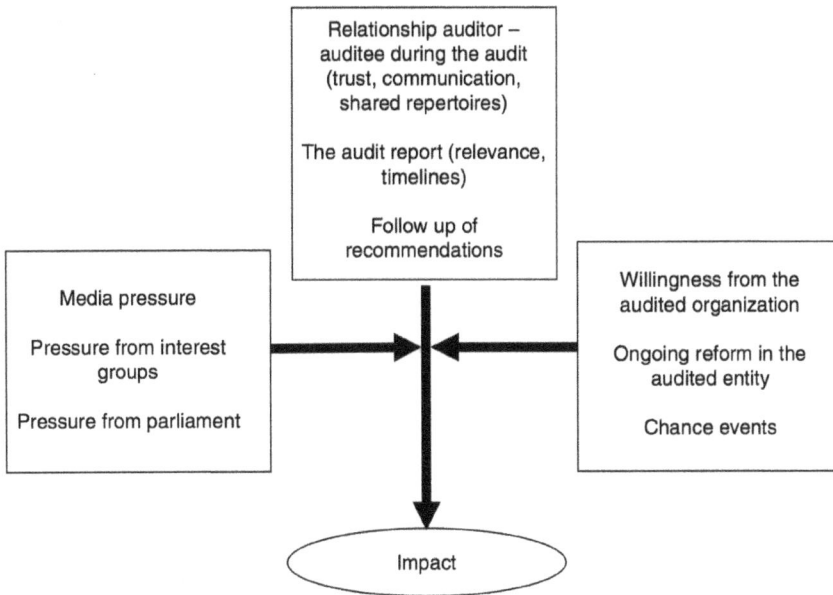

Figure 8: Factors that determine the impacts of performance audits

Source: Van Loocke and Put 2011, p. 202.

The most comprehensive study on impacts to date (Van Loocke and Put 2011), develops a framework for reflecting on the factors that influence audit impacts, and poises the field for further study in this area (See Figure 8). The study found that while performance audits do elicit positive impacts, they reaffirm Pollitt et al.'s (1999) earlier observation that these impacts are difficult to measure due to the inability to isolate cause and effect. While Pollitt et al. (1999) did outline several impacts including changes and improvements to public administration, cost-savings, and promotion of better practice, Van Loocke and Put (2011, pp. 202–203) identified four ways to improve upon those impacts: optimising the auditor–auditee relationship; managing its reputation through 'advocacy coalitions' with research institutions and media; investing more resources into audit selection and planning to boost audit relevance; and improving efforts to disseminate results and consult with relevant stakeholders.

Critics

The practice of performance auditing is not without its critics. Authors have accused the practice of having various deficiencies and, in some cases, as having adverse effects (Sutherland 1986, 2001; Pollitt et al. 1999; Shand and Anand 1996; Bowerman et al. 2003) or even no effect (Morin 2001). Performance audits typically increase the workload of audited agencies, creating inefficiencies (Pollitt et al. 1999), but some authors have suggested that they can actually cultivate negative behaviour changes in public managers, such as making them more risk-averse or anti-innovative. In the early days of performance auditing, some critics complained that the lack of standards and 'obscurity of methods' made it difficult to trust the findings as reliable (Sutherland 1986; 2002 p. 23), supposedly because it is based upon a subjective and 'utopian framework' (Clark and Swain 2005, p. 460). In a recent review, Kells (2011, p. 390) summarised many of these criticisms raised over the years into seven main categories of performance audit behavior: promoting anti-innovation; being too nit-picky; creating an expectations gap; behaving as a lapdog; encouraging unnecessary systems; hunting headlines in the media; and performing a hollow ritual. From Kells' (2011) perspective, each of these criticisms should be considered as a risk that can be managed in the design and operation of the audit institutions themselves, and Kells discusses several approaches to doing so. In other words, performance auditing is challenging work, but so long as risks are managed, the outcomes are ultimately good.

Current challenges to performance audit and recent trends

Although performance audit owes much of its existence to the cultural changes driven by the NPM reforms, its application has been ironically or paradoxically limited (Hood and Peters 2004) by many of the new forms of public sector management that emerged under these same conditions. The rise in privatisation, outsourcing and joint ventures for the delivery of public services are all well known to have challenged traditional accountability relationships in government. For auditors-general, their legislative powers of access were designed during a time when public services were delivered in-house by governments, and who have since been cut out from accessing or assessing the performance of government's partners in public service delivery, including when those partners are the departments of state and territories governments. Murray (2011, p. 131) explains that the problem is that 'third parties have been spending the money, but the Commonwealth has been carrying the risk', which means that Parliament is unable to obtain a full picture of how public services are being delivered.

This process is often referred to as an 'erosion of mandate' and cited as the reasoning behind the need for amendments to auditing legislation. The need to close such accountability gaps has been highlighted by auditors-general for many years, and has been well documented in the literature (see Funnell 1997, 2003). In a report commissioned by the Victorian Auditor-General's Office, Robertson (2009, p. 14) argued that the mandates of Auditors-General, 'should, *de facto*, be empowered to audit the use of public moneys, resources, or assets by any recipient or beneficiary regardless of its legal nature', and that any ability to 'circumvent' those powers ultimately undermines their purpose.

In Australia, requests to close this gap had been refused by successive governments (Barrett 2010), and even when access came it proceeded only incrementally. For example, GBEs were not audited until the most recent amendments in 2011. However, as Barrett (2010, p. 272) explains, 'even with reasonable access to premises and records, there is limited opportunity for performance auditors to establish 'value' either in the delivery processes or in the outcomes being achieved'.

Cooperative performance audits

Cooperative performance audits are an emerging concept in government auditing as a way to address inter-jurisdictional issues. Only limited academic and gray literature can be found on the subject, typically on government and professional association websites, or as the performance audit reports themselves. Initial reviews of the available documents reveal an inconsistency in cooperative audit terminology by various SAIs and academics, so the emphasis here is placed primarily on two guidance documents obtained from INTOSAI (1998, 2007). Several working definitions of the types of cooperative audits are drawn out, and are applied in a performance audit context.

A cooperative performance audit can be defined as an audit involving two or more audit institutions (INTOSAI 2007).[5] There are three main types of cooperative audit including concurrent, coordinated, and joint, with each involving varying degrees of cooperation between the audit institutions involved and outlined below.

- *Concurrent audits*: Also known as parallel audits, a concurrent audit can be defined as an audit conducted simultaneously by two or more audit agencies, after agreeing on a common issue to audit. Concurrent audits use separate audit teams from each agency and table separate reports only to their own legislature. The findings and recommendations contained in the reports are only those relevant to the agency's own government. The independence of each agency involved in a concurrent audit means that each may adopt a different audit approach, including different criteria, scope, and methods, in order to accommodate the needs of each jurisdiction. The extent of ideas and experiences exchange often varies.

5   Some audit agencies and organisations use the term 'collaborative' in place of 'cooperative'. For the purposes of consistency, this report will refer to 'cooperative audits' as the catch-all term.

- *Coordinated audits*: A coordinated audit falls somewhere in between concurrent and joint audits, and in practice tend to have a wide variety of configurations. Often there is some kind of collaboration in the planning stages of the audit, but agencies still operate with separate audit teams. Other examples include a joint team with separate reports, or concurrent audits with joint and individual reports.

- *Joint audits*: A joint audit is an audit conducted by a single audit team composed of auditors from two or more audit agencies. A joint audit involves a much greater degree of involvement between the two agencies and results in preparing a single audit report tabled in the legislatures of each participating jurisdiction. In practice, joint audits are rare.

Based on guidelines from INTOSAI (1998, 2007), these variations can be best illustrated on a spectrum from less to more cooperation, as presented in Figure 9. There are various audit elements that offices can cooperate on, including audit planning, developing criteria and methodology, sharing information, and sharing audit activities (such as client interviews or report writing). As more of these elements are shared, the more integrated the cooperation becomes.

Interest in cooperative auditing arose primarily out of the desire of SAIs to audit compliance with international environmental accords and other treaties and agreements that span multiple jurisdictions. For the agencies involved, 'cooperative audits facilitate mutual sharing and learning, capacity building, networking, and identification of best practices' (INTOSAI 2007, p. ix). At the same time, cooperative audits may offer a more complete picture of the issue or program examined by including information about performance from other jurisdictions that would otherwise be left out of a traditional audit — sometimes described as an 'end-to-end' audit (McPhee 2012).

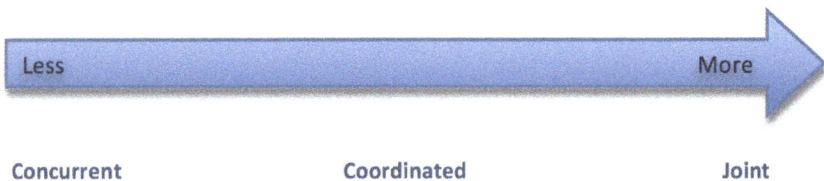

Less   More

Concurrent   Coordinated   Joint

Figure 9: Cooperative auditing from less to more integration

Source: Author's research.

The opportunities of cooperative audits outlined by INTOSAI and some auditors-general are echoed in the few academic articles that were located in the literature. Van Leeuwen (2004) argues that joint audits are the preferred approach because they have the potential for better quality and impact than a single audit alone. Likewise, Mayne (2010, p. 4) believes that joint approaches make the most sense when auditing federal-provincial programs in Canada, because 'this matches how the programs are being delivered and would be a more cost-effective way of auditing the joint program than having separate federal and provincial audits being undertaken, likely at different points in time'.

In his writing about auditing in Australia, Nicoll (2005, p. 70) observed that the lack of joint audits was 'surprising given the potential benefits to all levels of administration from cooperation in planning, especially in light of the limited resources available for performance auditing and the importance of services funded through these programs'.

There are also challenges associated with cooperative audits, many of which have been identified by auditors after taking part in cooperative audits. Mayne (2010, p. 4) admits that performance audit practices can vary significantly among audit offices, making cooperative work challenging, not to mention the value placed on independence by audit agencies, which is 'tightly guarded'.

When choosing a type of cooperative audit to undertake, INTOSAI guidelines recommend that primary consideration should be given to the availability of resources and time, the competency and experience of staff, and general knowledge base of each agency. The approach used also might depend on the topic of the audit and the priorities of each jurisdiction. While concurrent audits only require enough consultation between audit offices to set a topic, scope, and possibly a rough timeline, this approach lacks integrated conclusions, and therefore may have less impact for legislators. In contrast, joint audits are comprehensive, integrated, and have the potential for significant impacts; but there are many practical challenges stemming from jurisdictional differences. Finally, coordinated approaches are the most flexible, and can be altered to suit the degree of integration desired by both parties. Ultimately, successful cooperative audits require the commitment of both jurisdictions because 'whatever type of audit is chosen, the parties involved must have a sincere desire to cooperate with one another for a common purpose' (INTOSAI 1998, p. 19).

Cross-jurisdictional performance audits

In the most general sense, a cross-jurisdictional performance audit (CJPA) can be defined as an audit conducted by a single audit agency of an entity that lay outside the audit agency's typical jurisdiction. This type of audit can be used to assess the performance of an entity in receipt of government funding where there is a corresponding or reciprocal responsibility to deliver specified outcomes in accordance with agreed arrangements, such as financial transfers, grants, or contracts (ANAO 2012a). This can apply to non-governmental organisations, private contractors and sub-contractors, publicly owned companies, as well as national and sub-national governments — depending on the mandate granted to the auditor. The term 'cross-jurisdictional performance audit' was developed by the researcher to use in place of 'follow-the-money' audits in order to emphasise the jurisdictional element involved in this type of application of performance audit.

Though there is little explicit reference in the academic literature to CJPAs in the context of sub-national governments, gray literature indicates they do occur. Pinpointing cases of CJPAs where a national audit agency is accessing jurisdictions already covered by sub-national auditors-general has been difficult, however this process will be reported in later sections of this chapter. When compared to cooperative audits, CJPAs of sub-national governments are another way to address issues shared between levels of government. The main difference is that there is little, if any, formal cooperation with other audit agencies in undertaking audit work in a government jurisdiction outside of its own. However, despite any formal agreements or involvement of a second audit agency in the conduct of CJPAs, there is still space for consultation and sharing of information between the auditors-general and the audit offices, depending upon the willingness of the other office to cooperate.

Examinations of preliminary ANAO documents suggest that CJPAs will involve at least some consultation or contact with the audit agency representing the audited jurisdiction. For example, in a recent presentation, the Commonwealth Auditor-General stated his intent to consider 'the views of the JCPAA and other stakeholders, including those in state and territory jurisdictions' (McPhee 2012b, p. 5). He also suggested the possibility of 'utilising the expertise of the state and territory Auditors-General and participation in state and territory Parliamentary inquiries' (McPhee 2012b, p. 5).

Summary

This section provided a review of the literature relating to key areas of performance audit theory and practice considered most relevant to this study. The literature on the origins, development and expansion of performance audit clearly illustrate how the practice developed alongside the reforms of NPM, and that it represented one part of a greater shift in perspective on accountability in the public sector. At the same time, these changes have also impacted the Auditor-General's ability to provide such assurance, and therefore constant review of the mandate and governing legislation is necessary to ensure appropriate access is provided.

Due to the network of relationships that an auditor-general is typically subject to, it is not surprising that the practice of performance audit also operates within a system of constraints. The primary stakeholder relationships of the Auditor-

General can all have an influence on performance audit, and likewise they can themselves be influenced by a performance audit. This network of influences means that changes to any one part of the system are likely to have implications for the other parts.

New trends in performance audit, such as CJPAs or follow-the-money powers, as well as more cooperative approaches amongst audit offices, are on the rise in order to address areas identified as gaps in accountability and oversight and show promising potential for improving performance audit impacts and public administration more broadly.

Informed by the literature review, a conceptual framework is set out in Figure 10 to help guide this study. Drawing on Pollitt et al. (1999) and Van Looke and Put (2011), the framework has been modified to include other potential relationships which may be affected with the addition of CJPAs. The framework depicts the relationships of influence on the performance audit process at the ANAO, as well as the outward influence that performance audits can have on the broader organisational environment.

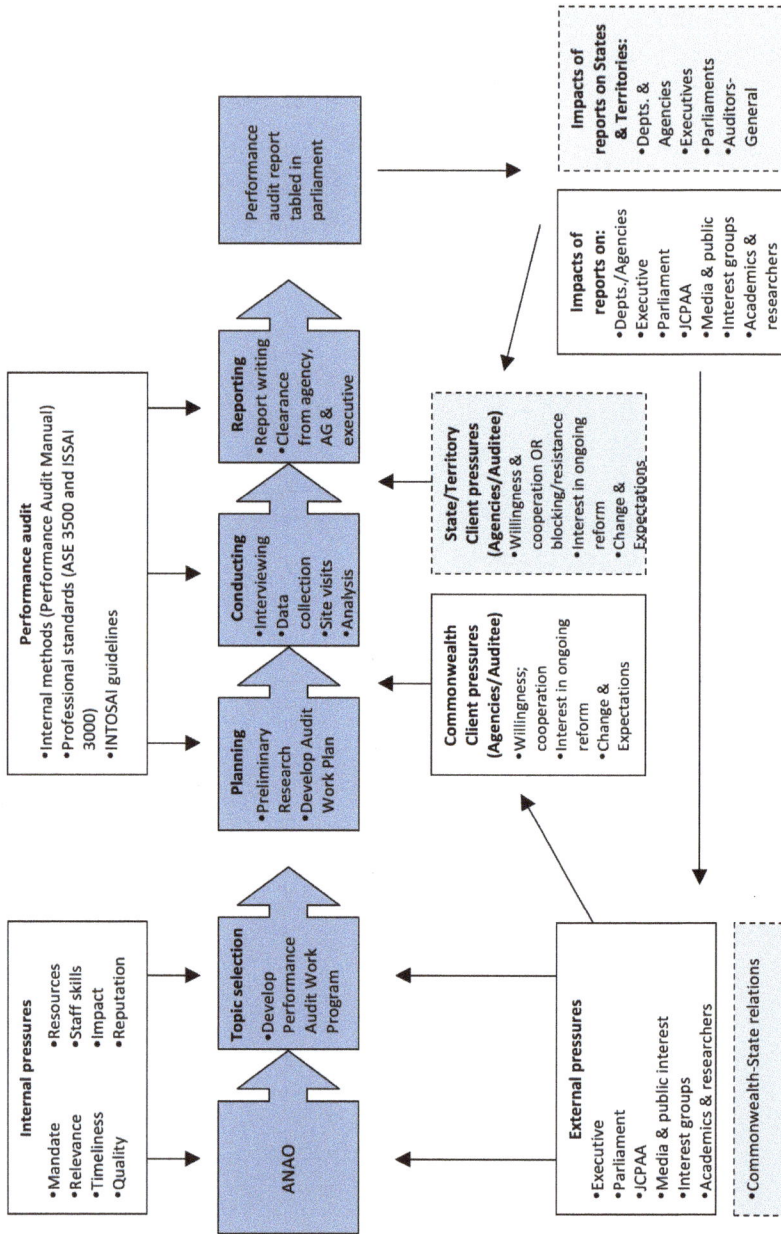

Figure 10: Cross-jurisdictional performance auditing at the ANAO: Process and influences

Source: Adapted from Pollitt et al. 1999, and Van Loocke and Put 2011.

Methodology

The research design for this study relied on a qualitative methodology consisting of three discreet approaches including a jurisdictional scan, interviews, and an online survey.

The jurisdictional scan identifies other national audit agencies that have experience in the conduct of CJPAs or cooperative performance audits and to gain insight into how they are applied and how often.

Semi-structured elite interviews were conducted with key stakeholders and selected experts in the field of public sector audit or involvement in the JCPAA Inquiry, including six current and two former auditors-general in Australia, the Chair of the JCPAA, the Committee Secretary of the JCPAA, and two senior audit office personnel (see Appendix 1). The aim of the interviews was to explore Australian perspectives on the new CJPA powers as well the various cooperative performance audit alternatives.

An online survey of national audit agencies was conducted to solicit international perspectives on the advantages and disadvantages of CJPAs and cooperative performance audits.[6]

Data collected from each of the three approaches is analysed together to arrive at a comprehensive and well-balanced assessment of the issues central to this study, and is presented later in this chapter.

International jurisdictional scan

The jurisdictional scan determines whether other national audit agencies were involved in CJPAs or other cooperative approaches to address inter-jurisdictional audit issues. The goal is to identify good practices to consider. The literature review establishes working definitions for CJPAs and the three types of cooperative audits, and these definitions are used to analyse the findings from the jurisdictional scan.

---

6   More detail on interview and survey methodology, including a list of draft interview questions and online survey questions, can be found in the original full-length report (Gerald 2012).

Canada: Cooperative audits with sub-national audit agencies

The responsibility for external public audit in Canada rests with the Office of the Auditor-General, while all provincial governments have their own external auditors general. While the Auditor-General of Canada may have some follow-the-money powers, communications with office staff have confirmed that CJPAs are not conducted by the federal Office of the Auditor-General in any areas under the exclusive jurisdiction of provincial or municipal governments. Though federal audits of the territories do occur, they are not considered to be CJPAs because the Office of the Auditor-General is actually mandated as the responsible external auditor in for the territories, as they do not have their own auditors general.

Although no instances of joint audits were identified in Canada, 12 instances of concurrent audits occurred (18 including follow-up audits), either between the federal Office of the Auditor-General and provincial audit offices or amongst provincial offices.

United States: CJPAs through a federal lens

The Government Accountability Office (GAO) is the public sector auditor for the US federal government, while each of the states also has their own independent audit offices. The GAO has a clear mandate to conduct CJPAs of state government administration in cases of federal transfers, but they are not undertaken that often, and typically only in cases where there is a substantial federal involvement (personal communication, GAO, 28 October 2012). When GAO audit staff examine a federally funded program such as education or work training programs, 'it is through the lens that focuses on how those goals may differ from federal goals and how that performance needs to be improved … from a federal perspective' (personal communication, GAO, 28 October 2012). While the GAO may have a real interest in how states are spending federal funds, it is clear that their assessments are focused on how well federal departments are managing their state-level contractors or agents, and does not extend to include any assessment of state-level performance.

The GAO indicated that direct involvement of state audit offices in CJPAs is rare, and limited to consultation and coordination activities to ensure they are not duplicating audit work (personal communication, GAO, 29 October 2012). A representative explained that the GAO is much larger size and resource capability than most state audit offices, and therefore it makes more sense that CJPAs do not draw on the resources of the state level auditors (personal communication, GAO, 29 October 2012).

Cooperative audits with the state level audit offices do occur, on occasion, relating to topics that are of mutual concern. The only involvement in an international cooperative performance audit that could be identified was an audit on invasive species undertaken in 2003 in partnership with the Office of the Auditor General in Canada.

United Kingdom: An integrated, joint audit approach to CJPAs

The external public auditor for the United Kingdom is the Comptroller and Auditor-General, an independent officer of the House of Commons supported by the National Audit Office (NAO). On occasion, the NAO conducts CJPAs of the devolved governments of Northern Ireland, Scotland, and Wales, although each of these also has their own independent auditors general. Since funding transfers from the UK government to the devolved governments are not conditional, these CJPAs are not for the purposes of assessing performance against national objectives (since there are none), and instead are used for the purposes of performance comparison across the four countries of the UK (Paun and Hazell 2008). Typically these CJPAs involve active collaboration with the audit offices of the devolved governments, allowing the NAO to draw on their resources and expertise while at the same time providing them a role in the process.

Occasionally, the NAO undertakes joint audits with the Audit Commission, the external public auditor for local government in England and Wales (personal communication, NAO, 16 October 2012).[7] In these cases the two agencies come together to examine conditional grants provided from the UK government directly to local governments in England of Wales, which are attached to UK government outcomes.[8] Similar to their CJPA approach, the NAO draws upon the expertise and local knowledge of the Audit Commission.

The NAO has been involved in cooperative audits in the past, but the only recent one that could be identified was a concurrent audit in 2000, with the Netherlands, Sweden, and England (personal communication, NAO, 16 October 2012). Apart from this example, no other international cooperative audits with the NAO could be located.

---

7 At the present time, the future of the Audit Commission in England is unclear, following a decision by the UK Department for Communities and Local Government to disband it. For more information please visit: http://www.audit-commission.gov.uk/. Audit oversight for local government in Scotland and Northern Ireland is provided by their national audit offices respectively.

8 For example, in 2005 a joint audit was undertaken in with the Audit Commission entitled, 'Delivery Chain Analysis for Bus Service in England', where a joint audit team comprised of members from both the NAO and the Audit Commission worked together to produce a single joint report.

Norway: Unrestricted access from a unitary perspective

The initial review of Norway revealed that it does not operate under a federal system of government, but rather as a multi-tiered government based on a unitary constitution (Boadway and Shah 2007). This means that ultimate control for government functions rests with the central government, and responsibilities can be delegated to lower levels by means of legislation. Norway's national public auditor is known as the Riksrevisjonen, or the Office of the Auditor-General of Norway, but it is not responsible for providing oversight to the local governments because they each have their own requirements for an external public audit function. Nevertheless, the Office of the Auditor-General can conduct CJPAs of financial transfers to local governments at their discretion when the funds are tied to specific national policies, and these audits do not have any involvement from the local audit agencies. Provisions for such audits are enshrined in the Office of the Auditor-General's governing legislation, which provides the right to access information and carry out investigations of anyone, 'to whom central government tasks have been delegated or who supply goods or services to the state' (Riksrevisjonen 2011, p. 16).

Cooperative audits in Norway were identified, typically between the Office of the Auditor-General and other Nordic countries, and relating to environmental issues. However, more recently a concurrent audit with Russia relating to the management of fish resources was conducted in 2008.

Switzerland: CJPAs with a role for sub-national cooperation

The Swiss Federal Audit Office is the independent federal public auditor of Switzerland. The Federal Audit Office's mandate allows for CJPAs to be conducted of the sovereign cantons (state governments), in areas where federal financial aid has been provided. The mandate also recommends that the cantonal level audit offices should be involved in any CJPA, but that such audits are to be led by the Federal Audit Office, and duties can be delegated at their discretion. The Federal Audit Office reports a high degree of cooperation with the canton level audit offices in this regard, which suggests that there might be advantages to working with the sub-national audit offices in the CJPA process in order to share the workload, access their specified knowledge base, and take advantage of their existing relationships with audit subjects. The Swiss case therefore provides a good example of how to integrate sub-national audit agencies into the CJPA process.

Few cooperative audits were located for the Swiss Federal Audit Office, however one concurrent audit with Hungary was located from 2005 concerning tunnel and bridge infrastructure.

Germany: Cooperation with respect for autonomy

The federal external public audit function in Germany rests with the Federal Court of Audit, the Bundesrechnungshof, while each of the 16 autonomous Länder (state governments) also have their own independent audit agencies. The Bundesrechnungshof has legislated powers to conduct CJPAs of the Länder governments in cases where 'they implement parts of the federal budget or have expenses reimbursed from the federal exchequer, if they manage federal funds or assets, or if they receive grants from the federal exchequer' (Bundesrechnungshof 1997, p. 7).

However, since tax revenues are shared in Germany, many programs are funded jointly by the federal and state governments, which result in overlaps in responsibility. In these cases the public auditors at each level of government must cooperate with one another to 'seek harmonization on fundamental issues' (Bundesrechnungshof 2012). This harmonisation is enshrined in the federal audit legislation, which refers specifically to joint audits and clarifies that 'where both the Bundesrechnungshof and a State Court of Audit are responsible for the audit, this should be carried out jointly' (German Federal Budget Code, Part V, Sec. 93, Art. 1).

While the joint approach is enshrined in legislation, the same legislation also states that 'the Bundesrechnungshof may agree to transfer any of its audit functions to the State Courts of Audit', and 'may also agree to take over audit functions from the State Courts of Audit', which provides the federal auditor with the maximum flexibility to address shared issues relating to jointly delivered programs, and adjust the workload to accommodate one another's priorities.

The Bundesrechnungshof has also been involved in cooperative audits with other SAIs, the most recent of which was conducted with the SAIs of Belgium and the Netherlands on intra-community value-added tax fraud.

Austria, South Africa and India: A national approach

Reviews of Austria, South Africa and India reveal that while their political arrangements as federal systems had much in common with Australia, their public sector audit function did not. All three of these countries have only one national auditor-general responsible for auditing the entire public sector, including national and sub-national government departments and agencies. Rather than having independent sub-national level auditors-general, the national audit-offices have regional offices across each country's sub-national districts that specialise in auditing their regional and local affairs. As a result, CJPAs of sub-national jurisdictions in these cases are not possible in the same way as they are in Australia, as they do not have same complicating factors of sub-national sovereignty and sub-national audit jurisdictions.

In terms of cooperative audits, Austria and South Africa have both been involved with cooperative performance audits with other SAIs relating to environmental issues. Most recently Austria has been involved with an audit on climate change with several other European countries (WGEA 2012). Cooperative audits involving India and other SAIs were unable to be located.

Summary

The jurisdictional scan and resulting cases reveal several important findings. First, the conduct of CJPAs is not entirely uncommon internationally. Second, there is a wide variation in how sub-national audit agencies can be integrated into the CJPA process. Some countries, such as Norway, do not provide any role for sub-national auditors, while others such as Germany actually make cooperation between audit offices mandatory. Switzerland and the US appear to take a more flexible and voluntary approach to sub-national involvement, while retaining the control of the audit. At the extremes, Canada does not conduct any CJPAs of its provinces, while the UK has opted for the most integrated approach of joint audits with the local government Audit Commission, consisting of joint audit teams and a single joint report.

The occurrence of cooperative audits was also found to a varying degree across the jurisdictions examined. Canada is of particular note with respect to frequency of concurrent audits.

Interviews

This section reviews the findings from interviews conducted with 12 key individuals possessing specialised knowledge about public sector audit in Australia.[9] For a list of participants see Appendix 1. Responses have been summarised and any direct quotes that have been included are not attributed

---

9   One interview included two participants — the Commonwealth Auditor-General and the senior ANAO staff member — and their responses have been considered as one, reducing the total number of interviews to 11.

due to the small sample size and the high-profile roles of those interviewed. Responses were organised by key themes that emerged following data analysis and only those most relevant to the current study are reported below.

Cross-jurisdictional performance audits

The majority of participants viewed the new CJPA powers as a valuable addition to the Commonwealth Auditor-General's mandate, however, a few stated that this was so long as these powers were not used to assess the states and territories themselves. Several commented that the mere possession of the new powers gave the Commonwealth Auditor-General more clout, suggesting that their looming threat will be enough to foment changes to both federal and state level management practices. As one participant explained, people have now been 'put on notice' that the federal auditor may come to examine their practices.

Participants highlighted a variety of potential benefits that will flow from the conduct of CJPAs, including the ability to tell the full story about how financial transfers are managed, the ability to provide proper assurance to Parliament, and the opportunity to compare and contrast the delivery approaches of the states and territories. Several also suggested that the new powers would mark the beginning of improved relationships amongst all auditors-general in Australia, both through the increased consultation required for CJPAs and through stimulation of debate about a possible return to exploring cooperative audit approaches.

Most participants viewed follow-the-money powers more generally as an important tool for all auditors-general in Australia, describing them as a way to 'catch up' or 'keep in step' with changes in public management. At the same time, almost half of participants admitted that they felt they were unable to oppose the new powers because they had already advocated for the states and territories to have those same powers, explaining that it might be hypocritical not to support the changes and difficult to argue against the proposal in terms of good public policy and governance.

Cooperative audits

References to cooperative audit approaches, either in addition to CJPAs, or as an alternative to them, arose frequently in all interviews. More than half of all participants suggested that the Commonwealth Auditor-General should have both approaches at his disposal, representing another tool in the toolkit, to be used depending upon the context and circumstances.

Despite overwhelming interest in the cooperative audit approach, participants pointed to several barriers that remain before more work can be done in this area, including legislation limitations, priority conflicts, and timing of performance audit cycles. Legislation issues cited by more than half of the participants relate to limitations on information sharing between audit offices.[10] A few participants pointed out that their audit legislation is currently under review to allow for more cooperation, while others suggested that there are already ways to work around these issues. Differing priorities and performance audit cycles were indicated as impediments because, as one participant explained, 'just trying to get agreement, you know, in very good faith, between all the jurisdictions, around a suitable topic, is not easy to do.'

Joint audits

The joint audit approach was strongly supported by half of participants. One cited it as an 'aspiration', one as the 'preferred approach', while yet another stated that it 'made an enormous amount of sense' for the average citizen, who is not concerned with the jurisdiction of an audit so long as they find out whether there is value being achieved for their tax dollar. Supporters of joint audits identified several advantages to its integrated approach, including the ability to pool resources and leverage expertise using a joint audit team.

Other participants identified barriers to joint audits, including information sharing restrictions, and administrative and personnel issues that could arise when composing an inter-jurisdictional team. Questions about which legislation team members would work under, which set of rules would they be held accountable to, and by whom they would be paid, were all identified. Others downplayed these concerns, explaining that many offices already support secondments, exchange programs and other arrangements, so administratively they would find solutions.

The nature of federal transfers

The most prominent area of disagreement amongst participants concerned the true meaning of the federal transfers, and how they are or should be perceived in the context of Australian federalism and the current vertical-fiscal imbalance.

---

10   One participant summarised the issue as follows: 'The ability for audit offices to share information is a good thing from an audit perspective, but it's another thing for governments and parliaments to be comfortable with that, because you need to appreciate that on the one hand, auditors-general have got quite wide powers of access — for instance we have access to Cabinet information, and other information — and so, if you just have sort of a sharing provision ... that suggests an auditor could pass on information about sensitive government matters to one of their colleagues ... and parliaments are sort of saying we need to think very carefully about how any such provisions are framed.'

On the one extreme, some participants pointed to the states and territories as simply agents of the Commonwealth when in receipt of the federal transfers, rendering them no different from any other contractor, private or otherwise. As one participant put it: 'grants are grants ... I don't think there should be any equivocation about that'. On the other extreme, some participants pointed to the transfers as merely flows of revenue back to the states and territories, which had been collected by the Commonwealth on their behalf. As one explained: 'it's not actually a payment for buying a particular item of activity'. Participants with the latter view seemed to suggest that these monies were somehow different in that once transferred to the states and territories, they became state and territory money and therefore only subject to audit in the state jurisdiction. The remaining participants fell somewhere in the middle, admitting they did not fully understand how the money transformed once it changed hands or how the accountability mechanisms attached to the transfers would change.

Key stakeholder impacts

The majority of participants referred to the state and territory governments as being 'suspicious' of the new powers, and described them as 'concerned', 'threatened', 'worried', 'apprehensive' or 'uncomfortable' about the prospect of their implementation. While most participants expected this initial resistance to CJPAs by state and territory governments, most believed that it was unlikely they would ever pursue a constitutional challenge over their use. Most participants anticipated the eventual socialisation and acceptance of the new process and that concern would begin to diminish as the ANAO develops its credibility and legitimacy through practice. Relationship management through consultation, education and sharing of information were cited as several participants as the best strategies to minimise negative impacts on the state and territory governments.

An overwhelming majority of participants felt that there was a role for state and territory auditors-general in the conduct of CJPAs, primarily through consultation, information exchange, and the sharing of previous experiences in the subject area, such as background information, previous audit reports or risk analysis that might have already been conducted on that particular agency. However, there were also a few participants who believed that any involvement in CJPAs would simply divert scarce resources away from state and territory auditors-general.

Challenges to CJPA implementation

The majority of participants identified the same key challenges to the implementation of CJPAs including the ANAO's unfamiliarity with state and territory systems and administration; potential relationship issues with their bureaucracies; and potential retaliation from state and territory governments if a CJPA is deemed to be too politically sensitive. One participant explained that 'state government activities are not their bread and butter so they will have difficulty efficiently doing those audits as they gain an understanding of the environment and operating area'.

Similarly, almost half of participants identified building and managing relationships with the state and territory bureaucracies as another major challenge to CJPAs, characterising the potential for turf wars, rivalries, obstruction, push-back, and interference. One participant explained that there will always be a 'political issue around a national office auditing a state agency' that will not easily be accepted by the states and territories without a concentrated communications campaign directed at their departments and agencies.

A few participants also identified resourcing as an issue, explaining that securing resources for a CJPA would be a challenge since state and territory level parliaments would have difficulty understanding why their resources were being diverted towards the conduct of an audit for the Commonwealth.

Details on the CJPA process

All participants surveyed unanimously agreed that in a CJPA, the state and territory auditees should be extended the same privileges of natural justice as those given to Commonwealth auditees, including copies of draft issues papers, an opportunity to respond to the issues papers, as well as the inclusion of their response (or a summary) in the final report. Participants spoke to these features as important to ensure audit quality and credibility. The majority of participants also indicated that CJPA reports should only be tabled in the Commonwealth Parliament.

More than half of the interview participants indicated that they did not feel it was appropriate for the Commonwealth Auditor-General to make direct recommendations to state and territory entities. However, they did support indirect recommendations so long as they are framed as recommendations to the responsible Commonwealth departments. This distinction, they explained, is because 'the Commonwealth should be accountable for their officials discharging their obligations', and that CJPAs are really meant to be about 'looking at the Commonwealth administration, oversight and monitoring of the states and not necessarily the delivery by the states of the services'. Three participants said it would simply not be possible to hold a state agency to account in the Commonwealth and so there was no point in making a recommendation to them.

In contrast, a few participants stated that direct recommendations should be made to the state and territory agencies involved in a CJPA. One noted that, 'if you see opportunities where they might make improvement, it seems to me that it would be a bit unusual not to', while another suggested they do so only after a couple of years of putting CJPAs into practice.

Summary

Data collected through the interviews uncovered several important insights. While participants generally viewed the new CJPA powers as a positive addition to the Commonwealth Auditor-General's mandate, some felt that CJPAs should not reach so far as to assess state and territory performance. The conduct of CJPAs is anticipated to impact state and territory stakeholders the most, but also the ANAO as they adjust to the addition of a new audit program. Several challenges to the implementation of CJPAs were highlighted, but none seemed insurmountable by the ANAO so long as they are proactive in their approach. Most participants showed a high degree of interest in pursuing cooperative audits, and although most admit these involve more work, time and resources, it was generally agreed that the benefits of these approaches are worth the effort.

Survey

Findings from the online survey are summarised into two categories, including those that relate to CJPAs and those that relate to cooperative performance audits. The nine audit agencies that responded to the survey and key information about their performance audit practices are summarised in Table 1.

Cross-jurisdictional performance audits

Of the nine audit agencies who responded to the survey, all indicated that they have conducted CJPAs of other levels of government, except for Mexico and Ireland. Canada explained that they only do so in the case of their three territory governments because they do not have their own auditors general. Similarly, New Zealand indicated they are the only public sector auditor and therefore are responsible for auditing all public sector entities, including the local authorities. The Netherlands clarified that they do not have an official mandate to access the sub-national departments and agencies, but instead their involvement is voluntary. Overall, the responses suggested that involvement by sub-national audit agencies in the CJPA processes is typically limited, although two agencies did report closer involvement (the UK and Switzerland).

Several challenges to conducting CJPAs were reported, including difficulties in accessing information, variations in agency capacity and expertise, more time consuming process, and differences in timing and scheduling. However, respondents also identified a range of opportunities associated with CJPAs, including the ability to examine the full picture of national spending, improved audit impacts, the ability to compare performance across multiple jurisdictions, and occasions to improve relationships with other audit agencies.

Cooperative performance audits

Seven participants indicated they have taken part in some form of cooperative performance audit, with two stating they have experience with all three (UK, The Netherlands), while others (Canada) were involved in only the concurrent variety. Only New Zealand and Mexico stated that they had not been involved in cooperative audits, but that they would like to in the future.

Most participants stated that the biggest challenge to cooperative audits is that the process can take longer and involves a large degree of coordination and consultation between the agencies involved at each of the performance audit phases. However, despite these challenges, respondents identified many opportunities that arise from cooperative audits, again supporting the ability to see the complete picture, improve impacts of the audit, as well as the advantages of pooling knowledge and expertise from two audit agencies.

Summary

The key results from the online survey have been summarised into Table 1.

Table 1: Online survey summary: International CJPA and cooperative audit practices

	CJPA of other level of government?	Involvement of audit agency responsible for that jurisdiction?	Cooperative performance audits?	Which types?
New Zealand	Yes	No, OAGNZ is the only audit agency (i.e. no local gov. auditor)	No	N/A
UK*	Yes	Yes, through joint working, combined visits	Yes	All three
Canada	Yes, but territories only (NWT,YK, and NVT)	No, OAG is only audit office, none in the territories	Yes	Concurrent

	CJPA of other level of government?	Involvement of audit agency responsible for that jurisdiction?	Cooperative performance audits?	Which types?
The Netherlands	Yes, but cooperation is voluntary	No	Yes	All three
US	Yes	Yes, through information exchange	Yes	Concurrent and coordinated
Norway	Yes	No	Yes	Concurrent, coordinated
Mexico	No	N/A	No	N/A
Ireland	No	N/A	Yes	Coordinated
Switzerland	Yes	Yes, through information exchange; optional involvement	Yes	Coordinated and joint

*In August 2010, the UK government announced its intention to abolish the Audit Commission, which was the agency responsible for auditing local government spending. As of 24 September 2012, the NAO website reports that the new audit arrangements will see the NAO not auditing the performance of individual local authorities, but producing a number of value for money reports each year on issues affecting the sector. However, it should be noted that the participant responding on behalf of the UK did so relative to past practices.

Discussion

The purpose of this chapter is to assess the impacts of the addition of CJPA powers to the mandate of the Commonwealth Auditor-General for Australia, which allows for audits to be conducted of states and territories when in receipt of federal transfers with attached Commonwealth objectives or outcomes. The assessment of impacts is conducted with a view to external stakeholders and internal considerations of the performance audit process at the ANAO, as well as consideration of cooperative approaches to performance audit as an alternative or additional approach to the ANAO's overall mix of audit activities.

This section includes a discussion of the implications of the key interview and survey findings in the context of the background, literature review, and jurisdictional scan, and is organised into three main parts: the first part discusses the implications of the findings relating to CJPAs and their impact on the various stakeholders identified throughout this study; the second part discusses the implications of key findings associated with cooperative audits; the third part summarises the overall discussion.

Cross-jurisdictional performance audits

Overall, the interview data was consistent with the information presented in the background section with respect to the anticipated concerns about the introduction of CJPA powers. Participants tended to view the addition of CJPA powers as a valuable tool for the Commonwealth Auditor-General because it will allow him to conduct end-to-end performance audits of federal transfers to states and territories, and provide Parliament with the full story in their final report. According to the interview data, the impacts of this power will also have effects further afield, since the mere possession of CJPA access effectively puts the states and territories on notice for a possible audit from the Commonwealth auditor, and this might encourage state and territory agencies to tighten up some of their practices in advance of any announced audits, in the same way that this can occur with federal auditees.

The interview data has also made it clear that there are many differences in opinion and understanding of the nature of the federal transfers that take place under SPPs and NPPs and that these underlying differences may be at the root of the disagreements over the conduct of CJPAs. For example, several participants referred to the transfers as being a payment for a service, equivalent to the exchange that takes place with a contractor. At the same time, several other participants indicated that they perceived the transfers as a redistribution of tax revenue collected by the Commonwealth on behalf of the states and territories, and that these transfers are not actually a payment for a service, but instead merely a flow of revenue. So clearly there remains some confusion as to the status of the federal financial transfers and the interview data seems to support this notion that one's perspective on the value of CJPAs is dependent upon what jurisdiction you represent. It is in this vein that it appears easier to rationalise the practice of CJPAs of sub-national governments in countries such as Norway, the Netherlands, and the UK, since they take place within unitary systems where sub-national governments really are more like service delivery conduits for national policy as opposed to the independent, autonomous units that are present in federations such as Australia.

Interview findings were also consistent with the literature on the issue of 'erosion of mandate' of auditors-general, which refers to the loss or impairment of an auditor-general's ability to assess or provide assurance of public sector performance in cases where services have been contracted out of the government sector and into either private or non-profit organisations. More than half of the interview participants indicated that follow-the-money powers in general were critical to ensuring auditors-general can continue to assess performance in these cases, because ultimately governments are still responsible for the provision of public services, despite their being outsourced. However, the conflation of the various types of cross-jurisdictional access into one access power — the ability to audit any Commonwealth partner — also made it difficult for many of the auditors-general to oppose the amendments, particularly when they had advocated for these powers in their own mandates. The interview data shows that although most participants supported CJPAs or follow-the-money audits of third parties, including local governments, NGOs and private businesses, several had indicated that they were less certain about CJPAs of states and territories, due to the impacts this might have on their autonomy.

Finally, more than half of those interviewed felt that that while the Commonwealth Auditor-General should have sufficient oversight powers, external audits exist to provide oversight; the intent is not to scrutinise all Commonwealth government operations. Strong internal assurance and accountability mechanisms must be built in to all government operations and managed from the inside, with the external auditor reviewing them from time to time to assess if they are in need of improvement. Most interview participants suggested that the overall accountability framework of the Commonwealth could be best strengthened through the COAG forum, particularly the COAG Reform Council and the National Partnership Agreements. Improving the clarity and roles and responsibilities in these agreements could help bring about better value for money spending and ultimately improved state and territory outcomes.

Impacts of CJPAs on external stakeholders

The process of performance audit was identified in the literature as being both influenced by, and having an influence on the various stakeholder relationships of the Auditor-General (Pollitt et al. 1999; Lonsdale 2008; Lonsdale et al. 2011). The importance of these relationships was generally supported in the interview data, which suggested that a change in the Auditor-General's mandate, such as the addition of the CJPA power, will have flow-on effects for a variety of external stakeholders, particularly state and territory auditors-general, state and territory governments, and state and territory auditees — each of which is discussed below. Regular stakeholders of the Commonwealth Auditor-General will be impacted to a lesser extent, and are discussed all together in one final paragraph.

One of the most impacted stakeholder groups discussed in the interviews is that of the state and territory auditors-general. For the most part, impacts were considered to be positive, in that CJPAs could promote partnerships amongst auditors-general through added consultation and information sharing, placing the state and territory auditors-general in a supportive role particularly at the front end of the audit planning process. Likewise, several interview participants suggested that CJPAs are likely to act as a catalyst to promote a renewed interest in cooperative approaches to performance audit, ultimately impacting the topic selection activities of all audit offices. There were also concerns about diverting state and territory resources to consult and provide information to the Commonwealth Auditor-General. Whether this would divert more priorities than requests from an MP or JCPAA to investigate a particular matter is an open question.

A second group of impacted stakeholders are the state and territory executive coordinators and central agencies. Interview participants generally felt that the reaction of the state and territory governments to the CJPA powers was not positive, and that they felt threatened, worried or apprehensive about the prospects. Not surprisingly, the state and territory governments have perceived this process as an infringement on their constitutional rights as sovereign and autonomous political units. On the other hand, as one interview participant pointed out, this type of vocal reaction is actually business as usual when it comes to Commonwealth–state relations, and perhaps this sentiment should not be interpreted as seriously as it was earlier in the process. In fact, most interview participants indicated that that they did not expect anything to come of the threats of constitutional challenges — unless, as two participants indicated, the topic was politically sensitive enough. Once CJPAs begin to occur, so long as they are not overly contentious, they will gradually begin to build their credibility with the states and territories, and potentially begin to add value through positive improvements. In the meantime, these sentiments will remain at the government level and could have flow-on effects to the departments and agencies that will eventually become the subjects of CJPAs. Interview data indicates that the extent of these effects can be best mitigated through direct consultation, education and information sharing with the state and territory governments.

A third stakeholder group impacted by CJPAs is the state and territory auditees. The introduction of CJPAs at the Commonwealth level will add another layer of audit to the state and territory bureaucracies, which will likely be greeted with similar sentiment to that of the state and territory governments as described in the previous paragraph. Although the impacts on this relationship were not discussed in detail in the interviews, it is easy to extrapolate from the literature on the auditor–auditee relationship to anticipate some of the impacts on this group. If we consider Funnell and Wade's (2012) study on the auditor–auditee relationship at the ANAO, characterised by animosity, it would be expected that the auditor–auditee relationship between the Commonwealth auditors and state auditees to be potentially worse. Several authors (Lonsdale et al. 2011; Put and Turksema 2011) point to the need for performance audits to be seen to add value to the auditees, and therefore the ANAO must make sure their product is of high quality in order to justify the effort.

The remaining stakeholders identified earlier in this chapter will also be impacted by the addition of CJPAs to the Commonwealth Auditor-General's mandate, however the findings from the various methods in this study suggest that they will be to a much lesser extent than the previous three groups identified at the state level. At the Commonwealth level, Parliament and the JCPAA will be impacted positively due to the increased confidence that CJPA access will bring through improving their understanding of how Commonwealth funding is being spent under NPPs and SPPs. Commonwealth auditees might be positively impacted during a CJPA if the additional state and territory information helps to better explain their actions or the quality of information they were given by the states and territories. Central agencies and the executive government at the Commonwealth level do not appear to be majorly impacted by these changes, which is of little surprise considering the endorsement of the amendments by the executive following the JCPAA's recommendations. The media, the public, academics, and professional associations will be impacted by a CJPA no more than by the tabling of a standard performance audit, although in the early days of the launch of CJPAs, the new access provisions might become newsworthy.

Internal stakeholders

As mentioned above, a change in mandate, such as the addition of CJPA powers, can have flow-on effects for an audit agency's internal process of performance audit, similar to those conceptualised in the literature by Pollitt et al. (1999) and Van Loocke and Put (2011). The findings from the interviews and the survey are generally consistent with this notion, and when applied to the ANAO it is clear that the addition of cross-jurisdictional powers has the potential to impact a range of performance audit activities, from planning through the conducting and reporting phases, and additional considerations will need to be made at each phase in the CJPA process.

During the pre-planning phase, it is clear from the interview data that the ANAO ought to begin with CJPA topics that are not too politically sensitive for state and territory governments, in order to allow time to build up the credibility and legitimacy of the process. Some low-risk and positive outcome audits that have little implications for the state and territory level bureaucracies could be a good place to start. A concentrated communications and education campaign from the ANAO about CJPAs was also indicated as essential to reducing the resistance of the state and territory governments. Once the planning phase has begun, the audit team will need to allot additional time to collect background information and to learn about state specific legislation, policies, rules and regulations. Auditors may also want to consult with the state and territory Auditors-General about their knowledge and experience about the audit topic or if they have previously conducted audits in this area, although some interview participants indicated there might be varying degrees of cooperation from auditors-general.

In the conducting phase, unfamiliarity is once again the biggest consideration for the audit team. They will be accessing new premises, working with new auditees, and learning about new systems. This may take additional time and auditors could be faced with resistance or less cooperative staff. On the other hand, if this is done well, the ANAO auditors may face less resistance and animosity on the part of the state territory agencies by demonstrating that they are across the issues and have a sound understanding of the state and territory level processes. Additional time considerations might be necessary during the development of issues papers, as all interview participants indicated the necessity of providing the state and territory agencies with issues papers and opportunity to comment. The consultation and negotiation period that follows might take more time, especially if findings are less than desirable.

In the reporting phase, auditors will have to consider very carefully whether or not they will make recommendations to the state and territory agencies. More than half of the interview participants felt that direct recommendations to states and territories should not be made, and that instead they should be directed at the responsible Commonwealth department or agency. On the other hand, some interview participants felt that if there were areas identified for improvement, that recommendations are a natural part of the performance audit process, so clearly there remains some disagreement as to the best approach to recommendations in CJPAs.

Finally, the tabling of reports also needs to be considered. Although most interview participants felt that the reports should only be tabled in the Commonwealth Parliament, several others indicated they believed there should be some mechanism or forum for the states and territories to discuss the findings of the report relevant to them. It would seem that the ANAO should consider producing alternate forms of the report for the state and territory auditees, or otherwise make them available upon request.

Table 2: CJPA considerations during the performance audit process at the ANAO

Phase	Activity	Standard	CJPA
ANAO performance audit planning	**Planning and development of annual audit work program**	Consideration of: • portfolio risks • potential benefits to public administration • potential to improve performance • financial materiality • risks to reputation and service delivery extent of previous audit coverage • ANAO capacity priorities of the Parliament, as determined by the JCPAA • views of entities and other stakeholders	Same as standard, plus consideration of: • areas where additional CJPA inquiry might be needed and these highlighted in annual work program as a possibility • additional views of state and territory stakeholders • possibility of political pressure from states depending on topic • whether one of the cooperative approaches would be a better fit than a CJPA
Individual audit planning	**Preliminary study (if required)**	• in cases of a complex audit, sometimes preliminary study is conducted to assist in setting of scope, objectives and methodology to be used	Same as standard, plus: • investigate whether state and territory audit offices already have coverage of the topic • consider the early notification of state and territory auditees as a way to build confidence and plan for communication and education about the process so it becomes familiar; • consider contact with state and territory auditors-general to solicit contact information, or auditee insights • begin background research to learn about state legislation, agencies, frameworks, compliance, systems, etc.
	Individual audit work plan	• define scope and objectives; set methodology, schedule, and budget • staff allocated to audit team	• consider that CJPAs might cost more due to larger scope, more people to talk to, and could take longer

Phase	Activity	Standard	CJPA
Evidence gathering and analysis	Entry interview	• entry interview held with senior management of entity responsible for the program or activities that are subject to the audit • discussion of access to relevant systems, documentation and facilities • agreement on administrative and contact arrangements	• same as standard
	Evidence gathering and analysis	• collection of evidence, electronic and paper documentation review, systems access, interviews with managers and staff, site visits, inspection of physical assets, staff observation, process demonstrations	• be prepared for unanticipated challenges at the state and territory agencies, as processes and practices can be quite different from those of the Commonwealth • consider possible resistance or push-back from state and territory agency staff evidence collection could take longer or be more challenging if ANAO staff do not know where to look or if systems are unfamiliar
	Prepare issues papers	• evidence gathered is analysed against the test criteria set in the planning phase and prepared in the form of issues papers, which outline the issues identified through the analysis.	• Issues papers might take longer to draft or be more complex in nature
	Exit interview and entity response	• interview with senior managers to discuss findings and conclusions and feasibility of recommendations tested • consensus reached • draft issues papers to entity for comment; comments to be considered in drafting final report	• more time might be needed for consultation process and coming to consensus
Reporting	Proposed report under Section 19 of AG Act	• final report for Parliament drafted and sent to entity for comment	• prepare for a potentially longer vetting process internally • consider recommendations to states and territories very carefully as they will not likely be accepted that easily at first
	Entity response	• entity's comments considered and incorporated into the final report	• consider whether it might be more challenging to bring multiple entities to agreement • prepare for possible negative response or disagreement from states to any direct recommendations
	Final report to Prime Minister, responsible ministers and chief executive of the agency		• consider whether copies or version of the report should be given to state level actors including premier, responsible ministers and agency chief executives
	Final report tabled in Parliament		• as final report tabled to Commonwealth Parliament, consider whether state or territory parliaments should be notified

Source: Adapted from ANAO 2008.

Overall, the conduct of a CJPA will require a variety of additional considerations to be taken at each step in the performance audit process, and these are summarised and presented in Table 2. It is anticipated that many of these considerations will diminish over time, as the practice of CJPAs becomes more frequent and better understood.

Cooperative approaches

The benefits of engaging in cooperative approaches to performance audit were generally supported across all methods including the literature review, jurisdictional scan, interviews, and online survey. Much of the professional literature and guidance from INTOSAI indicated that many SAIs have had success with cooperative approaches to environmental audit, and that the practice has increased substantially in recent years (WGEA 2012). The jurisdictional scan and survey data also indicated that the cooperative approach has spread beyond environmental audits and is being used by many SAIs to tackle a range of problems shared by multiple jurisdictions, including those shared between national and sub-national governments. The interview data was generally supportive of the benefits that a cooperative approach could offer to Australia and demonstrated a desire to further pursue these approaches more often. However, it was also clear that some hesitation remains as to the efficacy and practical realities that may arise in the development of such an approach.

In the most general sense, the barriers to pursuing cooperative audits in Australia relate primarily to priorities, resources, secrecy provisions, and timing, and are consistent with those and others identified in the literature and the survey. The latter two — secrecy provisions and timing — appear to be the easiest to resolve through legislation amendments and the demonstration of flexibility by audit agencies with respect to their timing and tabling programs (see Appendix 2 for current information-sharing capabilities of Australian auditors-general). The sharing of Cabinet-in-confidence information and other sensitive information amongst auditors has also been identified as a real concern by parliaments, however others believe that internal policies can be developed to ensure that these items are not shared by auditors between jurisdictions in cases where they are not deemed necessary. Auditors already operate with high-level security clearances and are familiar with their responsibilities relevant to the protection of sensitive information, so it seems that this barrier can be overcome.

With respect to differing priorities, coming to an agreement on an audit topic may well face resistance due to the various demands of the parliaments in each participating jurisdiction. On the other hand, as independent officers of the Parliament, it is also an auditor-general's responsibility to identify areas of priority, and if there are gaps, black spots or other areas they believe are worthy of audit, then they are within their rights to pursue such topics. In the context of federal transfers to states and territories, often they are supplemented by state and territory funds, potentially producing programs of interest to both the Commonwealth and State or Territory auditors-general, so surely it would not be difficult to identify areas of mutual interest. Resourcing these areas of mutual interest, however, might be difficult due to the variations in resource capacity, particularly with performance audit budgets, so a policy of voluntary participation might be optimal. For example, as a larger organisation with a substantial performance audit budget, the Commonwealth Auditor-General may have substantially more resources and flexibility at his disposal as compared to some state and territory audit offices that conduct only a handful of performance audits annually.

Despite these concerns with the difficulties associated with cooperative audits, the cooperative approach was still identified in the interview data as the preferred approach to the CJPA or 'go-it-alone' approach that has been adopted by some national audit agencies to assess the spending of national financial transfers to sub-national levels of government. In particular, the coordinated and joint audit approaches seemed able to remedy one of the most commonly reported difficulties of the CJPA approach — that being the unfamiliarity of the national audit agency with the business and processes of the sub-national departments and agencies. The coordinated and joint approaches also allow for the legitimisation of the process by providing a role for the sub-national audit agencies. These agencies act as experts in the sub-national government field, and allow for more information exchange, as well as the division of labor to maximise areas of expertise.

Concurrent

The specific application of the concurrent approach was identified in the literature (INTOSAI 1998, 2004) and survey data as being the easiest of the cooperative approaches to performance audit due to the minimal extent of integration required by participating audit agencies. Apart from topic selection and a rough timeline, concurrent audits allow for greater coverage of an issue area without much deviation from an audit agency's typical performance audit process and cycle. The jurisdictional scan revealed Canada as a frequent practitioner of concurrent audits and a proponent of the approach as an opportunity for the national audit office to share their capacity with the provincial audit offices. In Australia, concurrent audits were identified as a good starting point for a more cooperative approach to be taken between audit agencies, however many of the interview participants identified a preference for a more integrated approach, one resembling a coordinated or joint audit. Both interview and survey data were consistent with the literature regarding the limitations of the concurrent approach — that being their overall limited impact.

Joint

The data from the interviews and the survey were also consistent with the literature on the joint approach, suggesting the overall desirability of joint audits over all other approaches, but at the same time acknowledging the various barriers that some agencies might face in realising this approach — reiterating why they are quite rare in practice. In Australia, interview participants identified barriers such as confidentiality and secrecy provisions in the governing legislation of auditors-general as a barrier to joint audits, along with administrative concerns, such as how to integrate employees from two different jurisdictions under one set of rules and regulations, salary, and methodological approaches to performance audit. Nevertheless, these concerns do not appear to be insurmountable — as legislation can be amended and policies and regulations can be altered — particularly in light of joint audits having occurred elsewhere in the world (UK, Germany), pointing to opportunities for guidance or advice to be obtained through contact with international partners. Furthermore, it appears that joint audits are perceived to be the most credible approach to auditing federal transfers to states and territories in Australia, as they legitimise any recommendations arising from the audit due to the direct involvement of the state and territory audit offices — neutralising any cries of infringement on sovereignty or constitutional rights. Finally, joint audits were indicated in the literature and the interviews as being perceived as the most comprehensive approach to shared issues due to the maximised integration of the two jurisdictions via a single audit team, and despite their greater time commitments, they ultimately hold the most potential to produce a high quality audit with the greatest impact.

Coordinated

The coordinated approach was portrayed in the literature as a good middle path approach between concurrent and joint audits, one that is flexible enough to be adjusted to suit the desires of the participating audit agencies (INTOSAI 1998, 2004). The survey data also seemed to support this and was indicated as a practice undertaken by several of the surveyed audit agencies (UK, Netherlands, US, Ireland, Norway, and Switzerland). Naturally, the coordinated approach will take more time overall, as it requires frequent consultation and coordination by all participating audit agencies throughout each phase of the audit, and consensus has to be reached on a variety of significant decisions, including choosing the scope, methods, timelines and reporting style. The tradeoffs, however, were indicated in the literature and the survey data, pointing to a better quality audit product with greater impact than a concurrent audit, as well as much closer relations between audit offices and greater opportunities to collaborate and improve relationships. An overall summary of the advantages and disadvantages of all approaches to inter-jurisdictional performance audit are presented in Table 3.

Summary

This section presented a discussion of the main findings from the literature review, jurisdictional scan, interviews and online survey within the broader Australian context. Overall, it is clear that CJPAs are viewed as a positive addition to the Auditor-General's mandate, as they will finally enable the full story through end-to-end performance audits of Commonwealth financial transfers to states and territories, and will provide the Commonwealth Parliament with a renewed sense of confidence in the accountability process. An impacts assessment was also presented indicating that the majority of impacts from this new power will be felt at the state and territory levels as well as internally at the ANAO. Finally, a discussion of the advantages and disadvantages of the cross-jurisdictional and cooperative approaches to performance audit was presented, which concluded that that the choice of audit type is ultimately contingent upon audit circumstances.

The discussion section also revealed additional insights into the original conceptual framework presented earlier, particularly with respect to the more specific challenges the ANAO might face as it begins to fold in this new set of powers to its current mandate, and how these juxtapose themselves with the alternate approaches (namely cooperative audits), which appear to have widespread interest. With these new considerations in mind, an overlay to the conceptual framework has been developed to outline the more detailed decisions that the ANAO must make when considering a CJPA moving forward (see Figure 11).

Taken together, the findings suggest that there are several challenges to the unilateral introduction to CJPAs, particularly in first one or two years, that could be ameliorated by the involvement of the state and territory auditors to some extent, possibly through staff exchanges or secondments, to aid the ANAO in building their capacity and experience at the state and territory level. The widely supported cooperative approaches, while popular, do continue to retain barriers to their use that will require time, resources and legislation amendments prior to their use. However, cooperative audits do appear to be an optimal approach to be pursued for use in the medium to long term.

Options and recommendations for the Commonwealth Auditor-General and the ANAO are presented in the following section.

Table 3: Summary: Advantages and disadvantages to various audit approaches

Audit Type	Advantages	Disadvantages
Cross-jurisdictional	• ability to audit the entire funding process end-to-end • better sense of the impacts of federal funding • federal MPs, Parliament and PACs more confident in the process by having the full story about government performance • few, if any, coordination and consultation concerns with other audit agencies • do not have to compromise on areas of interest and priorities • ability to compare implementation processes across sub-national entities • opportunity to build better working relationships and connections between levels of government	• scope limited to federal portion of programs, so may not get overall picture • might become politicised if one level of government found to be outperforming another • longer planning phase and more background information needed • steep learning curve for audit staff: unfamiliarity of the sub-national levels of government will require more time to learn different processes, key people, and key systems • access to information can be difficult or more complicated • risk of perpetuating myths of the Commonwealth government as a bully and promoting suspicion and distrust • risk potential animosity of sub-national agency relating to diversion of their resources toward federal audit • risk of offending state or territory audit office by not involving them or suggesting an area they may have missed • cooperation by sub-national auditees is not guaranteed
Concurrent	• closest to the regular performance audit process • minimal legal problems (remains within respective jurisdictions) • each jurisdiction has the freedom to determine resources it will make available to the audit • disputes over scope, content, observations, resources, deadlines, publication, etc. are eliminated • easier information exchange low political sensitivity • fewer problems associated with tabling time, since report deals only with own jurisdiction • greater impact and media attention if tabling occurs within a few months of each other	• alignment of priorities challenging in pursuing a common topic • limited information exchange • harder on the auditee — for example, having multiple audit offices approach them for interviews and ask the same questions • the only observations and/or conclusions reported are those that pertain to that particular jurisdiction (i.e. narrower impact) • might be less impact on legislators, particularly if tabled far apart from one another or if they contain dramatic differences in scope

Audit Type	Advantages	Disadvantages
Joint	• more coordinated and directed scope • improved planning and criteria development • better understanding of program complexities and risks • improved exchange of information and methodology • access to shared resources and expertise • joint audits can reduce costs and streamline logistics and travel • joint interviews are more efficient and acceptable to auditees • more points of view brought to the audit which may result in more findings or more fair findings • reporting can be more focused and have greater impact • credibility of report increased with two jurisdictions speaking as one • most potential for identification of good practices amongst jurisdictions and contribution to best practices in audit community	• alignment of priorities challenging in pursuing a common topic potential legal limits on information access and sharing (e.g. cabinet-in-confidence documents) • variations in available resources, priorities, and expertise • compromises to achieve consensus amongst the audit team may weaken logistics, scope, methodology, resources, timing, findings, reporting and reviewing of each other's files • challenge of ensuring scope remains within each jurisdictions power • political sensitivities in participating jurisdictions may have to be considered • how to handle difficult findings • risk of strained relations amongst participating audit institutions
Coordinated	• the most flexible type of cooperative audit because various elements can be adjusted to suit the circumstances of the audit • provide a broader sense of whole picture than provided by a concurrent audit • greater knowledge and experience sharing between offices • perceived as more legitimate than CJPAs • report or reports have greater impact than concurrent audits • better take up of recommendations	• audits take longer overall • frequent coordination between audit teams required • alignment of priorities not always easy • differences in availability of resources, different skill sets, qualifications and experience, training • challenges to roles and responsibilities — who is leading the audit? • challenges in determining whose processes, audit tools, and standards to use • barriers to information-sharing between jurisdictions • challenges to reporting including format, tone, timing • if tabling is out of sync it will have less impact

Source: Adapted from INTOSAI 1998, pp. 10–15; CCOLA 2007, p. 1; interviews 2012; online survey 2012.

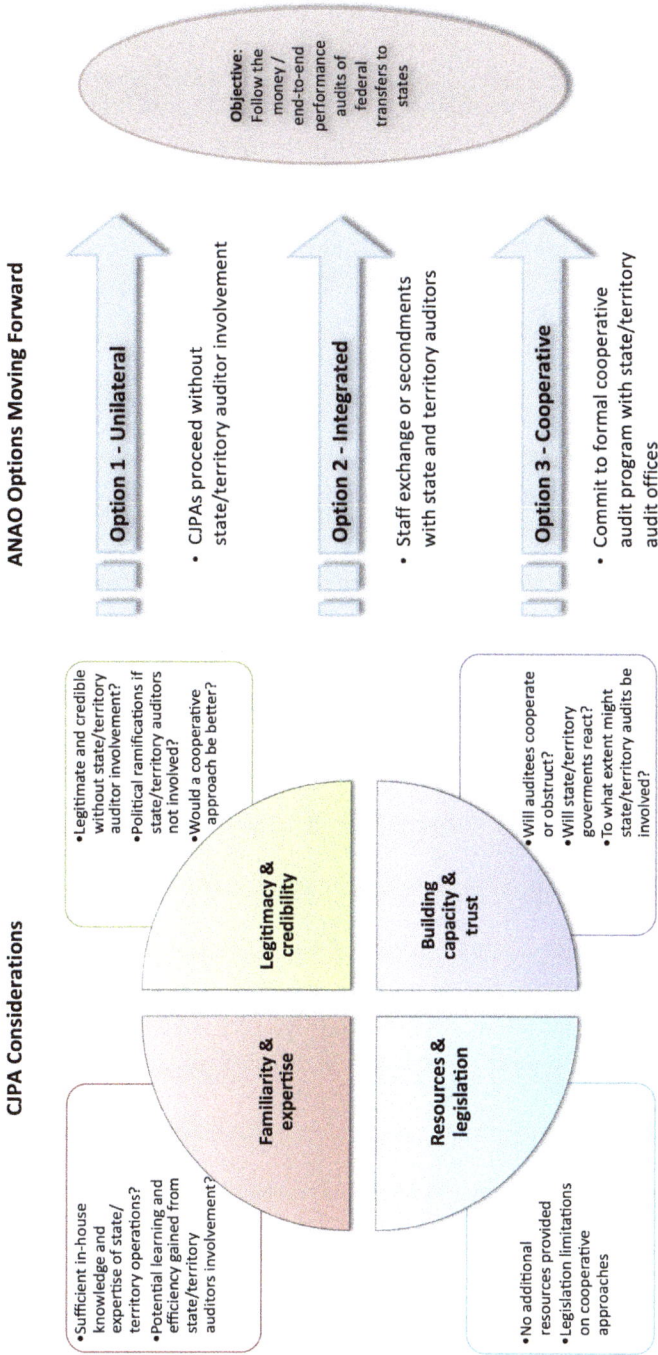

Figure 11: Framework overlay: Considerations from findings for options analysis

Source: Author's research.

Options, recommendations and implementation

This section explores the researcher's recommendations to the Commonwealth Auditor-General and the ANAO as they begin to move forward with their new program to conduct CJPAs of state and territories when in receipt of Commonwealth funds for a specific Commonwealth purpose. The recommendations are presented in the form of three options and have been carefully considered in light of the findings from this research, as well as the current realities of resource and legislation limitations. A summary of the option considerations is presented in Figure 12. The options are presented in order of less to more program development and integration with the state and territory auditors-general.

Option 1 — Unilateral: Proceed with a small CJPA program integrated into the annual performance audit program

Commitment to the status quo would see the ANAO proceed as close to normal as possible when beginning to conduct of CJPAs unilaterally, working in a handful of unique CJPAs to their overall performance audit program. For example, out of approximately 55 performance audits per year, three of these could be identified as having cross-jurisdictional components. This would require no additional resources, and no additional staff, as the new CJPAs would simply take the place of previously allocated standard performance audits.

Minimal engagement with stakeholders would take place such as courtesy notifications to the auditors-general of the relevant jurisdictions when a CJPA is about to begin. Contact with premiers or chief ministers could also be made, while contact with state and territory level auditees would be as normal, through designation letters at the beginning of an audit. As shown in the literature review and interview findings, the advantage of a CJPA is that few if any coordination and consultation commitments are required with key stakeholders beyond the initial notifications of the audit. This frees up the ANAO to pursue audits of their choice and on the timelines of their choice.

Topic selection would have to be carefully considered. Topics of low sensitivity to the state and territory governments could be prioritised for the early years and, as confidence is built by the auditees over time, the program could begin to include higher risk audits. There is also the possibility that the pre-planning work could take some additional time for the audit team members to familiarise themselves with the state and territory jurisdiction, so the Annual Audit Work Plan should account for the potentially longer performance audit process.

Overall, this is a realistic option for the ANAO to move forward, because it will require minimal cost and resources by the ANAO and the legislation is already in place to conduct such audits. This approach also allows the ANAO to retain control over the audit and guide it through the audit process according to their own criteria, scope, methods, reporting and timelines — with no compromises. The disadvantages of this approach are that the risks associated with the ANAO auditors not attaining a sufficient understanding of the state and territory systems, and producing a poor audit or otherwise difficult debates during the issues paper and recommendation phases. Likewise, if the ANAO ends up with a CJPA audit request from the JCPAA or responsible minister that is of high political sensitivity, they may find themselves insufficiently prepared and facing push-back from the states, making for a difficult and lower quality audit if accurate information is not obtained. If a poor audit is tabled, this could further undermine the credibility of the ANAO and their audit reports.

Option 2 — Integrated: Development of a formal CJPA program that is committed to the direct involvement of the state and territory audit staff through staff exchange or secondments to the ANAO

The integrated approach would see the ANAO pursue an approach similar to Option 1, but with a more significant commitment to involving state and territory audit staff in the process through audit-specific secondments or direct staff exchange. The knowledge and expertise gained through involvement of the state and territory auditors will help ensure that the new CJPA audits are conducted smoothly. Issues of information sharing are also circumscribed because seconded staff will be subsumed under federal legislation, and governed as federal public service employees. For example, if the ANAO wants to do a CJPA in the area of education, then they could liaise with the state or territory office involve and see if there are any staff available to come to the ANAO that usually work in the state level education portfolio.

To do this, the Auditor-General could begin to liaise with state and territory level auditors-general, and draw up a memorandum of understanding. This will secure in principle commitment from the state and territory audit offices as to their willingness to be involved when they are able. Since this study has shown that the majority of auditors-general in Australia believed there was a role for them in the ANAO's conduct of CJPAs, securing their involvement in some way should not be too difficult. Where possible, the ANAO should pursue direct staff exchanges in order to replenish any staff members drawn on at the state or territory level. If this is not possible and a secondment is pursued, then the ANAO will need additional resources to compensate the seconded staff, as well as the state or territory audit agency for their loss in capacity. Alternately, the ANAO could fund these secondments out of already existing secondment budgets, relieving the need for additional resources other than state compensation. The ANAO should develop a compensation plan to address the issue of capacity loss at the state level.

There are several advantages and disadvantages to this option. On the one hand, commitment to an integrated approach will allow the Auditor-General to capitalise on the knowledge and expertise of the state and territory auditors — one of the biggest challenges to implementation identified in this study — and minimise resistance on the part of state and territory governments through improved legitimacy. In cases where involvement by state or territory audit staff can be secured, the resulting impacts are likely to be more comprehensive, have more impact and be perceived as more credible — ultimately increasing the uptake of recommendations and improving public management practices.

Furthermore, the direct secondment of staff helps the ANAO retain control over the audit, and avoid all the coordination and alignment difficulties that are associated with more cooperative approaches. There will also be benefits to the state and territory level staff, who will return to their offices with additional insight and learning about the practices of performance audit at the Commonwealth level. This has the potential for flow-on effects in the future if a cooperative audit program is pursued at a later date. On the other hand, it might be difficult to secure resources from some of the smaller audit offices or those that have small performance audit programs and it might be difficult to justify the loss of two staff members to an ANAO audit that is not a state or territory priority, despite the learning opportunities available for the state and territory auditors. Financial compensation from the ANAO, however, could ameliorate this problem by allowing state and territory audit offices to retain additional staff.

Option 3 — Cooperative: Commit to the development of a formal cooperative audit program, to be pursued alongside the CJPA program

The cooperative approach would see the Auditor-General proceed in a similar way as presented in Option 1, but with a formal commitment to pursuing a program of cooperative audits. Since there still remain some legislative barriers to cooperative audits, the Auditor-General could pursue an amendment to the *Auditor-General Act 1997*, to allow for the ability to share information with other audit agencies within Australia. This would require prior consultation and bargaining with Parliament, followed by a request to the JCPAA. The Auditor-General should also advocate for the state and territory audit offices to pursue similar changes to their legislation.

Through the Australasian Council of Auditors-General forum, the Commonwealth Auditor-General could lead the way on the development of a formal cooperative audit program that would involve the movement towards coordinated and joint approaches to audits that relate to the federal financial transfers. Once a list of topics has been identified, joint working groups composed of performance auditors from participating jurisdictions could begin to meet regularly and discuss options moving forward.

There are various costs associated with this option and significant investment of time and resources required. The ANAO will need to request funding from the JCPAA and receive approval. In the pre-development stages, ANAO staff will be required to meet with state and territory staff to work out guidelines for the cooperative audit program that are satisfying to all parties. Once the guidelines are set, the focus will shift to topic selection and participation. A forward plan should be developed to identify topics and participating jurisdictions.

There are several advantages and disadvantages to this option. Through formal cooperation, it will allow better audit coverage of the service delivery, particularly in cases where federal money is combined with state or territory funding — an area where CJPAs do not have coverage as it is only capable of auditing the spending of federal funds. The interviews conducted in this study indicate significant support for the cooperative approach and a preference for it over the CJPA approach, in part because the cooperative approach will have more meaning for the states and territories, and will be of more interest to their parliaments. On the other hand, it is clear that cooperative audits are time-consuming and will cost more than standard audits, and they require a high degree of coordination and consultation between offices.

Recommended option

Option 2 is recommended for the ANAO as it begins to move ahead with its CJPA program. Option 2 incorporates all the basic considerations contained in Option 1, with the additional links to the state and territory audit office through a formal secondment program, but does not go so far as requiring the significant time and resource investments that come with a formal cooperative audit program. Bringing in staff from the state and territory agencies will improve the knowledge base of the ANAO in the early days, and mitigate many of the risks associated with entering new audit terrain at the state and territory level. In addition, involvement of the state and territory auditors will improve uptake of the recommendations and improve audit legitimacy.

While this approach appears to be the most realistic at the present time, it does not preclude the eventual development of a cooperative audit program, which has clearly garnered significant support and offers additional incentives that may not be captured in the secondment approach alone. The recommended approach should be considered the best course of action in the early days, but with an eye towards the future development of a cooperative audit program following necessary legislation amendments and budget increases.

Option 1 - Unilateral

- CJPAs proceed without state/territory auditor involvement
- no additional resources or legislation amendments required
- lack of specific knowledge and expertise;
- risks of push-back by auditees
- reputation risks if they get it wrong
- legitimacy risks if direct recommendations to state/territory agencies made

Option 2 - Integrated

- staff exchange or secondments with state and territory auditors
- capitalize on knowledge and expertise of state/territory staff
- boost legitimacy, credibility; reduce resistance from state/territory auditees
- minimal additional resources
- optimal in the early 1-2 years, as CJPAs are unfamiliar

Option 3 - Cooperative

- commit to formal cooperative audit program with state/territory audit offices
- additional time and resources required
- approval from JCPAA required
- improved audit outcomes
- opportunities to build capacity, relationships and share knowledge
- cooperative approach widely supported
- optimal in the long-term 5-10 years out

Objective: Follow the money / end-to-end performance audits of federal transfers to states

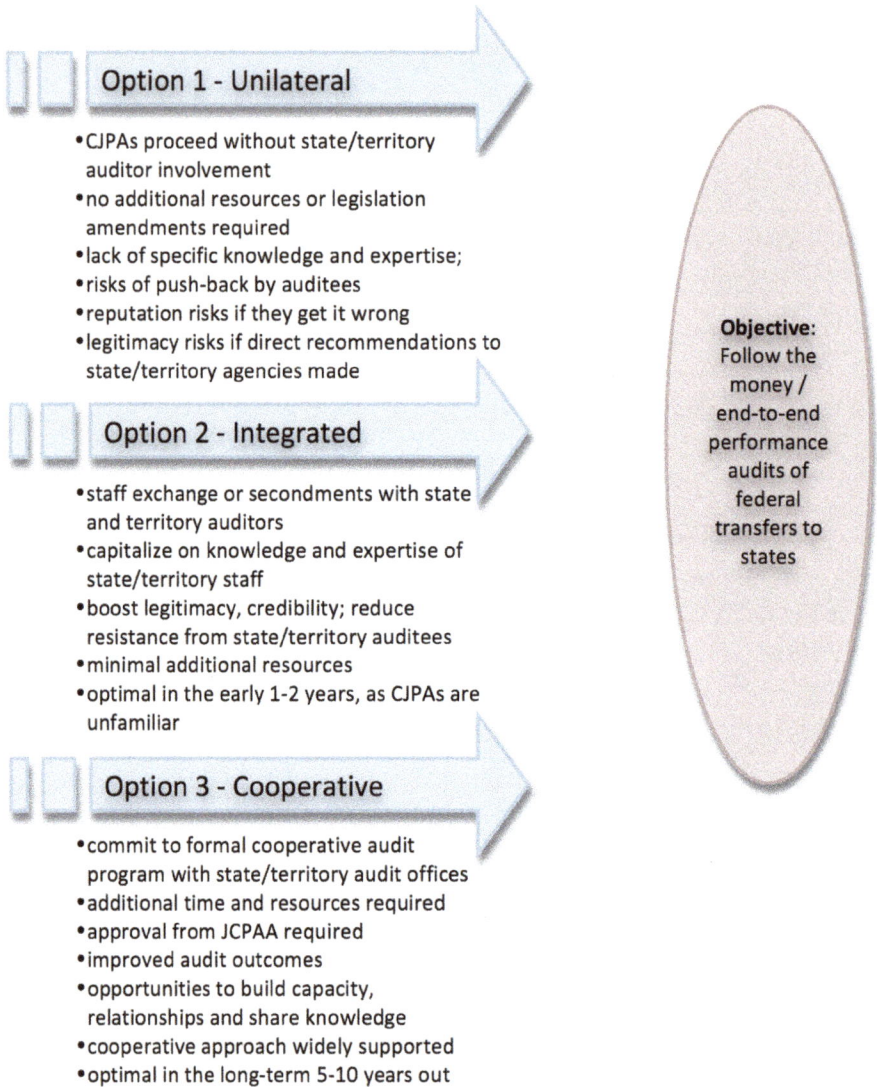

Figure 12: Options summary: Strengths and limitations

Source: Author's research.

Implementation

Discussed below is a brief implementation strategy for Option 2, including key components to be addressed before the ANAO moves forward with CJPAs.

The first step will be for the ANAO to begin liaising with the state and territory audit offices and work towards the development of a memorandum of understanding relating to secondments and staff exchanges for the purposes of CJPAs. This will help the ANAO determine which of the agencies would have immediate capacity and which might be more limited. It could also be used to clarify some of the terms and conditions of the secondments or exchanges including agency preferences, however individual employment contracts can also be used as in regular secondment and exchange situations.

The next step will be to develop a compensation plan to be used when secondments are used instead of direct staff exchange. This plan will outline how state and territory agencies would be compensated in the event that a secondment takes place and will include detailed financial information to allow the ANAO to best estimate costs when beginning to pursue a secondment.

The current secondment policy and budget should be reviewed immediately in order to determine how much flexibility exists within the current budget for additional secondments, as well as earmarking potential CJPA secondments for the upcoming year. A review of previous years' annual reports reveals that secondments can fluctuate from year to year, which suggests there is some flexibility in the budget.

Once the previous planning documents are in place, the ANAO can move ahead with any CJPA identified by a minister, the JCPAA or by the Auditor-General Once approval has been secured, the ANAO should immediately approach the relevant state or territory audit office, to notify them and inquire about possible staff exchange or secondment for the audit. This should allow ample time for the state or territory audit office to prepare for incoming ANAO staff or otherwise loss of their own. Compensation can then be pursued. Once secondment or staff exchange is agreed upon, the ANAO can begin making preparations for the secondees' arrival. Once secondees arrive, the audit team can begin to develop the Audit Work Plan and proceed with their performance audit as normal, but with the additional expertise of the state or territory audit staff.

Following the conclusion and tabling of the performance audit, the ANAO should conduct an evaluation of the CJPA process using the secondment or staff exchange components, to determine whether it was an effective approach. The evaluation should include input from all stakeholders involved in the new CJPA process.

Conclusion

The aim of this study was to assess the impacts of the new cross-jurisdictional performance audit powers of the Commonwealth Auditor-General on key stakeholders, including the ANAO, and to explore alternative approaches, such as cooperative audits. First, a review of background information outlining the Australian context was provided, followed by a review of the relevant performance audit literature. Next, a jurisdictional scan was conducted to explore performance audit practices of other national audit agencies, followed by interviews with a range of experts in the field of public audit. Finally, an online survey was administered to solicit international perspectives on CJPAs and cooperative audit approaches.

Findings from the study suggest that impacts of the new CJPA powers are anticipated to be widespread and not without their challenges, but will be concentrated at the state and territory levels, with the bulk of the effects felt by central agencies, auditees and auditors-general. While earlier fears of constitutional challenge on the part of the states appear to have diminished, both the credibility and reputation of the ANAO depend upon the outcomes of these audits. Therefore the ANAO must be diligent in its efforts to mitigate the risks associated with CJPAs through appropriate stakeholder management and by focusing on low sensitivity audits in the early days.

One of the best approaches to mitigating these risks would be to involve the state and territory audit staff through staff exchange or secondments, particularly in the first one to two years of the new CJPA program. This would help address the biggest concerns on the ground that relate to how well and how quickly ANAO staff can familiarise themselves with the state and territory operations, as well as how their new auditees will respond to the presence of federal auditors. It will also satisfy the desire of the state and territory auditors-general to be involved in the CJPA process, while providing overall legitimacy to the federal presence in state and territory jurisdictions. This approach will also be low in cost and does not require additional legislative amendments.

Although the evidence collected here presents a substantial case for the pursuance of more cooperative approaches to performance audit, particularly with respect to the issue of federal financial transfers, it is also clear that these approaches can be time and labor intensive, and still face legislative barriers that restrict information-sharing amongst audit offices. In order to pursue this approach, the ANAO will need to seek additional funding, as will the state and territory auditors-general, and some amendments to information sharing will have to be made at the state and territory level. However, in the medium to long term of 5–10 years, this approach holds promise for improved working relationships between audit offices and levels of government more generally, and ultimately improved performance audit outcomes.

References

Adams, N. 1986, 'Efficiency auditing in the Australian National Audit Office', *Australian Journal of Public Administration* 45(3), pp. 189–200.

ANAO (Australian National Audit Office) 2008, 'Performance Auditing in the Australian National Audit Office'. Available at: http://www.anao.gov.au/uploads/documents/Performance_Auditing.pdf.

ANAO 2009, 'Submission to the JCPAA Inquiry into the *Auditor-General Act 1997*', Submission No. 3. Available at: http://www.aph.gov.au/parliamentary_business/committees/house_of_representatives_committees?url=jcpaa/agact/subs.htm.

ANAO 2011, 'About us'. Available at: http://www.anao.gov.au/About-Us.

ANAO 2012a, 'Guidelines for the conduct of performance audits'. Available at: http://www.anao.gov.au/Publications/Corporate-Publications/Guidelines-for-the-Conduct-of-Performance-Audits.

ANAO 2012b, 'Annual Report 2011–2012'. Availble at: http://www.anao.gov.au/~/media/Files/Annual%20Reports/Annual%20Reports/2011_2012_Annual_Report/ANAO%20Annual%20Report%202011%202012.pdf.

Aucoin, P. 1990, 'Administrative Reform in Public Management: Paradigms, principles, paradoxes and pendulums', *Governance* 3(2), pp. 115–137.

Australian Government 2012, 'Final Budget Outcome 2011–12, Part 3: Australia's Federal Relations'. Available at: http://www.budget.gov.au/2011-12/content/fbo/html/index.htm.

Barrett, P. 2002, 'Auditing in a Changing Governance Environment', in *Papers on Parliament No. 39*, Department of the Senate, Canberra.

Barrett, P. 2010, 'Performance auditing: What value?', *Journal of Public Money and Management* 30(5), pp. 271–278.

Barrett, P. 2011, 'Commentary: Where you sit is what you see: The seven deadly sins of performance auditing: Implications for monitoring public audit institutions', *Australian Accounting Review* 21(4), pp. 397–405.

Barzelay, M. 1997, 'Central Audit Institutions and Performance Auditing: A comparative analysis of organizational strategies in the OECD', *Governance (Oxford)* 10(3), pp. 235–260.

Boadway, R. and Shah, A. (eds) 2007, *Intergovernmental Fiscal Transfers: Principles and practice*, The World Bank, Washington DC. Available at: http://documents.worldbank.org/curated/en/2006/11/7242002/intergovernmental-fiscal-transfers-principles-practice.

Bowerman, M., C. Humphrey and D. Owen 2003, 'Struggling for Supremacy: The case of UK public audit institutions', *Critical Perspectives on Accounting* 14(1), pp. 1–22.

Bundesrechnungshof 1997, 'Audit Rules of the Bundesrechnungshof'. Available at: http://bundesrechnungshof.de.

Bundesrechnungshof 2012, 'Institutional relations'. Available at: http://bundesrechnungshof.de/international-relations.

CCOLA (Canadian Council of Legislative Auditors) 2007, 'Collaborative audit general guidelines', internal document.

Chelimsky, E. 1985, 'Comparing and Contrasting Auditing and Evaluation: Some notes on their relationship', *Evaluation Review* 9(4), pp. 483–583.

Clark, I. and H. Swain 2005, 'Distinguishing the Real from the Surreal in Management Reform: Suggestions for beleaguered administrators in the government of Canada', *Canadian Public Administration* 48(4), pp. 453–476.

English, L. and J. Guthrie 2000, 'Mandate, Independence and Funding: Resolution of a protracted struggle between parliament and the executive over the powers of the Australian Auditor-General', *Australian Journal of Public Administration* 59(1), pp. 98–114.

English, L. and P. Skaerbaek 2007, 'Performance Auditing and the Modernization of the Public Sector', *Financial Accountability and Management* 23(3), pp. 239–241.

Fenna, A. 2008, 'Commonwealth Fiscal Power and Australian Federalism', *UNSW Law Journal* 31(2), pp. 509–529.

Funnell, W. 1996, 'Executive Encroachments on the Independence of the Commonwealth Auditor-General', *Australian Journal of Public Administration* 55(4), pp. 109–123.

Funnell, W. 1997, 'The Curse of Sisyphus: Public sector audit independence in an age of economic rationalism', *Australian Journal of Public Administration* 56(4), pp. 87–105.

Funnell, W. 1998, 'Executive Coercion and State Audit: A processual analysis of the responses of the Australian Audit Office to the dilemmas of efficiency auditing 1978–84', *Accounting, Auditing and Accountability Journal* 11(4), pp. 436–458.

Funnell, W. 2003, 'Enduring Fundamentals: Constitutional accountability and auditors-general in the reluctant state', *Critical Perspectives on Accounting* 14(1), pp. 107–132.

Funnell, W. 2011, 'Keeping Secrets?: Or what government performance auditors might not need to know', *Critical Perspectives on Accounting* 22(7), pp. 714–721.

Funnell, W. and M. Wade 2012, 'Negotiating the Credibility of Performance Auditing', *Critical Perspectives on Accounting* 23(6), pp. 434–450.

Furubo, J. E. 2011, 'Performance Auditing: Audit or misnomer?', in J. Lonsdale, P. Wilkins and T. Ling (eds), *Performance Auditing: Contributing to accountability in democratic government*, Edward Elgar, Cheltenham, pp. 22–47.

Gendron, Y., D. Cooper and B. Townley 2007, 'The Construction of Auditing Expertise in Measuring Government Performance', *Accounting, Organizations and Society* 32, pp. 101–129.

Gerald, P. 2012, 'Cross-Jurisdictional Performance Audits at the Australian National Audit Office: Impacts and alternatives'. Available at: https://dspace.library.uvic.ca:8443//handle/1828/4383.

Glynn, J. 1985, 'Value for Money Auditing: An international review and comparison', *Financial Accountability and Management* 1(2), pp. 113–128.

Guthrie, J. 1987, 'Public Sector Audits of Programmes and Management in Australia', *Managerial Auditing Journal* 2(16), pp. 10–16.

Guthrie, J. 1989, 'The Contested Nature of Performance Auditing in Australia', *International Journal of Public Sector Management* 2(3), pp. 56–66.

Guthrie, J. and L. Parker 1999, 'A Quarter of a Century of Performance Auditing in the Australian Federal Public Sector: A malleable masque', *Abacus (Sydney)*, 35(3), pp. 302–332.

Hamburger, P. 1989, 'Efficiency Auditing by the Australian Audit Office: Reform and reaction under three Auditors-General', *Accounting, Auditing and Accountability Journal* 2(3), pp. 3–21.

Hood, C. 1991, 'A Public Management for all Seasons?', *Public Administration* 69(1), pp. 3–19.

Hood, C. and G. Peters 2004, 'The Middle Aging of New Public Management: Into the age of paradox?', *Journal of Public Administration Research and Theory* 14(3), pp. 267–282.

INTOSAI (International Organisation of Supreme Audit Institutions) 1998, 'How SAIs May Cooperate on the Audit of International Environmental Accords'. Available at: http://www.issai.org/media/13180/issai_5140_e.pdf.

INTOSAI 2004, 'Standards and Guidelines for Performance Auditing Based on INTOSAI's Auditing Standards and Practical Experience'. Available at: http://www.intosai.org/issai-executive-summaries/view/article/issai-3000-implementation-guidelines-for-performance-auditingstandards-and-guidelines-for-perf.html.

INTOSAI 2007, 'Cooperation Between Supreme Audit Institutions: Tips and examples for cooperative audits'. INTOSAI Working Group on Environmental Audit. Available at: www.nik.gov.pl/plik/id,2334,vp,2948.pdf.

INTOSAI 2010, 'Performance Audit Guidelines: Key principles'. Available at: www.issai.org/media/13220/issai_3100_e.pdf.

INTOSAI 2012a, 'Australia: Amendments to the Auditor-General Act 1997', *International Journal of Government Auditing* 39(4), p. 6.

INTOSAI 2012b, 'Fundamental Principles of Public Sector Auditing'. Available at: www.intosai.org/issai.../issai-100-fundamental-principles-of-public-sector- auditing.html.

INTOSAI 2012c, 'Fundamental Principles of Performance Audits'. Available at: www.issai.org/media/69911/issai-300-english.pdf.

Jacobs, K. 1998, 'Value for Money Auditing in New Zealand: Competing for control in the public sector', *The British Accounting Review* 30(4), pp. 343–360.

JCPAA (Joint Committee of Public Accounts and Audit) 2010 'Report 419: Inquiry into the Auditor-General Act 1997', Commonwealth of Australia.

Justesen, L. and P. Skaerbaek 2010, 'Performance Auditing and the Narrating of a New Auditee Identity', *Financial Accountability and Management,* 26(3), pp. 325–343.

Keen, J. 1999, 'On the Nature of Audit Judgments: The case of value for money studies', *Public Administration* 77(3), pp. 509–525.

Kells, S. 2011, 'The Seven Deadly Sins of Performance Auditing: Implications for monitoring public audit institutions', *Australian Accounting Review* 59(21), pp. 383–396.

Leeuw, F. L. 1996, 'Auditing and Evaluation: Bridging a gap, worlds to meet?', *New Directions for Evaluation* 71, pp. 51–60.

Lonsdale, J. 2000, 'Developments in Value-for-Money Audit Methods: Impacts and implications', *International Review of Administrative Sciences* 66 (1), pp. 73–89.

Lonsdale, J. 2008, 'Balancing Independence and Responsiveness: A practitioner perspective on the relationships shaping performance audit', *Evaluation* 14(2), pp. 227–248.

Lonsdale, L., R. Mul and C. Pollitt 1999, 'The Auditor's Craft: In performance or compliance?', in C. Pollitt (ed.), *Performance or Compliance?: Performance audit and public management in five countries,* Oxford University Press, Oxford. Available at: http://www.oxfordscholarship.com/view/10.1093/acp rof:oso/9780198296003.001.0001/acprof-9780198296003-chapter-7.

Lonsdale, J., P. Wilkins and T. Ling 2011, *Performance Auditing: Contributing to accountability in democratic government,* Edward Elgar, Cheltenham.

Mayne, J. 2010, 'Performance Auditing: Cozy, comfortable, and in need of a challenge', *Optimum Online* 40(3), p. 2.

McPhee, I. 2010, 'Public Hearing 8/02/10', JCPAA Inquiry into the Auditor-General Act 1997, p. 8. Available at: http://www.aph.gov.au/Parliamentary_Business/Committees/House_of_Representatives_Committees?url=jcpaa/agact/hearings.htm.

McPhee, I. 2011, 'GOTCHA! Or improving administration: The impact of oversight and review agencies', paper delivered at IPAA (ACT) Forum, 23 August 2011. Available at: http://www.anao.gov.au/Publications/Speeches.

McPhee, I. 2012, 'The Evolving Role and Mandate of the Australian National Audit Office Since Federation', Papers on Parliament No. 57, Australian Senate. Available at: http://www.aph.gov.au/About_Parliament/Senate/Research_and_Education/pops/pop57/c04.

McPhee, I. 2012b, 'Audits of Commonwealth Partner', ANAO presentation at the Australasian Council of Pubic Accounts Committees Mid-Term Meeting, 25 May 2012. Available at: www.anao.gov.au/~/media/Files/Speeches/ACPAC.pdf.

Morin, D. 2001, 'Influence of Value for Money Audit on Public Administrations: Looking beyond appearances', *Financial Accountability and Management* 17(2), pp. 99–117.

Morin, D. 2008, 'Auditors General's Universe Revisited', *Managerial Auditing Journal* 23(7), pp. 697–720.

Murray, A. 2011, 'Budgets and Finance: Sunlight and the dark arts', Papers on Parliament No. 56, Australian Senate. Available at: http://www.aph.gov.au/About_Parliament/Senate/Research_and_Education/pops/pop56.

Nicoll, P. 2005, *Audit in a Democracy: The Australian model of public sector audit and its application to emerging markets*, Oxford University Press, Oxford.

Office of the Auditor-General of Canada 2007, '2007–08 Estimates — Reports on Plans and Priorities', p. 4. Available at: http://www.tbs-sct.gc.ca/rpp/2007-2008/oag-bvg/oag-bvg-eng.pdf.

Paun, A. and R. Hazell 2008, 'Centralised Power and Decentralised Politics in the Devolved UK', paper delivered at International Association of Centres for Federal Studies Conference, Barcelona, 20 September 2008.

Podger, A. and J. Wanna 2012, 'Accountability for National Funding Agreements', Thinkpiece Discussion Paper, COAG Reform Council. Available at: https://www.coagreformcouncil.gov.au/.../Think_piece_Podger_Wanna_ 2012.pdf.

Pollitt, C. 2006, 'Performance Information for Democracy: The missing link?', *Evaluation* 12(1), pp. 11–55.

Pollitt, C. and H. Summa 1996, 'Performance Audit and Evaluation: Similar tools, different relationships?', *New Directions for Evaluation,* 1996(71), pp. 29–50.

Pollitt, C. and H. Summa 1999, 'Performance Audit and Public Management Reform', in C. Pollitt, X. Girre, J. Lonsdale, R. Mul, H. Summa and M. Waerness (eds), *Performance of Compliance? Performance audit and public management in five countries,* Oxford University Press, Oxford.

Pollitt, C., X. Girre, J. Lonsdale, R. Mul, H. Summa and M. Waerness 1999, *Performance or Compliance? Performance audit and public management in five countries,* Oxford University Press, Oxford.

Power, M. 1997, *The Audit Society,* Oxford University Press, Oxford.

Pugh, C. 1987, 'Efficiency Auditing and the Australian Audit Office', *Australian Journal of Public Administration* 46(1), p. 55.

Put, V. and R. Turksema 2011, 'Selection of Topics', in J. Lonsdale, P. Wilkins and T. Ling (eds), *Performance Auditing: Contributing to accountability in democratic government*, Edward Elgar, Cheltenham, pp. 51–74.

Quiggin, J. 2005, 'Untangling the Web of Commonwealth/State/Local Government Funding: What did your GST buy?', presentation at the Housing Industry Association's Home and Building Expo, Brisbane, 26 May 2005.

Riksrevisionen 2011, 'The Act and Instructions Relating to the Office of the Auditor General: With comments'. Available at: https://www.riksrevisjonen. no/en/AboutRR/RoleAndTasks/Documents/ActAndInstructions.pdf.

Robertson, G. 2009, 'Independence of Auditors General: A survey of Australian and New Zealand legislation: A report commissioned by the Victorian Auditor General's Office'. Available at: http://www.acag.org.au/Independence_ANZ_20090702.pdf.

Shand, D. and P. Anand 1996, 'Performance Auditing in the Public Sector: Approaches and issues in OECD member countries', in *Performance Auditing and the Modernization of Government*, OECD, Paris, pp. 57–78.

Sharma, N. 2007, 'Interactions and Interrogations: Negotiating and performing value for money reports', *Financial Accountability and Management* 23(3), pp. 289–311.

Sutherland, S. L. 1986, 'The Politics of Audit: The federal office of the Auditor General in comparative perspective', *Canadian Public Administration* 29(1), pp. 118–148.

Sutherland, S. L. 2001, 'Biggest Scandal in Canadian history: HRDC audit starts probity war', School of Policy Studies Working Paper No. 23, Queens University.

Sutherland, S. L. 2002, 'The Office of the Auditor General of Canada: Government in exile?', School of Policy Studies Working Paper No. 31, Queen's University.

Talbot, C. and J. Wiggan 2010, 'The Public Value of the National Audit Office', *The International Journal of Public Sector Management,* 23(1), pp. 54–70.

Taylor, J. 1996, 'What Should be the Role of the Auditor-General in the Context of Managerialist Government and New Public Management?', *Australian Journal of Public Administration* 55(4), pp. 147–156.

Twomey, A. and G. Withers 2007, 'Australia's Federal Future: Delivering growth and prosperity: A report for the Council for the Australian Federation', Federalist Paper 1. Available at: http://www.caf.gov.au/documents/australiasfederalfuture.pdf.

van der Knaap, P. 2011, 'Sense and Complexity: Initiatives in responsive performance audits', *Evaluation* 17(4), pp. 351–363.

Van Leeuwen, S. 2004, 'Auditing International Environmental Agreements: The role of supreme audit institutions', *The Environmentalist* 24(2), pp. 93–99.

Van Loocke, E. and V. Put 2011, 'The Impact of Performance Audits: A review of the existing evidence' in J. Lonsdale, P. Wilkins and T. Ling (eds), *Performance Auditing: Contributing to accountability in democratic government*, Edward Elgar, Cheltenham, pp. 175–208.

Wanna, J., C. Ryan and C. Ng 2001, *From Accounting to Accountability: A centenary history of the Australian National Audit Office*, Allen & Unwin, Sydney.

Wanna, J. and A. Podger 2009, 'IPAA Submission to the JCPAA Inquiry into the *Auditor-General Act 1997*', Submission No. 5. Available at: http://www.aph.gov.au/parliamentary_business/committees/house_of_representatives_committees?url=jcpaa/agact/subs.htm.

WGEA (Working Group on Environmental Auditing) 2012, 'Audits by Country: Austria'. Available at: www.environmental-auditing.org/tabid/126/CountryId/346/Default.aspx.

Wilkins, P. 1995, 'Performing Auditors: Assessing and reporting the performance of national audit offices: A three country comparison', *Australian Journal of Public Administration* 54(4), pp. 421–430.

Appendix 1: List of interview participants

Biography information for interview participants has been gathered from the various audit office websites as well as through general internet searches.

- Ian McPhee (ANAO) — Ian McPhee was appointed as Auditor-General for Australia in March 2005. His previous position was as Deputy Secretary, Financial Management Group, Department of Finance and Administration, where his responsibilities included managing and providing policy advice to the Finance Minister on the budget and financial management framework; budget and financial reporting, and analysis for whole of government purposes; public sector superannuation; and the Office of Evaluation of Audit. From 1998 to January 2003, Ian was Deputy Auditor-General at the ANAO, where he was responsible to the Auditor-General for the delivery of the performance and assurance audit programs.

- Russell Coleman (ANAO) — Russell Coleman is a senior staff member at the ANAO and has worked for the office in various capacities for close to 30 years.

- Andrew Greaves (QLD) — Andrew Greaves became the Auditor-General of Queensland in December 2011. Prior to this appointment, Andrew had been an Assistant Auditor-General at the Victorian Auditor-General's Office since 2006 and headed both the Financial Audit Group and the Performance Audit Group. Andrew has over 27 years experience in public sector external and internal audit, at the Commonwealth, state and local government levels.

- Colin Murphy (WA) — Colin Murphy was appointed Auditor-General for Western Australia in June 2007. Colin has extensive experience in finance and administration in State and Commonwealth government roles. He has held senior positions within the state government in the Departments of Justice, Treasury and Finance, Land Administration, and the Building Management Authority. He has also worked for the Commonwealth Department of Finance in Perth and Washington DC, and as Business Manager for Murdoch University. Colin is a member of the Australian Auditing and Assurance Standards Board. He holds a Bachelor of Commerce degree from the University of Western Australia. He is a Fellow, former board member and past State President of CPA Australia and a Fellow of Chartered Secretaries Australia and the Institute of Chartered Accountants in Australia.

- Des Pearson (VIC) — Des Pearson was appointed Auditor-General of Victoria in October 2006. He was previously Auditor-General of Western Australia from 1991 to 2006. He has been an involved member of CPA Australia, the Institute of Public Administration, and the Australian Institute of Management.

- Mike Blake (TAS) — Mike Blake was appointed Tasmanian Auditor-General in May 2004. Prior to accepting the position, he was Auditor-General for the Northern Territory and had previous worked as the Deputy Auditor-General of Western Australia. Mike has been an active member of the Public Sector Accounting Standards Board from 1994 to 1999, a member of the Urgent Issues Group representing Auditors-General from 2003 to 2005 and was appointed to the Auditing and Assurance Standards Board on 1 January 2006. Mike is a Fellow of ICA Australia and of CPA Australia.

- Frank McGuiness (NT) — Frank McGuiness was appointed as the Auditor-General of the Northern Territory in September 2004. He previously held senior positions in the Northern Territory and South Australian Treasuries.

Originally from South Australia, Frank completed an undergraduate degree in economics and a Master of Financial Management degree.

- Megan Young (ACT) — Megan Young is a Senior Audit Manager at the ACT Auditor General's Office.

- Rob Oakeshott, MP — Rob Oakeshott is an independent member of Parliament for Lyne, an electorate situated on the mid-north coast of New South Wales. Since joining federal Parliament in September 2008, Rob has invested heavily in committee work, including his current chairmanship of the Joint Committee of Public Accounts and Audit and the Standing Committee on the National Broadband Network. Rob played a figurative role in the amendments to the Commonwealth Auditor-General Act both as Chair of the JCPAA and after introducing a private member's bill supporting the amendments in 2011.

- Russell Chafer, former Secretary of the JCPAA — Russell Chafer was the Secretary for the JCPAA during the time of the *Inquiry into the Auditor-General Act 1997*, but has since moved to the Clerk's Office at the House of Representatives.

- Pat Barrett, former Commonwealth Auditor-General — Pat Barrett served a 10-year term as Auditor-General for Australia until 2005. He is now a Senior Fellow at ANU Australian National Centre for Audit and Assurance Research and has expertise in numerous areas including public sector management, information technology, and financial, auditing and budgeting issues. He is a member of the Board of Governors of the International Federation of Accountants, the peak body of accountants in the world responsible for the International Auditing and Assurance Standards Board and the International Public Sector Accounting Standards Board. Mr. Barrett is also a prolific writer on the subject of auditing, accounting, and public management, and many of his papers have been published in either books or journals.

- Glenn Poole, former Auditor General for Queensland — Glenn Poole served as Queensland's Auditor-General from 2004 to 2011. Prior to that he was a senior executive in the Queensland Treasury Department for over 15 years. Glenn is now Executive in Residence at the Australian Centre for Philanthropy and Nonprofit Studies at Queensland University of Technology in Brisbane.

Appendix 2: Comparison of legislative powers of Australian auditors-general

	CW	ACT	NT	NSW	QLD	SA	TAS	VIC	WA
Explicit right to conduct joint audits	No	No	No	No	Yes (2011)	No	No	No	No
Right to share information	No	No	Not explicit but flexible*	No	Yes (2011)	No	Yes (2011)	No	Yes (2006)
Right to follow-the-money into third parties (NGOs, private contractors)	Yes (2011)	Pursuing (2012)	Yes (2011)	No	Yes (2011)	No	Yes, (2008)	No	Yes (2006)
Power to follow-the-money into local government	Yes	Yes	Yes	No	Yes	No	Yes	Yes	No

* This possibility was outlined in an interview with the Auditor-General for the Northern Territory